California
HMH SCIENCE DIMENSIONS™

Grade 6

Watch the cover come alive as you explore the body systems of a snail.
Download the HMH Science Dimensions AR app available on Android or iOS devices.

This Write-In Book belongs to

_____

Teacher/Room

_____

Houghton Mifflin Harcourt™

Consulting Authors

Michael A. DiSpezio

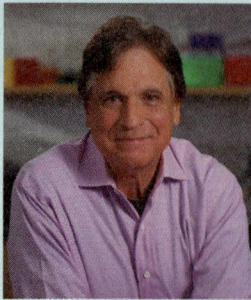

Global Educator
North Falmouth,
Massachusetts

Michael DiSpezio has authored many HMH instructional programs for Science and Mathematics. He has also authored numerous trade books and multimedia programs on various topics and hosted dozens of studio and location broadcasts for various organizations in the United States and worldwide. Most recently, he has been working with educators to provide strategies for implementing the Next Generation Science Standards, particularly the Science and Engineering Practices, Crosscutting Concepts, and the use of Evidence Notebooks. To all his projects, he brings his extensive background in science, his expertise in classroom teaching at the elementary, middle, and high school levels, and his deep experience in producing interactive and engaging instructional materials.

Marjorie Frank

Science Writer and Content-
Area Reading Specialist
Brooklyn, New York

An educator and linguist by training, a writer and poet by nature, Marjorie Frank has authored and designed a generation of instructional materials in all subject areas, including past HMH Science programs. Her other credits include authoring science issues of an award-winning children's magazine, writing game-based digital assessments, developing blended learning materials for young children, and serving as instructional designer and coauthor of pioneering school-to-work software. In addition, she has served on the adjunct faculty of Hunter, Manhattan, and Brooklyn Colleges, teaching courses in science methods, literacy, and writing. For *California HMH Science Dimensions™*, she has guided the development of our K–2 strands and our approach to making connections between NGSS and Common Core ELA/literacy standards.

Acknowledgments

Cover credits: (garden snail) ©Johan Swanepoel/Alamy; (poison dart frog) ©Dirk Ercken/Alamy.

Section Header Master Art: (machinations) ©DNY59/E+/Getty Images; (rivers on top of Greenland ice sheet) ©Maria-José Viñas, NASA Earth Science News Team; (human cells, illustration) ©Sebastian Kaulitzki/Science Photo Library/Corbis; (waves) ©Alfred Pasieka/Science Source

Printed in the U.S.A.

ISBN 978-1-328-91485-9

7 8 9 10 0877 27 26 25 24 23 22 21 20 19

4500758899   A B C D E F G

Michael R. Heithaus, PhD

Dean, College of Arts, Sciences & Education
Professor, Department of Biological Sciences
Florida International University
Miami, Florida

Mike Heithaus joined the FIU Biology Department in 2003 and has served as Director of the Marine Sciences Program and Executive Director of the School of Environment, Arts, and Society, which brings together the natural and social sciences and humanities to develop solutions to today's environmental challenges. He now serves as Dean of the College of Arts, Sciences & Education. His research focuses on predator-prey interactions and the ecological importance of large marine species. He has helped to guide the development of Life Science content in *California HMH Science Dimensions*™, with a focus on strategies for teaching challenging content as well as the science and engineering practices of analyzing data and using computational thinking.

Bernadine Okoro

Access and Equity Consultant

S.T.E.M. Learning Advocate & Consultant
Washington, DC

Bernadine Okoro is a chemical engineer by training and a playwright, novelist, director, and actress by nature. Okoro went from working with patents and biotechnology to teaching in K–12 classrooms. A 12-year science educator and Albert Einstein Distinguished Fellow, Okoro was one of the original authors of the Next Generation Science Standards. As a member of the Diversity and Equity Team, her focus on Alternative Education and Community Schools and on Integrating Social-Emotional Learning and Brain-Based Learning into NGSS is the vehicle she uses as a pathway to support underserved groups from elementary school to adult education. An article and book reviewer for NSTA and other educational publishing companies, Okoro currently works as a S.T.E.M. Learning Advocate & Consultant.

Cary I. Sneider, PhD

Associate Research Professor
Portland State University
Portland, Oregon

While studying astrophysics at Harvard, Cary Sneider volunteered to teach in an Upward Bound program and discovered his real calling as a science teacher. After teaching middle and high school science in Maine, California, Costa Rica, and Micronesia, he settled for nearly three decades at Lawrence Hall of Science in Berkeley, California, where he developed skills in curriculum development and teacher education. Over his career, Cary directed more than 20 federal, state, and foundation grant projects and was a writing team leader for the Next Generation Science Standards. He has been instrumental in ensuring *California HMH Science Dimensions*™ meets the high expectations of the NGSS and provides an effective three-dimensional learning experience for all students.

Program Advisors

Paul D. Asimow, PhD
Eleanor and John R. McMillan
Professor of Geology and
Geochemistry
California Institute of Technology
Pasadena, California

Joanne Bourgeois
Professor Emerita
Earth & Space Sciences
University of Washington
Seattle, WA

Dr. Eileen Cashman
Professor
Humboldt State University
Arcata, California

Elizabeth A. De Stasio, PhD
Raymond J. Herzog Professor of
Science
Lawrence University
Appleton, Wisconsin

Perry Donham, PhD
Lecturer
Boston University
Boston, Massachusetts

Shila Garg, PhD
Emerita Professor of Physics
Former Dean of Faculty & Provost
The College of Wooster
Wooster, Ohio

Tatiana A. Krivosheev, PhD
Professor of Physics
Clayton State University
Morrow, Georgia

Mark B. Moldwin, PhD
Professor of Space Sciences and
Engineering
University of Michigan
Ann Arbor, Michigan

Ross H. Nehm
Stony Brook University (SUNY)
Stony Brook, NY

Kelly Y. Neiles, PhD
Assistant Professor of Chemistry
St. Mary's College of Maryland
St. Mary's City, Maryland

John Nielsen-Gammon, PhD
Regents Professor
Department of Atmospheric
Sciences
Texas A&M University
College Station, Texas

Dr. Sten Odenwald
Astronomer
NASA Goddard Spaceflight Center
Greenbelt, Maryland

Bruce W. Schafer
Executive Director
Oregon Robotics Tournament &
Outreach Program
Beaverton, Oregon

Barry A. Van Deman
President and CEO
Museum of Life and Science
Durham, North Carolina

Kim Withers, PhD
Assistant Professor
Texas A&M University-Corpus
Christi
Corpus Christi, Texas

Adam D. Woods, PhD
Professor
California State University,
Fullerton
Fullerton, California

English Development Advisors

Mercy D. Momary
Local District Northwest
Los Angeles, California

Michelle Sullivan
Balboa Elementary
San Diego, California

Classroom Reviewers & Hands-On Activities Advisors

Julie Arreola
Sun Valley Magnet School
Los Angeles, California

Pamela Bluestein
Sycamore Canyon School
Newbury Park, California

Andrea Brown
HLPUSD Science & STEAM TOSA
Hacienda Heights, California

Stephanie Greene
Science Department Chair
Sun Valley Magnet School
Sun Valley, California

Rana Mujtaba Khan
Will Rogers High School
Van Nuys, California

Suzanne Kirkhope
Willow Elementary and Round
Meadow Elementary
Agoura Hills, California

George Kwong
Schafer Park Elementary
Hayward, California

Imelda Madrid
Bassett St. Elementary School
Lake Balboa, California

Susana Martinez O'Brien
Diocese of San Diego
San Diego, California

Craig Moss
Mt. Gleason Middle School
Sunland, California

Isabel Souto
Schafer Park Elementary
Hayward, California

Emily R.C.G. Williams
South Pasadena Middle School
South Pasadena, California

Contents

UNIT 1 Science and Engineering   1

Lesson 1 • Engineering, Science, and Society Are Related 4

Hands-On Lab Investigate a Technology Inspired by Nature 19

Lesson 2 • Engineer It: Defining Engineering Problems 26

Hands-On Lab Design a Model Car, Part 1 37

Lesson 3 • Engineer It: Developing and Testing Solutions 44

Hands-On Lab Design a Model Car, Part 2 54

Lesson 4 • Engineer It: Optimizing Solutions 62

Hands-On Lab Design a Model Car, Part 3 71

People in Science Ellen Ochoa, Electrical Engineer 73

Unit Review 79

ENGINEER IT Unit Performance Task 83

UNIT 2 Systems in Organisms and Earth   85

Lesson 1 • Models Help Scientists Study Natural Systems 88

Hands-On Lab Model Tissue Structure and Function 94

Lesson 2 • Cells Are Living Systems 108

Hands-On Lab Observe Cells with a Microscope 113

Hands-On Lab Use Cell Models to Investigate Cell Size 120

People in Science Lynn Margulis, Biologist 123

Lesson 3 • Plants Are Living Systems 128

Hands-On Lab Observe Transport 135

Lesson 4 • Animals Are Living Systems 144

Hands-On Lab Measure System Response to Exercise 150

Hands-On Lab Measure Reaction Time 159

Unit Review 167

ENGINEER IT Unit Performance Task 171

Stone/Getty Image; (b) ©Kotangens/Adobe Stock

v

Contents

UNIT 3 The Flow of Energy in Systems   173

Lesson 1 • Energy Flows and Causes Change 176

Hands-On Lab Investigate the Transfer of Energy 185

Lesson 2 • Heat Is a Flow of Energy 198

Hands-On Lab Compare Thermal Energy in Objects 204

Lesson 3 • Engineer It: Using Thermal Energy Transfer in Systems 216

Hands-On Lab Examine the Transfer of Thermal Energy through Radiation 222

Hands-On Lab Design and Test an Insulated Container 229

Careers in Engineering Energy Conservationist 231

Lesson 4 • Changes in Energy Drive the Water Cycle 236

Hands-On Lab Model the Formation of Clouds and Rain 243

Careers in Science Hydrologist 253

Unit Review 259

ENGINEER IT **Unit Performance Task** 263

Flash floods can occur suddenly after a heavy rainfall. A lot of energy is released during a flash flood.

Contents

UNIT 4 Weather and Climate   265

Lesson 1 • Air Moves in Patterns in Earth's Atmosphere 268

Hands-On Lab Model the Formation of Wind 271

Lesson 2 • Water Moves in Patterns in Earth's Oceans 288

Hands-On Lab Explore Density Differences in Water 295

Careers in Science   Physical Oceanographer 305

Lesson 3 • Interactions in Earth's Systems Cause Weather 310

Hands-On Lab Model an Air Mass Interaction 320

Lesson 4 • Weather Predictions Are Based on Patterns 332

Hands-On Lab Predict Costs Using a Model 337

People in Science   J. Marshall Shepherd, Meteorologist and Climatologist 345

Lesson 5 • Earth Has Different Regional Climates 350

Hands-On Lab Model Your Climate 363

Unit Review 373

ENGINEER IT   **Unit Performance Task** 377

Foggy summer mornings in San Francisco happen as water from the Pacific Ocean evaporates into the air and then condenses. Wind carries the foggy air over land.

vii

Contents

UNIT 5 Environmental and Genetic Influence on Organisms 379

Lesson 1 • Organisms Are Adapted to Their Environment 382

Hands-On Lab Compare the Drought Tolerance of Plants 389

People in Science Gary Bañuelos, Soil Scientist. 395

Lesson 2 • Organisms Inherit Traits from Their Parents 400

Hands-On Lab Model Genes and Traits. 406

People in Science Genetic Engineers 411

Lesson 3 • Reproduction Affects Genetic Diversity 416

Hands-On Lab Model Asexual and Sexual Reproduction. 426

Lesson 4 • The Environment and Genetics Affect Plant Survival 434

Hands-On Lab Investigate Flower Structures 443

Lesson 5 • The Environment and Genetics Affect Animal Survival 456

Hands-On Lab Model the Growth of an Animal 471

Unit Review 479

ENGINEER IT Unit Performance Task 483

This plumage display of a male bird of paradise attracts the female. With their needs met by the rich tropical rain forest, birds of paradise can spend extra time and energy on reproduction.

Contents

UNIT 6 Human Impacts on the Environment 485

Lesson 1 • Human Activities Cause Changes in the Environment 488

🖐 Hands-On Lab Model Ocean Pollution from Land 494

Lesson 2 • Human Activities Influence Climate Change 508

🖐 Hands-On Lab Model the Greenhouse Effect 512

People in Science Geeta G. Persad, Postdoctoral Research Scientist 527

Lesson 3 • Climate Change Affects the Survival of Organisms 532

🖐 Hands-On Lab Map Monarch Migration 540

People in Science Shayle Matsuda, Marine Biologist 547

Lesson 4 • Engineer It: Reducing Human Effects on the Environment 552

🖐 Hands-On Lab Design a Method to Monitor Solid Waste from a School 561

🖐 Hands-On Lab Evaluate a Method to Reduce the Impact of Solid Waste on the Environment 569

Unit Review 577

ENGINEER IT **Unit Performance Task** 581

A lot of plastic trash ends up in the oceans, where it affects many organisms, such as plankton, corals, fish, and whales.

Claims, Evidence, and Reasoning

Constructing an Argument

Constructing a strong argument is useful in science and engineering and in everyday life. A strong argument has three parts: a claim, evidence, and reasoning. Scientists and engineers use claims-evidence-reasoning arguments to communicate their explanations and solutions to others and to challenge or debate the conclusions of other scientists and engineers. The words *argue* and *argument* do not mean that scientists or engineers are fighting about something. Instead, this is a way to support a claim using evidence. Argumentation is a calm and rational way for people to examine all the facts and come to the best conclusion.

A **claim** is a statement that answers the question "What do you know?" A claim is a statement of your understanding of a phenomenon, answer to a question, or solution to a problem. A claim states what you think is true based on the information you have.

Evidence is any data that are related to your claim and answer the question "How do you know that?" These data may be from your own experiments and observations, reports by scientists or engineers, or other reliable data. Arguments made in science and engineering should be supported by empirical evidence. Empirical evidence is evidence that comes from observation or experiment.

Evidence used to support a claim should also be relevant and sufficient. Relevant evidence is evidence that is about the claim, and not about something else. Evidence is sufficient when there is enough evidence to fully support the claim.

Reasoning is the use of logical, analytical thought to form conclusions or inferences. Reasoning answers the question "Why does your evidence support your claim?" So, reasoning explains the relationship between your evidence and your claim. Reasoning might include a scientific law or principle that helps explain the relationship between the evidence and the claim.

Here is an example of a claims-evidence-reasoning argument.

Claim	Ice melts faster in the sun than it does in the shade.
Evidence	Two ice cubes of the same size were each placed in a plastic dish. One dish was placed on a wooden bench in the sun and one was placed on a different part of the same bench in the shade. The ice cube in the sun melted in 14 minutes and 32 seconds. The ice cube in the shade melted in 18 minutes and 15 seconds.
Reasoning	This experiment was designed so that the only variable that was different in the set-up of the two ice cubes was whether they were in the shade or in the sun. Because the ice cube in the sun melted almost 4 minutes faster than the one in the shade, this is sufficient evidence to say that ice melts faster in the sun than it does in the shade.

To summarize, a strong argument:

• presents a claim that is clear, logical, and well-defended
• supports the claim with empirical evidence that is sufficient and relevant
• includes reasons that make sense and are presented in a logical order

Constructing Your Own Argument

Now construct your own argument by recording a claim, evidence, and reasoning. With your teacher's permission, you can do an investigation to answer a question you have about how the world works. Or you can construct your argument based on observations you have already made about the world.

Claim	
Evidence	
Reasoning	

For more information on claims, evidence, and reasoning, see the online **English Language Arts Handbook.**

Whether you are in the lab or in the field, you are responsible for your own safety and the safety of others. To fulfill these responsibilities and avoid accidents, be aware of the safety of your classmates as well as your own safety at all times. Take your lab work and fieldwork seriously, and behave appropriately. Elements of safety to keep in mind are shown below and on the following pages.

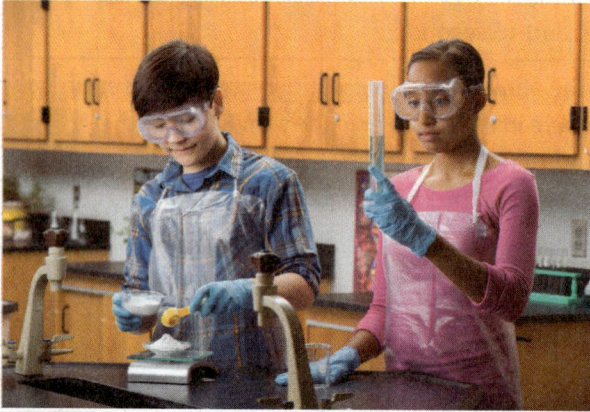

Safety in the Lab

- ☐ Be sure you understand the materials, your procedure, and the safety rules before you start an investigation in the lab.

- ☐ Know where to find and how to use fire extinguishers, eyewash stations, shower stations, and emergency power shutoffs.

- ☐ Use proper safety equipment. Always wear personal protective equipment, such as eye protection and gloves, when setting up labs, during labs, and when cleaning up.

- ☐ Do not begin until your teacher has told you to start. Follow directions.

- ☐ Keep the lab neat and uncluttered. Clean up when you are finished. Report all spills to your teacher immediately. Watch for slip/fall and trip/fall hazards.

- ☐ If you or another student are injured in any way, tell your teacher immediately, even if the injury seems minor.

- ☐ Do not take any food or drink into the lab. Never take any chemicals out of the lab.

Safety in the Field

- ☐ Be sure you understand the goal of your fieldwork and the proper way to carry out the investigation before you begin fieldwork.

- ☐ Use proper safety equipment and personal protective equipment, such as eye protection, that suits the terrain and the weather.

- ☐ Follow directions, including appropriate safety procedures as provided by your teacher.

- ☐ Do not approach or touch wild animals. Do not touch plants unless instructed by your teacher to do so. Leave natural areas as you found them.

- ☐ Stay with your group.

- ☐ Use proper accident procedures, and let your teacher know about a hazard in the environment or an accident immediately, even if the hazard or accident seems minor.

Safety Symbols

To highlight specific types of precautions, the following symbols are used throughout the lab program. Remember that no matter what safety symbols you see within each lab, all safety rules should be followed at all times.

Dress Code

- Wear safety goggles (or safety glasses as appropriate for the activity) at all times in the lab as directed. If chemicals get into your eye, flush your eyes immediately for a minimum of 15 minutes.
- Do not wear contact lenses in the lab.
- Do not look directly at the sun or any intense light source or laser.
- Wear appropriate protective non-latex gloves as directed.
- Wear an apron or lab coat at all times in the lab as directed.
- Tie back long hair, secure loose clothing, and remove loose jewelry. Remove acrylic nails when working with active flames.
- Do not wear open-toed shoes, sandals, or canvas shoes in the lab.

Glassware and Sharp Object Safety

- Do not use chipped or cracked glassware.
- Use heat-resistant glassware for heating or storing hot materials.
- Notify your teacher immediately if a piece of glass breaks.
- Use extreme care when handling any sharp or pointed instruments.
- Do not cut an object while holding the object unsupported in your hands. Place the object on a suitable cutting surface, and always cut in a direction away from your body.

Chemical Safety

- If a chemical gets on your skin, on your clothing, or in your eyes, rinse it immediately for a minimum of 15 minutes (using the shower, faucet, or eyewash station), and alert your teacher.
- Do not clean up spilled chemicals unless your teacher directs you to do so.
- Do not inhale any gas or vapor unless directed to do so by your teacher. If you are instructed to note the odor of a substance, wave the fumes toward your nose with your hand. This is called wafting. Never put your nose close to the source of the odor.
- Handle materials that emit vapors or gases in a well-ventilated area.
- Keep your hands away from your face while you are working on any activity.

Safety Symbols, continued

Electrical Safety

- Do not use equipment with frayed electrical cords or loose plugs.
- Do not use electrical equipment near water or when clothing or hands are wet.
- Hold the plug housing when you plug in or unplug equipment. Do not pull on the cord.
- Use only GFI-protected electrical receptacles.

Heating and Fire Safety

- Be aware of any source of flames, sparks, or heat (such as flames, heating coils, or hot plates) before working with any flammable substances.
- Know the location of the lab's fire extinguisher and fire-safety blankets.
- Know your school's fire-evacuation routes.
- If your clothing catches on fire, walk to the lab shower to put out the fire. Do not run.
- Never leave a hot plate unattended while it is turned on or while it is cooling.
- Use tongs or appropriately insulated holders when handling heated objects.
- Allow all equipment to cool before storing it.

Plant and Animal Safety

- Do not eat any part of a plant.
- Do not pick any wild plant unless your teacher instructs you to do so.
- Handle animals only as your teacher directs.
- Treat animals carefully and respectfully.
- Wash your hands throughly with soap and water after handling any plant or animal.

Cleanup

- Clean all work surfaces and protective equipment as directed by your teacher.
- Dispose of hazardous materials or sharp objects only as directed by your teacher.
- Wash your hands throughly with soap and water before you leave the lab or after any activity.

Student Safety Quiz

Circle the letter of the BEST answer.

1. Before starting an investigation or lab procedure, you should
   A. try an experiment of your own
   B. open all containers and packages
   C. read all directions and make sure you understand them
   D. handle all the equipment to become familiar with it

2. At the end of any activity you should
   A. wash your hands thoroughly with soap and water before leaving the lab
   B. cover your face with your hands
   C. put on your safety goggles
   D. leave hot plates switched on

3. If you get hurt or injured in any way, you should
   A. tell your teacher immediately
   B. find bandages or a first aid kit
   C. go to your principal's office
   D. get help after you finish the lab

4. If your glassware is chipped or broken, you should
   A. use it only for solid materials
   B. give it to your teacher for recycling or disposal
   C. put it back into the storage cabinet
   D. increase the damage so that it is obvious

5. If you have unused chemicals after finishing a procedure, you should
   A. pour them down a sink or drain
   B. mix them all together in a bucket
   C. put them back into their original containers
   D. dispose of them as directed by your teacher

6. If electrical equipment has a frayed cord, you should
   A. unplug the equipment by pulling the cord
   B. let the cord hang over the side of a counter or table
   C. tell your teacher about the problem immediately
   D. wrap tape around the cord to repair it

7. If you need to determine the odor of a chemical or a solution, you should
   A. use your hand to bring fumes from the container to your nose
   B. bring the container under your nose and inhale deeply
   C. tell your teacher immediately
   D. use odor-sensing equipment

8. When working with materials that might fly into the air and hurt someone's eye, you should wear
   A. goggles
   B. an apron
   C. gloves
   D. a hat

9. Before doing experiments involving a heat source, you should know the location of the
   A. door
   B. window
   C. fire extinguisher
   D. overhead lights

10. If you get chemicals in your eye you should
   A. wash your hands immediately
   B. put the lid back on the chemical container
   C. wait to see if your eye becomes irritated
   D. use the eyewash station right away, for a minimum of 15 minutes

Go online to view the Lab Safety Handbook for additional information.

Science and Engineering

How do humans explore and design our world?

Unit Project 2

Lesson 1   Science, Engineering, and Society Are Related 4

Lesson 2   Engineer It: Defining Engineering Problems 26

Lesson 3   Engineer It: Developing and Testing Solutions 44

Lesson 4   Engineer It: Optimizing Solutions 62

Unit Review 79

Unit Performance Task 83

This rocket car was developed and engineered for optimized speed. Each year people gather in Black Rock Desert, Nevada, to watch cars similar to this break the world land-speed record.

You Solve It How Can You Plan Efficient Cargo Shipping? Design an efficient way to deliver cars to two different ports by choosing the sizes of your ships, their shipping routes, and the size of your shipments.

Go online and complete the You Solve It to explore ways to solve a real-world problem.

Optimize a Race Track

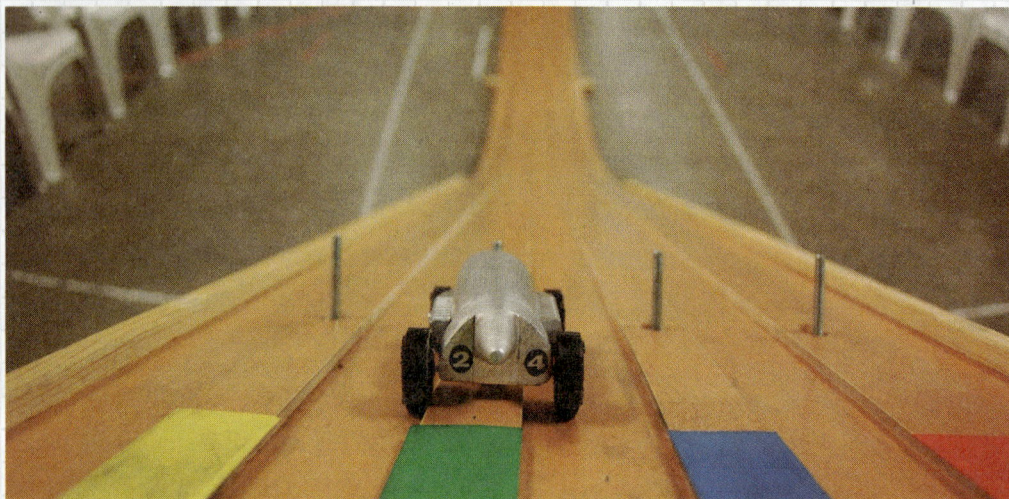

This wooden track is designed to keep the model race cars moving in a straight line.

A. Look at the photo. On a separate sheet of paper, write down as many different questions as you can about the photo.

B. **Discuss** With your class or a partner, share your questions. Record any additional questions generated in your discussion. Then choose the most important questions from the list that are related to designing, testing, and improving a track design. Write them below.

C. Choose a feature of the track you can test to see if and how it influences the speed of cars that use the track. Remember, in any iteration of the track, the finish line needs to be lower than the starting point, as the cars depend on the force of gravity to move them. What design feature of the track, or variable, will you investigate?

D. Use the information above, and your research, to develop a solution that will improve the speed of cars on the track.

Discuss the next steps for your Unit Project with your teacher and go online to download the Unit Project Worksheet.

Language Development

Use the lessons in this unit to complete the network and expand your understanding of these key concepts.

🟦	Similar term
🟩	Phrase
🟧	Cognate
🟨	Example
🟥	Definition

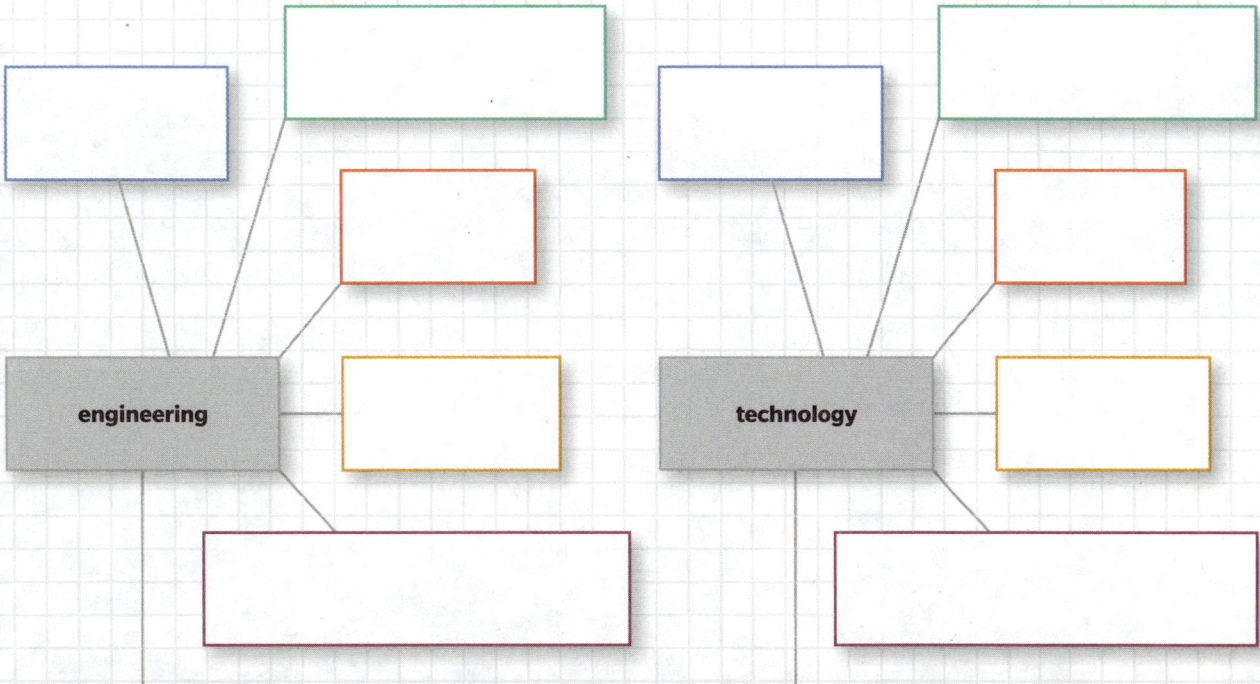

engineering

technology

How do humans explore and design our world?

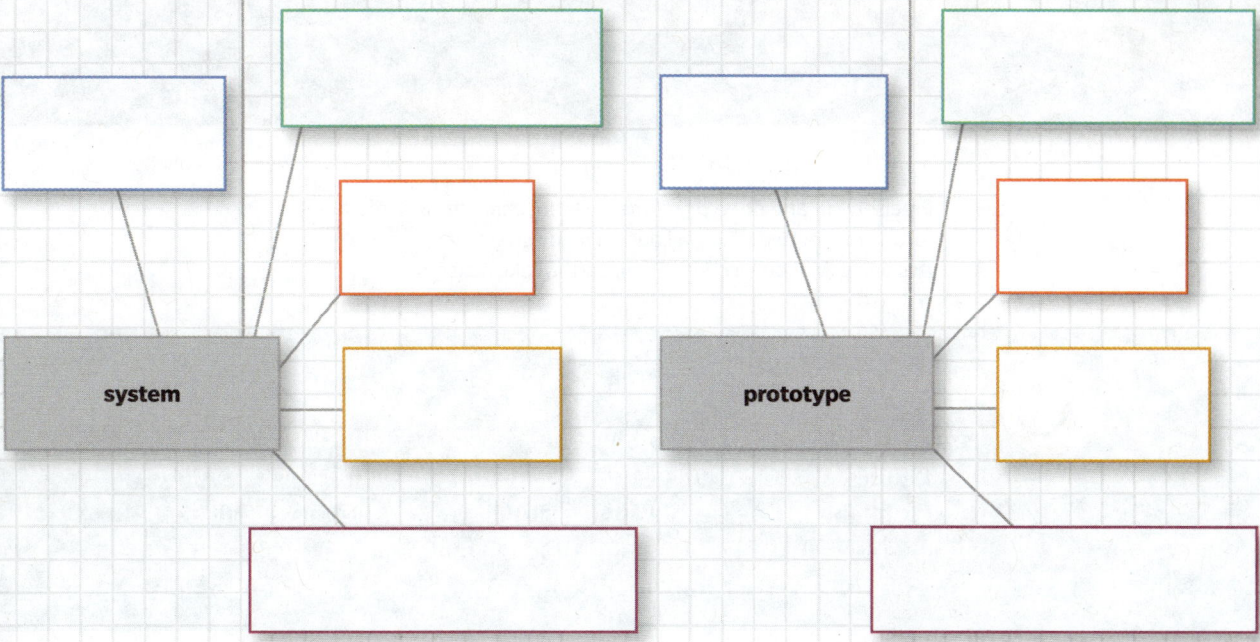

system

prototype

Engineering, Science, and Society Are Related

Precisely cut and fitted dry stone walls are characteristic of Incan architecture. The wall design made structures, such as this one in Machu Picchu in Peru, earthquake resistant.

Explore First

Comparing Wall Structures Model several rectangular bricks out of modeling clay. Construct a small wall using half of the bricks. Sculpt the remaining bricks so they fit in a similar way to the carved, fitted stones shown in the photo. Then, construct a wall with these bricks. How can you test the stability of each wall? Which one is more stable?

Go online to view the digital version of the Hands-On Lab for this lesson and to download additional lab resources.

CAN YOU EXPLAIN IT?

What needs influenced the development of mosquito netting?

Insecticide-treated mosquito nets help prevent the spread of malaria in developing countries. Malaria is spread by mosquito bites. The nets must meet the needs of the people who use them.

1. Does the solution to an engineering problem have to address every need of its users? Explain your answer.

2. Does a successful engineered solution to a problem have to be electronic? Explain your answer.

EVIDENCE NOTEBOOK As you explore the lesson, gather evidence to explain the needs that would influence the development of mosquito netting.

Relating Science, Engineering, and Technology

Science is the study of phenomena. It is a search for explanations of events, processes, or objects based on logic and evidence. Scientific discoveries help explain systems and phenomena. Engineering is related to science. **Engineering** is the systematic practice of solving problems with designed solutions. Solutions designed and built by engineers are examples of technology. **Technology** is any tool, process, or system that is designed to solve a problem. The designed world includes all parts of the environment that were made by people. You are surrounded by the designed world. You depend on it. The designed world exists within the natural world.

Explore Online

A volcanologist walks near the vent of an active volcano. Lava can range in temperature from 700 °C–1,250 °C (approximately 1,200 °F–2,200 °F).

3. **Discuss** Together with a partner, review the photo above. This scientist is using several engineered items to carry out his or her research. What are some of the items, and what might their purpose be?

Scientists Use Engineered Tools to Explore the Natural World

Scientific discoveries help increase our understanding of the world around us. Scientists often rely on engineered tools, such as computers and measuring devices, to carry out research. These tools "extend" our senses and abilities. They allow us to sense and process events that would otherwise be invisible to us. For example, telescopes allow us to study phenomena that are too far away for human eyes to see. Computers quickly carry out calculations that would take a human brain much longer to do.

Many phenomena are difficult to observe directly. Engineers may design materials and systems to aid scientific study. For example, special clothing, vehicles, and breathing devices allow scientists to stay underwater to study aquatic life. Satellites collect images and other data from great heights above Earth's surface. Microscopes visualize objects that are too small for the human eye to see. Advances in engineering such as these have greatly changed scientific exploration.

Scientists Rely on Technology

Technology is all around us. It is needed in schools, homes, stores, and communities. We all depend on technology. Many different tools are used in scientific investigations.

Glassware has many uses in the lab. Glassmaking is a very old technology. The earliest examples of glass date back to about 3000 BCE.

Digital scales are used to measure weight. Digital scales were first developed in the 1940s–1950s. Mechanical scales have been used for thousands of years.

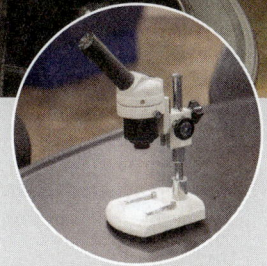

Light microscopes are used to see objects too small for human eyes to see. They were first developed in the 1590s.

4. What are the basic scientific principles the engineers who designed the digital scales would have needed to understand to design this tool? Choose all that apply.

   A. electric currents

   B. physical properties of metals

   C. influence of gravitational force on objects

   D. physical and chemical properties of materials used in building circuits

5. Identify two tools in the lab classroom: one that is used to measure volume and another that is used to observe objects. How would not having those tools affect your ability to carry out lab assignments?

To build cars, engineers must have a strong understanding of science and math principles that relate to cars, such as:

human anatomy and physiology, to design safe and comfortable interiors and exteriors.

forces and energy, to understand the effects of gravity, friction, and collision forces on cars and the materials of which they are made.

aerodynamics, including thrust and drag, to design sleek and efficient car bodies.

energy transmission by waves, for functioning of radio, interactive screens, and wireless software.

Engineers Use Science to Solve Practical Problems

Before a solution can be developed, the problem itself must be accurately defined. This can be done by identifying precisely what the solution needs to do. For example, the request that a car horn be "loud" is not precise. "Loud" is not a measurable value. However, "a car horn that is 95 decibels" is a more precise design description that will help engineers develop a better product.

Imagine a team of engineers working to design a new car for a car manufacturer. The car has to meet certain safety requirements and the needs of the market, and not be too expensive to manufacture. Consumer safety laws require car makers to build safe cars for their customers. The engineers might like to build a car that can reach high speeds, and customers might like that too. However, if the design of a car makes it dangerous, the car would have difficulty meeting safety laws.

In order to evaluate different car designs and materials, the design team needs to apply knowledge of many scientific principles. Qualities such as the physical properties, chemical properties, and the strength of materials are tested. In this way, engineers depend on science to develop new technologies. Discoveries made by scientists can also inspire engineers. For example, carbon fiber was discovered by a scientist studying the physical properties of carbon. Carbon fiber is made from long strands of carbon atoms that are woven together. It is light, strong, and resists high temperatures. These properties made carbon fiber suitable for use in cars and car parts.

6. Use the word bank to complete the table below by identifying the type of design concern that each question addresses. Some of the questions may address more than one engineering concern.

- resource availability
- environmental concerns
- safety concerns
- production costs
- consumer demands

Question	Type of Design Concern
How can chemical pollutants emitted by the car be minimized?	environmental concerns
How can the supply of steel and other raw materials be obtained for the best price?	
How do different parts of the car withstand collisions?	
How can reliable wireless connectivity be added to the car design?	

Solve a Food Storage Problem

The modern canning process was developed in the early 19th century as a safe way to preserve, store, and transport food while minimizing spoilage. Canning was originally developed to feed an army, but it was quickly adapted for nonmilitary purposes. A preservation method that minimized the number of harmful microbes in the food, kept it relatively tasty, and made it easy to store and transport was a need society had too, and canned food was an answer. Canned foods remain fresh for much longer than fresh foods. Before refrigeration was common, canned foods were in great demand as a way of keeping food at home. Modern canning is made possible by applying knowledge of many sciences, including biology, chemistry, and physics, to a real-life problem. Cans also created the need for another engineered object: the can opener!

Canning technology has many parts.

1. Sealing the cans to make them air tight.

2. Making the cans tough enough to withstand knocks and bumps.

3. Heating the foods to high enough temperatures to kill harmful microbes.

4. Ensuring that material from the can doesn't dissolve into the food.

5. Designing the lids and bottoms of the cans so they are easy to stack.

7. Many modern can designs include a ring pull that allows the lid to be pulled off by hand instead of cut off with a can opener. What need might have led to such a design change?

_____

_____

_____

_____

_____

_____

Harcourt

Analyzing Systems and Models

Scientists and engineers work with systems. A **system** is a set of parts, or *components*, that interact. A video game system includes game controls with computer graphics and sound. Your immune system helps your body fight disease. Some systems are natural. Other systems are engineered, or designed by people. Scientists study natural and designed systems to understand how they function, while engineers design or improve systems to solve problems. The lock and dam shown below is a system that engineers designed to help boats travel up and down rivers with large slopes.

The Parts of a System

Systems are made up of parts, or *components*. They may be made up of smaller *subsystems*, such as the movable dam gates in the example below. The gate subsystem is made up of strong metal doors and the motors that move them. Systems also have *inputs*, *processes*, and *outputs*. Boats are one of the inputs to the lock and dam system. They move into it, then move out of it at a different level. Systems also have *boundaries*. The boundaries of the lock and dam system are the gates that separate it from the river.

A Simplified Lock and Dam System

Explore Online

This engineered system has solved transportation problems for hundreds of years.

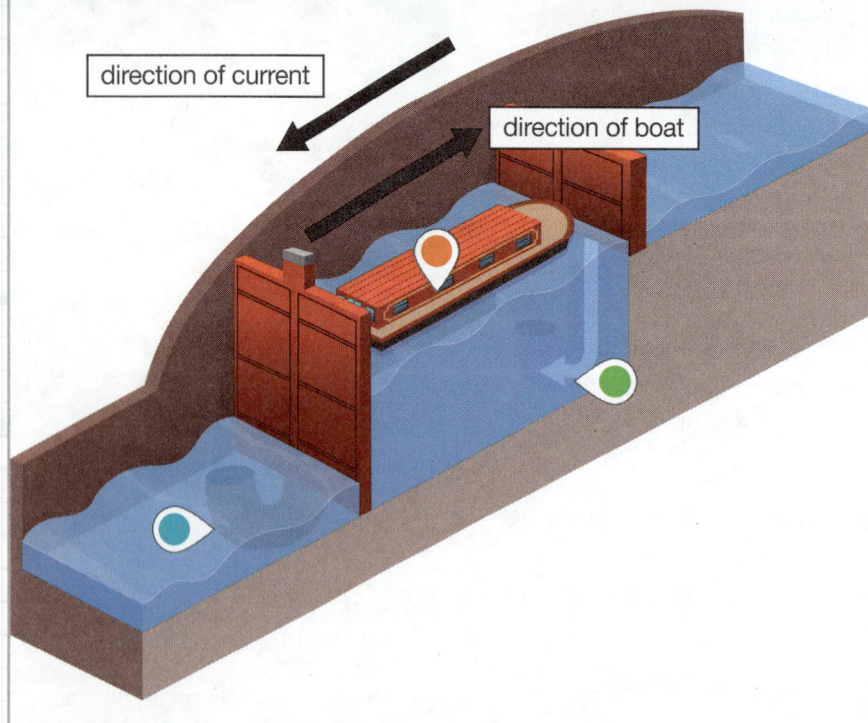

direction of current

direction of boat

🟠 A boat enters the lock system when the gate is open. Once the gate is closed behind the vessel, water is pumped into the lock through the filling valve. This causes the water level in the lock to rise.

🟢 Filling valves also release water from a lock to lower the water level. Lowering the water level in the lock allows the vessel to move smoothly downstream.

🔵 When a vessel is moving upstream, water is added to the lock by the filling valve to equal the upstream water level. This allows the vessel to travel upstream against the direction of the current.

8. Fill in the blanks to best complete the following statements.

The lock and dam together form a(n) _____ with _____ at the higher and lower river levels. Water moving through the lock starts as a(n) _____ and ends as a(n) _____.

WORD BANK
- system
- boundaries
- output
- input

System Models

Systems and their interactions can be very complex. Scientists and engineers often rely on models and simulations to better understand and predict the behavior of systems. A scientific model shows the structure of an object, system, or concept. Simulations use models to imitate the function, behavior, or process under different conditions.

Engineers use system models to explore how a designed system works. They may also discover what might be going wrong in a system. Investigating a system model is usually safer, less expensive, and easier than carrying out investigations on the real-world system. For example, carrying out earthquake tests on scaled-down building models is much cheaper, easier, and safer than carrying out tests on a full-scale building. Testing scale models like this can help identify potential problems with structural designs or materials.

Two scale models of buildings are tested on a shake table. One of the models is of an earthquake resistant design.

9. Do the Math Though models and simulations have many benefits, some factors or conditions must be approximated. Others cannot be reasonably included at all.

Imagine you are an engineer who needs to test a scale model of a footbridge. It will be a $\frac{1}{20}$ scale model. The footbridge will cross over a busy road and allow people to cross the road safely. How could a relatively small design error of 2 centimeters in the model system cause a significant problem in construction of the bridge?

Different Models Meet Different Needs

Different types of models allow scientists and engineers to test ideas and find solutions to difficult problems. A physical model represents the physical structure of an object or system. Physical models often look and work like the object or system they represent. Mathematical models are made up of numbers and equations. These models can often be shown as graphs and may be used to predict future trends. A conceptual or mental model is a way of thinking about how parts of a system are related in order to simplify complex relationships. Some computer models are like physical models in that they show the physical structure of an object. Other computer models are more like mathematical models.

The proportions, scale, and quantities used in a model must reflect the real-life object or system. For example, in modeling the piers and beams of a bridge, the scaled-down models must have the same proportions as the full-scale bridge. If not, the data collected while testing the model will not be valid. Models are also useful to run scenarios that would be impossible to test in real life, such as what may happen if Earth's temperature increased by 10 °C.

🔖 **EVIDENCE NOTEBOOK**

10. Keeping mosquitoes away from people is one of the needs mosquito netting should address. What type(s) of models might be useful in testing a solution to that need? Record your evidence.

Evaluate Benefits of Crash Testing

Seat belts and airbags are two technologies that have been demonstrated to be effective in crash simulations. These simulations, or crash tests, use physical, full-size models of cars, drivers, and passengers. They are very expensive to conduct, so a lot of data is gathered during these tests to make them worthwhile. Automotive crash tests and the data collected from them have led to stricter safety guidelines for car manufacturers. This has reduced injuries in car accidents over time.

👉 **Explore Online**

11. What are the benefits of crash tests? Select all that apply.

   A. They do not put people in danger.

   B. They allow engineers to test new designs.

   C. The type and speed of the crash can be controlled.

   D. There is very little cost in performing the test.

12. What solutions would you propose to a car manufacturer if its car rated poorly in a crash test?

   _____

   _____

   _____

Analyzing Influences on Technology

Technology helps people to meet needs such as food, shelter, and clothing. The ways we communicate, play, and move from place to place are also shaped by technology. The bicycle is an example of a technology that has changed over time, for several reasons. Many bike design changes resulted from safety concerns, ease of use, or society's demands and needs. For example, societal changes such as the increasing independence of women led to the development of "safety bicycles." These bikes were designed to be safer and easier to ride than the large-wheeled penny farthings. The increased popularity of safety bikes caused a "bicycle craze" in the 1890s.

Influences on Bike Design

Today's bicycles are products of many changes over time. Each design change solved a problem that was present in previous designs.

1817

The earliest bicycles, such as the draisine, were made of wood and did not have pedals, brakes, a chain, or adjustable seats. They were designed to be propelled by the user pushing his or her feet off the ground.

1890s

Safety concerns about the awkward penny farthing led to the development of safety bicycles. These bikes had chains, gears, brakes, and air-filled tires, which allowed for easier steering and pedaling and increased comfort.

1960s–1970s

Increasing interest in exercise influenced the design of road bikes, BMX roadsters, mountain bikes, and commuter bikes.

1870s

The penny farthing had a large front wheel and a tiny rear wheel. They moved when the rider pushed on pedals that were attached directly to the large front wheel. The seat of the bike was quite high off the ground. The bike did not have brakes. It was difficult to steer and pedal, and remaining balanced was difficult. Cyclists often fell off and got hurt.

Today

Materials technology has advanced so much that some bicycles are made of wood and bamboo— a return to materials the earliest bikes were made of!

13. In 1887, a Scottish vet named John Boyd Dunlop designed an air-filled bike tire after his son had difficulty learning to ride a tricycle with hard rubber tires. This is an example of a technology being inspired by a(n) *societal* / *individual* need.

Scientific Understanding Influences Technology

Scientific discoveries result in new kinds of technology. One modern example of this can be seen in the development of computer technology. Computing advanced rapidly in the 20th century. These advances were due to improved scientific understanding of such things as electric circuits and the physical properties of materials called semiconductors. The components used to control the flow of electric current in computers are now much smaller and more efficient than the large components used in the earliest computers. Over time, computers became smaller, faster, and more efficient because their components were made smaller, faster, and more efficient. Today's computers process data more rapidly and are able to share data more easily than earlier computers.

The earliest computers, such as this UNIVAC 1103, were very large and expensive. They were often the size of a room. They were mostly used by the government and military to perform complex calculations from large amounts of data.

Modern computers are thousands of times faster and have far more memory than the earliest household computers. Although the Internet was originally developed for scientists, people now use it for everyday activities.

14. List one positive influence and one negative influence that computers have on society.

15. Write What would happen if every piece of technology around you were to disappear?

The Environment Influences Technology

The environment has influenced the development of technologies for thousands of years. For example, archaeologists found evidence that early farmers developed ways to capture rainwater to irrigate their crops. People living in cold climates drove the development of heating technologies, while people living in hot climates drove the development of air conditioning. The presence of fast-flowing rivers led to the development of hydroelectric power. The understanding that burning fossil fuels is changing climates has led to the development of wind turbines and solar cells, which help generate electrical energy without the use of fossil fuels.

Society Influences Technology

Technology is everywhere. Technology is an important part of modern life. Humans have been engineering solutions to practical problems for a long time. The earliest forms of technology, such as lighting fire, spears, cutting tools, and clothing, helped people gather food efficiently and stay warm. The basic needs for food, shelter, safety, and warmth influenced the development of many technologies, and still do today.

Some modern technologies, such as snack foods, continue to be developed due to consumer interests or wants rather than needs. Consumer demand for watching movies on their phones has led to the design of phones with larger screens and the development of faster online streaming services. Many other technologies have been developed in response to changing attitudes and cultural norms.

For example, social awareness of the needs of people with physical disabilities has increased over time. Current laws require that schools, public transport, and living spaces be accessible to people who use wheelchairs and other assistive devices. Such requirements have led to the development of different assistive technologies such as chairlifts, showering benches, and assistive listening devices.

Laws that affect the mining and processing of materials can influence technology. Environmental laws such as the U.S. Clean Air Act and the Clean Water Act limit the amount of pollution that can be produced during manufacturing processes. Safety and health laws limit employees' exposure to hazardous conditions that could happen during mining or manufacturing processes.

16. In the 1970s, the U.S. Environmental Protection Agency put limits on vehicle emissions because pollution from vehicle exhausts was linked to human diseases. As a result, car makers had to develop technologies that reduced pollutants in vehicle exhausts. What limit to technology does this situation represent? Choose all that apply.

   A. a social change that resulted in a natural change

   B. a new technology that was informed by a scientific finding

   C. a change in the law that resulted in society limiting technology

   D. a technological change that resulted in a scientific discovery

Consumer demand for more interactive entertainment has influenced the size of TV screens and the development of smart TV technology.

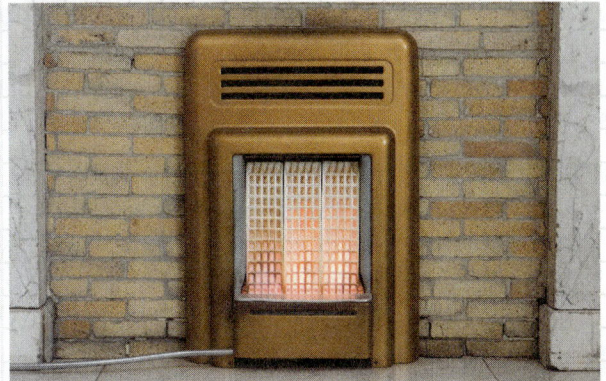

Unvented gas space heaters were once commonly built into new homes. They have been banned in most U.S. states due to the risk of carbon monoxide poisoning.

Indoor bathrooms were once a luxury. Before the early 20th century, homes did not usually have toilets. People used outdoor toilets in small sheds called outhouses.

EVIDENCE NOTEBOOK

17. Mosquitoes that spread diseases such as malaria are more common in climates that are very warm. How would the climate of an area affect the design of a mosquito net to be used there? Record your evidence.

Language SmArts
Identify Influences on Technology

Transportation is a vital part of modern life. But meeting the transportation needs of a community can be difficult. Extreme landscapes, rough terrain, and the need to preserve sensitive ecosystems all add to that challenge. Bridges, railways, and roads are transportation systems that require careful engineering. These technologies must meet complex environmental, physical, and societal needs, from minimizing the impact on the environment to maximizing the safety for users of the roadways. Civil engineers who design roadways consider factors such as material availability, motorist safety, and the effects of the structures and road system on wildlife.

The invention of different technologies influenced the design of roadways over time. Bicycles, asphalt, concrete, steel, cars, expanding business markets, and laws have all influenced the design of roads in different ways.

Dirt roads once connected many American cities. These paths, originally designed for traveling on foot, by horse, or by stagecoach, were simple to make and maintain, but could quickly become uneven, muddy, or dangerous.

Highways allow billions of vehicles to travel across great distances. Modern highway systems are also impressive feats of civil engineering. The U.S. highway system was one of the largest engineering projects ever built in the country.

18. Many factors have driven the development of roadway technology throughout history. What factor do you think likely had the greatest influence? Would you describe it as a social, scientific, or environmental factor? Use what you have read in this lesson to support your claim.

_____

_____

_____

_____

_____

_____

Assessing the Impact of Technology on Society

Technology and Society Affect Each Other

The development of a technology does not guarantee its widespread use. A community's values and environmental conditions play a role in determining which technologies are developed and used. As shown below, identifying the effect of technology on society calls for an understanding of social and environmental factors.

Water Supply Infrastructure

● Processes for supplying water to a community can differ depending on the abundance and quality of water in the region.

● People in a community may have different expectations of the water supplied to their homes. Is it safe? Is it free of harmful organisms? Does it contain harmful substances? These expectations may change over time, or vary from person to person.

● Town and cities in dry or hot climates may have higher water needs than towns or cities in wet, rainy climates. For example, in dry climates, more water may be needed for growing crops and gardens.

● The cost of repairing or replacing an existing water supply network is an important factor in maintaining access to clean water for residents. A technology is not useful to a community that cannot afford to purchase, maintain, or repair it.

19. How does climate most likely affect the water distribution system?

   A. If the area has a dry climate, water resources are likely to be limited or need to be pumped from farther away.

   B. If the area has a dry climate, people will need less water.

   C. If the area has a dry climate, the community cannot afford to replace cracked or rusted pipes.

   D. If the area has a dry climate, people in the community are more concerned about contamination of the water supply.

Technology Can Improve Quality of Life

Technology helps people accomplish everyday tasks. Technology allows people to travel by land, air, and sea, and to communicate with others all over the world. Medical technology has made many diseases easier to control or even cure. For example, controlling diabetes with medicine was once thought to be impossible, and organ transplants were experimental technologies. Today, both type of treatments are commonplace.

Assistive and adaptive technology plays a very important role in helping people in their daily lives. This type of technology includes devices such as hearing aids, wheelchairs, and titanium rods used to set broken bones. Other examples include devices that replace damaged or lost limbs, help keep hearts beating with a regular rhythm, and focus blurry vision.

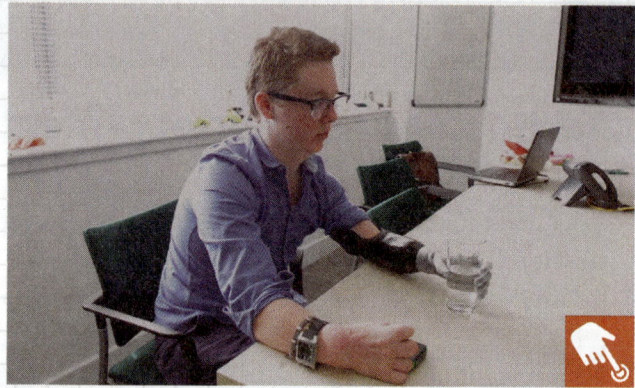

Some prosthetics have electrodes that connect to a person's nerves. These devices are controlled by the user's brain.

20. Identify the human needs that are addressed by the technologies listed in the table.

Technology	Issue to be addressed
hearing aid	
wheelchair	
glasses	
medicine	

21. Name two benefits that a modern electronic prosthetic device might have over an older, nonelectronic one.

EVIDENCE NOTEBOOK

22. Mosquito netting is most commonly used in developing countries. It is relatively cheap to make and is often distributed for free. What societal needs would demand that a tool be inexpensive to make or to buy? Record your evidence.

Investigate a Technology Inspired by Nature

Investigate a design problem that was solved with a nature-inspired solution, and identify a need that could also be met by a nature-inspired solution.

Biomimicry is the design and use of tools or solutions that copy natural structures or processes. For example, in 1941, a Swiss engineer named George de Mestral noticed that burs got stuck in his dog's fur and in his own clothes. De Mestral was very curious about what made them so "sticky." He viewed the burs under a microscope. What he saw inspired him to invent a hook-and-loop fastener he called Velcro®. In this investigation, you will observe the structure of burs to see how it influences their function and how they inspired such a useful tool.

Cockleburs produce a fruit called a bur, which contains seeds. Burs are covered in tiny hooks that attach to animals' fur, which helps disperse the seeds.

Procedure

STEP 1 Obtain a bur and square of fun fur. Take turns observing how the bur sticks to the fun fur.

STEP 2 Observe the bur and the fur, using the magnifying lens. Describe their structure in the first column of the table.

MATERIALS
- artificial animal fur (fun fur)
- cocklebur fruit (bur)
- hook-and-loop fastener
- magnifying lens

	Structure	Function
Bur and fur		
Hook-and-loop fastener		

STEP 3 In the second column of the table, describe how the bur's structure affects its function.

STEP 4 Observe the hook-and-loop fastener, using the magnifying lens the same way.

STEP 5 Identify a different need that could be solved by a nature-inspired solution.

Analysis

STEP 6 What features of your chosen object or process make it suitable to solve the problem or need you identified?

Analyze the Impact of a Technology on Society

Some types of technology have had a greater impact on society than others. Agriculture is one area in which technological advancements have had far-reaching effects. Agricultural technologies have increased the amount of food that can be grown per acre. Growing the same amount of crops but using less space means fewer existing habitats need to be cleared to make space for farmland to feed growing human populations. The areas of land that are being farmed are far more productive than they used to be. This is due to improvements in things such as plant breeding, soil preparation, harvesting, storage, and transportation.

Global Wheat Production and Area of Land Harvested from 1961 to 2014

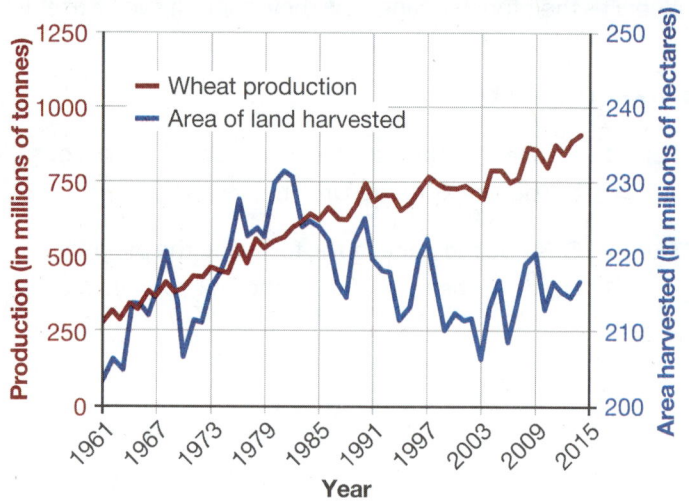

Credit: Adapted from *Global wheat production*, 1961–2014 from http://www.fao.org/faostat/en/#data/QC. Copyright © 2017 by Food and Agriculture Organization of the United Nations. Adapted and reproduced by permission of Food and Agriculture Organization of the United Nations.

23. From 1979 to 2014, the amount of wheat harvested worldwide
    decreased / increased / stayed relatively constant while the area
    of land use decreased / increased / stayed relatively constant.

24. The human population is projected to increase by 1 billion people by 2044. How will an increased demand on resources affect the need for agricultural engineering?

_____

_____

_____

_____

_____

_____

_____

_____

Continue Your Exploration

Name: _____   Date: _____

Check out the path below or go online to choose one of the other paths shown.

Designing an Efficient Lunch Line

- **Careers in Engineering**
- **Hands-On Labs** 🖐
- **Propose Your Own Path**

Go online to choose one of these other paths.

In many situations, the solution to an engineering problem is not an object or tool but a process or a system. For example, consider a cafeteria lunch line. A school lunch line is a process that is designed to serve meals to hundreds of people in a relatively short period of time.

Examine the Needs to Be Met

This is probably a familiar sight: the school cafeteria. Have you ever thought about all the steps that go into preparing and serving school lunches every school day? The food must be transported, prepared, cooked, and served to many people. Ingredients must be monitored for freshness and nutritional content. And the meals should taste good too!

Define the Problem

Suppose that you have been challenged to improve the efficiency of your school's cafeteria. Think about the cafeteria as a system. Identify the key people, processes, and technologies that keep it running. Then, think like an engineer by asking specific questions that will help you define the design problem you will address.

Angeles Times/Getty Images

Continue Your Exploration

Developing Solutions by First Asking Questions

Asking very specific questions about the problem or issue you are trying to solve will help you identify the problem. Identifying the problem precisely will help you come up with more or better solutions. Asking questions will also help you identify the important and nonimportant factors of the problem. For example, asking, "How many people use the cafeteria each day?", "What are the most popular meals and foods the cafeteria serves?", or "How long is the average wait for food on the busiest day?" will help you pinpoint possible problems that you can work toward solving.

1. What needs are not being met by a slow-moving or busy line at a school cafeteria?

2. Identify the people, processes, and technologies that play a role in the issue you identified. Now, identify a factor that is *unlikely* to influence the length of time people wait in the lunch line.

3. Identify one change in the cafeteria process that might make the lunch line more efficient.

4. **Collaborate** Serving fresh, nutritious food to several hundred people every day in a cafeteria is a design challenge. How might nutrition science and engineering affect each other?

Can You Explain It?

Name: _____   Date: _____

What needs influenced the development of mosquito netting?

> **EVIDENCE NOTEBOOK**
>
> Refer to your notes in your Evidence Notebook to help you construct an explanation of the needs that influenced development of mosquito netting.

1. State your claim. Make sure your claim fully explains how the needs you mention are related to the development of mosquito netting as a solution to the spread of disease.

2. Summarize the evidence you have gathered to support your claim and explain your reasoning.

All of Us/Corbis

Checkpoints

Answer the following questions to check your understanding of the lesson.

Use the photo to answer Questions 3 and 4.

3. What need is addressed by the simple technology the girl in the photo is using?

   A. keeping hair untangled

   B. keeping teeth healthy

   C. maintaining a clean home

   D. determining what programs are showing on television

4. A *positive / negative* impact this technology could have on society is that it makes it *easier / more difficult* for people to avoid costly and painful dental problems.

Use the diagram to answer Questions 5 and 6.

5. What information does this model of a water infrastructure provide?

   A. the flow of the system's inputs and outputs

   B. the number of people the system can support

   C. how the system would perform in a flood

6. What positive impact(s) will the construction of this water infrastructure have on the town for which it is built? Select all that apply.

   A. provide a clean and reliable water supply

   B. decrease the precipitation in the mountains

   C. create more jobs for people in the town

   D. prevent the river from flooding

7. A toothbrush is an example of a technology. Which of the following are important criteria for choosing a material for the bristles? Choose all that apply.

   A. The material comes in fashionable colors.

   B. The material is flexible and able to withstand wear.

   C. The material is able to support a large amount of weight.

   D. The material is nontoxic.

8. Which of the following is a form of technology?

   A. a lollipop stick

   B. a city park

   C. a public transit system

   D. a television

Interactive Review

Complete this section to review the main concepts of the lesson.

Scientists and engineers rely on technology to study phenomena and develop solutions to engineering problems.

A. Explain how engineering and science are related.

The concept of natural and engineered systems, and models of such systems, allow scientists and engineers to study how the natural and designed worlds operate.

B. Why can models of systems represent only certain aspects of the system under study? Explain your answer.

The use of technology is influenced by factors such as scientific discoveries, cultural values, and economic conditions.

C. Identify how scientific discoveries may influence the development and use of a technology.

Small-scale and large-scale technologies can improve quality of life.

D. Give an example of how a large-scale, technology-based industry such as agriculture has benefited society.

Defining Engineering Problems

Trebuchets were medieval weapons designed to hurl objects weighing 100 kilograms a distance of up to 300 meters. Their design was based on the sling.

Explore First

Exploring the Design Process   What might you do if your teacher handed you craft sticks, rubber bands, glue, and string, and asked you to build a working model of the trebuchets shown in the photo? What questions would you need to ask before starting the project?

Go online to view the digital version of the Hands-On Lab for this lesson and to download additional lab resources.

CAN YOU EXPLAIN IT?

How does the purpose of a treehouse affect how you would design and build it?

Before you start to build a treehouse, you have to figure out what structural design will allow it to serve the purpose you need it to as well as what resources you have available to you.

1. What are some questions that you might need to ask as you plan and design your treehouse?

2. Is "having access to a tree" an important factor in planning and building a treehouse? Why or why not? Explain your answer.

EVIDENCE NOTEBOOK As you explore the lesson, gather information to help explain how the treehouse's purpose is related to its design and construction.

Solving a Design Problem

Engineers use scientific principles and knowledge to address practical problems. The engineering process begins when a problem, need, or desire is identified. Scientists and engineers work to develop a solution to the problem, need, or desire. Engineering problems can be as small as designing a new type of pen or as large as designing and building a spacecraft to explore Mars. The solution can be an object, a process, or even a system involving many tools and processes.

Indoor open fires release harmful products such as soot and carbon monoxide into the air. People in the home then breathe these in, which can cause diseases.

3. **Discuss** Look carefully at the photo. What needs are suggested by the photo?

Engineering Begins with a Problem, a Need, or a Desire

The way people in developing countries cook food and warm their homes is a practice that often leads to serious health problems. In much of the developing world, people cook food over open fires or open stoves inside their homes. These stoves are usually poorly ventilated, which causes the fuel to burn incompletely. The fires and stoves do not usually have chimneys or stovepipes to remove smoke from the home. People who live in the house are exposed to smoke and gases from the fire. Gases, smoke, and soot from the fires cause illness and lead to the death of millions of people each year. There is a need to find practical ways to decrease this harmful exposure. Millions of lives could be saved each year. This is an example of a need that could be solved through an engineering solution.

4. To help guide an engineer to develop a safe way to meet this person's needs, identify a problem in this situation.

Questions Help Define the Engineering Problem

To develop a solution, the engineering problem must first be carefully defined. Engineers ask questions about the need. Then they conduct research to help form a precise definition of the engineering problem. For example, addressing the large-scale health problem of open fires and open stoves in the developing world requires precisely identifying the parts of the social and physical systems in which the problem occurs. Questions that help to develop a solution will also identify the systems in which the problem exists as well as other factors, including:

- the individuals or groups that are affected by the problem
- the scientific issues relevant to the problem
- potential impacts of solutions on the environment and society
- the cost-effectiveness of the design process and availability of resources
- the economic realities of the people for whom the solution will be developed

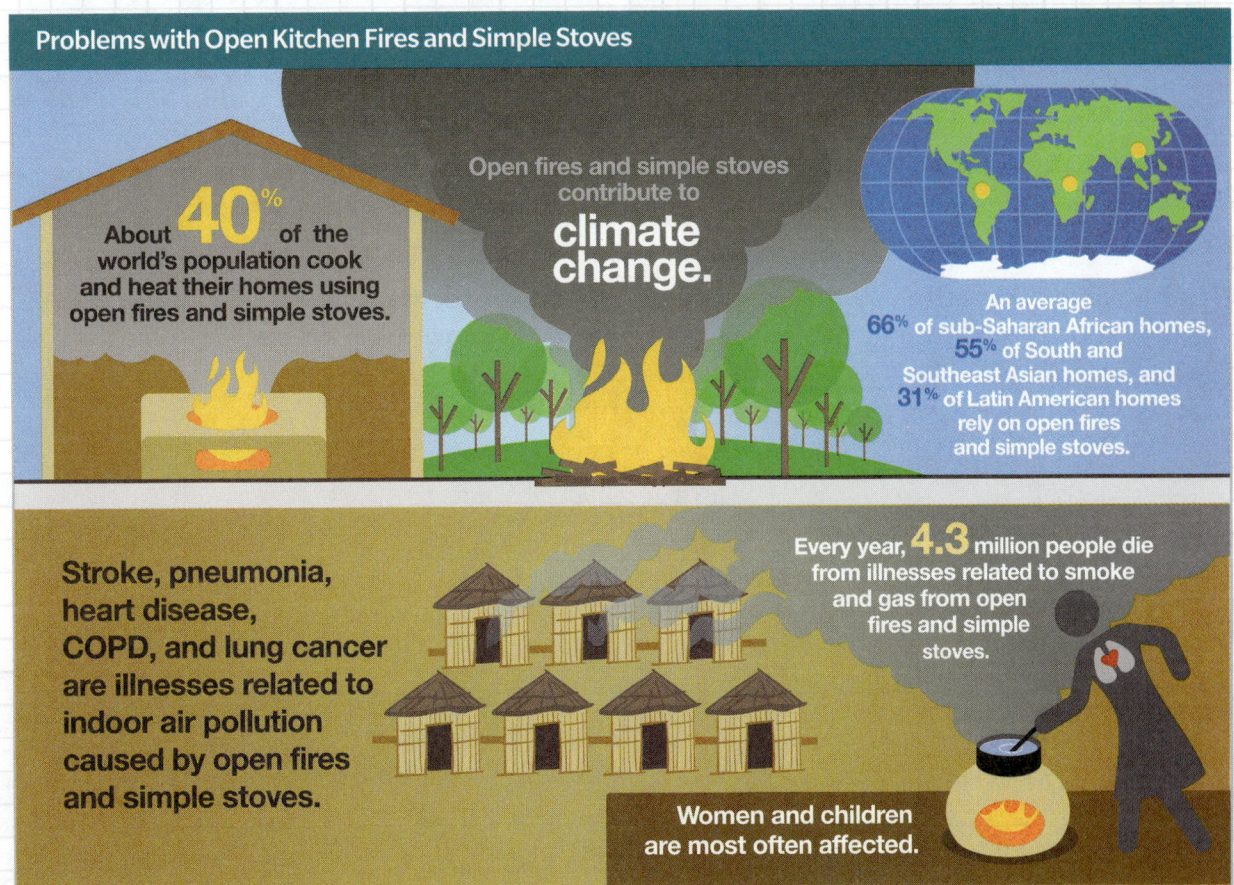

Problems with Open Kitchen Fires and Simple Stoves

About **40**% of the world's population cook and heat their homes using open fires and simple stoves.

Open fires and simple stoves contribute to **climate change.**

An average **66**% of sub-Saharan African homes, **55**% of South and Southeast Asian homes, and **31**% of Latin American homes rely on open fires and simple stoves.

Stroke, pneumonia, heart disease, COPD, and lung cancer are illnesses related to indoor air pollution caused by open fires and simple stoves.

Every year, **4.3** million people die from illnesses related to smoke and gas from open fires and simple stoves.

Women and children are most often affected.

Source: World Health Organization Media Center, *Household Air Pollution and Health* Fact Sheet. Accessed on January 5, 2016.

5. Which questions would help define this problem? Choose all that apply.

   A. How do open fires in homes cause health problems?

   B. What types of buildings usually have kitchens with open fires?

   C. What treatments are available for diseases caused by open fires and stoves?

   D. What is the household income of families with open fires in the home?

6. Draw The engineering problem related to open indoor fires can be represented as a system. Illustrate the problem of open indoor fires as a system. Don't forget to add the components, processes, inputs, and outputs of this system.

Language SmArts

Describe Smartphone Requirements

Suppose you want to develop a smartphone for older adults to use. This is a smaller-scale problem than redesigning how millions of people around the world cook and heat their homes. Even so, the problem needs to be described in detail before designing a solution.

7. In the table, each stated problem identifies a smartphone need or desire. The precisely stated problem gives further detail about the engineering problem, which then guides a designed solution. Fill in the blank sections of the table with details that address a more specific need or desire from that of the stated problem.

Stated Problem	Precisely Stated Problem
Develop a phone that can be used by adults with special needs.	Develop a phone for use by people who are vision or hearing impaired.
Develop a phone that is "eco-friendly."	Develop a phone that contains at least 25% recycled materials.
Develop a phone that has a camera.	
Develop a way to protect a phone from damage.	
Develop a phone that is affordable.	

Defining Problems Precisely

If an engineering solution is to be useful, the problem must first be defined precisely. Imagine designing an umbrella to keep someone dry while they are walking in light rain. Your umbrella design must address the need for the umbrella to stop rain from falling on a person's head. It must also allow the person to carry other things at the same time. With these needs in mind, design criteria might include that the umbrella must be light. Therefore, the umbrella must be made of lightweight, waterproof materials. The criteria that define this umbrella design do not necessarily apply to all umbrella designs, though. Think about how criteria for a shade umbrella, or an umbrella that can stand up to hail, might be different.

Umbrellas and other rain gear must all meet specific needs of the users to be useful.

8. Which of these requirements are things you would need to consider when designing an umbrella that will keep a person dry in rain showers? Choose all that apply.

   A. fabric that is water repellent or waterproof

   B. colorful fabric print

   C. fabric that you cannot see through

   D. lightweight materials

EVIDENCE NOTEBOOK

9. How would the engineering design problem of a treehouse to be used by young children differ from that of a treehouse to be used by teenagers? Record your evidence.

Specific Needs and Limitations Define Engineering Problems

Lighted city streets are much safer than dark streets. Until gas lamps were developed in the late 18th century, oil or kerosene lamps were used to light up streets and pathways. Then gas-fueled lights improved upon those lamps. However, gas lamps caused fires and explosions. In addition, the light from these lamps was not bright enough to light large areas. Many gas lamps were then replaced by carbon arc lights. These lights used a glowing carbon electrode that made the light very bright. They were placed high above street level. Unfortunately, arc lights needed a lot of maintenance.

The invention of the incandescent bulb improved the technology of outdoor lighting. Both streetlights and traffic signal lights used these bulbs. Today, streetlights and signal lights often use light-emitting diodes (LEDs). LEDs are more energy efficient and last much longer than incandescent bulbs. Each new streetlight design was developed to meet the changing needs of society, such as an increased focus on safety. In addition, changes to design were made as more resources became available.

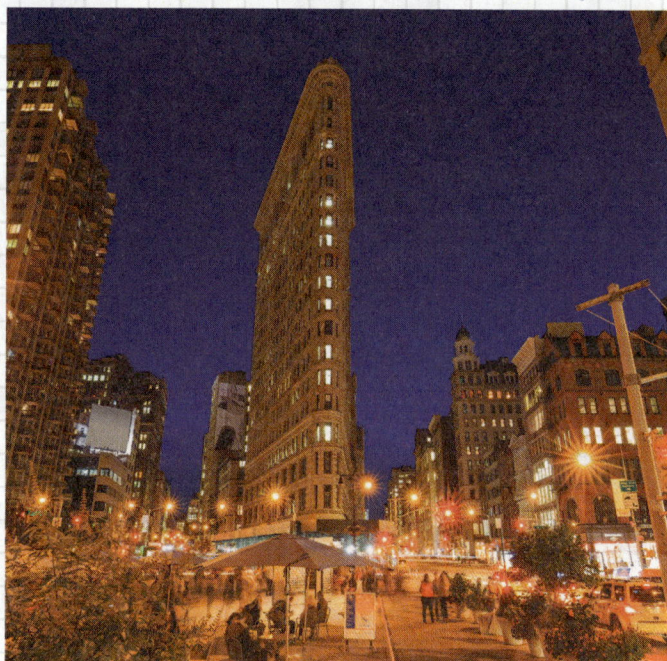

Many criteria of the engineering problem of lighting up city streets have not changed in more than 100 years. Streets still need to be "brightly lit." However, today's constraints may be very different.

Criteria

Engineers usually begin defining a problem by talking with people who are experiencing the problem and who will use the solution. They might also observe the current technology in use to see how it might be improved and to find out how other people solved similar problems in the past. Improvements in street lighting, for example, came about because electrical engineers talked with people about the need for good lighting and observed the problems with the current lighting technology. The engineers developed criteria that helped define the problem. **Criteria** are the desirable features a solution should have. Criteria (singular, *criterion*) of the street lighting problem included that the lights be bright enough to light up a large area, easy to maintain, and relatively inexpensive. New lighting technologies were developed that met those criteria and that eventually replaced the older technologies.

Constraints

The limits on the design of a solution are called **constraints**. They are the limitations on the solution's design. Constraints may be expressed as having a value or limit, such as, "It cannot cost more than $10 to make," or "It must withstand the force of a car crashing into it at 55 kilometers per hour." Constraints can also be limiting factors that exist because of such things as the availability of raw materials, current scientific understanding, or a country's laws. If a proposed design solution does not meet a constraint, it is unacceptable or unusable. For example, when incandescent light bulbs were invented, they were not immediately used in streetlights. They could not be used until a system to provide electrical energy to city blocks was developed. The absence of a reliable energy source was a constraint. Other constraints include time limitations, cost of materials, and environmental concerns. Precisely defining the criteria and constraints of the problem increases the likelihood of finding a successful solution.

10. Imagine you are designing streetlights for your town. The table below lists the criteria the solution should address. Score the criteria in order of importance to your design problem so you can design the best street lighting, with six being the most important and one the least important. Compare your order of criteria with your classmates'. Discuss reasons for the order of your criteria.

Criteria	Order of Importance
The lights should light up all areas of the street.	
The lights should be cost-effective to run.	
The lights should not shine into drivers' eyes.	
The light poles should be made of strong, sturdy materials.	
The lights should be made of environmentally safe materials.	
The lights should be of vintage style to match town buildings.	

11. Street lighting was originally developed to improve public safety. List the criteria from the table that relate to public safety concerns. Explain your reasoning.

Redefine Criteria and Constraints

What happens if you change the problem? When you do that, you need to define new criteria and constraints. This cyclist is trying to stay dry in the rain using an umbrella. Think about the criteria and constraints that were used to design a rain umbrella. The umbrella was a good design solution. Does the same solution work for keeping a rider dry while cycling? Think about how to define the criteria and constraints of this problem. The solution should keep a rider dry and safe while cycling in the rain.

12. Suppose you are leading a design team that is working on ways to keep cyclists dry in the rain. A standard rain umbrella creates some safety concerns. Your first task is to make a list of at least three criteria and three constraints that will help your design team to state the problem before they begin developing a solution.

Criteria	Constraints

13. Write a precisely defined engineering problem for a design solution that protects a bicycle rider from the rain. Use the criteria and constraints that you identified above.

_____

_____

_____

_____

_____

_____

_____

Researching to Define Engineering Problems

Soapbox car racing, also known as gravity racing, is an annual event in many places in the United States. In these races, sleek, motorless cars race downhill. Drivers race against each other or against the clock. The cars do not have engines, but they can reach speeds of up to 56 kilometers per hour (35 miles per hour). Gravity racing events began in the United States in the mid-1930s and were open to male racers only. Since 1971, female drivers have also raced. Anyone between the ages of 7 and 20 years old can compete in these annual races. The challenge for participants to build the fastest car possible is a good example of the need to precisely define an engineering problem.

Imagine that you have entered a soapbox car race. You will use the engineering design process to state the engineering problem and then design a solution.

14. Research will help you identify how this problem was addressed in the past. Your goal is to make the fastest car along the given course. First, identify questions you need to answer to precisely define the design problem you face. Then, identify the information and data you will need to plan the next steps of the design process.

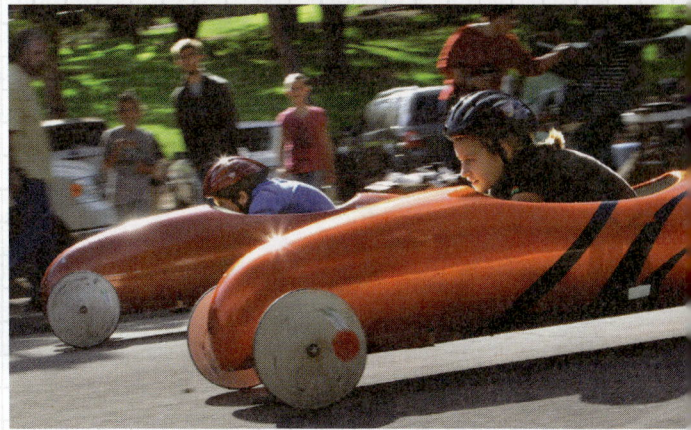

The design of soapbox cars, also called gravity racer cars, has changed over time. The availability of different materials and safety concerns are just two influences on the design.

Questions	Information and Data Needed

Engineering Problems Can Be Reframed

An engineering question builds on initial research. Sometimes, though, new information may require engineers to change, or reframe, the engineering question. This new information may mean that the question needs to be restated and a new solution proposed.

When Criteria or Constraints Change

Reframing may be needed when there is a change in the criteria or constraints of a problem as well. For example, after your research on the soapbox car, you might find out that cars are scored on appearance as well as speed. This new criterion requires that you reframe your question. A new criterion, such as a change in the maximum width of the car body, means your design question needs to be reframed. Your design problem now has different dimensions that affect the amount of material needed.

Reframing an engineering problem in the early stages of the solution development is better than doing so later, after the testing phase begins. Defining the engineering problem so that it best describes the problem without having to consider time or cost would be ideal. But it usually does not work that way. Engineers need to research production costs, schedules, market pressures, new scientific discoveries, and customer likes and dislikes before they can clearly define engineering problems. This type of research helps identify the criteria and constraints for a successful solution.

These wooden derby cars look different from one another, but they all were designed to meet the same constraints and criteria to make the race fair.

15. After you start planning the design for your soapbox racecar, you find out that the maximum weight for the car has changed. What new information do you need and what changes to your design plan would you have to make in order for your design to fit the new criterion?

EVIDENCE NOTEBOOK

16. Suppose the treehouse was at first meant to be big enough for three people, but then the builder decided it should fit five instead. How would this change affect the treehouse design? Record your evidence.

Design a Model Car, Part 1

Define an engineering problem for a model car design.

You will build a model car in class over several lessons. Your challenge is to build a car that will travel the farthest after being rolled down a three-foot-long ramp slanted at 30°. In developing a solution, you need to think about how limits such as the materials available to you, the time you have to complete the solution, and scientific principles will affect the available solutions.

Here are the criteria and constraints that define your design problem:

- The mass of the car must not be greater than 120 g.
- The length of the car must not be greater than 15 cm.
- The width of the car must not be greater than 7 cm.
- The car must have a 4.5-cm distance between the axles.
- The car must have a 1-cm clearance underneath the body.
- The car must be made only from materials provided by your teacher.
- The car body may have any shape.
- The car must be reusable.
- The car must have four wheels.
- The axles, axle housing, and wheels supplied with the kit must be used.
- The axles, axle housing, and wheels may not be changed in any way.
- The only weights that may be added to the car are washers supplied in the kit.
- The car should include a to-scale model driver.

> **MATERIALS**
> - corrugated cardboard
> - digital scale
> - measuring tape
> - metal washers (weights)
> - smoothie straws
> - scissors
> - tape
> - wooden axles (2)
> - wooden wheels (4)

Procedure

STEP 1 Criteria are features the solution should have. Constraints are the limitations the designers need to work within. What are the criteria of this design problem?

STEP 2 Identify the constraints of the design problem.

STEP 3 Clearly state the design problem. What need will the design address?

STEP 4 Think of at least three body plans for the shape of your car. Choose the one most likely to meet the criteria. Give reasons for your decision.

Analysis

STEP 5 **Do the Math** As part of your design, you will cut out a paper driver to attach to the top of your car. You want the driver to be correctly scaled to the car. The length of a typical soapbox derby car is 1.2 m. Your model soapbox derby car is 14 cm long. To the nearest centimeter, how tall should your model driver be in order to represent a 1.67-m-tall driver?

STEP 6 Why is it important to define the design problem more precisely than "design a small, fast model car"? Explain your answer using what you have learned about the engineering design process.

Reframe an Engineering Problem

If the race's rules were changed to say that each car should have three wheels instead of four, you would need to reframe the problem. Your design would have to include changing the locations of the wheels and changing the car's weight distribution.

17. Suppose a student wants to use the same car design in a new competition. She discovers that the guidelines for the new competition are different. For each new guideline, indicate whether reframing of the problem will be needed.

A. Reframing may be needed
B. Reframing not needed

_____ The car must have a 2-cm clearance below the body.

_____ Wheels may be made from any material.

_____ To prevent accidental poisoning, lead weights cannot be used in the car design.

Continue Your Exploration

Name: _____   Date: _____

Check out the path below or go online to choose one of the other paths shown.

| Redefining a Design Problem | • Learning from Design Failures
• Hands-On Labs ✋
• Propose Your Own Path | Go online to choose one of these other paths. |

Harnessing Wind Energy

Wind is a renewable energy source because it is generated continually. Wind turbines use wind to produce electrical energy. In many places around the world, giant windmill-like turbines stand on top of ridges, in wide prairies, or offshore. In these fairly isolated places, the structures do not generally interfere with the lives of people. These large turbines are not designed for use in urban areas because they take up a lot of space and require strong winds to move their blades.

Adjustments for Societal and Environmental Needs

How could you use engineering design to develop a way to harness wind energy in a city while meeting the constraints of urban needs? One solution is the Wind Tree shown in the picture. This artificial tree has "leaves" that are lightweight wind turbines. Generators and cables are located inside the branches and trunk. The Wind Tree silently produces electric power even in a light breeze.

Jérôme Michaud-Larivière, a French entrepreneur, developed the design after observing how even a very light wind rustled the leaves on trees. Michaud-Larivière wondered whether a wind-energy device based on several mini spinning turbines could generate enough energy to be useful in cities. The Wind Tree design has a relatively low power output of about 3.1 kW from light breezes when compared to the 2.5 to 3 mW output of traditional, large, land-based turbines. Michaud-Larivière suggested that a street lined with Wind Trees could power city streetlights or help offset the power use of nearby buildings.

Continue Your Exploration

1. Explain, in terms of criteria and constraints, why the design of a traditional wind turbine might not be suitable for use in a city.

2. For the mini turbines to operate properly, which of the following criteria are important in choosing the material for their construction?

   A. lightweight

   B. recycled

   C. realistic leaf colors

   D. attracts insects

   E. waterproof

The "leaves" of Wind Trees are miniature turbines. They can move in light breezes.

3. **Do the Math** The kilowatt (kW) is a measure of power. Wind Tree turbines have a power output of 3.1 kW. The lightweight leaf turbines can move in light breezes. A traditional, large wind turbine can have a power output of up to 3 megawatts (mW), but strong winds are needed to move the large turbines. The large turbines are more powerful machines than the smaller Wind Trees because they can do the same amount of work over a shorter period of time.

   How many Wind Trees would it take to match the power output of five large turbines? Remember that 1 mW equals 1,000 kW. Round your answer to the nearest whole number.

4. **Collaborate** As a team, learn about how changes to environmental and health laws have affected issues that engineers and designers of city infrastructure technologies deal with today.

Can You Explain It?

Name: **Date:**

How does the purpose of a treehouse affect how you would design and build it?

EVIDENCE NOTEBOOK

Refer to the notes in your Evidence Notebook to help you explain how the purpose of a treehouse is related to its design.

1. State your claim. Make sure your claim fully explains how the purpose of an object is related to the engineering problem of designing and building it.

2. Summarize the evidence you have gathered to support your claim and explain your reasoning.

Checkpoints

Answer the following questions to check your understanding of the lesson.

Use the photo to answer Questions 3 and 4.

3. The ladder for this treehouse has been removed because the wood was rotting. You need to design a new way to get into the treehouse. Which questions would help define this engineering problem more precisely? Choose all that apply.

   A. How much do the users of the treehouse weigh?

   B. What materials and tools can I use?

   C. Is the rope on the tire swing strong enough to be safe if two people are on the tire?

   D. Is there a way to close the window for privacy?

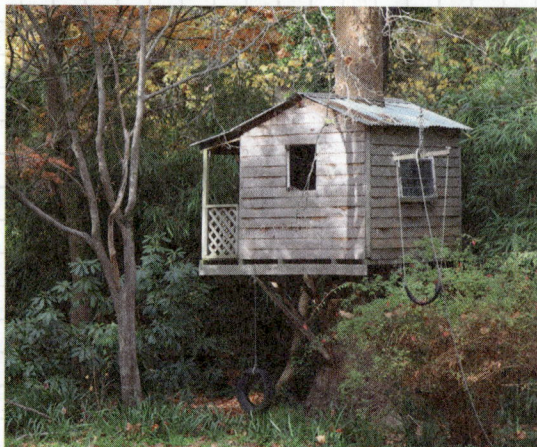

4. Each statement below refers to the engineering problem of designing and building a new way of accessing the treehouse. In the blank cells of the table, classify each statement as a *criterion*, a *constraint*, or *neither* a criterion nor a constraint of the problem.

Availability of tools and boards	
Desire to remove treehouse access after entry into it	
Treehouse to be made of wood	
Availability of roofing materials	

Use the photo to answer Questions 5 and 6.

5. The candles in the photo are a solution to a defined engineering problem. What problem do these candles solve?

   A. Warm up the room for the diners.

   B. Light up the entrance to the room.

   C. Light up the dinner table without relying on electricity.

   D. Light up the table brightly enough to read a book.

6. One hundred fifty years ago, the solution illustrated in this photo was the best solution to the need to provide light in a home at night. Today, it is not the best solution to this problem. What has likely changed? Choose all that apply.

   A. Most modern houses have electric lighting.

   B. Electric lights are safer and more convenient.

   C. Most modern houses have indoor plumbing.

Interactive Review

Complete this section to review the main concepts of the lesson.

A well-defined engineering problem identifies the needs or wants it is intended to address.

A. Why is it important to identify the right questions when developing a solution to an engineering design problem?

In order to develop a usable solution to a design problem, the problem must state specific needs and limitations that must be met.

B. How are criteria and constraints used to make a precisely stated solution to an engineering design problem?

Researching how similar problems were addressed in the past can help engineers define the design problem precisely.

C. Sometimes an engineering problem must be reframed. What might occur that would require an engineer to reframe an engineering problem?

Developing and Testing Solutions

Thomas Edison did not invent the incandescent light bulb, but he improved its design and made it more practical.

Explore First

Comparing Solutions Obtain a wooden pencil and a mechanical pencil. Identify a specific task for which you can test both pencil designs, such as consistency in drawing lines. Carry out your test and record the results. How well did each pencil do in the test?

Go online to view the digital version of the Hands-On Lab for this lesson and to download additional lab resources.

CAN YOU EXPLAIN IT?

How can you develop and test ways to get a kite out of a tree?

Oh no! Your favorite kite is caught in a tree and its string is tangled in the branches. What can you do to free it? A workable solution is one that keeps you safe and keeps the kite and tree as intact as possible.

1. Provide an example of a criterion and a constraint of this problem.

2. How might the material the kite is made of affect the solution of retrieving it from the tree?

EVIDENCE NOTEBOOK As you explore this lesson, gather information to explain how to develop a solution to the problem of the kite stuck in the tree.

Developing Solutions

There is not always one clear solution to an engineering problem. After the criteria and constraints of a problem have been defined, engineers brainstorm ideas for solutions. After the brainstorming step, you may have several design solutions you think will meet the criteria and constraints. You can test one or two of the solutions to see if that is true. You may decide to modify or combine solutions to develop a better solution.

For example, imagine your class is planning a field trip to study a stream ecosystem. Part of your study includes analyzing the water quality of the stream using delicate electronic equipment. Eight sets of equipment will be used by the class. It is not possible to drive directly to the stream, so you need to carry the fragile equipment from the school bus. The distance from the bus parking lot to the stream is a quarter mile. Defining this transportation problem using criteria and constraints and then prioritizing the criteria will help develop a solution.

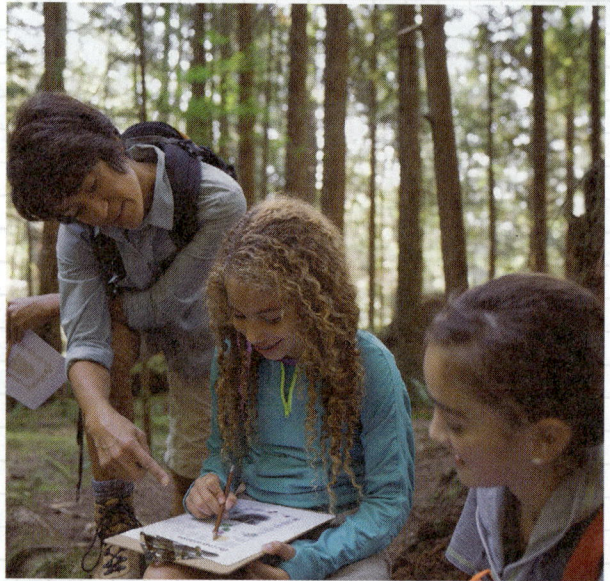

After identifying the important requirements of a problem, you can use brainstorming and planning to develop solutions.

3. Using a scale of 1–5, identify the importance of each criterion of the problem, with 5 being the most important and 1 being the least important.

	Rating (1-5)
Must be easy for a student to use, carry, or hold	
Must not damage the electronic equipment	
Must be reusable	
Must be inexpensive	
Must not be damaged by being used on a rocky trail	

4. **Discuss** Before the field trip, your class discusses the best ways to move the equipment. One student suggests using the janitor's hand-pulled, metal wagon. You test this idea and discover that the equipment would get dented if placed on the metal bottom of the wagon. What could you do to address the issue with denting?

Brainstorm Solutions

One way to generate ideas is to brainstorm with other people. When you work with others to think about and generate ideas quickly, you are **brainstorming**. You can brainstorm in different ways, but the most important thing is to suggest as many ideas as possible while avoiding judgments about any suggestions. The goal of a brainstorming session is to identify many solutions in order to find a few to refine further. Some ideas may turn out to be unusable, but brainstorming is not the time to figure out which ideas may or may not work. Brainstorming many ideas can often result in a much better solution than starting with a single idea alone. Considering only one option from the start can limit the creativity of the solution.

Brainstorming sessions can generate a lot of ideas.

5. The goal of brainstorming is to generate a number of possible solutions. Which statements are advantages of brainstorming many ideas instead of focusing on one initial solution? Choose all that apply.

   A. Multiple ideas increase the chance of finding a workable solution.

   B. Larger groups can reach a conclusion about a solution faster.

   C. Several different ideas might combine to form a better solution.

   D. New ideas may be generated from others' suggestions.

The Importance of Being Open-Minded

All ideas are considered valuable during brainstorming sessions. The ideas proposed in a brainstorming session are not completely random, though. As possible solutions are suggested, it is important that the criteria and constraints are kept in mind. One very important constraint to any solution is the budget. A solution such as using drones to carry the equipment to the stream is not a workable solution. It would be too expensive for the school to afford. However, if each student already had their own drone they could bring with them, using drones might be a workable solution.

When brainstorming, participants also have background knowledge about how similar problems were solved in the past. They can also use what they know of scientific principles and legal requirements related to the problem and the proposed solutions. For example, there are several laws that restrict the use of drones. If the use of drones is prohibited in the area where the field trip is, then it is not a suitable solution even if the school could afford to use them.

The Importance of Background Research

In order to find the best design solution for an engineering problem, research is also needed. If you jump straight into brainstorming without researching solutions that are already available or how similar problems were solved in the past, you do extra work and waste time. Part of the solution may already exist. By researching the problem, you start with a background of knowledge. Sometimes background research helps reframe the problem so that it is better focused. Research into a solution often continues after ideas are generated by brainstorming.

Use Decision-Making Tools

Some of the brainstormed solutions may not meet all the criteria of the problem, or maybe all of the solutions meet the criteria. Some solutions may be more effective or safer than others. Possible solutions are evaluated against the criteria and constraints. Less-effective solutions are rejected, and the remaining solutions are refined.

Workable solutions must meet the constraints of the problem. If a solution does not meet a constraint, it is eliminated. For example, renting a satellite phone to send data home from a field trip would be beyond your budget. But for a research team in a ship on the ocean, a satellite phone might be the best option to stay in contact with others.

Decision Matrix

Several decision-making tools can help you choose among the solutions to find the best option. A **decision matrix** is one tool for evaluating several options at the same time. In a decision matrix, each criterion is assigned a number that rates its importance in a successful design solution. For example, suppose students are asked to design a container to take soup to school for lunch. After brainstorming solutions, they can use a decision matrix like the one below to rate each idea to see which one best meets the criteria. In this example, students have decided that "does not leak" is the most important criterion of the design solution. They assign it a rating of five points.

The higher the point value, the more important the criterion is to a successful solution. Each solution is then scored on how well it meets each criterion. Points are awarded for each solution up to, but no more than, the maximum rating given to the criterion. The result is a numerical ranking of the proposed solutions based on the importance of the criterion for a successful solution. The solution that has the highest total score is the one that best addresses the problem.

Criteria	Rating (1–5)	Soup Container Solutions			
		Plastic container with screw-on lid	Foam container	Glass jar with lid	Plastic zipper bag
Easy to reuse	4	4	2	3	1
Does not leak	5	5	3	4	2
Not expensive	4	2	4	1	4
Unlikely to break	3	3	2	1	1
Totals		14	11	9	8

6. Which solution meets the criteria the best? Explain how the matrix provides useful information for evaluating the solution to the problem.

EVIDENCE NOTEBOOK

7. Brainstorming ways to get the kite out of the tree might lead to many potential solutions. How can you determine which solutions are most likely to succeed? Record your evidence.

Tradeoffs

Making a decision about the best solution nearly always involves making a tradeoff. In the case of the best container for carrying soup, the plastic container with the screw-on lid was the best solution. But the plastic foam container is cheaper and does a good job of not leaking, so you might choose it instead, because it would be a more affordable option for you. A tradeoff involves giving up something you like about one solution in order to have a more desirable feature in another solution.

Risk-Benefit Analysis

Another tool engineers often use to evaluate options is a risk-benefit analysis. A risk-benefit analysis compares the risks, or unfavorable effects, of a solution, to the benefits, or favorable effects. A solution that has greater benefits and fewer risks is favored over one with fewer benefits and greater risks. For example, x-ray machines are tools that doctors use to see inside the body to evaluate and diagnose health problems. However, as x-rays pass through the body, they can damage living cells. Medical x-rays expose patients to very small doses of radiation. The risk of harm to cells is considered much smaller than the benefit of being able to diagnose health problems.

Select Promising Solutions

8. You have drawn a decision matrix to help assess how well several solutions meet the criteria of the problem: "What item is best to bring to the beach to sit on?" Five criteria and four solutions are written into the decision matrix. Your next step is to rank the importance of each criterion for a successful solution. Then, fill out the matrix by awarding points to each solution based on how well it meets each criterion.

Criteria	Rating (1–5)	Solutions			
		Folding camp chair	Inflatable beach float	Beach towel	Metal patio chair
Not expensive					
Easy to carry					
Washable					
Comfortable for sitting					
Waterproof materials					
Totals					

Which solution was the "best"? Explain your answer.

_____

_____

_____

What type of tradeoff would you need to make if you were to choose the second-highest-scoring solution? Explain your answers.

_____

_____

Evaluating Solutions

A decision matrix helps you evaluate possible solutions. However, it does not provide every answer to address a design problem. The top-rated proposed solution to taking soup to school for lunch is the plastic container with the screw-on lid. This may well be the best way to carry soup to school. However, there are additional things you need to do before deciding this is the best solution. Solutions that seem to be perfectly workable sometimes do not actually solve the problem. After a solution or several possible solutions to a problem are identified, they are tested to identify whether they meet all the criteria and constraints of the problem. Testing several types of screw-top plastic containers that hold different volumes or have different styles of screw-top lids will help identify the best solution to your problem.

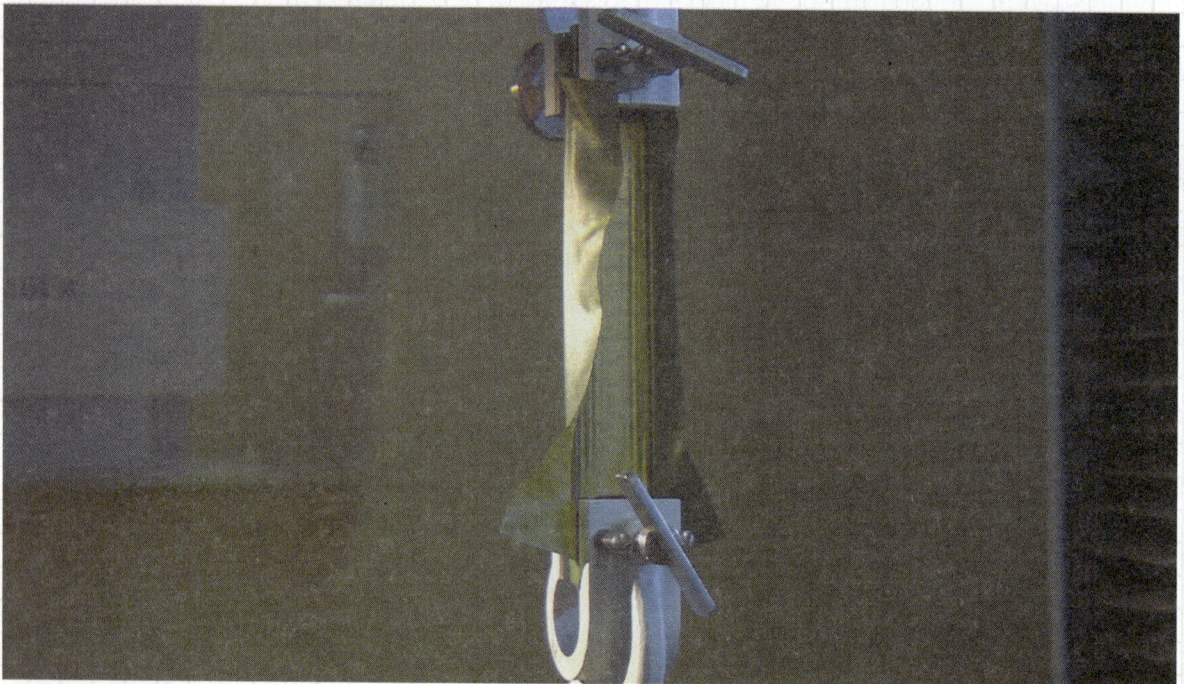

A universal testing machine is used to test the tensile strength and compressive strength of materials. It can apply pulling (tensile) or pushing (compressive) forces on the test material. This fabric is undergoing a tensile strength test.

Explore Online

9. An engineering team proposes a new water-resistant fabric for use in backpacks. Several different fabrics have been recommended. Why would it be helpful for the team to test each of the proposals before manufacturing the new backpacks? Choose all answers that apply.

   A. Testing can help engineers determine whether one option is better than the others.

   B. Engineers can use test results to confirm whether the fabrics actually work in real situations.

   C. Testing may help engineers discover ways in which the fabrics perform better or worse than predicted.

   D. Engineers may use testing to obtain information on ways to improve the performance of the fabrics.

Test Solutions

Similar to scientists, engineers rely on reproducible data in order to make and defend conclusions. Analyzing test results helps engineers identify which solution is best and whether the best solution solves the problem. In order to be useful, a test should measure one variable at a time. This provides information to evaluate the proposed solution and often leads to improvements in the design.

Some tests can be carried out using the solution exactly as proposed. For example, you can test which container best holds soup by testing the containers themselves. Sometimes, however, the actual solution cannot be tested directly. For example, engineers designing a large suspension bridge cannot build the bridge and then test it to see whether the design was right. Instead, they test a model of the bridge. A working test model of a solutions is called a **prototype**. Engineers use prototypes during the design process to test the design and make improvements to it.

The Systematic Steps of Developing and Testing Solutions to Engineering Problems

The "developing and testing solutions" portion of the design process is highlighted in yellow.

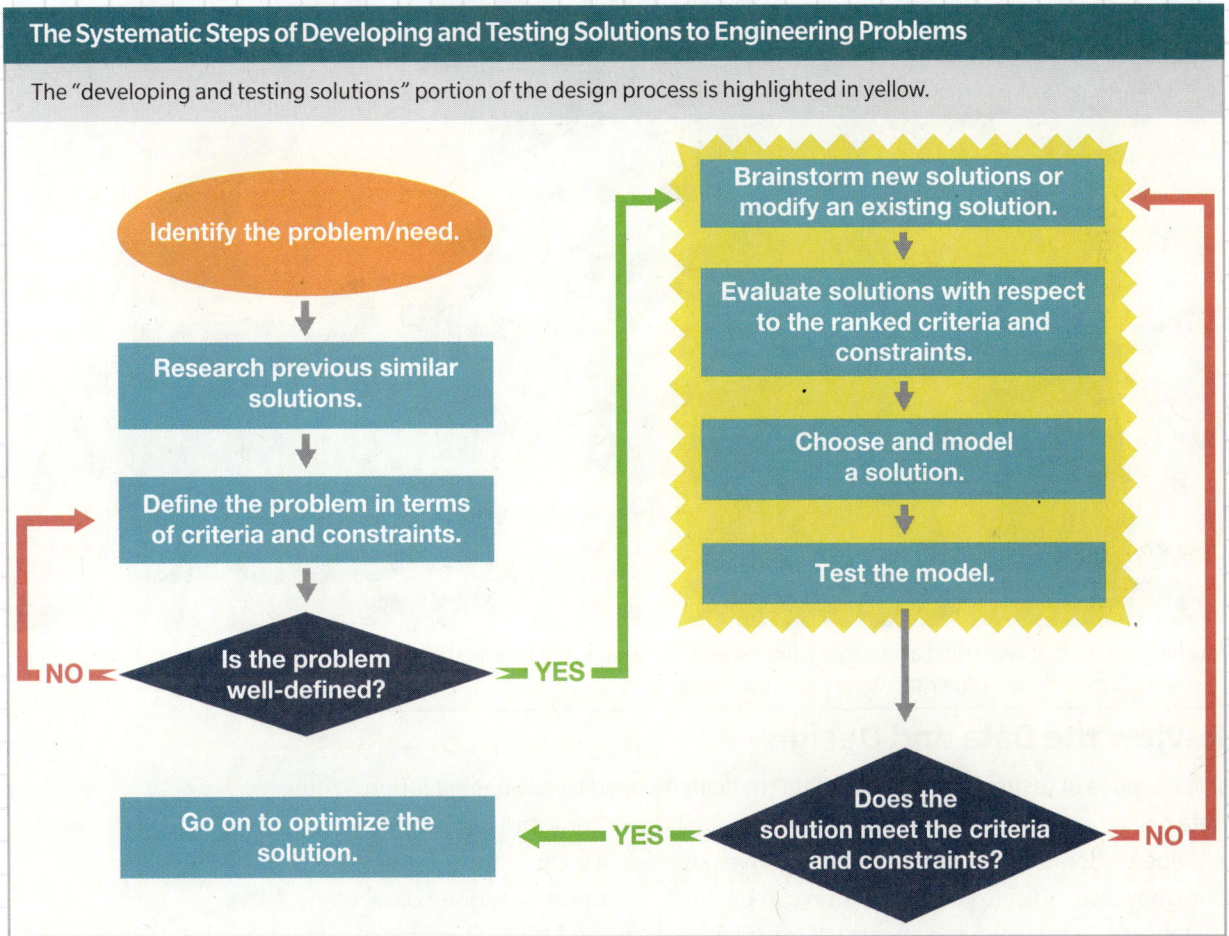

10. A decision matrix can be used to narrow down solutions. Often two or three solutions appear to be equally promising. When that happens it will be important to test each of the top designs to see which ones best meet the criteria. Why is it important that each of the top designs be tested in the same way?

Evaluate Test Data

Once engineers use a design matrix to identify the top two or three solutions, they build prototypes for testing. Many tests provide numerical data that can be compared mathematically. Every aspect of a solution can be tested, including the cost of materials and the time needed to implement the solution. These students are testing a parachute design model to see how long it takes to drop from the balcony. They want to develop a parachute that takes the longest time possible to drop. They will compare data from several tests and different designs to identify the best solution.

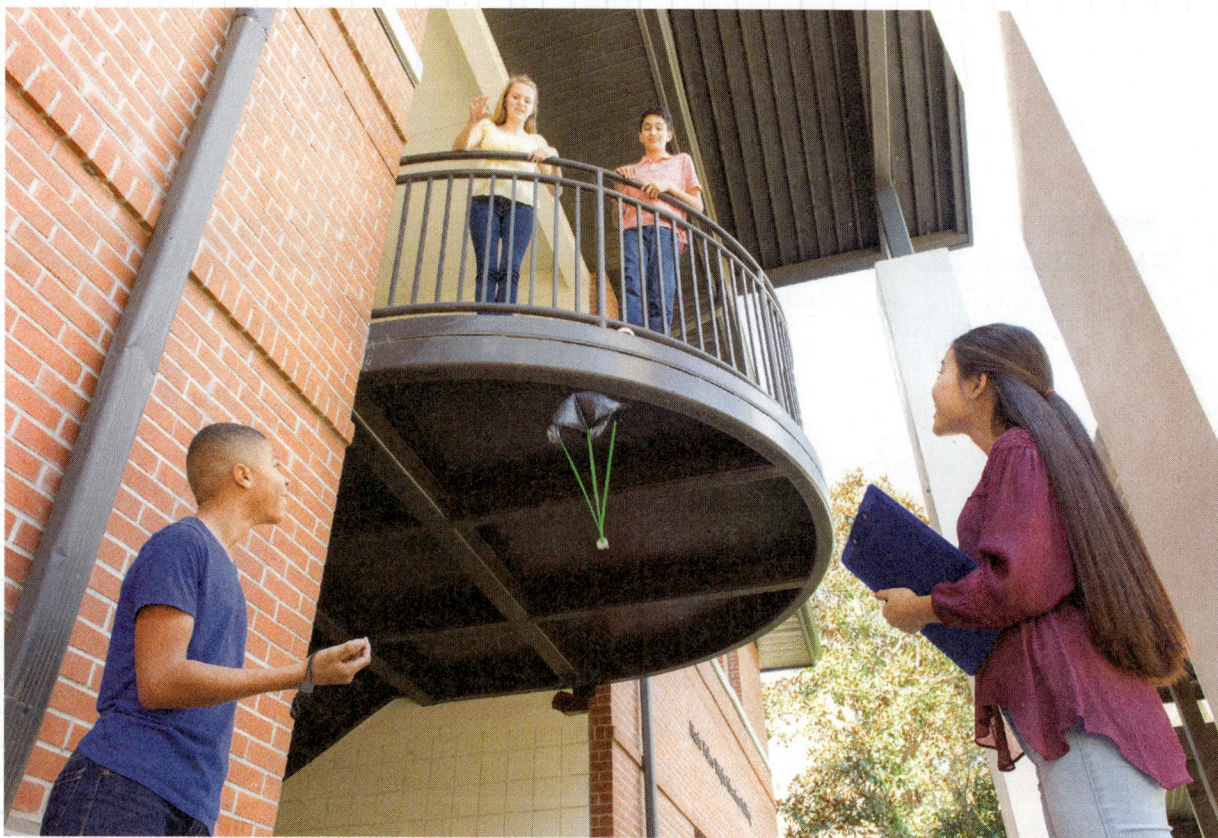

An important part of evaluating a design is building a design model and testing the model to measure the design's performance against criteria and constraints.

Review the Data and Design

The purpose of testing is to provide data that can be used to evaluate solutions. After data collection, each solution is evaluated against the criteria and constraints. The data provide evidence about the strengths and weaknesses of each proposed solution. The data may also indicate ways a solution can be improved upon. Using the data, team members can then provide constructive criticism of each solution. This analysis, which is based on evidence, helps to improve solutions.

11. Sometimes parts of different solutions can be combined to make a better solution. What benefit does this offer? Choose all that apply.

   A. It allows for the best part of each solution to be used in a final design.

   B. It gives the design team time to redefine the problem.

   C. It allows the designers to meet customer demands for new designs every year.

   D. It allows a solution to be developed that is better than earlier solutions.

   E. It allows each test variable to be tested fully in each test model.

Do the Math
Evaluate Parachute Designs

A group of students is designing a parachute system to drop an egg from a height of 3 meters without breaking the egg. The purpose of the first test was to compare the effectiveness of different parachute materials and sizes. To avoid making a mess, they tested their designs using a wooden block with a mass similar to that of an egg.

The variables in the tests were the parachute material and the parachute size. All of the test designs were dropped from the same point on the balcony using the same mass. The table below shows the averaged results after testing each design three times. Students then evaluated the data to determine which solution would be most likely to keep an egg from breaking.

Type of Parachute Material	Area of Parachute (cm²)	Time to Reach the Floor (s)
Cloth	500	1.7
Cloth	1,000	2.2
Plastic film	500	2.7
Plastic film	1,000	3.5
Paper	500	2.0
Paper	1,000	2.5

12. Based on the evidence from the tests, make a recommendation about the type of material the students should use for their parachute. Explain your reasoning.

13. A wooden block was used as a model egg in evaluating the parachute design. What could the students do to determine whether their design will work on a real egg?

EVIDENCE NOTEBOOK
14. Suppose you have identified two promising potential solutions to the kite problem. How can you further evaluate and choose a solution? Record your evidence.

Design a Model Car, Part 2

Propose design solutions based on your earlier work defining the problem.

You are designing and building a model car over several sessions. In Part 1, you defined the engineering problem. Now, in Part 2, you will propose design solutions. Later, in Part 3, you will evaluate the proposed solutions against the criteria.

Your challenge is to build a model car using the supplied materials and specifications. Refer to the criteria, constraints, and materials listed in Part 1 of this Hands-On Lab, which is in Lesson 2.

MATERIALS

• See materials from Design a Model Car, Part 1

Procedure

STEP 1 Brainstorm with your group to come up with several car designs to meet the challenge.

STEP 2 Identify three car design options that you want to explore further. Analyze how well these three design options meet the criteria of the problem using a decision matrix similar to the one shown below. Three criteria are listed in the sample matrix.

STEP 3 On a separate piece of paper, draw a decision matrix similar to the one shown below that lists the criteria of your design. Then, rank the importance of each criterion for the solution to be acceptable using a scale of 1 to 5 for each criterion with 1 meaning "least important" and 5 meaning "most important." Then, score each solution based on how well it meets each ranked criterion. Remember that points are awarded for each criterion up to, but no more than, the maximum value given to that criterion.

Criteria	Rating (1–5)	Solutions		
		Car design 1	Car design 2	Car design 3
Max mass of 120 g				
Has four wheels				
Is reusable				
Totals				

STEP 4 **Draw** Based on your decision matrix, choose the design solution that scores the highest. This is the design that best meets the criteria. Draw a sketch of the design on a separate sheet of paper. Then, build your chosen design! Remember, you may use only the materials supplied by your teacher to build the car.

STEP 5 Any complex design project involves carrying out a number of tests to see how variables affect the performance of the design. There are several design variables that may affect the performance of the car. Some of these variables include the shape of the car, the weight of the car, and the location of the weights (washers) on the body.

Choose one variable to test to identify how it affects the distance traveled by the car. Remember to check the race specifications to be sure you are testing only values of the variables that are within the allowed range for your car.

STEP 6 Design a test to evaluate the effect of the one variable on the distance the car travels. Explain how the test will be carried out.

STEP 7 Using a test ramp, conduct the test. Record your results on a separate sheet of paper.

STEP 8 You may, if time allows, identify and test another variable to see how it affects your car's performance.

Analysis

STEP 9 On a separate sheet of paper, draw a graph showing the relationship between the change in your variable and the distance the car traveled. Draw a graph for each variable tested. Remember to label the axes. Evaluate the effect of the variable on the distance traveled. State a conclusion about the effect the variable had on the distance the car traveled.

STEP 10 Suppose one member of your group suggests that to save time, two variables that may affect the distance traveled can be tested at the same time. Is this an acceptable way to test a design solution? Explain your answer.

STEP 11 Ideally, several tests that investigate the effect of different variables on the performance of the design solution are carried out. What is the purpose of carrying out so many tests on a design solution?

Engage in Argument from Evidence

Analysis of solutions includes using data to make suggestions for improvement to the solution. A conclusion that is not supported by data is not useful to the design process.

After deciding to use a plastic film parachute to slow the fall of an egg, students tested different parachute sizes and tested them by dropping the parachute and mass from a height of 3 m. Each parachute was tested three times. The average time to reach the floor is recorded in the table.

Area of Parachute (cm²)	Time to Reach the Floor (s)
100	1.0
250	1.5
500	2.2
1,000	3.0
1,500	2.7
2,000	2.1

15. One student argued that a parachute with a larger area is always better because it provides more air resistance. Explain how the data supports or does not support that argument.

_____

_____

_____

_____

_____

16. What size parachute would be the most suited to slow the fall of an egg? Use data from the table to support your conclusion.

_____

_____

_____

_____

_____

17. Why is systematic testing of possible solutions needed before choosing a design to refine?

_____

_____

_____

_____

_____

Continue Your Exploration

Name: Date:

Check out the path below or go online to choose one of the other paths shown.

| Building on Earlier Solutions | • Using Data to Make Informed Decisions
• Hands-On Labs 🖐️
• Propose Your Own Path | Go online to choose one of these other paths. |

Design of the Incandescent Light Bulb

The incandescent light bulb is a common technology. Thomas Edison is often thought of as its inventor, but he did not invent it. However, in 1878, he and his team developed the first practical and commercially successful incandescent bulb.

Edison approached the design of the light bulb as an engineering problem. He needed to develop a bulb that would produce enough light but not burn out quickly. He and his assistants tested thousands of materials and setups. In fact, Edison stated, "I have not failed. I've just found 10,000 ways that won't work."

Many Solutions Tested

Some of Edison's designs used a filament. A bulb filament is the part that lights up. It is a thin wire through which electric current flows. Some of the filament designs did not work because the material did not carry enough electric current. Others worked for a short period and then burned out. By combining what Edison and his team had learned in many tests, they eventually found a solution—a metal filament in a vacuum tube.

Edison's success in making a light bulb included using data collected from numerous experiments to help brainstorm new ideas. His team tested many different materials and configurations to find a workable solution. Brainstorming was part of the process, although Edison and his team would not have used that term. By remaining open to many possible solutions and knowing that "failure" was an important part of the learning process, Edison eventually solved the problem.

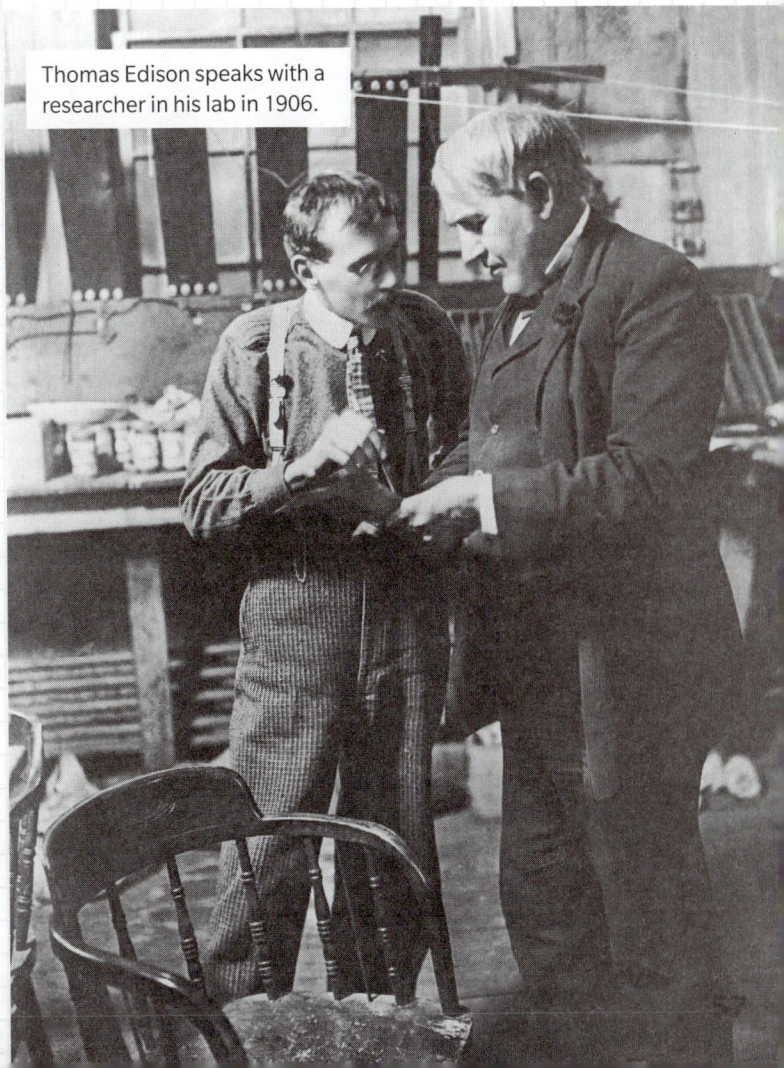

Thomas Edison speaks with a researcher in his lab in 1906.

Continue Your Exploration

1. How would the usefulness of the incandescent bulb have been affected if electrical supply systems had not been developed?

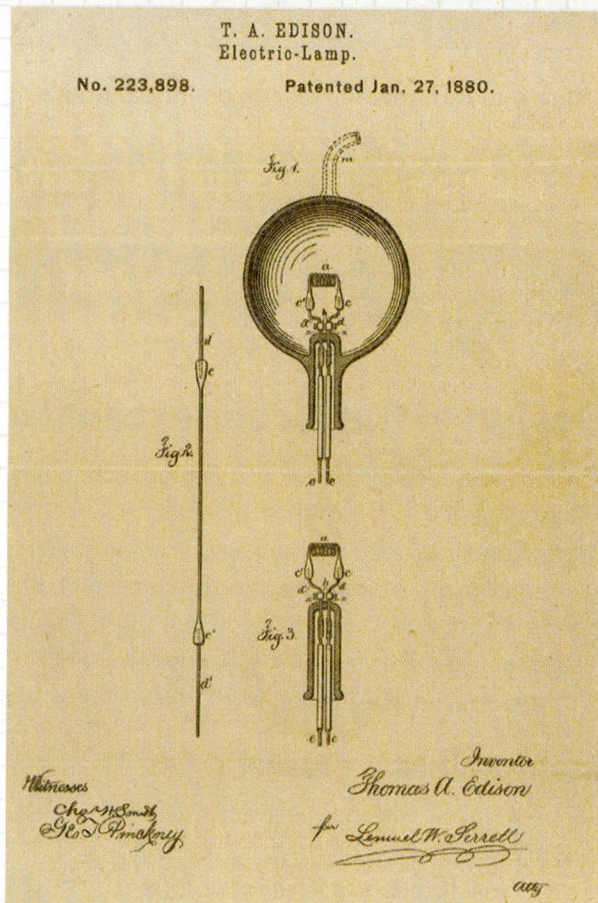

T. A. EDISON.
Electric-Lamp.

No. 223,898.   Patented Jan. 27, 1880.

This is Edison's patent filing for his light bulb design. A patent is a license from the government that legally protects an invention from being copied or sold by others.

2. Explain how Edison and his team used test evidence from failed tests to find the best material for the light bulb elements.

3. The term *brainstorming* was not used in Edison's time, but the descriptions of his research imply that his team used the technique. What aspect of Edison's research supports this idea?

4. **Collaborate** Work with your group to research the solution to an engineering problem that has had an impact on society. Find out who developed the first workable solution and how ideas were tested during the design process.

Can You Explain It?

Name: _____   Date: _____

How can you develop and test ways to get a kite out of a tree?

EVIDENCE NOTEBOOK

Refer to the notes in your Evidence Notebook to help you construct an explanation for how to develop solutions for a kite stuck in a tree.

1. State your claim. Make sure your claim fully explains how to develop and evaluate potential solutions to the problem.

2. Summarize the evidence you have gathered to support your claim and explain your reasoning.

Checkpoints

Answer the following questions to check your understanding of the lesson.

Use the photo to answer Question 3.

3. How does ranking criteria help designers develop a better helmet? Choose all that apply.

   A. It automatically ranks constraints because they are the same as criteria.

   B. It identifies the most important criteria that a solution must meet.

   C. It helps in assessing several solutions that meet the criteria of the problem.

   D. It helps to eliminate solutions that do not meet the constraints.

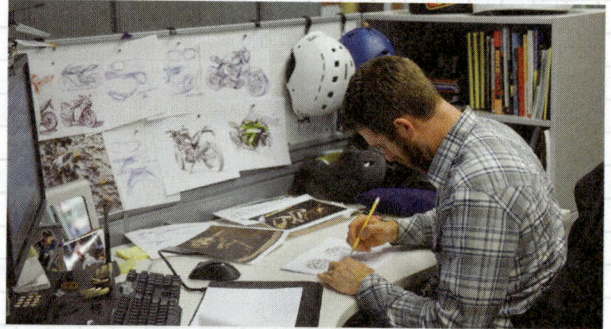

Use the photo to answer Question 4.

4. Calligraphy requires a writing tool that can make very precise and fine marks. Identify things you would do to help identify the best calligraphy pen from several different types of pens. Choose all that apply.

   A. Identify whether each pen meets the criteria of your calligraphy writing problem.

   B. Identify pens that do not meet the constraints of your writing problem.

   C. Test the pens to see which one best meets the criteria.

   D. Rank the criteria of the problem in their order of importance for a successful solution.

5. Why is using models an important part of the testing process? Choose all that apply.

   A. They allow designers to brainstorm better ideas.

   B. They allow the design solution to be tested when the actual solution itself cannot be tested.

   C. They allow design solutions to be tested in a systematic way.

   D. Their use provides engineers with lots of data to evaluate the performance of a possible design solution.

6. A team of students is designing a robot to compete in a race. They select three ideas to develop further. Which statements describe the steps the team might take to identify the best robot design? Choose all that apply.

   A. Build and test models of each design.

   B. Choose a team leader who will choose the design to build.

   C. Evaluate test data for each design and see how each one meets the criteria and constraints of the problem.

   D. Use the design that looks the best and discard the others.

Interactive Review

Complete this section to review the main concepts of the lesson.

Engineering solutions are developed by proposing ideas and then comparing how well those ideas meet the criteria and constraints of the problem.

A. How is a decision matrix useful during the development of a solution to an engineering design problem?

Testing provides data that can be used to rank proposed solutions and evaluate the effects of changes to design solutions.

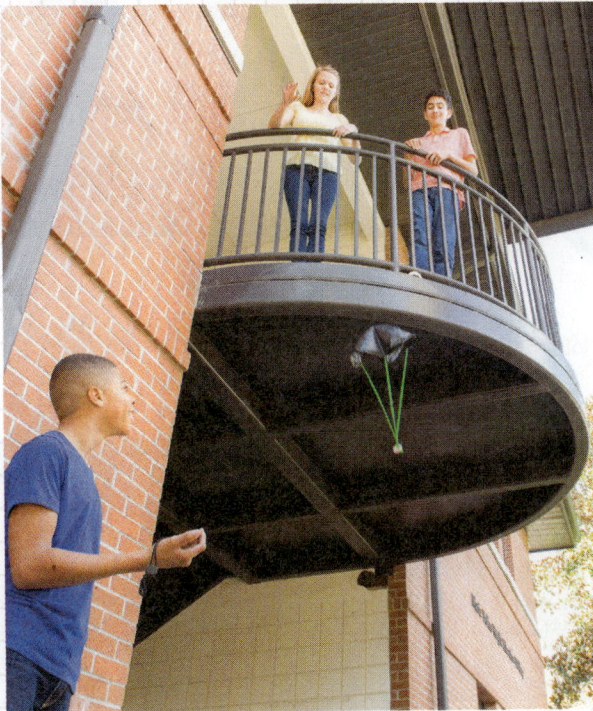

B. Why is analyzing data from tests important to improving a design solution?

Optimizing Solutions

The Akashi Kaikyō Bridge spans 3.9 km (2.43 miles) across the Akashi Strait. It links the city of Kobe with Awaji-shima Island in Japan. It is the longest suspension bridge in the world.

Explore First

Avoiding Cracked Screens Conduct a class survey to gather data on what causes the screens of students' phones to crack. Identify whether the phones had covers or screen covers when they fell or cracked. Are there cover designs that are more successful at protecting the screen?

CAN YOU EXPLAIN IT?

How can you determine the best way to keep plates from breaking on hard floors?

Most kitchens have hard floors, which are easy to clean. However, if a plate is dropped on a hard surface, it will break. Several solutions to prevent breaking plates are available. Identifying the solution that works the best and making it better is called optimization.

1. Imagine you are a chef in a busy kitchen. You need to reduce the number of plates that break because broken plates are a safety hazard and they need to be replaced. What are five potential solutions to this problem?

2. Choose the solution you think might work best for the problem above. Identify ways you could test it in order to make it the best solution for your problem.

EVIDENCE NOTEBOOK As you explore this lesson, gather information to help explain how you would choose a solution for this problem.

Improving a Promising Design Solution

Treats, such as muffins, are designed to taste delicious. Some muffin recipes make large and fluffy muffins. Other recipes make smaller, denser muffins. Each recipe uses different amounts of ingredients, such as baking powder, that make them light or dense. Imagine that you found a recipe for blueberry muffins that is rated as "delicious" by reviewers. You want to make the muffins for a party. Your design problem is to create muffins that are bite-sized and do not crumble, so you want to test the recipe first. If the muffins are too dense, people might not like them. If they are too fluffy, they will likely break apart when people bite into them. You follow the recipe. Then you test your design by tasting a muffin. It falls apart. It is too crumbly. It needs to be denser.

Build on the Most Promising Design

You have a design solution (a recipe), but it is currently not the best solution to your problem (to make small muffins for the party). You need to experiment to optimize the recipe. You decide to make several batches of muffins and change the amount of baking powder in each batch. The only way to know what such changes might do is to test the recipes and check the results.

Design optimization is the process of making an object or system as effective and useful as possible. A design solution, whether it is a blueberry muffin recipe or an engine part, is always tested to determine whether it is a better solution than any of those previously tested. Improvements to a design are made in response to test results.

Testing the recipe and modifying it based on your results will lead to a recipe that best meets your needs.

3. Optimizing a design solution always involves testing the modified solution. Why is it helpful to replicate these tests? Use the example of the muffin recipe in your answer.

Make Tradeoffs

Analysis of test data gives information about how a solution will perform in real-life situations. Data analysis also helps determine whether a design solution can be built within a given budget or whether it can meet constraints on the retail cost. These types of analyses do not always provide definite answers as to which solution is best. Sometimes tradeoffs are necessary to come to the solution that is most likely to meet the criteria. For example, a metal case for a cell phone might increase the lifetime of the phone. However, a plastic case is much less expensive and is lighter in weight, which customers prefer. The designer must identify which criteria are most important, such as "lower cost" and "lighter weight," instead of "a longer lifetime," before moving to the next steps in the optimization process. In this example, the designer might choose to go with a plastic case. The designer has made a tradeoff, giving up a longer lifetime for the product in favor of a lower cost and a lighter weight.

4. Why is making a tradeoff an important part of optimizing a design? Choose all that apply.

   A. It helps to identify more criteria.

   B. It gets rid of unnecessary constraints.

   C. It helps identify what the designer needs to do next.

   D. It helps identify the most important features the design solution should have.

Test Models

In selecting the best solution, engineers often perform tests on a type of model called a prototype. A **prototype** is a test model of a design solution. Prototypes are usually the first working models of a new design. They are built for testing and may be shown to others to get feedback for improving the design. Sometimes a prototype is an actual working example of the design, but often, especially for large or complex designs, it may be a scale model of the object or even just a part of the object.

Prototypes can also be tested for design flaws, safety, and ease of use. These tests help ensure that everything works the way it should and that customers can figure out how to make it work. Otherwise, the product may become an expensive design failure.

Engineers use prototypes to identify precise changes to the design. This shoe prototype was printed using a 3D printer.

Evaluate Advantages and Disadvantages

After testing, solutions can be further evaluated using tools such as a cost-benefit analysis. A *cost-benefit analysis* is a method of identifying the strengths and weaknesses of a design solution. One example is comparing the production costs to the benefits the solution offers. A cost-benefit analysis helps determine which solutions are most promising. This kind of analysis can be used to develop and refine solutions at several points throughout the design process.

Use Math for Design Improvement

In order to minimize costs for the manufacturer, processed food is often packaged in containers that allow the maximum storage volume but use the minimum amount of material. The best design solution for a cereal box can be chosen by calculating the box dimensions that best meet the criteria of maximum volume and the least amount of cardboard.

The table below shows some calculations that engineers made while creating a cereal box. Your task is to find the cereal box size that has the maximum volume and the least surface area (has the largest volume-to-surface-area ratio), or that uses the least amount of cardboard. The design criteria are as follows:

- The volume must be between 3,400 cm^3 and 3,425 cm^3.
- The height must be between 25 cm and 27 cm.
- The length must be between 18 cm and 20 cm.
- The width must be between 6 cm and 8 cm.

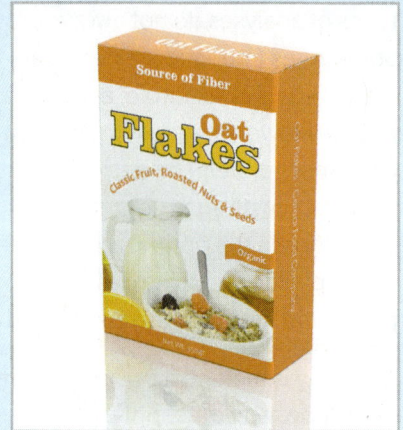

Containers with a large surface area also allow the manufacturer to better advertise their product.

Height (cm)	Length (cm)	Width (cm)	Volume (cm^3)	Surface Area (SA) (cm^2)	Volume to SA (ratio)
25.5	20.0	6.6	3,417	1,630	
27.0	19.0	6.7	3,437	1,642	
26.5	19.0	6.8	3,424	1,626	
26.0	19.0	6.9	3,409	1,609	
25.5	19.0	7.0	3,392	1,592	
27.0	18.0	7.1	3,451	1,611	
26.5	18.0	7.2	3,434	1,595	
26.0	18.0	7.3	3,416	1,578	
25.5	18.0	7.4	3,397	1,562	

5. For each set of box dimensions, determine the volume-to-surface-area ratio. Round the results to two decimal places. Choose the box that best meets the criteria and explain your reasoning.

6. Why do design engineers test promising solutions to a problem, such as preventing plates from breaking, before finalizing the design? Record your evidence.

Identify the Characteristics of the Best Solution

One design may not perform the best across all tests, so identifying the best-performing characteristics of the designs can help design the best solution to the problem. This is an important step in optimizing solutions.

A raincoat designer wants to make raincoats that teenagers would like. The company's engineers tested three different designs that performed well in three different tests. However, no design performed the best in all the tests. The design criteria are identified as follows:

- It must be as lightweight as possible.
- It must to be easy to close and open.
- It must be as water resistant as possible.
- It must be made of fabrics with fashionable designs and colors.
- It must have pockets.

Optimizing a raincoat design involves working with a design that combines the most favorable characteristics.

	Weight (g)	Closure	Fabric Water Resistance (minutes of exposure)
Raincoat A	250	Snaps: hard to use	11
Raincoat B	410	Zipper: easy to use	27
Raincoat C	500	Zipper: easy to use	>60

The three criteria identified as the most important for a successful design were: being lightweight, being easy to close, and having high water resistance. Engineers made a new design that combined the best features of each raincoat. This redesign had the weight range of Raincoat A, the water-resistant fabric of Raincoat C, and the zipper of Raincoats B and C. The redesigned raincoat was then tested. Tests showed that the most water-resistant fabric worked in the new design, but it was a little heavier because of the heavier fabric.

7. Imagine you are in charge of further optimizing the raincoat design. What next steps would you take in the optimization process?

_____

_____

_____

Adobe Stock

Using Data to Optimize Solutions

Some engineering problems involve designing a process or system rather than designing an object. The assembly line is an example of a system that has become an important manufacturing system. In an automotive assembly line, a car's frame moves on an automated belt system. As the cars or its parts move by, each worker along the line performs a specific task. At the end of the assembly line is a finished car. The assembly line is process-designed to solve an engineering problem—making many similar or identical objects as efficiently as possible. Assembly lines are used to produce many things, such as clothing, tools, food, and vehicles. Engineers whose job it is to optimize industrial systems are called *systems engineers*.

Process and System Optimization

Engineered systems are designed to solve a well-defined problem. Although assembly line systems were used during the Industrial Revolution to speed up the manufacturing process, it was not until the early 20th century that they were optimized to include the types of processes that are used today.

Henry Ford and his team designed the first modern assembly line to produce large numbers of cars. Each major car part was produced on a separate line. Then a final line assembled the vehicle. Every worker carried out a specific task. The time needed to build a single car dropped from 12 hours to about 90 minutes. Optimizing assembly lines allowed Ford's main factory to increase production from fewer than 20,000 cars a year to more than a million cars per year in just 10 years. Ford was able to reduce the price of his cars by reducing the time, cost, and number of people it took to build them.

The assembly line has changed through continual optimization. Today, assembly lines are often made up of rows of robots doing repetitive tasks for long periods of time instead of rows of human workers doing the same thing.

8. The assembly line has changed over time. How is the optimization of engineered processes similar to the optimization of engineered products?

The Iterative Design Process

Part of design optimization includes iterative testing of a prototype. The results of iterative tests are used to improve the next design version. For example, suppose a company that makes bicycle parts is designing a new gear sprocket. Bicycle sprockets are most often made from an alloy of aluminum and zinc. The alloy is light and is available in a variety of strengths. The sprocket design works well, but designers now want to make it from the strongest alloy they can. To identify the most suitable alloy, designers will test the sprocket design using different alloys. Strength tests will identify the strongest alloy. The sprocket design will be modified to use the new, stronger alloy.

Several sprockets make up the gears of a bicycle.

The Systematic Steps of Optimizing a Design Solution

This diagram represents the "ideal" engineering design process. In reality, engineers may skip steps or do things in different orders. Iterative design processes are used to optimize the solution. The optimizing steps are highlighted.

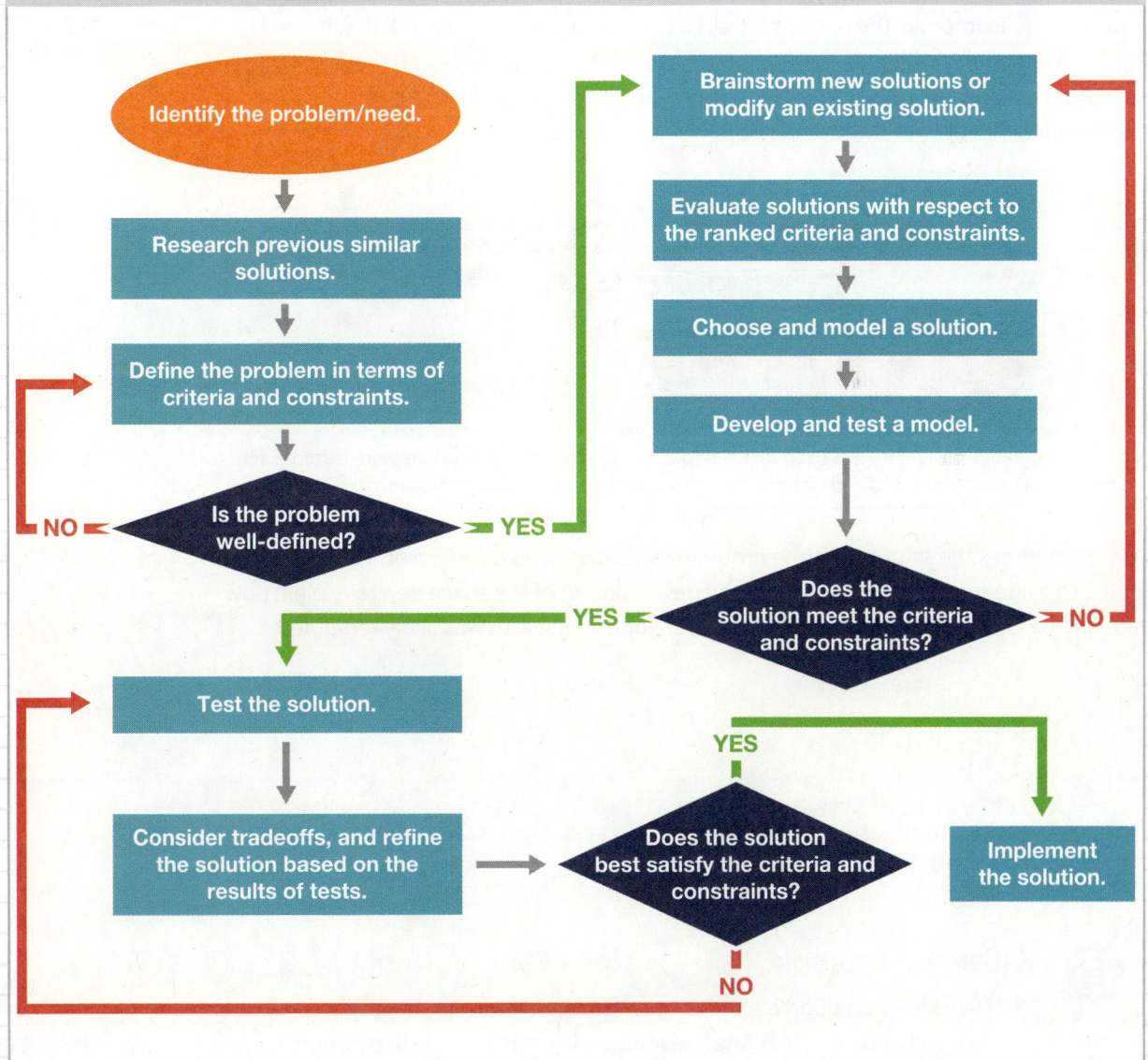

Identify the problem/need.

Research previous similar solutions.

Define the problem in terms of criteria and constraints.

Is the problem well-defined? — NO / YES

Brainstorm new solutions or modify an existing solution.

Evaluate solutions with respect to the ranked criteria and constraints.

Choose and model a solution.

Develop and test a model.

Does the solution meet the criteria and constraints? — YES / NO

Test the solution.

Consider tradeoffs, and refine the solution based on the results of tests.

Does the solution best satisfy the criteria and constraints? — YES / NO

Implement the solution.

Getty Images Plus/Getty Images

9. What are some characteristics of the iterative design process? Choose all that apply.

   A. Each iteration incorporates features that worked in previous tests.

   B. Useful features of different solutions can be combined.

   C. Solutions are tested during every iteration of the design process.

   D. Each iteration starts with a completely new idea or solution.

The Space Pen

An example of a product of the iterative design process is the "space pen," a ballpoint pen that can work in zero gravity. Astronauts on early space missions used pencils to keep notes, but using pencils created problems. Broken tips and graphite dust floated around the cabin and interfered with instruments. The developer of the space pen, Paul Fisher, used the iterative process to optimize the design solution for writing in space. In the freefall conditions of space, the ink in a regular pen dried out or it did not flow in the right direction. Fisher designed a cartridge to hold the ink. However, a vacuum formed in the cartridge, and the ink stopped flowing. To solve this problem, he pressurized the ink cartridge. Then the ink flowed well. However, sometimes it leaked because of the air pressure. To improve the performance, Fisher developed a gel-like ink that flowed well and did not leak. The result was a pen that can be used in space and that can write upside down on Earth. In each iteration, the features that worked were improved, and the features that did not work were not developed further.

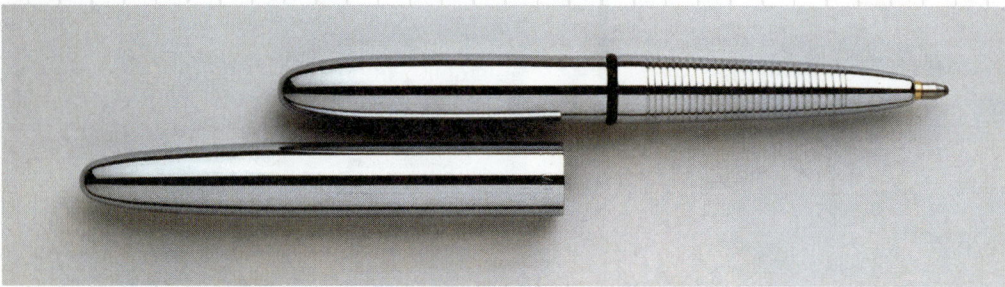

During the iterative design process used to develop the space pen, many solutions were tested. Each iteration of proposed solutions and test results led to more improvements in the pen's design.

10. Sometimes the solution for one problem leads to new solutions to other problems. Use evidence from the example of the development of the space pen to explain how the problem of developing a ballpoint pen for use on Earth was likely redefined.

EVIDENCE NOTEBOOK

11. Even after a solution is used, engineers often return to the original problem and work to refine the solution. How is the iterative design process helpful in developing a solution to breaking plates? Record your evidence.

Hands-On Lab
Design a Model Car, Part 3

Evaluate test data and optimize a design.

In Part 2 of this lab, you built your model car. Now, in Part 3, you and other groups in your class will evaluate and optimize your car designs. The exact steps of your optimization process can vary depending on the number of cars built and the time available. Refer to the instructions in Part 1 of this lab (in Lesson 2) for the criteria and constraints for the car designs and the materials list.

MATERIALS
- See materials from Design a Model Car, Part 1.

Procedure and Analysis

STEP 1 Compare your test results from Part 2 of this lab with the results of other groups who tested the same design variables. Describe how those variables are related to the distance traveled.

STEP 2 Are there characteristics of other groups' cars that performed better in the tests than your car's? Based on your comparison of the class results, propose three design changes that could improve your car's performance, if needed. List your proposed design changes. Identify how you think the proposed design change will improve the car's performance. If you believe your car design does not need improvement, explain your reasoning.

STEP 3 With your teacher's approval, apply one design change to your car. Repeat the test and record your data on a separate sheet of paper. Compare the data from your modified design to the data from your original design.

STEP 4 How did the design change affect performance?

STEP 5 As a class, discuss and evaluate all of the test results and make suggestions for a new iteration of the design that uses the best characteristics of each design.

Lesson 4 Engineer It: Optimizing Solutions **71**

STEP 6 Each component of the solution must relate to the problem as it is defined. For example, unless the clearance the car body from the ground meets specifications for the ramp on which the cars will roll down, the car might get stuck as it leaves the ramp. How do the car's wheels and body clearance relate to the car as a solution to the engineering problem?

STEP 7 How might taking the best-performing characteristics of different car designs and using them to redesign your car help improve it?

Combine the Best Parts of Solutions

After a product is introduced, the iterative process continues, often leading to development of new models or styles. Each new style is a solution to a restated design problem that is influenced by successes and failures of the previous solutions. For example, cell phones have changed over time, as shown in the photo. Touchscreens have replaced keypads, and antennas are now contained within the phone. Optimization of the phone's built-in camera has added a major new function to cell phones. Point-and-shoot cameras, once popular devices, have been almost entirely replaced by cell phones.

During the optimization of cell phones, tradeoffs were necessary.

12. Improvements to one function frequently lead to worse performance of another function. Which of these statements describes a tradeoff that was needed as cell phones changed to meet new criteria and constraints? Choose all that apply.

A. Larger cell phone screens allow new functions, such as viewing videos.

B. Adding more applications shortens the life of a battery.

C. Bigger screens have a larger glass surface area, making them easier to shatter.

D. Internal antennas increase portability but decrease signal reception.

E. Touchscreens increase viewing area but can be harder to use than buttons.

F. Thinner cases decrease the weight of the phone and make it easier to handle.

13. How might starting the engineering design process with only one idea affect the ability to optimize that design later on?

_____

_____

_____

_____

_____

Continue Your Exploration

Name: _____   Date: _____

Check out the path below or go online to choose one of the other paths shown.

People in Engineering

- **Rapid Prototyping (3D Printers)**
- **Hands-On Labs** 🖐
- **Propose Your Own Path**

Go online to choose one of these other paths.

Ellen Ochoa, Electrical Engineer

Ellen Ochoa is an astronaut who became the director of the Johnson Space Center in Houston, Texas, in 2013. As a student working on her doctorate in electrical engineering, and later as a researcher at NASA, she designed optical data systems for processing information using light signals. She became an astronaut in 1991 and flew on four Space Shuttle missions. Her jobs included developing software and computer hardware for space flights and robotics development and testing. Besides being an astronaut, a manager, and a research engineer, Ochoa is a classical flutist.

Electrical engineers design, develop, and test electrical equipment, such as electric motors, radar and navigation systems, communications systems, and power-generation equipment. They also supervise the manufacturing of this equipment. Electrical engineers who work in industrial careers often have bachelor's degrees. Electrical engineers who direct research at university and government labs frequently have a doctorate. As Ellen Ochoa has shown, the sky is not the limit for electrical engineers.

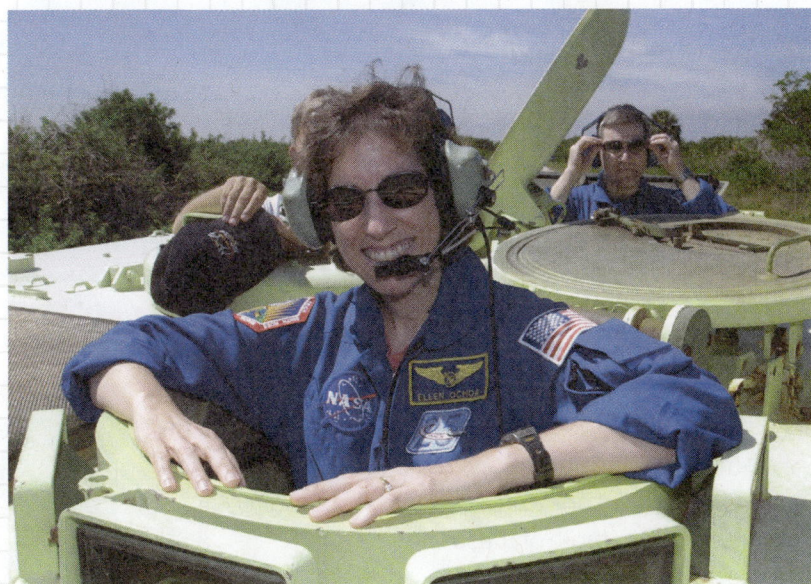

Ellen Ochoa became the first Hispanic woman to go to space when she served as a mission specialist aboard the Space Shuttle Discovery in 1993.

Continue Your Exploration

1. List three industries that would likely employ electrical engineers. Then describe one job that would likely involve electrical engineering in each industry.

2. Why might a person who is thinking about studying electrical engineering need to think about whether they enjoy solving problems?

3. Ellen Ochoa was accepted by NASA as an astronaut after she established her career as an electrical engineer. Why would a career in electrical engineering be a useful background for an astronaut?

4. **Collaborate** Research one or more electrical engineers who are involved in research. On a sheet of paper, generate a list of questions to ask the engineers about their work. With your teacher's help, contact one or more of these engineers to interview. Present your findings to the class.

Can You Explain It?

Name: _____   Date: _____

How can you determine the best way to keep plates from breaking on hard floors?

> **EVIDENCE NOTEBOOK**
>
> Refer to the notes in your Evidence Notebook to help you describe how to optimize a solution to the problem of plates breaking on floors.

1. State your claim. Make sure your reasoning fully explains how a solution may be optimized to solve the problem.

2. Summarize the evidence you have gathered to support your claim and explain your reasoning.

Science Source/Getty Images; (r) ©Bunkers/abourPictures/Alamy

Checkpoints

Answer the following questions to check your understanding of the lesson.

Use the data in the table to answer Questions 3–5.

3. Your team is building a rocket to enter into a national competition. Scoring is based on three factors: how high the rocket flies, time of flight before the parachute opens, and how safely it delivers a cargo of three eggs. These criteria are of equal importance to your design. You test four different design solutions and record the results, which are averaged here. Evaluate the test results to decide which design is the best one for you to optimize.

	Height (m)	Time of flight (s)	Number of eggs unbroken
Rocket A	260	49	3
Rocket B	220	57	1
Rocket C	240	66	3
Rocket D	275	58	2

   A. Rocket A **C.** Rocket C

   B. Rocket B **D.** Rocket D

4. The iterative process involves testing the _most promising / rejected_ solutions and modifying the _size / design_ based on test results. Iterative testing can be carried out to _redesign / optimize_ the most successful design.

5. You want to improve the height your rocket can reach. Which of the following features should you use in your new design?

   A. the dimensions of Rocket A

   B. the dimensions of Rocket B

   C. the dimensions of Rocket C

   D. the dimensions of Rocket D

Use the photo to answer Question 6.

6. This engineer is testing scale models of bridge components. Why might he use scale models in his tests rather than full-scale models? Choose all that apply.

   A. Scale models are less expensive to construct than actual pillars.

   B. Using models allows the engineer to test many different combinations of materials.

   C. The engineer will be able to find the best combination of materials for the bridge.

   D. Models are able to exactly reproduce the function of a pillar, but the testing is faster.

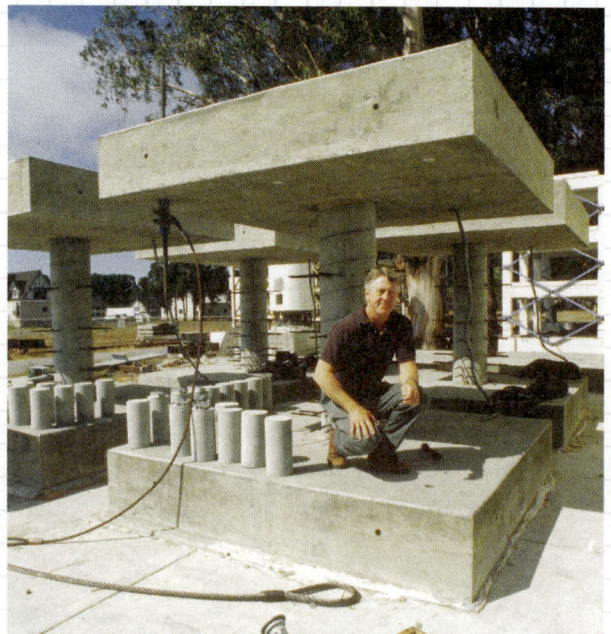

Interactive Review

Complete this section to review the main concepts of the lesson.

The solution that best addresses the ranked criteria of the engineering problem is chosen to further refine.

A. Why is it important to compare test results when making decisions about what design to develop further?

The iterative design process is a tool that engineers use to build the best solution. It is used to identify ways a solution can be improved further to better address the criteria and constraints of the design problem.

B. After a solution has been built, why might engineers want to optimize it further? What design process would they likely use to optimize a solution?

Choose one of the activities below to explore how this unit connects to other topics.

☐ People in Science

Luis von Ahn, Computer Scientist Luis von Ahn researches problems that can be solved by many people working together, an area he calls *human computation*. Von Ahn grew up in Guatemala City and became interested in computers at a young age. He earned degrees in math and computer science. His work on Internet security tests and the digitizing of data shows that humans and computers can work together to solve complex problems.

Present a human-computation project to your class. Explain the project goal, the roles of humans and computers in the project, and why its goals are possible only through human-computer collaboration.

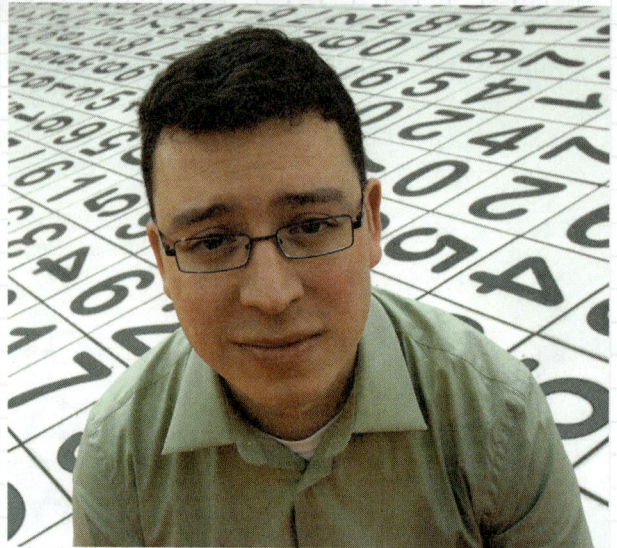

☐ Social Studies Connection

Epic Failures Many inventors and scientists "failed" before making a big discovery. The Wright brothers became successful only after experimenting with hundreds of glider flights and airplane designs.

Conduct research and make a verbal presentation about another person in history who persevered through adversity before having his or her invention succeed. Describe how the inventor refined the device using the engineering design process.

☐ Life Science Connection

Biomedicine Medical biology, or biomedicine, is the application of biological research to medical practices. This field of study includes specialties ranging from laboratory diagnostics to vaccine development and gene therapy. Engineers in the field of biomedicine work to design biomedical devices and develop biotechnologies.

Research a biomedical invention, therapy, or process and the history of its development. Prepare a multimedia presentation describing how the engineering design process contributed to the development of a successful treatment solution.

Name: _____   Date: _____

Complete this review to check your understanding of the unit.

Use the diagram to answer Questions 1–3.

1. This diagram is an example of information flowing through a system. What is an example of this system's output?

   A. brainstorming solutions

   B. a successful solution

   C. evaluation of potential solutions

   D. evaluation of test data

2. Which step in the engineering design process comes after precisely describing the problem?

   A. brainstorming solutions

   B. evaluating solutions with respect to criteria

   C. choosing solutions for testing

   D. any of the above

3. Testing and evaluating solutions is a(n) *iterative / linear* process.

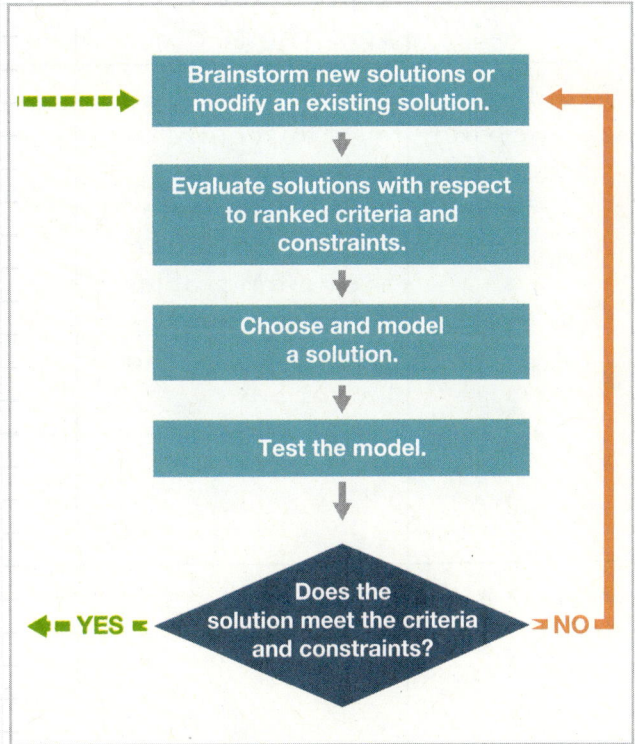

Brainstorm new solutions or modify an existing solution.

↓

Evaluate solutions with respect to ranked criteria and constraints.

↓

Choose and model a solution.

↓

Test the model.

↓

YES ← Does the solution meet the criteria and constraints? → NO

Use the decision matrix to answer Questions 4–5.

Decision Matrix: The Best Screen Protector			
Criteria	**Materials**		
	TPU	Tempered glass	PET film
Does not scratch	2	4	4
Reduces glare	2	3	2
Lightweight	2	2	1
Durable	1	4	4
Not expensive	3	1	2

4. This decision matrix ranks screen protector materials according to several specifications. Which material would make the best screen protector if the most important features were *Not expensive* and *Reduces glare*?

   A. TPU (thermoplastic polyurethane)

   B. Tempered glass

   C. PET film (polyethylene terephthalate)

5. The materials are the *criteria / solutions* in the decision matrix. The specifications about each option are the *criteria / solutions*.

6. Think about the engineering design process as you fill out this chart. Describe how each of the steps involves aspects of each of the big-picture concepts.

Process Steps	Criteria and Constraints	Research and Data Analysis	Systems and System Models
Defining an engineering problem	Determining the most important criteria and constraints helps to precisely define the design problem by identifying specific needs and limitations.		
Testing a solution			
Making tradeoffs			

Name: _____   Date: _____

Use the photo of the mind-controlled prosthetic arm to answer Questions 7–10.

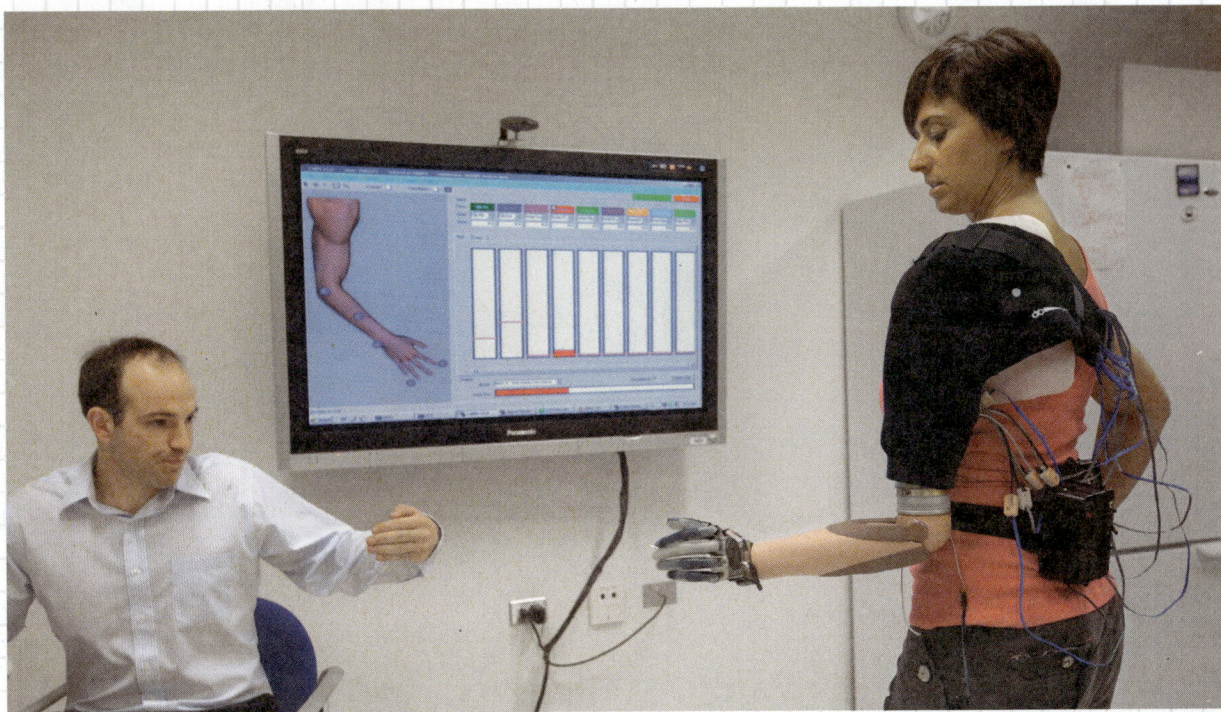

7. The photo shows a woman controlling the movements of her prosthetic arm using brain signals. Describe the problem that this tool solves.

8. People using this new type of prosthetic have noticed that some of their needs are not met by the current design. Based on these comments, the engineers are working to address these issues and are developing a new prototype. Explain why a new prototype is necessary.

9. What criteria do you think the inventors determined were important when developing their prototype?

10. What scientific principles might have guided the inventors of this prosthetic arm?

Use the photos to answer Questions 11–14.

11. What needs does each suitcase address? Are they the same needs? Explain your answer.

12. What kinds of data could you collect about suitcase designs to compare the needs each different style meets? What tests would be the most helpful in comparing how each design solution solves a problem or need?

13. After analyzing the data from suitcase design tests, you may find that both options have good features. Explain how engineers might use these results to develop an improved solution.

14. Suitcase designs have changed over time. Use evidence to explain how suitcase design has benefited from the engineering design process.

Name: _____   Date: _____

What is the best feature for a new pool entry ramp?

An inspector has determined that the entrance ramp for your community pool does not meet current safety requirements. The pool management board is looking at ways to upgrade the current ramp to meet the standards. They are looking at reducing the slope of the ramp, coating the ramp with non-slip surface material, and/or installing railings.

Your team has been asked to analyze design solutions to determine which ramp modification is the most appropriate and affordable choice for your community pool. You will present your findings to the pool directors as they decide how to proceed.

The steps below will help guide your research and develop your recommendation.

Engineer It

1. **Define the Problem** Define the design problem using the criteria and constraints. How might each type of ramp modification increase safety for different types of pool patrons?

Engineer It

2. **Conduct Research** Consider each of the three pool ramp feature options (changing the ramp angle, the surface material, and/or the railings). Explain what types of work would have to be done in order to make that type of ramp modification. How might each of these changes help the pool meet current safety rules?

3. **Analyze Data** On a separate sheet of paper, create a decision matrix to analyze the modification options. Describe the strengths and weaknesses of each modification option.

4. **Identify and Recommend a Solution** Based on your research, construct a written explanation about which pool ramp feature change is the best choice for your community pool. Describe any tradeoffs involved in your decision.

5. **Communicate** Prepare a presentation of your recommendation for the community pool directors as they decide which design is best for the ramp. Include an argument for your recommendation based on evidence and an explanation of the benefits and drawbacks associated with the design.

✓ **Self-Check**

	I precisely defined the criteria and constraints that helped define the problem of improving pool ramp safety.
	I researched the design features to determine how well they met the criteria and constraints of the problem.
	I analyzed my research and data to create a decision matrix.
	My solution is based on evidence from research, and an analysis of my decision matrix.
	My solution and recommendation were clearly communicated to others.

Systems in Organisms and Earth

How do interactions among natural systems make life on Earth possible?

Unit Project 86
Lesson 1   Models Help Scientists Study Natural Systems 88
Lesson 2   Cells Are Living Systems 108
Lesson 3   Plants Are Living Systems 128
Lesson 4   Animals Are Living Systems 144
Unit Review 167
Unit Performance Task 171

Rock climbing requires a combination of muscle strength, balance, and hand-eye coordination.

You Solve It How Can You Design a Satellite's Orbit?

Design and test orbits for two satellites that will be put into orbit around the Earth and Mars systems.

Go online and complete the You Solve It to explore ways to solve a real-world problem.

Investigate an Animal Behavior

Dolphins locate the size and position of prey using sound waves.

A. Look at the photo of the dolphin. On a separate sheet of paper, write down as many different questions as you can about the photo.

B. Discuss With your class or a partner, share your questions. Record any additional questions generated in your discussion. Then, choose the most important questions from the list that are related to animal behavior. Write them below.

C. Identify an animal that has an interesting behavior that you would like to research. List some of the sources you might use in your research.

D. Use the information above and your research to produce a multimedia presentation or science magazine article describing the animal's behavior. Include body and sensory adaptations involved in the behavior.

Discuss the next steps for your Unit Project with your teacher and go online to download the Unit Project Worksheet.

Language Development

Use the lessons in this unit to complete the network and expand your understanding of these key concepts.

■	Similar term
■	Phrase
■	Cognate
■	Example
■	Definition

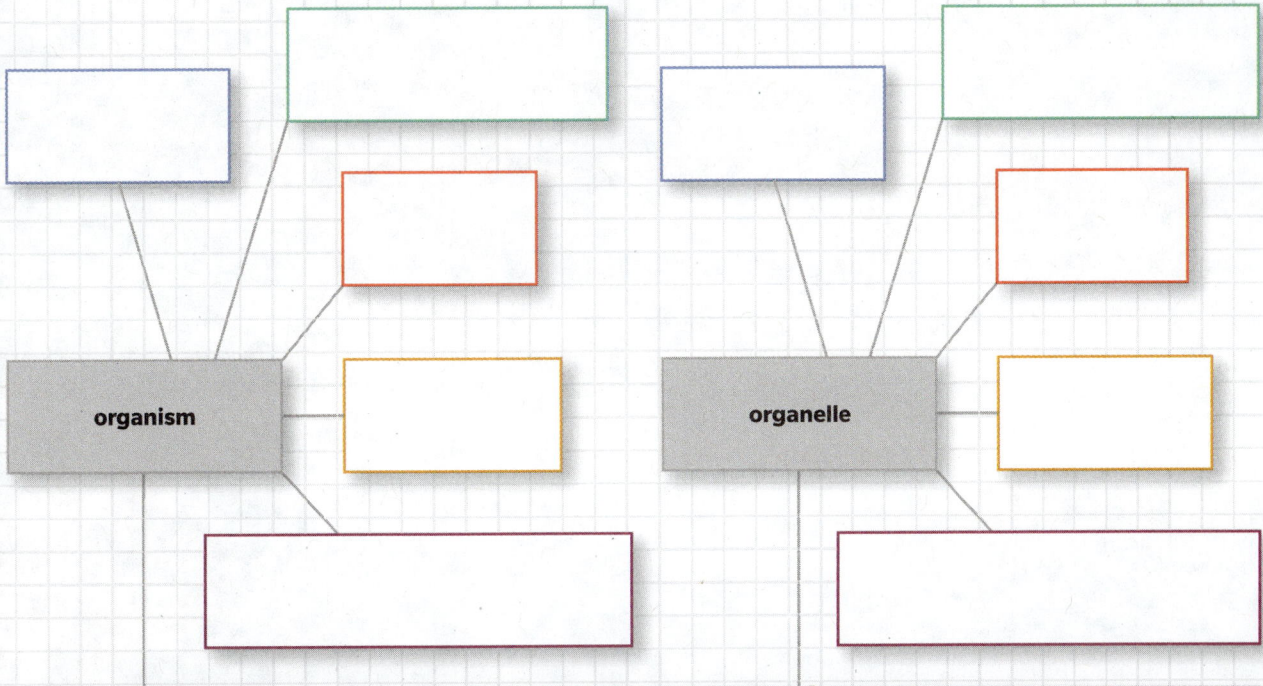

organism

organelle

How do interactions among natural systems make life on Earth possible?

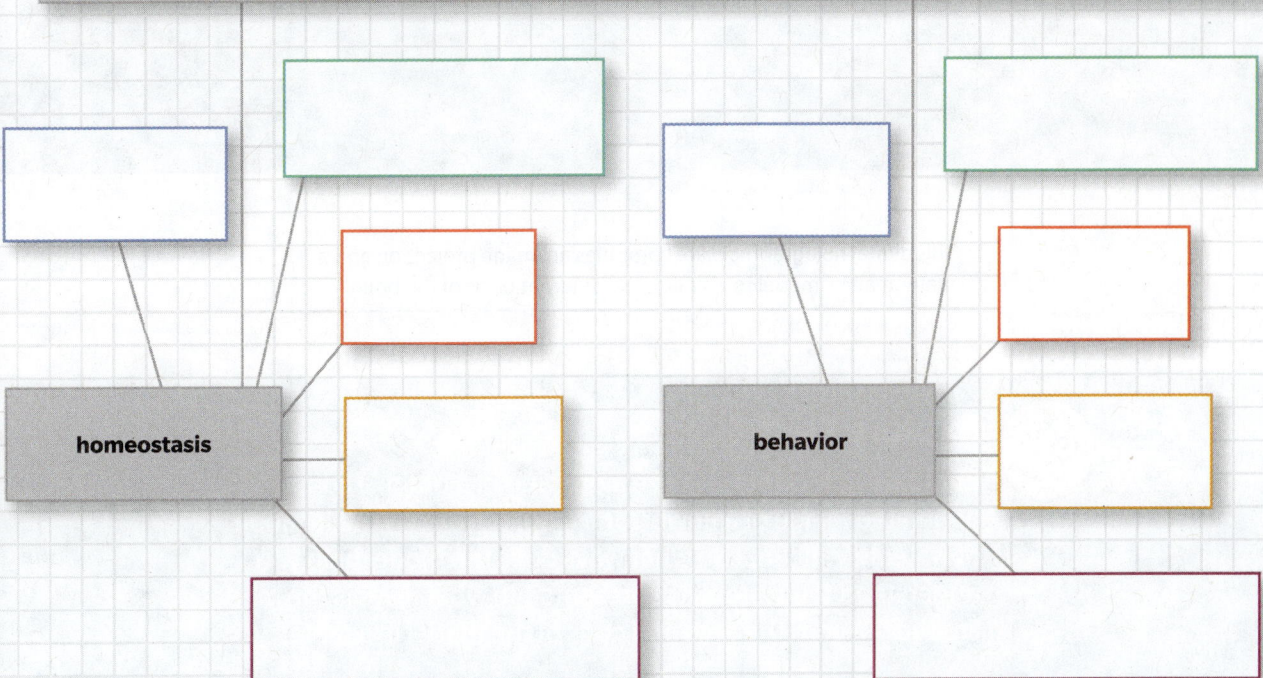

homeostasis

behavior

Models Help Scientists Study Natural Systems

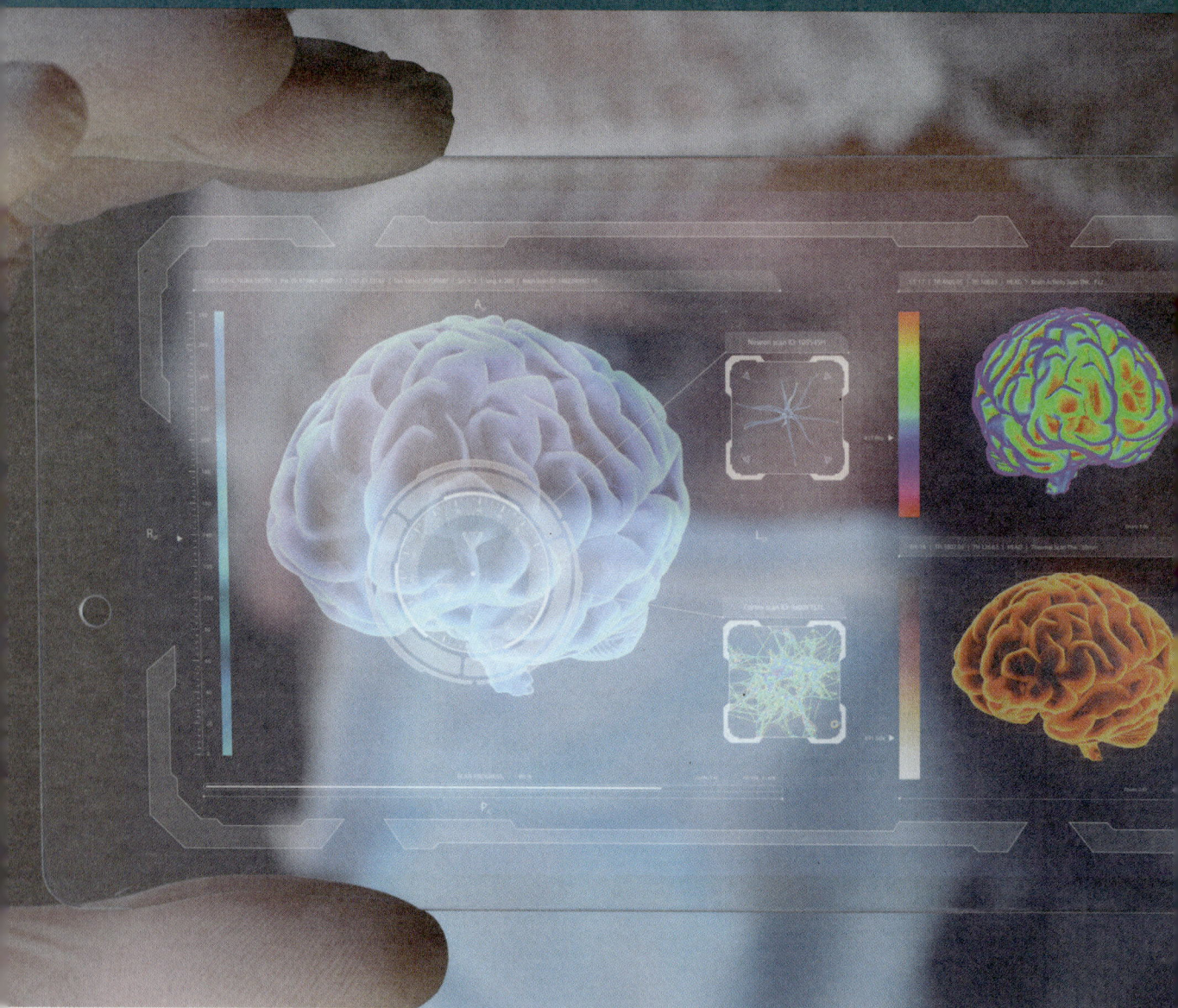

This digital holographic plate combines an image projection and a mathematical model to visualize the different parts of the brain.

Explore First

Evaluating Models Analyze a drawing of a brain, a computer-generated image of a flower, or a map that shows the location of water in your area. In what ways does the model help you understand the system it represents? In what ways is the model limited? Record the pros and cons of the model in a table.

Go online to view the digital version of the Hands-On Lab for this lesson and to download additional lab resources.

CAN YOU EXPLAIN IT?

How can this model help scientists study natural systems?

Biosphere 2 was built to determine if a physical model of the Earth system could sustain life. Today, the facility is an education and research center.

Biosphere 2 was designed to support a small team of researchers for two years, completely sealed off from the outside environment. It contained thousands of species of plants and animals in different environments, including an ocean with a coral reef. However, low oxygen and high carbon dioxide levels resulted in many problems and endangered the lives of the researchers. Although the project did not achieve its goals, scientists gained an understanding of how systems on Earth interact.

1. **Discuss** Study the photo that shows Biosphere 2 from the outside. What do you think it would be like to live inside for two years?

2. Why might scientists and engineers want to find out if a system like Biosphere 2 can sustain life?

EVIDENCE NOTEBOOK As you explore the lesson, gather information to help explain how the Biosphere 2 model helps scientists study natural systems.

Defining Systems

What do you think of when you hear the word, "system"? You might think of a video game system, the solar system, or your digestive system. Scientists define and study systems to help them construct explanations and make predictions. For example, scientists study coral reef systems to explain interactions between organisms and to analyze the effects of human activities on the environment.

3. There is no hard boundary between a coral reef and the open ocean. How does defining a boundary help scientists to better study a coral reef? Select all that apply.

   A. Defining a coral reef boundary allows scientists to explain all ocean parts and interactions by studying the reef as a system.

   B. Defining a coral reef boundary allows scientists to focus on a smaller set of parts and interactions.

   C. Defining a coral reef boundary allows scientists to see how the parts of the reef interact with the parts of the rest of the ocean.

   D. Defining a coral reef boundary allows scientists to decide that the reef is not part of the ocean.

Coral skeletons form the reef structure that many animals, including fishes, urchins, and crabs, rely on for food and shelter.

Explore Online

Systems

A **system** is a set of interacting parts working together. Corals, fishes, and seawater are all parts, or *components*, of a coral reef system. Organisms in the system interact with each other, their environment, and components of other systems. One organism can be food or shelter for other organisms. For example, algae growing on reefs use energy from sunlight to make food by photosynthesis. Parrotfish eat the algae and hide from predators in the reef openings. Sharks visit the reef to prey on parrotfish and other animals. All of these interactions result in transfers of matter and energy.

Matter and energy flow into, within, or out of systems. Matter or energy that enters a system is called an *input*. A coral reef system relies on inputs of seawater and sunlight. Some inputs harm reefs. Pollution from industry or runoff is an example of a harmful input. A product of a system is an *output*. The output of one part of the system can become the input for another part. For example, algae and other producers release oxygen during the process of photosynthesis. Organisms in the coral reef system use the oxygen in the process of cellular respiration.

Natural Systems

A coral reef is a *natural system,* because it occurs in the natural world and was not designed by people. Scientists are interested in understanding how natural systems function and change while engineers are interested in studying and solving problems. For example, scientists might study a coral reef system to determine how pollution affects coral reef health. Engineers might develop a computer model to identify the source of the pollution and design and test affordable methods to reduce or stop the pollution.

In order to study a system, a scientist starts by imagining a *boundary,* or surface that encloses the system. In a natural system, like a coral reef, matter and energy pass into and out of the boundary. When fish, crabs, and bits of drifting seaweed flow through the imaginary boundary, they become components of the reef ecosystem.

Natural systems have *properties,* or characteristics, that result from the interactions of their parts. For example, temperature and salinity are properties of a coral reef system.

4. **Discuss** Your body is another example of a natural system. Brainstorm parts of your body system and record them to complete the model below.

Boundary		Inputs/Outputs
		oxygen

Components		
organs		

Interactions

breathing

Properties

personality

EVIDENCE NOTEBOOK

5. What is the boundary of the Biosphere 2 system? How is this boundary similar to a natural system? How is it different? Record your evidence.

Modeling Systems

Scientists and engineers use models to represent natural systems. When scientists and engineers construct models of systems, they include only the parts and interactions that are most important for their intended purpose. Then they can improve the model by comparing it with the real system. For example, the diagram on this page is a conceptual model intended to communicate the parts of the human respiratory system. It shows some of the system features, but does not include details at the microscopic scale.

Models can be physical, mathematical, digital, or conceptual, or combinations of these different model types.

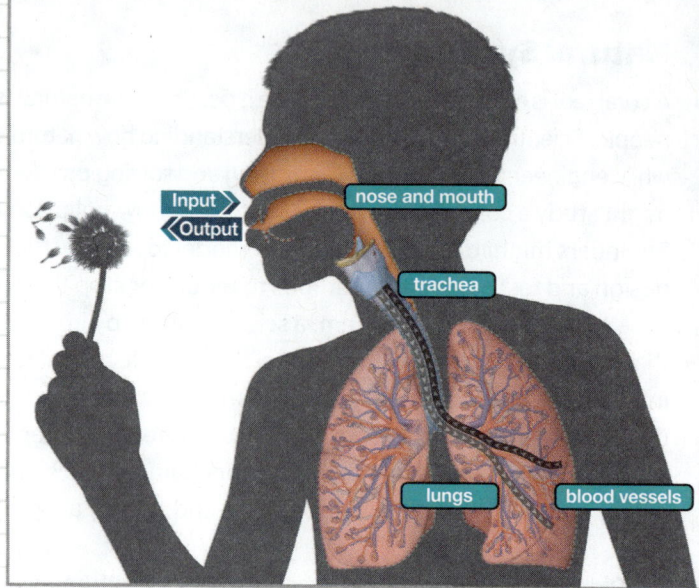

This diagram is a conceptual model of the respiratory system.

Define a System

Think of something that you could define as a system to help you study how it works. It could be your classroom, favorite animal, or sports team. List the features of your system including the boundary, inputs and outputs, components, and interactions.

6. Record your system and system features in the graphic organizer.

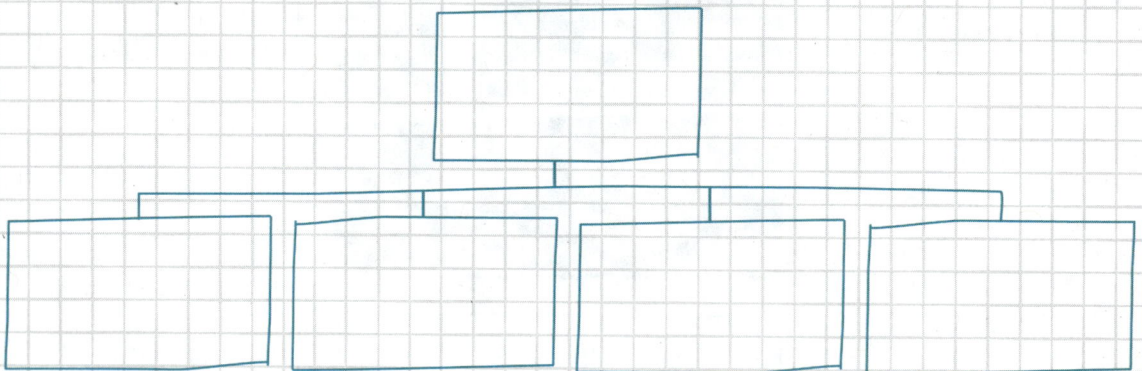

7. Summarize the evidence you collected to define your system.

Modeling Living Systems

Organisms Are Living Systems

A bacterium, a tree, and a rat are all living things, yet they look very different and perform different activities. However, all living things, or organisms, perform basic life functions. An **organism** is a living system made up of one or more cells that perform all the functions needed for life and growth. The body of a complex organism can be organized into subsystems that interact to perform functions. For example, your body has a circulatory system and a respiratory system that work together to deliver oxygen and nutrients to all the cells in your body.

Cells

All organisms are made of cells. A **cell** is the smallest subsystem of an organism. Organisms that are made up of a single cell are called *unicellular* organisms. *Multicellular* organisms are made of more than one cell. The cell types that make up multicellular organisms are specialized and organized to carry out specific functions.

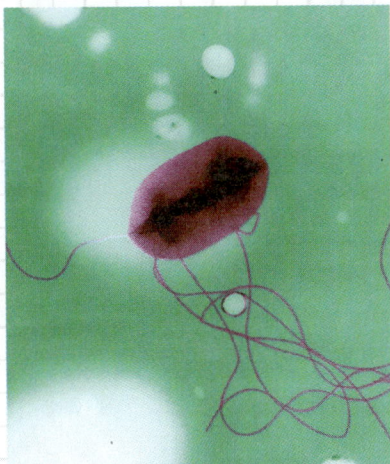

E. coli bacteria are unicellular. They have whip-like structures that help them move and attach to host cells.

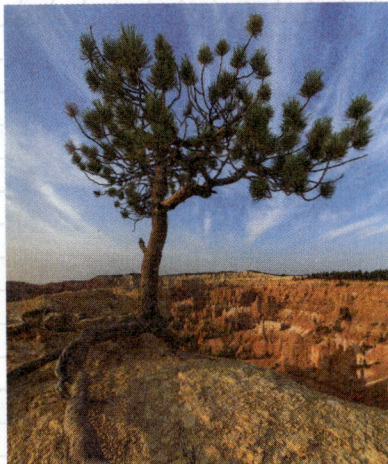

Ponderosa pine trees are multicellular plants. They have a thick outer layer, or *bark*, that protects them from the sun.

The kangaroo rat is a multicellular animal. Its specialized body system allows it to survive with very little water.

8. Each cell in unicellular organisms performs *some/all* of the functions required for life. Each cell in a multicellular organism performs *some/all* of the functions required for life.

Tissues

In organisms, such as plants and animals, specialized cells are grouped together in tissues. A **tissue** is a subsystem made up of a group of similar cells that are organized to perform a specific function. For example, certain specialized cells in a plant are small and hollow. These cells connect together to form a tissue, called *vascular tissue*, that transports water throughout the plant.

Model Tissue Structure and Function

You will model two different tissue types and relate their structure to their function.

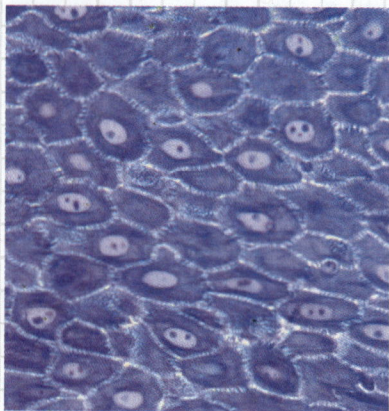

This tissue protects the skin from scraping. It can be especially thick on the heels of your feet.

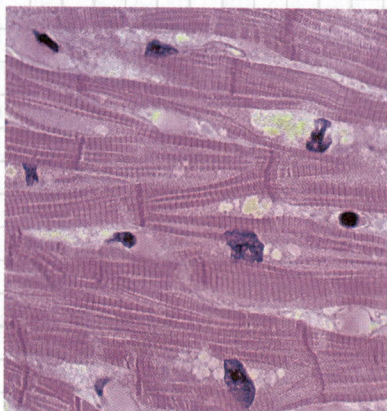

This tissue is located in the heart. It stretches and contracts to make the heart pump blood.

MATERIALS
- adhesive putty
- beads
- cardboard
- construction paper
- foam peanuts
- glue
- markers
- modeling clay
- pom poms
- rice
- rubber bands
- scissors
- sponges
- tape

Procedure and Analysis

STEP 1 Look at the tissues in the photos. Record your observations about the structure and shape of the cells.

STEP 2 Select the materials that you think will best model the cells and how they are connected to form the tissues. Construct a model of each tissue.

STEP 3 Describe how your models represent groups of cells working together to form tissues.

STEP 4 Use your models to make a claim about how the role played by different types of tissues within an organ depends on the structure of its cells.

Organs

An **organ** is a subsystem made up of different tissue types that work together to perform a function. For example, the stem of a plant is an organ that is made up of vascular tissue that transports water and nutrients, ground tissue that provides support, and epidermal tissue that protects the outside of the stem. Blood vessels are organs in animals made up of epithelial tissue that controls the passage of blood cells, layers of smooth muscle tissue that control the diameter of the vessel, and a tough wall of connective tissue.

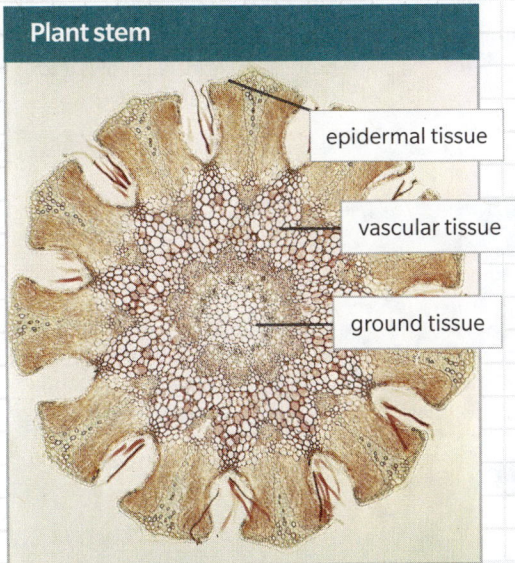

Plant stem

epidermal tissue

vascular tissue

ground tissue

Stems are plant organs that transport materials and provide support for the plant.

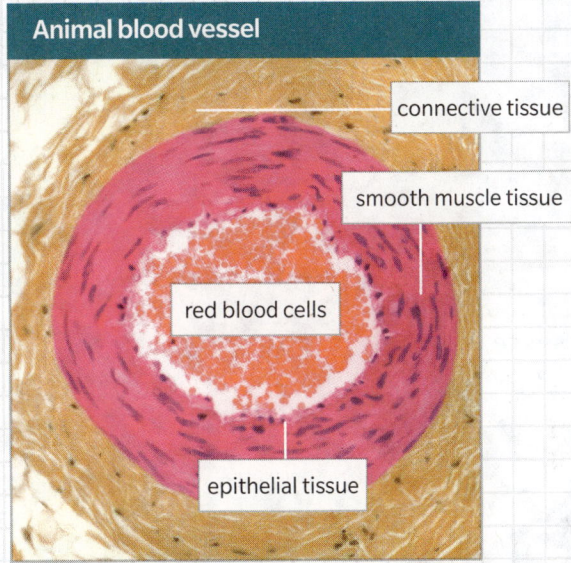

Animal blood vessel

connective tissue

smooth muscle tissue

red blood cells

epithelial tissue

Blood vessels transport blood and nutrients and remove wastes in the body.

Organ Systems

An **organ system** is a subsystem made up of a group of organs that work together to perform body functions. For example, in animals the heart, lungs, and blood vessels are organs of the *circulatory system* that takes in oxygen from the air through the process of respiration and delivers it to all the cells in the body. In plants, the leaves, stems, and flowers are organs of the *shoot system*, which transports water and nutrients from the roots to the leaves and uses carbon dioxide from the air and sunlight to produce food through the process of photosynthesis. An organism can have many organ systems that work together to perform all the functions the organism needs to survive.

9. Draw a model that shows the relationship between cells, tissues, organs, and organ systems.

10. When this frilled lizard is threatened, its heart rate increases to prepare to fight or run. Label the subsystems to complete the lizard circulatory system infographic.

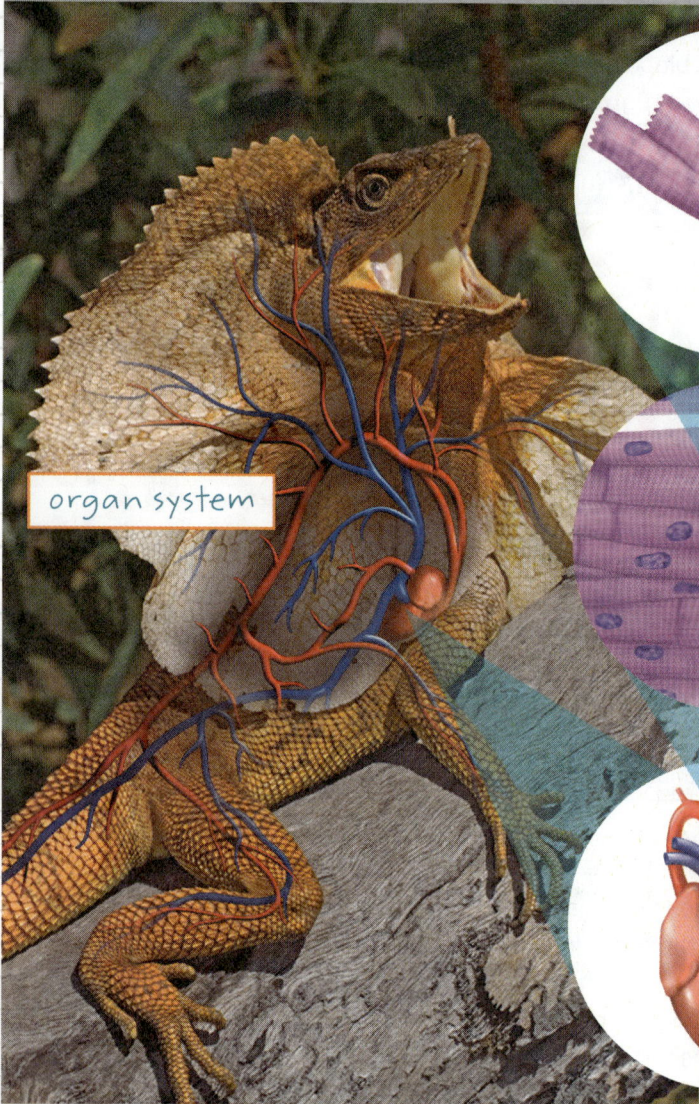

organ system

This subsystem is specialized for contraction. The structure of protein fibers inside allows it to stretch and contract.

Special junctions where cells connect allow all the cells in this subsystem to contract at the same time.

Several tissue types work together in this heart to perform the function of pumping blood throughout the body system.

Language SmArts

Use Evidence to Support an Argument

11. Use evidence from the text and the lizard diagram to support an argument that living things are made up of subsystems that can be part of larger systems.

_____

_____

_____

_____

_____

_____

_____

_____

Modeling Earth Systems

Earth Is a System

The boundary of the Earth system surrounds the entire planet, including the atmosphere. The system includes all the matter, energy, and processes within this boundary. The Earth system includes nonliving things, such as water, rocks, and air. It also includes living things, such as trees, animals, and people.

The Earth system is made up of smaller subsystems that constantly interact as matter and energy cycle and flow among them. The transfer of energy from the sun and Earth's interior drive the transfer of matter among the subsystems. Energy can also be transferred by the action of waves and moving objects. These interactions can happen in just a fraction of a second or over billions of years.

The Earth system can be divided into four major subsystems: the geosphere, the hydrosphere, the atmosphere, and the biosphere.

12. Identify the components of each subsystem as living or nonliving things.

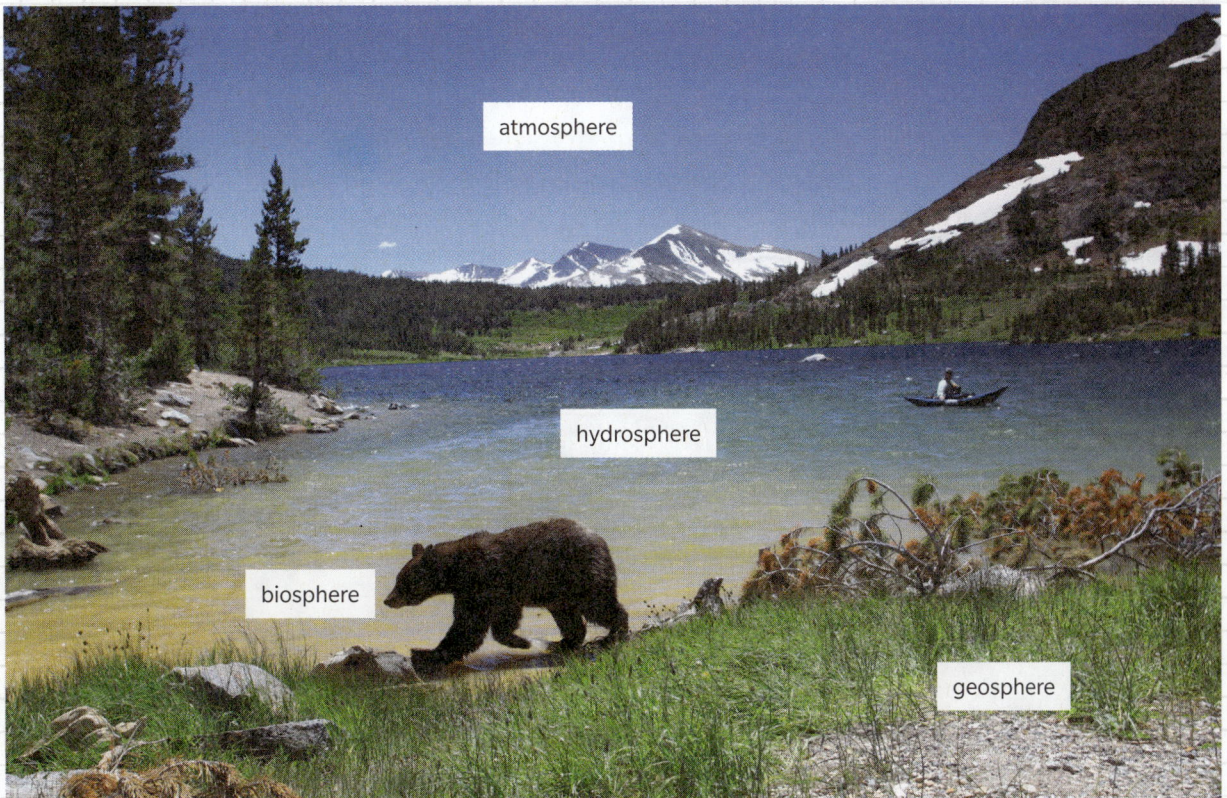

biosphere _____   atmosphere _____

hydrosphere _____   geosphere _____

13. Discuss Brainstorm ways in which the components of the different subsystems interact with each other.

Geosphere

Nearly all the mass of Earth is in the *geosphere*, the Earth subsystem that includes all rocks, minerals, and landforms on Earth's surface and all the matter in Earth's interior.

The geosphere is constantly changing. Thermal energy from Earth's formation and the decay of radioactive rocks drive changes on the surface that we experience as earthquakes, volcanoes, and the gradual buildup of mountains. Erosion by wind and water wears away landforms, and shapes rivers, lakes, and canyons.

These *tufa* pinnacles formed underwater 10,000 to 100,000 years ago.

Hydrosphere and Cryosphere

The *hydrosphere* is all the water on Earth. Ninety-seven percent of the hydrosphere is salt water found in the oceans. The hydrosphere also includes the fresh water in lakes, rivers, and underground. Rain and water droplets in clouds are also part of the hydrosphere. The *cryosphere* is a subsystem of the hydrosphere, made up of all the frozen water on Earth, such as glaciers, sea ice, and the snow shown in the photo.

Water on Earth is constantly moving as it flows through rivers, rocks, and living things. Energy from the sun drives the water cycle, which circulates water between Earth's surface and the atmosphere.

Liquid and frozen water are present at Lake Tahoe during the winter months.

Atmosphere

The *atmosphere* is the mixture of gases and particles that surround Earth. Nitrogen makes up about 78% of the atmosphere. Oxygen makes up nearly 21% of the atmosphere. The remaining 1% includes carbon dioxide, water vapor, and trace amounts of other gases. The atmosphere absorbs some of the energy from the sun. This energy warms Earth and makes life possible. Earth's rotation and uneven warming by the sun results in winds and air currents that move air and thermal energy around Earth.

Water Moves Between the Atmosphere and Hydrosphere

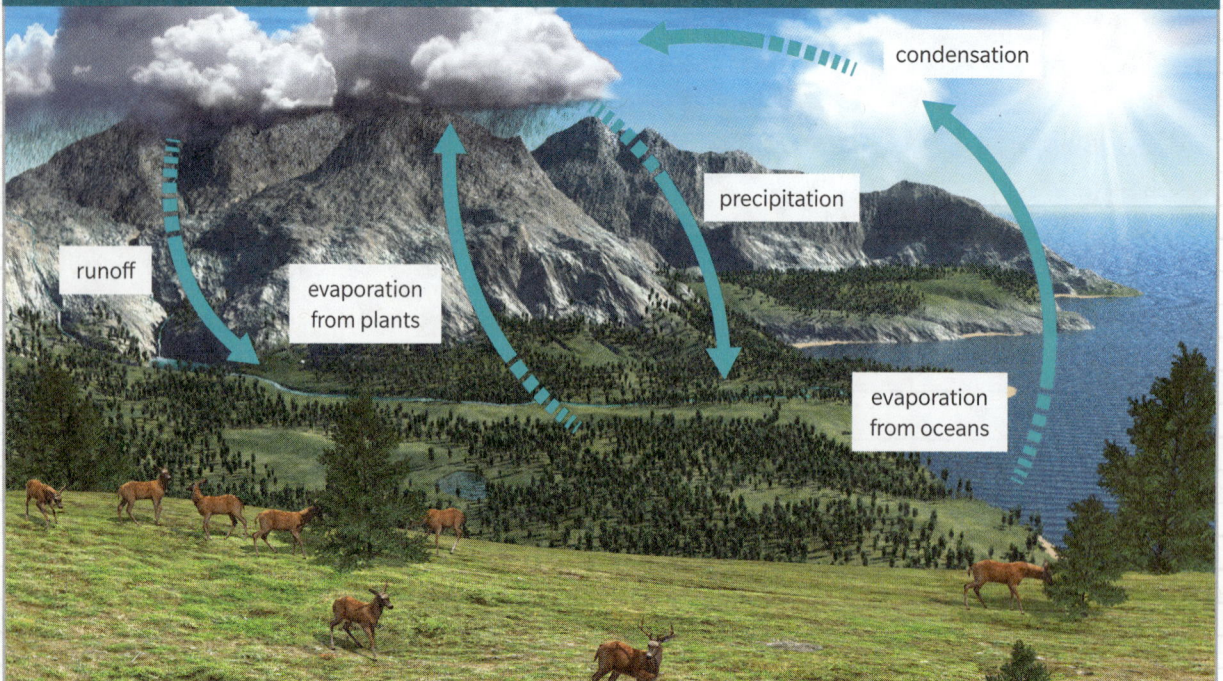

condensation

precipitation

runoff

evaporation from plants

evaporation from oceans

14. The diagram shows some of the interactions between the atmosphere and the hydrosphere. Identify the inputs and outputs of each system. Use your observations to explain how the inputs of one subsystem can be outputs of another subsystem.

Biosphere

The biosphere is made up of living things, including all the plants, animals, and microorganisms found everywhere on Earth. The biosphere extends upward about ten kilometers, and down to the deepest ocean trenches. Living things depend on other living things and nonliving things in their environment to exist.

The sun is the source of energy for green plants and other organisms that produce food using photosynthesis. Almost all life depends on these producers, since animals and most other organisms cannot make their own food. Animals and other consumers get food by eating plants or other organisms. Matter and energy move through the biosphere and other Earth subsystems as living things eat, grow, breathe, and move.

15. Wildfires occur naturally or are caused by human negligence. They spread quickly and emit harmful carbon particles into the air. Describe the ways a wildfire can affect the biosphere.

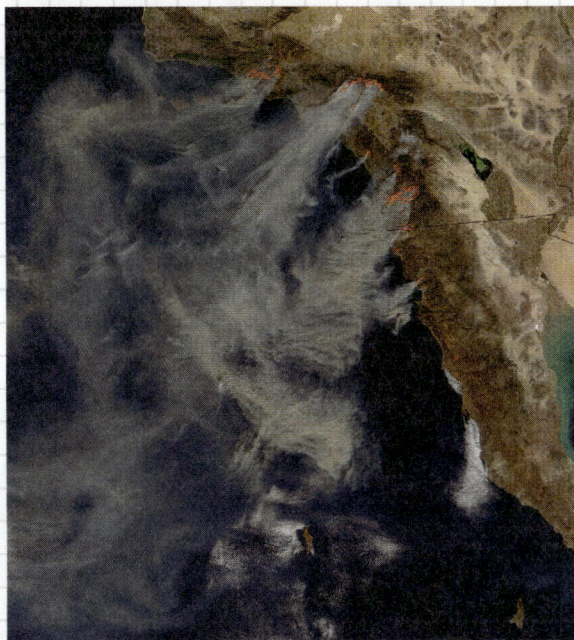

This satellite image shows the clouds of smoke from massive wildfires moving over the ocean.

16. *Decomposition* occurs when bacteria, fungi, or worms in the soil break down the matter in an organism that has died. Decomposition transfers matter from the geosphere / biosphere to the geosphere / biosphere.

EVIDENCE NOTEBOOK

17. All of Earth's subsystems are represented in Biosphere 2. How can this help scientists understand interactions between subsystems? Record your evidence.

Anthroposphere

A recently recognized Earth subsystem is the anthroposphere. The *anthroposphere* includes the total human presence on Earth, including built structures, technologies, activities, economy, and culture.

The anthroposphere is greatly affecting other Earth subsystems at a rapid rate. Human activities are changing carbon dioxide levels in the atmosphere and the amount of sea ice in the cryosphere. Human populations and the use of natural resources place stresses on the biosphere and geosphere.

Human-built cities are part of the anthroposphere.

18. List the Earth subsystem most affected by the activity described.

clear-cutting rainforest to make way for a railroad	
burning gasoline in cars	
draining wetlands to make space to build housing	
mining for coal and minerals	

Model Agricultural Runoff

Agricultural runoff occurs when water moves from farms to other areas due to rain, melting snow, or irrigation. Runoff collects the added nutrients from farm fields and carries them to lakes, coastlines, and groundwater.

If farms are not managed well, nutrient pollution is a problem. Manure and fertilizers high in nitrogen and phosphorus affect water quality.

19. Draw and label a model showing how the products of agricultural runoff travel through the Earth's subsystems. Indicate the transfer of matter between the subsystems, impacting fish and other living things.

Using Models to Analyze Systems

Studying Natural Systems Using Models

Natural events and human activities can result in changes to living and Earth systems over time. These changes can occur rapidly or very slowly over millions of years. Scientists use models to monitor changes that are occurring and to predict changes that might occur in the future. Scientists can compare predictions of their models with changes in the real world to refine their models so they will be more accurate.

Case Study: Modeling Changes to Coral Reefs

Coral reef systems are changing in response to human activities. Carbon emissions into the atmosphere result in increased global air and water temperatures. Algae that live in the tissues of coral provide food to the corals and are also responsible for the coral color. High temperatures stress the coral and cause them to release their algae partners. This appears as "bleaching", or lack of color, and eventually leads to coral death.

Coral Bleaching Alert

This map shows the risk of coral bleaching around the world. Satellite sea surface temperature monitoring data is used to construct a mathematical model that represents coral bleaching risk.

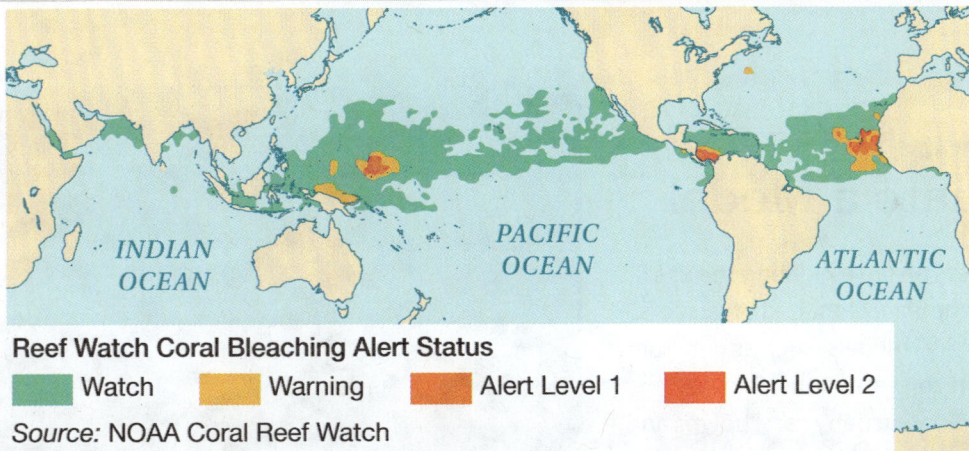

Reef Watch Coral Bleaching Alert Status

Watch   Warning   Alert Level 1   Alert Level 2

Source: NOAA Coral Reef Watch

20. **Discuss** How can scientists use this model to better understand how climate change affects interactions in coral reef systems?

EVIDENCE NOTEBOOK
21. How could Biosphere 2 be used to make predictions about the effects of climate change on natural systems? Record your evidence.

22. Do the Math What is the projected temperature increase by 2099 if carbon emissions are not reduced? What is the projection if carbon emissions are reduced?

Carbon Emissions and Temperature Increase

This model shows the relationship between carbon emissions in the atmosphere due to human activities and the projected increase in global temperature over time.

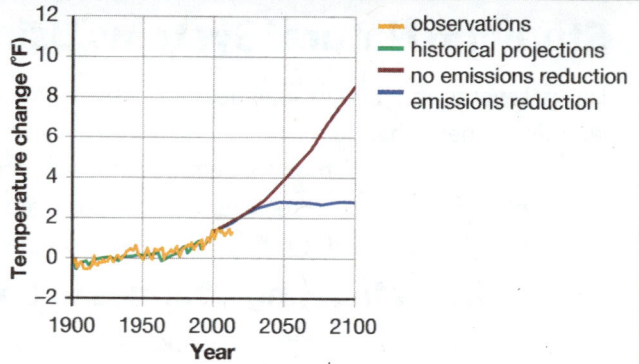

Legend:
- observations
- historical projections
- no emissions reduction
- emissions reduction

Source: NOAA Technical Report NESDIS 144, 2015

23. Carbon emissions in the atmosphere can enter the hydrosphere and cause acidification of ocean water, which can negatively affect the health of coral reefs. What can scientists infer about the future health of coral reef systems based on this climate change model?

24. Discuss How can conservation scientists use the bleaching risk and climate change models to improve strategies for protecting coral reef ecosystems?

Engineer It
Evaluate a Model

Scientists and engineers are investigating the use of artificial reefs to repopulate damaged coral reefs. Engineers design physical models, such as concrete blocks and 3-D printed coral skeletons, that will attract algae and free-floating baby coral polyps and begin a new reef.

Divers are setting up concrete reef balls to build an artificial reef.

25. What criteria and constraints do engineers need to consider when designing and constructing a physical reef model?

26. Describe ways that engineers can test different models to determine the one best suited for forming a new reef.

Continue Your Exploration

Name: _____   Date: _____

Check out the path below or go online to choose one of the other paths shown.

Systems and Organ Donation

- **Biosphere 2**
- **Hands-On Labs** ✋
- **Propose Your Own Path**

Go online to choose one of these other paths.

The human body is a complex system. Interactions among all your body systems are necessary for your body to breathe, play soccer, digest your lunch, and study for a test. But sometimes a component, such as a heart, lung, or kidney, is damaged because of injury or disease, disrupting body system interactions and functions.

Transplantation

A failing tissue or organ can be replaced with one that is healthy. This procedure is called *transplantation*. A tissue or organ from a donor is transplanted to the body of the recipient. Donor tissues and organs, such as skin, bone, or a heart, can come from people who have agreed to donate them after they die. It is also possible to remove some tissues and organs, such as bone marrow and kidneys, from living donors.

A donor is evaluated as a match for the transplant recipient by blood or tissue analysis. The diseased organ, such as a heart, is surgically removed from the recipient and replaced with the healthy organ from the donor.

Heart Transplant Procedure

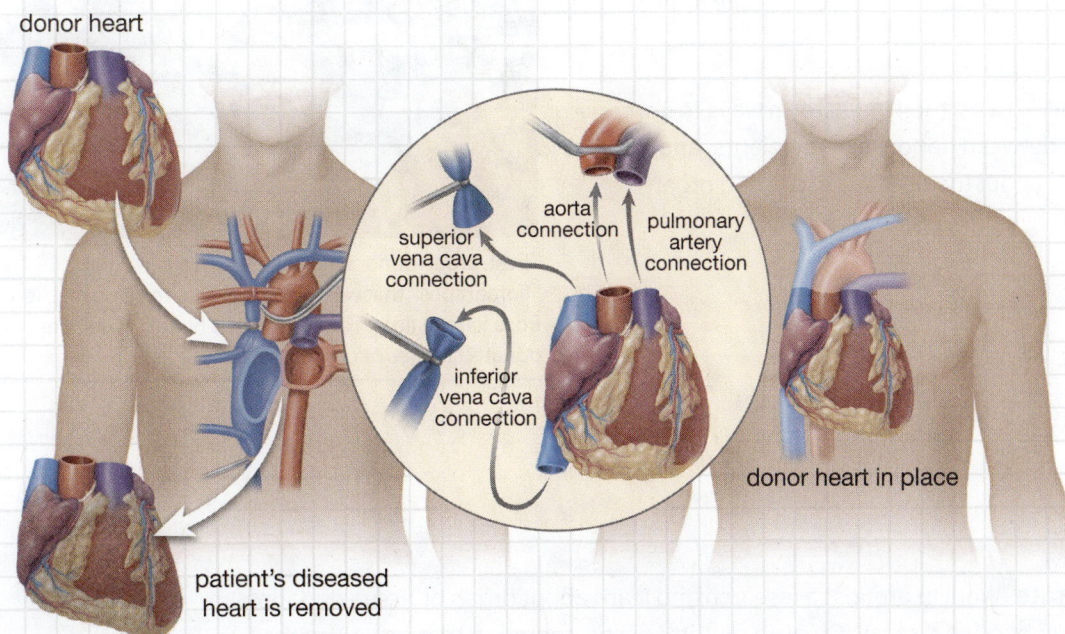

donor heart

superior vena cava connection

aorta connection

pulmonary artery connection

inferior vena cava connection

donor heart in place

patient's diseased heart is removed

Credit: Mayo Foundation for Medical Education and Research

Continue Your Exploration

1. Explain how the failure of one organ can affect the healthy function of the entire body system.

2. The immune system is a subsystem of the body that fights against infection. It recognizes the cells that make up a person's body but attacks invaders, such as bacteria and viruses. How might the function of this system affect tissue and organ transplant success?

Soliciting and Identifying Donors

Unfortunately, there is a shortage of tissue and organs available for donation. A well-organized donation system can maximize the chances of matching people willing to donate with compatible recipients, and ensure rapid delivery of donated organs to waiting recipients. Educating the public about the importance of tissue and organ donation can help to increase the pool of potential donors.

3. **Discuss** With a partner, brainstorm ways to improve matches between donors and recipients, and inform the public about the need for tissue and organ donors.

These organ donor family members are making "floragraphs" that will become part of the Donate Life Rose Parade float. The floragraphs honor loved ones who donated tissues or organs to save a life.

4. **Collaborate** Work in groups to research and learn about organ or tissue donation related to a specific disease. Create a multimedia presentation that describes the disease, the body systems affected, and the transplantation procedure.

Can You Explain It?

Name: _____   Date: _____

How can this model help scientists study natural systems?

EVIDENCE NOTEBOOK

Refer to the notes in your Evidence Notebook to help you construct an explanation for how Biosphere 2 can help scientists study natural systems.

1. State your claim. Make sure your claim fully explains how Biosphere 2 can help scientists study natural systems.

2. Summarize the evidence you have gathered to support your claim and explain your reasoning.

Checkpoints

Answer the following questions to check your understanding of the lesson.

Use the diagram to answer questions 3 and 4.

3. Kidneys are components of the urinary system, a subsystem that filters waste from the blood. A kidney is made up of millions of smaller units, called *nephrons*. Based on this information, which of the statements could be true? Select all that apply.

   A. A nephron is a subsystem.

   B. A kidney is a subsystem.

   C. A kidney is an organ system

   D. A kidney is an organ.

4. The human body has two kidneys, one on each side of the body. Failure of one kidney will / will not result in failure of the urinary system. Failure of both kidneys will / will not require a(n) tissue / organ transplant.

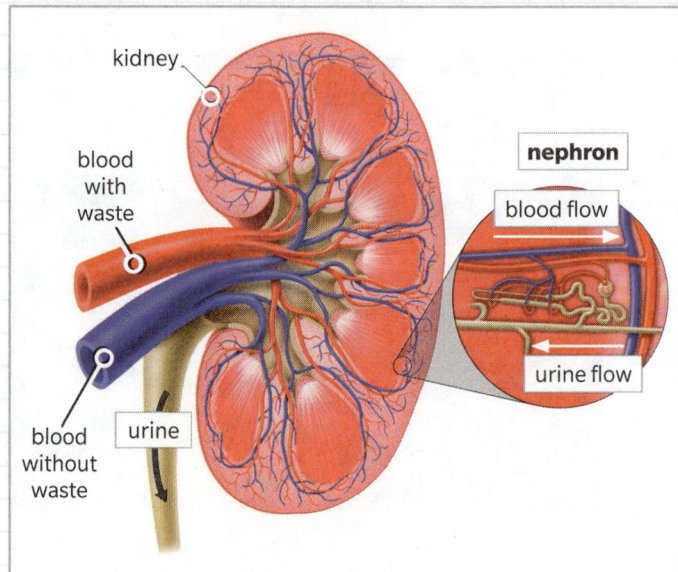

Use the photo to answer Questions 5-6.

5. Palm Jumeirah is a human-engineered island made of sea-floor sand constructed into the shape of a palm tree. Millions of tons of rock were placed around the island to protect it from waves and storms. Draw lines to connect a change caused by the Palm Jumeirah construction to the Earth subsystem affected.

The rocky barriers have changed wave patterns.	geosphere
The shape has led to increased algae and mosquitoes.	anthroposphere
The islands provide shopping, hotels, houses, and restaurants.	hydrosphere
The islands have caused increased erosion of beaches on the coast.	biosphere

6. The Palm Jumeirah is an example of the anthroposphere / geosphere. This structure is likely to have a positive / negative effect on the health of the Earth system.

Interactive Review

Complete this section to review the main concepts of the lesson.

A system is a set of interacting parts that work together. A natural system is a system that occurs in nature.

A. Describe the features that define a system.

Organisms are living systems made up of subsystems that interact to perform functions.

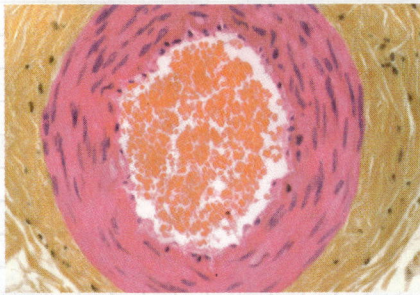

B. Construct a diagram or concept map to describe the subsystems that make up a multicellular organism.

Earth is a system made up of subsystems that interact to make life on Earth possible.

C. Explain why a change to one of Earth's subsystems can have an effect on other Earth subsystems.

Models can be used to study and predict changes to natural systems.

D. Why might scientists use a model of a natural system to predict results of interactions instead of studying the system directly?

Cells Are Living Systems

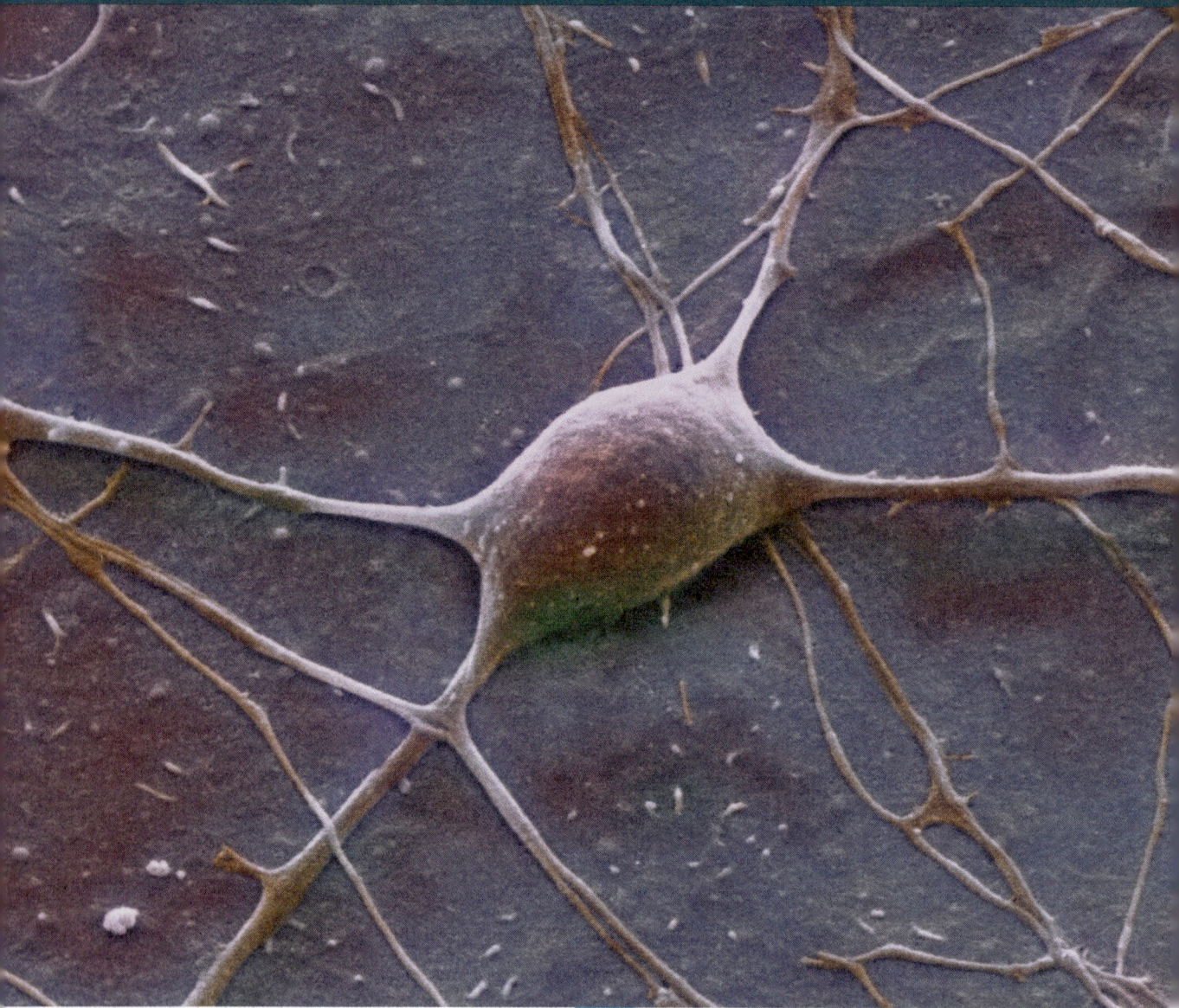

Nerve impulses are relayed to this nerve cell through its numerous thread-like branches, called *dendrites*.

✋ Explore First

Modeling System Interactions Cut a ten-word sentence into its different words and mix the pieces. Put the sentence back in order. Next, remove two words. Does the sentence make sense? Return the removed pieces and arrange the words in a different order. Does the sentence make sense? Discuss why or why not.

Go online to view the digital version of the Hands-On Lab for this lesson and to download additional lab resources.

CAN YOU EXPLAIN IT?

How does a virus make you sick?

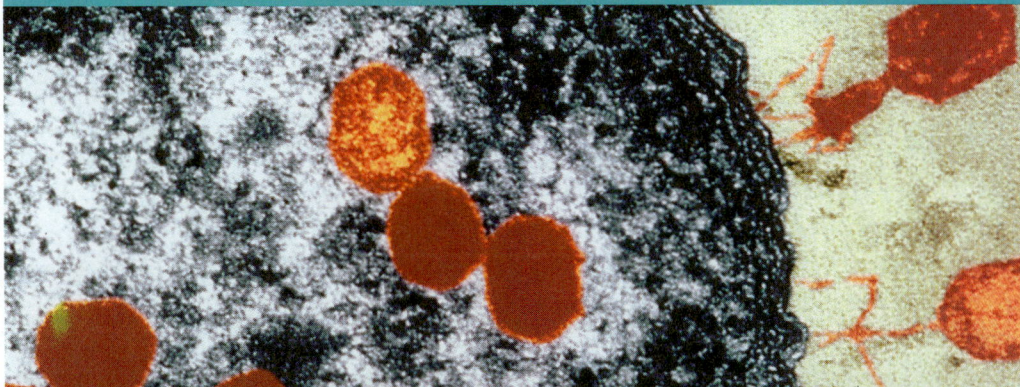

The virus particles (red) attacking this bacterium need a host cell in order to reproduce, or *replicate*.

Do you remember the last time you had a cold? Your runny nose and scratchy throat were signs that your body was responding to an infection caused by a virus. Different types of viruses can infect bacterial, plant, and animal cells.

1. Look at the photo of the viruses attacking the bacterium. What can you conclude about the relative sizes of the virus particles and the host cell?

2. **Discuss** Brainstorm ways that a virus can penetrate the human body's protective boundaries.

EVIDENCE NOTEBOOK As you explore the lesson, gather evidence to explain how a virus makes you sick.

Identifying Cells

When you were very young, you may have played with blocks. You could build almost anything from these blocks —from an insect to a tree or even a person. But, did you know that nature has its own building blocks? Unlike the blocks you played with as a child, the "blocks," or *cells*, that make up all living things can grow, move, and change.

Living Things Are Made of Cells

What makes living things different from nonliving things? The *cell theory* is one way to define living things. The theory states that all living things are made of one or more cells. These cells divide to produce new, identical cells. In this way, all cells are produced only from existing cells. Nonliving things are not made of cells.

Other characteristics are used to define living things. Living things grow, use energy, respond to the environment, and reproduce to make more of their own kind. They can be unicellular, such as bacteria, paramecia, and organisms called *archaeans* that live in extreme environments. Multicellular plants, fungi, and animals are also living things. Nonliving things, such as rocks, oxygen, and water, do not grow, reproduce, or behave in response to the environment.

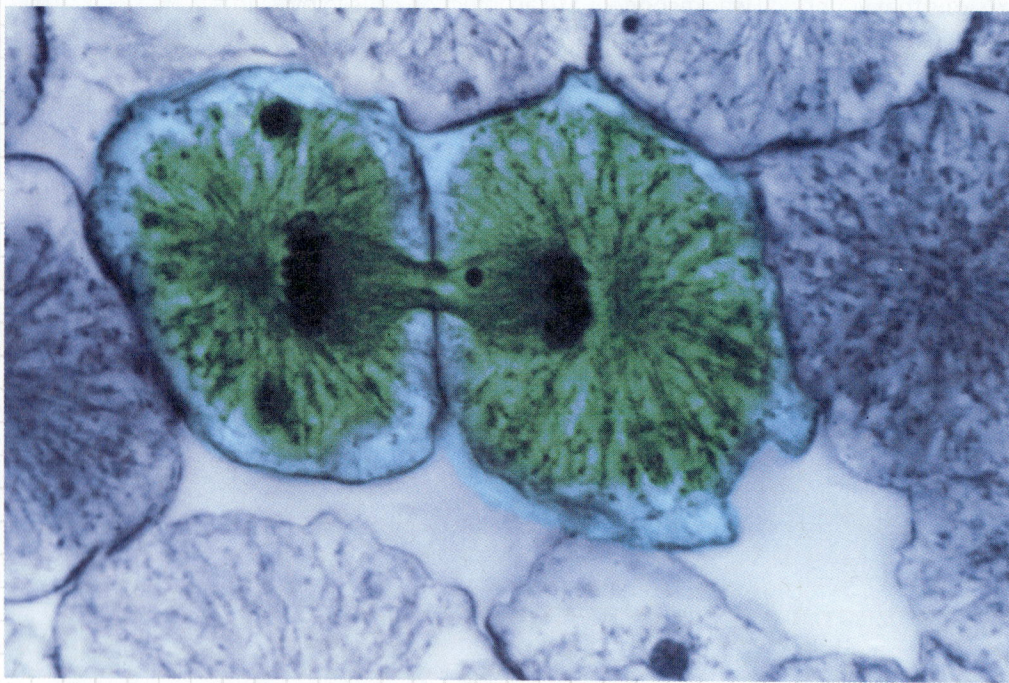

This light microscope image shows two new cells resulting from the division of the original cell.

3. **Discuss** Why is the cell theory an important tool for classifying unknown objects?

Microscopes Are Used to Observe Cells

Most cells are too small to see with the unaided eye. Because of their extremely small size, most cells can be observed only by using technology, such as a microscope. A microscope allows visualization of cells and cell structures that is not possible with the human eye.

Scientists use several types of microscopes to view cells. For example, light microscopes form magnified images by directing light through thin layers of cells and one or more lenses. Light microscopes can be used to view living or dead specimens. Electron microscopes form images with a beam of electrons. Electron microscopes can only be used to view dead specimens, but provide much greater magnification and visualization of details within the cell than light microscopes.

A butterfly's wing is made up of thousands of scales. Here, wing scales are visualized at 10 times larger than actual size and 100 times larger than actual size using an electron microscope.

4. The magnified photos show more / less detail of smaller / larger portions of the butterfly wing.

5. The invention of the microscope resulted in the discovery of cells and the development of the cell theory. How does this demonstrate the relationship between science and technology?

Observe Magnified Objects

These images show three different objects as they appear when observed through a microscope. As you explore the images, think about how cells relate to each object.

Paramecium A paramecium is an organism made up of a single cell. Tiny hairlike structures, called *cilia*, surround the cell. The cilia beat back and forth, allowing the paramecium to sweep prey microorganisms into its cell mouth.

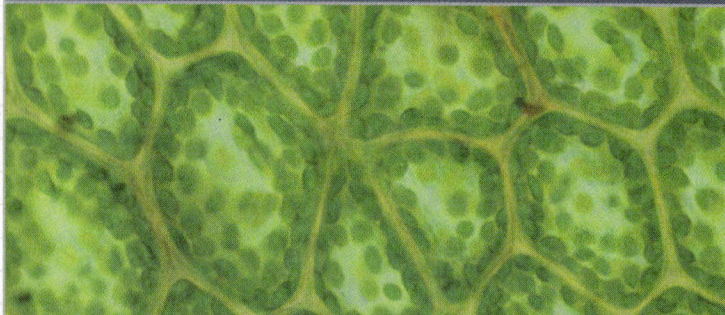

Plant Plants use sunlight to make their own food. The leaf of a plant is an organ made up of specialized cells that contain the structures that absorb sunlight.

Glucose Glucose is a simple sugar made of carbon, hydrogen, and oxygen atoms. Each of these crystals is a grain of sugar.

6. Decide whether each object is a living or a nonliving thing.

   A. Paramecium _____

   B. Plant _____

   C. Glucose _____

7. Select one of the objects in the table. Use evidence to write an argument for why you think the object is a living or a nonliving thing.

EVIDENCE NOTEBOOK

8. Viruses are not made of cells, but they do respond to their environments. They have their own genetic material, but need a host cell to reproduce. Do you think a virus is a living or a nonliving thing? Record your evidence.

Hands-On Lab
Observe Cells with a Microscope

Use a microscope to observe objects and determine if they are made of cells. Microscopes use lenses to magnify objects. The way that the lenses bend light toward your eyes makes the objects appear larger. The scale on a microscope at which you are viewing an object is called *magnification*.

Procedure and Analysis

STEP 1 Describe an investigation that you could conduct with the materials provided that would demonstrate that living things are made of cells and nonliving things are not made of cells. What data would be collected and what evidence might the data provide about living things and cells?

MATERIALS
- celery stalk
- celery leaf
- cork, thin slice
- eyedropper
- human hair
- light microscope
- microscope slides with coverslips
- pond water
- sand
- tissue paper
- water

STEP 2 On a separate sheet of paper, build a data table to collect data from your investigation. Include fields to record data from observations without a microscope, with 10x magnification, and with 40x magnification.

STEP 3 Look at the cork sample without a microscope and record your observations.

STEP 4 Put the cork sample on a slide and add a drop of water. Carefully place the coverslip on the slide so that the cork sample is in the middle.

STEP 5 Make sure that the 10x lens of the microscope is in place. Put the prepared slide on the microscope stage.

STEP 6 Look through the microscope's eyepieces. Adjust the position of the lens until the image of the cork is sharp.

STEP 7 Observe the cork. Write your observations in the 10x column of the table.

STEP 8 Now click the 40x lens into place. Use only the fine focus (never the coarse focus) to adjust the image. View the cork sample and write your observations in the 40x column of the table.

STEP 9 Repeat Steps 3–8 with the remaining samples.

STEP 10 Evaluate the data you collected. Which items contained cells? Which objects do you think were part of living things? Which objects do you thing were part of nonliving things?

STEP 11   How do your observations support the cell theory?

STEP 12   **Engineer It** Identify the needs filled by the microscope in this activity. What are the limitations of the microscope you are using?

Draw to Scale

To draw microscopic and very small objects it is useful to *scale up*, or calculate the size of the objects to be larger than what they actually are. The table below shows the actual sizes and scaled up sizes of a few cell types.

object	actual size (mm)	size in mm if scaled up 100x	size in cm if scaled up 100x
bacterium	0.002	0.2	0.02
cheek cell	0.050	5	0.5
onion cell	0.250	25	2.5

Credit: Adapted from Amazing Cells by Maureen Munn et al. Copyright © 2007 by University of Washington. Adapted and reproduced by permission of Maureen Munn, Ph.D. and Phyllis Harvey-Bushel Ed. D.

9. Use a metric ruler to draw each of the cells scaled up 100 times in either millimeters or centimeters. Compare and contrast the sizes of the cells with each other, an onion, and a person.

Analyzing Cell Systems

Types of Cells and Their Structures

Every cell is a system made up of interacting parts. There are different types of cells, but they all have some structures in common. The **cell membrane** surrounds and protects the cell. The cell membrane regulates the matter that enters and exits the cell. Cytoplasm is a liquid substance that fills the inside of the cell and supports cell structures. Genetic material contains all the information a cell needs to function.

Some cell types also contain **organelles,** membrane-bound structures in the cytoplasm that each perform a specific function. Mitochondria, chloroplasts, and nuclei are examples of organelles. Not every cell contains every type of organelle, and different types of cells may have different organelles and other specialized structures. Although many kinds of cells exist, all cells can be organized into two categories: prokaryotes and eukaryotes.

Prokaryotic Cells

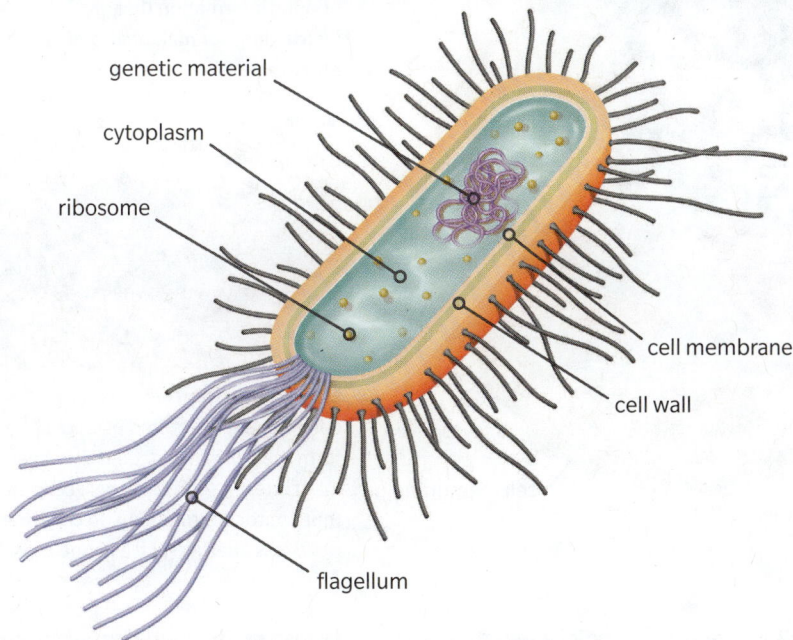

A prokaryotic cell contains its genetic material in the cytoplasm. Most prokaryotic cells do not have membrane-bound organelles, although they do have other structures called *ribosomes* that make proteins. Prokaryotic cells are unicellular organisms. Bacteria and archaeans are prokaryotes.

Prokaryotic Cell

genetic material

cytoplasm

ribosome

cell membrane

cell wall

flagellum

genetic material Genetic material contains information that directs all of the cell's functions.

cytoplasm The cytoplasm surrounds and supports organelles inside the cell.

ribosome Ribosomes make proteins inside the cytoplasm.

cell membrane The cell membrane surrounds and protects the cell and controls what materials go into and out of it.

cell wall The cell wall provides structural support for some prokaryotic cells.

flagella These projections move the prokaryote through its environment.

10. Which structure is the boundary of this cell system?

Eukaryotic Cells

Eukaryotic cells are generally larger and more complex than prokaryotic cells. In a eukaryotic cell, genetic material is enclosed in a membrane-bound organelle called the **nucleus.** Eukaryotic cells also have additional membrane-bound organelles.

Animals and plants are both made of eukaryotic cells. Both have organelles called **mitochondria,** which convert the energy stored in food to a form of energy that cells can use. Plant cells and animal cells also have some different structures. For example, plants make their own food using a process called *photosynthesis*. Therefore, plant cells have organelles called **chloroplasts,** where photosynthesis occurs. Animals do not make their own food, so animal cells do not have chloroplasts. Each plant cell also has a rigid **cell wall** that supports the cell. The extra support of a cell wall is not needed in animal cells because most animals have some type of skeleton that supports the body.

Animal Cell

An animal cell has some of the same structures as a prokaryotic cell, such as a cell membrane and cytoplasm, and some different structures.

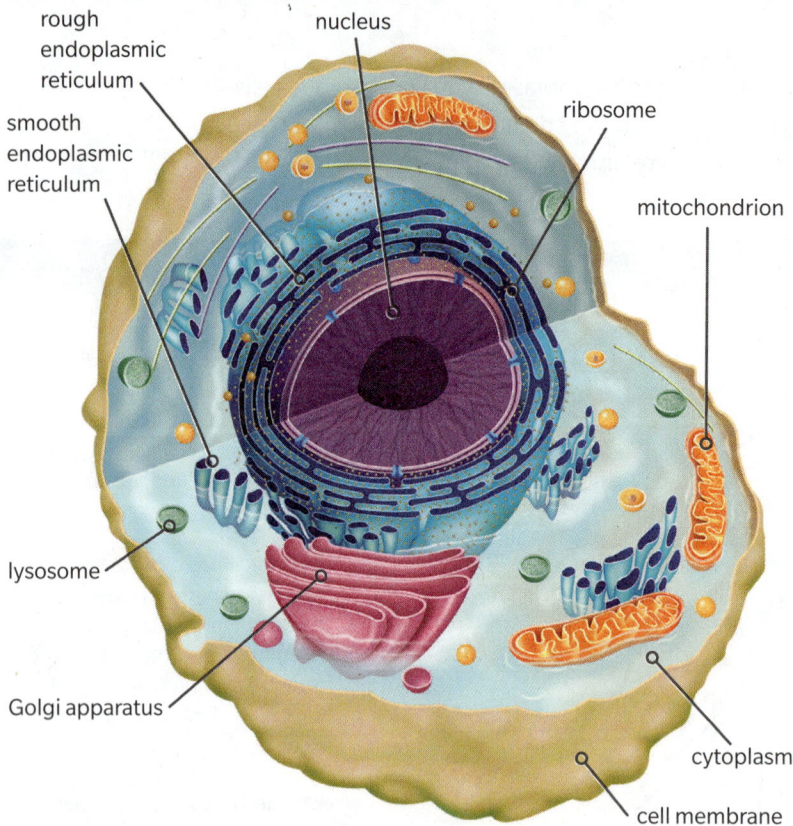

rough endoplasmic reticulum
nucleus
smooth endoplasmic reticulum
ribosome
mitochondrion
lysosome
Golgi apparatus
cytoplasm
cell membrane

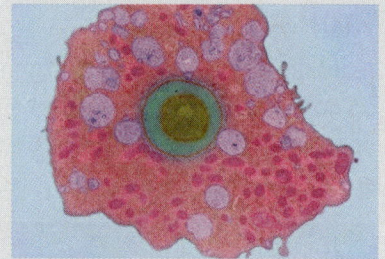

Nucleus The cell nucleus contains genetic information that gives instructions for making proteins and other materials the cell needs.

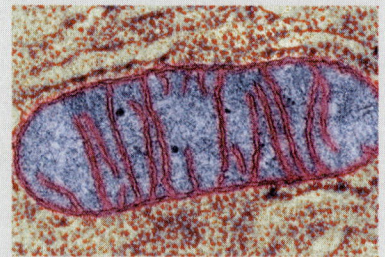

Mitochondrion This organelle converts energy stored in food into a form the cell can use. Cells that need a lot of energy, such as muscle cells, have more mitochondria than do cells that need less energy, such as bone cells.

Rough ER The rough ER is located near the nucleus and contains ribosomes on its surface. It is involved in making and processing proteins.

Smooth ER The smooth ER does not contain ribosomes. It makes fat-based molecules called lipids that are used to make membranes.

Golgi apparatus The Golgi apparatus takes proteins from the ER and moves them to different parts of the cell.

Lysosome These structures contain powerful chemicals known as enzymes that break down food and recycle proteins, carbohydrates, lipids, and nucleic acids inside the cell.

Plant Cell

In addition to a cell membrane, cytoplasm, nucleus, and mitochondria, a plant cell also has a cell wall and chloroplasts.

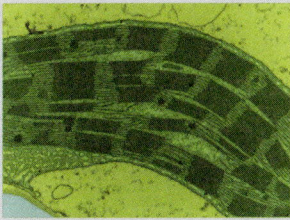

Chloroplast In the cells of plants and a few other kinds of organisms, chloroplasts capture energy from sunlight and change it into food that stores energy for the cell to use.

Cell wall A cell wall surrounds the entire plant cell, including its cell membrane, and supports the plant cell. Most bacterial cells, which are prokaryotic, also have cell walls.

Vacuole A large central vacuole is bound by a membrane and contains materials and waste. It also maintains adequate pressure inside the plant cell.

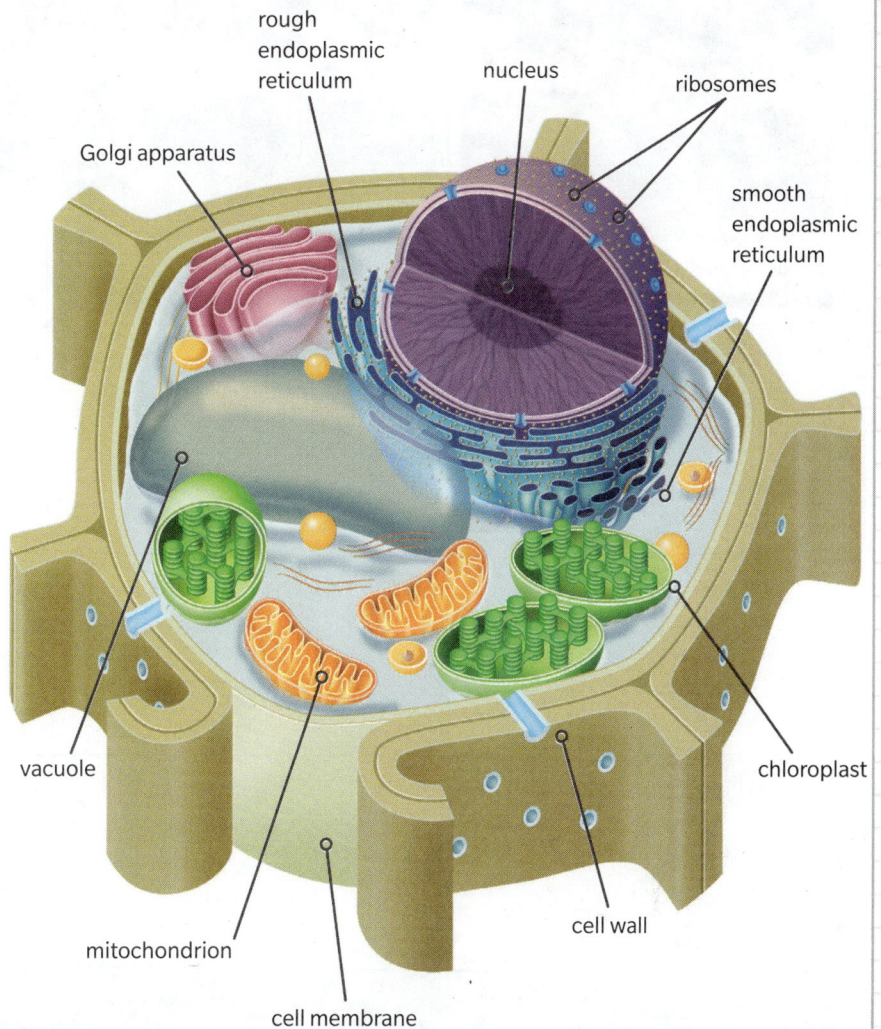

Labels: rough endoplasmic reticulum, nucleus, ribosomes, Golgi apparatus, smooth endoplasmic reticulum, vacuole, chloroplast, mitochondrion, cell wall, cell membrane

11. Read these cell observations. In the space next to each answer choice, write whether the cells described are prokaryotic cells, animal cells, plant cells, or there is not enough information to determine.

   A. Cell has a membrane and ribosomes but no organelles. _____

   B. Cell has many chloroplasts. _____

   C. Cell has a cell membrane and mitochondria but no cell wall. _____

   D. Cell has a nucleus. _____

   E. Cell has a nucleus and cell wall. _____

Identify Different Cell Systems

12. Define each cell system. Identify the cell system boundary, two or more components, and one or more functions that result from system interactions.

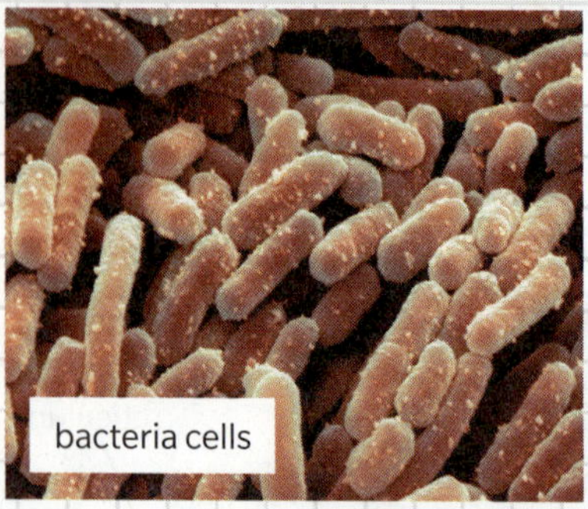 bacteria cells	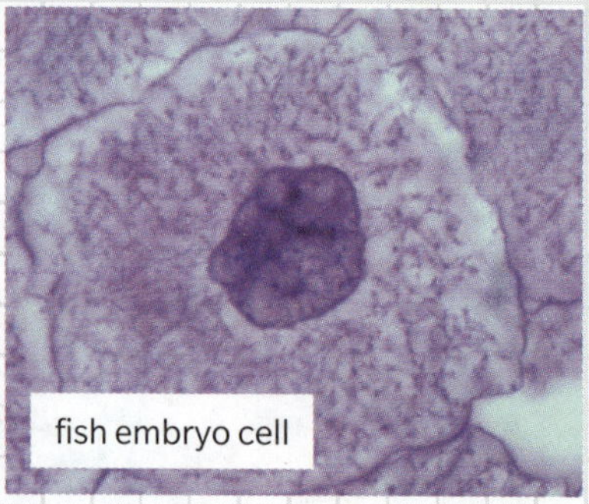 fish embryo cell	 moss leaf cells
Boundary:	Boundary:	Boundary:
Components:	Components:	Components:
Functions:	Functions:	Functions:

13. What types of inputs and outputs do these cell systems share?

_____

_____

_____

_____

_____

_____

EVIDENCE NOTEBOOK

14. Viruses inject their own DNA into a host cell. The viral DNA uses the host cell's components to make more viruses. How might this affect the function of the host cell system? Record your evidence.

Modeling Cells

Imagine that a friend asks you how the sizes of planets in our solar system compare to each other. A map of the solar system would show you the planets and the shapes of their orbits, but it would be difficult to see how their sizes compare. However, if you built a model of the solar system, you could show your friend many things about the solar system. You could show planet sizes in relation to each other and to the sun, and you could show how far away the planets are from each other.

Scientists use both two-dimensional (2D) and three-dimensional (3D) models to study cells. Examples of a 2D cell model are an illustration or a photograph. Examples of a 3D cell model are a physical model that can be touched and moved around, or a computer model that includes the dimensions of width, height, and depth.

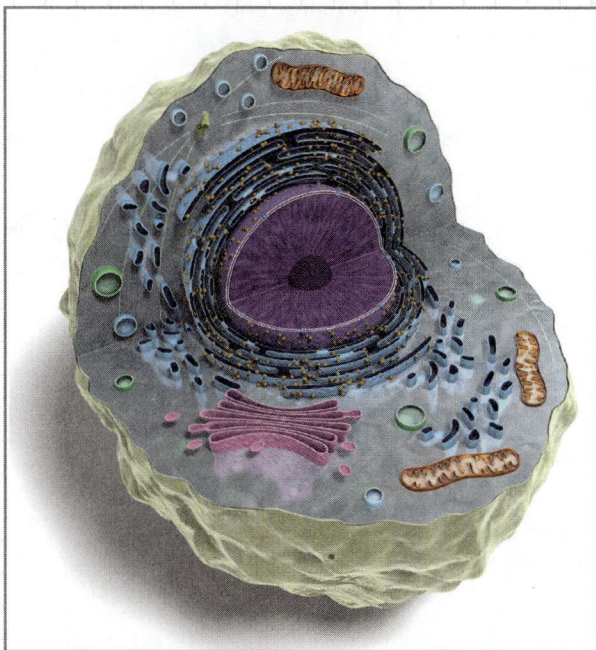

This illustration uses perspective to represent three dimensions of a cell.

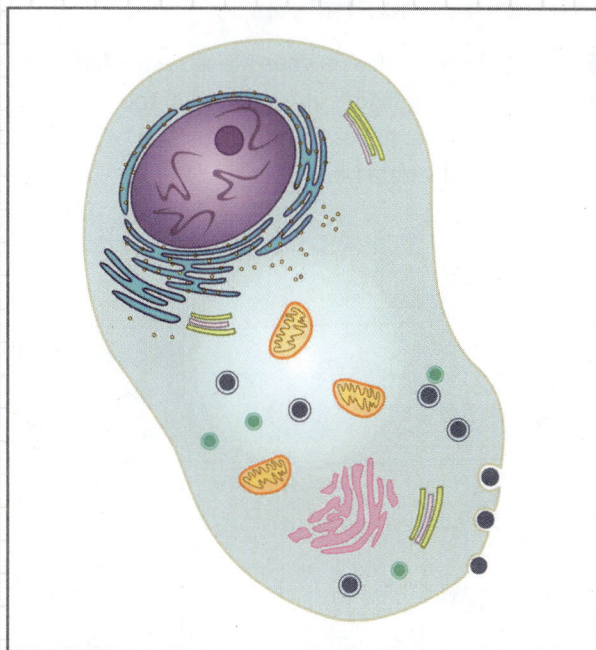

This illustration is flat and represents two dimensions of a cell.

15. There are advantages and disadvantages to different models. Examine the two models, note the types of information each provides, and list the pros and cons of using each model.

Hands-On Lab
Use Cell Models to Investigate Cell Size

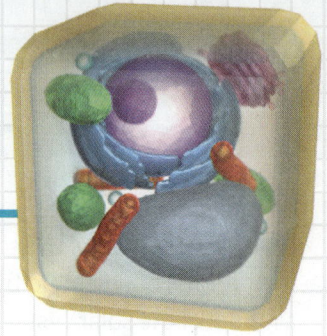

Use large and small cubes of gelatin to model cell function in cells of different sizes. Use evidence to support an explanation of how cell size affects function.

The gelatin cubes that you will work with represent a model of a cell. Using a cube allows you to easily calculate its dimensions, such as its surface area and volume. A cell's surface area-to-volume ratio is an important factor in its functioning.

Procedure and Analysis

STEP 1 Work with a partner. Measure the length of each side of the large gelatin cube and one of the smaller cubes. (All of the smaller cubes are the same size). Record the measurements in the data table.

MATERIALS
- beaker, 250 mL (2)
- calculator (if desired)
- container, plastic, 473 mL (2)
- gelatin cubes, prepared (1 large and 27 small)
- ruler, metric
- stopwatch or clock with second hand
- water, warm

	Cube sides (cm)	Surface area (cm²)	Volume (cm³)	SA:V ratio	Time to dissolve
Large cube					
Smaller cube					

STEP 2 Place the large cube in one of the plastic containers. Place the 27 smaller cubes in the other container.

STEP 3 Ask your teacher to fill your beakers with warm water to the same level. Then pour the water from the beakers into both plastic containers at the same time. Make sure all the gelatin cubes are submerged in the water. Start the timer. If any water has spilled, clean it up immediately to avoid slips.

STEP 4 **Do the Math** While you wait for the cubes to dissolve, calculate the surface area, volume, and surface area-to-volume ratio for the large cube and the smaller cubes. Enter this data into the data table.

To calculate the surface area (SA) of a cube, first multiply the cube's length (L) by its width (W). Then multiply the answer by 6 (for the 6 sides of the cube).

Formula: SA = L × W × 6

To calculate the volume (V) of the cube, multiply the length (L) by the width (W) by the height (H).

Formula: V = L × W × H

A ratio compares two quantities. One way to write the surface area-to-volume ratio is to use a colon between the surface area (SA) and the volume (V).

SA to V ratio = SA : V

STEP 5 Record the length of time it took for the gelatin cubes to completely dissolve.

STEP 6 Which of the cubes has the largest total surface area and the largest total volume? Which has the highest surface area-to-volume ratio?

STEP 7 Describe the relationship between surface area-to-volume ratio and the time it took for the cubes to dissolve.

STEP 8 Remember that all cells must take in materials and get rid of wastes through the cell membrane. Think about how the surface area-to-volume ratio affected the time it took for the different-sized cubes to dissolve. What can you infer about the relationship between the surface area-to-volume ratio and the movement of materials into and out of a cell?

Language SmArts
Explain Limits to Cell Size

Imagine you are looking at a small mouse. You know that both the mouse and your own body are made of cells because all living things are made of cells.

Cell sizes can vary based on their function. For example, red blood cells that transport blood throughout your body are small. But muscle cells in your leg are much larger. A human contains more than 37 trillion cells. Given how much larger you are compared to a mouse, how do your cells compare in size?

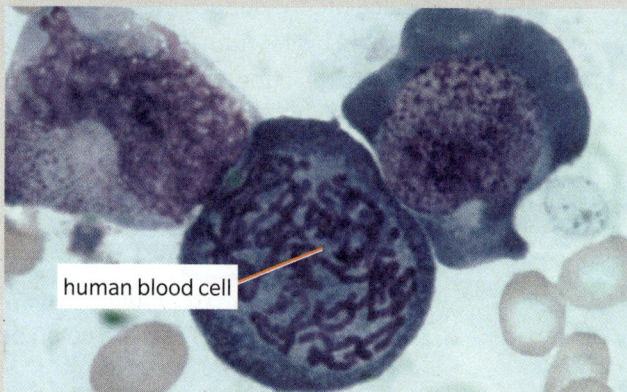

human blood cell

This purple human red blood cell is roughly 6-8 μm. One micron, or 1 μm, is 1/1,000 the size of 1mm.

16. Humans must have *more / larger* cells than mice.

17. Given your answer, explain your reasoning for the difference in cell size or cell number between humans and mice.

_____

_____

_____

_____

_____

_____

18. What problems might result if a cell gets too large? Use evidence from your cell modeling lab to explain why cells are unable to perform important functions if they become too large.

_____

_____

_____

_____

_____

_____

_____

_____

_____

EVIDENCE NOTEBOOK

19. Viruses are much smaller than living cells. Many viruses form inside a single cell, causing the cell to burst open and die. How might this affect the function of the organism as a system? Record your evidence.

Continue Your Exploration

Name: _____   Date: _____

Check out the path below or go online to choose one of the other paths shown.

People in Science

- **Making a Microscope**
- **Hands-On Labs** ✋
- **Propose Your Own Path**

Go online to choose one of these other paths.

Lynn Margulis, Biologist

American biologist Lynn Margulis at work in a greenhouse in the 1990s.

Lynn Margulis (1938–2011) was a biologist who made many important contributions to science. Her most well-known contribution was her proposal in 1966 that eukaryotic cells evolved through the process of endosymbiosis. She proposed that billions of years ago, smaller prokaryotes began living inside larger host prokaryotic cells. In some cases, smaller prokaryotes entered larger cells as parasites. In others, smaller cells were engulfed by larger cells. Margulis proposed that mitochondria and chloroplasts of today's eukaryotic cells are descended from free-living bacteria.

Eventually Margulis outlined her ideas in her 1970 book *Origin of Eukaryotic Cells.* Most scientists of the time were skeptical of the ideas because they thought the organelles of eukaryotic cells evolved from materials found inside the cells.

Today, most scientists accept Margulis's hypothesis. She and other scientists showed that, like a cell nucleus, mitochondria and chloroplasts contain DNA. Also, the DNA of mitochondria and chloroplasts is different from the DNA in a cell's nucleus. Instead, the DNA of mitochondria and chloroplasts resembles the DNA of bacteria.

Continue Your Exploration

1. Which statements provide evidence to support Lynn Margulis's hypothesis of endosymbiosis? Arrange the statements below into the order that accurately shows the sequence of events described in Margulis's hypothesis by writing the number 1, 2, 3, or 4 next to each statement.

_____ Prokaryotes inside other prokaryotes evolved into organelles.

_____ Prokaryotes lived inside other prokaryotes in a symbiotic relationship.

_____ Prokaryotes that had engulfed other prokaryotes evolved into eukaryotes.

_____ Free-living prokaryotes engulfed other free-living prokaryotes.

2. How do the findings of Margulis and other scientists—that mitochondria and chloroplasts have their own DNA, like a cell's nucleus—support the hypothesis of endosymbiosis?

3. Explain how Lynn Margulis's hypothesis changed scientific ideas about cell development.

4. **Collaborate** Research the prokaryotic organism that most likely evolved into a chloroplast. Develop a model of a chloroplast and the prokaryote and describe the similarities and differences in the structure and function of individual components and the whole system.

Can You Explain It?

Name: _____   Date: _____

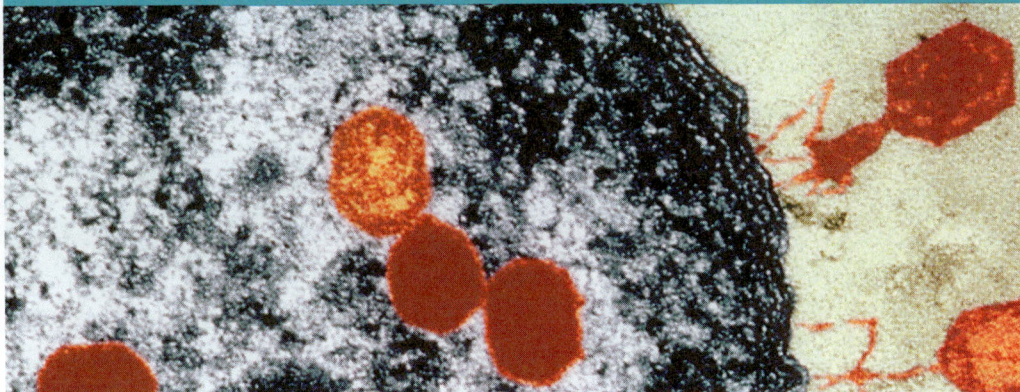

How does a virus make you sick?

EVIDENCE NOTEBOOK
Refer to the notes in your Evidence Notebook to help explain how a virus makes you sick.

1. State your claim. Make sure your claim fully explains how a virus makes you sick.

2. Summarize the evidence you have gathered to support your claim and explain your reasoning.

Checkpoints

Answer the following questions to check your understanding of the lesson.

Use the photograph to answer Question 3.

3. Study the photograph. What would happen to these cells if the green components were not functional? Select all that apply.

   A. The cells would not have a source of energy.

   B. The cells would function normally.

   C. The cells would eventually die.

   D. The cells would not be able to control inputs and outputs.

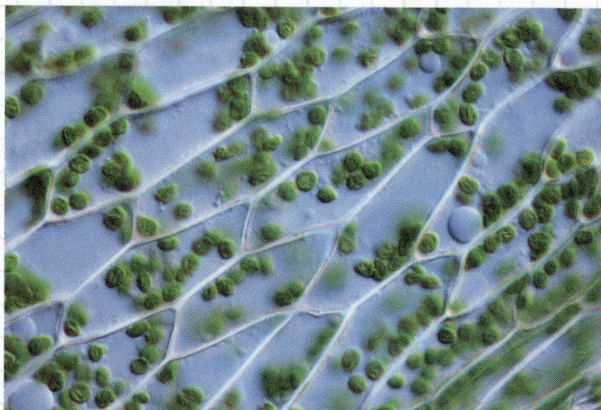

4. If a cell's surface area-to-volume ratio increased from 3:1 to 4:1, what impact would that have on the transport of materials across the cell membrane?

   A. it would be unchanged

   B. transport would increase

   C. transport would decrease

   D. none of the above

Use the illustration to answer Questions 5 and 6.

5. An analogy is a model of a relationship. Match each cell organelle to the analogy of its function.

nucleus	power plant
cell membrane	control center
mitochondrion	solar panel
chloroplast	border between countries

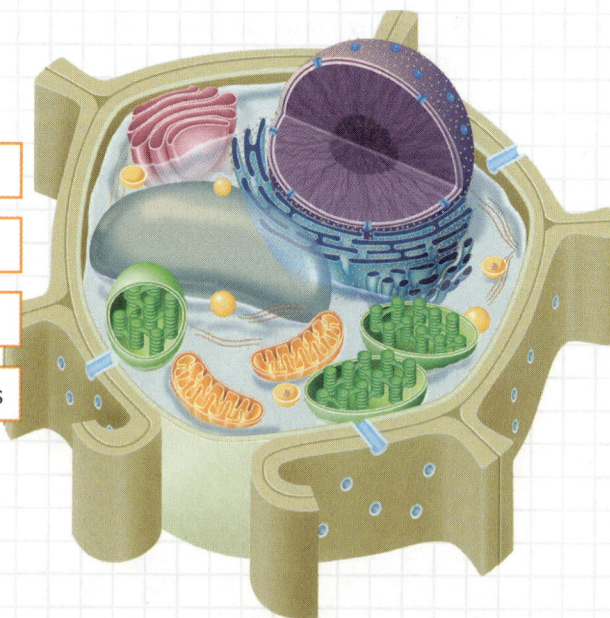

6. The cell system shown in the diagram is a prokaryotic / eukaryotic cell. The evidence supporting this is that the cell has chloroplasts / flagella and a nucleus / cell wall.

Interactive Review

Complete this section to review the main concepts of the lesson.

All living things are made of cells.

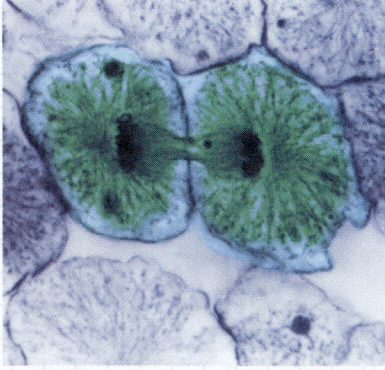

A. List two statements of the cell theory.

All cells are systems made of components that interact to perform functions.

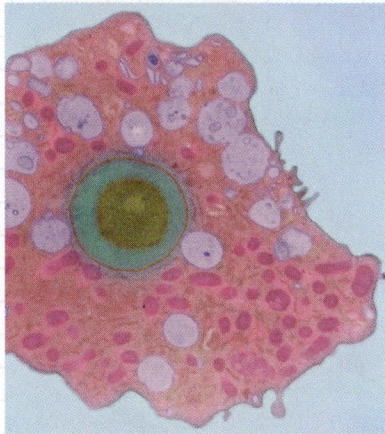

B. Draw a concept map to show the parts that make up an animal cell system.

Examining 3D models of cells can enhance understanding of how cell structures work together to maximize function.

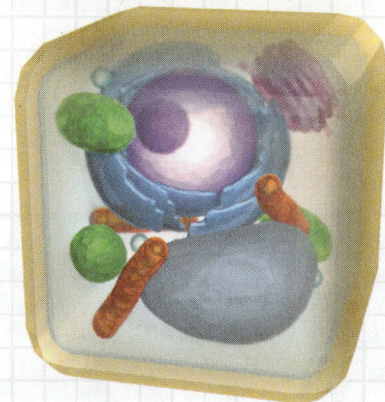

C. Explain how using 3D models of cells can help scientists gain a better understanding of cell structure and function.

Plants Are Living Systems

Dragon's blood trees have a wide, dense canopy of leaves that protects the soil below from the hot sun.

Explore First

Modeling Leaves Cut two identical, leaf-shaped pieces from a paper towel. Use a spray bottle to wet, but not soak, both shapes equally with water. Wrap one in wax paper and set both near a sunny window or other warm location. Which "leaf" do you think will dry faster? Record your observations at the end of class.

Go online to view the digital version of the Hands-On Lab for this lesson and to download additional lab resources.

CAN YOU EXPLAIN IT?

How can the onyanga survive in the harsh conditions of the Namib Desert?

The onyanga grows in the Namib desert, where there is little rain but regular, dense fog develops at night.

For many hundreds of years—and possibly even thousands of years—this plant has been growing where not much else can grow. It grows only two leaves that become ragged and torn over time, a stem, and roots. It may not look like much, but it can go without rain for up to 5 years. The largest onyanga plants are estimated to be nearly 2,500 years old!

1. **Discuss** Study the photo of the onyanga. Record as many observations as you can about the plant.

EVIDENCE NOTEBOOK As you explore the lesson, gather evidence to help you explain how the body systems of the onyanga help it survive in the desert.

Exploring Plant Body Systems

Plants live on every continent on Earth. They live in lush forests and expansive grasslands. They also live in places you might not expect, such as dry deserts and frozen tundra. They range in size from the tallest giant sequoia trees, reaching more than 80 meters, to the smallest flowering plant, which can fit on the tip of your finger.

All plants are multicellular. They are also eukaryotes—their cells contain membrane-bound organelles, including a nucleus that contains the cell's genetic information. All plants have cells with cell walls and large vacuoles. All plants use energy from sunlight to make their own food by a process called *photosynthesis*.

This maple tree has a central stem, called a *trunk*, that connects the roots to the branches of the tree.

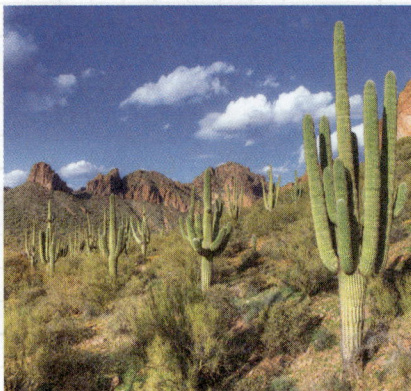

The root system of the saguaro cactus is shallow, but it reaches out as far as the plant is tall.

The water lily's broad, flat leaves float on the water to maximize the amount of sunlight they can capture.

2. **Discuss** With a partner, gather information from the text and the photos to compare the plants shown above. Record your observations in the table.

Similarities	Differences

The Plant Body System

Plants can be divided into two major groups based on the structure and function of their body systems. Most of the land plants on Earth today have a vascular system. A *vascular system* transports materials and provides support to the plant body. Plants that have a vascular system are called *vascular plants*. Plants that do not have a vascular system are called *nonvascular plants*.

Plant Cells

Like all living things, plants are made of cells. Plant cells have rigid cell walls, which help to provide structure and support for the plant.

Plant Tissues

The cells in a vascular plant are organized into three tissue types. *Dermal tissue* protects the plant, *vascular tissue* transports materials, and *ground tissue* provides support and storage.

Plant Organs

Leaves, stems, roots, and flowers are all plant organs made up of the three tissue types. For example, the stem is protected by dermal tissue. Inside the stem, the vascular tissue that transports water and nutrients is surrounded by ground tissue. Ground tissue gives the stem support and stores materials.

Plant Organ Systems

Plant organs are organized into two organ systems. The *shoot system* includes the leaves, stems, and flowers. The *root system* takes up water and nutrients from the soil. These two systems work together to deliver water and nutrients to all parts of the plant body.

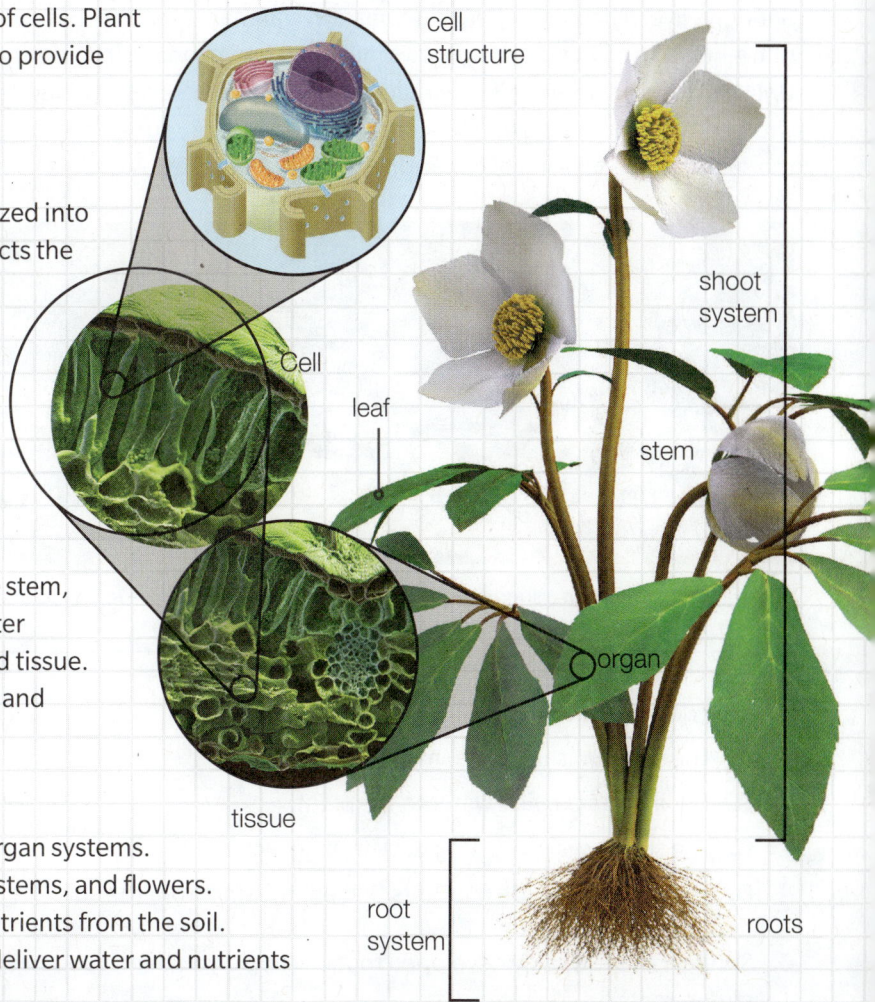

cell structure

Cell

leaf

tissue

shoot system

stem

organ

root system

roots

3. Use the diagram of the vascular plant as evidence to support the claim that the root system and shoot system interact to deliver water and nutrients to all parts of the plant body.

EVIDENCE NOTEBOOK

4. The onyanga has a wide, shallow root system. How might this type of root system help the onyanga collect nightly fog? Record your evidence.

Analyze a Plant Body System

Sundews live in habitats where sunlight and water are plentiful, but the soil has few nutrients. Like most plants, sundews make their own food using energy from sunlight. Unlike most plants, sundews also capture and digest insects. Sundew leaves are covered with tentacle-like structures that contain a sweet, sticky substance. Insects attracted to the sundew for a tasty meal get trapped in the leaf and are digested by the plant.

When an insect lands on a sundew, it gets stuck on the sticky leaf. The leaf curls around the trapped insect, which is digested by the plant.

Explore Online

5. Why do you think sundews need to capture insects?

   A. The sundew is unable to make enough food.

   B. The insects provide water to the plant.

   C. The sundew is protecting itself from insects.

   D. The insects provide nutrients that are missing from the soil.

6. Sundews have weakly developed roots. Why do you think sundews do not need strong roots?

   _____

   _____

   _____

   _____

7. How does the structure of the sundew leaf relate to its function?

   _____

   _____

   _____

   _____

   _____

Describing How Plant Systems Process Nutrients

Plants bodies are systems that perform all the processes needed for a plant to live. Plants need sunlight, water, and carbon dioxide to make and transport the food they use as a source of matter. They also need oxygen to convert the food to energy that is used by all parts of the plant. Nutrients from the soil, such as nitrogen and phosphorus, are used for cellular processes and growth. All of these processes produce unwanted products, so plants also need to get rid of wastes to stay healthy.

Making Food

Like you, plants need food that cells can use for energy. But unlike you, plants do not get their food by eating. Instead, plants make their own food by the process of photosynthesis. *Photosynthesis* is the process that uses energy from sunlight to convert water molecules and carbon dioxide into sugars and oxygen. A **leaf** is the plant organ that is the main site of photosynthesis. The sugars produced in leaf cells are transported from the leaves to all parts of the plant's body.

Inputs and Outputs of Photosynthesis

8. Complete the diagram by labeling the inputs and outputs of the process of photosynthesis. Use evidence from the text.

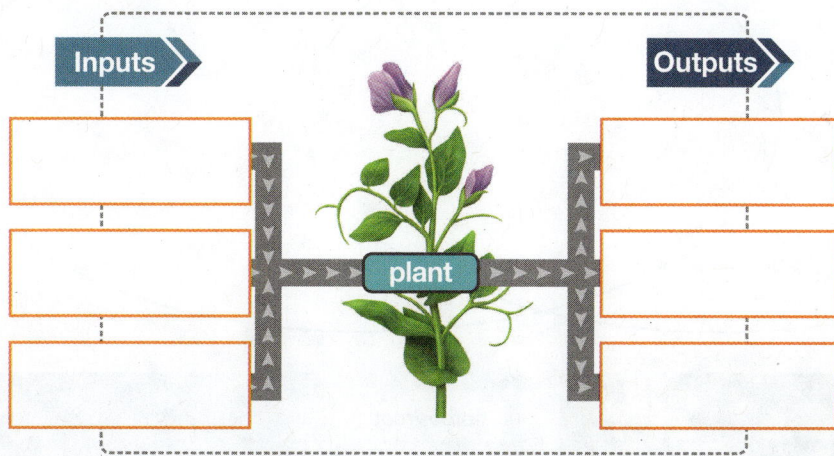

---

9. Engineer It Solar cells are devices that collect energy from sunlight and convert it into electricity. What plant structure might engineers look at when they are designing the way that solar cells are arranged? Explain your reasoning.

Moving Materials

Materials move through a plant through two kinds of vascular tissue—xylem and phloem. Water and dissolved nutrients enter the plant through the **roots**, organs that absorb water and dissolved nutrients from soil. Roots also anchor the plant in the ground. Roots connect to **stems**, organs that transport nutrients to all parts of the plant body and provide support to the plant. Water moves from the roots to the stems through tube-shaped cells in the xylem tissue. Sugars made during photosynthesis move throughout the plant in the phloem.

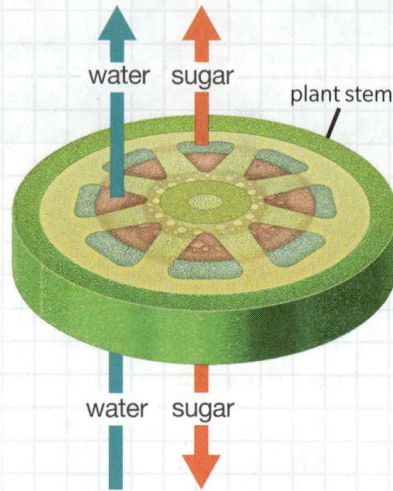

water   sugar   plant stem

water   sugar

Compare Root Systems

10. Using the word bank, complete the Venn diagram by entering the functions you think best describe the root systems.

WORD BANK

- absorbs nutrients
- stores nutrients
- drought tolerant
- absorbs water
- anchors plant
- protects soil

taproot   both   fibrous root

taproot

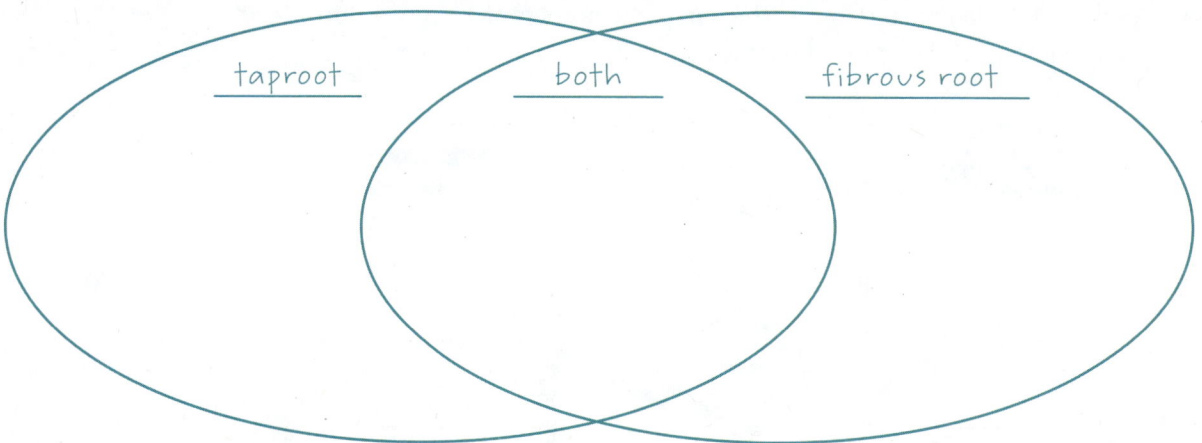

Some plants have a root system called a taproot. As you can see in the photo, these plants have one large main root structure with many smaller branch roots. Taproots can grow deep into the soil.

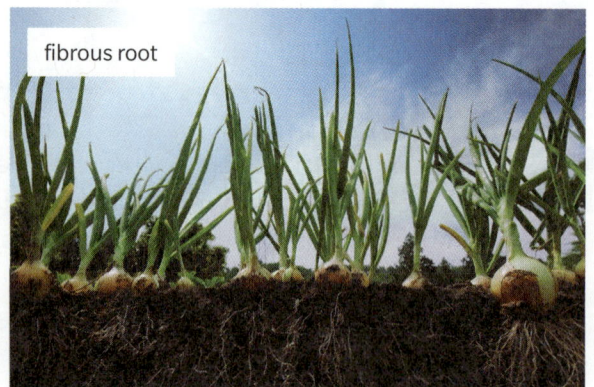

fibrous root

Other plants have a fibrous root system, in which many branching roots grow close to the soil surface. Fibrous roots can spread wide and form mats that anchor the plant very firmly in the soil.

Hands-On Lab
Observe Transport

You will compare and contrast the movement of water through the stems of two different plants.

Procedure

STEP 1 Fill two 16 oz cups with 100 mL of water each. Add 10–15 drops of red food coloring and mix thoroughly.

STEP 2 Use the knife to cut 8 cm sections of the broccoli stem and the asparagus spears. Be sure to cut the stems horizontally.

STEP 3 Place one or two pieces of broccoli stem in one cup and one or two pieces of asparagus spears in the other cup. Be sure the stems stand upright in the water and will not fall over.

STEP 4 Allow the stems to sit in the water for 24 hours. Cut your stems at 1–2 cm intervals to see how far the water traveled up the stems.

STEP 5 Record your observations in the data table below.

MATERIALS
- asparagus spears
- broccoli stems
- clear plastic cups, 16 oz (2)
- graduated cylinder
- knife
- red food coloring
- stir stick

Asparagus	Broccoli

Analysis

STEP 6 How do your observations from this activity provide evidence for the function of a plant's vascular system?

STEP 7 Through which vascular tissue did the water move in the broccoli and asparagus stems?

Disposing of Wastes

Plants produce waste as a result of cell processes, such as photosynthesis. Water, carbon dioxide, and oxygen enter and exit a plant through tiny openings in the leaf surface, called stomata (*sing.* stoma).

Plants also need to get rid of unwanted substances, such as pollutants, that may enter their systems through water. Some plants store wastes in living cells, such as leaves. These unwanted materials are removed when the leaves fall from the plant.

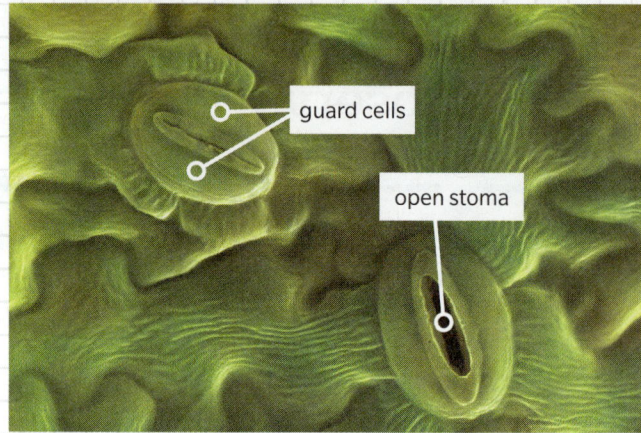

guard cells

open stoma

The size, shape, and placement of stomata allow water and gases to efficiently move in and out of the plant.

11. A plant system must balance its need for water with its need for carbon dioxide and oxygen. If too much water is lost, the stomata will close. How does this affect a plant's ability to regulate levels of carbon dioxide and oxygen?

12. Discuss What would likely occur if most of a plant's stomata became blocked? Explain your reasoning.

Use Observations to Develop an Argument

13. This plant has shallow roots, short stems, and leaves that are covered in fuzzy hairs. In what type of environmental conditions might this plant live? Use your observations as evidence to support your argument.

Describing How Plant Systems Respond to the Environment

Unlike many animals, plants cannot move to a new place when their environment changes. Plant bodies respond to a variety of environmental factors. Many of these responses happen very slowly. Other responses are surprisingly fast! The Venus flytrap will respond to the touch of an insect in a few seconds by snapping its leaf shut. Two factors that plants respond to are light and water.

14. Why do you think it is important for plants to be able to regulate the level of water in their bodies?

Regulating Water

Plants regulate the water in their bodies in response to environmental conditions. Plants do this mostly by opening and closing their stomata. Two guard cells control the opening and closing of each stoma. Stomata open to allow air to move in and out. They close to prevent water loss. Some plant leaves also have a waxy coating that helps prevent water loss. Plants may also store water in their stems, leaves, or roots.

Do the Math
Calculate Stomata Percentage

The percentage of stomata on a leaf surface can be calculated using the equation:

$$\text{Stomatal percentage} = \frac{S}{S+E} \times 100$$

where S = the number of stomata and E = the number of epidermis cells, which form the outer layer of a leaf.

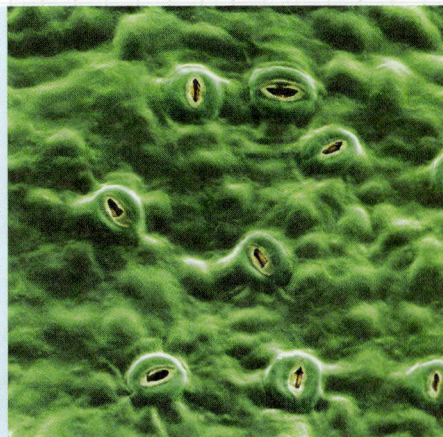

Look at the photo of the leaf.

15. Count and write the number of open stomata that you can see. _____

16. If the number of epidermis cells in this area is 150, what is the percentage of stomata in this area of the leaf?

17. Stomata percentage on a plant varies, depending on the environment where the plant lives. What environmental factors might influence the percentage of stomata? Explain your thinking.

18. The onyanga opens its stomata only at night for necessary gas exchange. How might this adaptation help the plant survive in its environment? Record your evidence.

Responding to Light and Gravity

Have you ever noticed your houseplant growing toward the window? One way that plants respond to their environment is by growing toward a light source. This process is called *phototropism*. Chemical messengers build up on the shaded side of the plant's stem. These messengers cause the cells to grow longer. As the cells on the shaded side grow longer, they cause the stem to bend toward the light source.

A change in the direction of plant growth in response to gravity is called *gravitropism* or *geotropism*. Most stems grow upward, away from the pull of Earth's gravity. Most roots grow downward, toward the pull of gravity.

19. What advantage do you think growing toward a light source gives a plant?

20. What might happen to a plant if the roots grew away from the pull of Earth's gravity?

Construct an Explanation

Explore Online

21. Water pressure in stems and leaves helps to keep a plant rigid. A plant wilts when there is a lack of water. How do interactions at the cell and tissue levels cause a plant to wilt? Explain your reasoning.

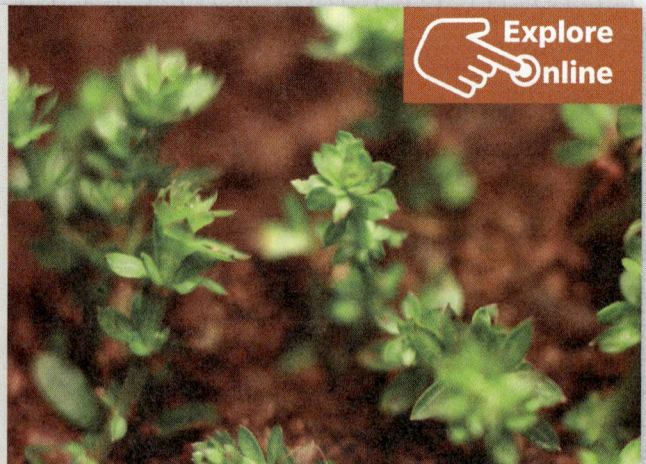

_____
_____
_____
_____
_____
_____
_____

Continue Your Exploration

Name: _____   Date: _____

Check out the path below or go online to choose one of the other paths shown.

| Growing Plants in Space | • **Feeding the World Using Less Water**
• **Hands-On Labs** 🖐️
• **Propose Your Own Path** | *Go online to choose one of these other paths.* |

The International Space Station is a research laboratory that travels at a speed of 8 kilometers per second and orbits Earth every 90 minutes. Solar panels provide power to the station, and life support systems supply oxygen and remove unwanted gases from the enclosed space. The water supply is supplemented by capturing and recycling the water vapors that enter the cabin when the crew members exhale and sweat! The crew members are researching ways to grow food on the space station in the hope that they will be able to have fresh food available for extended periods of time in space.

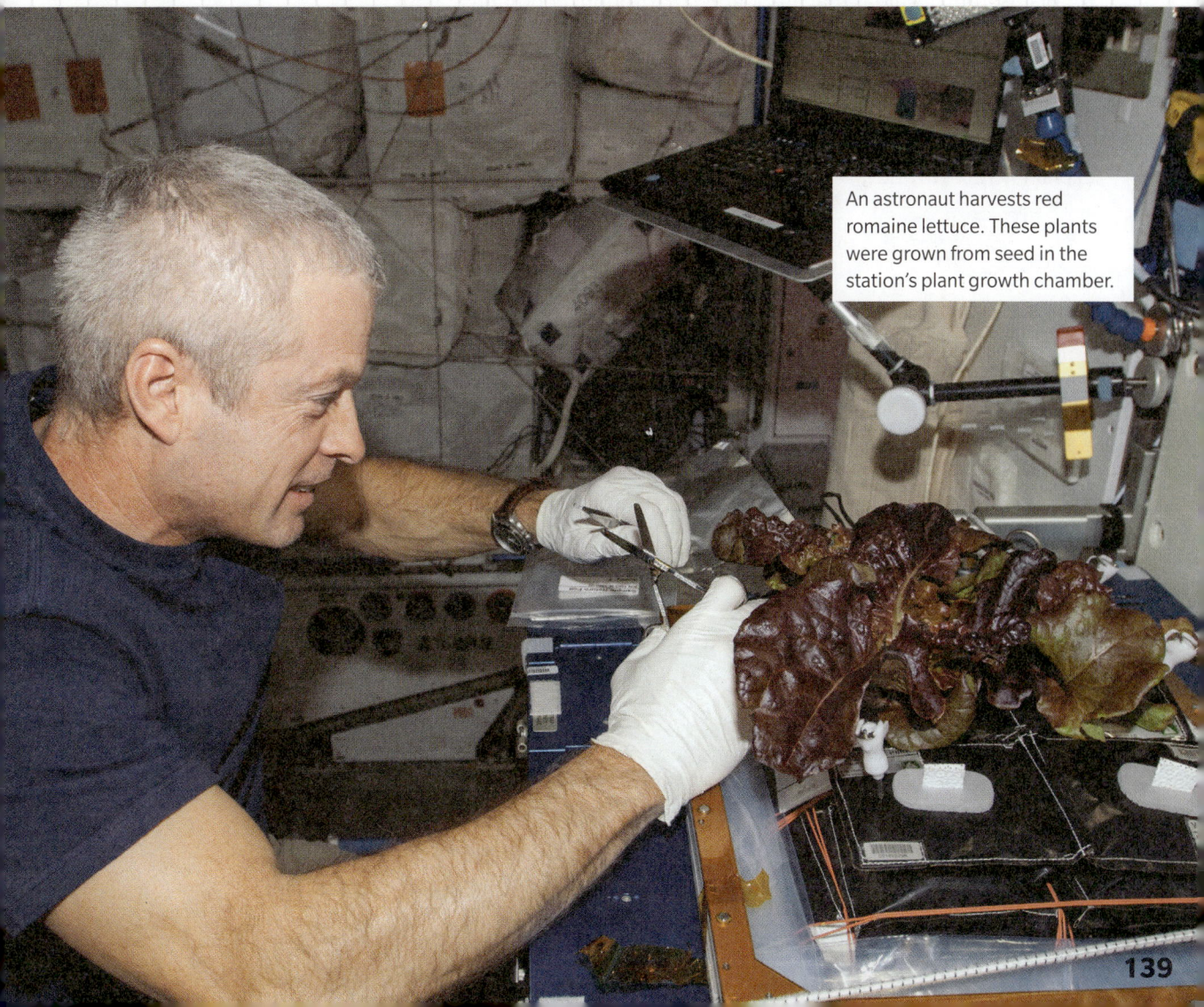

An astronaut harvests red romaine lettuce. These plants were grown from seed in the station's plant growth chamber.

Continue Your Exploration

1. The force of gravity is very weak on the space station, a condition referred to as microgravity. How might microgravity affect the growth of plants on the space station? Select all that apply.

   A. The length and shape of the roots and stems of the plants grown in space might be different than the same plants grown on Earth.

   B. The plant may not be able to absorb and transport water and nutrients in microgravity.

   C. The plant would not be able to respond to light in microgravity.

   D. The growth of the plant would not be affected by microgravity.

2. One of the biggest challenges of long-term space travel is having a sufficient supply of fresh water. Water must be recycled and used sparingly to ensure that the crew will have enough water to drink and to bathe. What types of plants from Earth would be good candidates for food plants for the crew of the space station? Select all that apply.

   A. plants from dense areas of vegetation that are adapted to crowded conditions

   B. plants from dry areas that are adapted to drought conditions

   C. plants from shady areas that are adapted to low light conditions

   D. plants from coastal areas that are adapted to saltwater conditions

3. Do you think the plants on the space station are able to conduct photosynthesis? Explain why or why not.

4. **Collaborate** Research plant growth in space. You may also find out more about the space garden on the International Space Station. Gather information about the types of questions researchers are asking about growing plants in space and the research being conducted to answer these questions. Develop a multimedia presentation or informational brochure that communicates your findings.

Can You Explain It?

Name: _____   Date: _____

How can the onyanga survive in the harsh conditions of the Namib Desert?

EVIDENCE NOTEBOOK

Refer to the notes in your Evidence Notebook to help you construct an explanation of how the onyanga can survive in the Namib Desert.

1. State your claim. Make sure your claim fully explains how the onyanga's body systems help it survive the harsh conditions of the Namib Desert.

2. Summarize the evidence you have gathered to support your claim and explain your reasoning.

Checkpoints

Answer the following questions to check your understanding of the lesson.

Use the photo to answer Questions 3 and 4.

3. Prickly pear cacti live in hot, dry habitats. The spines are modified leaves that do not have stomata. The green stems of the cactus store water and are covered in stomata. The site of photosynthesis in the prickly pear is likely to be the spines / stems .

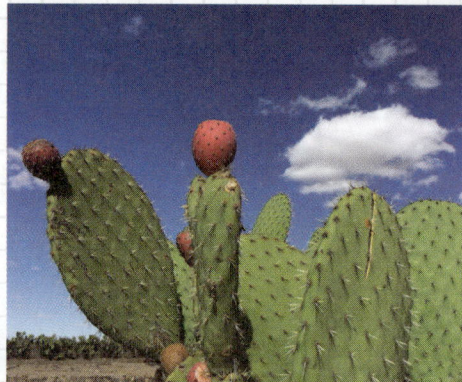

4. Which statement best describes the relationship between structure and function in the prickly pear cactus? Select all that apply.

   A. The stems are wide to maximize the capture of sunlight.

   B. The spines are narrow because they do not have stomata.

   C. The spines protect the stem from animals that try to eat the cactus.

   D. The stems are wide to maximize the amount of water that can be stored.

Use the photo to answer Questions 5 and 6.

This red mangrove tree has specialized roots, called prop roots, that extend above the ground.

5. The specialized roots of the mangrove tree help the tree to anchor / float in the sandy soil. The aboveground portions deliver gases / sunlight to the roots that are under the water.

6. Mangrove trees live in saline conditions that would kill most other types of plants. How do you think the mangrove tree is able to tolerate this environment?

   A. The mangrove tree needs more salt than other plants to live.

   B. The mangrove tree disposes of salt through its leaves.

   C. Animals that live on the tree eat the salt from the tree.

   D. The mangrove tree does not grow as well as trees that do not live in saltwater conditions.

Interactive Review

Complete this section to review the main concepts of the lesson.

Plant are living systems made up of cells that form tissues, organs, and organ systems.

A. Describe why the interaction of the different components in the plant body are necessary for the plant body system to function.

Plant body systems interact to perform all the functions needed for survival.

B. **Draw** Make a diagram to explain how a plant's root system and shoot system work together to provide the plant with food, water, and soil nutrients.

Plant body systems respond to the environment.

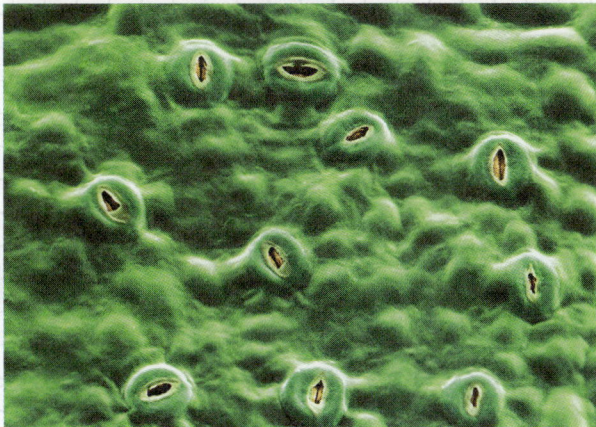

C. Describe the cause-and-effect relationships between conditions in the environment, such as light and a plant's response to light.

Associates/Science Source. Colorization by: Mary Martin

Animals Are Living Systems

The pangolin is the only mammal that has scales. The scales protect the pangolin from predators such as leopards and hyenas.

Explore First

Exploring Senses Fill a paper bag with items that have different textures. In groups, take turns feeling one item without looking and identify what it is. How did each person determine what the item was by only using the sense of touch?

CAN YOU EXPLAIN IT?

Why is it so difficult to catch a fly?

Houseflies can be found anywhere there are animals. They feed on garbage, manure, or softened food, like this biscuit left on the counter.

1. **Discuss** Have you ever tried to catch a fly? If so, you know that it isn't easy. Look at the photo of the fly. Write down your observations about its body and think about how the parts might be involved in evading your grasp.

EVIDENCE NOTEBOOK As you explore the lesson, gather evidence to help you explain why it is so difficult to catch a fly.

Analyzing Animal Body Systems

When we think of animals we often think of feathered or furry creatures, but sponges, corals, and worms are animals too. Animals live on land, underground, in freshwater and in salt water—in nearly every place on Earth where there is life. Some animals even live in or on other animals!

The Animal Body

Animal bodies come in many shapes and sizes, but they have some characteristics in common. All animals are multicellular. Animals can have four basic tissue types: nervous, epithelial, connective, and muscle. Nervous tissue functions as a messaging system within the body. Epithelial tissue protects and forms boundaries, and is found in organs such as skin. Connective tissue, including bones and blood, holds parts of the body together and provides support. Muscle tissue produces movement.

The organs in an animal are made up of two or more of these tissue types. For example, the human heart is made up of muscle, nervous, and epithelial tissues. Organs are organized into systems that perform specific functions, such as digestion of food or delivery of oxygen. The types of tissues, organs, and organ systems present in an animal depend on the type of animal and its environment.

2. **Discuss** Look at the photos and read the captions. With a partner, discuss the ways that these animals are similar and the ways they are different.

This **nautilus** moves by "jet propulsion." Water is pulled into its shell and forced out of a muscular, flexible tube.

The unusual looking **okapi** has large, upright ears that can detect the slightest sound.

This **red rock crab** has five pairs of legs that grip rocks and help the crab avoid being swept away by powerful waves.

Digestive and Excretory System Interactions

Animals get the energy they need from food. The *digestive system* and *excretory system* interact to process food and eliminate wastes. Digestion begins with the teeth or other structures that break down food mechanically. Digestive enzymes in the saliva and stomach chemically break down the food, which is absorbed into the bloodstream in the small intestine. Solid wastes are processed and expelled by the large intestine.

The excretory system removes liquid wastes from the body. The skin, lungs, and kidneys are organs in the excretory system. For example, excess salts are released through the skin when an animal sweats. Waste products are filtered from blood as it flows through the kidneys. When you breathe out, or exhale, carbon dioxide and water vapor are released from your lungs.

3. The crabeater seal is an aquatic mammal that eats krill, tiny shrimp-like crustaceans. It filters the krill from the water as it swims. A tiger shark is a fierce predator that eats a wide variety of prey. Which teeth do you think belong to the *crabeater seal* and which belong to the *tiger shark*? Write the name in the box provided.

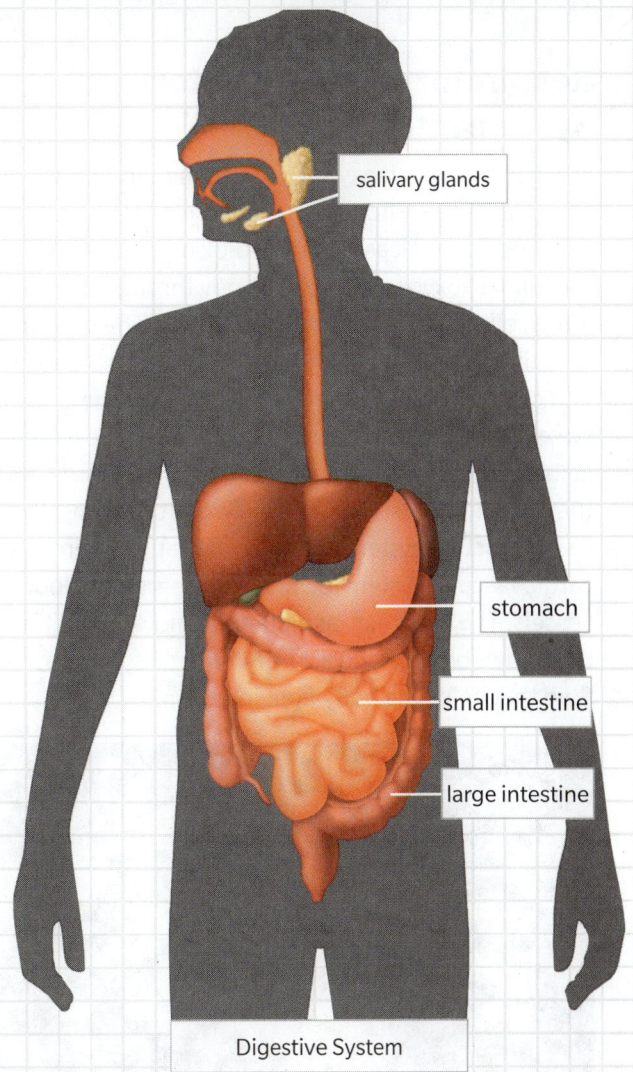

salivary glands

stomach

small intestine

large intestine

Digestive System

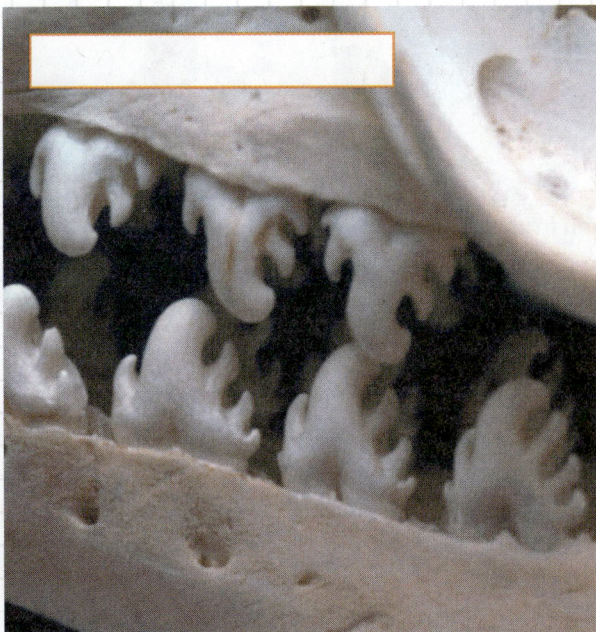

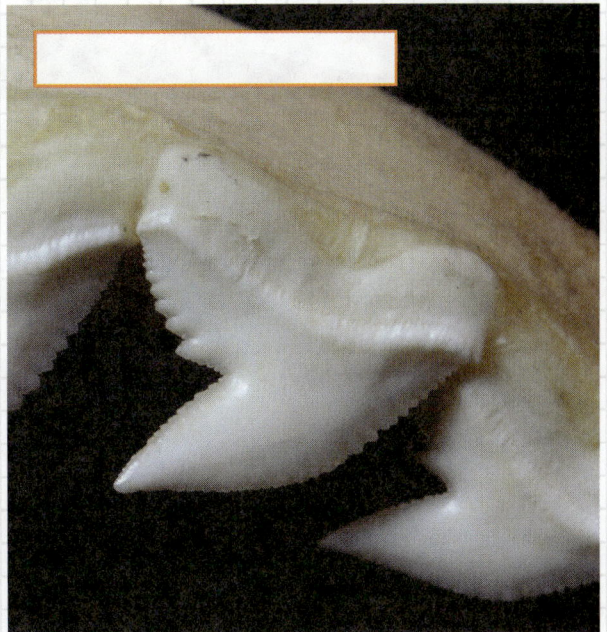

Respiratory and Circulatory System Interactions

Most animals need oxygen to live. Animal cells use oxygen to release energy from food. The *respiratory system* takes in oxygen and releases carbon dioxide. Depending on the animal, oxygen enters the body through the skin, lungs, gills, or other specialized organs. The oxygen can be delivered directly to the tissues and cells of the body, or it can be sent to the circulatory system. The *circulatory system* carries oxygen, water, and nutrients to all the cells of the body. In some animals, such as mammals, the circulatory system includes two subsystems: the cardiovascular system and the lymphatic system. The cardiovascular system includes the heart and blood vessels. The heart acts as a pump to move blood through the body's blood vessels. The lymphatic system transports fluid that helps the body fight infection.

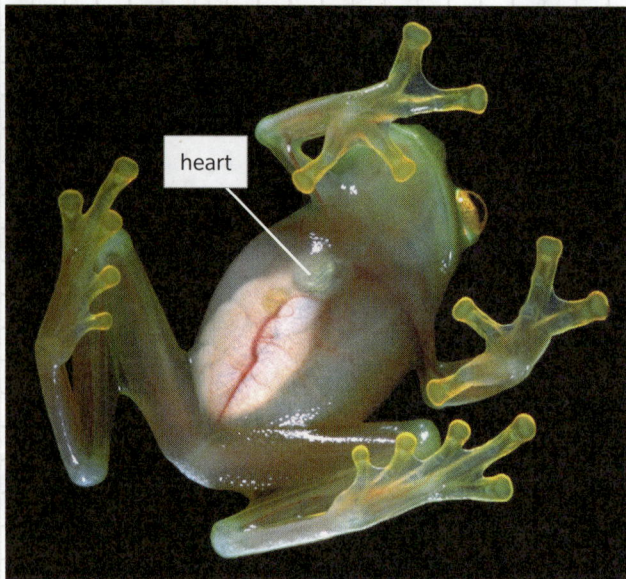

lung

heart

Cardiovascular System

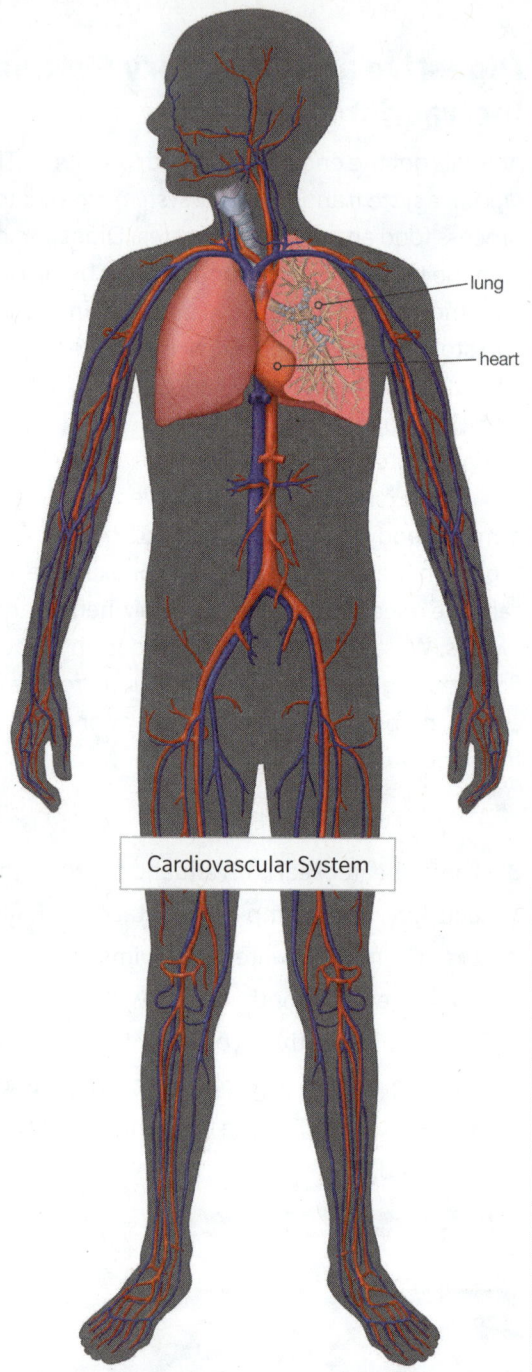

heart

Frogs have a circulatory system and a respiratory system but can also absorb oxygen through their skin.

4. A layer of water just under a frog's skin captures oxygen from air or water and delivers it to blood vessels at the skin's surface. How might this function relate to the fact that frogs are very sensitive to environmental pollution?

Skeletal and Muscular System Interactions

All animals are able to move at some point in their life cycle. The *muscular system* is a body system that provides internal and external movement for an animal. Most animals use muscles for movement, but some animals use other body structures, such as hair-like cilia.

Muscles attached to the skeleton produce movement. An animal skeleton can be made of bones or other hard, nonbony structures, such as spines or crystals. A skeleton can be external, like the exoskeleton of insects. An internal skeletal system, or endoskeleton, is a framework that provides support for the body.

This cicada is *moulting*, or shedding its exoskeleton.

5. The exoskeleton of an insect provides a stiff, protective armor. What might be some disadvantages of an exoskeleton?

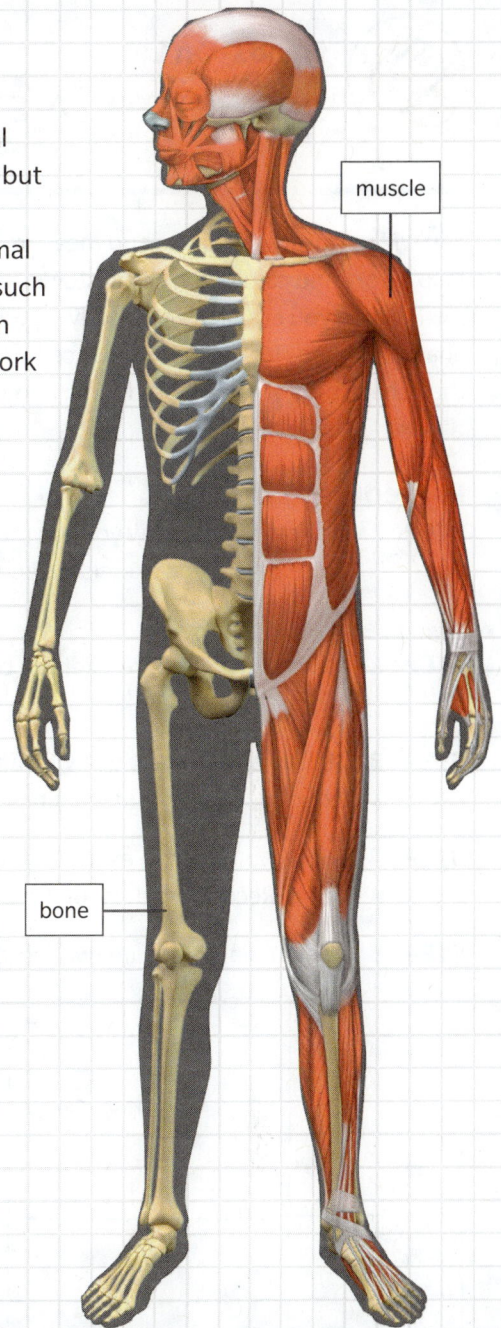

Skeletal and Muscular Systems

Information Processing

All animals must be able to detect and react to conditions in their environments. The *nervous system* collects and processes information. The nervous system in most animals is a network of branching nerves that communicate messages between the brain and other parts of the body. In some animals, the brain is simply a cluster of nerve cells, while in others, it is complex and made up of many structures that work together.

Animals use a variety of structures to gather information from the environment. Eyes and ears are familiar organs, but animals also use hairs, skin, and antennae to collect information. Butterflies taste with their feet, and snakes smell with their tongues!

Geographic Magazines/Getty Images

Hands-On Lab
Measure System Response to Exercise

You will perform an exercise and measure the responses of your respiratory and cardiovascular systems.

When you exercise, your body systems work together to respond to changing needs for oxygen in your cells. Animals need more oxygen when they chase prey, run from predators, and travel long distances.

MATERIALS
- chair or other space to rest
- small space for exercising (for example, running in place)
- stopwatch

Procedure

STEP 1 Make a plan for how you will measure your breathing rate and pulse before you exercise. Decide how long you will rest before collecting the data.

STEP 2 Measure your before-exercise breathing rate and pulse. Record the data in the table below.

STEP 3 Make a plan for how you will measure your breathing rate and pulse after you exercise. Think about what type of exercise you will do and for how long.

STEP 4 Follow your plan to exercise. Measure your after-exercise breathing rate and pulse. Record the data for 3 trials in the table below.

STEP 5 Repeat the procedure two more times.

	Before Exercise		After Exercise	
	breathing rate	pulse	breathing rate	pulse
Trial 1				
Trial 2				
Trial 3				
Average				

Analysis and Conclusions

STEP 6 **Do the Math** For each column in your table, calculate the average of the three trials. Are the values recorded for each trial the same?

STEP 7 How did the change in pulse compare to the change in breathing rate? Did one change more than the other?

STEP 8 Look at the diagram that shows the connection between the circulatory and the respiratory systems. Use the diagram and your data to explain why pulse and breathing rates change when you exercise, and how the two systems are working together.

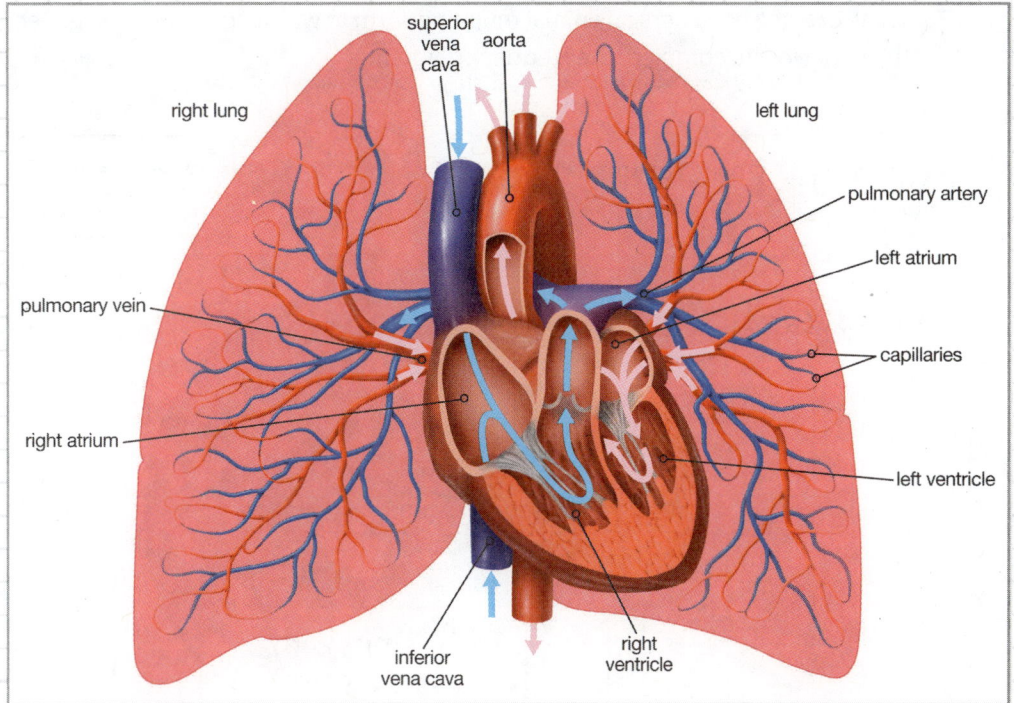

This diagram shows the path that blood takes through the human heart and lungs. Blood is pumped from the right side of the heart to the lungs. From the lungs, it returns to the left side of the heart. The blood is then pumped from the left side of the heart to the body. It flows to the tiny capillaries around every part of the body before returning to the right side of the heart.

Design a Video Game Character

6. **Draw** Using drawing materials or digital tools, plan and draw a video game character based on an animal. The animal can have any features or functions you choose. Label the features and functions of your character.

Describing Information Processing in Animals

Think about what your body is doing right now. What can you see, feel, smell, and hear? Without even thinking about it, you are constantly receiving and processing information. Information processing causes you to respond to your environment, regulate the internal processes of your body, and learn and form memories from your experiences. The nervous system collects and processes information.

Animal Responses to Changes in Temperature

7. Think of some behaviors an animal might perform to warm up or cool down. Record the behaviors to complete the feedback diagram.

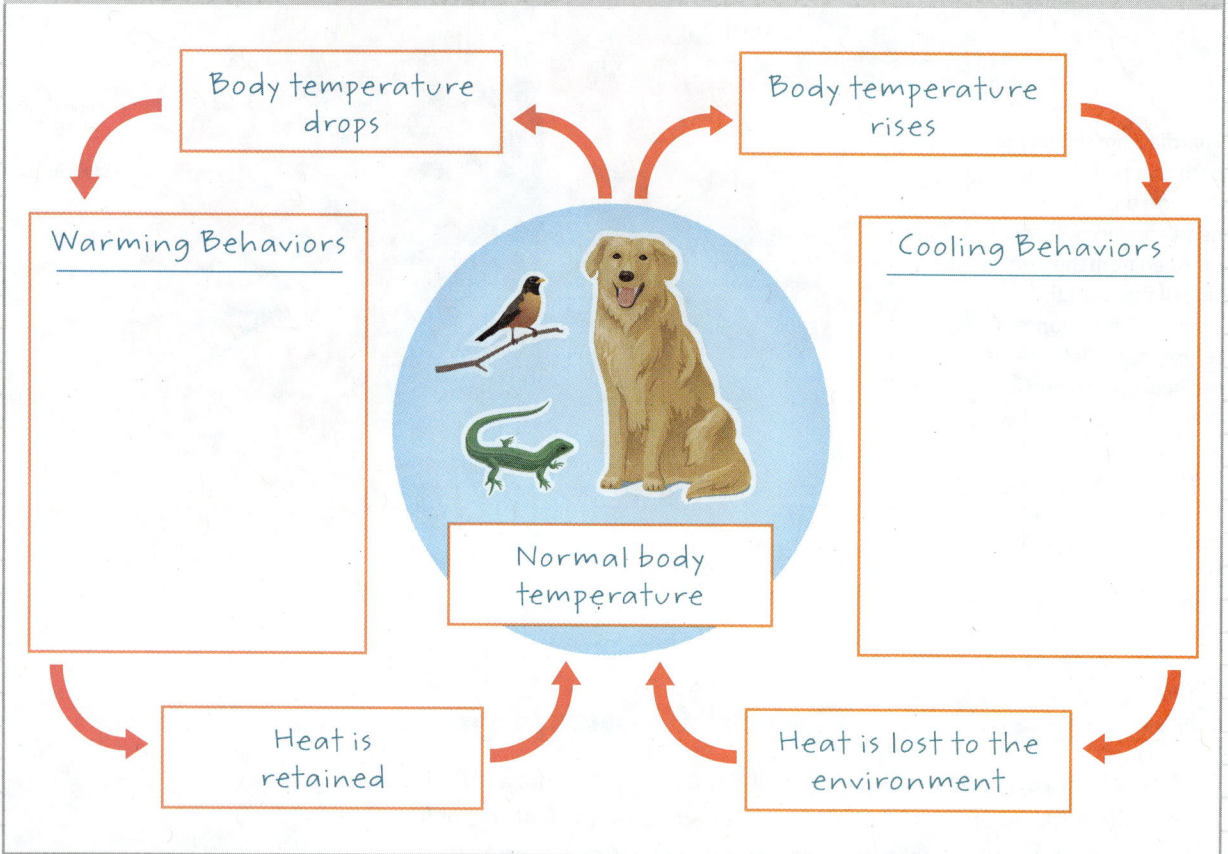

Body temperature drops

Body temperature rises

Warming Behaviors

Cooling Behaviors

Normal body temperature

Heat is retained

Heat is lost to the environment

Homeostasis

In order to survive, an animal might need to respond to danger, the need for food and water, or changes in temperature. These responses help an animal maintain homeostasis. When internal and external environments change, **homeostasis** is the process by which the inside of the body maintains stable conditions. Homeostasis is controlled through feedback. Feedback is a cycle of events in which information from one step controls or affects a previous step. Feedback can be positive or negative. Negative feedback occurs when the body senses a change in its internal environment and activates processes that will slow or prevent the change. Positive feedback occurs when the body activates processes that increase or reinforce the change.

8. A dog responds to the stimulus of feeling hot by panting. When the dog cools down, the dog will stop panting. This way of controlling body temperature is an example of negative /positive feedback.

To help cool off, this dog is panting. Water evaporates from the dog's mouth, resulting in heat loss.

Sensing and Transmitting Information

Specialized cells in an animal's nervous system are called sensory receptors. **Sensory receptors** help an animal gather information about its environment. Sensory receptors are especially plentiful in sensory organs—the skin, ears, nose, mouth, and eyes—but they also occur in other parts of the body. Different types of sensory receptors respond to different environmental messages, such as light, heat, or pressure. This type of environmental message is called a *stimulus*. For example, a sensory receptor could detect pressure from a butterfly landing on your finger. When a sensory receptor detects a stimulus, it sends the information to the brain in the form of electrical energy. The information travels through specialized cells called *neurons*.

One group of neurons carries information from sensory receptors to the brain. Another group of neurons carries information from the brain to various parts of the body, telling them how to respond.

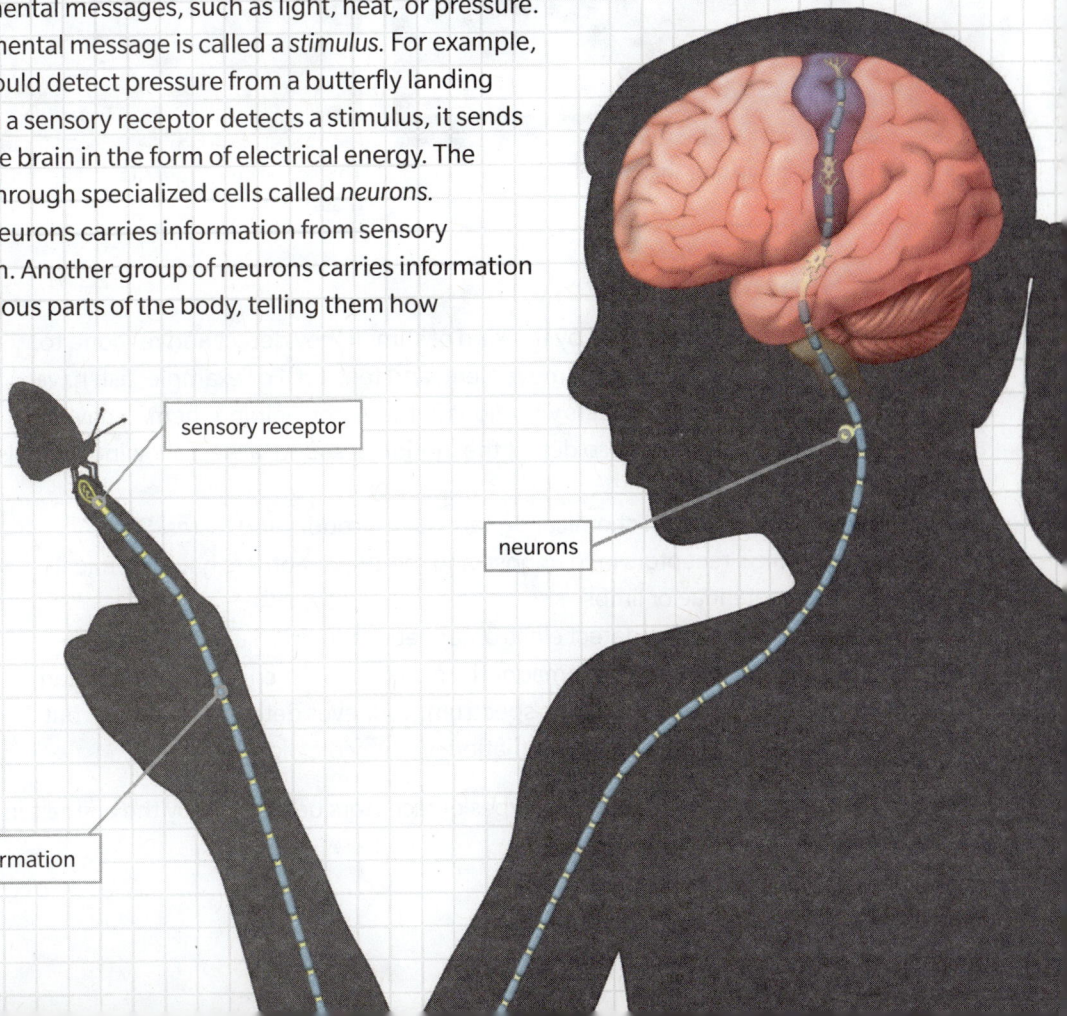

sensory receptor

neurons

path of sensory information

9. Read the descriptions about each animal below. Which stimulus might each of these animals be responding to? Use the terms in the Word Bank.

word bank	
• light	• odor
• motion	• sound

This male silkworm moth can detect very small concentrations of chemicals given off by a female.

Chameleons use highly coordinated eye movements to target their prey.

This spider is wrapping up prey that got caught in its web.

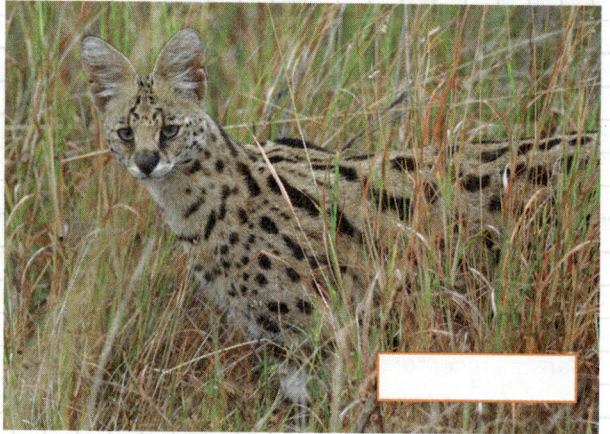

This serval hunts rodents that are scurrying through the grass.

Types of Sensory Receptors

Sensory receptors can be organized by the kind of stimuli they detect and respond to. *Mechanical receptors* detect pressure, movement, and tension. For example, fish have a specialized sense organ that detects vibrations in the water, helping them to navigate and hunt. Mechanical receptors also detect the motion of sound waves, allowing animals to hear.

    Chemical receptors detect chemical signals, such as odors and tastes. Some animals have chemical receptors in their nose and mouth, but others have chemical receptors on their antennae or limbs.

    Electromagnetic receptors detect electromagnetic radiation, such as light. Different kinds of animals have different electromagnetic receptors, so each kind of animal can see specific parts of the electromagnetic spectrum. Your eyes detect visible light, but some other animals can detect infrared radiation or ultraviolet light.

10. **Discuss** With a partner, discuss the types of receptors being used by the animals in the table.

Processing Sensory Information

Most animals have a brain that organizes and processes information from sensory receptors. Animal brains can be just a cluster of neurons, or they can be made up of many structures that work together. Different animals process information at different rates. For example, quick moving insects and small birds process visual information more rapidly than leatherback turtles do. Insects and birds need to respond quickly to catch prey or avoid being eaten by predators. Leatherback turtles move slowly and feed on slow-moving jellyfish, so fast visual processing does not provide a survival advantage.

Major Areas of the Human Cerebral Cortex

The illustration and the magnetic resonance image (MRI) both show the cerebral cortex of the human brain.

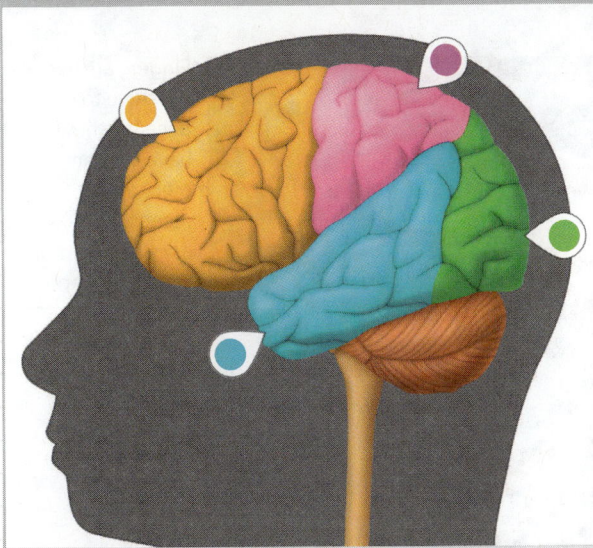

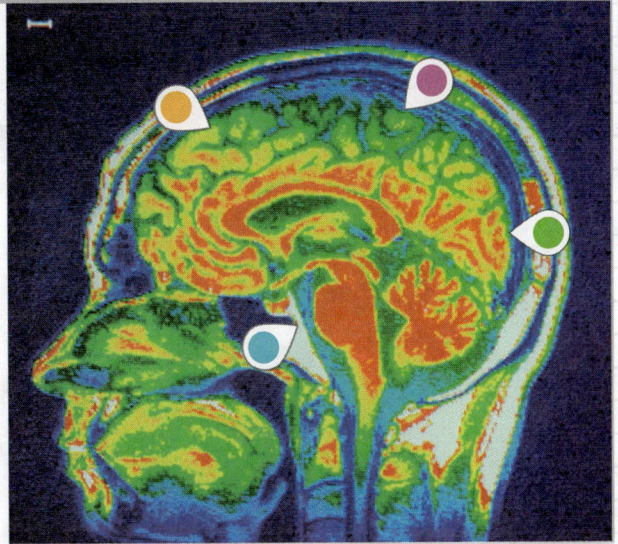

Frontal lobe
The frontal lobe is the "boss." It coordinates planning, organization, behaviors, and emotions.

Parietal lobe
The parietal lobe processes sensory information related to taste, temperature, and touch.

Temporal lobe
The temporal lobe is associated with hearing, language, and olfactory senses.

Occipital lobe
The occipital lobe is involved in the reception of visual stimuli.

11. You are walking down a busy street. The smell of freshly baked bread is coming from a bakery up ahead. You move to your right as a bike zooms past you. Suddenly, you hear a loud car horn directly behind you. Make a list of the information your brain is receiving in this scenario. Identify the areas of the brain that are involved in processing the different stimuli.

EVIDENCE NOTEBOOK

12. What types of stimuli is the fly responding to when you try to catch it? Which body systems might be involved in the response? Record your evidence.

Language SmArts

Explain Sensory Receptor Patterns

Not all parts of your body are as sensitive to touch as others. Your fingers, for example, have many sensory receptors, so they are very sensitive to touch. Other body parts—your back and your calf, for example—have fewer sensory receptors and are much less sensitive to touch.

Fingers are very sensitive to touch because they have so many mechanical receptors, as well as other types of sensory receptors.

13. Why do you think the parts of the body have different sensitivities? Write an argument to support your explanation.

_____

_____

_____

_____

_____

_____

_____

_____

_____

_____

_____

Analyzing Animal Responses to Information

When the brain receives sensory messages, it determines what to do with the information. Sensory inputs can result in an immediate response, and they can also be stored in the brain for use in the future. For example, an animal might perform the immediate behavior of spitting out a bad-tasting prey. The animal might also store that information as memory and avoid the prey when they meet again.

14. Look at the lion and the porcupines. What immediate behaviors might each animal perform? What might be stored as memory for each animal? Record your answers.

	behavior	memory
lion		
porcupines		

Behavior

The set of actions taken by an organism in response to stimuli is called **behavior**. Animals perform behaviors to survive. Some animal behaviors do not require learning or experience. For example, newborn whales know how to swim as soon as they are born. Behaviors that do not require learning or experience are called *innate* behaviors. Animals are born knowing these behaviors, but they are triggered by things that happen in the animal's environment.

Other behaviors develop through memories and experience, and from observing the actions of other animals. These behaviors that depend on memory are *learned* behaviors. For example, some birds learn their songs by listening to other individuals. Young animals can learn to hunt and even use tools by watching adults.

Analyze Hibernation

Hibernation is a behavior that allows animals to survive in their habitats during the winter months when food may be scarce. Animals that hibernate store body fat when food is plentiful. When food becomes scarce, they enter a period of inactivity, surviving off of their stored body fat. The graph below shows how two variables—weight gain and month of the year—relate to each other.

The hazel dormouse is a tiny rodent that hibernates for about half the year, from fall to spring.

15. The independent variable is the month of the year. The dependent variable is the average weight of the dormice. How are the two variables related to each other?

16. During which time period do both the males and females gain weight most rapidly?

Average Weight of Adult Dormice

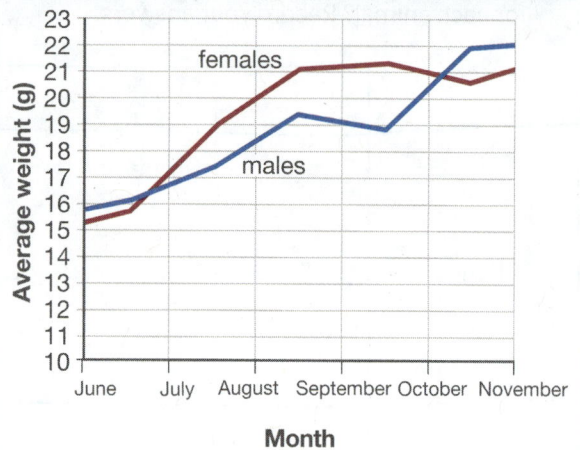

Source: Surrey Dormouse Group, 2014

17. Write a short summary that explains the relationship between weight and hibernation.

Memory

Information can be stored in the brain as **memory**. Information that gets stored as memory can be an event, such as an encounter with predator or prey. Animals can also remember information related to sensory stimuli. Odor memory can help animals identify their infants or other family members. Visual memory can help them remember locations of food sources or migration routes. Memory allows an animal to respond to its environment more efficiently. For example, an animal that can remember the location of a food source will spend less time searching for food and more time eating!

Hands-On Lab
Measure Reaction Time

You will measure your reaction time in response to a falling object and compare your data with other groups.

Behaviors are the result of systems working together. To catch an object, your brain sends a message to the muscles in your arm. The time it takes for the message to travel from your brain to your arm is called your reaction time.

MATERIALS
• chair
• meterstick

Procedure and Analysis

STEP 1 One person should sit in a chair with one arm in a "handshake" position. The other person should stand facing the person in the chair, holding the meterstick vertically, so that the lower end is between the sitting person's thumb and forefinger. Observe where on the meterstick's scale the sitting person's thumb and forefinger are. Record the data in the table.

STEP 2 Make sure the sitting student has the thumb and forefinger far enough apart for the meterstick to fall through. The person holding the meterstick should drop it without warning. The person sitting should catch the meterstick as quickly as possible. Record the location of the sitting person's thumb and forefinger on the meterstick's scale after catching the meterstick.

STEP 3 Determine the distance the meter stick fell and record the data in the table.

STEP 4 Repeat Steps 1–3 two more times. Calculate the average distance the meterstick fell in the three trials.

	Finger position before drop (cm)	Finger position when caught (cm)	Distance meterstick fell (cm)
Trial 1			
Trial 2			
Trial 3			

Average distance meterstick fell: _____

STEP 5 Describe the flow of information from sensory receptors to behavioral response. Make note of all the body systems that are involved in the response you tested in this activity.

Lesson 4 Animals Are Living Systems **159**

STEP 6 Compare your group's data with the data of another group. How did the data compare? What factors might explain any differences in reaction times?

STEP 7 **Discuss** In the activity, your reaction time probably got faster each time you caught the meterstick. With a partner, discuss how memory and experience contribute to a faster reaction time.

EVIDENCE NOTEBOOK

18. Look back at the photo of the fly. Does the fly have a fast reaction to your hand or a slow reaction? What effect might memory and experience have on the fly's reaction time in the long-term? Record your evidence.

Engineer It
Evaluate Biomimetics

Animals are often capable of sensing different information than humans. *Biomimicry*, or *biomimetics*, uses design solutions found in nature to solve human design problems. For example, brittle stars are covered in lenses that help them avoid predators. These lenses transmit light more perfectly than any human-made lens. Engineers designed improved lenses based on the brittle star lens structure that are soft, providing better fine-tuning and complexity than conventional hard lenses.

19. Why is it advantageous for engineers to look to animals for engineering design solutions?

_____

_____

_____

20. Bats detect objects using sound waves. The bat emits a sound from its mouth or nose. The sound wave hits an object and the echo returns to the bat's ear, which the bat uses to locate the object. Describe how this ability could be applied to the design of a cane used by visually-challenged people to navigate through their environments.

_____

_____

_____

_____

Continue Your Exploration

Name: _____   **Date:** _____

Check out the path below or go online to choose one of the other paths shown.

| Migration | • Sensory Organ Adaptations
• Hands-On Labs 🖐
• Propose Your Own Path | Go online to choose one of these other paths. |

Animals travel long distances in response to seasonal weather changes and change in the availability of food. This type of travel is called *migration*. Migration is a seasonal movement from one place to another. Many birds, mammals, reptiles, fish, and even insects migrate. Animals make long journeys to escape harsh weather conditions, to find more abundant food, or to find more suitable locations for reproduction.

Unlike humans, animals do not have maps or instruments to navigate long distances. Animals might use the position of the sun or Earth's magnetic field to navigate. They can also use odor, sound waves, or the sight of familiar landmarks.

Monarch butterflies travel from the United States to Mexico to avoid the cold winter temperatures.

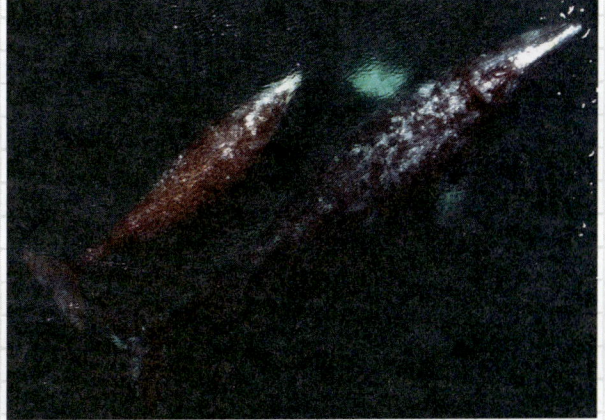

This gray whale and her calf are migrating north from California to summer feeding grounds in the Arctic.

1. If migration is thought of in terms of cause and effect, migration can be considered the effect. What is the cause of the monarch migration? What is the cause of the gray whale migration?

Continue Your Exploration

2. Scientists are not certain why the little Arctic tern makes the migration journey of 70,000 km round trip each year. Which statement below do you think is the most likely explanation?

    A. The Arctic terns are following patterns of food availability and favorable wind conditions from pole to pole.

    B. The Arctic terns are being carried from pole to pole by wind currents.

    C. The Arctic terns are traveling from pole to pole to find mates.

The Arctic tern makes the longest known annual migration—from the South Pole to the North Pole and back again.

3. Odor, or *olfactory*, memory plays a role in the migration of salmon, as well as some other animals. What type of sensory receptors do you think the salmon are using to navigate their migration path? Explain your answer.

Salmon hatch in fresh water and then migrate to the ocean. When salmon are ready to reproduce, they migrate back to the freshwater areas where they were hatched.

4. **Collaborate** Research a migration pattern of one of the animals from the previous page or another animal of your choice. Describe whether the cause of the migration is well-established, or if scientists have different opinions. Explain the possible role of memories in the behavior. Collaborate to make a visual summary or map of the pattern of migration.

Can You Explain It?

Name: _____ **Date:** _____

Why is it so difficult to catch a fly?

EVIDENCE NOTEBOOK

Refer to the notes in your Evidence Notebook to help you construct an explanation for why it is so difficult to catch a fly.

1. State your claim. Make sure your claim fully explains how the fly's body system works to respond to your grasp.

2. Summarize the evidence you have gathered to support your claim and explain your reasoning.

Checkpoints

Answer the following questions to check your understanding of the lesson.

Use the image to answer Questions 3–4.

3. The *muscular / excretory* system is interacting with the *digestive / skeletal* system to move the racer's arms.

4. Which body systems will interact to provide the energy the racer needs to keep pushing the wheels of the chair?

    A. digestive/excretory

    B. circulatory/respiratory

    C. muscular/skeletal

    D. digestive/circulatory

Use the image to answer Questions 5–6.

5. A scallop has as many as 100 bright blue eyes along the edges of its valves. What is the best explanation for having so many eyes?

    A. The scallop is able to detect the best time to reproduce.

    B. The scallop is able to detect predators from many directions.

    C. The scallop is able to detect a mate while swimming.

    D. The scallop is able to detect changes in water conditions.

6. Scallops use their shell valves to feed and move. A scallop opens its valves when it sees a *food particle / predator* nearby. It moves by clapping its valves together when it sees a *food particle / predator* nearby.

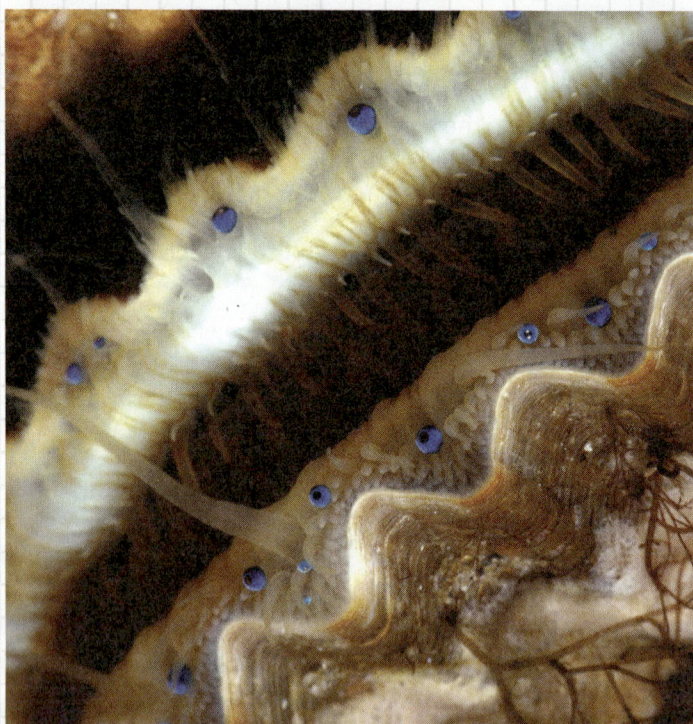

Interactive Review

Complete this section to review the main concepts of the lesson.

Animals are living systems made up of interacting subsystems that perform functions.

A. Describe the interaction of two body systems that perform a function needed by an animal to survive.

Animals gather and process information from their environment.

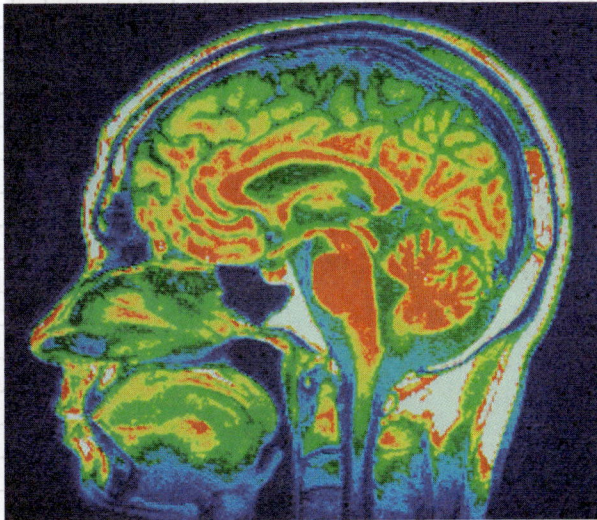

B. Draw a concept map or flow chart to show the path of an environmental stimulus to the brain.

Animals respond to stimuli by performing behaviors.

C. What is the relationship between memory and behavior?

Scientific/Getty Images

Choose one of the activities to explore how this unit connects to other topics.

People in Science

Garfield Kwan, Marine Biologist Garfield Kwan grew up in Hong Kong and Los Angeles. He studies marine biology at University of California in San Diego and is interested in how fish will respond to increased carbon dioxide levels in the ocean. Garfield knows that scientific concepts are often complex and that adding illustrations can make science easier to understand. He founded a company that creates infographics – a combination of illustrations and text – as a way to communicate complex scientific concepts in an interesting way. Research a natural system and create an infographic to explain the relationships among its components. Present your infographic to the class.

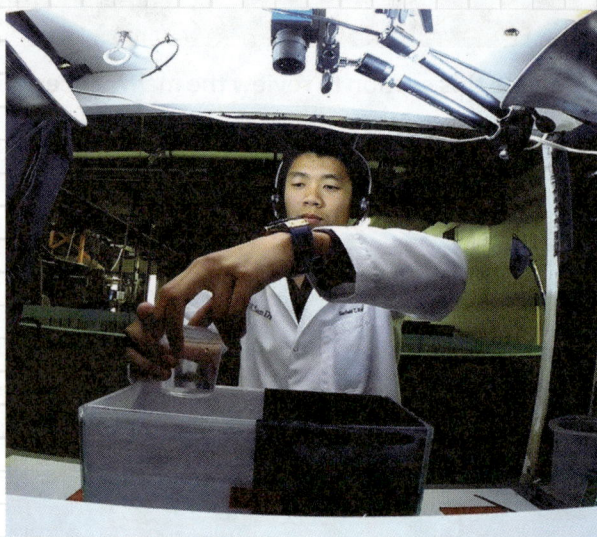

Garfield Kwan at work in the laboratory.

Physical Science Connection

Scanning and Transmission Electron Microscopes In order to examine the smallest parts of cells in detail, scientists can use a scanning electron microscope or a transmission electron microscope. These types of microscopes use beams of electrons, rather than light. Using library or Internet resources, research how scanning electron microscopes (SEMs) and transmission electron microscopes (TEMs) work. Investigate the advantages and disadvantages of both types of microscope. Compare what is visible in a cell with a light microscope versus what is visible in a cell with a SEM or TEM. Create a multimedia presentation with your findings to share with the class.

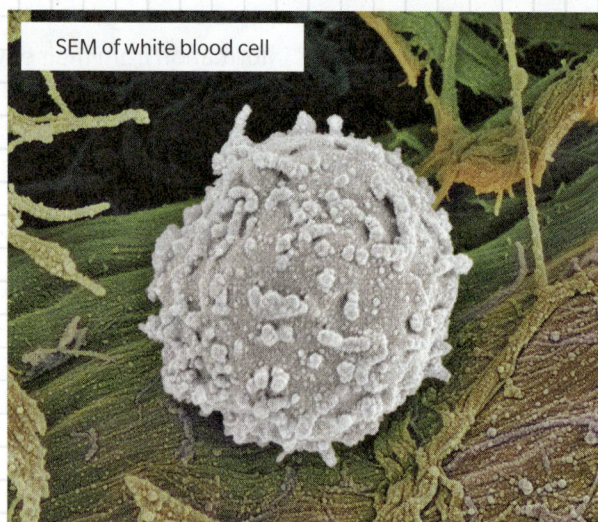

SEM of white blood cell

Health Connection

Medical Research Neurological diseases affect components of the nervous system, including the brain, spinal cord, and neurons. Advances in gene mapping, stem cell therapy, and imaging technologies have improved understanding, diagnosis, and treatment of these diseases. Research a neurological disease, such as Alzheimer's disease or amyotrophic lateral sclerosis (ALS). Identify the causes and symptoms of the disease, and how current technologies are helping medical researchers diagnose and treat the disease. Write a magazine article to present your research.

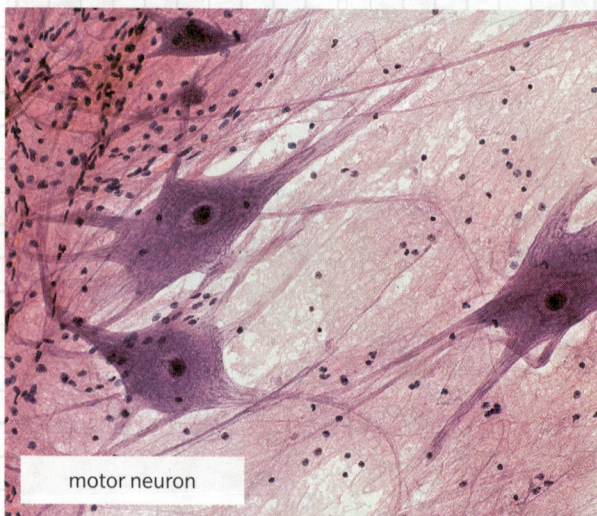

motor neuron

Name: _____   Date: _____

Use the diagram of the snake to answer Questions 1–3.

skull

1. Snakes have a wide range of movement because their backbones are very flexible. Which body subsystems working together result in movement of the snake?

    A. digestive and skeletal

    B. digestive and muscular

    C. respiratory and excretory

    D. muscular and skeletal

heart

muscles

2. The snake's skin performs specialized functions for the body, including protection from injury and disease. The skin is made up of several tissue types. The snake's skin is an example of a(n)

    A. organelle.

    B. tissue.

    C. organ.

    D. organ system.

vertebrae (backbones)

stomach

lungs

ribs

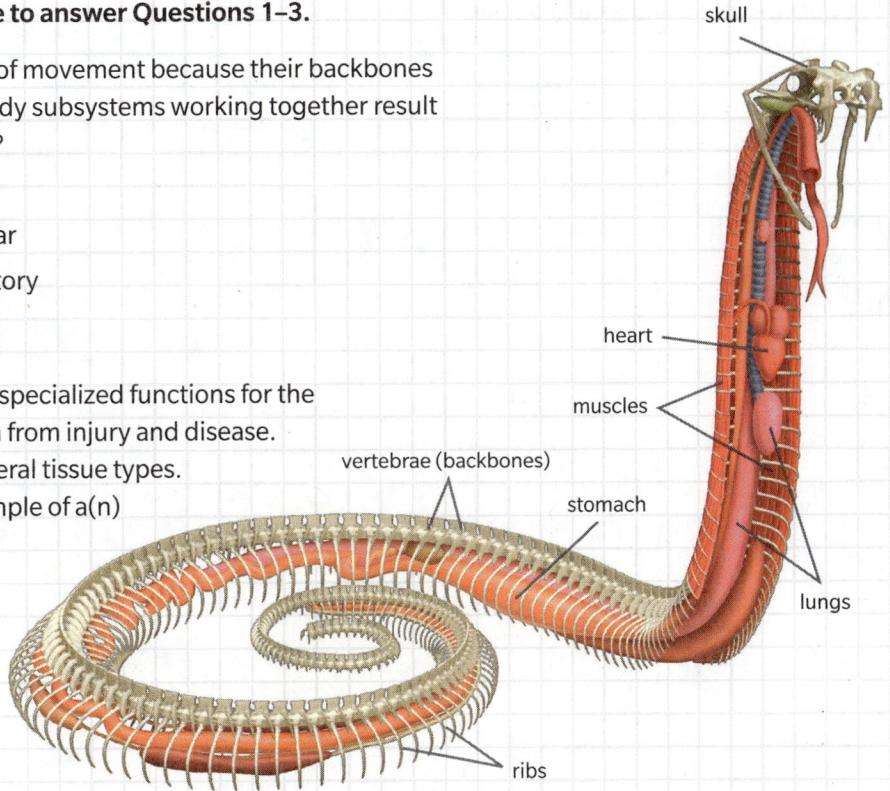

3. The snake's skeletal system provides the function of *transport / support*, just as the *root / shoot* system does for a plant.

Use the photo to answer Questions 4–5.

4. Which Earth subsystem is not represented in the photo?

    A. geosphere

    B. hydrosphere

    C. cryosphere

    D. atmosphere

5. The Golden Gate Bridge is part of the *geosphere / anthroposphere*. It connects two sections of land previously separated by the *biosphere / hydrosphere*. The movement of animals across the bridge has resulted in changes in populations in the *biosphere / atmosphere* on each side of the bridge.

6. For each of the body functions listed, describe the function in terms of cause and effect. Identify the plant and/or animal systems involved, and describe any related patterns between plant and animal bodies.

Body Functions	Systems	Cause-and-Effect Relationships	Patterns in Plant and Animal Bodies
Moving water and nutrients throughout body			
Getting energy from food			
Providing support for the body			
Regulating oxygen and carbon dioxide			
Responding to the environment			

Name: _____   Date: _____

Use the illustration of the frog to answer Questions 7–11.

7. Identify the environmental stimulus that the frog is perceiving.

8. Explain how both electromagnetic receptors and mechanical receptors might be involved in sensing this stimulus.

9. Describe how sensory receptors transmit information about the stimulus to the frog's brain.

10. Describe the frog's possible responses to the information the sensory receptors have transmitted to the brain. Include a description of how the brain will cause the frog's body to act.

11. A frog's response to prey is innate. Explain how the response time might change over the life of the frog.

Use the illustration to answer Questions 12–15.

nucleus

mitochondrion

cell membrane

12. Is the cell shown in the illustration a bacterial, plant, or animal cell? Support your claim with evidence from the illustration.

13. Describe the cell as a system of interacting parts. Include the parts of the system in your description.

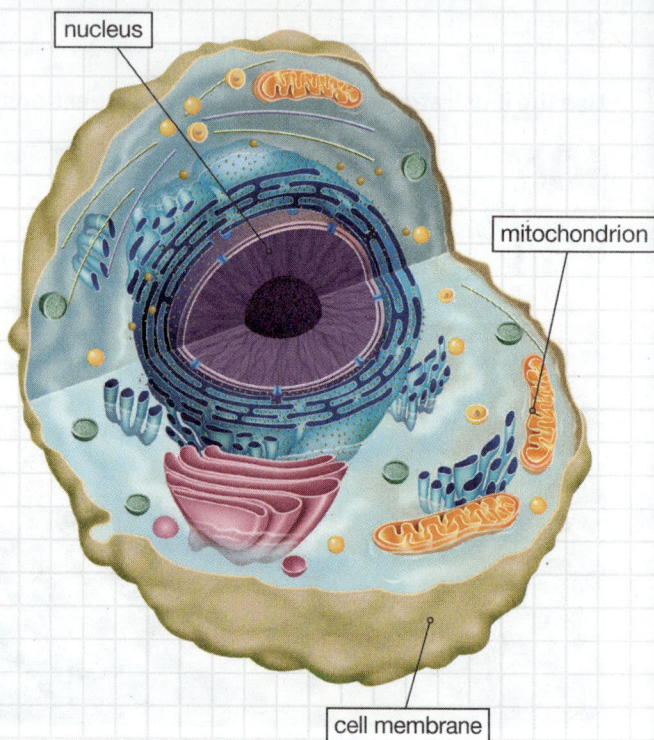

14. Describe how cell system function might be affected if one or more components were not functional.

15. What are some advantages of this cell illustration ? What are some limitations of this cell illustration?

Name: **Date:**

How can dehydration be prevented?

Your school district wants to find the best ways to keep student athletes from becoming dehydrated during afterschool practices. You have been asked to help school officials, coaches, and parent volunteers devise a plan for keeping student athletes hydrated. Study the diagram below, which shows some of the body systems involved in maintaining water balance in the body.

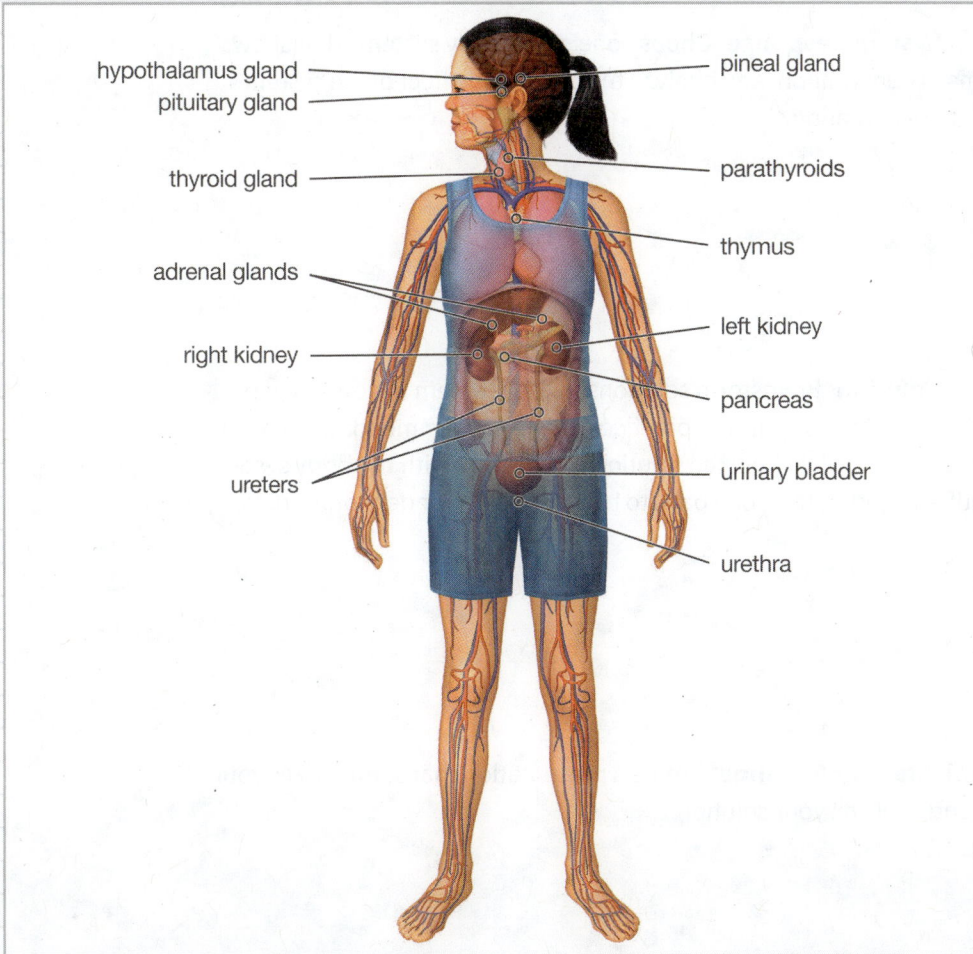

The steps below will help guide your research and develop your recommendation.

Engineer It

1. **Define the Problem** Investigate the importance of water in human body systems. Define the problem you are trying to solve.

Engineer It

2. **Conduct Research** Investigate the body systems involved in maintaining water balance in the body. Research the causes and symptoms of dehydration in the human body.

3. **Analyze a System Response** Choose one of the body systems that shows symptoms of dehydration, and analyze the cause and effect of the system's response to dehydration.

4. **Propose a Solution** Brainstorm solutions to the problem of how to keep student athletes hydrated during practices. Make a recommendation based on your research. Explain how the solution would work with the body system you identified to bring the body back to homeostasis after dehydration.

5. **Communicate Your Findings** Create a presentation that summarizes your findings and explains your solution.

✓ Self-Check

	I defined the problem of preventing dehydration in student athletes and investigated the importance of water to human body systems.
	I investigated the body systems involved in maintaining water balance in the body and researched causes and symptoms of dehydration.
	I analyzed the causes and effects of a body system's response to dehydration.
	I recommended a solution to the problem of preventing dehydration in student athletes and explained how the solution would work with the body system to bring the body back to homeostasis.
	I clearly communicated my findings and explained my solution.

The Flow of Energy in Systems

How does energy flow and cause water to cycle?

Unit Project 174
Lesson 1   Energy Flows and Causes Change 176
Lesson 2   Heat Is a Flow of Energy 198
Lesson 3   Engineer It: Using Thermal Energy Transfer in Systems 216
Lesson 4   Changes in Energy Drive the Water Cycle 236
Unit Review 259
Unit Performance Task 263

Flash floods can occur suddenly after a heavy rainfall. Flash floods release a lot of energy.

You Solve It How Can You Use the Sun's Energy?

Design a way to use the sun's energy to cook an egg and to heat water for people who are camping in the wilderness.

Go online and complete the You Solve It to explore ways to solve a real-world problem.

Explore Energy Flow in the Earth System

This rocky coastline is along Big Sur, California.

A. Look at the photo. On a separate sheet of paper, write down as many different questions as you can about the photo.

B. Discuss With your class or a partner, share your questions. Record any additional questions generated in your discussion. From the list choose the most important questions that are related to possible ways that energy could interact with different parts of the Earth system — atmosphere, geosphere, biosphere, and hydrosphere. Write them below.

C. What possible energy transformations or transfers will you research?

D. Use the information on this page, along with your research, to explore how surface materials interact with other surrounding materials.

Discuss the next steps for your Unit Project with your teacher and go online to download the Unit Project Worksheet.

Language Development

Use the lessons in this unit to complete the network and expand your understanding of these key concepts.

Similar term	
Phrase	
Cognate	
Example	
Definition	

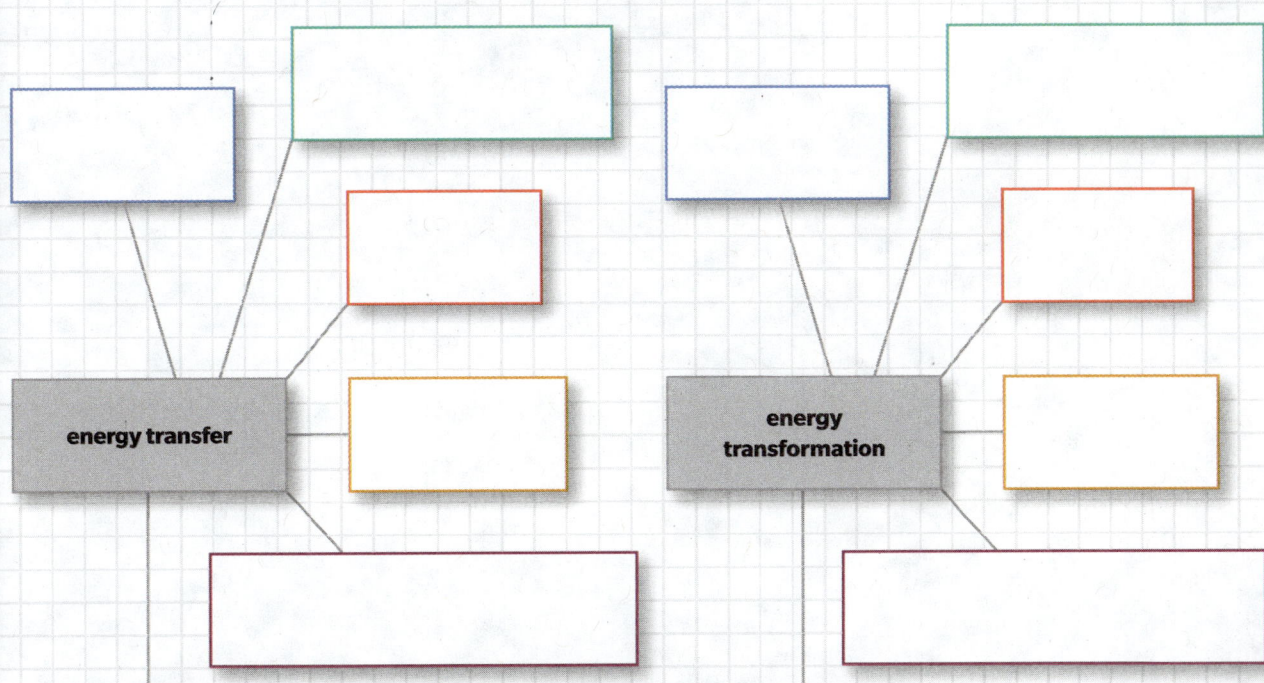

energy transfer

energy transformation

How does energy flow and cause water to cycle?

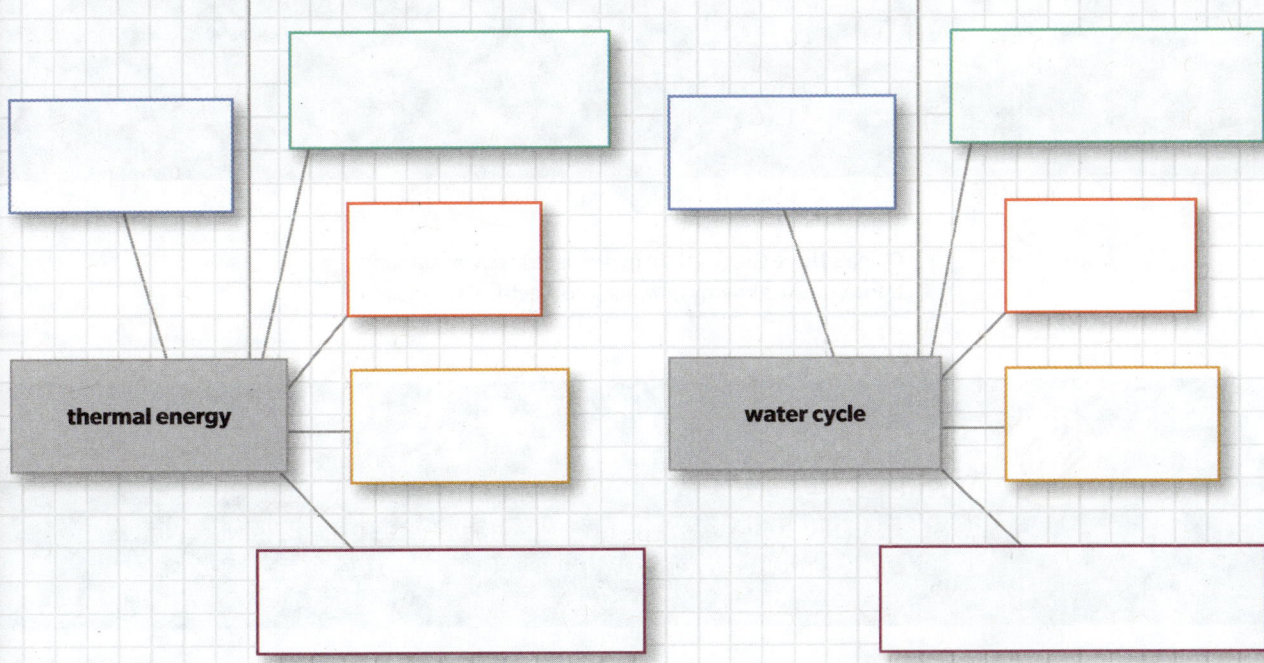

thermal energy

water cycle

Energy Flows and Causes Change

China's Three Gorges Dam hydroelectric power station transforms the energy of water into electrical energy.

Explore First

Moving Boxes Place three boxes of the same size on a table. In each box place a different size weight. Slide each box across the table. What do you notice about the energy that is required to move each box?

CAN YOU EXPLAIN IT?

How can energy from the motion of the crank on a hand-powered flashlight produce light?

Hand-powered flashlights are useful tools in an emergency. They do not need replaceable batteries or other sources of electric power. Instead, the user turns a crank on the side of the flashlight. This causes the light bulb in the flashlight to light up.

1. How would you define the flashlight as a system? What are its inputs and outputs? What are the parts of the system?

2. The crank has the energy of motion when it is turned. What other types of energy might the flashlight have when the light bulb is on?

EVIDENCE NOTEBOOK As you explore the lesson, gather evidence to help explain how turning the crank of a hand-powered flashlight produces light.

Identifying Different Forms of Energy

Energy is the ability to cause change. Processes and technologies that require energy are all around you. The movement of a clock's hands, the light from light fixtures, and the sounds made by electronic devices are all results of changes in energy. Understanding energy is important for making accurate weather forecasts. Weather prediction models account for energy transfers between the sun, our atmosphere, and oceans. This helps us understand when and where storms can develop.

Explore Online

You can observe many types of energy in a tornado.

3. **Discuss** What types of energy can you identify in the photo of the tornado?

The Energy of Matter in Motion: Kinetic Energy

A bowling ball rolling down a lane toward the pins is an example of a system that has energy. Evidence of this is the force that would be required to stop the rolling ball. A force was also used to send it rolling toward the pins. The energy that an object has due to its motion is called *kinetic energy*. All moving objects have kinetic energy. A bowling ball traveling down a lane, a skateboarder rolling down a ramp, and water rushing down a river are all systems that have kinetic energy.

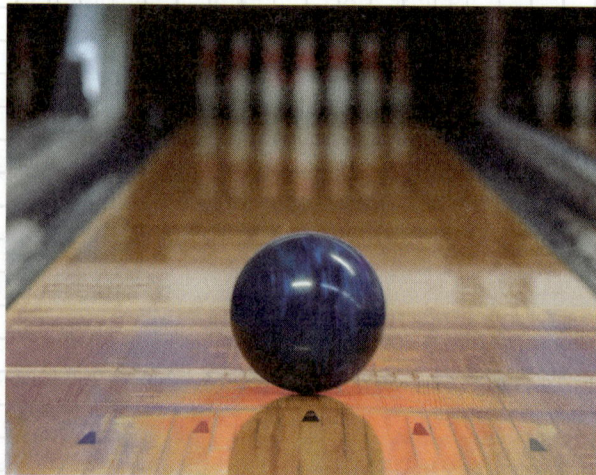

Energy applied by the bowler started this ball moving.

Kinetic Energy and Mass

A bowling ball has a much greater mass than the tiny ball used in a pinball machine. Think about what would happen if you rolled these balls down the same bowling lane at the same speed.

4. What evidence could you use to compare the energy of the two balls? Which ball do you think has more energy? Write your answer in the table.

Type of Ball	Mass of Ball	Both ball are rolling at 2 m/s.	Kinetic Energy
Bowling Ball	6 kg		
Pin Ball	0.08 kg		

Kinetic energy is directly proportional to the mass of an object. In the example above, the bowling ball has more kinetic energy than the pinball. They are traveling at the same speed, but the bowling ball has more mass. The bowling ball has more kinetic energy because more energy was put into the system.

Kinetic Energy and Speed

Two balls with different masses moving at the same speed have different amounts of kinetic energy. Now think about how different speeds might affect kinetic energy.

5. Two bowlers each roll a 6 kg bowling ball down a lane. One ball rolls very fast. The other rolls slowly. Predict what will happen when each ball reaches the pins. What does your prediction tell you about how much energy each ball has? Write your prediction in the table.

Type of Ball	Mass of Ball	The balls are moving at different speeds.	Kinetic Energy
Bowling Ball	6 kg		
Bowling Ball	6 kg		

Kinetic energy is also proportional to the square of the object's velocity. A ball traveling at a fast speed has more kinetic energy than a ball of the same mass traveling at a slow speed. It would require more force to stop the fast ball than it would to stop the slow ball.

Stored Energy: Potential Energy

A ball at rest at the top of a hill does not have kinetic energy. As it rolls down the hill, it gains kinetic energy. Where does the kinetic energy gained by the ball come from? When the ball is at rest at the top of the hill, its position gives it the potential to begin rolling and gain kinetic energy. The energy stored in an object due to its position or condition is called *potential energy*. For example, increasing the height of the ball on the hill will increase its potential energy.

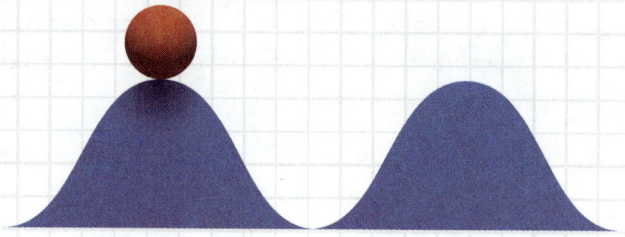

6. Think about how the ball's energy changes at different points on the hill.

At the top of the hill, the ball's potential energy is at its maximum / minimum.
As the ball rolls downhill, its kinetic energy increases / decreases and its potential energy increases / decreases. At the bottom of the hill, the ball's potential energy is at its maximum / minimum and its kinetic energy is at its maximum / minimum.

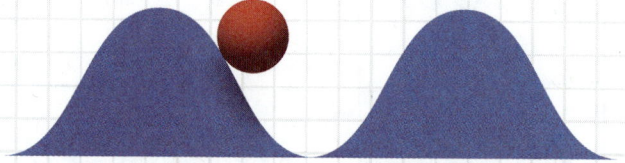

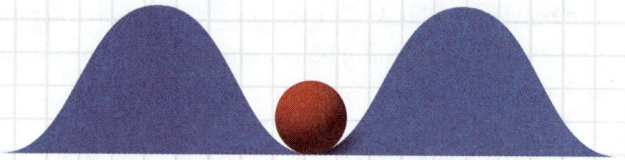

The ball speeds up as it rolls downhill. As the ball goes downhill, it gains kinetic energy and loses potential energy. The ball slows down as it rolls uphill. As the ball goes uphill, it loses kinetic energy and gains potential energy. The total energy does not change. Like matter, energy cannot be created or destroyed. That means that the total amount of energy in a system does not change unless energy is added to it or removed from it. This is known as the *law of conservation of energy*.

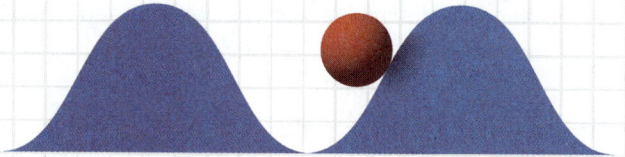

As the ball rolls downhill, its potential energy decreases. As the ball rolls up the next hill, its potential energy increases again.

Changes in Gravitational Potential Energy

Just as a ball on a hill will naturally roll downward because of gravity, the water at the top of a waterfall will flow downward. A pendulum released from the top of its arc will swing downward. Before they move downward, the ball, the water, and the pendulum have potential energy because of their positions.

The potential energy of an object due to its height, or its position relative to Earth's surface, is called *gravitational potential energy*. The higher an object is, the greater its gravitational potential energy.

For example, water a little bit upstream has more gravitational potential energy than it does at the top of the waterfall.

7. Rain drops move from clouds where they have more / less gravitational potential energy to Earth's surface, where they have more / less potential energy.

Imagine holding a ball in the air. If you let go, the ball will fall to the ground. It falls due to the pull of Earth's gravity. All objects tend to move from places where they have higher gravitational potential energy to places where they have lower gravitational potential energy. This means that balls do not roll uphill on their own. Pendulums do not spontaneously swing upward. Water does not flow up a waterfall on its own. However, you can make objects move upward by adding energy to them.

8. Where does the water in the photo have the least gravitational potential energy?

As water at the top of the waterfall flows downward, its potential energy decreases.

Forms of Energy

All energy is either potential energy or kinetic energy. Potential energy is due to an object's position or condition. Kinetic energy results from an object's motion. Each type of energy comes in different forms. Thermal energy, sound energy, electromagnetic energy, and electrical energy are forms of kinetic energy. Chemical energy, nuclear energy, gravitational potential energy, and elastic potential energy are forms of potential energy. All forms of energy are expressed in units of joules (J).

Mechanical Energy

Mechanical energy describes an object's ability to move—or do work on—other objects. It is the sum of the potential energy and kinetic energy of an object or a system. For example, a person swinging a hammer is providing kinetic energy to the hammer. The hammer does work on a nail. An object's mechanical energy can be all potential energy. It can be all kinetic energy. It can also be a combination of the two.

A hammer provides mechanical energy to do work on a nail.

Other Forms of Energy

You use many forms of energy every day. In fact, you are using several forms of energy as you explore this lesson. Electrical energy is a flow of negatively charged particles that generates the electric current that powers computers and lights. Chemical energy is the form of energy involved in chemical reactions. The battery on your cell phone uses chemical energy. Nuclear energy powers the sun. The sun gives off light energy that reaches Earth.

More than one form of energy can exist in a system at the same time. For example, fireworks explode because a huge amount of chemical potential energy is released. This energy becomes sound, light, and thermal energy.

The sun is the driving force behind many processes in Earth's systems. For example, energy from the sun causes the evaporation of water.

Thermal energy is the kinetic energy of the particles that make up matter. As its thermal energy increases, the glacier will melt at a faster rate and may retreat.

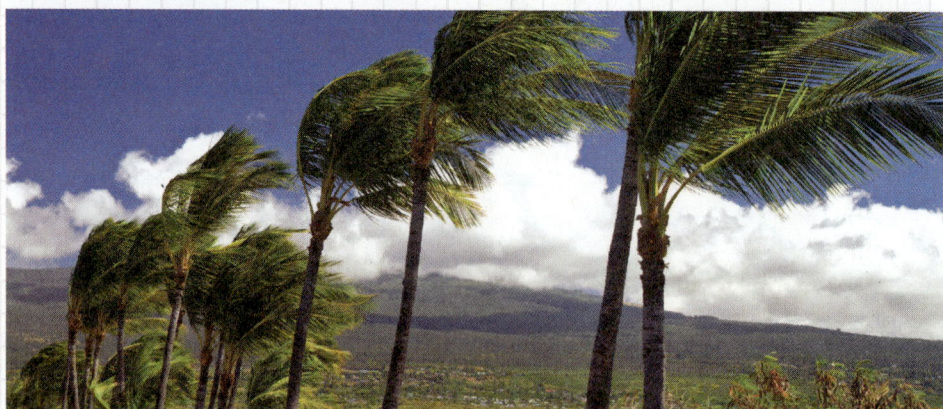

Sound energy is kinetic energy caused by the vibrations of the particles that make up matter. As the particles in the air vibrate, they transfer the sound energy to other particles. Your ears pick up the vibrations of particles in the air, which you hear as sound.

EVIDENCE NOTEBOOK

9. Think about the hand-cranked flashlight. What kinds of energy are involved in the operation of the flashlight? Record your evidence.

Analyze Applications of Mechanical Energy

Throughout history, people have designed machines that made the seemingly impossible possible. Many of these tools do work to increase the potential energy of an object or system. A simple lever can be used to lift a heavy boulder. Lifting it increases its potential energy. The lever can move the huge rock because the person using the lever adds kinetic energy by pushing the lever.

A towering 25-meter stone pillar called an obelisk stands in the center of St. Peter's Square in Rome. The 320,000-kilogram obelisk was put in place in 1586. The diagram shows how winches, shown as circles, were used. Some 900 workers and 75 horses pushed on levers to turn the winches, winding rope around their barrels. The ropes pulled on the obelisk to lift it into the place where it stands today.

10. Objects tend to come to rest at a position of lowest potential energy. Think of a machine or system that works against this tendency. Describe how kinetic energy is needed to increase the system's potential energy.

_____

_____

_____

_____

_____

_____

_____

11. How might your machine or system be improved? What constraints might be involved in its design?

_____

_____

_____

_____

_____

_____

_____

_____

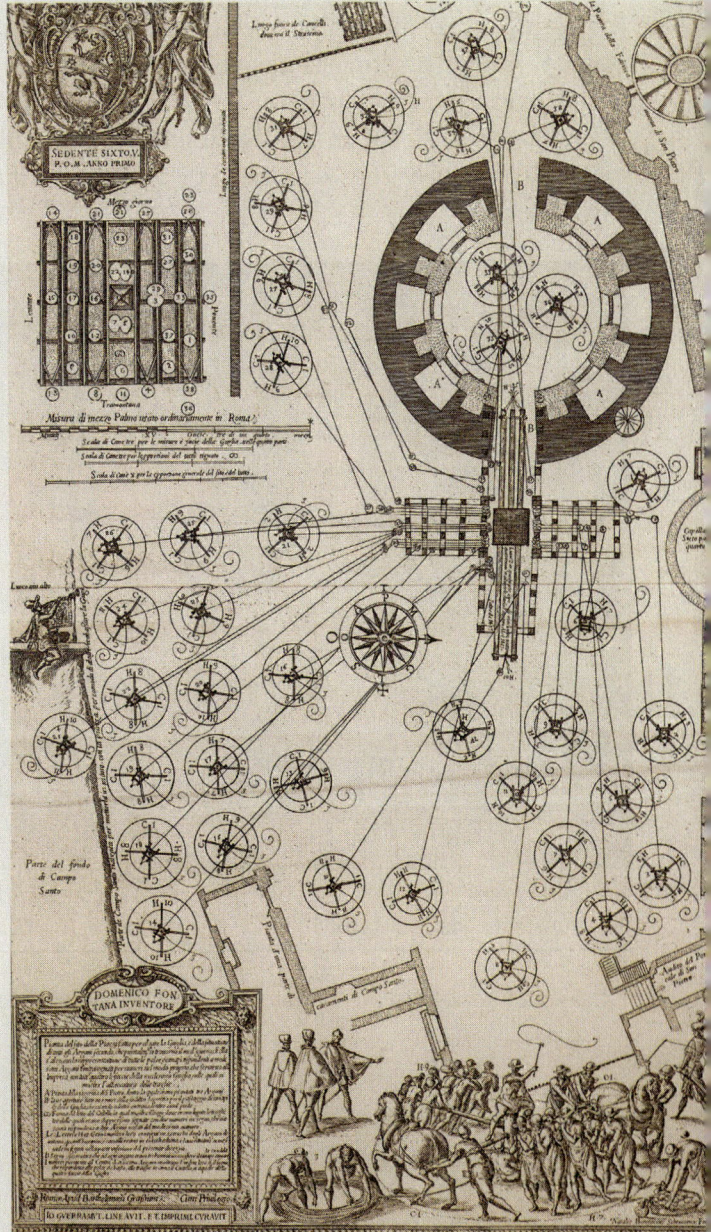

The Vatican Obelisk was first built by the Egyptians 3,200 years ago. This illustration shows how the obelisk was later installed in its current location in St. Peter's Square in Rome.

Observing Energy Transfer

All forms of energy fall into two main categories—potential energy and kinetic energy. The position or condition of an object determines its potential energy. The speed and mass of an object determine its kinetic energy. A heavier object has greater kinetic energy than a lighter object moving at the same speed. And an object moving more quickly has more kinetic energy than a slower object with the same mass.

The bowling ball has kinetic energy because it is moving. As the ball hits the pins, it slows.

The bowling ball has kinetic energy as it moves toward the pins. The pins scatter in different directions when the ball hits them.

12. What happens to the kinetic energy of the bowling ball when the ball hits the pins?

13. Predict what will happen if the ball rolls straight into an object with a greater mass than a bowling pin.

Hands-On Lab
Investigate the Transfer of Energy

You will roll balls with different masses down a ramp at different heights. You will record how these factors affect the distance a cup moves when the balls hit it.

MATERIALS
- balance
- balls, of different masses
- books
- cardboard panel or plastic racecar track
- cup, plastic, with a section of the side cut out
- masking tape
- meterstick

Procedure and Analysis

STEP 1 Stack the books until they are about 20 cm high. Place one end of the cardboard panel or plastic racecar track on the books to make a ramp. Use masking tape to mark a starting point at the top of the ramp. Use a second piece of masking tape to mark a position near the bottom of the ramp where the target cup will be placed.

STEP 2 Use the balance to find the mass of Ball 1. Record the mass in the table below.

Ball	Mass	Distance moved: low ramp	Distance moved: high ramp
1			
2			
3			

STEP 3 Place the target cup with its cut side down on the masking tape. The open top of the cup should face the ramp so it can catch the ball. Release Ball 1 from the starting point at the top of the ramp. Measure the distance the cup moves after it catches the ball. Record your data in the table.

STEP 4 Repeat Steps 2 and 3 with other balls that have different masses.

STEP 5 Add books to the stack to increase the slope of the ramp. Repeat Steps 3 and 4.

STEP 6 How did the distance the cup moved change as the mass of the ball changed? How did the distance change as the height of the ramp changed?

STEP 7 **Language SmArts** On a separate sheet of paper, use the results of the activity to construct a statement about how mass and speed affect the transfer of kinetic energy. How can this investigation serve as a model for collisions in the real world?

Energy Transfer in Collisions

Objects that are not moving need energy to set them in motion. They carry that energy with them as they move. They can pass this kinetic energy to other objects when they collide. The passing of energy from one object to another is known as **energy transfer.** Because energy cannot be created or destroyed, you can model energy flowing through a system as inputs and outputs. Think about the bowling ball. It received an input of energy from the bowler. The ball carried that energy as it rolled down the lane. When the ball collided with a pin, it transferred energy to the pin. Energy is transferred from the object with more kinetic energy to the one with less kinetic energy. The pin moves because energy was transferred to it.

Energy is transferred from the bowler's hand to the bowling ball. Then it is transferred from the bowling ball to the pin.

Energy transfers in other types of collisions can also be modeled. For example, energy is transferred within the system when a swinging pendulum hits a pendulum that is not moving. Transferring kinetic energy to an object can move it to a position with higher potential energy.

Energy Transfer between Objects of the Same Size and Mass

14. Two pendulums are set to collide. Identify where the swinging pendulum has the greatest potential energy and where it has the greatest kinetic energy. Draw an arrow in the second photo to show the transfer of energy between the pendulums during the collision.

• greatest potential energy	• greatest kinetic energy

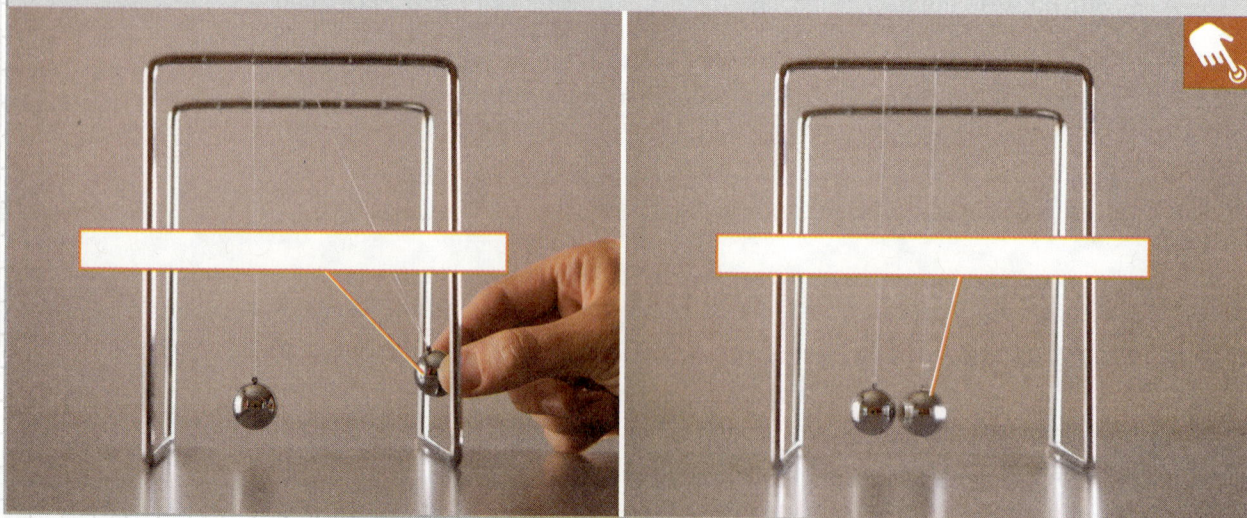

Energy Transfer in a Newton's Cradle

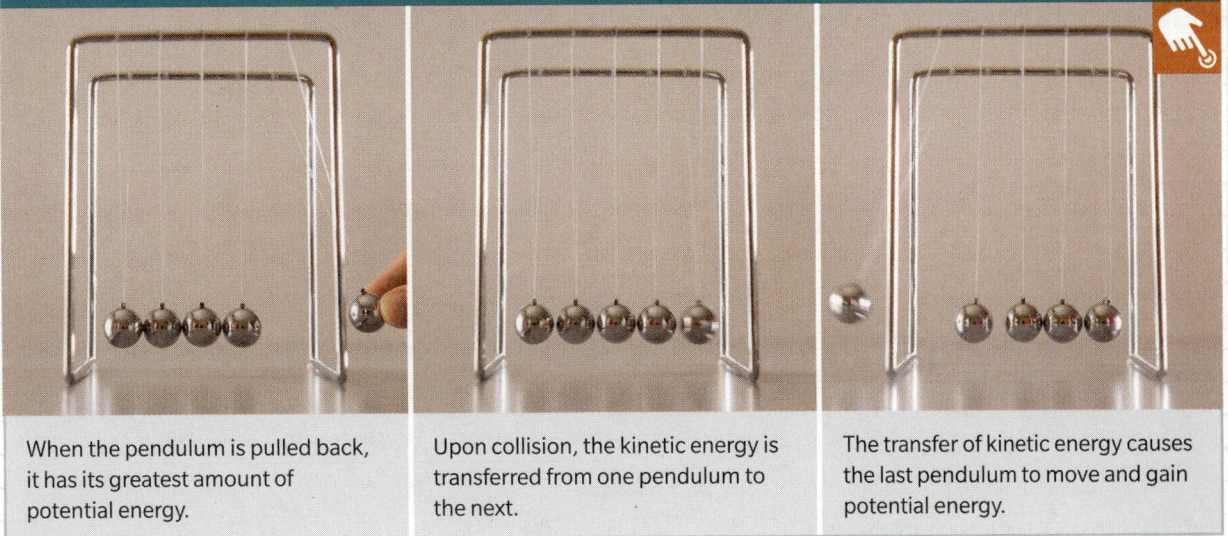

When the pendulum is pulled back, it has its greatest amount of potential energy.

Upon collision, the kinetic energy is transferred from one pendulum to the next.

The transfer of kinetic energy causes the last pendulum to move and gain potential energy.

In the earlier pendulum collision, the kinetic energy from the moving pendulum is transferred to the motionless one. The transfer of kinetic energy causes the stationary pendulum to move to a position of greater potential energy than it had at its starting point. That system only had two pendulums. Explore what happens when multiple objects are involved in a transfer of energy within a system. These photos show a Newton's cradle, a series of identical pendulums hanging side by side.

15. **Draw** Create a diagram showing the transfer of energy between two objects. You can base your diagram on a Newton's cradle .

Energy in Machines

Transfers of kinetic energy are used in devices and processes that reduce human effort. Energy transfer can also be used to do things that the human body alone would not be able to do.

The downward flow of water in a river is the result of the pull of gravity. As water moves downhill, its potential energy transforms into kinetic energy Kinetic energy can also be used to do other work, as in a water wheel. A water wheel can be used to turn a gristmill, which uses the energy to grind grains for flour.

Energy from flowing water is transferred to the water wheel, causing it to turn.

Energy Transfer in the Earth System

Energy transfers in the Earth system drive many processes, including weathering and erosion. For example, in rivers, the kinetic energy of flowing water can be transferred to sediment on the river bottom. If enough energy is transferred, rocks move along the river bottom or move downstream in the water. The moving rocks may collide with other rocks. Kinetic energy can be transferred during these collisions. The collisions can also cause the rocks to break down and become smoother.

Water transfers kinetic energy to the boulders in this river.

EVIDENCE NOTEBOOK

16. Describe the transfer of kinetic energy that occurs between a person and the crank of a hand-cranked flashlight. Record your evidence.

Analyze Meteoroid Deflection

Stony or metallic space objects, known as *meteoroids,* often enter Earth's atmosphere. Most are small. They burn up before they reach Earth's surface. Rarely, larger chunks traveling at extremely high speeds hit Earth's surface. Because of their high speeds, the objects have a large amount of kinetic energy. Such an impact can have disastrous results.

In 1908, a 91-million-kilogram space rock entered Earth's atmosphere above Tunguska, Siberia. The rock exploded in the sky, producing a huge fireball that destroyed 2,000 square kilometers of forest. A similar blast happened over another site in Russia in 2013, injuring 1,500 people and damaging thousands of buildings.

This photo shows a portion of the forest destroyed in the aftermath of the Tunguska event.

17. One idea for avoiding a catastrophic collision of space debris with Earth is the use of missile-like projectiles to knock the object off course, or deflect it. How can scientists be sure to create an impact with enough kinetic energy to change a meteoroid's course? What factors should they consider?

_____

_____

_____

_____

_____

Modeling Energy Transformations

As you observed with the Newton's cradle, kinetic energy is transferred between objects when one object collides with another. However, if you continued to watch the pendulums, you would observe that they gradually swing lower and lower until they eventually come to a stop.

18. Why do you think the Newton's cradle stops swinging? What does this imply about the energy in the system of pendulums?

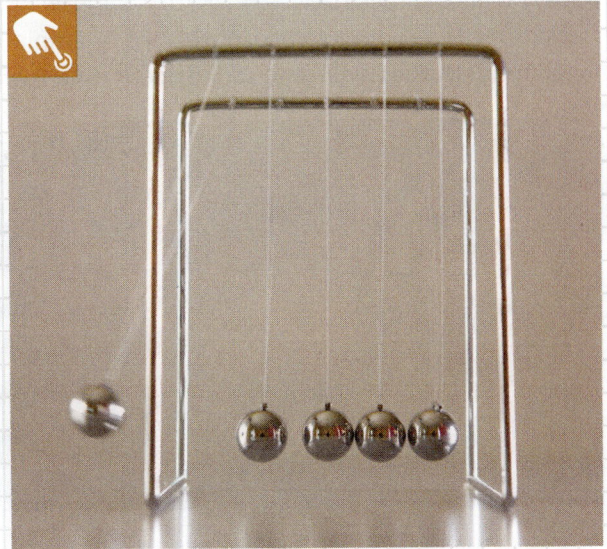

As the action of the Newton's cradle progresses over time, the pendulums gradually slow to a stop.

Transformations: Changes in the Form of Energy

You can see the transfer of kinetic energy when one pendulum hits another. Energy also seems to be lost gradually from the system as the pendulums lose speed and height with each swing. The law of conservation of energy says that energy cannot be created or destroyed, so the "lost" energy must transfer somewhere else or be changed in some way.

19. Think about collisions and what you know about different forms of energy. What other forms of energy might result from collisions in a Newton's cradle?

When the pendulums collide, they make a sound. This sound is evidence that some of the energy transferred during the collision changes form. Some of the energy becomes sound energy. The collisions also increase the kinetic energy of the particles that make up the pendulums. This increases the thermal energy of the system. The process of one form of energy changing to another form is known as **energy transformation.** It differs from simple energy transfer in which energy moves from one object to another, or from one place to another while staying in the same form.

Everyday Uses of Energy Transformations

The process of energy transformation happens all the time and everywhere. In fact, all of the electronic technologies you use every day need energy transformations to work. Refrigerators, microwave ovens, lights, batteries, and cars all rely on energy transformations. These devices make use of the fact that any form of energy can transform into any other form of energy. For example, a personal music player transforms electrical energy to sound energy and thermal energy.

The chemical energy stored in fireworks is transformed into electromagnetic, sound, and thermal energy.

Electrical energy is transformed into electromagnetic energy and sound energy in a television or computer monitor.

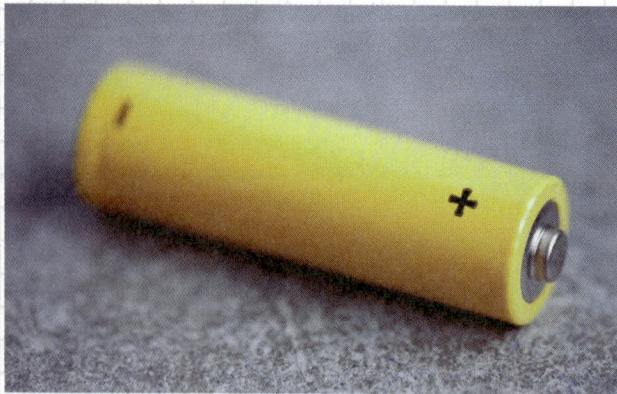

Batteries power electronic devices by transforming chemical energy into electrical energy.

People can also generate electrical energy. Wind-up radios work by converting kinetic energy from a person to electrical energy.

Alternative Energy and Energy Transformations

Today, many people are looking for energy sources other than fossil fuels. Many alternative energy sources transform mechanical energy into electrical energy. In hydroelectric dams, the kinetic energy of flowing water is transferred to a generator that transforms that energy into electrical energy. Windmills work in a similar way and use the kinetic energy of wind to generate electrical energy. Tidal energy provides power by converting the kinetic energy of ocean waves into electrical energy. Solar panels do not use kinetic energy. Instead, they transform light energy from the sun directly into electrical energy.

EVIDENCE NOTEBOOK

20. What energy transformations occur in the hand-cranked flashlight? Record your evidence.

Energy Loss in a System

Think about a Newton's cradle again. During the collisions, some energy is transferred between the pendulums as mechanical energy. Some energy is also transformed into sound and thermal energy. What happens to the energy that is converted into sound and thermal energy?

21. Draw Reconsider the diagram of energy transfer within the Newton's cradle system you created earlier in this lesson. How would you revise your model to account for the transformations of energy that also occur during the collisions between the pendulums? Where are the additional forms of energy transferred?

The energy from the pendulum collisions that is transformed into sound energy is carried through vibrations of the molecules in the air around the pendulums. The energy that is transformed into thermal energy is also transferred to the surrounding air. With each collision, this energy is transferred away from the Newton's cradle.

Because energy cannot be created or destroyed, transfers of energy away from a system to its surroundings result in an overall loss of energy from the system. The loss of energy from a system may seem minor, but over time it adds up. The motion of the pendulums in a Newton's cradle decreases as the system loses energy. Eventually, the cradle comes to a complete stop. An input of kinetic energy is needed to start the cradle swinging again.

Do the Math | Energy Efficiency The ratio of useful energy ouput to the overall energy input in a system is known as *efficiency*. Incandescent light bulbs are not efficient. They transform a large portion of electrical energy into thermal energy instead of light. To save energy, these bulbs have been replaced with compact fluorescent lamps (CFLs) and light-emitting diodes (LEDs). CFLs and LEDs use less electrical energy to produce the same amount of light.

The flow of energy through a system can be expressed in watts (W). One watt is equal to the flow of one joule of energy for one second. This table shows data for three bulbs that produce the same amount of light. Electrical energy is often measured in kilowatt-hours (kW•h), or the amount of energy used in one hour at the rate of 1,000 W (J/s).

Energy Used by Light Bulbs		
Bulb type	Watts (J/s)	Energy used over 2,000 hours (kW•h)
Incandescent	60	120
CFL	14	28
LED	10	20

22. Suppose the price of electricity is 12.75 cents per kW•h. What is the difference in cost in dollars between the use of an incandescent bulb for 2,000 hours and an LED bulb for the same amount of time?

23. How much more energy (in J) does an incandescent bulb use than a CFL in one minute?

Describe Efficient Energy Use

Laptops and other electronic devices become warm when they are in use. Some of the chemical energy from the battery is transformed into thermal energy instead of electrical energy. Much of the electrical energy produced by the battery becomes thermal energy as it flows through the computer parts. The electrical energy is useful, but the thermal energy is not. The battery loses chemical energy in both useful and non-useful transformations as it is used.

A laptop battery produces thermal energy.

24. Hand-cranked flashlights transform mechanical energy into other forms of energy. Which energy transformations are useful, and which are not? Explain why most hand-cranked flashlights are made with LEDs.

Continue Your Exploration

Name: _____   Date: _____

Check out the path below or go online to choose one of the other paths shown.

Moving Water Uphill

- **Hydroelectric Power**
- **Hands-On Labs** 👏
- **Propose Your Own Path**

Go online to choose one of these other paths.

A water wheel uses kinetic energy from flowing water to power machinery. In this use, mechanical energy supplied by moving water is used to power another process. Another type of water wheel, called a *noria*, is not used to supply mechanical energy for other processes. A noria's only purpose is to raise water to a higher location.

A noria is similar to other water wheels, except that it has open containers along the outer rim of its wheel. The containers fill with water when they are lowered into a body of flowing water, such as a river, as the wheel turns. As the wheel continues to turn, the containers of water are lifted. During this upward movement, the containers overturn and empty the water into a higher trough or aqueduct. The water can then be transported to another location for irrigation or use in towns and villages.

1. Kinetic energy from water flowing in the river is transferred to the noria, which lifts water from the river to the aqueduct. How does the gravitational potential energy of the water change as it approaches the top of the wheel?

A. Its gravitational potential energy does not change.

B. Its gravitational potential energy increases.

C. Its gravitational potential energy decreases.

The norias of Hama, Syria, are the largest in the world. They were used for centuries to lift water from the Orontes River. Today, they are mostly unused.

Continue Your Exploration

As water reaches the top of the wheel, it pours into a collecting trough.

2. The norias of Hama are known for creaking loudly as they turn. Which statements about a noria is correct?

   A. Some kinetic energy of the noria is transformed into sound energy.

   B. Some kinetic energy of the noria is transformed into light energy.

   C. The kinetic energy of the noria does not change.

   D. The noria does not have any input or output of energy.

3. Paddle boats are boats that are propelled by a paddle wheel using similar mechanics as a water wheel. A water wheel is propelled by flowing water. A paddle boat can be operated using human power, a steam engine, or solar power. Describe the energy transfers and transformations that take place within the paddle wheel system.

4. **Collaborate** Water wheels can be good sources of renewable energy. Norias help people use water resources. Because these devices rely on running water to function, they are not always reliable. Discuss how the availability of flowing water affects the usefulness of a water wheel. Discuss how you might plan ahead to deal with changes in conditions, such as a drought.

Can You Explain It?

Name: _____   Date: _____

How can energy from the motion of the crank on a hand-powered flashlight produce light?

EVIDENCE NOTEBOOK

Refer to the notes in your Evidence Notebook to help you construct an explanation for how the input of mechanical energy with the crank is able to produce an output of light.

1. State your claim. Make sure your claim fully explains the transfers and transformations of energy within the system.

2. Summarize the evidence you have gathered to support your claim and explain your reasoning.

Checkpoints

Answer the following questions to check your understanding of the lesson.

Use the photo of the roller coaster to answer Questions 3 and 4.

3. As the cars move downward on the loop, their kinetic energy decreases / increases . The cars have the greatest amount of potential energy when they are at the bottom / top of the loop.

4. A roller coaster car requires an input of energy from an electric motor to reach the top of the first hill. Which statement describes the transformation of energy involved in this process?

   A. Mechanical energy is transformed into electrical energy.

   B. Electrical energy is transformed into chemical energy.

   C. Electrical energy is transformed into mechanical energy.

   D. No energy transformation occurs.

Use the table to answer Question 5.

5. Each of the balls in the table collided with a stationary object of the same mass. Which statements about the transfer of kinetic energy are correct? Choose all that apply.

   A. Ball A and Ball B transfer the same amount of energy.

   B. Ball B transfers more energy than Ball A.

   C. Ball B and Ball C transfer the same amount of energy.

   D. Ball C transfers more energy than Ball B.

Ball	Mass (g)	Velocity (m/s)
Ball A	45	30
Ball B	45	40
Ball C	60	40

6. When a meteoroid strikes Earth, mechanical energy is transformed into which of these forms of energy? Choose all that apply.

   A. sound energy

   B. thermal energy

   C. electrical energy

   D. chemical energy

Interactive Review

Complete this section to review the main concepts of the lesson.

Kinetic energy is the energy of an object due to its speed and mass. Potential energy is the energy of an object due to its position or condition.

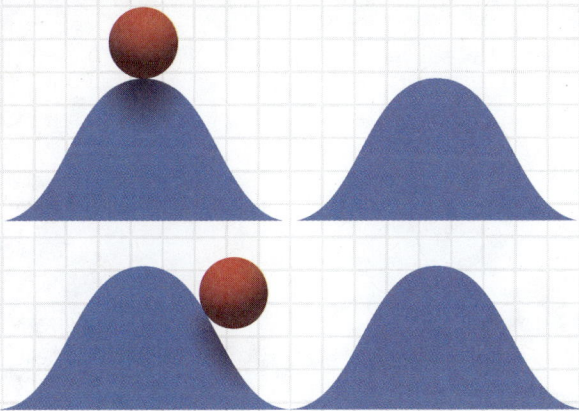

A. Describe how the speed and mass of an object affect the amount of kinetic energy of the object.

Changes in kinetic energy involve a transfer of energy to or from an object.

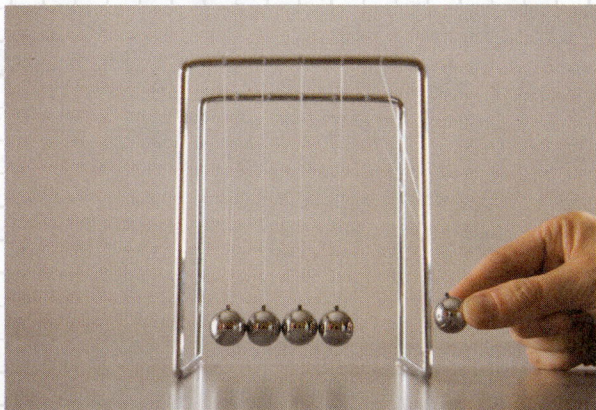

B. Describe the transfer of energy between the pendulums in a Newton's cradle.

A change in energy from one form to another is known as an energy transformation. Any form of energy can transform into any other form of energy.

C. Explain how evidence of energy transformations in fireworks supports the law of conservation of energy.

Lesson 1 Energy Flows and Causes Change **197**

Heat Is a Flow of Energy

Even when the temperature outside is very low, an insulated coat can keep you warm.

Explore First

Comparing Temperatures Fill a glass beaker and a paper cup each with warm or hot water that is at the same temperature. Touch the outside of each container. What do you observe?

Go online to view the digital version of the Hands-On Lab for this lesson and to download additional lab resources.

CAN YOU EXPLAIN IT?

What allows us to visualize temperature differences?

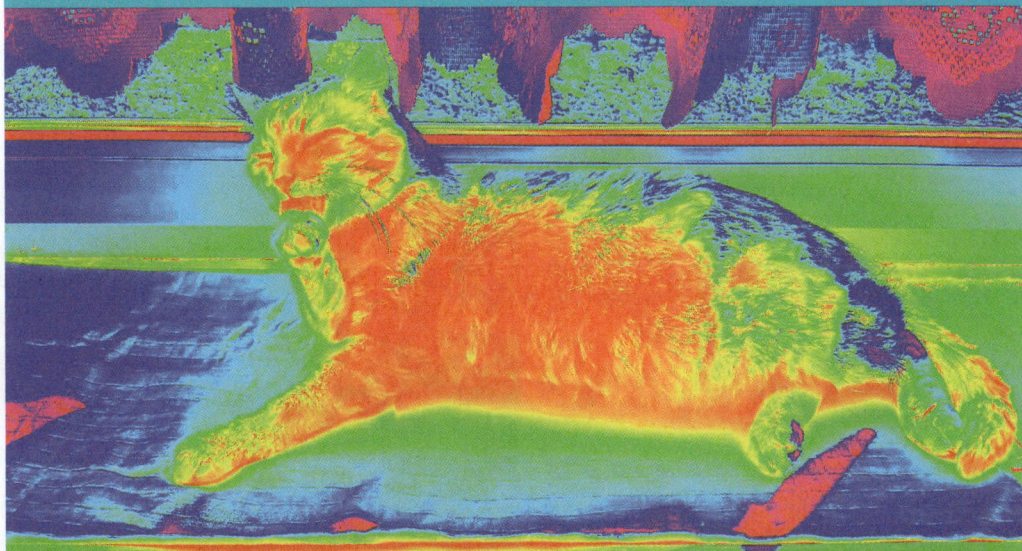

Most photographs use visible light to make an image. These images are similar to what we see with our eyes. Infrared photography, though, can generate an image that shows temperature differences. In this image, different colors indicate different temperatures.

Explore Online

1. What does it mean for objects to be at different temperatures? What is different about them physically?

2. Why do you think different temperatures appear as different colors on an infrared image?

EVIDENCE NOTEBOOK As you explore the lesson, gather evidence to help explain how temperature differences could be visualized.

Comparing Hot and Cold Objects

You come into contact with hot and cold objects every day. Objects that are hot, relative to their surroundings, do not stay that way. They will eventually cool. For example, hot soup begins to cool as soon as it is taken off the stove burner. Objects that are cold, relative to their surroundings, will warm. An ice cube starts to warm and melt as soon as it leaves the freezer.

3. Ice cubes melt if you leave them out on a warm day. Describe this process in terms of energy and temperature.

4. Imagine you are holding an ice cube. Draw a diagram that shows how your hand, the ice cube, and the air around your hand and the ice cube are warming or cooling. Use arrows to show how energy is being transferred from one object or substance to another.

As the ice cubes warm, their particles have more kinetic energy.

The Direction of Energy Transfer

If a hot pan is placed on a cool counter, the pan will spontaneously warm both the countertop and the surrounding air. As the pan warms the countertop and air, the pan cools. This process continues until the pan, the air, and the countertop are all the same temperature. In the same way, if a cold pack is placed on your forehead, your forehead will cool and the cold pack will warm until they are the same temperature. When objects are at different temperatures, energy is transferred from the warmer object to the cooler object. This energy transfer can be modeled by using arrows to show how energy is flowing from warmer objects to cooler objects.

5. When two objects at different temperatures are in contact, thermal energy flows from the cooler / warmer object into the cooler / warmer object until the temperatures increase / are the same in both objects.

Hot and Cold

When you touch an object and it feels warm, it is because energy is being transferred from that object to you. When an object feels cold, energy is being transferred from you to the object. Energy flows from warmer objects to cooler objects. So, an object will usually feel warm to the touch if it is at a higher temperature than your hand. And if an object is at a lower temperature than your hand, it usually feels cool to the touch.

6. If you hold a glass of cold water, your hand will become cold. Describe how energy flows in this situation.

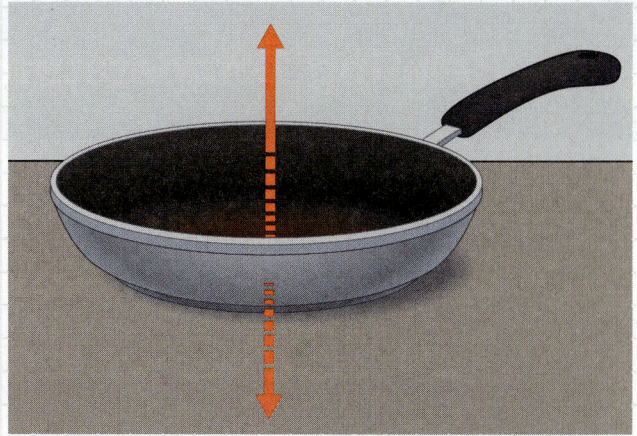

A hot pan on a countertop will transfer energy to the countertop and to the air around it until the pan, the countertop, and the air are all the same temperature.

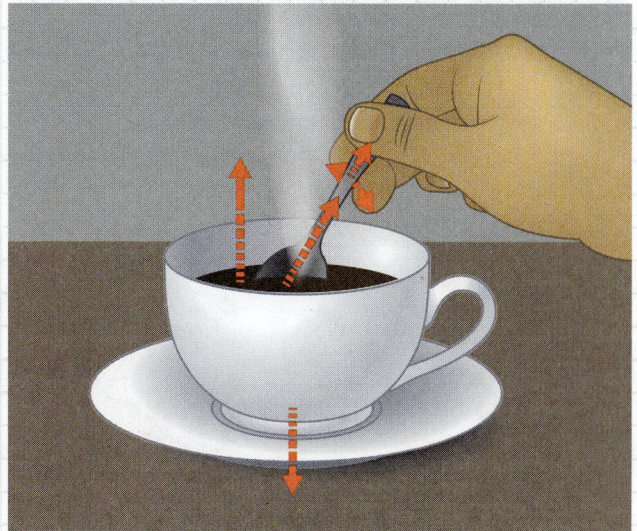

Energy is transferred from the hot liquid to the spoon and then from the hot spoon to your hand. This energy transfer causes the spoon to feel warm relative to your hand.

Analyze the Loss of Thermal Energy

7. Recall the photo of the melting ice cubes. If you put the water from the melted ice cubes back into the freezer, it will become solid again. Describe the transfer of thermal energy as the ice cubes melt and then as they become solid again. In both situations, describe which substances are gaining and losing energy.

_____

_____

_____

_____

_____

Relating Temperature and Thermal Energy

Suppose you have two similar rocks in front of you. One rock has been sitting in the shade, and the other has been sitting in the sunlight. The two rocks look the same, but if you touch them, you will observe a difference. One rock will feel cold and the other rock will feel warm because the temperatures of the rocks are different. When you touch the rocks, you will know right away which one was in the sunlight.

These rock outcrops are in the Mojave Desert in California.

8. **Discuss** How will the temperature of a rock in the desert change throughout the day and night?

Temperature

Think back to the hot and cold rocks. What makes one rock hot and the other cold? Like all matter, the rocks are made up of particles that are too small to be seen. These particles are in constant motion. Like all objects in motion, these particles have energy. The energy associated with their motion is kinetic energy. The faster the particles move, the greater their kinetic energy is.

9. The rock sitting in the sunlight feels hotter because its particles are moving
   faster / slower than the particles in the rock that is sitting in the shade.

   Temperature is a measure of the average kinetic energy of all the particles in an object or substance. Temperature does not depend on the material or the type of particles in a substance.

Thermal Energy

Temperature is a measure of the average kinetic energy of an object. **Thermal energy** is the measurement of the total amount of kinetic energy of all the particles in an object or substance. Thermal energy is measured in joules (J). All matter has thermal energy. When an object is hot, its particles are moving faster and it has more thermal energy than it has when it is cold.

A quarter and a dime are made of the same materials. If the two coins have the same temperature, the quarter has more thermal energy than the dime. Although the average kinetic energy of their particles is the same, the quarter has many more particles than the dime, so the quarter has more total thermal energy.

quarter

dime

10. If you warmed the dime until it melted, the melted dime would have *more /*
less thermal energy than the solid dime had. This is because the particles in the
melted dime are moving *faster / slower* than the solid particles were. So the
particles of the melted dime have *more / less* kinetic energy.

Consider a glass of ice water in which the water and ice are both close to the same temperature. The liquid water has more thermal energy than an equal mass of ice, even though they are at the same temperature. Liquid particles move much faster and have more energy than solid particles. Similarly, the particles in a gas have more energy than the particles in the liquid phase of the same substance.

Different kinds of matter are made up of different kinds of particles that do not interact with one another in the same way in each substance. Because of these differences, the amount of thermal energy in two different substances with equal mass can be different even if they have the same temperature.

11. If two objects have the same temperature, will they always have the same thermal
energies? Record your evidence.

Hands-On Lab
Compare Thermal Energy in Objects

You will plan an investigation to determine what properties affect the amount of thermal energy in an object.

Procedure

You will need to use a hot water bath for this investigation. Your teacher will guide you in making one.

As you develop your plan, consider these questions:

- How can you indirectly determine the thermal energy of the objects? (Hint: Think about how a hot object would affect water if placed in the water.)

- What data should you measure and record?

- Which objects will you test to provide data to answer your questions?

STEP 1 Plan and write your procedure to determine the properties that affect the amount of thermal energy an object. Your procedure should describe how to test the amount of thermal energy that four different objects have.

MATERIALS
- bowl, wide, flat bottom
- cups, small, plastic foam (5)
- graduated cylinder, 25 mL
- hot plate
- ice water
- thermometers, non-mercury (6)
- tongs
- washers, aluminum, 10 g
- washers, aluminum, 20 g
- water
- weight, brass, 20 g
- weight, rubber, 10 g

STEP 2 Get your teacher's approval before you begin your investigation. Make any changes to your procedure requested by your teacher.

STEP 3 Perform your investigation, following the steps you have written. Record your observations on a separate sheet of paper.

STEP 4 Rank the objects by the amount of thermal energy they seemed to contain.

1. _____

2. _____

3. _____

4. _____

STEP 5 Which factors seem to affect the amount of thermal energy an object has? Select all that apply.

    A. mass

    B. shape

    C. color

    D. material

STEP 6 **Language SmArts** Trade procedures with another group and follow the steps that they used. Did you get the same results? Why or why not?

STEP 7 If the water in two different lakes is at the same temperature, can the lakes have different amounts of thermal energy? Explain your answer.

Factors Affecting the Thermal Energy in an Object

Every object has thermal energy because every object's particles are moving. In the Hands-On Lab, when you placed a hot object in cold water, the temperature of the water increased. The change in water temperature was not the same for all of the objects. The object with the larger mass had more energy than the smaller object of the same material at the same temperature. Because it had more energy, the larger object warmed the water to a higher temperature after a certain amount of time.

The brass and aluminum objects that had the same mass warmed the water by different amounts, so this is evidence that the thermal energy of an object also depends on the material it is made of. Different materials of the same size and same temperature can have different amounts of thermal energy.

EVIDENCE NOTEBOOK

12. The infrared photograph indicates that the surfaces and air near the cat are warmer than the surfaces and air farther away. What factors might cause these temperature differences? Record your evidence.

Do the Math
Compare Objects' Thermal Energies

All matter has some amount of thermal energy—even the coldest object you have ever felt. But the actual amount of thermal energy varies among objects of different temperatures and of different materials. The thermal energy in any object is related to its mass, composition, state, and temperature.

13. Look at the photos of the two rocks and the information in the caption. Think about how the rocks are different. Which rock has a greater amount of thermal energy? Explain your answer.

These two rocks are made of the same substance and are the same temperature, but have different masses. The rock on the right has significantly less mass than the rock on the left.

14. Place these objects in order by the amount of thermal energy they contain. Number the boxes so that they are ordered from least thermal energy (1) to greatest thermal energy (5). Assume that the iceberg and the lake have similar masses.

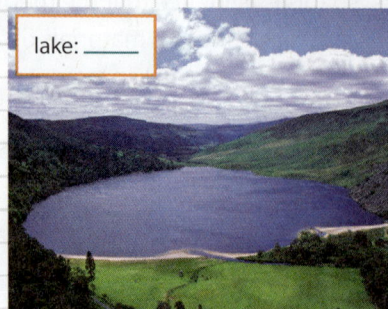

ice: __1__

iceberg: _____

boiling water: _____

water: _____

lake: _____

Engineer It
Explore Thermal Energy Storage

Energy from the sun can be captured in solar power plants and used by humans. At night and on some cloudy days, solar power plants do not generate any energy. At other times, solar power plants generate more electrical energy than people need. A thermal battery is one way to store the extra energy for use later. When the sun is shining, the system adds thermal energy to a solid, such as salt. As the thermal energy of the salt increases, it melts. The energy stored in the molten material is later used to warm other objects or produce an electric current.

This giant mirror focuses sunlight onto material in the box.

15. Some solar power plants use mirrors to focus sunlight on a central collector. The energy from sunlight causes water in the central collector to boil and produce steam. A generator uses the kinetic energy of the steam to produce electrical energy. How could a thermal battery help this type of power plant generate electrical energy 24 hours per day?

Analyzing Heat

Suppose that you are standing outside on a sunny day. The skin on your arms feels very warm in the sunlight. Suddenly a cloud comes between you and the sun. A thermometer would show that the temperature of the air near you has not changed very much. Your skin feels much cooler, though. As the cloud moves away, you start to feel warmer.

A sunny place usually feels warmer than a shady place, even if a thermometer shows little to no temperature difference in the air.

16. Why might you feel warmer in a sunny place than in a shady place, even though the air temperature is the same?

Heat

Think about what happens when you boil water on the stove. The pot of water becomes warmer while it is over the stove. This is because thermal energy is being transferred to the water. Energy flows from the stove to the pot of water as heat. You may have heard *heat* used in other ways in everyday language, but in science, heat has a specific definition. **Heat** is the energy that is transferred between two objects that are at different temperatures.

When thermal energy is transferred to an object as heat, the average kinetic energy of the particles in the object will increase. And so, the temperature of the object will rise. Heat always flows from an object at a higher temperature to an object at a lower temperature. Heat will flow as long as there is a temperature difference. If no energy is added to the system, both objects will eventually have the same temperature.

It is sometimes helpful to know how much thermal energy is needed to change the temperature of a substance by a certain amount. For example, a materials scientist might want to know how much energy it would take to melt a metal sample. The amount of thermal energy needed to change the temperature of a substance depends on the identity of the substance the mass of the sample, and the system surrounding the substance.

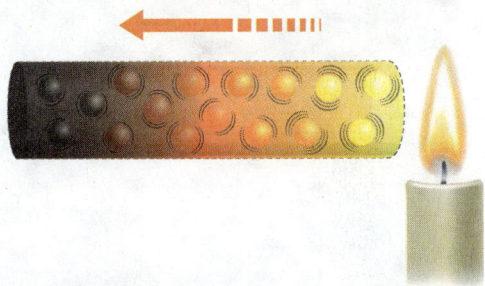

Conduction Thermal energy is transferred between particles through conduction. In this example, the candle is warming one end of the metal bar. The particles in the metal bar start to move faster as they gain more thermal energy. As the particles move faster, they bump into each other and transfer thermal energy through the metal rod.

Convection Thermal energy is transferred throughout liquids and gases through convection. In this example, the candle is heating the box. As air in the box warms, the air particles begin to move faster and the air becomes less dense. The colder, denser air sinks and pushes up the warmer air. This movement transfers thermal energy through liquids and gases.

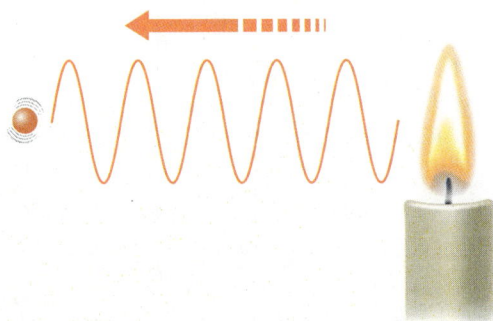

Radiation Radiation is the transfer of energy through electromagnetic waves. In this example, the candle produces infrared radiation. This radiation travels through empty space until it hits a particle. The particle then absorbs this radiation, and the radiation is converted into thermal energy. This process is how thermal energy is transferred through space.

Three Types of Thermal Energy Transfer

To remove a metal pan from a hot oven, you must use an insulated pad or glove. If you do not, energy will transfer quickly to your hand by conduction. The pan is much hotter than your skin, so its particles have a lot more thermal energy. When the particles of the metal bump into the particles of your skin, energy is transferred.

When the hot pan is on top of the stove, you can tell that it is hot by holding your hand above the pan. The moving air around the pan absorbs energy and carries it to your skin by convection. You can also absorb energy by holding your hand to the side of a stove's heating element. Energy is transferred through radiation to your skin.

Energy in the form of heat can be transferred by conduction, convection, and radiation. During all three types of energy transfer, the thermal energy of the warmer object decreases and the thermal energy of the cooler object increases. In all three types of energy transfer, energy is being transferred to a cooler object.

EVIDENCE NOTEBOOK

17. Infrared photography produces images showing the temperature ranges of different objects. What type of energy transfer is necessary for infrared photography? Explain your answer.

18. Explain how each of the three types of energy transfer occurs in a solar oven while it cooks a bowl of soup.

Radiation carries energy from the sun. In a solar oven, this energy is directed at a single object to cook food.

19. **Act** With your group, plan a short skit to model one of the three methods of thermal energy transfer. Focus on making your performance convey information as accurately as possible. Record the plan for your skit and then perform it for the class.

Compare Thermal Conductivities

Different substances can absorb or transfer energy at different rates. For example, cooks often prefer a wooden spoon to a metal spoon for stirring a hot liquid. This is because a spoon made of wood absorbs energy slowly and will not get very hot. A metal spoon will absorb energy quickly and become too hot to hold. Thermal conductivity is a property of matter that refers to how quickly a material transfers and absorbs energy as heat.

20. Suppose you are designing a heat exchanger to remove energy from a motor as quickly as possible. Energy will be transferred from the motor to the heat exchanger. Then the energy will be transferred from the heat exchanger to the air. The table shows the thermal conductivities of a few substances as measured in W/m·K. The greater the thermal conductivity, the faster the rate of energy transfer. Which material would be the best choice?

Substance	Thermal conductivity (W/m·K)
Copper	385
Glass	0.8
Polystyrene	0.033
Steel	50

   A. copper

   B. glass

   C. polystyrene

   D. steel

Continue Your Exploration

Name: _____   Date: _____

Check out the path below or go online to choose one of the other paths shown.

| Heat and Cooking | • **Heat and Computing**
 • **Hands-On Labs** ✋
 • **Propose Your Own Path** | *Go online to choose one of these other paths.* |

A good cook must understand temperature, thermal energy, and heat. The energy added to food during cooking causes chemical changes in the food. It is important to control the amount of energy absorbed by the food. Too much energy, and the food will be overcooked. Too little energy, and food will still be raw. It is also important to control the rate of energy transfer. If energy is added too quickly or too slowly, the food may have the wrong texture or it might cook unevenly.

1. How might using a pizza stone instead of a pan affect how the pizza cooks?

    A. The stone gets hotter than the rest of the oven, so the pizza cooks faster.

    B. The stone transfers energy slowly, so the crust cooks evenly.

    C. The stone absorbs energy, keeping the crust cooler than the pizza toppings.

2. Pizza restaurants often use large ovens lined with bricks. These ovens remain very hot, even though only a small fire is kept burning in the oven. Why might this be?

Pizzas can be cooked in an oven using a pizza stone, a pizza pan, or no pan at all. The pizza stone absorbs and releases energy more slowly than a pizza pan does.

Continue Your Exploration

If food is cooked too quickly, the outside can burn, while the inside of the food is still raw.

3. What might cause the food to not cook all the way through?

   A. Not enough energy reaches the center of the food.

   B. Energy flows into the food too quickly and is lost before the inside is cooked.

   C. The food conducts energy, so the energy passes through the food without cooking it.

   D. The energy cooks the outside of the food, and then the food begins to lose heat instead of cooking further.

4. If the oven is too hot, the bottom part of cookies on a metal tray can become hard and black. Why would the bottom of the cookies burn first?

5. **Collaborate** With a partner, research one or more recipes. Make a presentation that shows how the method of cooking described in the recipe or recipes affects the food.

Can You Explain It?

Name: _____   **Date:** _____

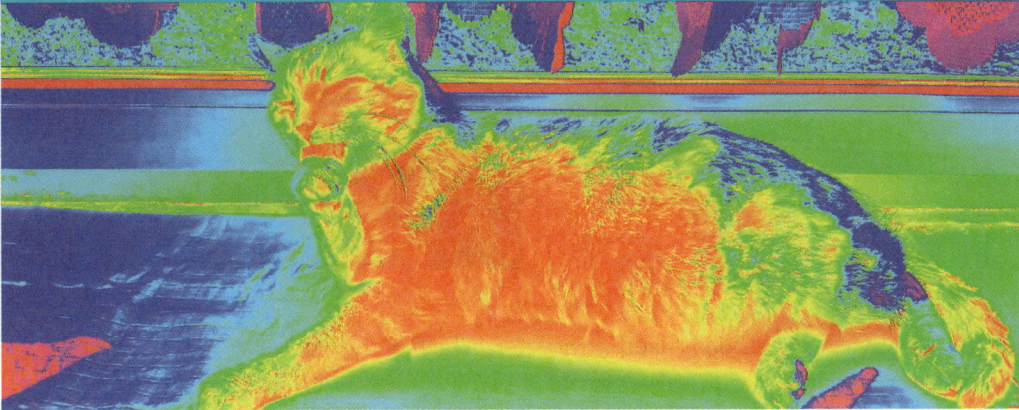

What allows us to visualize temperature differences?

Explore Online

EVIDENCE NOTEBOOK

Refer to the notes in your Evidence Notebook to help you construct an explanation for how infrared photography can be used to visualize temperature differences.

1. State your claim. Make sure your claim fully explains how infrared photography can be used to visualize temperature differences.

2. Summarize the evidence you have gathered to support your claim and explain your reasoning.

Checkpoints

Answer the following questions to check your understanding of the lesson.

Use the photo to answer Question 3.

3. Energy flows through a system that consists of the stove, the pan, the boiling water, and the air around these objects. Which of the following statements describe a direction that energy is moving in this system? Select all that apply.

   A. the stove to the pan

   B. the pan to the water

   C. the water to the pan

   D. the pan to the stove

4. Suppose you had a glass that was partially filled with water. Which of the following statements describe ways that you could raise the thermal energy of the glass of water? Select all that apply.

   A. Remove water from the glass.

   B. Add water of the same temperature to the glass.

   C. Warm the glass of water using a microwave.

   D. Cool the glass of water using a refrigerator.

Use the photo and table to answer Questions 5–6.

5. On a sunny day, the sidewalk and the street are both warmer than the atmosphere because they have more _heat / thermal energy_ due to energy transfer by _conduction / radiation_ from the sun.

6. A student used a thermometer to measure the temperature at three places and recorded the data in a table. Which statements represent conclusions that you can support with these data? Select all that apply.

   A. The temperature of the sidewalk is the same as the temperature of the street.

   B. Energy has been transferred from the street to the air above the street.

   C. Energy has been transferred from the lawn to the street and sidewalk through conduction.

   D. The street surface has absorbed more radiant thermal energy than the sidewalk.

Location	Temperature
0.5 m above street	38 °C
0.5 m above sidewalk	33 °C
0.5 m above grass lawn	27 °C

Interactive Review

Complete this section to review the main concepts of the lesson.

Humans perceive objects as hot or cold due to temperature differences and the transfer of energy.

A. Recall a situation when you felt a hot or cold object. Discuss the temperature differences involved and the direction in which the energy was being transferred.

Thermal energy is the total kinetic energy of the particles that make up a substance. Temperature is a measure of the average kinetic energy of the particles that make up a substance.

B. Describe how an object's thermal energy will change and how the particles in the object will be affected when the object's temperature increases.

Heat is the energy transferred between two objects that are at different temperatures. Energy in the form of heat can be transferred by conduction, convection, or radiation.

C. Describe situations in which energy is transferred through conduction, convection, and radiation.

Using Thermal Energy Transfer in Systems

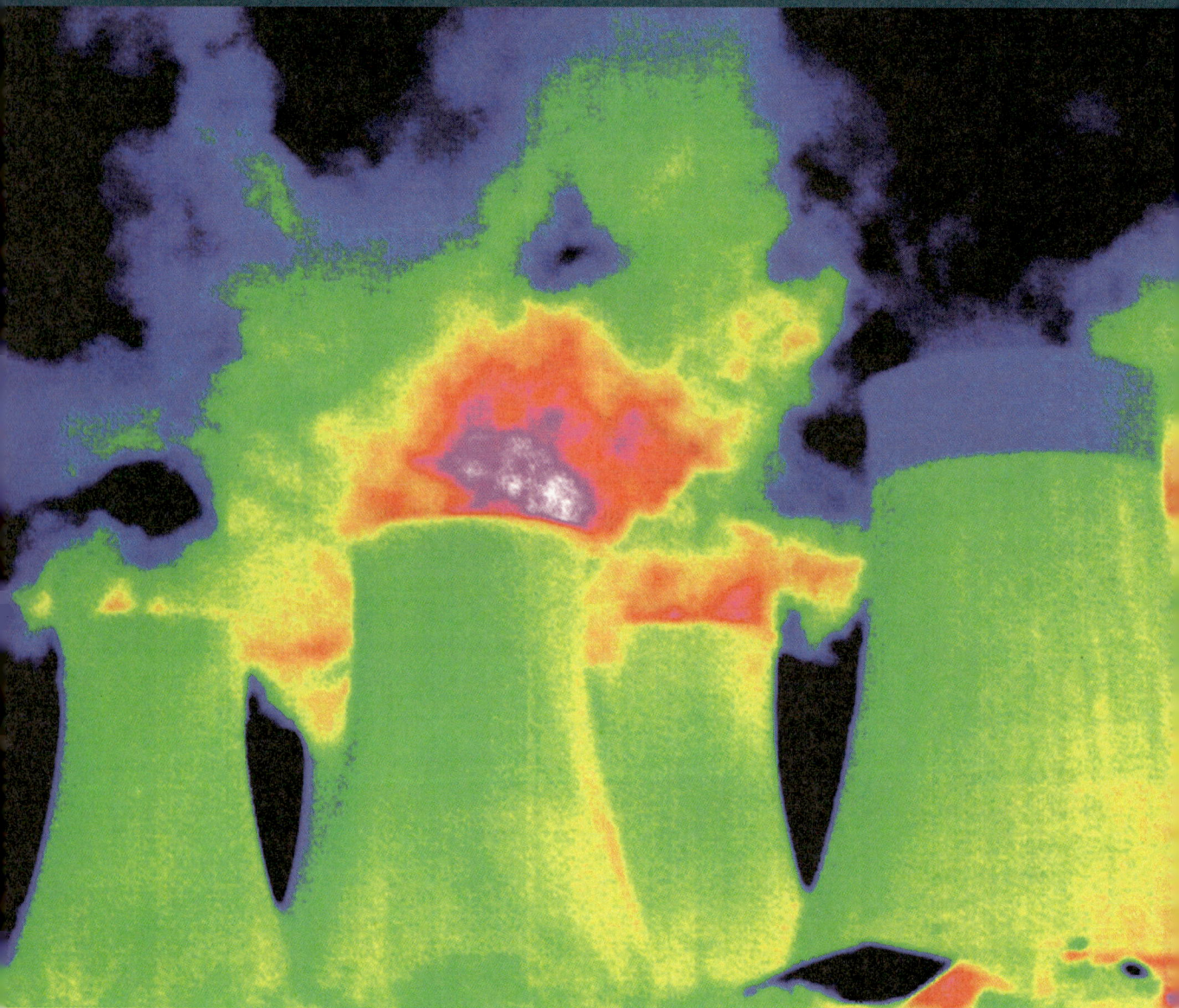

Used, or *spent*, nuclear fuel rods are stored at the bottom of a cooling pool at the nuclear power plant in Chinon, France.

Explore First

Observing a Thermal Energy Transfer Pour water into a beaker and add a few drops of food coloring. Warm the bottom of the jar. What do you observe about the movement of the food coloring and water in the jar?

Go online to view the digital version of the Hands-On Lab for this lesson and to download additional lab resources.

CAN YOU EXPLAIN IT?

Why are urban heat islands hotter than their surrounding regions?

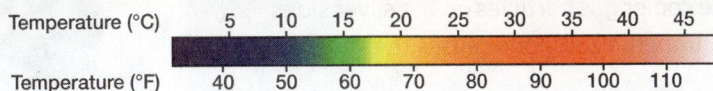

Temperature (°C)	5	10	15	20	25	30	35	40	45
Temperature (°F)	40	50	60	70	80	90	100	110	

These satellite images of suburban (left) and urban (right) Atlanta, Georgia, show the differences in daytime temperatures in the region. The images show the two areas at the same time and on the same day.

Using a variety of tools ranging from thermometers to satellite images, scientists have collected data about the average temperatures in many places. The data show that urban areas are often significantly warmer than the rural places nearby. These warmer areas inside cities are called *urban heat islands*.

1. Think about how surfaces in cities differ from those in the surrounding areas. Why might a central city contain more thermal energy than a farm or forest?

2. What might be some negative consequences of the increased temperatures within an urban heat island?

EVIDENCE NOTEBOOK As you explore the lesson, gather evidence to help explain the causes of urban heat islands.

Modeling the Flow of Thermal Energy through Systems

Energy Transfer

A radiometer, or light-mill, is a device that responds to light. When the radiometer is exposed to a bright light source, the vanes of the radiometer rotate.

The vanes of the radiometer are black on one side and silver on the other. The black surfaces absorb more energy from the light than the silver surfaces, so they become warmer. The gas particles near the black sides of the vanes warm up more than the gas particles near the silver sides. This increase in temperature indicates an increase in kinetic energy. This means the gas particles near the black sides of the vanes collide with the vanes more frequently and with more energy than the cooler gas particles on the silver sides do. The transfer of energy from the collisions causes the vanes of the radiometer to spin.

The vanes of a radiometer spin when they are exposed to bright light.

3. What is the energy input to the radiometer system? What form(s) of energy are present in the system as a result?

A transfer of energy happens when the energy in an object is added to or removed from that object. You can think of the entire radiometer as a **system**, or a set of interacting parts that work together. The vanes of the radiometer move because of a transfer of electromagnetic energy from a light source into the radiometer system.

The *law of conservation of energy* states that energy cannot be created or destroyed. The total energy of a system will increase if the input of energy from outside the system is greater than its output. Once a system's boundaries are defined, the inputs and outputs of energy can be modeled. The bulb is the boundary of the radiometer system. When the radiometer is exposed to a bright light source, the input of electromagnetic energy will be greater than the loss of thermal energy from the system.

EVIDENCE NOTEBOOK

4. Think about the energy inputs and outputs in an urban area. How do urban heat islands demonstrate the law of conservation of energy? Record your evidence.

The Flow of Thermal Energy

Thermal energy is a measure of the total kinetic energy of the particles in an object. This energy can flow as heat between parts of a system. Thermal energy is transferred three ways: conduction, convection, and radiation. Thermal energy is transferred by *conduction* when particles collide. *Convection* describes the transfer of thermal energy through the motion of particles of a fluid. In *radiation*, energy is transferred when electromagnetic waves are emitted by a warmer object and absorbed by a cooler object. Thermal energy always spontaneously flows from objects at higher temperatures to objects at lower temperatures.

Models of Thermal Energy Transfer in Systems

During the operation of a nuclear reactor, fuel rods in the reactor core produce a large amount of thermal energy. This energy is used to generate electrical energy. This energy is transferred to homes, schools, and businesses. After the used fuel rods are removed from a nuclear reactor, they are still very hot. These hot fuel rods are stored in cooling pools filled with water. Thermal energy from the hot fuel rods is transferred to the cooler water. As the fuel rods cool down, the temperature of the water in the pool increases. The rods eventually cool to just above the temperature of the warming water in the pool. Because the rods continue to produce thermal energy, they will always be a little warmer than the water.

Nuclear Cooling Pool

The used fuel rods from a nuclear reactor are stored in cooling pools, where thermal energy is transferred from the hot fuel rods to the cool water.

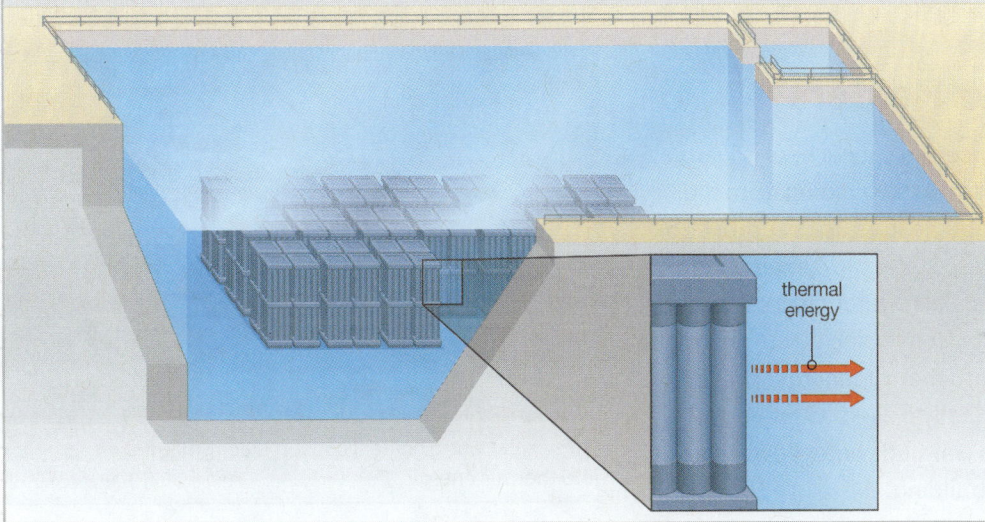

thermal energy

5. How would the temperatures of the components of this system change if additional hot fuel rods were placed in the pool after a steady temperature was reached?

   A. The temperature of the water and the original fuel rods would decrease.

   B. The temperature of the water and the original fuel rods would increase.

   C. The temperature of the water would decrease but the temperature of the original fuel rods would not change.

   D. The temperature of the water would increase but the temperature of the original fuel rods would not change.

Thermal Energy Transfer and Ambient Temperature

All parts of a system will eventually reach the same temperature if there are no inputs or outputs of energy. The temperature of an object's surroundings is called the *ambient temperature*. For example, a building is a system surrounded by the ambient outdoor environment. If thermal energy is not added to the building, the indoor temperature will eventually become the same as the ambient outdoor temperature. If you light a fire in a fireplace, the building will become warmer than the ambient outdoor temperature.

Without energy inputs, the buildings will cool down to the ambient temperature.

6. Think of a window in a house as a system boundary separating the air on opposite sides of the glass pane. Draw the flow of thermal energy through the window when the indoor temperature is 23 °C and the outdoor temperature is 15 °C. Then show how the system model would change if the temperature outside were warmer than inside. How would bright sunshine affect the system?

Analyze Solar Heaters

Hot water from the faucets in your school is warmer than water that comes into the building from the water supply. Most water heaters use a combustible fuel, such as natural gas, or electrical energy to raise the water temperature. Solar water heaters raise the temperature of water by converting electromagnetic energy from the sun into thermal energy. These water heaters are generally placed on the roof of the building. After it is warmed, water flows to a hot water tank inside the building.

These solar water heaters convert electromagnetic energy into thermal energy.

7. Sometimes, the hot water produced by a solar water heater is not warm enough to meet the needs of the occupants of a building. A traditional water heater inside the building supplies additional thermal energy to the solar-warmed water. How can this method still reduce the overall amount of natural gas or electrical energy a building uses?

_____

_____

_____

_____

_____

Describing the Thermal Properties of Materials

Pastry chefs around the world bake pies in plates with a similar shape, but they disagree on the best material for the plates. Some bakers claim they get the best results from shiny aluminum plates. Some chefs never use any material other than glass. A third group argues that ceramic is definitely the way to go.

8. Why might the material of a pie plate have an effect on the quality of the pie's crust?

A common problem when baking pies is burnt crust.

The Thermal Energy of an Object

The thermal energy of an object is the total kinetic energy of its particles. An object's thermal energy depends on the mass of the object, its temperature, its state of matter, and its chemical composition. Larger objects have more thermal energy than smaller objects of the same material and density at the same temperature. A liquid substance has more thermal energy than the same mass of the substance in its solid form.

9. Suppose you have two identical objects made of the same mass of the same material. If one object is 20 °C warmer than the other, which object has more thermal energy?

10. Suppose you have two objects made of the same material but with different masses. If both objects are the same temperature, which object has more thermal energy?

The amount of thermal energy an object has increases as its temperature increases because its particles are moving faster. A greater mass of the same substance at the same temperature will also contain more thermal energy. This is because it contains more moving particles. The composition of the object also affects the thermal energy because some materials are more likely to absorb thermal energy than others. Thermal energy is also related to a material's physical state, or phase. When a solid reaches its melting point or a liquid reaches its boiling point, its physical state changes.

Hands-On Lab
Examine the Transfer of Thermal Energy through Radiation

In this activity, you will investigate how the composition of an object affects its absorption of thermal energy through radiation.

Procedure and Analysis

STEP 1 Use a graduated cylinder to measure and pour the same amount of water into each of the two cans. The cans should be almost full.

STEP 2 Place a plastic foam cover on each can and insert a thermometer through the hole in the cover. Measure the temperature of the water in each can and record the value at time zero in the data table. The water in both cans should be approximately the same temperature.

STEP 3 Use the ruler to place each lamp the same distance from both cans. Turn on both lamps at the same time and begin timing the experiment.

STEP 4 Record the temperature of the water in both cans every 5 minutes for 30 minutes. On a separate piece of paper, graph your data showing the temperature of the water in each can over time.

STEP 5 Describe your observations about each can's absorption of radiation. Why does the water in the two cans have different temperatures at the end of the experiment?

MATERIALS

- adjustable desk lamps, each with at least 60-watt incandescent light bulbs (2)
- graduated cylinder, 100 mL
- plastic foam disks that can fit onto the tops of cans, each with a hole in the middle for a thermometer (2)
- ruler
- stopwatch or timer
- thermometers (2)
- tin cans of the same size (2), one painted matte black and the other painted matte white
- water

Time (min)	Temperature (°C)	
	White can	Black can
0		
5		
10		
15		
20		
25		
30		

EVIDENCE NOTEBOOK

11. How could the surfaces and structures in an urban area be related to the urban heat island effect? Record your evidence.

Changes in Thermal Energy

The total thermal energy of a particular component of a system depends on its temperature, mass, composition, and physical state. Different parts of a system can have different temperatures. Differences in thermal energy and temperature affect the transfer of energy to and from the system, as well as within the system. For example, water is able to absorb more thermal energy than the same amount of soil or rock. So, the temperature of land near large bodies of water is influenced by the temperature of the water.

The California current is a cold ocean current that runs south along the coast of California. During the summer this current becomes colder due to stronger global winds from the northwest. At the same time, air above the Central Valley is being heated by energy from the sun. Lower pressure over land leads to the wind blowing from west to east. This brings the moist air from over the Pacific Ocean toward California. The moist air is cooled by the California current. As the water vapor cools it condenses onto particles of salt in the air to form a thick layer of fog. The winds from the west often push this fog bank through the Golden Gate Bridge and into San Francisco Bay.

Fog forms in the San Francisco Bay area when moist air is cooled by a cold ocean current.

12. Different materials absorb and release thermal energy at different rates. How might you use this property to control the temperatures of components within a system?

The Thermal Properties of Substances

Think about baking something in a hot oven. When you take the pan out of the oven, you use a padded cloth potholder to hold the hot dish. Could you use a sheet of aluminum foil as a potholder? That would not be a good idea. It is likely that you would burn your hands. How an object absorbs and transfers thermal energy depends on the materials from which it is made. Some substances transfer thermal energy better than others. Aluminum foil rapidly transfers thermal energy from the pan to your hand. The cloth potholder does not.

You can also observe how different materials absorb and transfer thermal energy by touching a bicycle sitting in the sun on a hot summer day. The metal frame of the bike feels much hotter than the plastic handlebar grips. Metals, such as aluminum or steel, transfer thermal energy to your hand much faster than plastic.

Engineers consider differences in properties of materials during the design process. Because some materials conduct heat better than others, heat will flow differently depending on the materials used. The transfer of thermal energy to and from an object does not just depend on the difference between the temperatures of the object and its surroundings. It also depends on the material from which the object is made.

Differences in Thermal Energy Transfer

Aluminum, glass, and ceramic each transfer thermal energy differently. The table shows the thermal conductivity values for these materials. Thermal conductivity is a measure of how quickly a material transfers thermal energy, measured in watts per meter-Kelvin (W/m·K). The higher the value, the faster the material transfers energy.

The values in the table indicate that an aluminum pie plate will conduct heat much more quickly than a glass or ceramic plate. This means that thermal energy will transfer to the pie crust through conduction faster in an aluminum plate. A glass pie plate will conduct heat much more slowly. Because glass is clear, the transfer of radiant thermal energy will be greater in the glass plate than in the ceramic plate. Even though ceramic has a higher thermal conductivity value, a ceramic plate is likely to cook the crust more slowly than a glass plate. It does not transfer thermal energy by radiation.

13. **Discuss** Based on the thermal properties of aluminum, glass, and ceramic, how would you revise your recommendation for a pie-plate material? Would one material be preferable to the others based on the pie you are baking?

Thermal Conductivities	
Substance	**Thermal conductivity (W/m·K)**
Aluminum	205
Ceramic	1.5
Glass	1.1
Stainless steel	16

Engineer It
Analyze Evaporative Cooling

The thermal energy of a substance is related to its physical state. The particles of a gas move faster than those of a liquid. So, the gas carries more thermal energy compared to the same amount of liquid.

In dry climates, people often use evaporative coolers instead of air conditioners. In an evaporative cooling system, water is added to an evaporative pad. A fan pulls hot, dry air from the outside through the damp pad and into the building. The water in the damp pad changes from liquid to gas by absorbing some thermal energy from the hot, dry air. As the air loses thermal energy to the water, it becomes cooler.

Evaporative Cooler

14. Add the following labels in the correct spaces below to complete this general model of an evaporative cooling system. HD for hot, dry air and CM for cool, dry air.

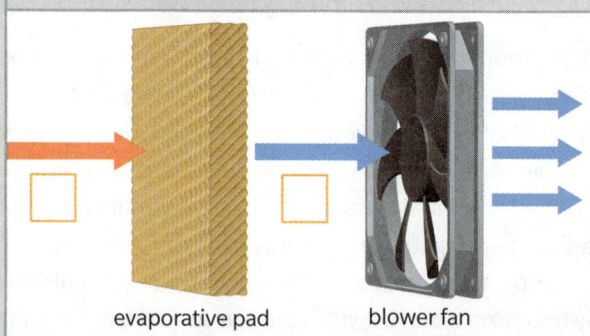

evaporative pad   blower fan

EVIDENCE NOTEBOOK

15. As plants grow, they release water vapor into the atmosphere around them. How might this be related to urban landscapes and surrounding areas? Record your evidence.

Applying the Concepts of Heat Transfer

The application of the transfer of thermal energy in real-world situations is often referred to as *heat transfer*. Engineers are often required to develop solutions to control heat transfer. For example, greenhouses are designed to maximize the amount of *radiant* thermal energy taken in during sunny hours. They also minimize the amount of *convective* thermal energy lost to the atmosphere at night. One way to store thermal energy is to use a thermal mass.

A *thermal mass* is a material that absorbs thermal energy when the air around it is warmer, and then slowly releases it when the air is cooler. Many greenhouses use big black barrels filled with water for this purpose. The barrels absorb thermal energy during the day and release thermal energy during the night.

In this greenhouse, the concrete floor acts as a thermal mass by absorbing radiant energy during the day and slowly releasing it after sundown.

Identify a Heat Transfer Problem: Design a Safe Lunch Carrier

People sometimes call a lunch that someone carries to work or school a "brown bag" lunch, but a paper bag is not always a safe way to carry food. Some foods must be kept cold to be safe, such as meats, cheeses, milk, sliced fruits, or salads. Bacteria that can make you sick grow quickly when the temperature of the food is between 4 °C and 60 °C. That means that the food carrier must keep chilled food almost as cold as a refrigerator at home. Hot food must stay above 60 °C to be safe.

The engineering process begins with defining the engineering problem. In this case, the problem is to design a container that keeps chilled food at a safe temperature long enough to last until lunch.

The next step in the engineering design process is to precisely define the criteria and constraints of an acceptable solution. The *criteria* for the problem are the properties that the product should have in order to successfully solve the problem. Think about what the container should do in order to solve the problem in this situation. *Constraints* are limitations on the solution. For example, a small refrigerator might meet the criterion of keeping food cold. It would not be a successful solution if there is a constraint that the container must be portable.

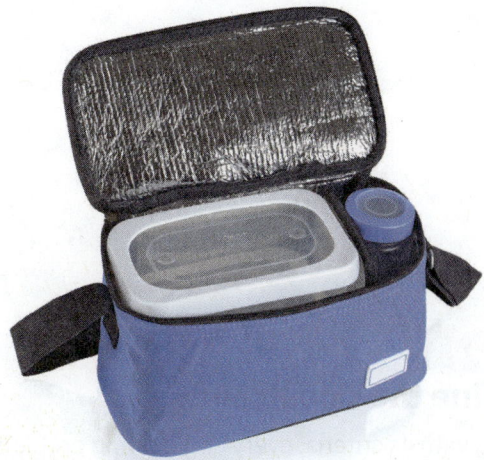

Insulated containers for hot and cold foods can help to keep packed lunches safe.

Define the Criteria

Because this engineering problem involves heat transfer, an important criterion is whether the heat transfer should be maximized or minimized. In this case, the goal is to minimize heat transfer. You can begin defining the criteria for this engineering problem by stating that the solution should reduce heat transfer as much as possible. Another criterion might be to make sure that any heat transfer that does happen will occur slowly. A specific statement could be that the solution will hold a chilled lunch that starts at 2 °C for five hours at a temperature of 7 °C or below.

16. The goals of the design are not only to minimize heat transfer. Because this is a design for a carrier for taking lunch to school, you might want to consider other criteria, such as appearance and size. What are some criteria that you would include to define the problem more precisely?

17. Consider your list of criteria for a lunch carrier design. Think about the purpose of the designed product. Which criterion is the most important one you should consider for possible solutions?

Define the Constraints

Along with its criteria, every engineering problem has constraints. Identifying the constraints helps you think about possible solutions more realistically. What kind of constraints might apply to a lunch carrier engineering problem? They might include the availability of materials, the amount of money that you have to spend, safety considerations, and environmental or societal impacts.

18. **Discuss** What are some of the constraints of the lunch container problem?

Design Heat Transfer Solutions

After you have clearly defined the problem and determined its criteria and constraints, you can begin to work on a solution. It is often helpful to brainstorm possible solutions based on background research. Before designing a safe lunch container, think about the thermal properties of different common materials you could use to construct a container. You have already identified minimizing heat transfer as an important criterion of the problem.

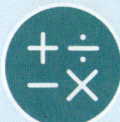

Do the Math
Compare Thermal Properties of Different Materials

Some materials transfer thermal energy very quickly. These materials are called *thermal conductors*. Other materials, known as *thermal insulators*, transfer energy slowly. The thermal conductivity values shown in this table compare how quickly the materials transfer heat. Recall that materials with higher thermal conductivity values transfer thermal energy more quickly than materials with lower thermal conductivity values.

Thermal Conductivities of Substances	
Substance	**Thermal conductivity (W/m•K)**
Aluminum	205
Cloth (wool)	0.07
Copper	401
Polyethylene plastic	0.42
Polystyrene foam	0.03
Tin	67
Wood (pine)	0.12

19. Based on the data in the table above, which materials might work the best in designing a safe lunch container? Use evidence to explain your answer.

20. **Collaborate** With a group, use information from the text and your own experiences to brainstorm design solutions. Besides the thermal properties of the materials you use to build your lunch container, consider other design features that might be important for your solution. Record every suggestion made by your group members.

Choose the Best Solutions

After brainstorming, your group will have a number of ideas that can be used for solutions. Some of them will be more likely to solve the problem than others. Now evaluate and critique each possible solution. First, eliminate any solutions that violate the constraints of the problem. Next, compare how successfully the remaining solutions meet the criteria.

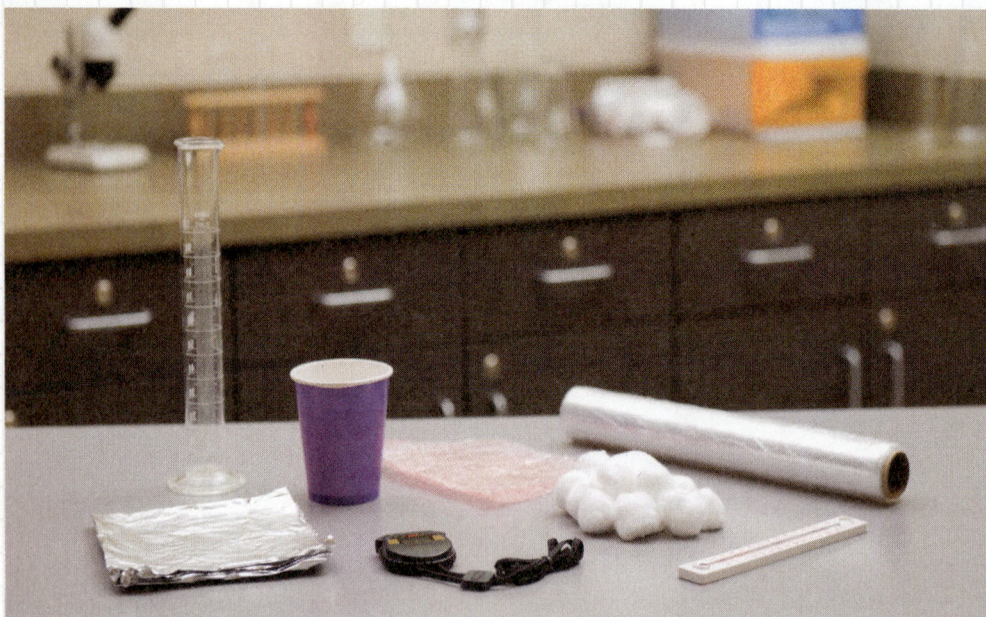

Some materials will perform better as thermal insulators than others. Testing a model will help to develop a solution.

Develop and Test a Model

Once you have determined that one or more of the solutions best meets the criteria and constraints, you need to test those solutions. In order to test solutions, you need to develop a model for each proposed solution. This model can be an actual device, a scale model, or a computer model. You also need to develop a method for testing how well the solution meets the design requirements. The test method should ensure that you obtain accurate data for comparing results.

Design and Test an Insulated Container

You will design a device to insulate a paper cup containing ice-cold water. After you design the device, you will build a model and test it by measuring the change in water temperature over a period of 30 minutes.

The engineering problem is to design a system that minimizes the transfer of thermal energy to the water from its surroundings. In this case, the criteria and constraints include the use of available materials and completion of the design and construction of the model in the time designated by your teacher.

MATERIALS

- aluminum foil
- bubble packing
- cardboard
- cotton balls
- cotton fabric
- drinking straws
- graduated cylinder, 100 mL or larger
- ice
- paper cup
- plastic film
- rubber bands
- sheets of paper
- stopwatch or timer
- string
- thermometer
- water
- wire
- other materials provided by your teacher

Procedure and Analysis

STEP 1 With your group, brainstorm ideas for building an insulation system to minimize change in temperature of the water in the cup.

STEP 2 Evaluate the solutions that were suggested during the brainstorming session. During evaluation, you may want to eliminate some ideas. You may also want to combine parts of two or more ideas. Then build a model of the selected solution for testing.

STEP 3 Test your model by measuring 150 mL of ice-cold water into the cup and placing the cup in the model. Be careful not to include any ice in the water. Measure the temperature of the water, and record it as time zero on the data table.

STEP 4 After 5 minutes, measure and record the temperature of the water. Repeat every 5 minutes for 30 minutes.

STEP 5 What did you observe during your investigation? How do your data show that a transfer of thermal energy did or did not occur?

Thermal Energy Transfer Data	
Time (min)	Temperature (°C)
0	
5	
10	
15	
20	
25	
30	

Analyze and Revise the Design

After completing the test, you need to analyze the data resulting from the test of the design solution. Compare your results with others in the class. Evaluate how different design solutions performed. With your group, discuss how each aspect of the design may have contributed to its success or failure.

21. **Language SmArts** Based on your analysis, suggest some modifications to improve your container. Support your argument using evidence from your experiment and the text.

Analyze Geothermal Heat Pumps

Geothermal technology uses the transfer of thermal energy to or from the ground beneath a structure. Just a few feet below the ground's surface, the temperature is almost constant all year long. Geothermal heat pumps take advantage of the difference between the above-ground air temperature and the soil temperature below the surface to warm and cool buildings. A liquid is pumped through underground pipes. To warm a room, the pump transfers thermal energy from the liquid to the building's heating system. Then the cooled liquid flows through the pipes underground where thermal energy flows into it again before returning to the indoor heating system. For cooling, the heat pump adds thermal energy to the liquid, which is cooled underground.

22. Geothermal heat pumps require a lot less energy than traditional heating and air conditioning systems. How do the energy inputs and outputs differ between a house with a heat pump and a house with a furnace that burns fuel? Explain why using this technology could lead to a reduction of the issues associated with urban heat islands and other problems.

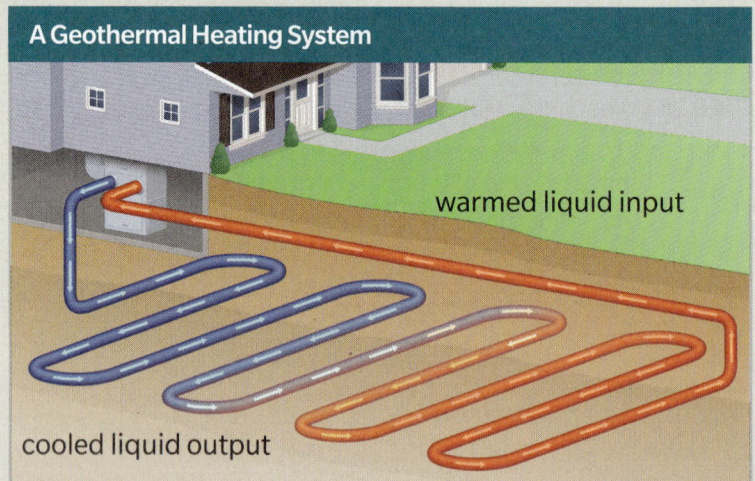

A Geothermal Heating System

warmed liquid input

cooled liquid output

Continue Your Exploration

Name: _____   Date: _____

Check out the path below or go online to choose one of the other paths shown.

Careers in Engineering

- **Maximizing Heat Transfer**
- **Hands-On Labs** ✋
- **Propose Your Own Path**

Go online to choose one of these other paths.

Energy Conservationist

Many modern systems such as buildings, transportation networks, and lighting systems consume a lot of energy. This energy usage is expensive, consumes a large amount of natural resources, and causes pollution that contributes to global climate change. Energy conservationists work to develop solutions to reduce energy consumption.

An energy conservationist may also be an engineer, an environmental scientist, or a building designer. The main goal of the job is to increase the efficiency of systems so they use less energy but still function well. To do this, the energy conservationist has to understand how energy is generated and transmitted and how it is used in the system. The best solution to the problem of energy conservation often saves money, even if it requires new equipment. Energy conservationists have to find ways to save energy in industries such as hotels, commercial properties, municipalities, and even in private homes. Then they make recommendations to solve the engineering design problem of reducing energy consumption.

An energy conservationist measures energy usage and designs ways to reduce it.

1. An energy conservationist often works as a consultant who makes recommendations that other people use to make decisions. What type of information would the energy conservationist have to consider in order to convince people that changes are a good idea?

Continue Your Exploration

An Energy-Efficient Home

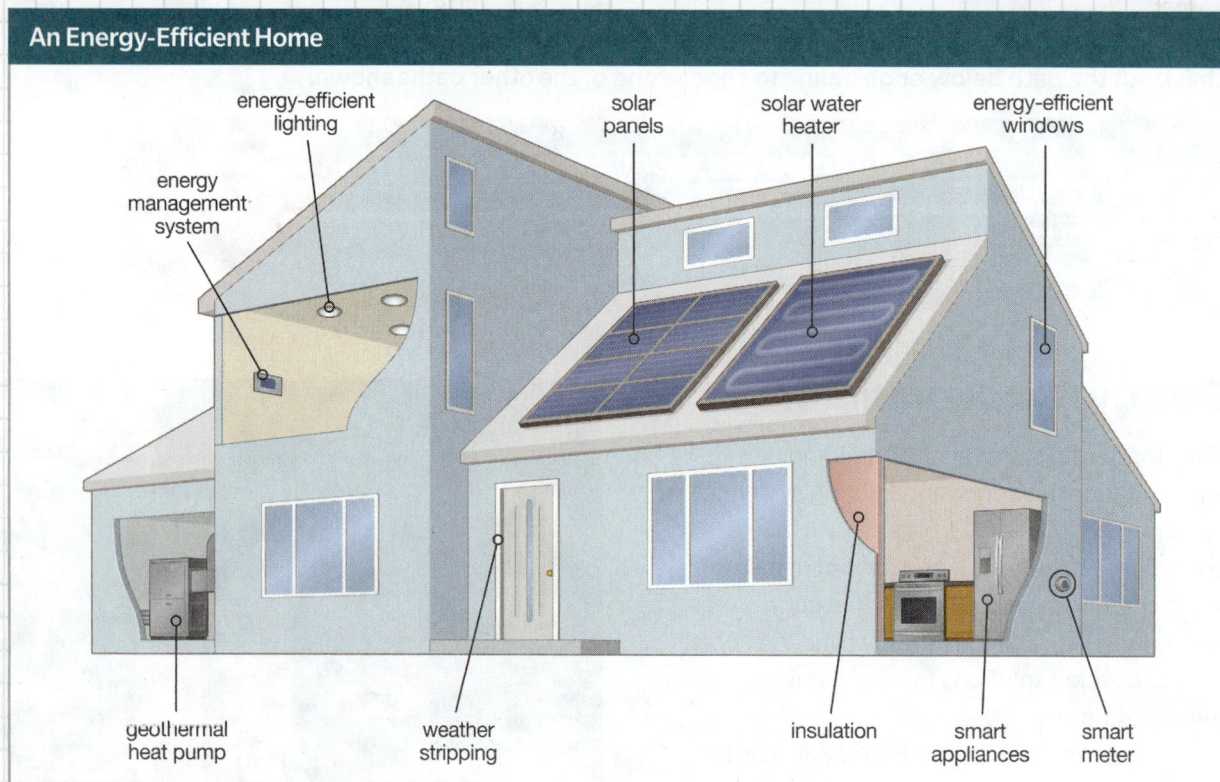

energy-efficient lighting

solar panels

solar water heater

energy-efficient windows

energy management system

geothermal heat pump

weather stripping

insulation

smart appliances

smart meter

One way to improve home energy usage is to use renewable resources such as solar energy or geothermal energy and to reduce fuel usage. Another approach is to reduce energy use. Efficient appliances, insulation, and well-designed windows and doors reduce impacts on the environment and the costs of providing energy.

2. Which of these changes might be suggested by an energy conservationist to reduce the transfer of thermal energy to a home's surroundings? Select all that apply.

   A. Add more insulation to the attic of the home.

   B. Use renewable energy sources instead of fossil fuels to heat the home.

   C. Install the most energy-efficient appliances available.

3. An energy conservationist studies a home and makes a suggestion that each room should have a separate thermostat instead of having one temperature control device in a central room. How could this suggestion help reduce energy usage in the home?

4. **Collaborate** Discuss with a group how you and your families can be "energy conservationists" in your own everyday lives. What steps do you take to make sure your use of energy is most efficient? As a group, make a poster showing things that you can do to minimize your energy use and share your ideas with the class.

Can You Explain It?

Name: **Date:**

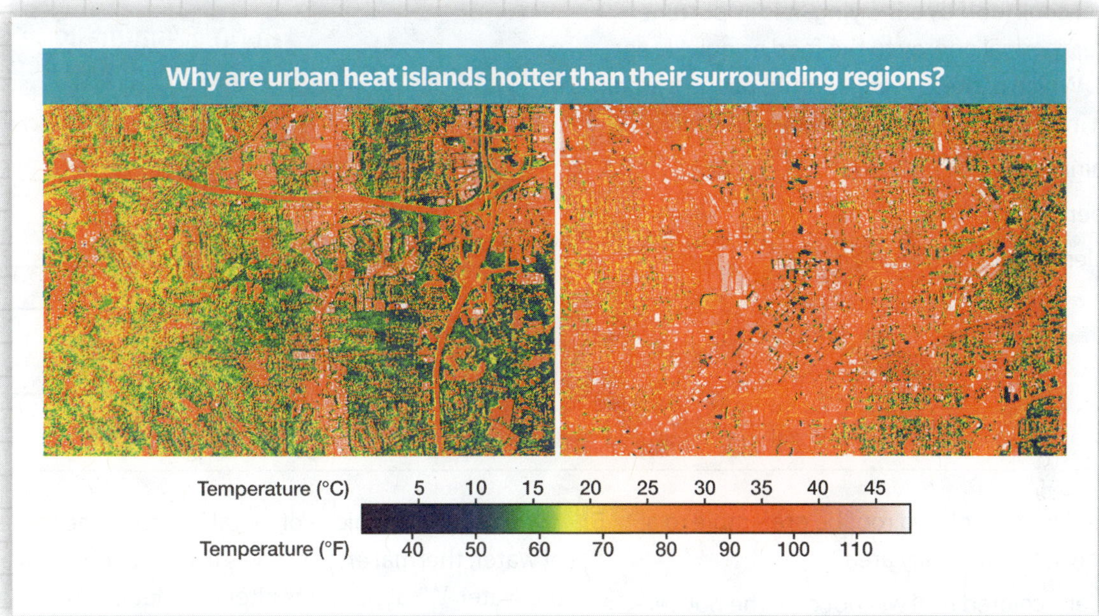

Why are urban heat islands hotter than their surrounding regions?

Temperature (°C) 5 10 15 20 25 30 35 40 45
Temperature (°F) 40 50 60 70 80 90 100 110

EVIDENCE NOTEBOOK

Refer to the notes in your Evidence Notebook to help you construct an explanation for the causes of urban heat islands.

1. State your claim. Make sure your claim fully explains why urban heat islands are hotter than their surrounding regions.

2. Summarize the evidence you have gathered to support your claim and explain your reasoning.

Checkpoints

Answer the following questions to check your understanding of the lesson.

Use the table to answer Question 3.

3. When you cook food by stir-frying, it is important to transfer thermal energy to the food as quickly as possible. Which of these metals would be the best choice for a pan intended for stir-frying vegetables?

   A. aluminum

   B. copper

   C. stainless steel

   D. tin

Thermal Conductivities of Substances	
Substance	**Thermal conductivity (W/m•K)**
Aluminum	205
Cloth (wool)	0.07
Copper	401
Polyethylene	0.42
Polystyrene foam	0.03
Stainless steel	16
Tin	67
Wood (pine)	0.12

4. Why would a light-colored roof be preferable to a dark roof in a warm, sunny area?

   A. The dark-colored roof will not cool the house as quickly at nighttime.

   B. The dark-colored roof absorbs more energy during the day and becomes hotter.

   C. The light-colored roof absorbs more energy and keeps it from entering the house.

   D. The light-colored roof cools the house faster than the dark-colored roof.

5. If you place a hot piece of metal in a container of water, thermal energy flows from the metal to the water. What happens after the metal and the water reach the same temperature?

   A. The flow of thermal energy stops, and the temperature remains constant.

   B. The flow of thermal energy continues and causes both substances to become warmer.

   C. The flow of thermal energy reverses and causes both substances to become warmer.

   D. The flow of thermal energy reverses, and the water becomes colder.

Use the diagram to answer Question 6.

6. There are two streams of liquid flowing through the heat exchanger. As these streams pass opposite sides of the tubes, thermal energy transfers from Liquid A/ Liquid B to Liquid A/ Liquid B .

Liquid A output (60 °C) Liquid B input (20 °C)

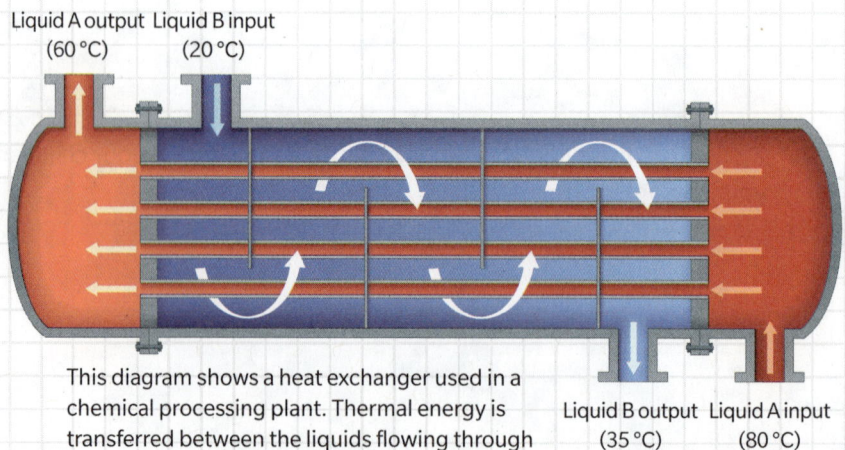

Liquid B output (35 °C) Liquid A input (80 °C)

This diagram shows a heat exchanger used in a chemical processing plant. Thermal energy is transferred between the liquids flowing through the tubes in the exchanger.

Interactive Review

Complete this section to review the main concepts of the lesson.

Thermal energy flows from a warmer object or substance to a cooler object or substance. The total amount of thermal energy in a system does not change unless energy transfers into or out of the system.

A. How does the flow of thermal energy in a solid object change when it is taken from a warm building out into the cold?

The amount of thermal energy that a substance or object contains depends on its temperature, composition, physical state, and mass.

B. How does the thermal energy of a pie fresh out of the oven compare to the thermal energy of a pie fresh out of the refrigerator?

Thermal conductors transfer thermal energy faster than thermal insulators.

C. How is a thermal mass in a building similar to a large body of water, such as a lake?

Changes in Energy Drive the Water Cycle

A dark storm approaches a wooden structure built in the water in the Maldives.

Explore First

Collecting Water   Remove a sealed container of water from a refrigerator where it had time to become cold to the touch. Place the container on a table and observe any changes. What is happening on the outside of the container? Where is the water coming from?

CAN YOU EXPLAIN IT?

How could the water in a dinosaur's drink end up in a raindrop today?

Some of Earth's water makes up your body as well as the bodies of all living things. A tiny drop of water can contain more than a trillion water molecules. Every water molecule has its own story, and some water molecules at Earth's surface today may have been ingested by a dinosaur 200 million years ago.

1. Think about the last drink of water you took. How do you think that water may have moved or changed before you drank it?

2. How do you think the physical state of water affects its movement?

EVIDENCE NOTEBOOK As you explore the lesson, gather evidence to show how water in a dinosaur's drink could end up in a raindrop today.

Analyzing Water on Earth

Where Water Is Found on Earth

Water is found almost everywhere on Earth, and it exists in many forms. From space, it is easy to see Earth's oceans. They cover about 70% of Earth's surface. Salt water makes up about 97% of Earth's total volume of water. For humans and for many animals, the salt dissolved in seawater makes it too salty to drink. It is also too salty to use to water crops.

Earth is known as "the blue planet" because most of its surface is covered with water.

3. Together with a partner, look at the photo for evidence of water. Besides the oceans, where else is water present on Earth? Is it always in liquid form?
   It is also in Antarctica. It is not always in liquid form; it can also be ice.

The Importance of Water on Earth

Water plays an important role in many processes in the Earth's system. It shapes Earth's surface and influences weather. Water is also essential for life. You depend on clean, fresh drinking water to survive. Only a limited amount of Earth's water—about 2.5%—is fresh water. The remaining water on Earth is salt water. Almost 70% of Earth's fresh water is frozen in ice and not readily available for us to use. Therefore, it is important to protect our water resources.

Water's Role on Earth

Water shapes Earth's surface through weathering and erosion, and it also influences Earth's weather.

Water is vital for sustaining all organisms on Earth.

4. **Discuss** Together with a partner or with your class, discuss at least four things you did or used today that would not be possible or would not exist without water.
   - Wash my hands - Take a shower -
   - Drink water - Used Toilet Brush my teeth

States of Water on Earth

Earth is the only planet in our solar system with abundant liquid water. The Earth system also contains water in two other states: gas and solid. Water (liquid), water vapor (an invisible gas), and ice (solid) all have the same chemical formula of H_2O.

The States of Water

Liquid Most of Earth's water is liquid. Gravity causes liquid water to flow downhill and rest in low-lying areas. As a result, Earth has rivers, lakes, and oceans.

Gas Most water vapor is in Earth's atmosphere. We cannot see water vapor, but our bodies take it in every time we inhale.

Solid Solid water forms ice crystals, snowflakes, and hail in Earth's atmosphere and ice and snow on Earth's surface.

5. Look at the scene in the photo. Describe two ways that the liquid water you see here could have come to this location on Earth.

It could have come from rain, or melted ice/snow

Water's Changing State

When the temperature of the environment that water is in rises, water can absorb thermal energy. As water absorbs energy, it can change from solid to liquid, from liquid to gas, or from solid to gas. The same amount of water that existed before the change of state exists after the change of state.

No, water can also be in the form of solids, like ice, or gas during evaporation

On the other hand, if the surrounding environment cools, water can lose energy to its surroundings and can change state in the opposite direction. As energy is released from water, the water may change from gas to liquid, from liquid to solid, or from gas to solid.

EVIDENCE NOTEBOOK

6. Think back to the dinosaur's drinking water. Was this water always in the liquid state? Did it remain in a liquid state after the dinosaur drank it? Record your evidence.

7. In each image, fill in the blank to indicate whether water gains or loses kinetic energy.

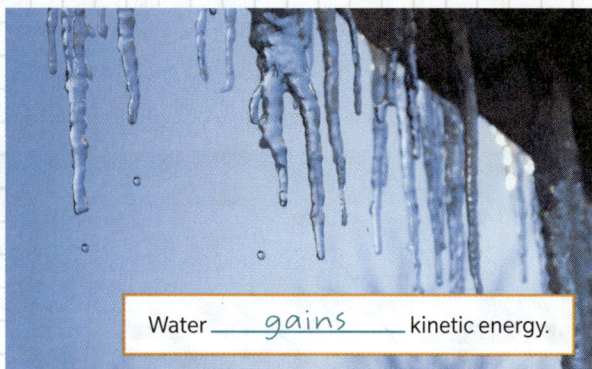

Water ___gains___ kinetic energy.

As air temperatures increase, the water molecules in this ice begin to vibrate just enough to break free and start to flow past one another to form a liquid.

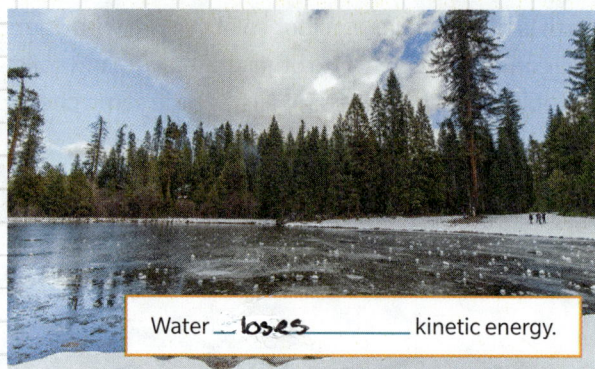

Water ___loses___ kinetic energy.

As air temperatures decrease, the molecules in liquid water begin to move more slowly until they only vibrate in place. The molecules form the rigid structure of solid water, or ice.

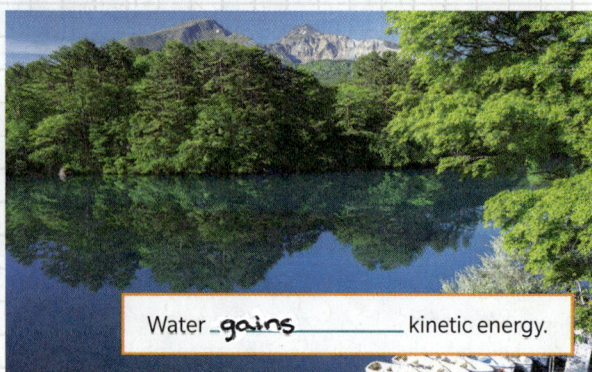

Water ___gains___ kinetic energy.

As air temperatures increase, liquid water molecules begin to vibrate enough that some will escape the liquid's surface into the air above as water vapor.

Water ___loses___ kinetic energy.

As water vapor molecules rise, they eventually enter colder air. This causes the molecules to vibrate at a slower rate and change to liquid water droplets.

Do the Math
Analyze Temperatures

When we find the temperature of something, we are really measuring the average kinetic energy of the particles in that object. The freezing point and the melting point of water are both 0 °C. When water cools to 0 °C or below, it is losing kinetic energy, and is likely to freeze. If ice warms to 0 °C or above, it is gaining kinetic energy and is likely to melt. And the boiling point of water is 100 °C.

8. In the United States and some other countries, temperature is generally measured in degrees Fahrenheit (°F). Scientists generally measure temperature in degrees Celsius (°C), so it is helpful to be familiar with both temperature scales. Use the equation to calculate the temperature in °F for each item below. The first one has been done for you.

$$F = \frac{9}{5}C + 32$$

a running stream	snow	boiling water
25 °C = 77 °F	0 °C = 32	100 °C = 212

Describing the Movement of Water in Earth's Atmosphere

A mixture of gases surrounds Earth and makes up its atmosphere. Earth's atmosphere contains nitrogen, carbon dioxide, oxygen, and water. At any given time there is about 12,900 km³ of water in the atmosphere. That's enough water to completely fill Lake Superior, the largest lake by volume in North America!

9. What evidence of water in the atmosphere can you see in the photo?

The water's color comes from the sky's reflection

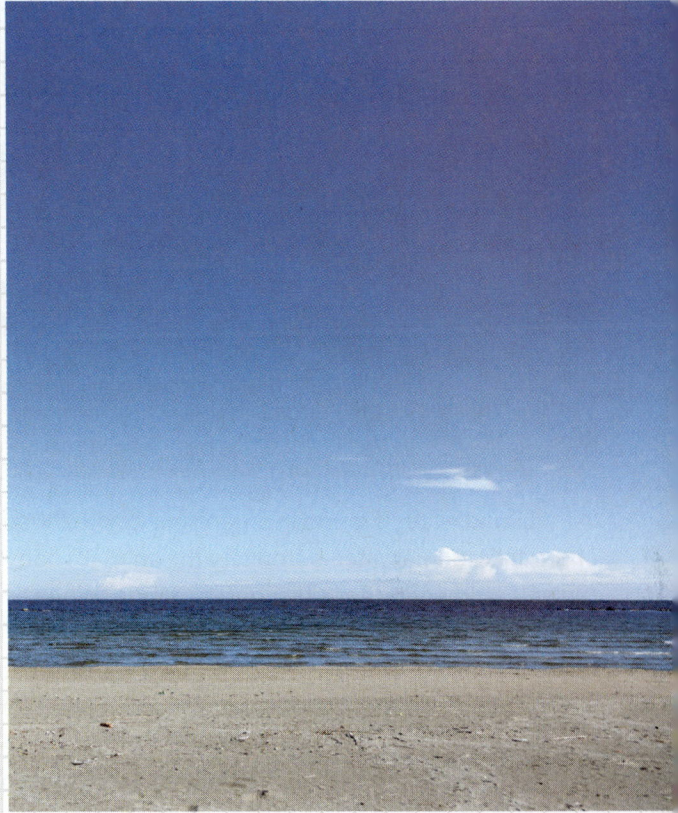

The atmosphere contains a lot of water vapor, which you cannot see.

How Water Reaches the Atmosphere

Water can exist in the atmosphere as a solid, a liquid, and a gas. In addition to evaporation, two other processes can move water into the atmosphere from Earth's surface. These processes are transpiration and sublimation.

10. Where can water in the atmosphere come from? Circle all possible answers.

A. oceans

B. plants

C. ice

D. puddles

When liquid water gains enough energy to escape the liquid's surface and form water vapor, the process is called **evaporation**. Some water evaporates from the water on land. However, most water evaporates from the surface of Earth's oceans. The amount of thermal energy needed to evaporate water from different parts of Earth's oceans depends on the kinetic energy of the ocean water. In some places, the ocean water is cold at the surface, and has less kinetic energy. Here, more thermal energy is needed for water to evaporate. In other places, the ocean water is warm at the surface and needs less thermal energy for evaporation to occur.

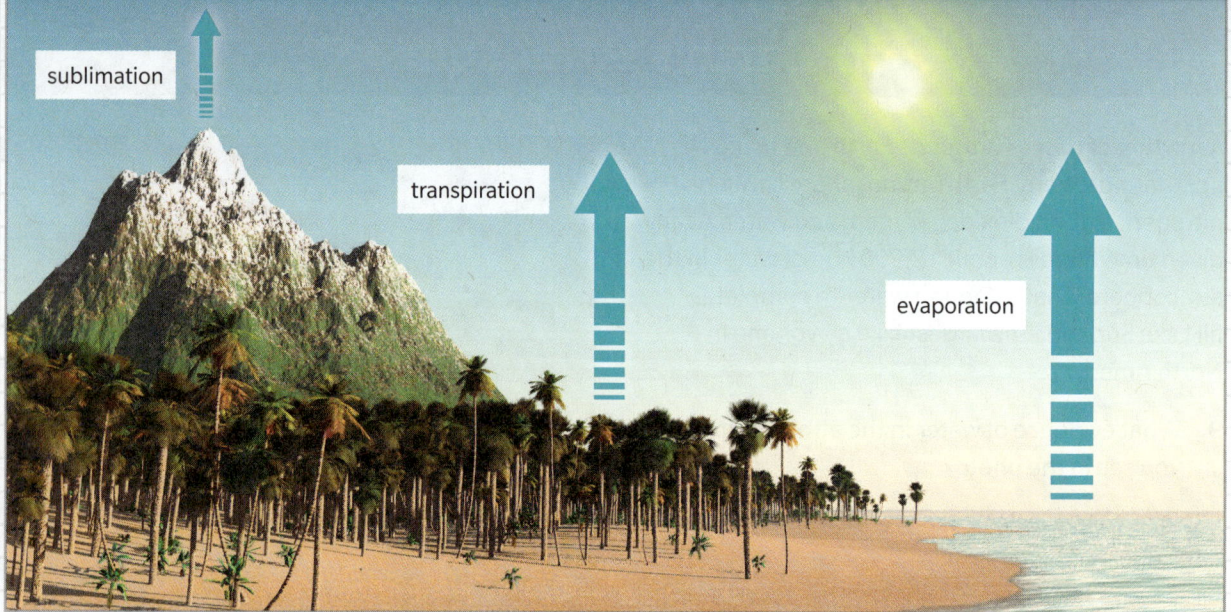

Ways Water Reaches the Atmosphere

sublimation

transpiration

evaporation

Liquid water is found in organisms' bodies. Water is ingested as an animal eats and drinks. Some water is stored in the animal's body and some is returned back into the environment by excretion or respiration. When an animal dies, its body decomposes and any water in the body is returned to the environment. Like many organisms, plants release water vapor into the environment. As water flows throughout a plant, some water changes to water vapor as it leaves the plant through small openings called stomata. This release of water vapor into the air by plants is called **transpiration**. This process requires the addition of kinetic energy to the water molecules, so they can break away from the liquid state.

When solid water changes directly to water vapor without first becoming a liquid, the process is called **sublimation**. Energy is required for this process to occur because the molecules of the solid water must gain enough kinetic energy to break free from the solid state.

How important are the contributions from each source of atmospheric water? About 90% of the water in the atmosphere comes from evaporation of Earth's liquid water, especially oceans. About 10% of the water in the atmosphere comes from transpiration. Less than 1% of the water in the atmosphere comes from sublimation.

Water in the Atmosphere

Water molecules in the atmosphere are in constant motion, bouncing against each other and against other gas molecules in the air. During these collisions, the water molecules spontaneously gain or lose kinetic energy. If a water molecule collides with a molecule that is warmer, and so has more kinetic energy, the water molecule will gain kinetic energy. If a water molecule collides with a molecule that is cooler, and so has less kinetic energy, the water molecule will lose kinetic energy.

The water could have been urinated from a dinosaur into a lake or river, which could have flowed into the ocean. From the ocean, the water could have been evaporated.

EVIDENCE NOTEBOOK

11. Through what processes might the water have changed and moved before and after the dinosaur drank it? Record your evidence.

Hands-On Lab
Model the Formation of Clouds and Rain

You will model Earth's atmosphere inside a jar.

Procedure and Analysis

STEP 1 Carefully fill a jar about half full by pouring 250 mL of hot water into it.

STEP 2 Place a dented lid on top of the jar so that it covers the entire opening and the raised bumps are facing down into the jar.

STEP 3 Place ice cubes, a little cold water, and a teaspoon of salt into the can and stir. Put the cold can on top of the lid of the jar.

STEP 4 Shine a flashlight through the jar. Record your observations. Repeat this step every few minutes for 10 minutes.

STEP 5 Use what you observed in this activity to explain some of the things that can happen to water in Earth's atmosphere. What might cause these changes?

MATERIALS
- can, empty
- flashlight
- ice cubes
- glass jar, medium size with a dented lid
- salt (1 tsp)
- water, very hot (250 mL)
- water, cold

Condensation and Clouds

As air cools, water vapor in the air may change to liquid water. The process of a gas becoming a liquid is called **condensation**. As water molecules bump into each other, they can stick together and form small water droplets or ice crystals, depending on the air temperature. At first, these droplets form around tiny particles in the air, such as sea salt, dust, and pollen. As more and more water molecules collect in the water droplets, the droplets become larger. Eventually, there may be enough water droplets to form visible clouds, fog, or mist.

High clouds that form at temperatures colder than those close to Earth's surface are made up of solid ice crystals and liquid droplets. At the ground level, water vapor may condense as dew or frost on cool surfaces, such as blades of grass and windows.

12. Microscopic droplets of water in the air grow larger as water vapor continues to condense. What might happen next?

It forms a cloud, then rains

Precipitation

As the water droplets in clouds become larger and larger, the pull of gravity on them increases. Eventually, the force of gravity can cause the water in clouds to fall to Earth's surface. **Precipitation** is any form of water that falls to Earth from clouds. Three common kinds of precipitation are rain, snow, and hail. Snow and hail form when the water in clouds freezes.

Hailstones are frozen balls of precipitation that form in some thunderstorms.

You can see the beautiful six-part crystals of snowflakes when they are viewed under magnification.

Rain falls when water droplets that form in clouds are pulled to Earth's surface by gravity.

Deposition

Deposition occurs when water vapor changes state directly from a gas to a solid. Deposition is the reverse of sublimation. One example of deposition occurs high in the atmosphere or on the top of high mountains where the temperature is very low. In these conditions, water vapor forms snow without becoming a liquid first.

13. Circle the best answer to complete each statement.

    A. When water vapor in the atmosphere condenses and forms water droplets, the water molecules absorb / ⟨release⟩ energy.

    B. When liquid water in the atmosphere form ice crystals, the water molecules absorb / ⟨release⟩ energy.

Describe the Formation of Hail

Sometimes, when ice crystals form in clouds and begin to fall, strong winds carry the ice crystals high into the clouds. When the crystals begin falling again, they grow larger as more water droplets freeze onto them. Clumps of ice, called hailstones, start to form. Eventually, the hailstones grow too heavy for the wind to carry and they fall to Earth.

14. Describe a time during the formation of hailstones when water releases energy.

    Inside the clouds, water droplets are formed in cold temperature. Then they clump together and then they freeze. When they come down, they become hail.

Describing the Movement of Water on Earth's Surface

Much of Earth's surface is covered with water. Most of this water is salt water, which makes up Earth's oceans, salt marshes, and salty lakes. Only a small amount of Earth's water is fresh water, and most of that is frozen as sea ice at the poles or as ice and snow on land.

15. From photos of Earth's surface can you see all the locations where water might be? Explain.

The Dungeness River in Washington State forks before entering the bay and the Strait of Juan de Fuca.

Ocean Circulation

While it is easy to observe water flowing on land after a rainstorm, remember that most of Earth's precipitation falls into the ocean. Just as water moves through Earth's rivers, water in the ocean also moves in patterns. The movement of ocean water in a particular direction and pattern is called a *current*. This diagram shows the main pattern of ocean circulation, but does not show all ocean currents. The light green paths show currents on the ocean surface. The dark green paths show currents below the surface.

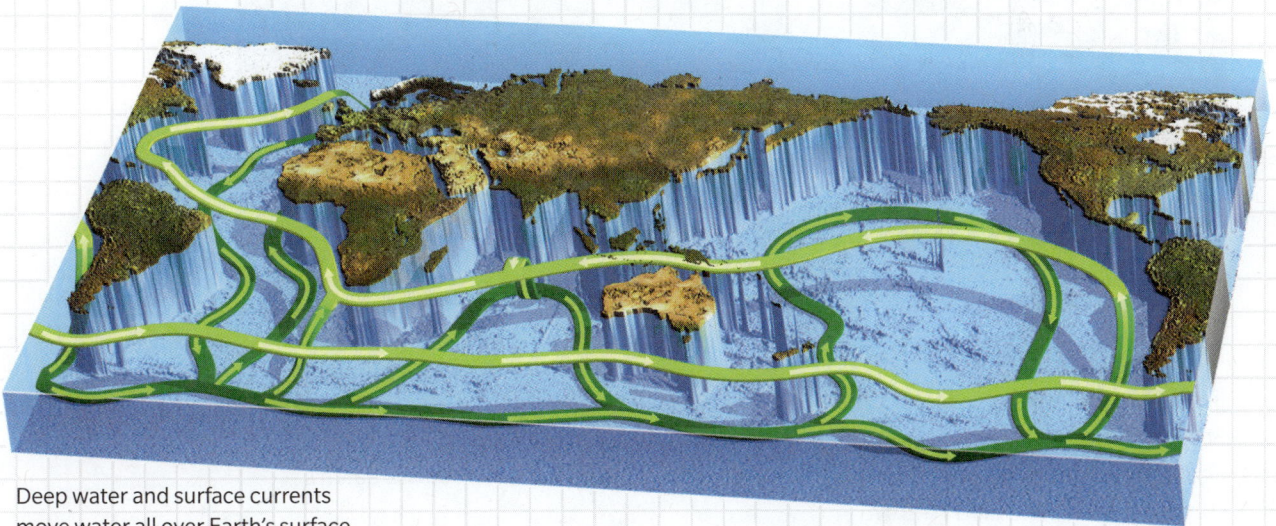

Deep water and surface currents move water all over Earth's surface.

16. In which ways might ocean currents be like streams and rivers on land?

Surface Currents and Deep Ocean Currents

Currents at or near the ocean surface are called *surface currents*. Surface currents are powered by wind. The wind is powered by thermal energy from the sun. The Gulf Stream that moves warm ocean water from the Gulf of Mexico northeast toward Europe is one example of a surface current. As this current moves toward Europe, it also moves the thermal energy found in the water.

Currents that flow below the ocean surface are called deep currents. These currents are driven by differences in water densities. Gravity causes denser water to sink below surrounding water in some parts of the ocean.

Deep currents flow at all levels of the ocean below the surface. Ocean currents transport large amounts of water as well as dissolved solids, dissolved gases, organisms, and energy around the Earth system.

Water Movement on Land

Water from the atmosphere falls to Earth's surface in the form of precipitation. Some precipitation forms coverings of snow and ice on mountains and other cold places. When this ice and snow melts, and when rain falls, the liquid water flows downhill. Some of the water may seep into the ground.

In the Highlands of Scotland, mountain streams flow down to lower elevations. As the water flows downhill it loses potential energy and gains kinetic energy.

17. What drives the movement of water in Earth's systems?

Runoff and Infiltration

Just as gravity pulls you and all other objects toward Earth's center, it also pulls on water. So, when precipitation lands on Earth's surface, some of the water will flow downhill across Earth's surface into wetlands, rivers, or lakes. Water that flows across Earth's surface this way is called **runoff**.

Some of the water on land may also seep below Earth's surface into spaces in soil and rock. This process is called *infiltration*. Water under Earth's surface is called *groundwater*. Groundwater can flow downhill through soil and some types of rock. Some drinking water in the United States comes from groundwater supplies. To use these supplies, people drill down into the ground to reach the groundwater. More than 75% of Earth's fresh water exists as ice and about 20% exists as groundwater.

Water Movement on and below Earth's Surface

Water flows over Earth's surface as runoff from precipitation, melting snow, and ice. Some of this water flows through streams and rivers. Because of gravity, some of this water seeps downward to form groundwater.

Explore Online

18. Which statement correctly describes the movement of water represented by arrows in the picture? Choose all that apply.

A. Water from melting snow runs down the mountainside.

B. Rainwater seeps into the ground.

C. Streams carry water to the mountain peaks.

D. Gravity prevents groundwater from reaching Earth's surface.

19. Engineer It In some rivers and lakes, dams are constructed to harvest energy by converting the mechanical energy of moving water into electrical energy. Dams also form reservoirs that can be used to supply fresh water, which is a valuable resource in California.

These reservoirs also disrupt natural systems and cycles. Ecosystems upstream are flooded and destroyed. Downstream, ecosystems that depend on seasonal flooding can suffer from a lack of water. What kinds of trade-offs need to be considered before construction of a freshwater reservoir can begin? Explain your reasoning.

Dams, such as the Glen Canyon Dam, can help control water movement on Earth's surface.

Ice on Earth's Surface

Most of Earth's fresh water is locked up in large ice caps in Antarctica and Greenland, or in ice floating in polar ocean water. Some ice is also found in glaciers. Glaciers are sometimes called "rivers of ice" because gravity causes them to move slowly downhill. Many glaciers never leave land. However, some glaciers reach the ocean, where pieces may break off and form icebergs.

Glacier Bay National Park, Alaska, is home to large glaciers that have carried ice over the land for thousands of years. This glacier flows to the ocean.

20. How might an iceberg move once it breaks off from a glacier?

Analyze Processes

21. Which of the following processes could have caused this cave to fill with water?

    A. evaporation

    B. sublimation

    C. infiltration

    D. transpiration

22. Together with a partner, think of a way water might exit this cave. Explain your reasoning.

A limestone cave beneath Earth's surface can fill with water over time.

Modeling the Water Cycle

You can use everyday experiences to observe and model the movement of water in Earth's systems. You can observe some changes in water after any hot shower you take. While much of the shower water goes down the drain, some evaporates into the bathroom air. You know this because the mirror fogs up as that water vapor condenses back into liquid. When returning to the bathroom after a day at school, you notice that the mirror and your wet towel are now dry. Think about what happened to the water.

Time

23. **Discuss** Together with a partner, examine the photos. The material inside the glass changes over time. What do you think happened? Did the ice and water just disappear?

The Water Cycle

On a global scale, water constantly moves through Earth's system. The movement of water among the atmosphere, land, oceans, and living things is called the **water cycle**. This cycling of water involves changes of state, the movement of water in different forms, and the transfer of matter and energy in Earth's system.

A Water Cycle Model

24. Complete the water cycle model by writing the correct process in the spaces provided. Write *condensation*, *runoff*, *infiltration*, or *evaporation*.

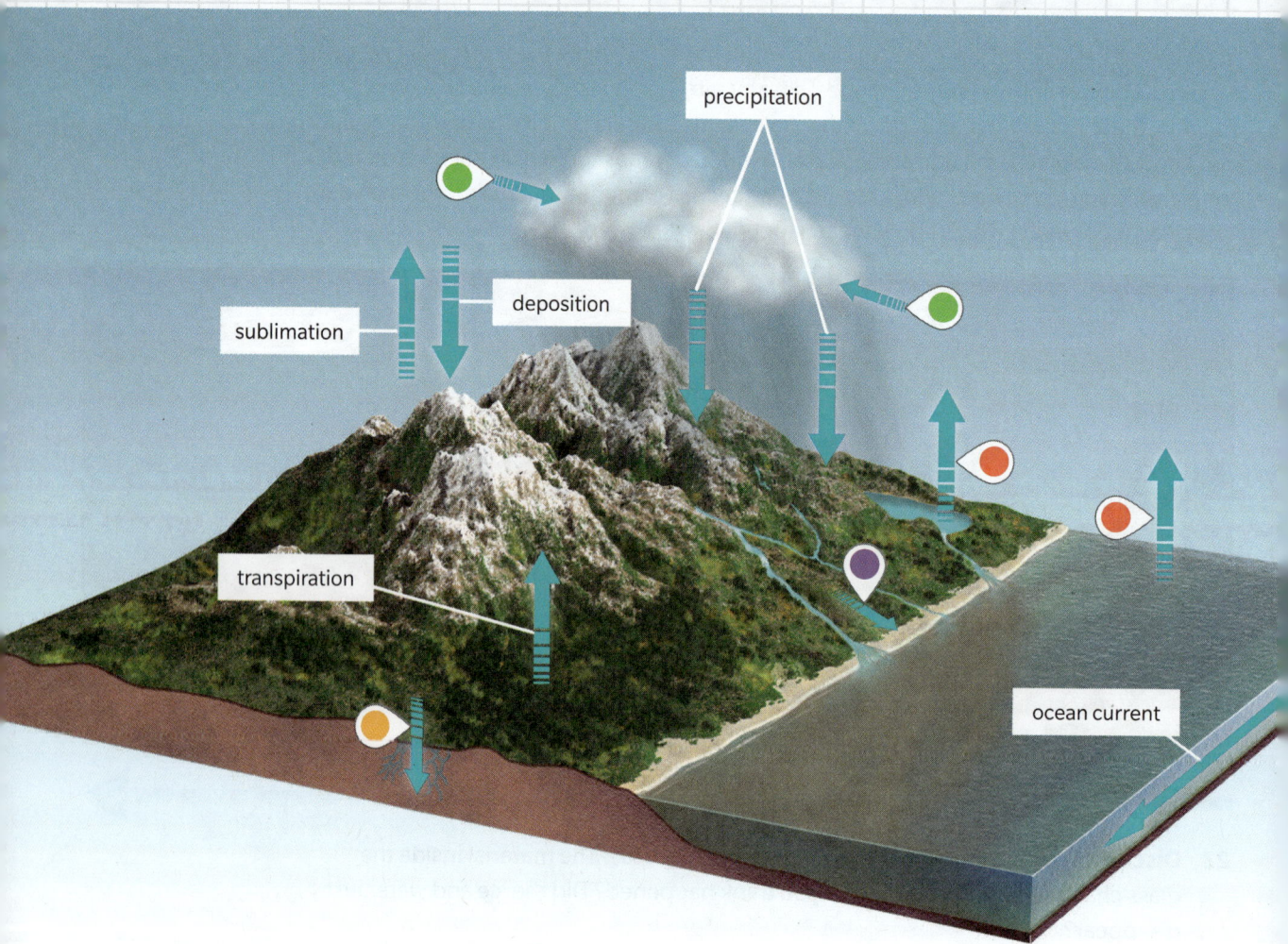

25. What other processes that involve energy in Earth's system are not shown in this model of the water cycle?

Sunlight and Gravity Drive the Water Cycle

Surface water, groundwater, and ice flow downhill because of gravity. Precipitation falls to Earth's surface because of gravity. Energy from the sun is the source of changes of state in which water absorbs energy, such as melting and evaporation. Solar energy also powers Earth's winds, which move air and water in the atmosphere.

26. Describe what might happen in the water cycle if the amount of solar energy entering the Earth system decreased.

The Flow of Energy in the Water Cycle

Energy flows through the Earth's system in the water cycle in two ways—when water changes state and when water moves from place to place. When water changes state, water molecules absorb energy from or release energy to their surroundings. For example, water can evaporate when it absorbs energy from sunlight or from surrounding air, water, or land. When water condenses to form clouds, the water molecules release energy to the surrounding atmosphere.

As water moves, it transfers energy from one location to another. For example, as a warm surface current in the ocean flows to a colder polar region, thermal energy from the equator is transported toward Earth's poles. When the warm water reaches areas where the air is colder, some energy in the warmer water is released into the cooler air. These energy transfers between the ocean and the atmosphere greatly influence Earth's weather and climate.

27. Imagine snow on top of a mountain. What are some ways energy could be transferred as the seasons change? Choose all answers that apply.

    A. Energy flows into the snow from sunlight.

    B. Cold snow melt flows into the warmer lake.

    C. Warmer air absorbs energy from snow.

    D. Energy flows into the snow from warmer air.

The Cycling of Matter in the Water Cycle

As water moves above, on top of, and below Earth's surface, it carries other matter with it. For example, streams and rivers carry sand, mud, and living things, which are deposited in a new place. As water moves over land, some substances will dissolve in the water and be carried along with it. When the water evaporates, the dissolved substances will be deposited. Precipitation can carry substances from the air to the ground, including gases, dust, ash, pollen, and pollutants.

28. What are some other examples of the cycling of matter that happen as a result of the water cycle?

EVIDENCE NOTEBOOK

29. How could a water molecule move through the water cycle over millions of years? Record your evidence.

Model the Water Cycle

The movement of water throughout Earth's systems is called the water cycle. However, this cycle is not a "circle" of events. A water molecule can take different paths as it moves through the cycle. The term *cycle* refers to the fact that water continuously moves from Earth's surface to the atmosphere and back.

30. Language SmArts Remember the water on the bathroom mirror that appears after you take a shower? Tell a story about how those droplets appear on the mirror and what could happen to a water molecule from one of the droplets as it moves through the water cycle. Describe at least four changes in the state of water, the processes that move the water, and how energy flows to and from the water. Be sure to include at least one living organism in the water cycle.

_____

_____

_____

_____

_____

_____

_____

31. Draw In the space below, draw a model to go with your story. Use arrows and labels to show processes in the water cycle. Present your story and model to the class.

Continue Your Exploration

Name: _____   **Date:** _____

Check out the path below or go online to choose one of the other paths shown.

People in Science

- **Investigating Water Sources**
- **Hands-On Labs** 🖐️
- **Propose Your Own Path**

Go online to choose one of these other paths.

Hydrologist

Hydrologists are scientists who study water. They study a wide variety of topics, including water quality and availability. Some hydrologists also study water's movement at different scales, from global ocean currents to local replenishment of reservoirs by spring snowmelt. Hydrologists use many instruments in their work, including depth gauges and flow meters.

Hydrologists take water samples along irrigation channels near the Rio Grande. They are looking for pharmaceuticals, nutrients, metals, and other characteristics to determine water quality.

Continue Your Exploration

The Rio Grande runs along the border between Texas and Mexico. The river is an important resource. It is a vital stop along birds' migration routes. It is central to many important desert ecosystems, and houses several dams used for purposes such as generating electrical energy and diverting water to irrigate cropland. However, the Rio Grande is polluted from human activities. Its water levels have significantly declined over the past century from human activities and changes in climate. Hydrologists play an important role in collecting data that shows how much water runs through the river, how much water is used for different human activities, and what pollutants are in the water.

1. A hydrologist needs to know how much water will run off into a river after an exceptionally rainy spring. What data will the hydrologist need to consider? Choose all that apply.

   A. air temperature

   B. amount of precipitation in the winter

   C. depth of snowpack on surrounding mountain peaks

   D. stream flow rates

   E. reservoir water depth

2. Why is the work of hydrologists important?

3. What type of information about water and the water cycle would be important for a hydrologist to focus on in your community?

4. **Collaborate** Work with a small group to list the sources of drinking water in your community, such as lakes, rivers, and reservoirs. Think about why that source was chosen for use. Then consider a scenario that could reduce the amount of clean, fresh water available to the residents of the community. Together, "think like a hydrologist" to describe the scenario and to make predictions about the outcome. Create a brochure to provide to the community explaining the situation.

Can You Explain It?

Name: _____   Date: _____

How could the water in a dinosaur's drink end up in a raindrop today?

> ### EVIDENCE NOTEBOOK
> Refer to the notes in your Evidence Notebook to help you construct an explanation for how some of the water molecules in a dinosaur's drink could be the very same ones in a raindrop today.

1. State your claim. Make sure your claim fully explains how the water molecules in a raindrop falling today also could have been ingested by a dinosaur millions of years ago.

2. Summarize the evidence you have gathered to support your claim and explain your reasoning.

Checkpoints

Answer the following questions to check your understanding of the lesson.

Use the photo to answer Questions 3–5.

3. What state(s) of water do you directly observe in this photo? Choose all that apply.

   A. liquid

   B. solid

   C. gas

4. As the snow forms in the atmosphere, the water molecules *gain / lose / neither gain nor lose* kinetic energy.

5. How will the environment shown in the photo change when summer arrives? Select all that apply.

   A. The snow will melt.

   B. The water will evaporate from the stream.

   C. Transpiration could occur.

   D. Snow will continue to fall and form large piles.

Use the photo to answer Questions 6–8.

6. Which of the following steps of the water cycle can you infer are taking place in this scene at the moment the photo was taken? Choose all that apply.

   A. evaporation

   B. sublimation

   C. condensation

   D. transpiration

7. Using numbers *1–4*, order the following events in a sequence that most logically describes the movement of water from the ocean to the bottom of a well in a village on the island.

   _____ condensation

   _____ infiltration

   _____ evaporation

   _____ precipitation

8. Water in the clouds in this scene eventually moves from the atmosphere to the land by *infiltration / precipitation / evaporation.*

   Next, *transpiration / melting / runoff* carries that water to the sea.

   Wind / Gravity drives both examples of water movement.

Interactive Review

Complete this section to review the main concepts of the lesson.

The water on Earth can be found in three states: as a solid, liquid, and a gas. Changes in thermal energy cause water to change states.

A. Explain how water changes state by using an example.

Water in the atmosphere affects cloud formation and precipitation.

B. Use a sequence of at least four events to describe some of the ways that water moves into, through, and then out of the atmosphere.

Water moves on Earth's surface, below Earth's surface, and in Earth's oceans.

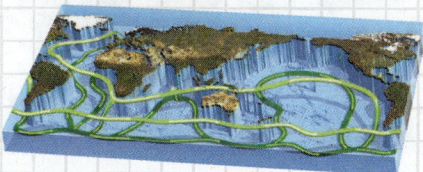

C. Make a table to describe at least one way that water moves in each of these parts of the Earth system: in the oceans, above ground, and below ground.

Water molecules can follow many different paths through the water cycle.

D. Explain the roles of sunlight and gravity in the water cycle.

Choose one of the activities to explore how this unit connects to other topics.

People in Engineering

Kaitlin Liles, Thermal Engineer Kaitlin Liles joined NASA while a student at Virginia Tech, where she later earned a degree in mechanical engineering. Liles uses computers models and conducts real-world tests in thermal vacuum chambers. Liles served as the lead thermal engineer on NASA's Stratospheric Aerosol and Gas Experiment III. Liles helped design the instrument to withstand the extreme temperatures of space during its mission on the International Space Station.

Research how spacecraft temperature is regulated. Create a short presentation to share your findings.

Environmental Science Connection

Passive Solar Design Heating and cooling a building requires a lot of energy and can be very expensive. Buildings designed to use the sun's energy for warmth in the winter and to minimize solar heating in the summer are becoming more popular. These passive solar buildings can reduce the need for energy and reduce heating and cooling costs.

Research the features of a passive solar building. Draw a diagram that explains how the features keep the building warm in the winter by maximizing energy transfer from the sun and cool in the summer by minimizing energy transfer from the sun.

Social Studies Connection

Chilling Out People often open and close refrigerator doors a dozen or more times a day. We count on refrigerators to minimize thermal energy transfer and keep our food cold, so it stays fresh and does not spoil. Today, most of us take the refrigerator for granted, but people did not always have easy access to fresh, cold food.

Research the history of the refrigerator. Create a timeline to show the progression from iceboxes to the modern-day refrigerator. Include key events along the way in developing this technology.

Name: _____   Date: _____

Complete this review to check your understanding of the unit.

Use the image of the fan to answer Questions 1 and 2.

1. To be more energy efficient, the fan should transform as much of the electrical energy input as possible into:

   A. kinetic energy of the fan blades

   B. sound energy in the fan's motor

   C. thermal energy in the fan's motor

   D. electromagnetic energy in the fan's blades

2. A transformation of chemical energy to electrical energy would occur if the fan were plugged into:

   A. a solar-powered generator

   B. a wind-powered generator

   C. a hydro-powered generator

   D. a fuel-powered generator

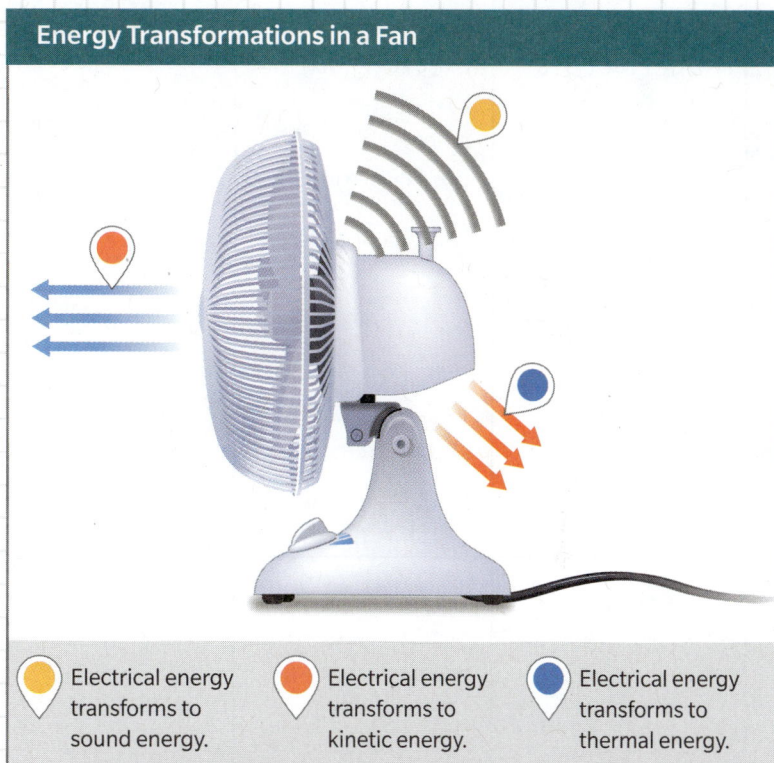

Energy Transformations in a Fan

Electrical energy transforms to sound energy.

Electrical energy transforms to kinetic energy.

Electrical energy transforms to thermal energy.

Use the photo to answer Questions 3 and 4.

3. Which processes are missing from this model of the water cycle? Select all that apply.

   A. sublimation

   B. transpiration

   C. evaporation

   D. precipitation

4. What labels would you add to this model to show how gravity drives water cycling between the Earth's surface and the atmosphere?

   A. evaporation on the surface of water

   B. precipitation falling from clouds to the water

   C. air current circulation

   D. ocean current circulation

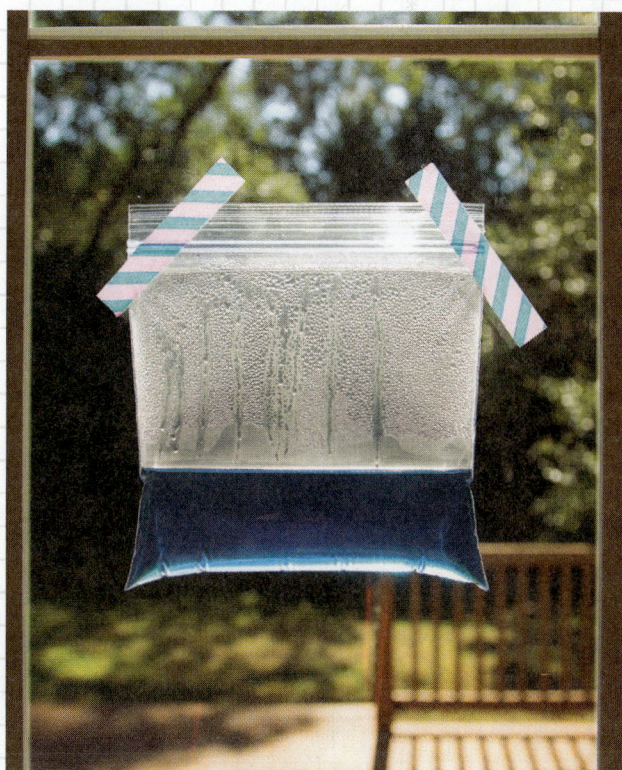

5. Complete the table by providing examples of how each system relates to each big-picture concept.

System	Forms of energy	Transfer of energy	Transformation of energy	Scale, proportio and quantity
Roller coaster	mechanical, kinetic, potential, electrical			
Diesel engine				
River				

Name: _____   Date: _____

Use the images of the fish tank and fish bowl to answer Questions 6–9.

6. Compare the thermal energy in each container if the water is the same temperature.

7. If you start with water at the same temperature in both containers without fish and add the same amount of ice to each tank, which container would cool more quickly?

8. Assume a heater is added to each container, again starting with water at the same temperature. How would the energy required to heat the containers to a new temperature differ? Explain your reasoning.

9. Suppose identical aquarium ornaments that are the same temperature, but warmer than the water, are added to each container. If the water in each container is originally the same temperature, which piece will cool more quickly? How would the overall change in water temperature differ between the two containers over time?

Use the body temperature graph to answer Questions 10–13.

Body Temperature vs. Ambient Temperature

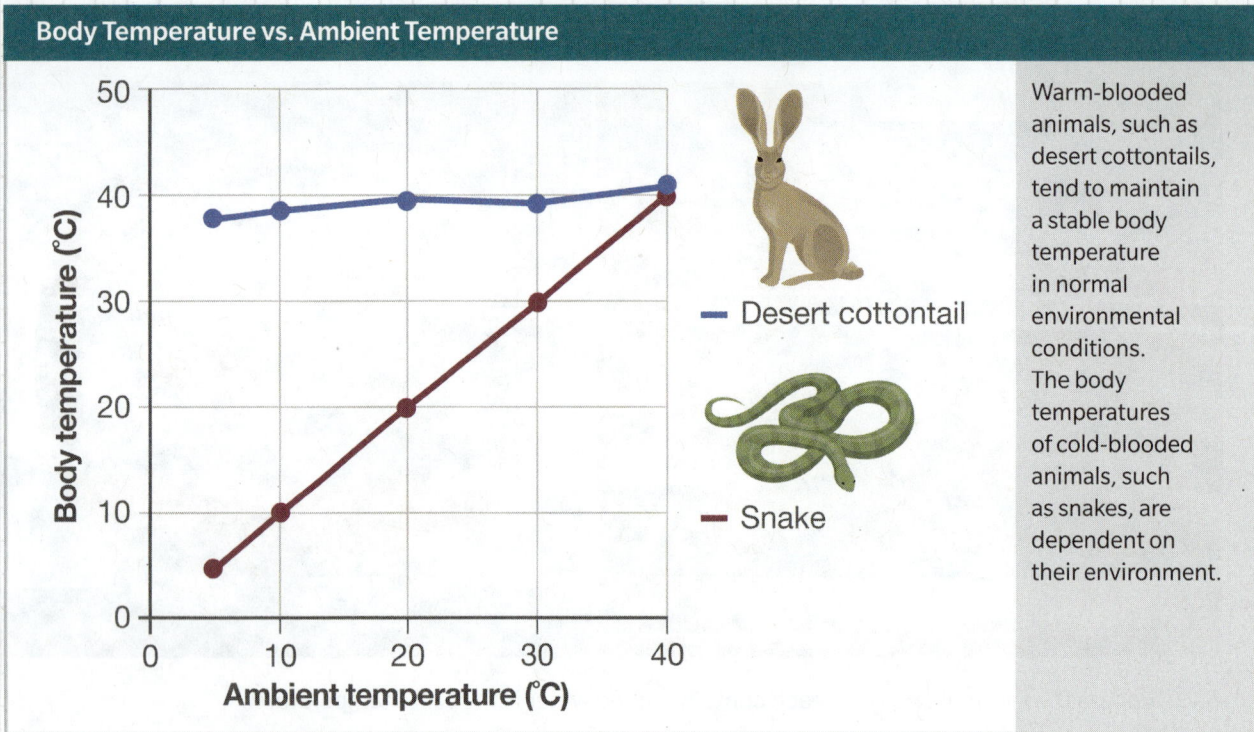

Desert cottontail

Snake

Warm-blooded animals, such as desert cottontails, tend to maintain a stable body temperature in normal environmental conditions. The body temperatures of cold-blooded animals, such as snakes, are dependent on their environment.

10. Describe the body temperatures of a desert cottontail and a snake compared to their surrounding (ambient) temperature.

11. When the snake's body temperature increases, where does the energy come from?

12. Snakes do not have an internal mechanism to regulate body temperature. How could a snake stay cool on a hot day?

13. Humans are able to maintain a nearly constant internal body temperature of about 37 °C even when it is very hot by perspiring. How does this process work to cool a person's body?

Name: _____   Date: _____

How can you cool water faster?

Hyperthermia, or heat stroke, is a life-threatening condition of elevated body temperature. Emergency medical providers know that the best way to treat people suffering from hyperthermia is to cool them very quickly by submerging them in cold water. This lifesaving process must be performed as quickly as possible to avoid deadly complications.

You are on a team of first responders tasked with developing a first aid station by the organizing committee of a local marathon. This first aid station will need to be prepared to treat runners suffering from hyperthermia. You will have large tubs of water available, along with two different forms of ice—crushed and cubed. Which type of ice should your team use to cool the tub of water as rapidly as possible? Prepare a report for the committee that includes your recommendation of which type of ice to use.

Crushed ice

Whole ice cubes

The steps below will help guide your research and recommend a solution.

Engineer It

1. **Define the Problem** What is the engineering problem you are trying to solve? Describe your criteria and constraints.

Engineer It

2. **Develop a Model** Prepare a diagram that shows how the transfer of energy occurs within the system. Describe how the problem could be modeled on a smaller scale for testing.

3. **Design an Investigation** Develop a procedure for testing the solutions to obtain measurable data. What could you use as your experimental control?

4. **Compare Solutions** Gather information from multiple sources about how to best treat hyperthermia. Consider possible biases in the sources. Describe how each type of ice would transfer thermal energy in a large water bath. What other factors might you need to consider when selecting the best solution?

5. **Identify and Recommend a Solution** Identify which type of ice to use at the first aid station, and share your recommendation with the organizing committee.

✓ **Self-Check**

	I defined the engineering problem, including the criteria and constraints.
	I developed a model representing the problem.
	I designed an investigation to meaningfully compare the solutions.
	I compared the solutions based on performance and other considerations.
	I identified and recommended a solution.

Weather and Climate

How do circulation of air and water affect weather and climate in California?

Unit Project 266
Lesson 1   Air Moves in Patterns in Earth's Atmosphere 268
Lesson 2   Water Moves in Patterns in Earth's Oceans 288
Lesson 3   Interactions in Earth's Systems Cause Weather 310
Lesson 4   Weather Predictions Are Based on Patterns 332
Lesson 5   Earth Has Different Regional Climates 350
Unit Review 373
Unit Performance Task 377

Foggy summer mornings in San Francisco happen as water from the Pacific Ocean evaporates into the air and then condenses. Wind carries the foggy air over land.

You Solve It **Can You Explain the Different Climate in Two California Cities?** Choose two cities for parks that will showcase different organisms and climates, and use data from maps to explain why the climate is different in the two locations.

Go online and complete the You Solve It to explore ways to solve a real-world problem.

Investigate Severe Weather

How does lightning form?
What comes first; thunder or lightning?
Can you see thunder and lightning?

What is the difference between thunder + lightning?
Where did this occur?
What type of storm?
Can lightning do good?
Is lightning predictable?
How far does it strike?
How strong is the electricity in each bolt?

Lightning can occur during thunderstorms, hurricanes, and heavy snowstorms.

A. Look at the photo. On a separate sheet of paper, write down as many different questions as you can about the photo.

B. Discuss With your class or a partner, share your questions. Record any additional questions generated in your discussion. Then choose the most important questions from the list that are related to severe weather. Write them below.

- How strong is the electricity in each bolt?
- Is lightning predictable?
- Can lightning cause power outages?
- How long does it last?

C. Choose a type of severe weather that you'd like to research. You will research one region affected by this type of severe weather.

D. Use the information above, along with your research, to develop a climate model and explain the causes of the severe weather you chose.

Discuss the next steps for your Unit Project with your teacher and go online to download the Unit Project Worksheet.

Language Development

Use the lessons in this unit to complete the network and expand your understanding of these key concepts.

■	Similar term
■	Phrase
■	Cognate
■	Example
■	Definition

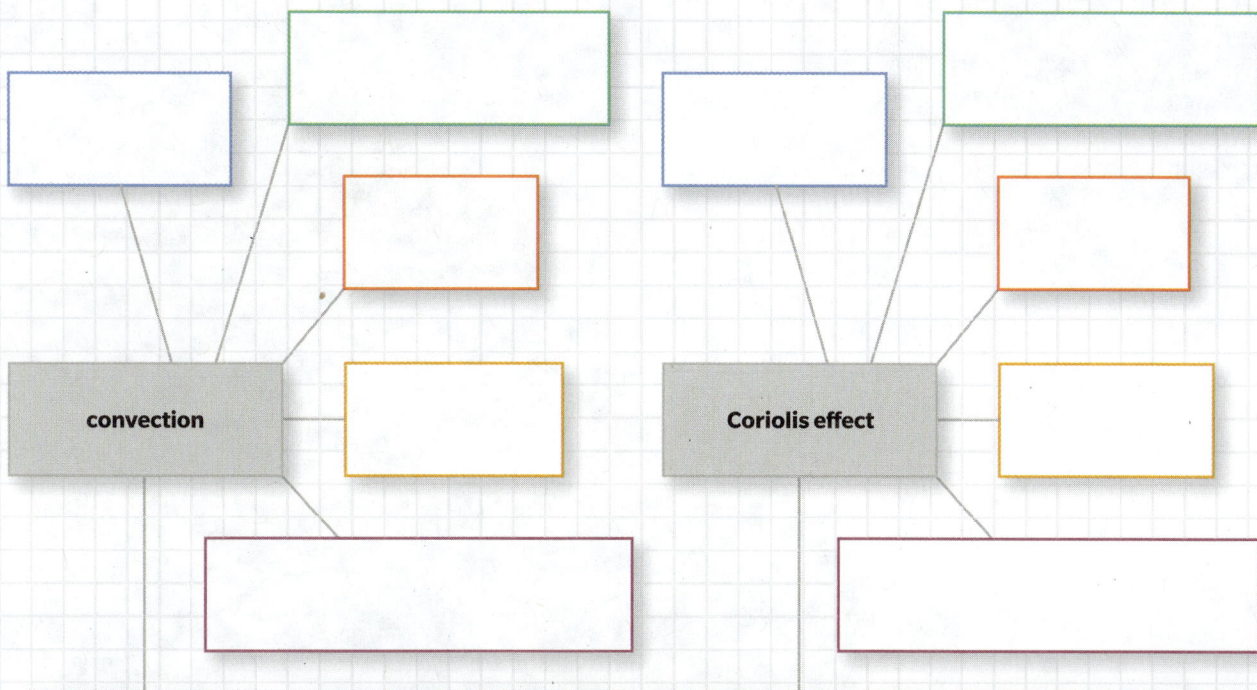

convection

Coriolis effect

How do circulation of air and water affect weather and climate in California?

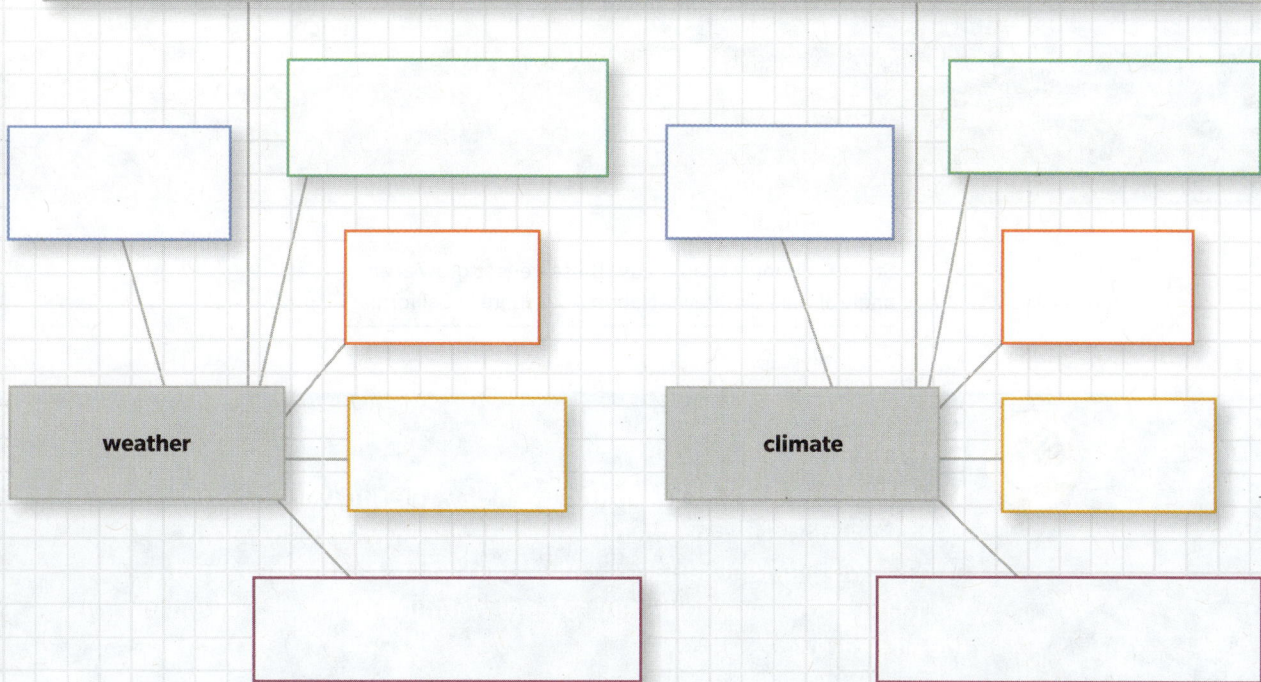

weather

climate

Air Moves in Patterns in Earth's Atmosphere

Strong continual winds cause these trees to grow at an angle at the Point Reyes National Seashore in California.

Explore First

Modeling the Rate of Warming Each day, the sun warms Earth. Develop a model to explore how quickly or slowly the sun warms at least two different surfaces. How could you measure the rate of warming? How might different rates of warming cause circulation in the air nearby?

CAN YOU EXPLAIN IT?

How is it possible for dust from the Sahara to end up in the Amazon?

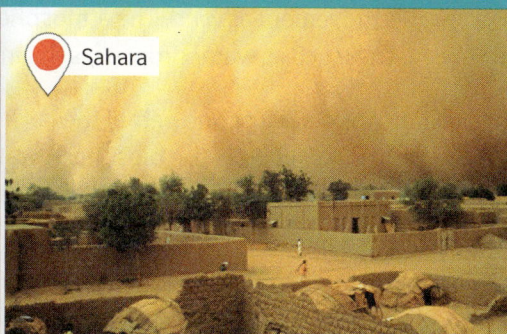

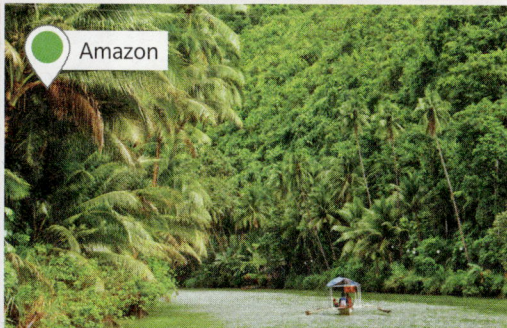

Sahara

Amazon

Scientists have discovered that about 22,000 tons of phosphorous is deposited in the Amazon every year. The strange thing is that the phosphorus comes from the Sahara! The middle of the Amazon in South America is more than 9,000 kilometers from the middle of the Sahara desert in Africa.

1. What explanation can you suggest for how dust from the Sahara can travel over 9,000 kilometers, across the ocean, and then settle in the Amazon jungle?

EVIDENCE NOTEBOOK As you explore the lesson, gather evidence to help explain how dust and other particles can travel so far.

Modeling Wind and Convection

The *atmosphere* is a mixture of gases that surrounds Earth. We often refer to this mixture of gases as *air*. Although you cannot see it, air is matter. Air moves from one place to another. We know this movement as *wind*. The atmosphere also contains small particles of liquid and solid matter, such as water droplets, ash, and ice.

2. **Discuss** The atmosphere is just one part of the larger Earth system. The Earth system also includes organisms in the biosphere, water in the hydrosphere, and rocks and minerals in the geosphere. Describe how the atmosphere interacts with other parts of the Earth system in each photo.

Winter winds in the Kronotsky Reserve, Russia

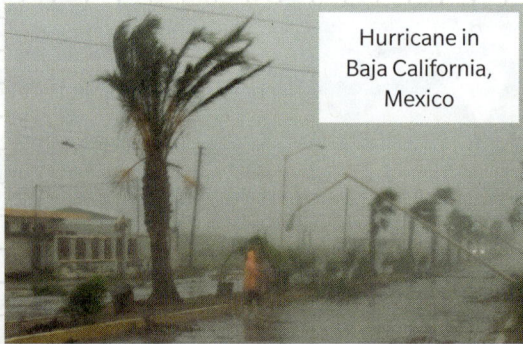

Hurricane in Baja California, Mexico

Wildfire in Santa Paula, California

Energy From the Sun and Wind

The sun emits energy that travels through space and enters the Earth system. Some of that energy can be seen as light, and some of it is invisible. Matter in the atmosphere and on Earth's surface absorbs, reflects, and transfers the sun's energy.

To understand why wind blows, you must first understand that Earth has temperature differences. Temperature differences occur because some areas receive more direct sunlight than others do. For example, the equator receives more direct sunlight than the poles, so the equator is generally warmer. Earth's temperatures also vary because some surfaces absorb more energy than others do. For example, the oceans absorb more solar energy than land does, and land absorbs more solar energy than air does. Surfaces also absorb and release energy at different rates. For example, land warms and cools faster than water does.

Convection

Cool, dense air sinks to Earth's surface and spreads out. As it spreads out, it pushes away warm, less dense air. This causes the warm air to rise. The cool air, now at the surface, begins to warm. The warm air that was pushed up begins to cool and become denser. If it becomes denser than the surrounding air, it sinks back toward the surface. This cycling of matter due to different densities is called **convection**.

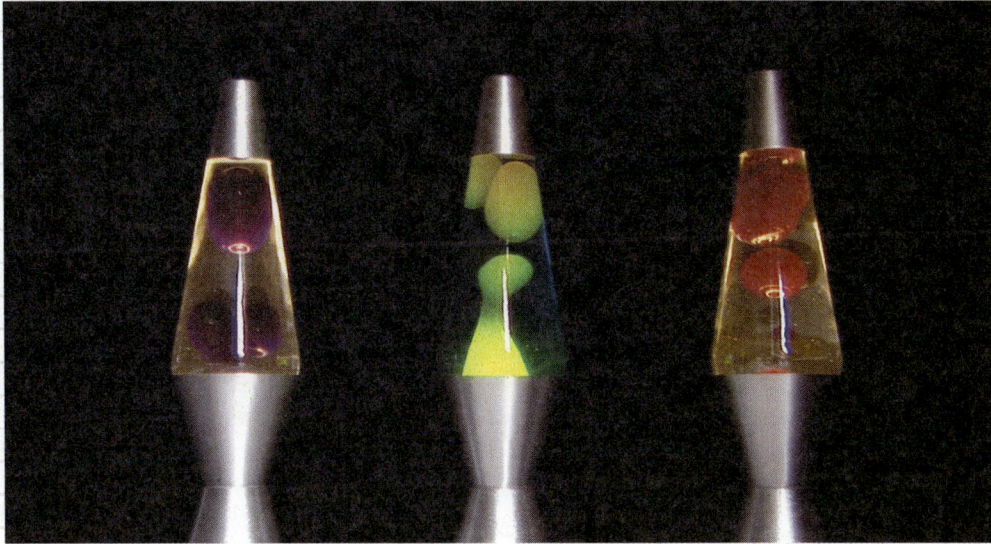

Explore Online

These lava lamps show convection. The colored wax at the bottom is warmed, becoming less dense. The more dense material surrounding the warm wax sinks. This pushes the wax up until it cools and becomes more dense than the surrounding material. The dense wax sinks.

4. Which statements about air in the atmosphere are true? For each statement, write T for "true" or F for "false."

   __F__ Warm air pushes cool air downward.

   __F__ Rising air cools and may become more dense than the air around it.

   __T__ Cool air pushes warm air upward.

   __T__ Air that is more dense than the air around it will sink.

5. **Engineer It** Modern houses have systems to control internal air temperatures in times of very cold or hot weather. In these homes, hot or cool air is pumped into the interior of the house to help keep the temperature comfortable. Based on what you know about how cool and warm air circulate in the atmosphere, what might an engineer need to consider when designing a heating/cooling system for a home in a cooler climate? How might the design differ for a house found in a warmer climate?

Convection Cells

Convection can occur on a large or small scale. Look at the air in the diagram. The air near the flame is warm and less dense than the air farther from it. The cool, denser air sinks and pushes the warm air upward. As the warm air moves upward, it loses energy to other air particles. As a result, the warm air becomes cooler and sinks. When the sinking air gets near the flame, it will become warm again. The process continues. This cyclic pattern of movement caused by density differences is called a *convection cell*. Large convection cells form in Earth's atmosphere because the sun heats Earth's surface unevenly.

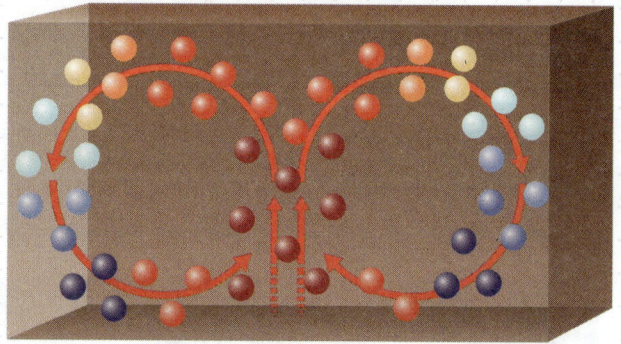

6. How does the density of air affect its movement in a convection cell?

   Colder and denser air sinks, making the warm air rise. Then the warm air gets denser, and colder. The cold air then becomes warm and gets less denser, causing it to rise. It is a cycle

7. **Act** Together as a group, act out the movement of air near a heat source. Assign roles to classmates, and have each participant explain what is happening to them as they move close to and away from a heat source.

Analyze Winds

Air, land, and water have different properties because they are made up of different materials. Land changes temperature more quickly than water does. Air changes temperature more quickly than either land or water. Air near the surface is warmed and cooled by being in contact with land or water at a different temperature.

8. Use the word bank to complete this paragraph and explain why the wind is blowing in the photo. You will only use some of the words in the word bank.

   When the sun shines on this area, the land warms _faster_ than the ocean. The air above the land becomes _warmer_ than the air above the water. The wind is blowing toward the _land_ because air generally moves from cooler, high-pressure areas toward warmer, low-pressure areas.

   WORD BANK
   - faster
   - slower
   - warmer
   - cooler
   - land
   - ocean

Explaining the Circulation of Air

Patterns of Air Circulation

Air moves in patterns in Earth's atmosphere. One reason for these patterns is the shape of Earth. Because Earth is spherical, the equator receives more energy from the sun than the north and south poles receive. This results in differences in temperature. Differences in temperature result in air pressure differences. Because air travels from high to low pressure, wind patterns result.

Earth's spin, or rotation, on its axis also affects the way that air moves across the planet's surface. The effects of Earth's rotation on the movement of air over long distances can be modeled. For example, explore the physical model shown in the photos below.

Model the Effects of Earth's Rotation on Matter in the Atmosphere

The photo at the left shows what happens to a drop of ink that is placed at the top of a stationary balloon. The photo at the right shows what happens to a drop of ink that is placed at the top of a rotating balloon. This balloon is being rotated clockwise the entire time that the ink runs down the balloon.

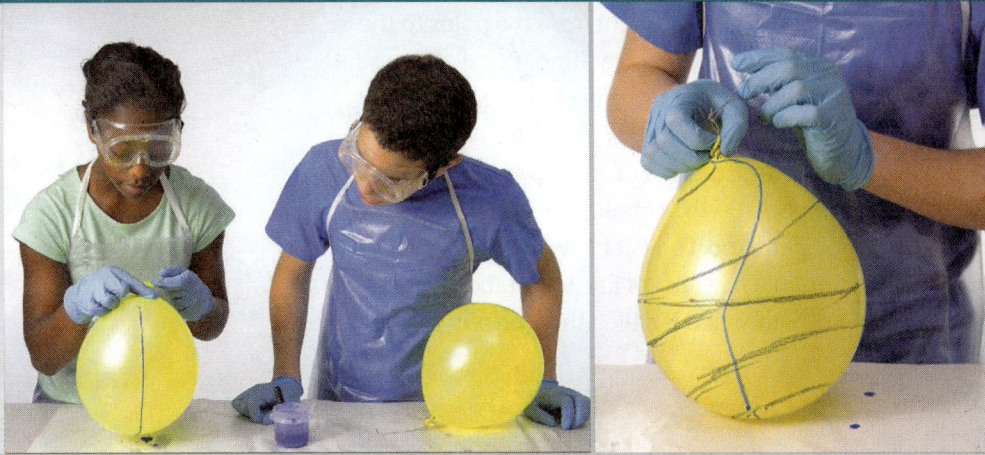

9. **Collaborate** With a partner, develop and use a different physical model to show how Earth's rotation affects matter in the atmosphere. Describe your model. What will you use to represent Earth? How will you model Earth's rotation? What will you use to represent matter in Earth's atmosphere? Before using your model, be sure it is approved by your teacher and you are wearing appropriate safety gear, such as gloves, goggles, and an apron.

Take a cake on a lazy suzan and drip ganache as it is spinning

10. **Language SmArts** Make a claim about how Earth's rotation affects matter in the atmosphere. Describe what evidence from your model supports your claim, and include a diagram or sketch.

If the wind is going straight, but the Earth is spinning, the wind will appear to curve, though it is just distributing itself into different places because of the Earth's movement.

If Earth Did Not Rotate

The sun warms the equator more than the poles. Because wind blows from cold, high-pressure areas to warm, low-pressure areas, surface winds would blow in a straight path from the poles to the equator. At the equator, the incoming cold air would push up warm air. The rising warm air would begin to cool as it flowed back toward the poles. By the time it reached the poles, it would be cold and dense enough to sink. As shown in the diagram, these motions would form two large convection cells between the equator and the poles.

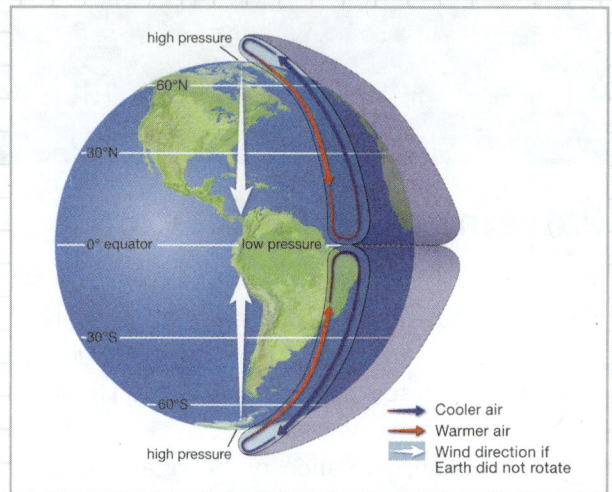

If Earth did not rotate, air would circulate in large convection cells between the poles and the equator.

The Effect of Earth's Rotation

Wind does not blow straight from the poles to the equator, because Earth is rotating. Recall the model of the rotating balloon. The ink followed a straight path when the balloon did not rotate. When the balloon rotated, the line of ink appeared to follow a curved path. Earth's rotation causes air to follow a curved path, too. Look at the white arrows on the diagram. The effect of Earth's rotation on the pathway of the wind is called the **Coriolis effect.**

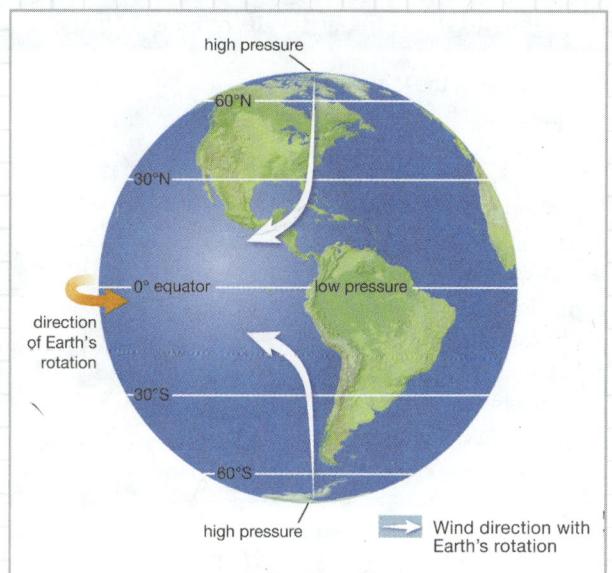

Earth's rotation causes air to deflect, or curve, away from a straight path.

The Formation of Global Wind Belts

Patterns of surface winds and convection cells change about every 30 degrees of latitude. The curving surface winds shown by the white arrows are part of the cycling air in the convection cells, shown by the red and blue arrows. Notice the bands of high and low pressure between the convection cells. Cooler, denser air sinks along bands of high pressure. Warmer, less dense air rises along bands of low pressure.

11. **Discuss** The diagram shows the result of the Coriolis effect. Compare it to the previous diagrams. Are these wind patterns what you expected? Why or why not?

yes they are because we did an experiment which proved it right. One thing rotates while one moves straight making it look like it's curving

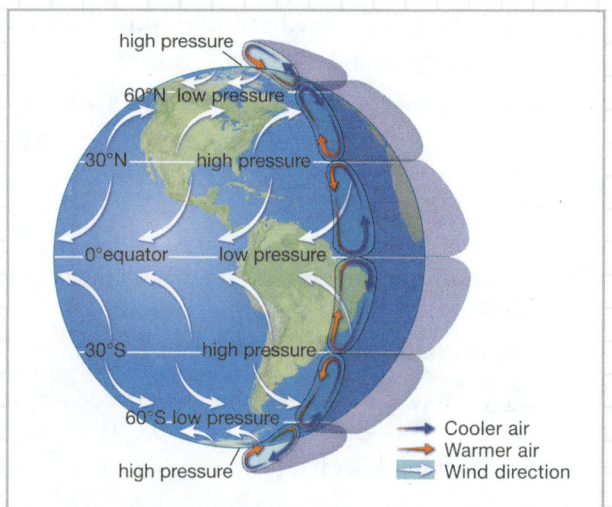

Because Earth rotates, there are global wind and pressure belts that change about every 30 degrees of latitude.

12. Use the diagram to explain how air the equator could eventually end up in North America. How would it change temperature along the way?

The cold air colides with warm air. As cold air enters a different hemisphere, the air temperature changes.

Global Wind Patterns

Why does the Coriolis effect result in patterns of air flow that change every 30° of latitude? Consider the white arrows showing surface winds flowing toward the low-pressure belt at the equator. This incoming cooler air pushes up the warmer air at the equator. The warm air rises, as you can see by the arrows in the two convection cells on either side of the equator. The rising air cools and begins to travel north or south. Once it reaches about 30°N or 30°S, the air is cooler and denser than the surrounding air. The air therefore sinks along 30°N and 30°S, forming high-pressure belts along these latitudes. From there, some air travels back toward the equator and some travels toward the low-pressure belts along 60°N and 60°S.

Model of Global Winds

Global winds blow in fairly consistent, steady directions across Earth. Each global wind belt has a specific name. Global winds are also known as *prevailing winds*.

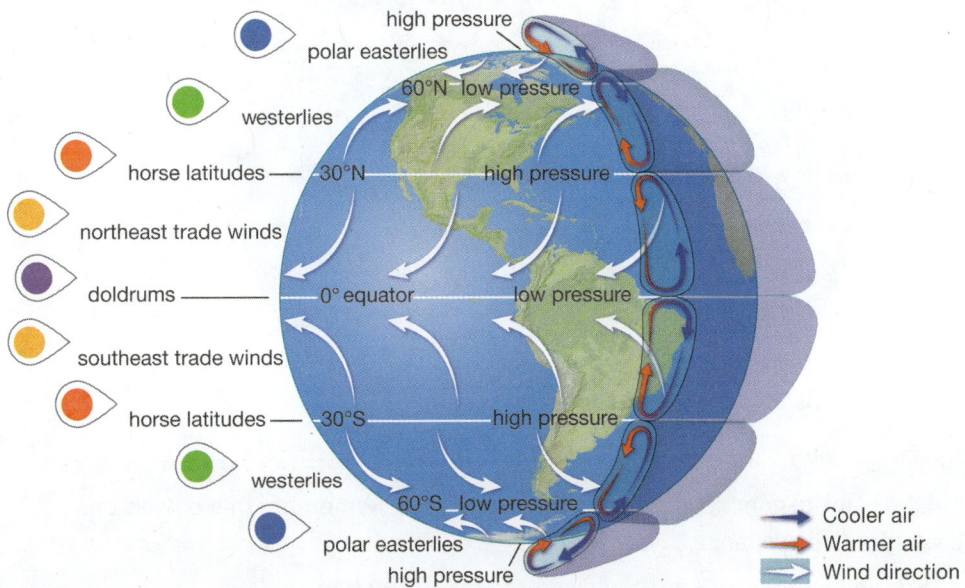

The cold *polar easterlies* blow from the northeast at the North Pole and from the southeast at the South Pole. They usually form at latitudes greater than 60°.

The *westerlies* are named for the direction from which they blow—from the west toward the east. They form between 30° and 60° latitude.

The *horse latitudes* are a narrow zone of warm, dry climates between the westerlies and the trade winds. Many deserts exist along the horse latitudes, which are found at about 30° north and south of the equator.

Warm *trade winds* blow constantly across the tropics from the east toward the west. The trade winds in the Northern Hemisphere are called the *northeast trade winds*, and those in the Southern Hemisphere are called the *southeast trade winds*. They are located between the equator and 30° latitude.

The *doldrums* are found where the trade winds of the two hemispheres meet. Winds in the doldrums are very weak, and the weather is consistently calm.

Do the Math
Compare the Hemispheres

Earth can be divided into *hemispheres,* or half spheres, in different ways. One way is to divide Earth at the equator. The Northern Hemisphere is from the equator to the North Pole, and the Southern Hemisphere is from the equator to the South Pole. Imaginary parallel lines measure north-south distances between the poles and the equator. The equator represents 0°, and the poles represent 90°N for the North Pole and 90°S for the South Pole. The distance between one of the poles and the equator is measured in 1° increments.

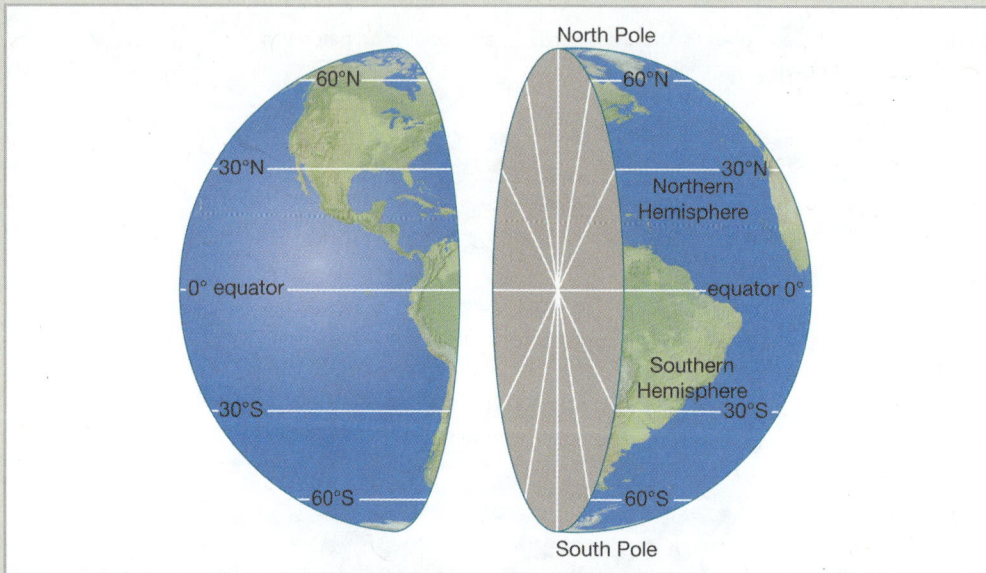

North Pole
60°N   60°N
30°N   30°N
Northern Hemisphere
0° equator   equator 0°
Southern Hemisphere
30°S   30°S
60°S   60°S
South Pole

The lines of latitude are named by the angle made by a line connecting the latitude and Earth's center and a line connecting the equator and Earth's center. The location of the latitude north or south of the equator is added to the angle to indicate its relative position on the globe.

14. Fill in the blank to complete each statement correctly. Remember that *equidistant* means "the same distance."

  A. 45°N and ___45___ °S are equidistant from the equator.

  B. ___78___ °N and 78°S are equidistant from the equator.

  C. 90°N and ___90___ °S are equidistant from the equator.

  D. ___15___ °N and 15°S are equidistant from the equator.

15. The city of Boulder, Colorado, in the United States, is about 40° north of the equator, and the city of San Carlos de Bariloche, in Argentina, is about 40° south of the equator. Which statement is generally true about the wind patterns of these two cities?

  A. Their prevailing winds blow in opposite directions.

  B. Their prevailing winds blow from east to west.

  C. Their prevailing winds blow from west to east.

Relating Air Circulation to the Earth System

When it is windy outside, you can feel the air blowing against you. You feel this because air is matter. You can not see the tiny particles of air around you, but they exist and move around due to differences in temperature and density. The average, organized motion of these tiny air particles results in wind.

Wind itself is moving matter, and wind moves matter around Earth. This includes invisible matter, such as gases and microscopic bacteria. Wind also moves visible matter, such as dust, clouds, and seeds. Wind also transfers energy and affects weather patterns.

The Witch Fire destroyed over one thousand buildings and almost two-hundred thousand acres of land in San Diego County in 2007.

16. The Witch Fire occurred when dry, high-speed winds were blowing through San Diego County. These winds, called the *Santa Ana winds*, can affect Southern California in the fall and winter. The winds are warm and sometimes are even described as hot. Why might the Santa Ana winds be related to high wildfire risk?

The hot air can dry the vegetation which will brush together. This will cause sparks, and eventually, wildfires

The Cycling of Matter in the Atmosphere

Wind can pick up matter from one place and deposit it in another place. Small particles, such as the tiny water particles in clouds, can be easily moved by wind. So can lightweight matter, such as ash and feathers. Larger or heavier matter can be transported by strong winds, such as the winds generated by tornadoes and hurricanes. These movements are part of the constant cycling of matter through the Earth system.

17. Discuss With a partner, make a list of all of the factors that might determine how far something is carried by wind. Compare your list with other pairs' lists.

     -sediment -dust -ash -fine particles

Wind can move large amounts of sediment in a short time.

Sediment, Dust, and Ash Eriana

Wind picks up dust and other sediment from the ground. Large volcanic eruptions can send ash many kilometers into the atmosphere. Global winds can spread the ash around Earth. Ash and dust in the atmosphere reflect some of the sun's incoming rays. This is why some large eruptions result in a temporary drop in the average global temperature.

Water Kaela

The atmosphere contains a lot of water. Water vapor enters the atmosphere from Earth's surface. Then, water in the atmosphere is carried by wind from one place to another, often hundreds of kilometers. Water falling from clouds in the form of precipitation soaks into soil and forms rivers and lakes. Organisms depend on this water to live. Water cycles constantly through these parts of the Earth system.

Organic Matter Maanasi

The atmosphere is also part of the cycling of organic materials. For example, winds can carry pollen, seeds, bacteria, and even insects. Animals, such as birds, bats, and butterflies, depend on prevailing winds to migrate.

Carbon, Nitrogen, and Phosphorus Lavanya

Other important substances that are cycled in the atmosphere are carbon, nitrogen, and phosphorus. Plants use carbon in the form of carbon dioxide during photosynthesis. You and other organisms release carbon dioxide during cellular respiration. Carbon dioxide enters the atmosphere when fossil fuels burn and when volcanoes erupt. Nitrogen is also released into the atmosphere when fossil fuels burn, during industrial processes, and when bacteria break down organic matter. Plants use nitrogen to make proteins. Animals use proteins to build body structures. Living organisms also contain the element phosphorus. As organisms excrete waste or die and decompose, phosphorous is released into soil and water. Water and wind can help cycle phosphorous through the Earth system.

> **EVIDENCE NOTEBOOK**
>
> **18.** How might the cycling of matter in Earth's atmosphere relate to dust traveling from the Sahara to the Amazon? Record your evidence.

The Flow of Energy in the Atmosphere

Matter is not the only thing that flows through Earth's atmosphere. Energy also flows through Earth's atmosphere and into, through, and out of Earth's subsystems.

The Transfer of Thermal Energy

The temperature of air is related to the random, disorganized motion of its particles. Air particles move more when air is hot and less when air is cold. *Thermal energy* is the energy something has due to the motion of its particles. A hot object has more thermal energy than a cold object does. As warm air cools, its thermal energy decreases.

The sun's energy travels in waves through space in a process called *radiation*. When the sun's energy is absorbed by Earth's surface, the surface becomes warmer than the air above it. The surface's thermal energy increases. When air particles and surface particles touch, thermal energy is transferred from the warmer surface particles to the cooler air particles. The energy transfer that happens when particles touch is called *conduction*. As air warms, its particles move farther apart. The air becomes less dense. The warmer, less dense air may rise if cooler, denser air flows in and pushes up the warm air. The flow of air due to differences in density is an example of convection. *Convection* is the transfer of energy due to the movement of matter.

Energy from the Sun and Energy Transfer

Radiation
Some radiation from the sun warms the atmosphere and some passes through it to warm the ground, water, and human-made structures.

Conduction
Thermal energy can be transferred to and from the atmosphere by conduction when air comes in contact with materials warmed by the sun.

Convection
Land warms faster than water does. As a result, the air over the water is cooler than the air over land. Convection transfers energy as the cool air flows toward land and causes warm air to rise.

The Transfer of Kinetic Energy

In addition to transfers of thermal energy in the Earth system, there are transfers of kinetic energy. *Kinetic energy* is the energy of motion. For example, the kinetic energy of wind is transferred to ocean water as wind forms waves. Waves help drive ocean surface currents. The kinetic energy of the wind also moves solid material, such as the sand in deserts. Therefore, over time, wind can shape Earth's surface.

19. How might the transfer of thermal energy and of kinetic energy by wind affect water molecules on Earth's surface and in the atmosphere?

   They can start to heat and move in different speeds

Case Study: The Santa Ana Winds

The Santa Ana winds are dry, warm winds that can blow at high-speeds through Southern California during the fall and winter. The winds can form when there is an area of cold, high-pressure air around the Great Basin, and an area of warm, low-pressure air near Southern California. The high-pressure air travels quickly toward the low-pressure air. Elevation decreases along the way, causing the winds to become drier. Wind speeds increase as the air travels through narrow canyons and valleys. The Santa Ana winds eventually reach Southern California, where they can damage trees and structures, dry out vegetation, and worsen the effects of wildfires.

Formation of the Santa Ana Winds

A cold mass of high-pressure air can form over the Great Basin during the fall and winter. If there is an area of low-pressure air off the coast of Southern California at the same time, the Santa Ana winds form, following the route shown by the arrows in this diagram.

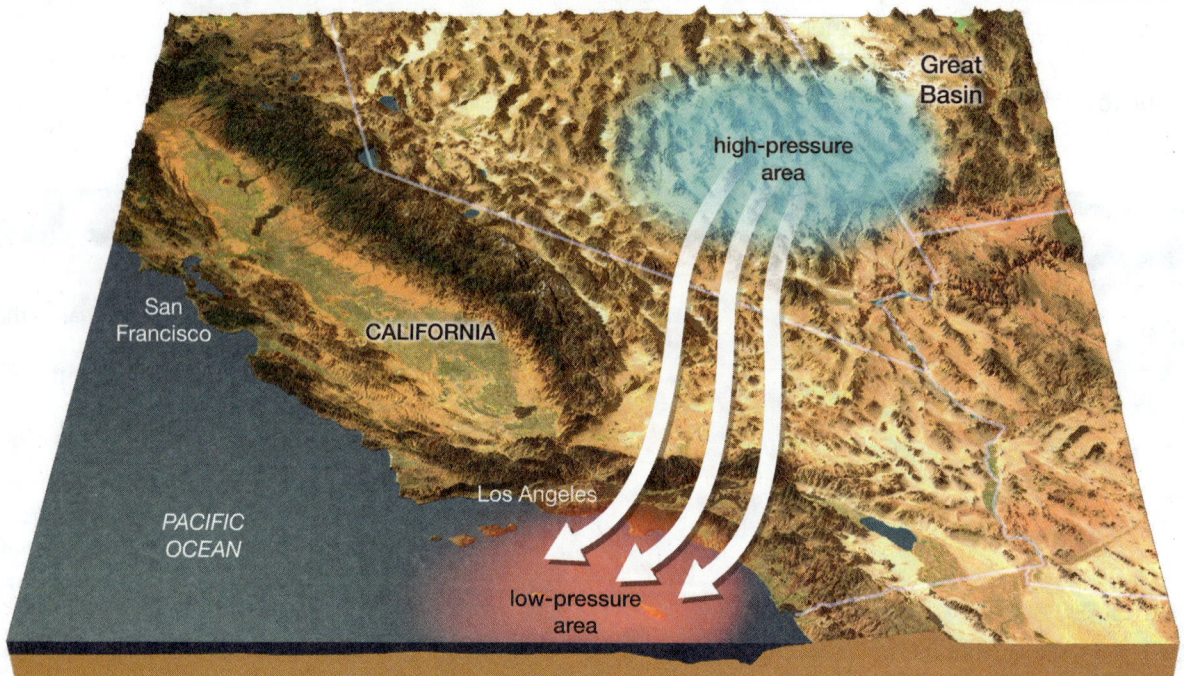

Explain the Santa Ana Winds

20. The atmosphere is interacting with the *geosphere / hydrosphere* as the Santa Ana Winds flow through canyons and valleys. These winds can cause fires to spread and burn vegetation in the *geosphere / biosphere*.

21. Language SmArts Think again about the Witch Fire in San Diego county. Explain how the Santa Ana winds can worsen the effects of wildfires like the Witch Fire. Use evidence from the diagram and the text to support your explanation.

_____

_____

_____

_____

_____

Continue Your Exploration

Name: _____   Date: _____

Check out the path below or go online to choose one of the other paths shown.

Jet Streams

- **People in Science**
- **Farming for Energy**
- **Hands-On Labs** ✋
- **Propose Your Own Path**

Go online to choose one of these other paths.

A *jet stream* is a narrow belt of fast-moving wind that forms several kilometers high in the atmosphere. Jet streams flow from west to east because of Earth's rotation. They travel at least 92 kilometers per hour (km/h) and sometimes up to 450 km/h.

Jet streams flow above the boundaries between warm and cool air. The greater the temperature difference between the bodies of air, the faster the jet stream will travel. Temperature differences are usually greater in the winter, so jet streams are strongest during this season. The locations of jet streams are also affected by the position of the sun during different seasons. For example, in the summer in the Northern Hemisphere, the temperature boundaries are farther north, so the jet stream is farther north. In the winter, the cold air moves farther south, so the jet stream is farther south.

Jet streams are above the surface winds you can feel near the ground. Even though jet streams do not flow along Earth's surface, they do affect you. Jet streams influence weather patterns. In the diagram you can see some of Earth's major jet streams.

1. Jet streams flow several kilometers above the surface where airplanes can fly. Therefore, the length of an airplane trip could be affected if the airplane traveled along a jet stream. For example, an airplane trip from Las Vegas to Orlando would be faster / slower than a trip from Orlando to Las Vegas if the jet stream moved over these cities.

Jet Streams

Both the Northern Hemisphere and the Southern Hemisphere have two main kinds of jet streams. The polar jet stream travels between 50° to 60° north or south of the equator. The subtropical jet stream is closer to the equator.

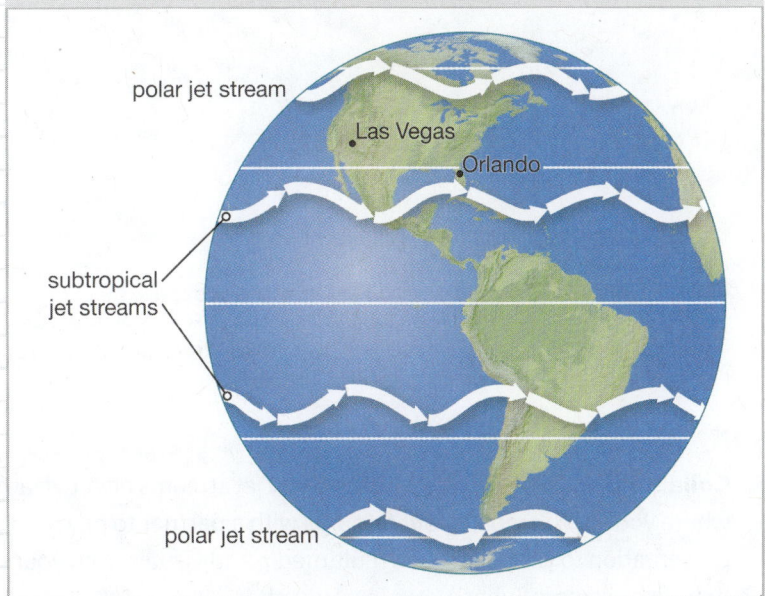

polar jet stream
Las Vegas
Orlando
subtropical jet streams
polar jet stream

Continue Your Exploration

2. Use evidence from the diagram to explain why the airplane trip is faster one way.

3. Would this airplane trip always be faster one way? Explain why or why not.

4. Explain why no jet stream exists at the equator.

5. Collaborate Do research to find out how jet streams affect weather patterns where you live. Compare your findings with a partner to plan and deliver an oral presentation to your class. Use multimedia and visuals from your research to explain how jet streams influence your local weather.

Can You Explain It?

Name: _____   Date: _____

How is it possible for dust from the Sahara to end up in the Amazon?

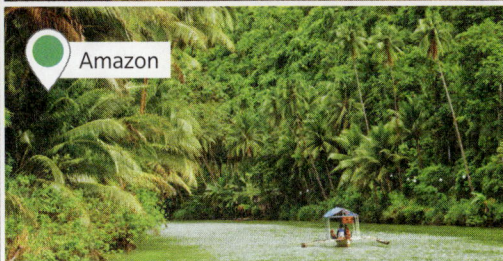

Sahara

Amazon

EVIDENCE NOTEBOOK

Refer to the notes in your Evidence Notebook to help you construct an explanation as to how it is possible for dust from the Sahara to end up in the Amazon.

1. State your claim. Make sure your claim fully explains how material from the Sahara ended up in the Amazon.

2. Summarize the evidence you have gathered to support your claim and explain your reasoning.

Checkpoints

Answer the following questions to check your understanding of the lesson.

Use the illustration to answer Questions 3–5.

3. Which of the following is a characteristic of all global winds?

   A. They all move from areas of high pressure to areas of low pressure.

   B. They all move from areas of low pressure to areas of high pressure.

   C. They all move in the same direction toward the equator.

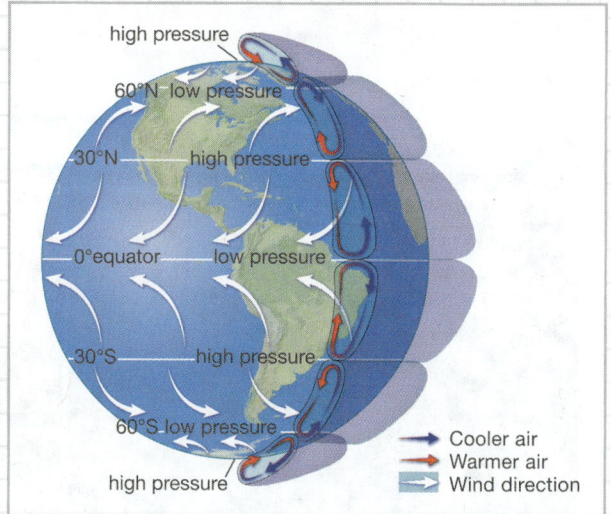

4. Which factors have the greatest impact on the direction of global winds? Choose one.

   A. air speed and the amount of daylight

   B. rotation of Earth and pressure differences

   C. length of the day and temperature of the air

   D. distance from the horse latitudes and size of the sun

5. Many dry desert climates are found around 30° N and 30° S latitude. Which factor has the most influence on the formation of desert climates?

   A. dry air rising at 30° latitudes

   B. dry air descending at 30° latitudes

   C. low amounts of rainfall at other latitudes

   D. high rates of evaporation at the equator

Use the illustration to answer Questions 6 and 7.

6. The sun warms the dark-colored road faster than the surrounding fields. Order the statements from 1–4 to describe what happens next.

   _____ The warm air above the road rises and loses energy as it cools.

   _____ The air above the road becomes warmer and less dense than the air above the fields.

   _____ The denser, cooler air over the fields sinks and flows toward the road.

   _____ The denser, cooler air sinks back down to Earth's surface.

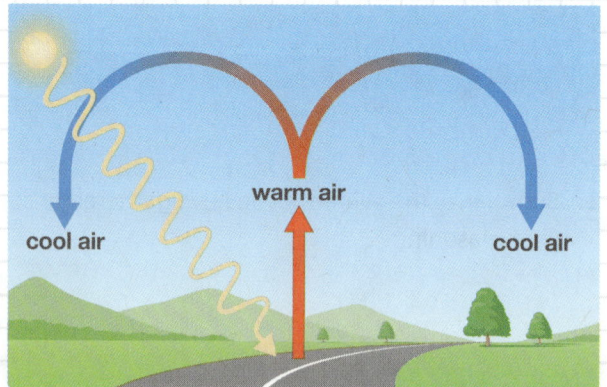

7. The red and blue arrows in the diagram represent the transfer of thermal energy by the process of *conduction / convection / radiation*.

Interactive Review

Complete this section to review the main concepts of the lesson.

Wind forms when air moves from an area of high pressure to an area of low pressure.

A. Draw a convection cell and label the source of thermal energy, the air temperature and density, and the directions of air flow.

The unequal heating of Earth's surface by the sun and deflection caused by the Coriolis effect cause distinct patterns of global winds.

B. On a large scale, what causes winds to move east and west in patterns across Earth's surface?

Circulation in Earth's atmosphere moves air around the planet and plays a role in the cycling of matter and the flow of energy in the Earth system.

C. How does wind transfer thermal and kinetic energy?

Water Moves in Patterns in Earth's Oceans

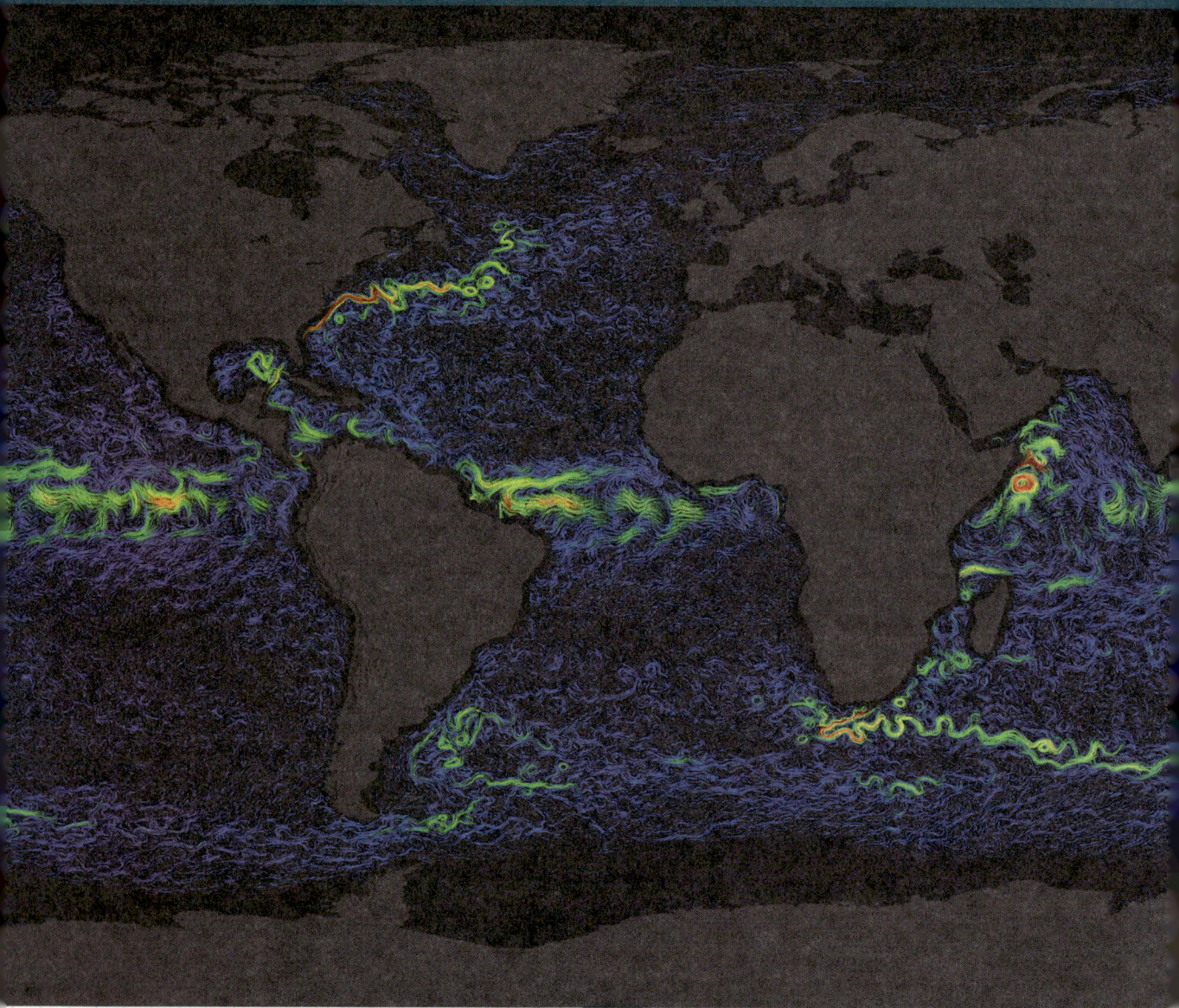

Scientists used satellite data to construct this map of ocean surface currents. Red and yellow represent faster currents. Green and blue represent slower currents.

Explore First

Determining Density When an object is less dense than water, it will float, but if the object is more dense, it will sink. Fill one plastic tub with salty water, and one with fresh water. Test five different objects to see if they sink or float in each tub. Does water's salinity affect whether each object sinks or floats? What is the relationship between the salinity and density of water?

CAN YOU EXPLAIN IT?

Why does floating garbage tend to build up in certain places in the ocean?

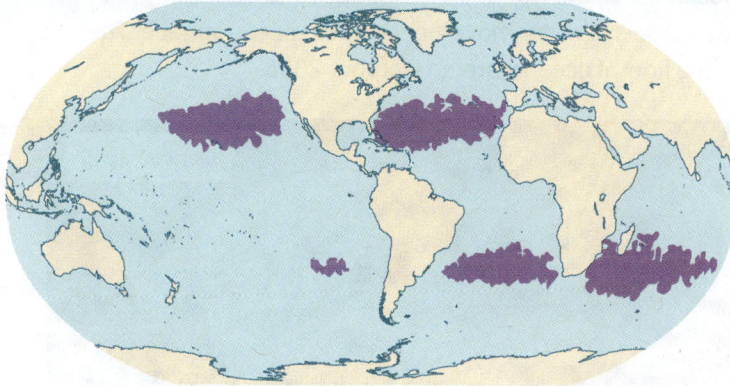

km 0   4,000

mi 0   2,000   4,000

Model shows predicted accumulation of floating garbage 10 years after release

Credit: Adapted from "Origin, dynamics and evolution of ocean garbage patches from observed surface drifters, Figure 1 (c) Tracer accumulation factor after 10 years, doi:10.1088/1748-9326/7/4/044040" from Environmental Research Letters, Volume 7 by Erik van Sebille et. al. Copyright © 2012 IOP Publishing Ltd. CC BY-NC-SA. Adapted and reproduced by permission of Erik van Sebille and IOP Publishing Ltd.

Have you ever wondered what happens when someone throws trash such as a plastic bottle into the ocean? This map shows where floating garbage is likely to collect. The purple areas show where floating garbage is most likely to be found ten years after it is dumped into the ocean.

1. What explanation can you suggest for how floating garbage could be moved around in the ocean?

2. What might cause floating objects to collect in one area in a body of water?

EVIDENCE NOTEBOOK As you explore the lesson, gather evidence to help explain how floating garbage could build up in certain areas of the ocean.

Patterns in the Ocean

Using satellite data about ocean water, the National Aeronautics and Space Administration (NASA) made models of water movements on the ocean surface. The white lines in the map show the flow of ocean water in October 2005.

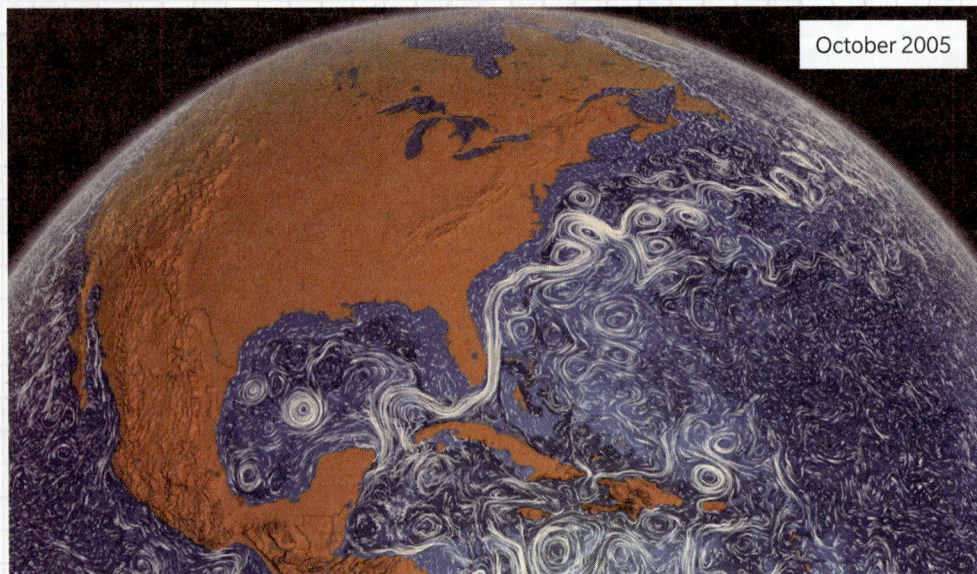

October 2005

Explore Online

3. What patterns do you see in the movement of the ocean surface?

4. Why do you think there is so much movement in the ocean?

The Formation of Surface Currents

When you look out over the ocean, you might see floating objects being carried along by the movement of water. Although it may be hard to see ocean water moving, it flows in regular patterns. The streamlike movement of ocean water in a regular pattern is called an **ocean current.** As you can see in the map, some ocean currents flow at or near the ocean's surface. This horizontal movement of water in a regular pattern at the ocean's surface is called a *surface current*.

km 0 2,000 4,000

mi 0 2,000 4,000

← Ocean surface wind direction

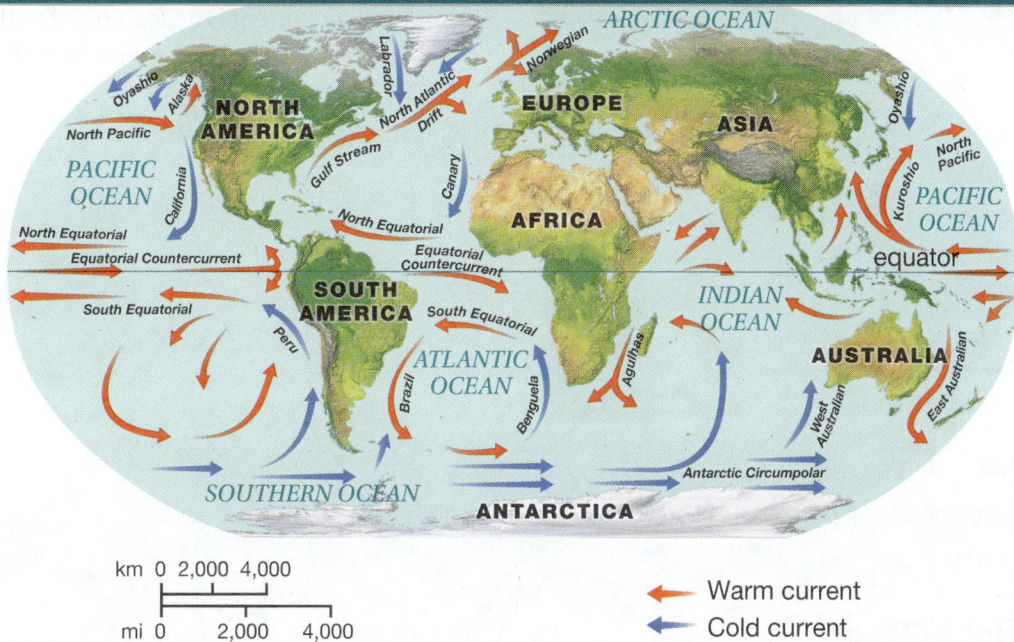

km 0 2,000 4,000

mi 0 2,000 4,000

← Warm current
← Cold current

5. What patterns do you see when comparing the global surface winds with the global surface currents in these maps?

   A. In most areas, the winds and the currents move in opposite directions.

   B. In most areas, the winds and the currents move in similar directions.

6. More of the sun's energy is received near the equator than near the poles. This uneven warming causes _____ differences in the atmosphere. The pressure differences cause _____. As wind blows, energy is transferred from the wind to the ocean. The energy transfer causes the water to move in surface ocean _____.

WORD BANK
• currents
• pressure
• wind

Factors That Affect Surface Currents

Surface currents in Earth's oceans are influenced by three factors: global winds, the locations of the continents, and Earth's rotation, which causes the Coriolis effect. These factors keep surface currents flowing in distinct patterns around Earth.

Global Winds

Surface winds cause surface currents by transferring kinetic energy to ocean water. Think about what happens if you blow across the surface of a liquid in a cup. The transfer of energy from your breath to the liquid causes liquid to move across the cup. In a similar way, winds that blow across the oceans cause ocean water to move, forming surface currents. The currents generally flow in the same direction as the winds.

Continents

As you can see in the map, when surface currents reach continents, the currents change direction. *Continental deflection* refers to the change in the direction of currents as they meet continents. For example, when the Peru Current reaches the coast of South America, it is deflected toward the west.

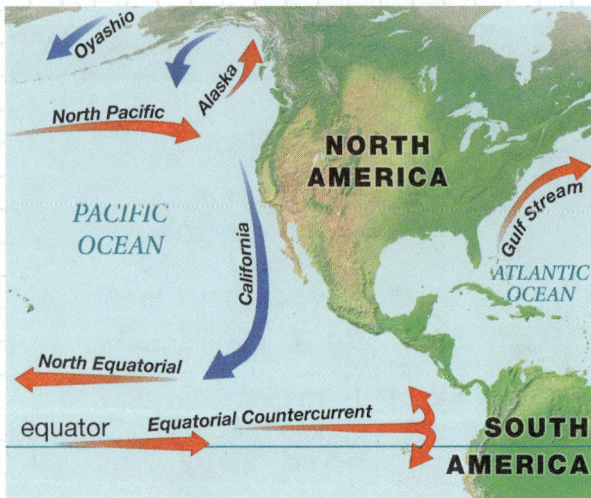

Warm current
Cold current

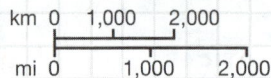

km 0 1,000 2,000
mi 0 1,000 2,000

7. The California Current travels *south / north / west* from where the North Pacific Current is deflected by North America. The California current eventually turns toward the *south / north / west* and joins the North Equatorial Current.

The Coriolis Effect

Earth's surface currents flow in huge circular patterns, called *gyres* (JYRZ). One reason for this circular flow is the rotation of Earth on its axis. Earth's circumference at the equator is larger than its circumference near the poles. So, points near the equator travel faster than points closer to the poles travel. As matter, such as a mass of air, moves from a pole toward the equator, the matter moves more slowly than the ground beneath it does. As a result, winds and water traveling south from the North Pole deflect in a clockwise direction to the right. And winds and water traveling from the South Pole deflect in a counterclockwise direction to the left. This deflection of moving objects from a straight path as a result of Earth's rotation is called the *Coriolis effect*. The Coriolis effect is only noticeable for objects that travel over long distances, such as Earth's wind and water. The Coriolis effect causes water to drift inward a bit toward the center of the gyres.

Surface Currents

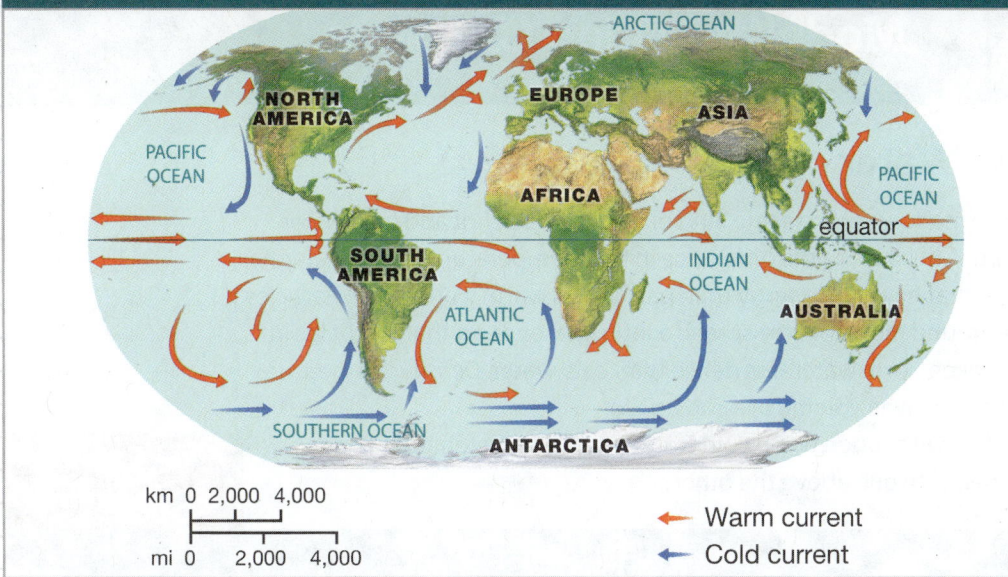

Warm current
Cold current

km 0 2,000 4,000
mi 0 2,000 4,000

8. What do you notice on the map about the pattern of the gyres in the Northern Hemisphere as compared to the gyres in the Southern Hemisphere?

EVIDENCE NOTEBOOK

9. Think about how ocean surface currents could affect floating garbage. Record your evidence.

Explain Sea Surface Temperatures

Scientists use infrared and microwave sensors to gather sea surface temperature data. From these data, they make color-enhanced maps that help them study ocean surface currents.

10. The sea surface temperature at the point labeled *east* is _____. The sea surface temperature at the point labeled *west* is _____.

11. The points *east* and *west* are at the same latitude, so they receive about the same amount of solar energy. Explain why points *east* and *west* have different ocean temperatures.

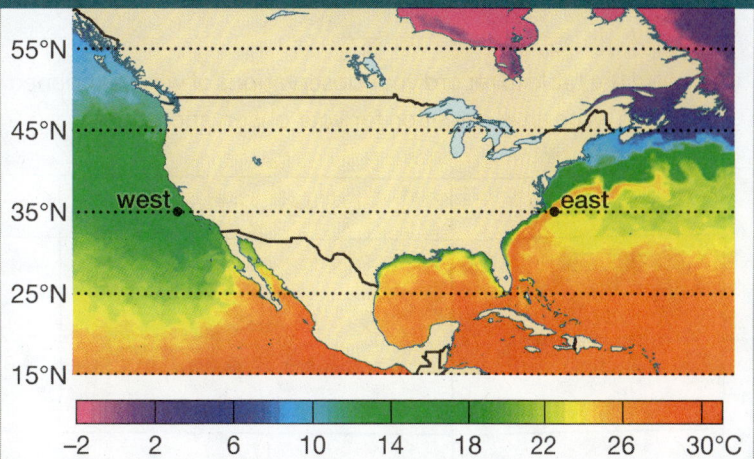

Sea Surface Temperature

−2   2   6   10   14   18   22   26   30°C

Source: National Oceanic and Atmospheric Administration, 2015

Modeling Deep Currents

Hot and Cold Water

Hot and cold water are made up of the same kind of particles. But hot and cold water have different properties because of the difference in their temperatures. Cold water has slow-moving particles that have less energy than particles in warm water have. Particles in warm water move around more and are spread a little farther apart than particles in cold water are. This makes warm water less dense than cold water. *Density* is a measure of the amount of mass in a given volume of a substance.

What do you think will happen when cold water and warm water are put in contact with each other, with one above the other?

Explore Online

Before	After
The blue water is cold. The red water is warm. Bottles of water at different temperatures are placed on top of each other with a plastic card separating the warm water from the cold. The plastic cards are removed from between the bottles. The cold and warm water come into contact.	This shows the same bottles a few minutes after the plastic cards were removed.

12. Use the table to record your observations of what happened in each pair of bottles. Then write an explanation for your observations.

Experiment	Observations	Possible Explanation
cold ⁄ warm		
warm ⁄ cold		

Hands-On Lab
Explore Density Differences in Water

Design and carry out an investigation to see why sometimes water moves relative to water nearby, and sometimes it does not. Test water at different temperatures and salinities. *Salinity* is a measure of the amount of salt in water.

Density can be measured in the units of kilograms per meter cubed (kg/m^3). Fresh water has a density of about 1000 kg/m^3. Density can be used to predict whether items will float or sink in water. For example, if a piece of metal has a greater density than that of water, the metal will sink in water. In gases and liquids, matter that is more dense than the matter that surrounds it will sink toward Earth's center.

Food coloring was added to the water in these bags.

Procedure and Analysis

STEP 1 Look at the photo. You can test how differences in temperature and salinity affect water's movement by putting your water samples in a zipper bag. Seal the bag so that there are no bubbles left in the bag. It is okay if a little water spills out of the bag as you are sealing it. Then gently place the bag in a large container of water and see where your bag comes to rest.

STEP 2 Write a plan for investigating the relationships of temperature and salinity to the density of water.

STEP 3 On a separate sheet of paper, design a table like the sample table shown or use another method to record data from your investigation.

Sample	Water Temperature	Amount of Salt Added	Results

STEP 4 Carry out your investigation and collect data.

STEP 5 What patterns do you see in your results?

STEP 6 Use what you learned in this activity to draw conclusions about the effects of temperature and salinity on the density of ocean water. State your conclusions. Summarize your evidence and explain your reasoning.

STEP 7 How might your conclusions relate to the movement of ocean water?

The Density of Ocean Water

Ocean water is not all the same. The density of ocean water changes when its temperature or salinity changes. Differences in density affect how ocean water circulates. Denser ocean water sinks and pushes up less dense water.

If you have ever accidentally swallowed some ocean water, you would say it is pretty salty. One way to express this saltiness, or salinity, is the number of grams of salt dissolved in one liter of water, or g/L. The average salinity of all the oceans is about 35 g/L, but ocean water has a range of salinities. The higher the salinity of ocean water is, the more dense it is.

The temperature of ocean water varies as well. The colder the ocean water is, the more dense it is. In polar regions, ocean temperature near the surface can be as cold as −1.9 °C. Near the equator, water temperature near the surface can be as high as 30 °C.

Analyze Water Density Data

Analyzing data in graphs can help you see patterns and discover relationships between variables. In each of the graphs below, one variable is held constant so that you can investigate the relationship between two other variables.

The Density of Water at 0 g/L Salinity

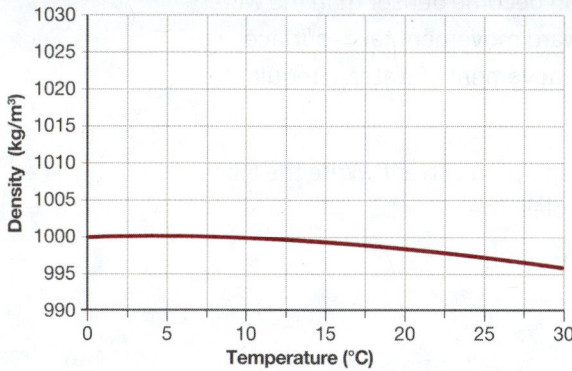

This graph shows how the density of fresh water changes as its temperature changes.

13. Water at a temperature of 10 °C has a density of about _____.

14. Water at a temperature of 25 °C has a higher / lower density than water at 10 °C does. As the temperature increases from 15 °C to 30 °C, the density of water decreases / increases.

The Density of Water at 20 °C

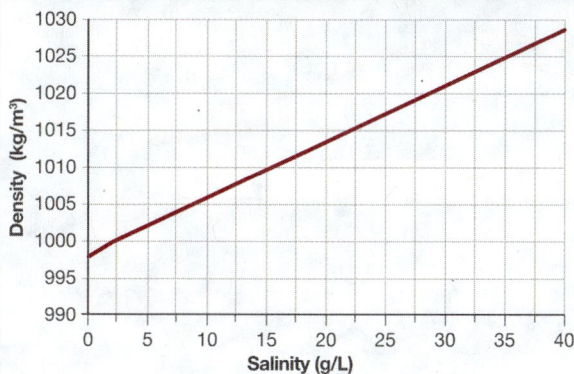

This graph shows how the density of water at 20 °C changes as its salinity changes.

15. Water with a salinity of 20 g/L has a density of _____.

16. Water with a salinity of 34 g/L has a higher / lower density than water with a salinity of 20 g/L does. As the salinity increases from 0 g/L to 40 g/L, the density of water decreases / increases.

Changes in Temperature

Temperature changes happen when ocean water absorbs or releases energy. The sun warms ocean water near the surface. When air above the ocean is at a different temperature than the water, energy is transferred and temperature changes result. Ocean water also changes temperature where ice melts and rivers flow into the ocean.

Changes in Salinity

The salinity of ocean water changes when fresh water is added or removed. For example, when rain falls into the ocean, fresh water is added, and the water's salinity decreases. During evaporation, liquid water changes to water vapor that enters the air, but dissolved particles, such as salts, remain behind. Ocean water's salinity increases during evaporation. When ocean water freezes, dissolved particles are left in the liquid part of the water, and the water's salinity increases.

17. When rivers flow into the ocean, the salinity of the ocean water
increases / decreases because the river adds salt / fresh water.

In an area of the ocean where a lot of evaporation but little precipitation happens, the salinity of the water is likely to increase / decrease. Therefore, the density is likely to increase / decrease.

The Formation of Deep Currents

The density of ocean water will increase if the water becomes colder or if the salinity increases. If this happens, ocean water at the surface can become denser than the water around or below it. The denser water sinks. This downward movement takes surface water into the deep ocean. *Deep ocean currents* are the movement of water in regular patterns below the surface of the ocean.

18. The diagram shows the circulation of water in a deep ocean current. Write the labels provided in the proper places on the diagram to explain the model.

- a surface current flows toward the pole
- water sinks and forms a deep current

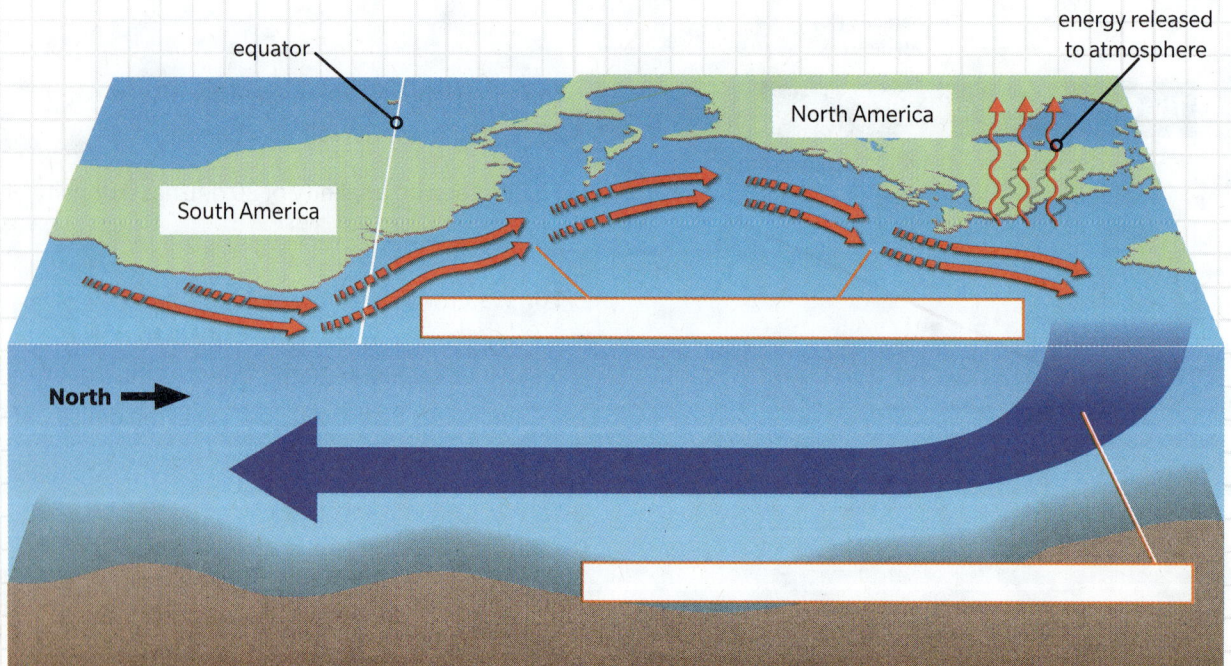

Factors that Affect Deep Currents

Deep currents are driven by density differences in ocean water and by gravity. At Earth's poles, surface water cools and becomes denser. The denser water is pulled toward the ocean floor by gravity more strongly than less dense water is. The denser water sinks and moves below the surface toward the equator, forming a deep current.

Deep currents flow along the ocean floor or along the top of another layer of water. As a result, several layers of deep currents can occur at any place in the ocean. Continents and the bottom topography of the ocean affect the path of deep ocean currents because deep currents are deflected whenever they flow toward land. And the Coriolis effect causes deep ocean currents to be deflected in the same way that surface currents are deflected.

19. **Engineer It** A water heater is a tank in which cold water is heated. Cold water flows into the tank to keep it full. A heating element warms the water inside the tank. The heated water can then be sent to hot water faucets in a building. Assume that a water heater design requires the hottest water possible to be sent to hot water faucets in a building. Where would be the best place for the hot water outlet pipe to be attached to the tank: the top, the middle, or the bottom of the tank? Explain your answer.

Analyze Currents in the Mediterranean Sea

Long ago, people observed water flowing into the Mediterranean Sea from the surface of the Atlantic Ocean, from the Black Sea, and from rivers. They noticed something very puzzling. No matter how much water flowed into the Mediterranean, its sea level remained the same. Some evaporation was occurring, but it was not enough to remove the amount of water that was entering the Mediterranean Sea.

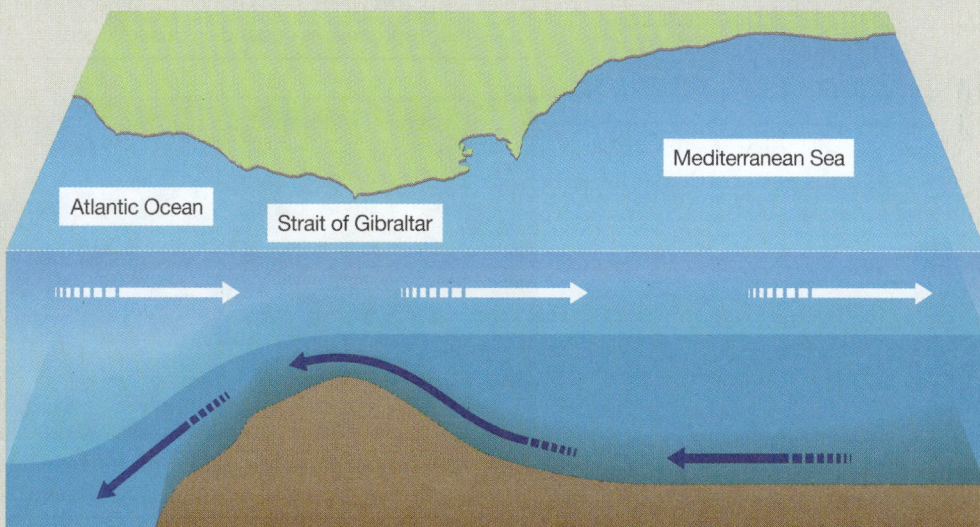

20. What processes in the Mediterranean Sea might explain why the water level of the Mediterranean did not increase, even though all the surface currents were flowing into that sea? The map and diagram may help you develop your explanation.

_____

_____

_____

_____

Relating Ocean Circulation to the Flow of Matter and Energy

The Earth system has four main subsystems. These subsystems interact in a complex and always-changing whole that we can think of as the *Earth system*. Earth's subsystems include

- the geosphere, which is the part of Earth that contains rocks, minerals, and sediment
- the biosphere, which is living things and the areas of Earth where they are found
- the atmosphere, which is the layer of air surrounding Earth
- the hydrosphere, which is all of Earth's water, including rivers, oceans, clouds, and precipitation

Oceans make up a large part of the hydrosphere because 97% of Earth's water is salt water.

21. Explain how Earth's subsystems are interacting in each photo.

A.

B.

C.

This kelp forest in the Channel Islands National Park in California provides a habitat for sea lions and other animals.

Deltas are places where rivers deposit sediment in the ocean. Some marine organisms depend on this sediment.

Ocean water evaporates, rises into the air, and then condenses. These processes can result in clouds and rain.

Convection Currents in the Ocean

The movement of matter due to differences in density is called *convection*. When denser material sinks, less dense material around it is pushed up. Convection also describes the transfer of energy due to the flow of matter. Convection can happen in gases, in liquids, and in solids that flow slowly. In the Earth system, convection happens in the atmosphere, in the ocean and other bodies of water, and in rock deep inside Earth. A convection current forms when convection happens repeatedly or in a cycle.

22. Add the following labels in the correct spaces below to complete this general model of a convection current in the ocean:
- deep current moves toward equator
- surface current moves toward pole

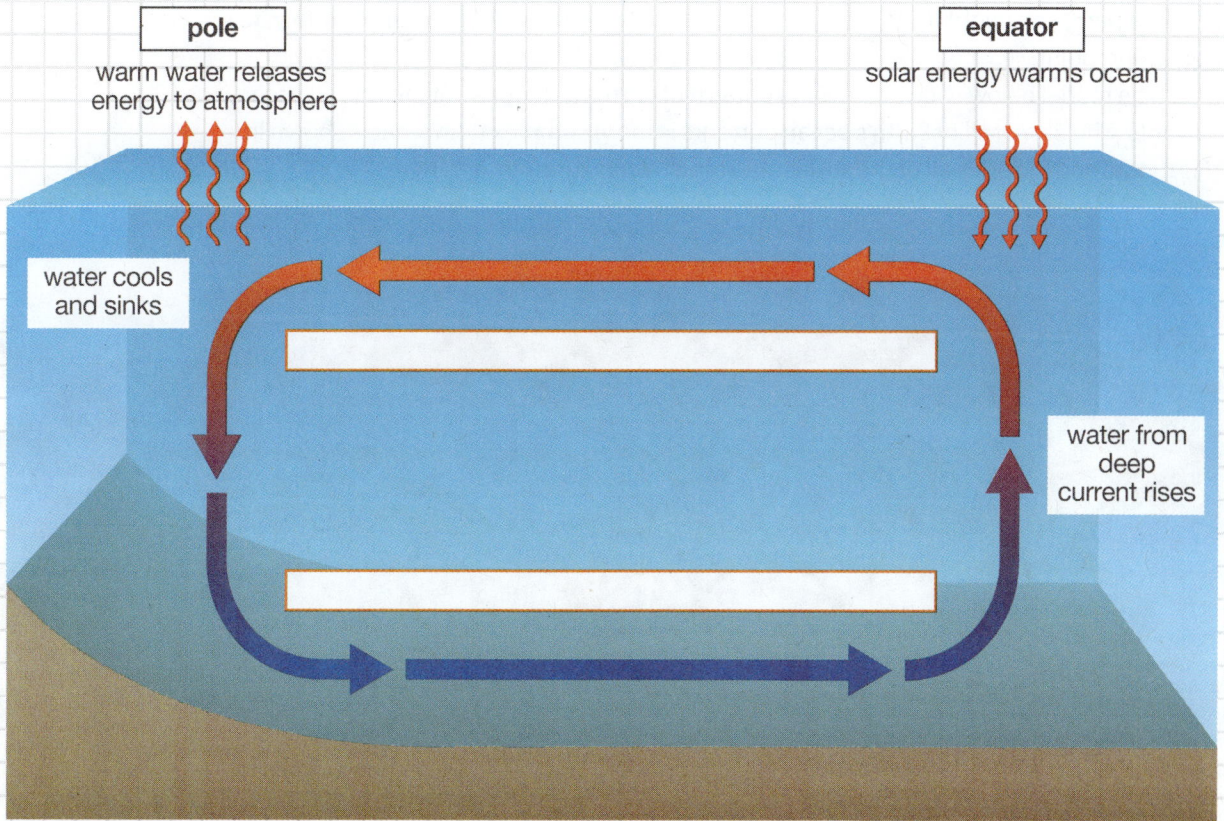

pole
warm water releases
energy to atmosphere

equator
solar energy warms ocean

water cools
and sinks

water from
deep
current rises

Convection currents involve the sinking of dense water and the rising of less dense water in a cycle. This process takes place all over Earth's oceans to form global circulation patterns. These patterns include surface currents that carry warm, less dense water away from the equator toward the poles. Water from the deep ocean near the equator rises to replace the water that is moving away on the surface. The patterns also include deep ocean currents that carry cool, denser water away from the poles toward the equator. These global circulation patterns affect the flow of energy and the cycling of matter in the Earth system.

23. Language SmArts Using what you have read and observed in the diagram, describe the path of a molecule of water in a convection current in the ocean. Include a description of the transfers and transformations of energy that would occur as the molecule travels in the convection current.

Global Ocean Circulation

When you put all of Earth's ocean currents together on a map or globe, you can see a pattern of water movement in the ocean. The model can be thought of as the main highway on which ocean water flows. If you could follow a molecule of water on one possible path, you might find that the molecule takes more than 1,000 years to return to its starting point!

The model below shows an overall pattern of currents. It does not include all ocean currents. The flow of all of Earth's ocean currents is more complex than what is shown in this model and includes all of the surface currents, deep currents, and gyres.

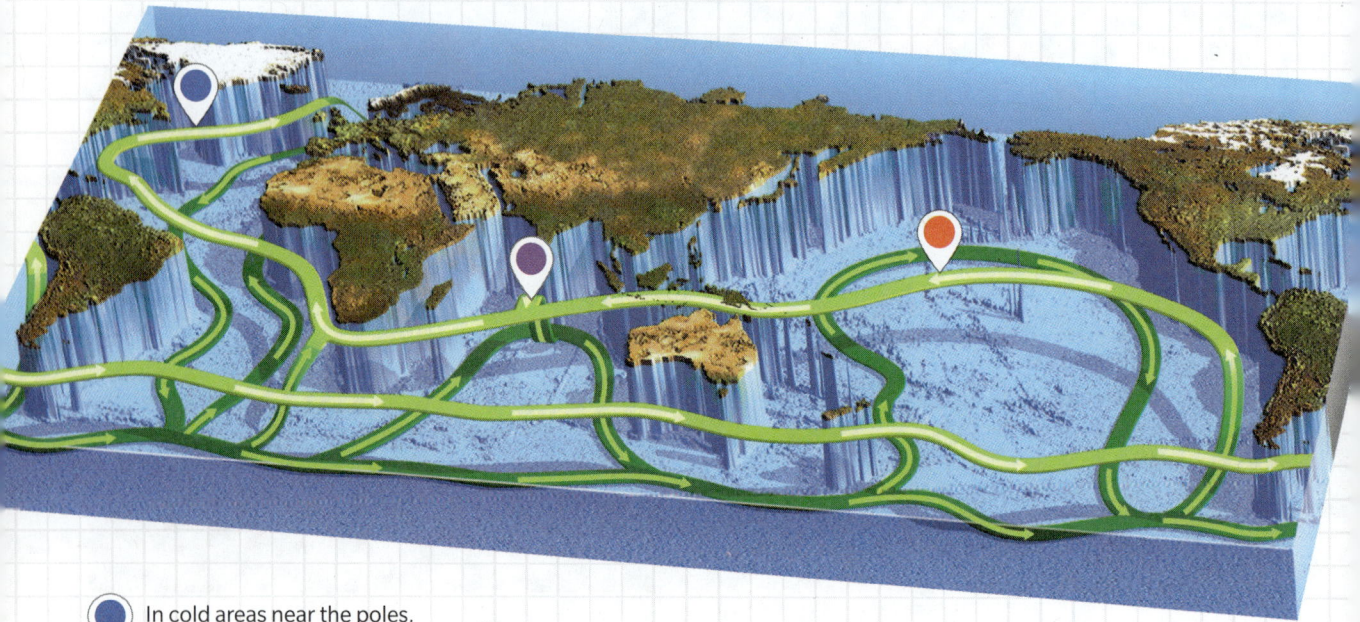

In cold areas near the poles, energy flows from the ocean into the atmosphere. The ocean water gets colder and more dense. This cooler, denser water sinks and then moves toward the equator along the ocean bottom.

In areas such as the Indian Ocean and the west coast of South America, deep water comes up to the surface. This upwelling of deep water brings cold, nutrient-rich water to the surface.

Near the equator, surface ocean water absorbs solar energy and gets warmer. This warm water tends to flow toward the poles and replace the cold water that is sinking there.

24. **Collaborate** In your school or community, there may be patterns of circulation that you can observe as groups of people move around during different times of the day. Work with a team to model these patterns with a map or drawing. Discuss with your team how the patterns you observe are like global ocean circulation and how they are different.

The Flow of Energy

The sun's energy enters Earth by the process of *radiation*. As the sun warms Earth's surface, solar energy is transformed into thermal energy. Weather and climate are affected as energy flows through the Earth system.

Energy is transferred from warmer to cooler objects. For example, when ocean water is warmer than the air above it, thermal energy flows from the water to the air by *conduction*. This process warms the air. Thermal energy is also transferred from warmer to cooler ocean water by conduction.

Energy is transferred from the equator toward the poles by *convection* as ocean water circulates around the globe. For example, cold and dense ocean water near the poles flows toward warmer, less-dense water near the equator. Warm water travels away from the equator and back toward the poles.

25. The greater the temperature difference between objects, the more quickly energy is transferred. In which location would energy be transferred more quickly?

    A. a lake at 5 °C where the air is 10 °C

    B. a lake at 2 °C where the air is 10 °C

    C. a lake at 2 °C where the air is 2 °C

26. Discuss Share your explanation with a partner. Together, determine whether energy is flowing from the air to the water or from the water to the air. Cite evidence for your explanations.

The Cycling of Matter

Ocean currents transport not only energy but also matter in the Earth system. This matter includes the ocean water itself, dissolved solids such as salt, and gases such as oxygen and carbon dioxide. Matter transported by ocean currents also includes marine organisms such as plankton. Some matter transported by ocean currents is harmful to the environment. Human waste, garbage, and other pollutants affect the environment everywhere that ocean currents carry these materials.

The cycling of matter in the Earth system also involves the chemical reactions and processes that take place in the ocean. For example, gases such as oxygen and carbon dioxide move back and forth between the ocean and the air depending on temperature, concentration of the gases, and other factors. Some marine organisms use carbon dioxide during the process of photosynthesis. During this process, organisms release oxygen into the water. The oxygen is then used by most living organisms during cellular respiration.

Diatoms are one type of plankton.

EVIDENCE NOTEBOOK

27. How might the cycling of matter in the ocean be related to the buildup of floating garbage in certain parts of the ocean? Why might some garbage float and not sink? Record your evidence.

The Carbon Cycle

This diagram shows the cycling of carbon through the Earth system, in living and nonliving subsystems. The ocean plays an important role in the carbon cycle.

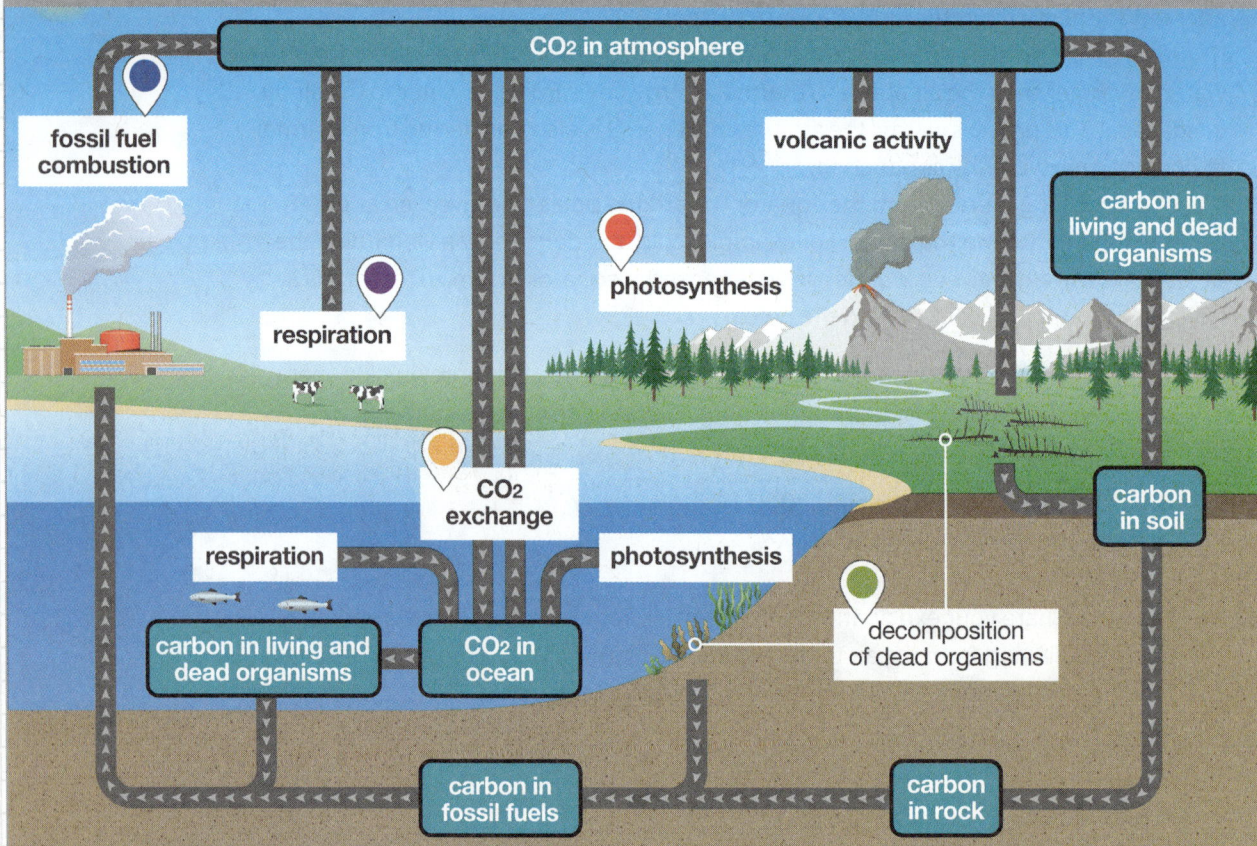

CO₂ in atmosphere

fossil fuel combustion

respiration

photosynthesis

volcanic activity

carbon in living and dead organisms

CO₂ exchange

respiration

photosynthesis

carbon in soil

carbon in living and dead organisms

CO₂ in ocean

decomposition of dead organisms

carbon in fossil fuels

carbon in rock

Respiration During cellular respiration, organisms take in oxygen (O_2) and release CO_2. Aquatic organisms release CO_2 into the water. Organisms on land release CO_2 into the atmosphere.

CO₂ exchange Ocean water can absorb carbon dioxide (CO_2). And CO_2 can be released from water into the air. So, the ocean plays an important role in regulating the amount of CO_2 in the air.

Photosynthesis Plants and algae use CO_2 in photosynthesis. The carbon in CO_2 is used to make sugars that are energy sources for the organisms and for the organisms that eat them.

Combustion of fossil fuels Fossil fuels contain carbon that originally came from the remains of dead plants and animals. When fossil fuels are burned, CO_2 is released into the atmosphere.

Decomposition As organisms die and decompose, carbon from their bodies goes back into the environment. This carbon may be used by other organisms, go into the soil or ocean, or form rock.

Predict Effects of a Change in Ocean Circulation

28. Describe at least two effects on the Earth system that might happen if ocean circulation stopped. Explain your reasoning.

_____

_____

_____

_____

_____

_____

Continue Your Exploration

Name: _____   Date: _____

Check out the path below or go online to choose one of the other paths shown.

Careers in Science

- **Upwelling in Earth's Oceans**
- **Hands-On Labs** 👋
- **Propose Your Own Path**

Go online to choose one of these other paths.

Physical Oceanographer

Oceanographers are scientists who study the ocean. There are many areas to study in oceanography. Some of these are marine ecosystems, ocean circulation, the geology of the sea floor, and the chemical and physical properties of ocean water. These topics are related. So, it is important that oceanographers have an understanding of biology, chemistry, geology, and physics to unravel the mysteries of the ocean. All oceanographers must have a four-year college degree. Most go on to earn a master's degree and a doctorate before becoming ocean scientists.

One type of oceanographer, a physical oceanographer, studies the physical conditions and processes in the ocean. This involves studying phenomena such as waves, currents, and tides; the transport of sand on and off beaches; coastal erosion; and the interactions of the atmosphere and the ocean. Physical oceanographers also study the relationships that influence weather and climate, the behavior of light and sound in water, and the ocean's interactions with the sea floor.

1. Why is it important for physical oceanographers to have studied several different fields of science?

Oceanographers work outside *Alvin*, one of the world's first deep-sea submersibles. *Alvin* can take scientists as far as 4,500 meters below the ocean surface.

A physical oceanographer brings a CTD instrument onto a research ship. The CTD takes many measurements of conductivity, temperature, and depth.

Continue Your Exploration

2. Which descriptions identify areas of science that a physical oceanographer might need to use to answer questions about the topic listed? Choose all that apply.

    A. chemistry and physics to study how currents and salinity are related

    B. physics and geology to study the transport of sand on and off beaches

    C. biology, chemistry, geology, and physics to study the interactions of the atmosphere and the ocean

3. Write at least three questions that you could investigate if you were a physical oceanographer.

4. **Engineer It** Today physical oceanographers can measure the speed of ocean currents with advanced technology. For example, floating buoys that have Global Positioning System (GPS) devices can be used to collect data about where the buoy is traveling and how fast it is going. These data can be used to calculate the speed of a current and to map its direction. Before computers and GPS devices, scientists managed to map and measure currents with fair accuracy. Propose one way you could measure the speed of a surface ocean current if you had a boat you could anchor, pieces of wood, string or rope, and a stopwatch.

5. **Collaborate** Research opposing claims about the causes of ocean acidification. Choose one claim and write an argument to support it. Be sure to use credible sources. Describe the claim, explain the evidence and reasoning behind the claim, and provide a concluding statement to support your argument.

Can You Explain It?

Name: _____   Date: _____

Why does floating garbage tend to build up in certain places in the ocean?

■ Model shows predicted accumulation of floating garbage 10 years after release

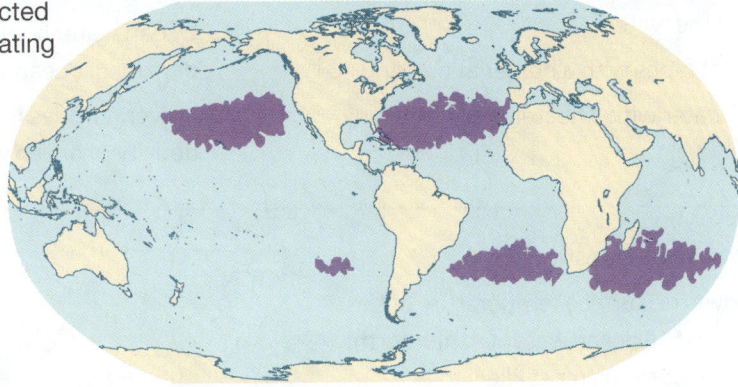

Credit: Adapted from "Origin, dynamics and evolution of ocean garbage patches from observed surface drifters, Figure 1 (c) Tracer accumulation factor after 10 years, doi:10.1088/1748-9326/7/4/044040" from Environmental Research Letters, Volume 7 by Erik van Sebille et. al. Copyright © 2012 IOP Publishing Ltd. CC BY-NC-SA. Adapted and reproduced by permission of Erik van Sebille and IOP Publishing Ltd.

EVIDENCE NOTEBOOK

Refer to the notes in your Evidence Notebook to help you construct an explanation for why floating garbage that comes mostly from the land tends to build up in certain places in the ocean.

---

1. State your claim. Make sure your claim fully explains how and why floating garbage builds up in certain areas.

2. Summarize the evidence you have gathered to support your claim and explain your reasoning.

Checkpoints

Answer the following questions to check your understanding of the lesson.

3. Which of the following would be the best choice to model what drives surface ocean currents?

   A. a tank of water with a block of ice attached to one end

   B. a tank of water with a fan blowing over the surface of the water

   C. a system of pipes with a heater at one end

   D. a tank of water with a heater under the tank

4. Fill in each blank with *increases* or *decreases* to show how the density of liquid ocean water can change.

   A. Rain falls into the ocean; the density of ocean water _____.

   B. Ocean water cools from 30 °C to 25 °C; the density of ocean water _____.

   C. A river empties into the ocean; the density of ocean water _____.

Use the map to answer Questions 5–6.

5. The map shows the surface temperature of the Gulf Stream and the ocean water farther north. Where are deep currents most likely to be forming as water from the surface sinks?

   A. south of 30° north latitude

   B. between 30° and 35° north latitude

   C. between 35° and 40° north latitude

   D. north of 40° north latitude

6. Thermal energy is transferred from the warm Gulf Stream ocean water to the cooler air above it by the process of *conduction / convection / radiation.*

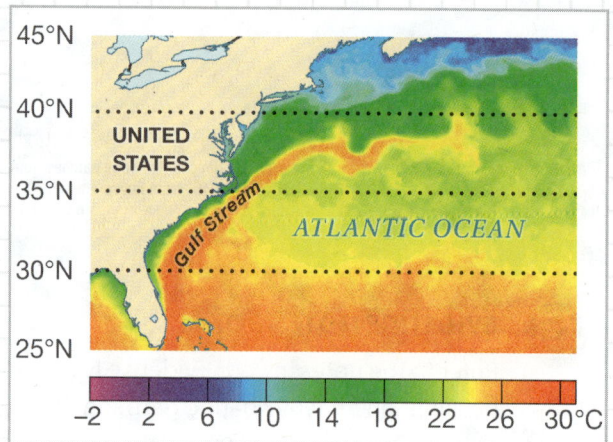

Use the map to answer Questions 7–8.

7. Which statement explains why the water in the South Pacific gyre begins to warm up as it moves away from the coast of South America?

   A. It receives more energy from the sun.

   B. It receives more rainfall from the atmosphere.

   C. It loses more thermal energy to the atmosphere.

8. Ocean water in the *cold / warm* Peru Current is deflected by the continent of *South America / Antarctica / Australia* and then joins the South Equatorial Current.

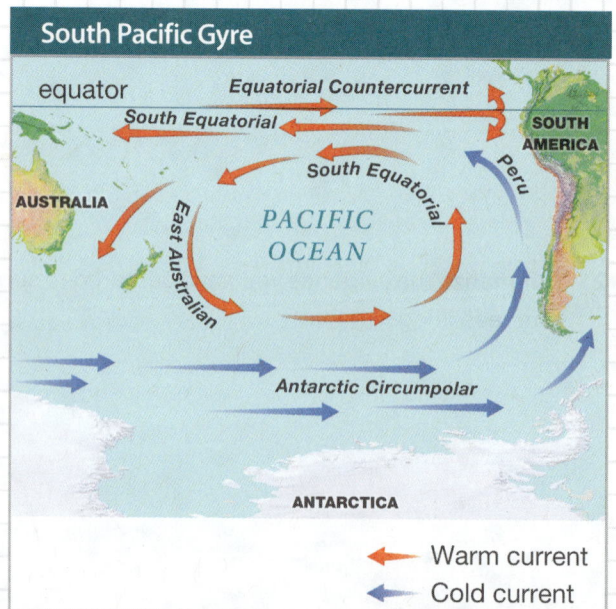

Interactive Review

Complete this section to review the main concepts of the lesson.

Surface currents are affected by wind, by the Coriolis effect, and by continental deflection.

A. Explain how energy that comes from outside the Earth system drives the flow of water in surface currents.

Deep ocean currents form when denser ocean water sinks. The flow of deep currents is also affected by the Coriolis effect and by continental deflection.

B. Draw a diagram that models one way a deep current could form.

Global ocean circulation moves water through Earth's ocean basins and plays an important role in the cycling of matter and the flow of energy in the Earth system.

C. Explain how the flow of matter and energy in global ocean circulation is related to interactions of the ocean with two other parts of the Earth system.

Interactions in Earth's Systems Cause Weather

Heavy rain falls from this dramatic storm cloud that formed where hot and cold air masses met.

Explore First

Measuring Wind Direction   Build a device that you can set up to measure wind direction outside your home or school. Be sure to place your device where objects such as buildings or trees will not influence your measurements. Does the wind blow in the same direction most of the time or does it change? How might you improve your device?

CAN YOU EXPLAIN IT?

What could cause a storm like this to happen suddenly?

It was a calm and cloudy spring day in this Utah town. Suddenly the clouds grew dark and heavy, and a storm covered the town in a blanket of snow.

Explore Online

1. What could cause the weather to change suddenly like this?

2. Draw Include a drawing to illustrate your explanation.

EVIDENCE NOTEBOOK As you explore this lesson, gather evidence to help explain what causes sudden changes in weather like this storm.

Describing Weather

Elements of Weather

Has weather ever caused your plans to change? **Weather** is a description of the short-term conditions of the atmosphere at a particular time and place. Reports of weather might include information about temperature, humidity, precipitation, air pressure, wind speed, and cloud cover.

3. What is the weather like right now? What is your favorite kind of weather? What is your least favorite kind of weather?

Temperature

Temperature is a measure of how hot or cold something is, which has to do with the motion of the particles that make up matter. So, the temperature of air is related to the kinetic energy of air particles. The faster the air particles move, the greater their kinetic energy is. Look at the models of cool and warm air particles within a cube. The air in each cube is under the same amount of pressure.

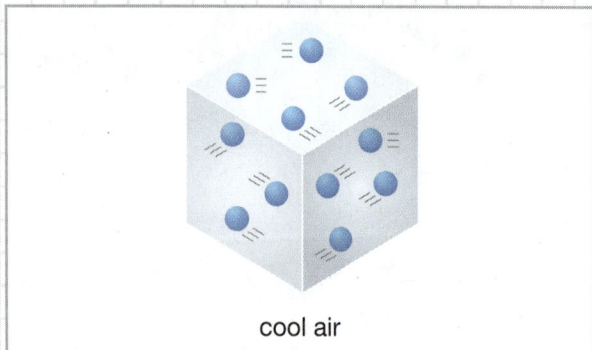

cool air

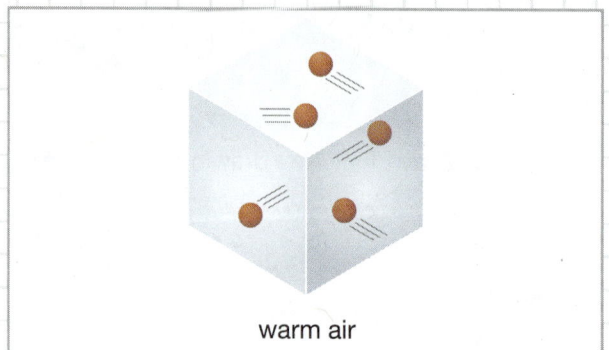

warm air

The cool air particles in this cube move more slowly and have less kinetic energy than the air particles in the warm air cube.

In the same volume of warm air, the particles move faster and are more spread out. Warm air is less dense than cool air.

Humidity

Humidity is a measure of the amount of water vapor in the air. Much of the water vapor in air comes from the evaporation of liquid water on Earth's surface. The more water vapor there is in the air, the higher the humidity of the air is. Humidity affects how warm or cool you feel. You might feel comfortable at 25 °C, but if the humidity rises, you may feel too warm, even if the temperature is the same.

Weather reports often refer to relative humidity. *Relative humidity* is the percentage of water vapor in air relative to the amount needed to saturate the air at the same temperature. For example, at 10 °C, air becomes saturated when there are 8 grams of water vapor per kilogram of air (g/kg). At this point, the relative humidity is 100%. If there were only 4 g/kg of water vapor in the air at 10 °C, then the relative humidity would be 50%. The warmer the air is, the more water vapor it can contain without reaching saturation.

Clouds and Precipitation

What happens when relative humidity exceeds 100%? At this point, more water vapor condenses than evaporates. The water vapor condenses onto particles in the air, such as dust and pollen, to form liquid water droplets or ice crystals. These droplets and crystals form clouds. The droplets and ice crystals in clouds grow and fall back to Earth as precipitation, such as rain, snow, hail, or sleet. The type of precipitation that forms and falls depends on the air temperature where the cloud formed and the changing air temperature as the precipitation falls to the ground.

Clouds themselves affect the air temperature. During the day, clouds can keep an area cool by reflecting more sunlight back into space. Clouds also affect temperatures overnight. During the day, energy from the sun is converted into thermal energy as it warms Earth. Earth radiates some of the thermal energy it absorbed during the day back toward space. If no clouds are present at night, much of this thermal energy escapes into space and cooler temperatures result. If clouds are present, they may absorb the thermal energy and radiate it back down to Earth's surface. This is why a cloudy night is often warmer than a clear night.

Do the Math
Describe Relative Humidity

The line on this graph shows how much water vapor is in the air at 100% relative humidity at different temperatures. For example, at 30 °C, relative humidity reaches 100% when there are 29 grams of water in each kilogram of air.

4. Use the graph to circle the word that correctly completes each sentence.

   A. As temperature increases, it takes more / less water vapor to reach 100% relative humidity.

   B. At 25 °C with 10 g/kg of water vapor in the air, precipitation is likely / not likely.

   C. If 10 g/kg of water vapor remained in the air and the temperature dropped to 10 °C, precipitation would be likely / not likely.

Amount of Water in Air at 100% Relative Humidity

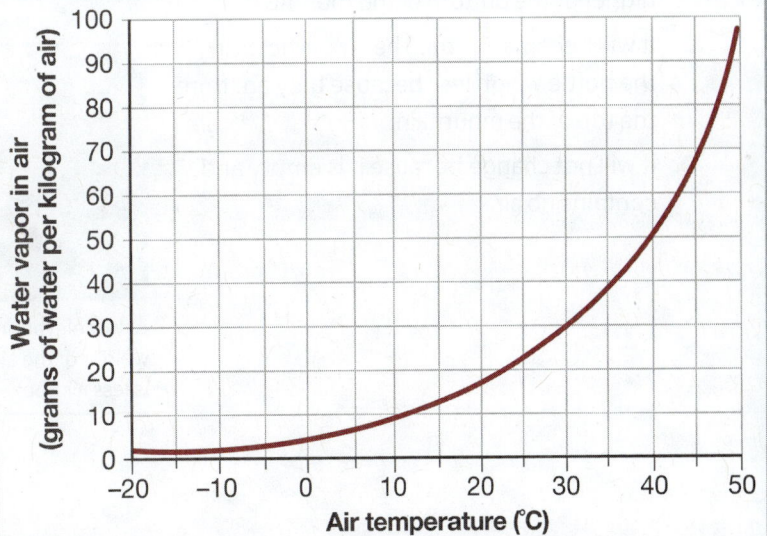

Air Pressure

Particles of air are invisible, but they do have mass. Gravity pulls the particles toward Earth's surface. Air particles press on objects from all sides. *Air pressure* is the force of air pushing on an object.

The air pressure on any one object on Earth depends on how much air exists above that object. The more air there is above an object, the greater the air pressure will be. Air pressure is measured in millibars (mb). At sea level, the air pressure is about 1,013 mb. Higher above sea level, less air is above you, so the air pressure will be lower. For example, the air pressure on the top of Mount Everest is only 300 mb.

6. A student drank a bottle of water during a car ride up a mountain. At the top of the mountain, the student capped the plastic bottle. During the drive back down the mountain, what might happen to the bottle?

   A. It will expand because the air pressure is lower at the bottom of the mountain.

   B. It will contract because the air pressure is higher at the bottom of the mountain.

   C. It will become lighter. The air particles in the bottle weigh less because they are from the top of the mountain.

   D. It will not change because it is empty and contains no air.

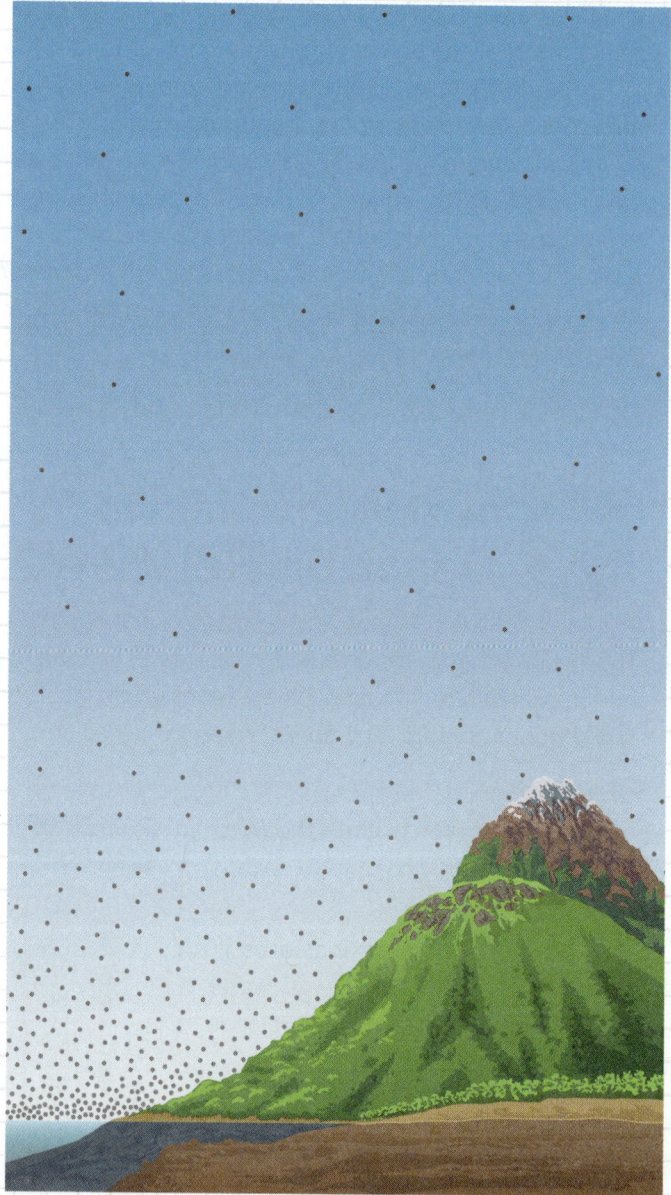

At low elevations, air particles are packed together because the weight of the air above them is greater. At high elevations, there is less air above, so the particles are more spread out.

Wind

Air flows from high to low pressure. For example, air from an opened balloon will escape from the high air pressure inside the balloon to the lower air pressure outside the balloon. This movement of air is called *wind*. The greater the air pressure difference is between two places, the faster the air moves and the stronger the wind is.

7. Draw an arrow in the middle box to show which way the wind is blowing. Add the labels high pressure and low pressure on either side of the photo.

Air moves because of differences in air pressure.

Language SmArts
Describe Weather

8. Think back to the descriptions you wrote about the current weather, your favorite weather, and your least favorite weather. Choose one description and apply what you have learned to rewrite that description. Include the terms *temperature, humidity, precipitation, wind,* and *air pressure*.

_____

_____

_____

_____

_____

9. What might have caused the type of weather in your description? For example, why might it have been sunny, rainy, or windy?

_____

_____

_____

_____

_____

Identifying Weather Associated with Pressure Systems

Air temperature varies because the sun warms Earth's surface unevenly. Because temperature affects pressure, differences in air temperature result in differences in air pressure. Differences in air pressure cause wind to blow. Wind moves clouds and precipitation from one place to another.

On weather maps, an "H" shows where the air pressure is highest. An "L" shows where it is lowest. An *isobar* is a line that connects points of equal air pressure. Observe the patterns in air pressure on the map.

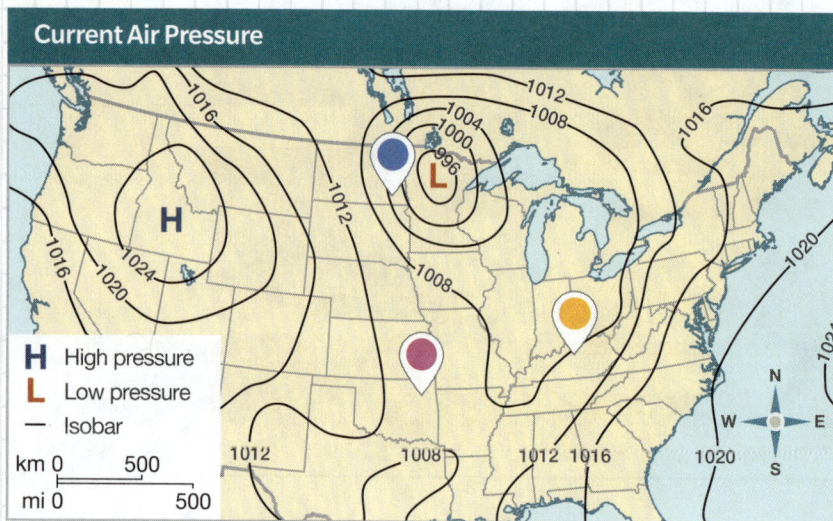

Current Air Pressure

Each isobar traces along the same air pressure. The numbers show the measured air pressure in millibars (mb).

Where isobars are spaced far apart, the air pressure change is slight, so wind speed is lower.

Where isobars are spaced closely together, the air pressure change is great, so wind speed is higher.

H High pressure
L Low pressure
— Isobar

km 0   500
mi 0   500

10. Draw a line across the map anywhere you choose. Describe how the air pressure and wind speed change as you go along this line.

11. Engineer It A team of engineers and meteorologists are working to identify the best places in the United States to build new wind farms. Because wind conditions can change from day to day, they conducted research to find the average wind speeds in the United States. What else might they need to consider to make a decision? Circle all that apply.

A. land ownership

B. average wind direction

C. frequency of storms

D. current wind speed

Pressure Systems

Examine the maps showing high- and low-pressure systems. A *high-pressure system* forms where air sinks toward the surface. As the air sinks, it spreads out from the high-pressure system toward areas of lower air pressure. Because Earth rotates, the air moves away from the high-pressure area in an outward spiral.

Where warm, less dense air rises from Earth's surface, a *low-pressure system* forms. This happens as air flows in from higher-pressure areas. The air moves into a low-pressure area as an inward spiral.

Pressure Systems and Weather

As air in a high-pressure systems sinks, it gets warmer. Relative humidity decreases, and if there were any clouds, they evaporate. These conditions usually bring clear skies and calm or gentle winds. In contrast, the air in a low-pressure system rises and cools. Clouds and rain form if the air is humid enough and the temperature drops enough.

Air Pressure Systems in the Northern Hemisphere

Earth rotates, so wind does not blow in a straight line. In the Northern Hemisphere, air spirals counterclockwise around a low-pressure system and clockwise around a high-pressure system.

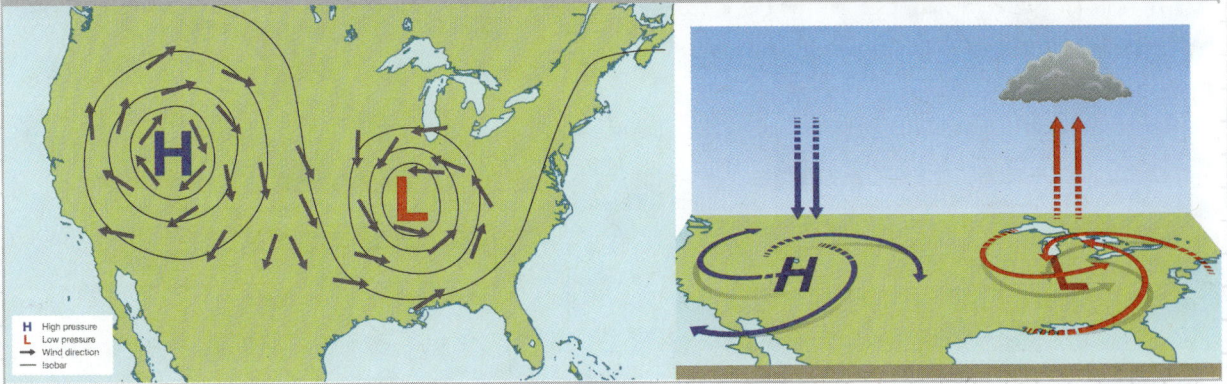

H   High pressure
L   Low pressure
→   Wind direction
—   Isobar

12. Write H or L to indicate whether each statement is associated with a high-pressure system or a low-pressure system in the Northern Hemisphere.

H	sinking air becomes warmer
	rising air becomes cooler
	clear, sunny weather

	cloudy, rainy weather
	clockwise winds spread out
	counterclockwise winds move in

EVIDENCE NOTEBOOK

13. Think again about the storm that blew over the town in Utah. What kind of pressure system was probably involved? Record your evidence.

Interpret a Weather Map

A weather map shows the weather conditions of an area at a particular time. The map may include information, such as temperature, humidity, wind, cloud cover, precipitation, and air pressure.

14. This map shows precipitation and air pressure. Use the descriptions in the word bank to label the map and describe the weather associated with each pressure system.

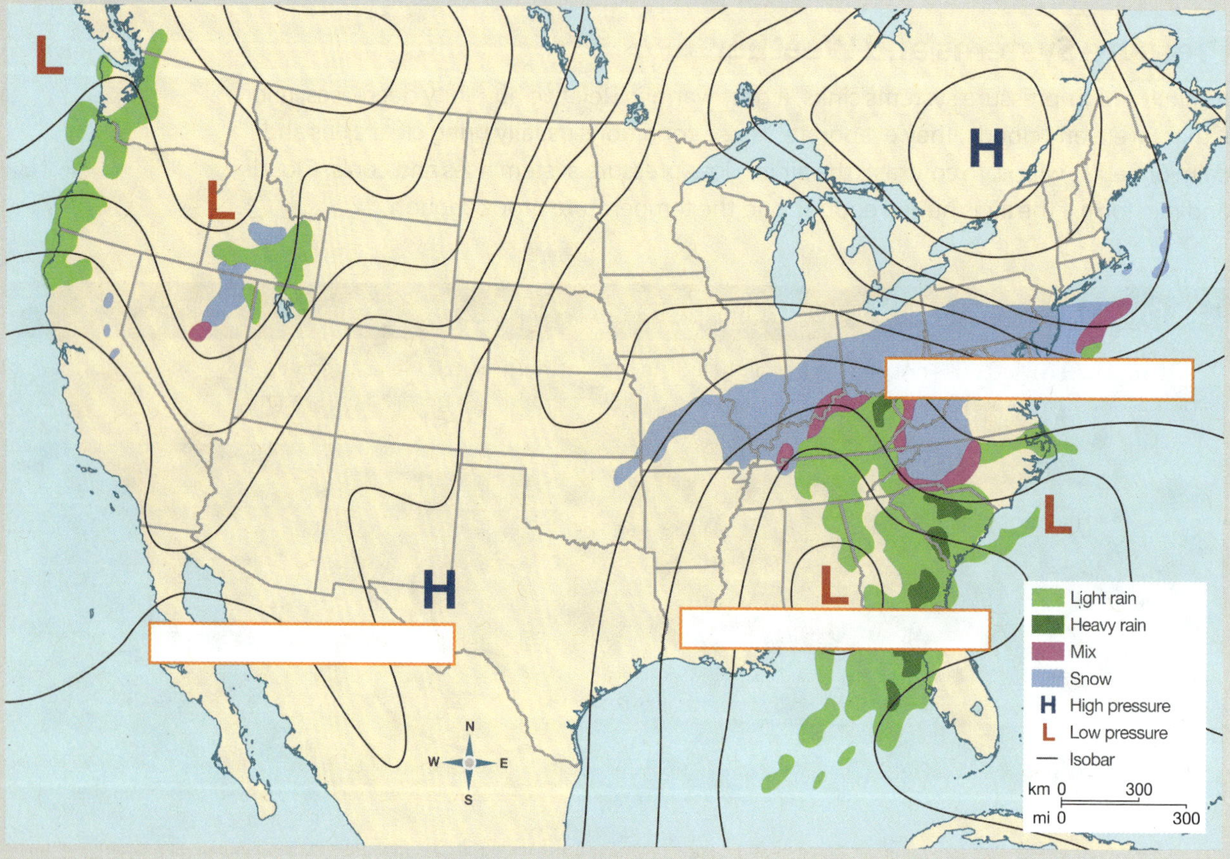

WORD BANK
- sunny and calm
- rainy
- snowstorms, windy

15. What patterns can you see in the map related to air-pressure systems and different weather conditions?

_____

_____

_____

_____

_____

_____

_____

_____

_____

_____

_____

_____

Explaining How Fronts Change Weather

The Formation of Air Masses

An **air mass** is a large body of air that has similar temperature and humidity throughout it. An air mass develops over Earth's surface when air stays in one region for many days or weeks. The air mass gradually takes on the characteristics of the water or land below it. An air mass that forms above a warm, dry desert will be warm and dry. An air mass that forms above Arctic waters will be cool and humid.

> **WORD BANK**
> ~~warm and dry~~
> warm and humid
> cool and dry
> cool and humid

16. What kind of air mass do you think forms over each region shown in the photos? Use the descriptions in the word bank to label each photo.

warm and dry

The Movement of Air Masses

Eventually, air masses move because of air pressure differences. As an air mass travels, its temperature and humidity can slowly change as conditions on Earth's surface below the air mass change. When two different air masses meet, the warmer air mass will generally rise over the cooler air mass.

Along the California coast in summer, the water is cool. Therefore, cool and humid air masses form over the area. These air masses often move toward land and run into hot and dry air masses. Think about how summer weather patterns might depend on distance from the coast.

Hands-On Lab
Model an Air Mass Interaction

You will make a prediction about how a model will show the interaction between a warm and a cool air mass. You will then construct the model and use your observations to explain how warm and cool air masses interact.

MATERIALS
- container, shoebox-sized, clear, plastic
- food coloring, red
- ice cubes that contain blue food coloring
- water, warm

Procedure

STEP 1 The melted blue ice cubes represent a cold air mass, and the warm red water represents a warm air mass. Read through this procedure, and then use what you know about air masses to write a prediction about what might happen when the blue and red water interact.

STEP 2 Fill the plastic container half full of warm water. Let the water settle and become still.

STEP 3 On one side of the container, carefully place the blue ice cubes into the warm water.

STEP 4 On the other side of the container, add a few drops of red food coloring.

STEP 5 Observe the interaction between the blue and red water. Record your observations.

Explore Online

Analysis

STEP 6 Was your prediction supported by your observations? Explain.

STEP 7 What type of weather might occur if these were two air masses interacting? Explain your thinking.

STEP 8 **Discuss** Is this a good model for showing how two air masses interact? Explain why or why not.

The Formation of Fronts

When two air masses of different temperatures and densities meet but do not mix, a front forms. A **front** is a boundary between air masses. The type of front that forms depends on the temperature, humidity, and motion of each air mass. The main types of fronts are cold fronts, warm fronts, stationary fronts, and occluded fronts.

Fronts commonly form as air masses rotate around low-pressure areas. As fronts move over Earth's surface, they cause changes in temperature and precipitation. A front might also change wind speed and direction as it passes over an area. Therefore, fronts have a strong effect on the weather.

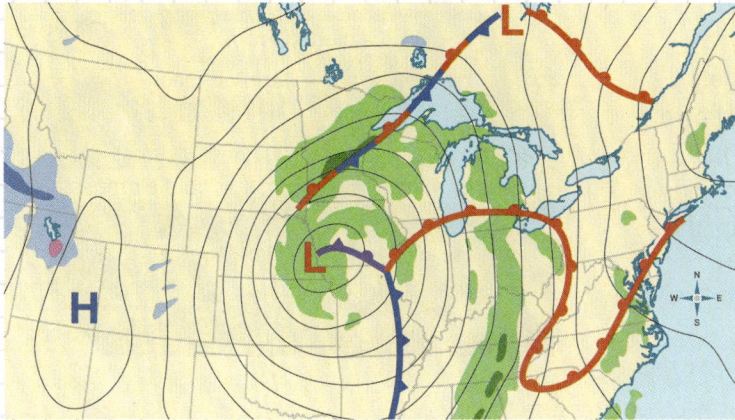

This weather map shows the air pressure, fronts, and precipitation on one day. Each type of front has its own symbol.

Cold Fronts

A *cold front* is a boundary that forms as a cold air mass pushes under a warm air mass. A cold front is shown on a weather map by a blue line of triangles that point in the direction that the front is moving.

If the rising warm air is somewhat humid, scattered clouds form. If the rising warm air is very humid, heavy clouds and precipitation can occur. Cold fronts usually move quickly and can bring rain, snowstorms, and even thunderstorms. Cool, fair weather often follows a cold front.

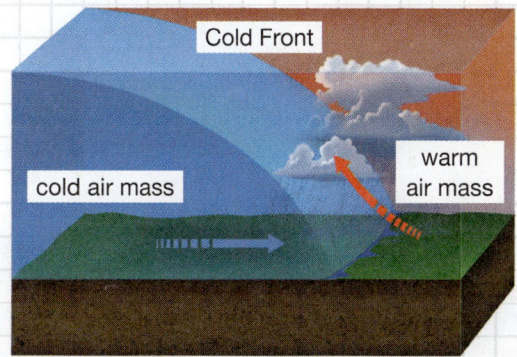

Warm Fronts

A *warm front* forms where a warm air mass overrides a cold air mass. A warm front is shown on a map by a red line of half circles that point in the direction that the front is moving.

Warm fronts generally bring drizzly rain if the warm air mass is humid or scattered clouds if the air mass is only somewhat humid. Because warm air masses move slowly, the weather may remain rainy or cloudy for several days. After a warm front passes, the weather often becomes warmer.

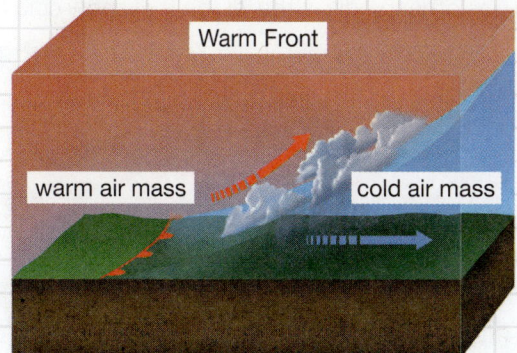

Stationary Fronts

A *stationary front* forms where a cold air mass and a warm air mass meet and become still. In other words, the air masses become stationary. A stationary front is represented on a map by alternating blue triangles and red half circles.

A stationary front often brings many days of clouds and precipitation. This happens as water vapor in the air along the boundary between the air masses rises and condenses.

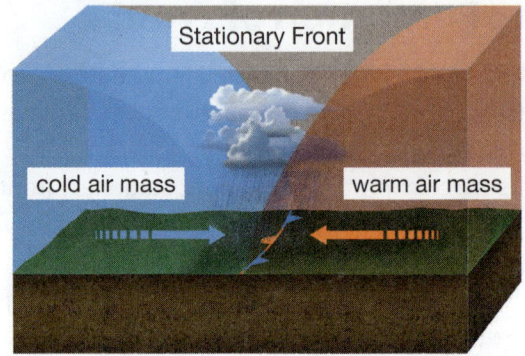

Stationary Front

cold air mass   warm air mass

Occluded Fronts

An occluded front forms when a warm front gets pushed up under two cooler air masses. It is shown on a map as purple alternating triangles and half circles pointed in the direction the front is moving.

Because the warm air mass is pushed up, the temperature drops as an occluded front forms. Heavy precipitation can occur as water vapor in the warm air mass cools and condenses.

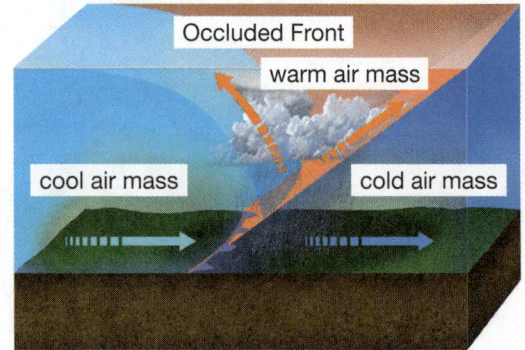

Occluded Front

warm air mass

cool air mass   cold air mass

17. Fronts often form around areas of high / low pressure. A sudden thunderstorm is most likely associated with the arrival of a cold / warm / stationary front.

EVIDENCE NOTEBOOK

18. Which type of front is most likely associated with the weather change in the town in Utah? Record your evidence.

Language SmArts
Compare and Contrast Information

19. In the experiment, you modeled a cold front. Compare and contrast your model to the other media in the lesson that show cold fronts. Compare their strengths and weaknesses.

_____

_____

_____

_____

_____

_____

_____

Describing Weather Patterns in California

At a single moment in California, it can be hot and dry in one place and freezing and snowy in another place. The southern part of the state is closer to the equator and is generally warmer than the northern part. On the western side of the state lies the Pacific Ocean. On the eastern side of the state, the Sierra Nevada mountains influence temperature and precipitation patterns.

20. This satellite image shows densely vegetated areas in green. Drier, less vegetated areas are shown by brown and tan colors. Complete the paragraph to describe the satellite image.

The satellite image shows dry / *vegetated* / hot areas along the Pacific coast and the eastern / *western* edge of the Sierra Nevada Mountains. These areas generally receive *more* / less precipitation than the brown areas *east* / west of California's Mountains, such as the Mojave Desert and the Great Basin.

21. With a partner, generate questions regarding the landforms and vegetation patterns you see in this satellite image. Think about how vegetation and precipitation are related.

Satellite Image of California and Nevada, July 2002

This satellite image of California shows areas where land is vegetated and where it is not.

Influences on Weather

Vegetation patterns can indicate the types of weather an area experiences. Weather is also influenced by vegetation. Trees can decrease wind speeds, release moisture into the air, and shade the ground. Several other interactions in the Earth system influence weather patterns as well. Driven by energy from the sun, these interactions between the biosphere, atmosphere, hydrosphere, and geosphere are constantly taking place. For example, California's weather patterns are influenced by interactions between the atmosphere and hydrosphere as solar energy causes ocean water to evaporate into the atmosphere. Upon cooling and condensing, the water vapor can form clouds, rain, fog, or snow that is brought to California by winds.

Prevailing Winds

Prevailing winds influence weather because they affect the speeds and directions of moving air masses. Prevailing winds tend to move west to east over the United States and Canada. These winds bring air masses from the Pacific Ocean toward California. Prevailing winds also drive ocean surface currents.

The Pacific Ocean

Along with gravity and differences in ocean water density, prevailing winds influence ocean currents that circulate around the globe. Just off the coast of California, a cold surface current called the California Current runs north to south.

Ocean surface currents affect weather in coastal cities. For example, the cold California Current carries cold water along California's coast. The air masses that form above this area are therefore cool and humid. Prevailing winds blow this air toward California. The cool, humid air interacts with landforms and inland air masses. The result is often fog, rain, and cool coastal temperatures in northern and central California.

Prevailing Winds and Ocean Surface Currents

Prevailing winds and continents influence the directions of ocean surface currents.

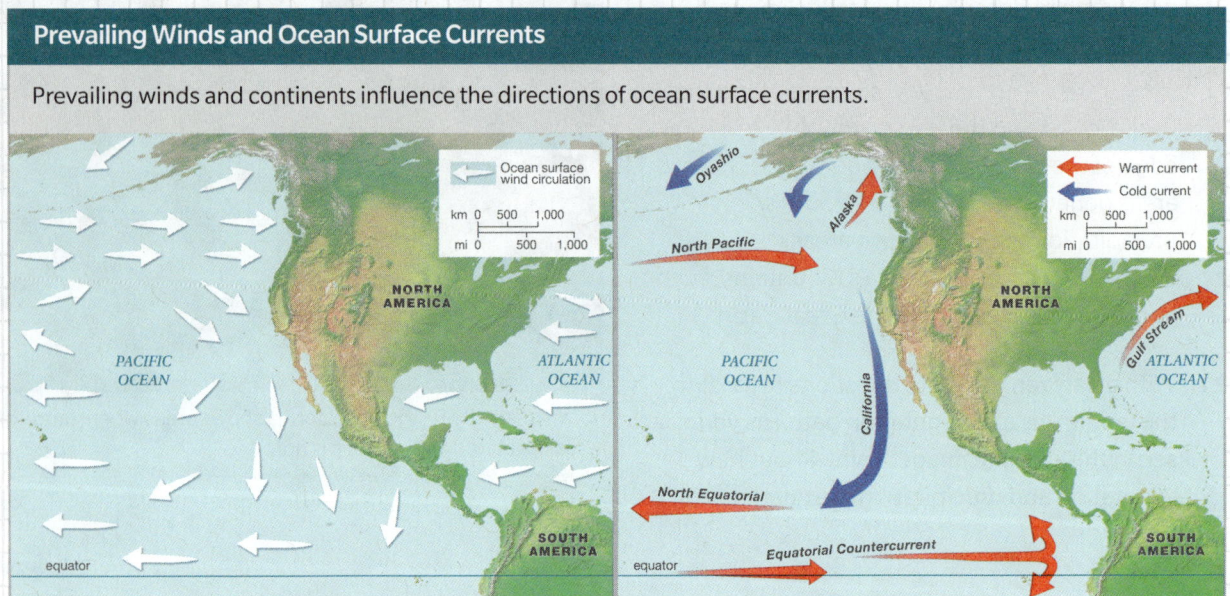

22. Circle the correct terms to complete each statement.

Both prevailing winds and the continent of North America influence the direction of the North Pacific Current and the California Current. The California Current brings _cold / warm_ ocean water along the coast of California.

Prevailing winds blow cool and humid air masses that form over the Pacific Ocean toward the _east / west_. Therefore, the Pacific Ocean _is / is not_ a major influence on California's weather.

Landforms

Both prevailing winds and ocean surface currents are redirected as they run into land. For example, the California Current is partly a result of the North Pacific Current being deflected toward the south as it runs into North America.

A phenomenon known as the *rain shadow effect* happens where prevailing winds bring humid air over mountains. As the humid air is forced to rise over the mountains, it cools and condenses into clouds and causes precipitation. Once the air reaches the other side of the mountain, it is drier. Therefore, one side of the mountain is cloudy and has more precipitation. On the other side, it is dry and the skies are often sunny.

Pineapple Express Precipitation

The Pineapple Express is an *atmospheric river* that brings a huge amount of moisture from the tropical Pacific Ocean toward the western United States.

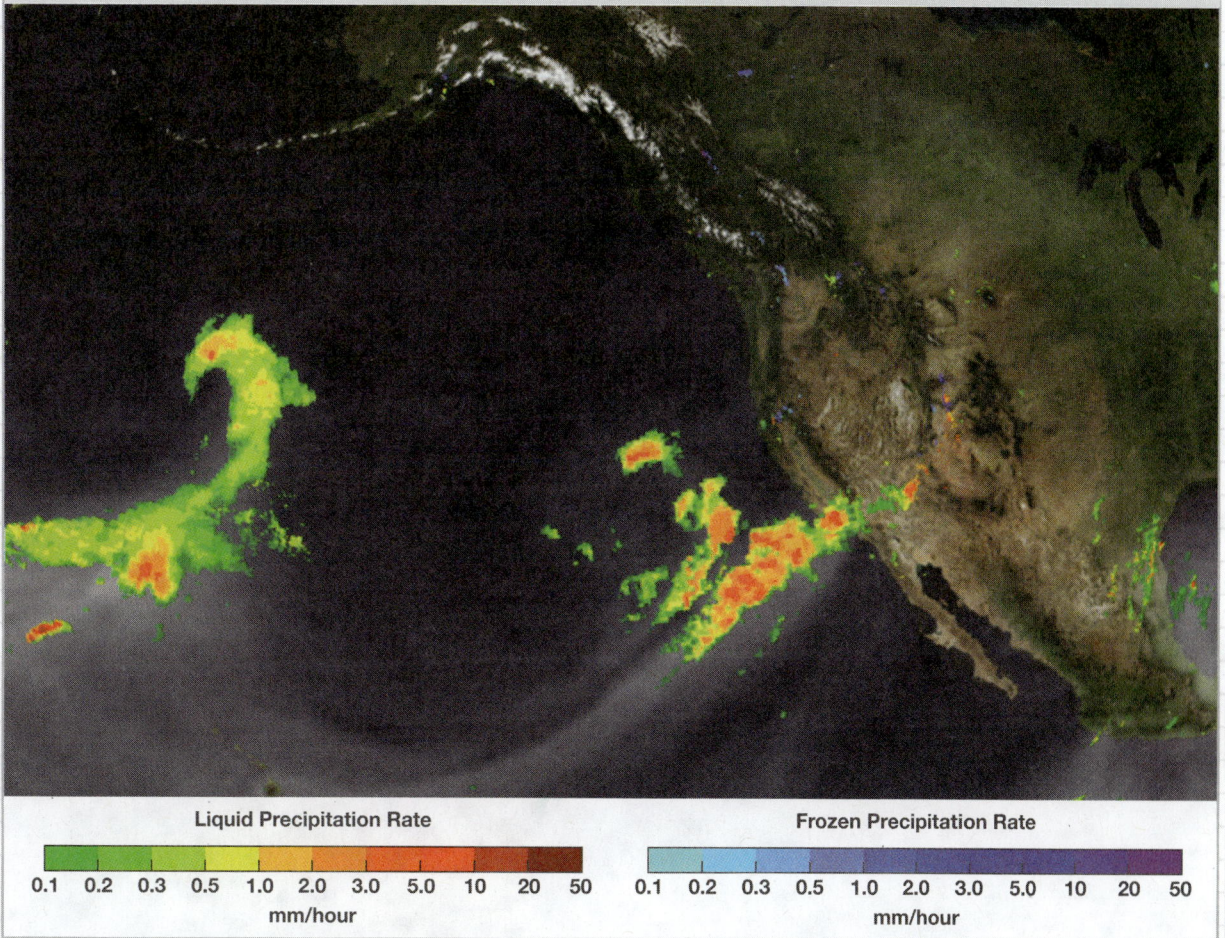

Liquid Precipitation Rate									
0.1	0.2	0.3	0.5	1.0	2.0	3.0	5.0	10	20	50

mm/hour

Frozen Precipitation Rate									
0.1	0.2	0.3	0.5	1.0	2.0	3.0	5.0	10	20	50

mm/hour

23. Complete the following paragraph to explain how the Pineapple Express can cause extreme rainfall and snowfall in California.

In the tropical Pacific Ocean, warm ocean water enters the atmosphere by the process of *evaporation / condensation / precipitation*. Prevailing winds bring the moisture-filled air toward California, where it cools as it rises to pass over mountains. Water vapor in the cooling air *condenses / evaporates / disappears*, and precipitation falls. This is one example of how landforms, winds, and the ocean influence California's weather.

24. Think back to the satellite image of California and use the word bank to complete the description. You do not have to use all of the words in the word bank.

California's Coast Range forces humid air masses from the Pacific Ocean to rise and cool. This brings ____________ weather and results in ____________ vegetation on the western side of the Coast Range. On the eastern side, ____________ air flows across the land and results in ____________ vegetation.

WORD BANK
- rainy
- dry
- dense
- little

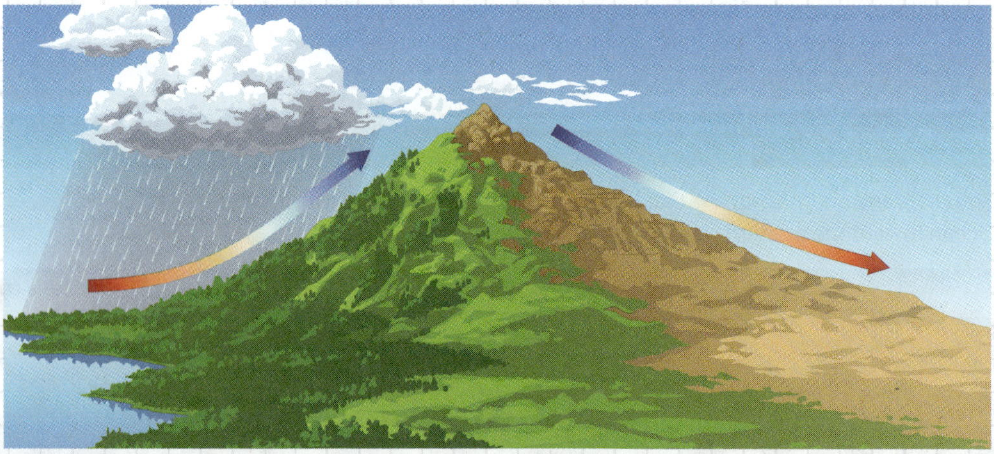

Analyze Air Masses

Air masses form over large regions and move to new places due to air pressure differences. Air masses can change as they move. For example, a polar air mass moving over warm land will become warmer. Explore the map of air masses that influence weather in North America.

25. Weather changes as air masses meet and interact. Which air masses most likely influence weather in California? Use the map and your knowledge of air masses and prevailing winds to support your claim.

Air Masses that Affect Weather in North America

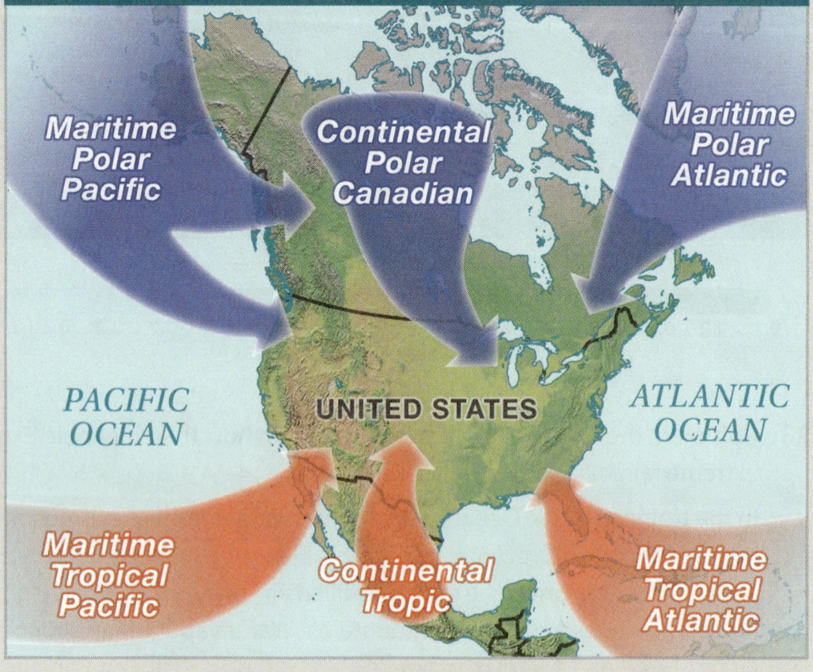
Maritime Polar Pacific
Continental Polar Canadian
Maritime Polar Atlantic
PACIFIC OCEAN
UNITED STATES
ATLANTIC OCEAN
Maritime Tropical Pacific
Continental Tropic
Maritime Tropical Atlantic

Continue Your Exploration

Name: _____   **Date:** _____

Check out the path below or go online to choose one of the other paths shown.

| Snowflake Sizes and Patterns | • **El Niño and La Niña: Effects on Local Weather**
 • **Hands-On Labs** ✋
 • **Propose Your Own Path** | *Go online to choose one of these other paths.* |

Although snowflakes have a variety of structures, they all form by the same process. As air temperature cools, tiny droplets of water freeze and form ice crystals. Many crystals have a symmetrical pattern with six "arms." As the crystals fall toward Earth, water vapor in the atmosphere freezes onto the crystals and they grow larger.

The unique shapes of individual snowflakes are a result of the temperatures in which they formed and fell to Earth. These ice crystals all have a similar 6-armed shape because they encountered similar conditions as the crystals fell through the atmosphere.

The Effects of Temperature and Humidity on Snowflakes

The variation in the shapes of snowflakes is a result of differences in air temperature and humidity. A crystal may begin to grow in one shape, but then as it falls through the atmosphere, changes in air temperature or humidity can cause it to grow in a different manner. For example, as air temperature increases during the snow crystal's descent, the sharper edges of a snowflake may become smoother.

The shape that the snow crystal has when it lands on a surface will determine the type of snow. Large snowflakes stack loosely on top of each other, leaving air pockets and producing fluffy, airy snow. Very cold temperatures and low humidity produce tiny snow crystals that can fall for hours and will barely build up. Warmer temperatures near freezing will produce heavy, wet snow.

Continue Your Exploration

The Effects of Temperature and Humidity on Snowflake Type

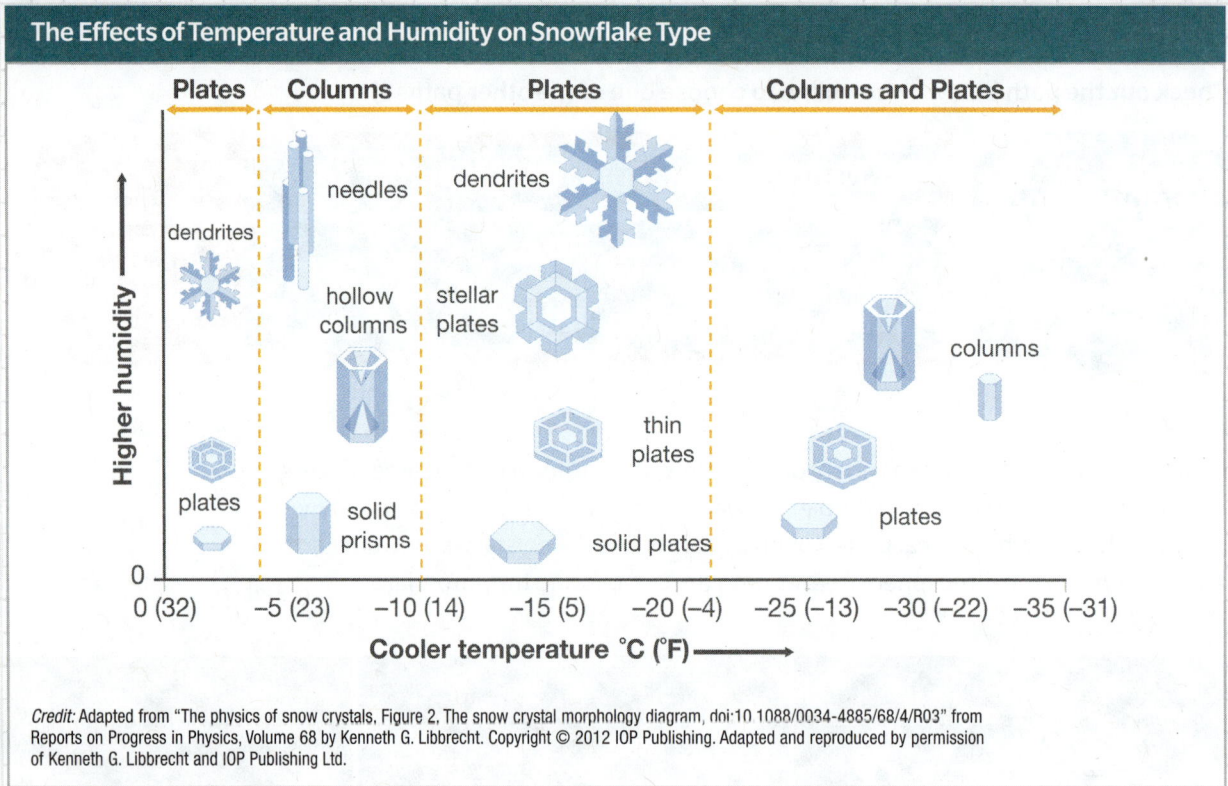

Credit: Adapted from "The physics of snow crystals, Figure 2, The snow crystal morphology diagram, doi:10.1088/0034-4885/68/4/R03" from Reports on Progress in Physics, Volume 68 by Kenneth G. Libbrecht. Copyright © 2012 IOP Publishing. Adapted and reproduced by permission of Kenneth G. Libbrecht and IOP Publishing Ltd.

1. What patterns do you notice in snowflake type and humidity across all temperatures?

2. **Do the Math** Over which temperature range do needles form? Tell whether these temperature ranges include *positive* or *negative* numbers.

   Needles form between _____ °C and _____ °C, or _____ °F and _____ °F. Even though the Celsius temperature range includes _____ numbers and the Fahrenheit temperature range includes _____ numbers, they represent the same below-freezing temperatures.

3. What weather conditions might bring snow that is good for building a snowman? Explain.

4. **Collaborate** Develop a list of interview questions and interview people about their experiences with winter weather. Take notes during each interview. Summarize your interviews into a short article, and be sure to use complete sentences.

Can You Explain It?

Name: _____ Date: _____

What could cause a storm like this to happen suddenly?

Explore Online

EVIDENCE NOTEBOOK

Refer to the notes in your Evidence Notebook to help you construct an explanation for what causes sudden changes in weather like this storm.

1. State your claim. Make sure your claim fully explains how the storm suddenly occurred.

2. Summarize the evidence you have gathered to support your claim and explain your reasoning.

Checkpoints

Answer the following questions to check your understanding of the lesson.

Use the photo to answer Questions 3–4.

3. Differences in air humidity / pressure / pollution cause wind that blows snow across this landscape.

4. How did the cold front that caused this snowstorm form?

   A. Two warm air masses met.

   B. A cold air mass pushed up a warm air mass.

   C. Two cold air masses met.

   D. A warm air mass pushed up a cold air mass.

Use the map to answer Questions 5–6.

5. What type of weather do you notice near low-pressure areas?

   A. precipitation

   B. heat waves

   C. dry weather

6. What does the distance between the isobars near the high-pressure area tell you?

   A. They are close together, so it is windy.

   B. They are far apart, so it is windy.

   C. They are far apart, so winds are calm.

   D. They are close together, so winds are calm.

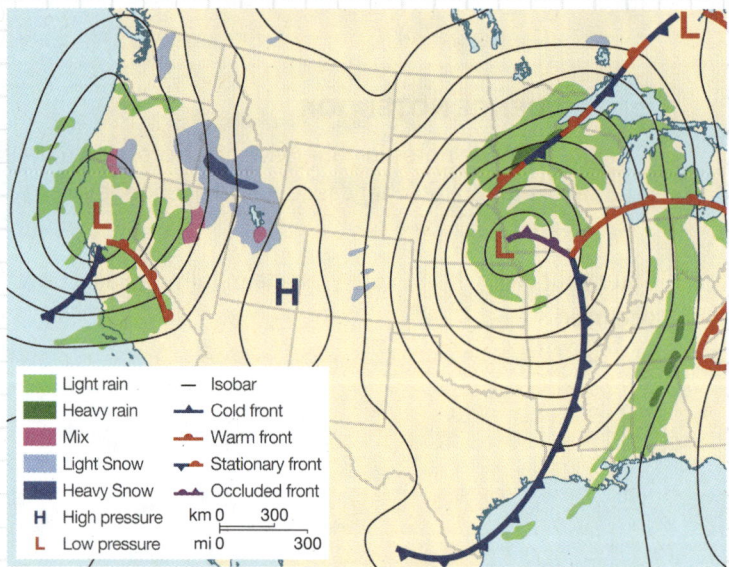

7. Which factors would most likely affect the weather on a small, flat island in the ocean? Select all that apply.

   A. the formation of dry air masses

   B. ocean surface currents

   C. the formation of humid air masses

   D. the rain-shadow effect

8. Which is true about factors that influence weather?

   A. Precipitation type depends on air temperature.

   B. The rain shadow effect causes equal precipitation on both sides of a mountain.

   C. As air sinks, it absorbs moisture and forms rain clouds.

Interactive Review

Complete this section to review the main concepts of the lesson.

Temperature, humidity, and air pressure are factors that influence the weather we experience daily.

A. Explain how temperature and humidity are related and how that relationship impacts the weather.

High- and low-pressure systems affect wind speed and direction and are related to specific types of weather.

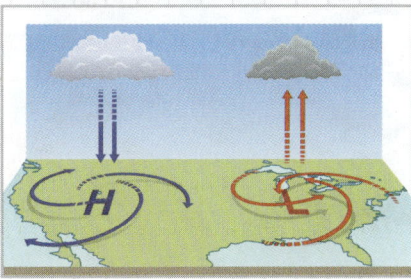

B. Why are low-pressure systems associated with rain but high-pressure systems are accompanied by clear skies?

Air masses take on characteristics of the regions over which they form. Moving air masses form fronts that affect the weather.

C. Provide an example of a front and explain how it forms.

California's weather is influenced by the Pacific Ocean, by landforms, and by prevailing winds.

D. How do mountains in California affect the weather?

Weather Predictions Are Based on Patterns

Weather prediction helps us prepare when we go outside.

Explore First

Analyzing Historical Weather Research what the weather was like on the day you were born. What was it like on your past birthdays? Describe any patterns you notice. Predict what the weather will be like next time your birthday comes around. What did you base your prediction on?

Go online to view the digital version of
the Hands-On Lab for this lesson and to
download additional lab resources.

CAN YOU EXPLAIN IT?

How does this forecaster know that stormy weather is coming?

This weather forecaster uses weather maps and charts to show her prediction that a cold front is going to bring heavy rain and storms to the area over the next five days.

Explore Online

1. How might this forecaster predict future weather conditions? Describe any data or tools she might use, and explain whether you think her prediction is likely to be accurate.

EVIDENCE NOTEBOOK As you explore this lesson, gather evidence to explain how weather predictions are made.

Using Mathematical Models to Make Predictions

Models in Science

How does an animal digest its food? Can a building withstand an earthquake? *Models* are tools that help scientists answer these kinds of difficult questions. Models are used in science to represent things that are large, small, dangerous, or complex. They help scientists make predictions and test ideas to find solutions to challenging questions.

It is possible for scientists to make models because events in nature often follow predictable patterns. For example, if you drop a ball from a certain height, you can predict how high it will bounce. Another pattern in nature is the yearly migration of some animals. Observing patterns in nature is the basis of science. These observations lead to explanations about the way the world works. Although these explanations are supported by observations, they may not be accurate. For example, the sun appears to move across the sky. For thousands of years, people observed this pattern and incorrectly concluded that Earth was the center of our solar system.

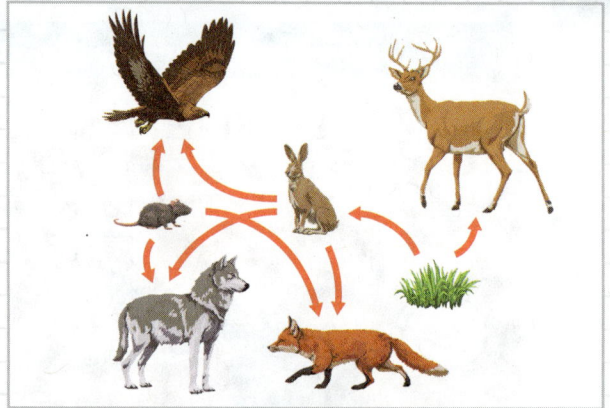

This model is called a *food web*. It uses arrows to show feeding relationships in an ecosystem. For example, rabbits eat grass and foxes eat rabbits.

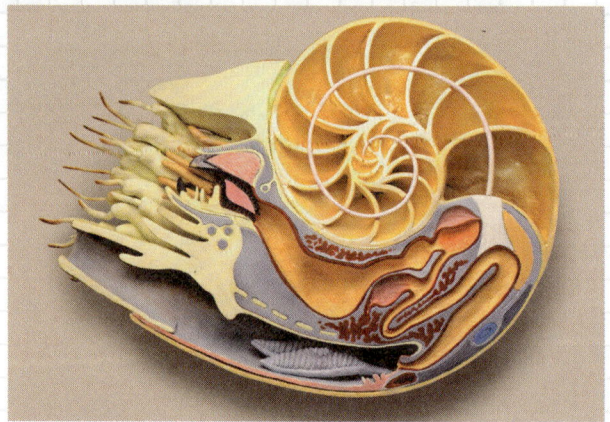

This model shows a cross-section of an animal called a nautilus. It has a shell made up of many chambers filled with gas to help the nautilus float. The nautilus fills its chambers with water when it wants to dive deeper.

2. Describe the food web by writing *increase* or *decrease*.

The rabbit population would _____ if the supply of grass became limited. This would happen because grass is a food source for rabbits. If the population of rabbits and mice decreased, the population of hawks would likely

_____.

3. Write one question that the nautilus model could be used to answer. Write one question that the satellite image could be used to answer.

This satellite image is a computer model that uses data about Earth. In the model, healthy vegetation stands out in red. Areas burned by wildfires are shown in black.

Mathematical Models

A *mathematical model* is a model that uses equations to represent the way a system or a process works. Some mathematical models are just a single equation. Others are more complex and involve many related equations. In order to use a mathematical model, data are collected. Next, data values are used to replace the variables of the equation or sets of equations in the model. Finally, calculations are made to get the results.

Mathematical Models and Prediction

Whether they are simple or complex, mathematical models can be used to make predictions. They can predict how something might work under different conditions. For example, you could use an equation to predict what an object would weigh on different planets. The equation is useful because we cannot easily travel to other planets and weigh the object. Mathematical models can also help to predict an event at a future time. Predictions can be shown on maps, graphs, and other displays.

Do the Math
Predict Run Times Using a Model

Dwayne has been training for cross-country tryouts. He has been tracking his progress by recording his run times in a table every Saturday. In the left column, Dwayne noted the week number. In the right column, he noted his run times.

4. Plot the data from the table onto the graph.

Dwayne's Weekly One-Mile Run Times

Time (week)	Run Time (min)
Week 1	11.95
Week 2	12.25
Week 3	11.40
Week 4	10.10
Week 5	9.25
Week 6	8.60

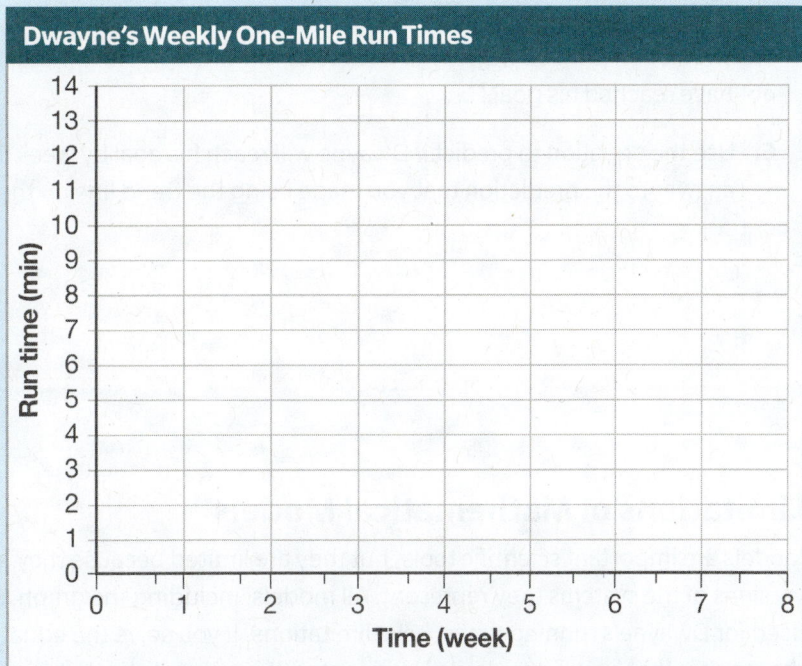

Dwayne's Weekly One-Mile Run Times

5. Dwayne's goal is to run 1 mile in 8 minutes or less. In order to predict when he will reach his goal, he drew a *trend line* that fits along the data points. Use a ruler to extend the trend line to week 8. According to the line, will he reach his goal by week 7? By week 8?

Trend in Dwayne's Weekly One-Mile Run Times

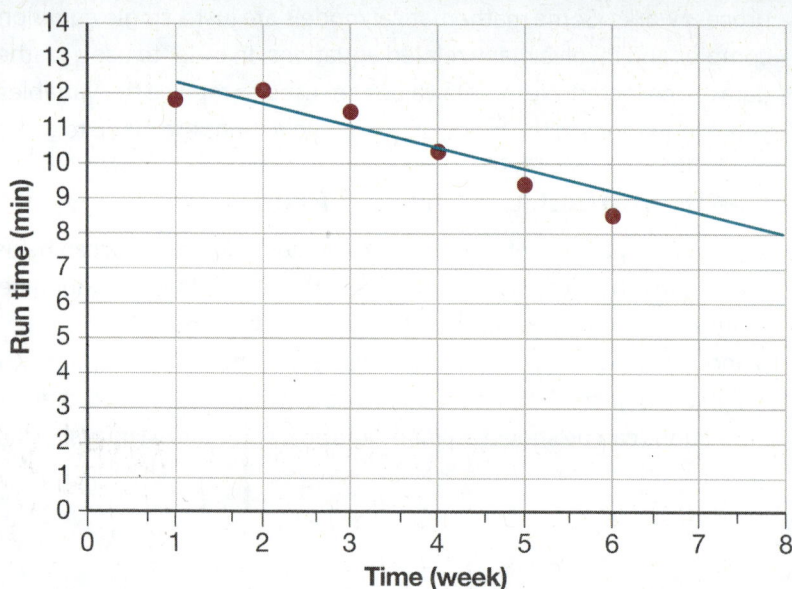

Did you know this line represents an equation? Another way to make a prediction about Dwayne's goal is to use the equation of the trend line:

$$y = -\frac{2}{3}x + 13$$

y = run time in minutes
x = time in weeks

The variable y represents Dwayne's run times. The variable x represents the week. To predict the run time for week 7, evaluate the equation for $x = 7$:

$$y = -\left(\frac{2}{3}\right)(7) + 13$$
$$y = 8.3 \text{ min}$$

The prediction is that Dwayne will be able to run a mile in 8.3 minutes by week 7. He will not have reached his goal.

6. Use the equation to predict if Dwayne will reach his goal by week 8. Compare your answer to the prediction that you made using the trend line on the graph.

Limitations of Mathematical Models

Models are important scientific tools, but they are limited because they are simplified versions of the systems they represent. All models, including the graph and equation used for Dwayne's running times, have limitations. If you solve the equation for week 15, the result is that he will run a mile in 3 minutes. It is not realistic that a person could run a mile in 3 minutes. Therefore, this model is only valid within a specific range of speeds.

Hands-On Lab
Predict Costs Using a Model

You will use a mathematical model to make predictions.

Suppose you are a manufacturer who must ship rope of four different lengths to a store. You would like to figure out your shipping costs. For this, you need to know the weight of each piece of rope. However, you do not have time to weigh each piece. You can measure a few samples of rope and use a mathematical model to predict the weight of materials and estimate your costs.

> **MATERIALS**
> • meterstick
> • rope, pieces of different lengths (4)
> • spring scale with 5 g increments

Procedure and Analysis

STEP 1 Select four pieces of rope of different lengths.

STEP 2 Measure the length in centimeters of all four pieces of rope. Record your measurements in the table.

STEP 3 Measure the weight in grams of three individual pieces of rope. Record your measurements in the table. Set those pieces of rope aside.

	Rope 1	Rope 2	Rope 3	Rope 4
Length (cm)				
Weight (g)	actual:	actual:	actual:	predicted: actual:

STEP 4 Make a graph that plots the length and weight of the three pieces of rope. Include a title and be sure to label your x-axis and y-axis.

STEP 5 Use your graph to predict the weight of the fourth piece of rope. Record your prediction in the table.

STEP 6 Explain how you used your graph to predict the weight of the fourth piece of rope.

STEP 7 You need to ship 10 pieces of each length of rope. Estimate the total weight of the ropes you will be shipping.

STEP 8 How much would the shipment cost if the shipping rate was $1.00 per 1000 grams? Round to the nearest cent.

STEP 9 Measure the actual weight of the fourth piece of rope. Record your measurement in the table.

STEP 10 Compare your prediction to the actual weight of the fourth piece of rope. Was your prediction accurate? Can you explain why or why not?

STEP 11 Would your estimate for the shipping cost change when using the actual weight of the fourth piece of rope? Explain why your prediction was still useful even if it was not completely accurate.

STEP 12 **Engineer It** If you were a manufacturer, you would want your method of prediction to be as accurate as possible. Can you think of a way to improve your method so that your predictions are more likely to be accurate?

Estimate Air Temperature with Cricket Chirps

Can crickets and a mathematical model help us estimate the temperature? Since the late 1800s, different equations have been developed to calculate the temperature based on the number of chirps a cricket makes over time. It was found that only certain species of crickets make reliable thermometers. The following equation works between 55–100 °F.

Snowy tree cricket chirp equation:
$T = N + 40$

Variables:

T = temperature (°F)

N = number of chirps every 13 seconds

This snowy tree cricket chirps at a different rate depending on the temperature outside! However, other things affect these crickets' chirp rates, such as age and mating behavior.

7. A student recorded 39 chirps in 13 seconds around 4 p.m. Use the equation to estimate the temperature.

8. The actual temperature was measured at 4 p.m., and it was 76.6 °F. Explain why your estimate may have been different. Note any other limitations this model might have.

9. The hourly temperature forecast for the evening is 70 °F at 5 p.m., 64 °F at 6 p.m., and 62 °F at 7 p.m. Predict the rate at which the crickets will chirp at these times as the sun sets. Start by rearranging the equation to solve for N: $N = T - 40$.

Explaining the Accuracy of Weather Prediction

Weather Prediction

Have you ever seen a weather forecast online or in a newspaper? A **weather forecast** is a prediction about the state of the atmosphere at a given place and time. Weather forecasts are commonly provided using maps and weather charts. They can include predictions about temperature, wind, precipitation, cloud cover, and humidity. Have you ever used a weather forecast to make plans or decide what to wear? Weather forecasts not only help people plan their day, but they also provide warnings about severe weather, such as blizzards and hurricanes. Pilots also rely on forecasts to navigate the planes we fly in. Who else might use weather forecasts?

10. This weather chart shows past and current temperatures. Try to predict the temperature for Friday.

Monday	Tuesday	Wednesday	Thursday (today)	Friday (tomorrow)
5 °F	0 °F	1 °F	−2 °F	

11. What did you base your prediction on? What other data would you want to use if you were asked to predict the weather?

12. Do you think your prediction would be within a degree of the actual temperature? Within three degrees? Within five degrees? Explain your answer.

Data Used in Weather Prediction

To make a weather forecast, past and current weather conditions are considered. This includes things such as wind speed, air pressure, humidity, cloud cover, precipitation, and temperature. Also taken into account are the current locations and movements of air masses, fronts, and high- and low-pressure systems.

Weather Forecast for Truckee, California			
Wednesday Nov. 25	**Thursday** Nov. 26	**Friday** Nov. 27	
HIGH **75 °F** LOW 50 °F Mostly Sunny	**60 °F** 22 °F Scattered Thunderstorms	**26 °F** 18 °F Freezing Rain and Windy	This row shows predictions for the high and low temperatures along with a description of the predicted weather for each day.
Chance of Precipitation 0%	Chance of Precipitation 60%	Chance of Precipitation 90%	**Precipitation** This is the predicted chance of precipitation.
Wind southwest 14 mi/h	Wind south 16 mi/h	Wind northeast 20 mi/h	**Wind** Predicted wind speed is shown in miles per hour. Wind direction is shown with an arrow.
Humidity 26%	Humidity 88%	Humidity 94%	**Humidity** This is the predicted relative humidity.

Weather Forecast Models

Past and current weather data are used to build weather forecast models. Weather forecast models are based on the physical laws that determine how the atmosphere works. They are mathematical models that contain many related equations. The equations represent the atmosphere and its interactions in the Earth system. Because so many factors influence weather, forecast models are very complex. For example, ocean currents affect humidity in some locations, and humidity impacts precipitation and cloud cover.

In the early 1900s, the first weather forecast model was used. It took so long to do the calculations by hand that, by the time the forecast was ready, the weather had already happened. By the 1950s, computers could do these calculations more quickly. Today, supercomputers do them even faster. Five-day forecasts can be made with about the same level of certainty as a two-day forecast could thirty years ago. This is due to the continual improvement of weather forecast models and the increased speed of supercomputers. Meteorologists and forecasters analyze weather forecast model results before the results are shared with the public.

EVIDENCE NOTEBOOK

13. How do forecasters use mathematical models to make predictions about future weather conditions? Record your evidence.

Limitations of Weather Forecast Models

All weather predictions contain some degree of uncertainty—that is, they rarely turn out to be 100% accurate. Weather is a complex phenomenon that is affected by many factors. One small change in a factor, such as wind direction, can affect many other factors and result in different weather conditions. Because it is hard to predict the exact timing or location of future weather events, weather forecasts involve probabilities and percentages. For example, you may see a forecast that describes the probability of rain occurring for a specific area and time. This probability is often given as a percentage.

Weather forecast models are constantly being improved. Predictions are compared to what actually happens with the weather. For example, if a forecast predicted the temperature on Friday, the observed temperature on Friday is compared to the prediction. This comparison process would be followed for many days. If the predictions mostly match the recorded temperatures, then the model is a good predictor of temperature. If the model often predicts that it will be warmer or cooler than it actually is, then adjustments are made to improve the model. This process repeats as models are constantly improved to make predictions more likely to be accurate. Models are also improved in order to make predictions further into the future.

14. Look back to the forecast chart and maps for Truckee. Compare these predictions to what actually happened with the weather. Describe your findings. If the forecast chart did not predict exactly what happened with the weather, explain why it is still useful.

Weather Observations in Truckee, California

This weather chart shows past weather in Truckee. These weather data were recorded for the same days the predictions were made.

Wednesday Nov. 25	Thursday Nov. 26	Friday Nov. 27
HIGH 76 °F	59 °F	29 °F
LOW 35 °F	28 °F	22 °F
Mostly Sunny	Fog, Rain, and Snow Mix	Rain and Snow Mix
Precipitation Amount 0.00 in.	Precipitation Amount 0.52 in.	Precipitation Amount 0.34 in.
Wind ↗ southwest 15 mi/h	Wind ↑ south 17 mi/h	Wind ↙ northeast 21 mi/h
Humidity 48%	Humidity 90%	Humidity 90%

EVIDENCE NOTEBOOK

15. Why do weather forecast models have limitations? Why are they still useful to people? Record your evidence.

16. Interpret the weather forecast maps to complete the descriptions.

These maps show the *past / predicted / current* weather. There is a *cold / warm / stationary* front moving toward Texas. This front is a boundary where a cold air mass is moving beneath a warm air mass and causing the warm air to rise. From Thursday to Friday, you can see that precipitation along this front *increases / decreases / stays the same*.

Two-Day Weather Forecast Model Results

These weather forecast maps were produced on a Wednesday. The maps show data resulting from a computer model that predicts the movement of fronts, pressure systems, and precipitation. The model also predicts how heavy the precipitation will be.

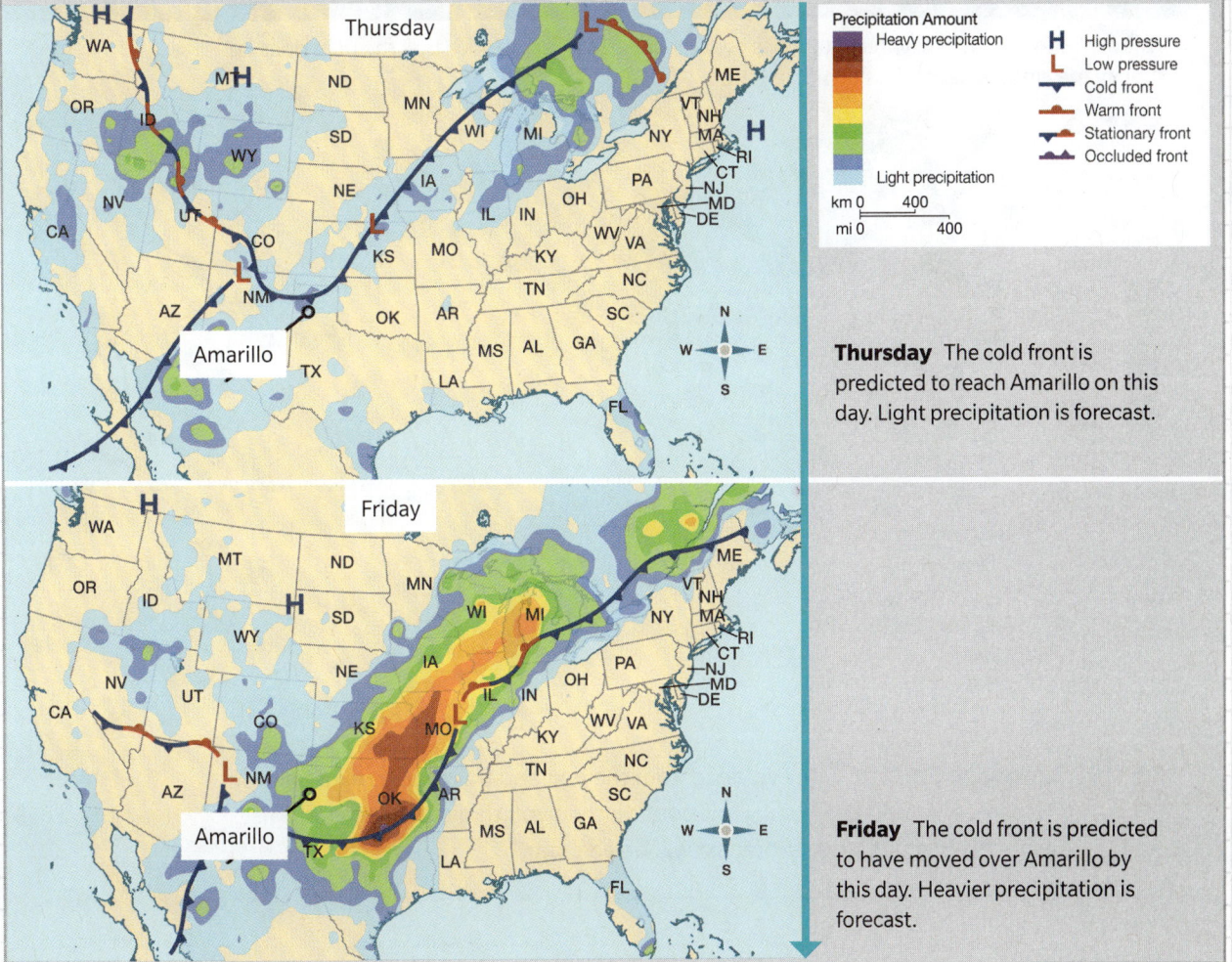

Thursday The cold front is predicted to reach Amarillo on this day. Light precipitation is forecast.

Friday The cold front is predicted to have moved over Amarillo by this day. Heavier precipitation is forecast.

17. Act Analyze the maps with a partner and act as meteorologists who are planning to deliver a weather forecast for Amarillo, Texas on Wednesday night. Explain how Amarillo's weather will change on Thursday and Friday.

18. Complete the descriptions to explain the limitations of the weather forecast model that produced these maps.

The accuracy of the model's results decrease with time into the future. Therefore, the forecast results for Thursday are likely to be *more / less* accurate than they will be for Friday. The model shows the *type / amount / rate* of precipitation with different colors, but the model does not give an exact quantity.

Analyze Weather Forecasts

Different models are used to predict weather for different ranges of time.

- Short-range weather forecasts make predictions for 0 to 3 days into the future.
- Medium-range weather forecasts make predictions for 3 to 7 days into the future.
- Long-range weather forecasts, or *outlooks*, range from weeks to months into the future.

In general, short-range forecasts are more likely to be accurate than forecasts made for longer periods of time. Given the continuous changes that occur in all of the factors that influence the weather, even short-range forecast results are not always accurate.

24-Hour Probability of Precipitation

This map shows how likely precipitation is over the next 24 hours. Notice that the map does not specify the amount or the type of precipitation.

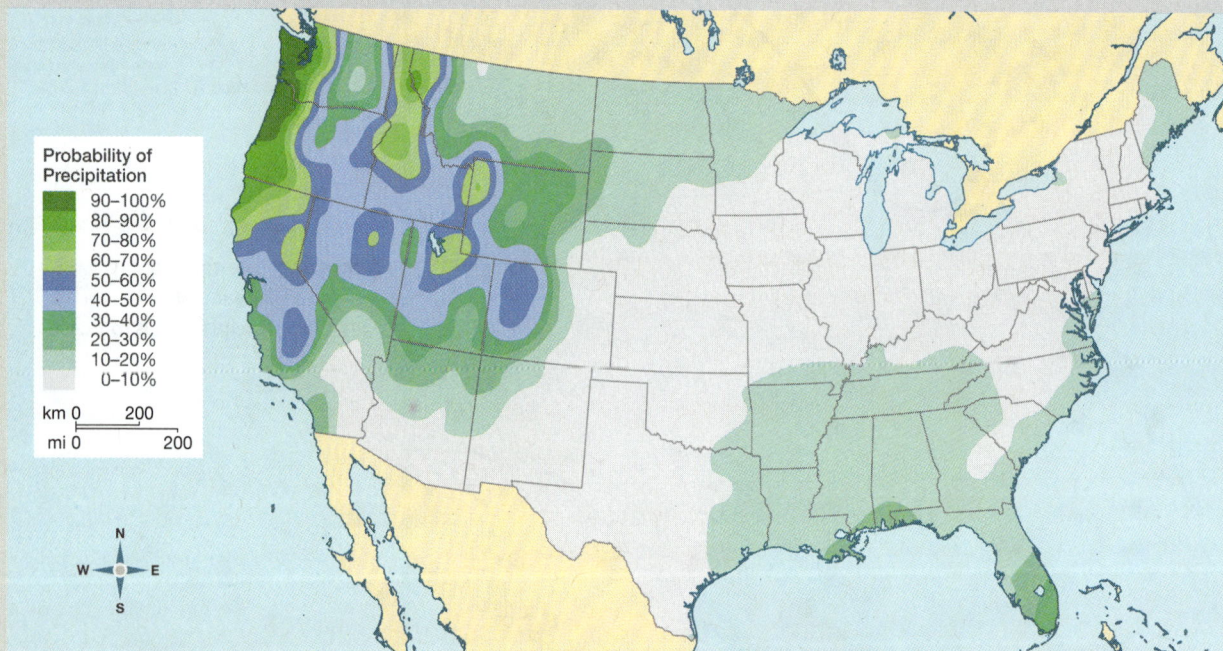

Probability of Precipitation

- 90–100%
- 80–90%
- 70–80%
- 60–70%
- 50–60%
- 40–50%
- 30–40%
- 20–30%
- 10–20%
- 0–10%

km 0   200
mi 0   200

19. **Language SmArts** Cite evidence from the text and this map to explain how this forecast could be useful. How confident do you think the meteorologist using this map is that this forecast will be accurate?

20. Based on this map, what travel advice would you give to someone planning to visit the beach in Oregon tomorrow?

Continue Your Exploration

Name: _____   Date: _____

Check out the path below or go online to choose one of the other paths shown.

People in Science

- **Hurricane Prediction**
- **Hands-On Labs** ✋
- **Propose Your Own Path**

Go online to choose one of these other paths.

J. Marshall Shepherd, Meteorologist and Climatologist

Dr. J. Marshall Shepherd, who works at the University of Georgia, has been interested in weather since he made his own weather instruments for a school science project. Although the instruments he uses today, such as computers and satellites, are much larger and much more powerful than the instruments he made in school, they give him some of the same information.

In his work, Dr. Shepherd tries to understand weather events and relate them to current weather and climate change.

Do Cities Affect Rainfall?

Rainfall patterns are influenced by many factors, such as latitude, prevailing winds, and ocean currents. Some places are rainy because they are near an ocean or because they are located at certain latitudes. Other places are dry. For example, many deserts exist at 30 degrees latitude, both north and south of the equator. Dr. Shepherd and other scientists noticed increased rainfall in cities and in areas downwind of cities. For example, there was a 10-year thunderstorm study done in Atlanta, Georgia. The results, given in 2010, showed that during the summer months, there was an increase in rainfall and lightning over the city and downwind of the city, but not over the surrounding areas.

Continue Your Exploration

One explanation for the increased rainfall in cities is that dark surfaces, such as asphalt, absorb more energy from the sun than surfaces in a natural landscape do. Average temperatures in cities can be 6–8°F (3–4°C) warmer than the temperatures in natural landscapes surrounding a city. The warmer city surfaces warm the air directly above them. Because cities affect air temperature, they affect rainfall patterns. As warm air rises into the atmosphere, it begins to cool down. Moisture in the air forms clouds and brings rain to the city and to places downwind of the city, as seen in the Atlanta, Georgia, study. Another explanation is that cities disrupt air flow because of the tall buildings. Just like air rises over a tall mountain and causes rainfall, city buildings may have a similar effect.

1. One of the cities Dr. Shepherd has studied is Houston, Texas. He found that it rains more in Houston than in surrounding areas. What do you think will happen to rainfall amounts if Houston grows larger?

   A. Rainfall amounts will likely decrease in the city.

   B. Rainfall amounts will likely increase in the city.

   C. Rainfall amounts will likely be the same in the city.

2. **Draw** Make a diagram to show how cities might affect rainfall patterns. Include how a city's landscape impacts the flow of energy and the cycling of water.

3. A physical model is a miniature version of some part of the real world. How could you model how a city affects weather? Describe your physical model. What might you use to represent the sun, wind, rain, city surfaces, and natural surfaces?

4. **Collaborate** Research the historical weather data for a city that has grown very quickly over the past century. Are there any patterns in the precipitation data over time? Do you notice any other weather patterns that change over time? Record your observations. Share your results with a partner.

Can You Explain It?

Name: _____   Date: _____

How does this forecaster know that stormy weather is coming?

EVIDENCE NOTEBOOK

Refer to the notes in your Evidence Notebook to help you construct an explanation about how weather predictions are made.

1. State your claim. Make sure your claim fully explains how this forecaster predicted the weather, including any data or tools she might have used. Describe how accurate you think her forecast will be.

2. Summarize the evidence you have gathered to support your claim and explain your reasoning.

Checkpoints

Answer the following questions to check your understanding of the lesson.

Use the graph to answer Questions 3–4.

3. Using a ruler, draw a single, straight trend line that comes as close as possible to all the points, and extend it to day 40. How tall will the seedling be on day 40 according to your trend line model?

   A. 42 cm

   B. 32 cm

   C. 38 cm

   D. 34 cm

4. All models have limitations / graphs. By drawing a straight trend line on this graph, we are assuming the rate of growth is constant / changing. If the rate of growth changes as the plant ages, the line would / would not be straight and this model would not make a reliable prediction.

Seedling Growth

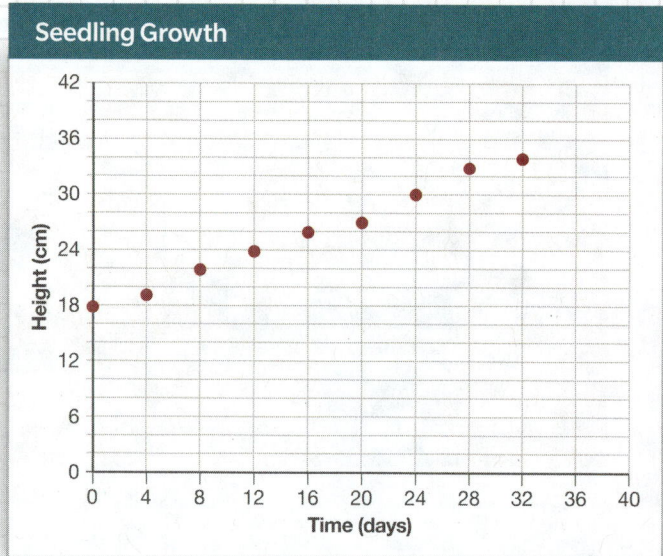

Use the map to answer Questions 5–6.

5. Currently, it is snowing in Fargo / Knoxville. It is likely to rain in Denver / Knoxville tomorrow because a cold / warm front is moving toward that area.

6. Rate the following forecast statements from 1 to 3, with 1 being the most likely to be accurate and 3 being the least likely to be accurate.

   _____ Tomorrow, it will be snowy in Fargo.

   _____ In seven days, it will be sunny in Denver.

   _____ In four days, it will be rainy in Knoxville.

Current Weather Conditions

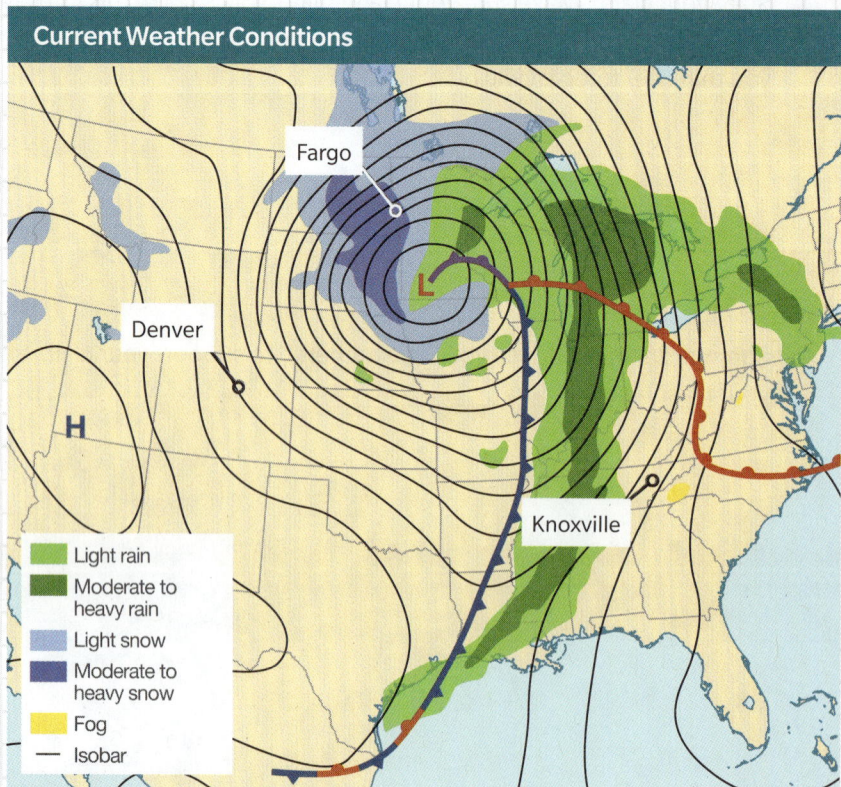

Interactive Review

Complete this section to review the main concepts of the lesson.

Mathematical models include equations that represent processes or phenomena. All mathematical models have limitations.

A. Why are mathematical models so valuable to scientists who study complex phenomena like weather?

Weather forecasts are made by analyzing various weather data and determining the probability that certain weather conditions will exist in the future based on patterns.

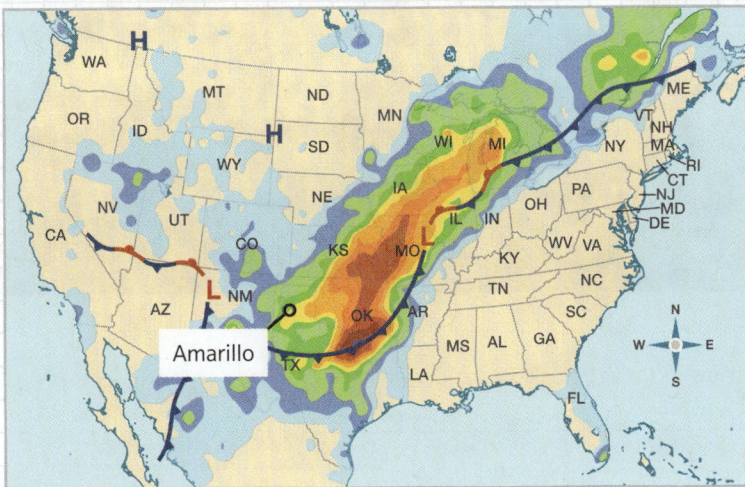

B. Weather forecast models have advantages and drawbacks. For example, one model may predict rain in a region with more accuracy than another model. Explain how the accuracy of a weather forecast model is tested.

Earth Has Different Regional Climates

These alpine wildflowers thrive in the cool and dry air in the Sierra Nevada Mountains.

Explore First

Observing Organisms Make a list of plants and animals you see in your local area. Compare your list with your classmates' lists. Discuss what factors might determine the types of plants and animals that live in your area. How are they affected by weather conditions? Do the plants and animals you see change with the seasons?

Go online to view the digital version of the Hands-On Lab for this lesson and to download additional lab resources.

CAN YOU EXPLAIN IT?

Why do these regions in California have such different climates?

Yosemite National Park is part of the Sierra Nevada Mountains. The park has cold, snowy winters and dry, short summers with temperatures that rarely reach 90 °F. There are pine forests, bears, deer, rivers of fish, and many kinds of birds. Two glaciers currently exist at the highest elevations.

Joshua Tree National Park is in the Mojave Desert. It is dry year-round. The park has very hot summers, and winters are mild with daytime temperatures in the 60s and 70s. Desert plants, such as this yucca, also known as a Joshua tree, are found here. The park is also home to many reptiles and birds as well as nocturnal animals such as coyotes, snakes, and rabbits.

1. Why do you think short-term and long-term weather conditions are different in different locations around the world?

2. Explore the photos and captions to identify differences between these parks. List your observations.

EVIDENCE NOTEBOOK As you explore the lesson, gather evidence to help explain why the climates in these two locations are so different.

Describing Climate

The world has many different climates. The average weather in an area over a long period is called **climate**. Descriptions of climate usually include temperature, precipitation averages, and sometimes information about winds, clouds, and seasons.

This area near Lake City, Colorado, is popular for ice climbers. The area has long, cold winters that are partially due to its high elevation.

The Tottori sand dunes in Japan exist because prevailing winds have continuously blown sand inland from Japan's coastline.

Surfers enjoy the Pacific Ocean and the mild, sunny climate in San Clemente, California. On average, there are 281 sunny days per year in this area.

3. **Discuss** Are there popular sports or outdoor activities where you live due to the climate?

Climate of San Francisco, California

This graph shows San Francisco's average monthly temperatures and precipitation totals. These averages were calculated over a long period of time, from 1981 to 2010.

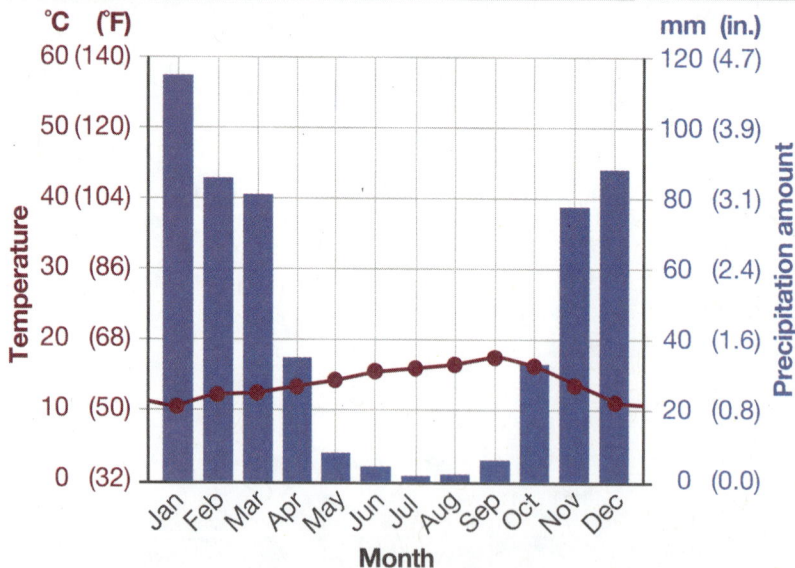

Temperature The red line on the graph shows that the average temperature does not vary much over the year. It stays between 10 °C and 20 °C.

Precipitation Unlike the average temperature, the average precipitation amount varies greatly over the year. The blue bars show that the precipitation amount is highest from November to March.

Credit: "Climate Graph San Francisco" from Climate: San Francisco by AM Online Projects. Copyright © AM Online Projects. Adapted and reproduced by permission of Alexander Merkel, AM Online Projects, © Climate-Data.org

4. This graph shows San Francisco's climate over a period of 1 / 10 / 30 years. The warmest month is January / July / September. The rainiest month is January / July / September.

Climate Descriptions

Climate descriptions include the average temperatures and precipitation amounts over many years. Precipitation is usually expressed as average monthly totals. Average monthly temperature is also included in climate descriptions, and sometimes includes the average high and low temperatures for each month. Climate may also be described by how windy, cloudy, or humid a place is. Finally, an area's climate description can include its seasons—or its lack of seasons.

Climate graphs are used to display average monthly rainfall and temperature data. By comparing climate graphs from two different places, we can describe similarities and differences about their climates. Climate graphs also allow us to make predictions. For example, a climate graph could help a person predict the best time of year to plan an outdoor event.

Do the Math
Analyze Climate Graphs

Imagine this: You won a trip to see the Great Wall of China, near the city of Beijing. To make sure that you can comfortably explore outside, you want to visit when the temperature is at or above 20 °C and when the chances of precipitation are low.

5. On the graph, circle the names of months with temperatures at or above 20 °C.

6. Of the months you circled, which month has the least amount of precipitation?

_____

7. The graph does not specify whether the precipitation is snow or rain. Use the graph to infer which time of year snow would fall and which time of year rain would fall. Explain your reasoning.

_____

_____

Climate of Beijing, China

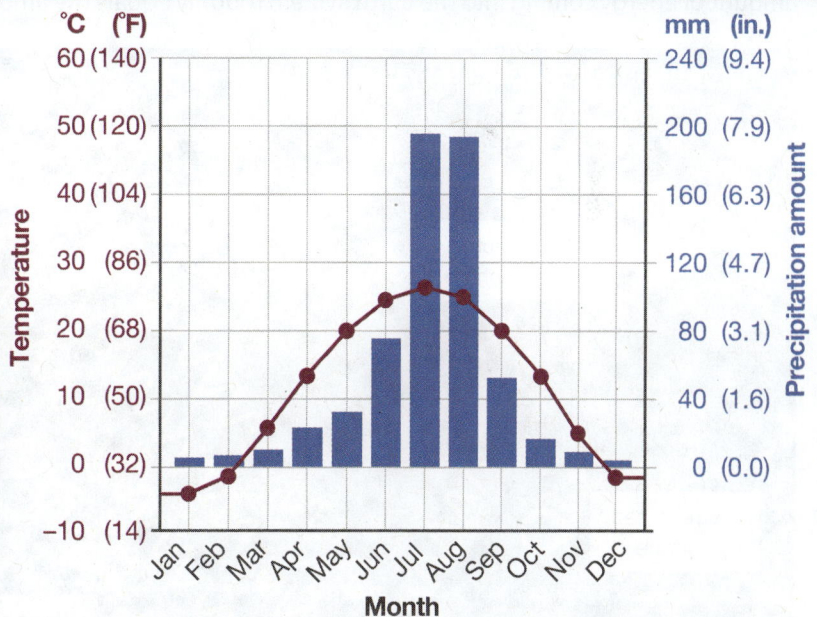

Credit: "Climate Graph Beijing, China" from Climate: Beijing, China by AM Online Projects. Copyright © AM Online Projects. Adapted and reproduced by permission of Alexander Merkel, AM Online Projects, © Climate-Data.org

_____

_____

_____

_____

_____

Describing How Sunlight Affects Climate

Energy from the sun powers the Earth system and Earth's climate. The sun radiates energy. This energy travels in the form of waves and has to go about 150 million kilometers (93 million miles) through space before it reaches Earth. Energy enters the Earth system during the day when the sun is shining. Some of the energy is reflected and some is absorbed by Earth's surface and atmosphere.

8. Think about how the ground might feel on your bare feet on a sunny day. Do you think different surfaces, such as the grass, a sidewalk, or sand, would have the same temperatures? Why or why not?

Earth's Energy Balance

Earth emits the energy it absorbs as radiation. This emitted energy drives currents in Earth's oceans and atmosphere and powers the climate system. Eventually, most of the energy emitted by Earth leaves the Earth system and goes back into space. So, the amount of energy coming into the Earth system roughly equals the amount going out.

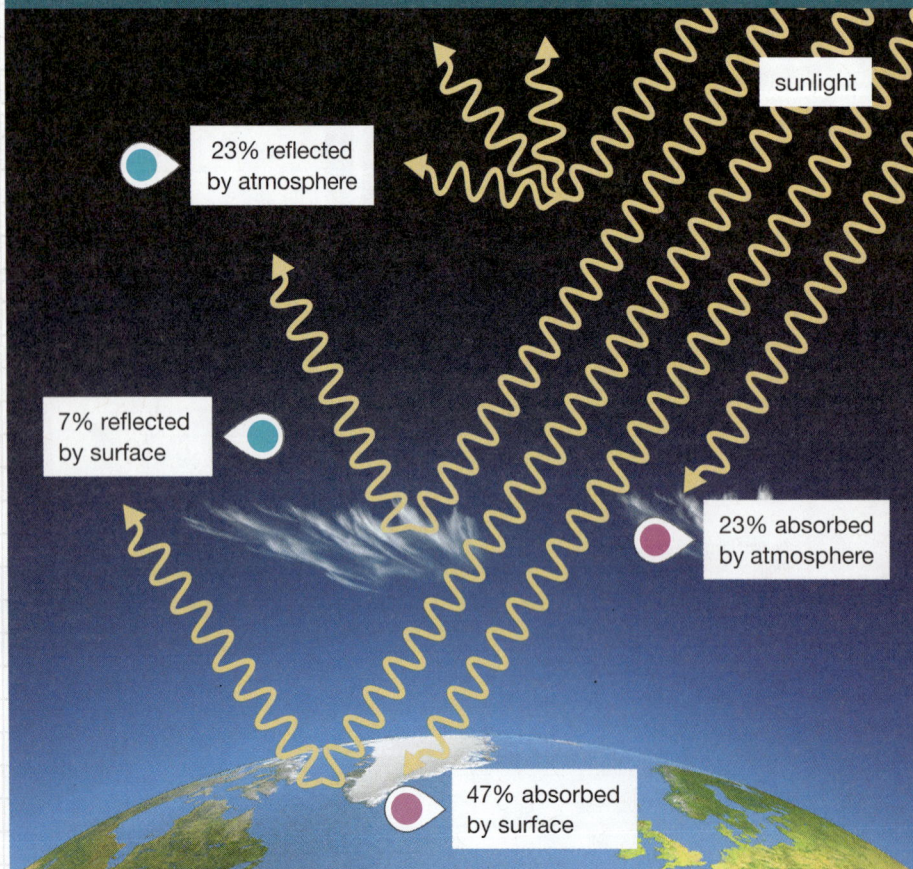

Energy Balance in the Climate System

sunlight

23% reflected by atmosphere

7% reflected by surface

23% absorbed by atmosphere

47% absorbed by surface

Sunlight is reflected. In total, about 30% of the sunlight that reaches Earth is reflected back into space. This energy is reflected by clouds and gases in the atmosphere and by light-colored materials on Earth's surface, such as snow and ice.

Sunlight is absorbed. Energy from the sun is absorbed by the atmosphere and by darker areas of Earth's surface, such as water, rock, and forests. The absorbed sunlight warms the surface. In turn, the surface warms the air above it.

Sunlight and Latitude

Latitude is the distance north or south of the equator. An area's climate depends on its latitude because latitude determines the intensity and amount of sunlight an area receives. Generally, areas that receive more direct sunlight are warmer than areas that receive less direct sunlight. Solar radiation arrives from the sun in essentially a straight line. However, because Earth's surface is curved, some of the sun's rays strike the surface more directly, while others strike at an angle.

9. **Collaborate** With a partner, model how sunlight strikes Earth. One person should shine a flashlight straight down onto a sheet of paper, and the other should trace the lighted area. Note the distance from the flashlight to the paper using a ruler. Next, shine the flashlight on a different area of the paper at the same distance away, but tilt the flashlight at an angle. Trace this shape. Explain how this models the way sunlight strikes Earth. Can you think of a way to improve this model? Explain.

Sunlight and Earth's Surface

sunlight

equator

Near the equator, sunlight hits Earth most directly. Therefore, a certain amount of solar energy strikes a relatively small area. So, areas near the equator have higher temperatures than areas farther from the equator do. When the flashlight is shined perpendicularly to the paper, the light strikes a relatively small area.

Near the poles, sunlight hits Earth indirectly. The same amount of sunlight is therefore spread over a larger area than at the equator. As a result, areas near the poles have lower temperatures than areas near the equator do. When the flashlight is shined at an angle, the light is spread over a larger area.

Albedos of Earth's Surface

Different materials absorb and reflect different amounts of sunlight. *Albedo* describes how much sunlight a surface reflects. Generally, dark-colored surfaces absorb a lot of sunlight. That means dark surfaces do not reflect much sunlight and have low albedos. The absorbed energy warms the surfaces and the surfaces warm the air above them.

Light-colored surfaces generally reflect a lot of sunlight, so they have high albedos. Surfaces with high albedos stay relatively cool because they reflect so much sunlight. Because these surfaces are cool, the air above them stays cool, too.

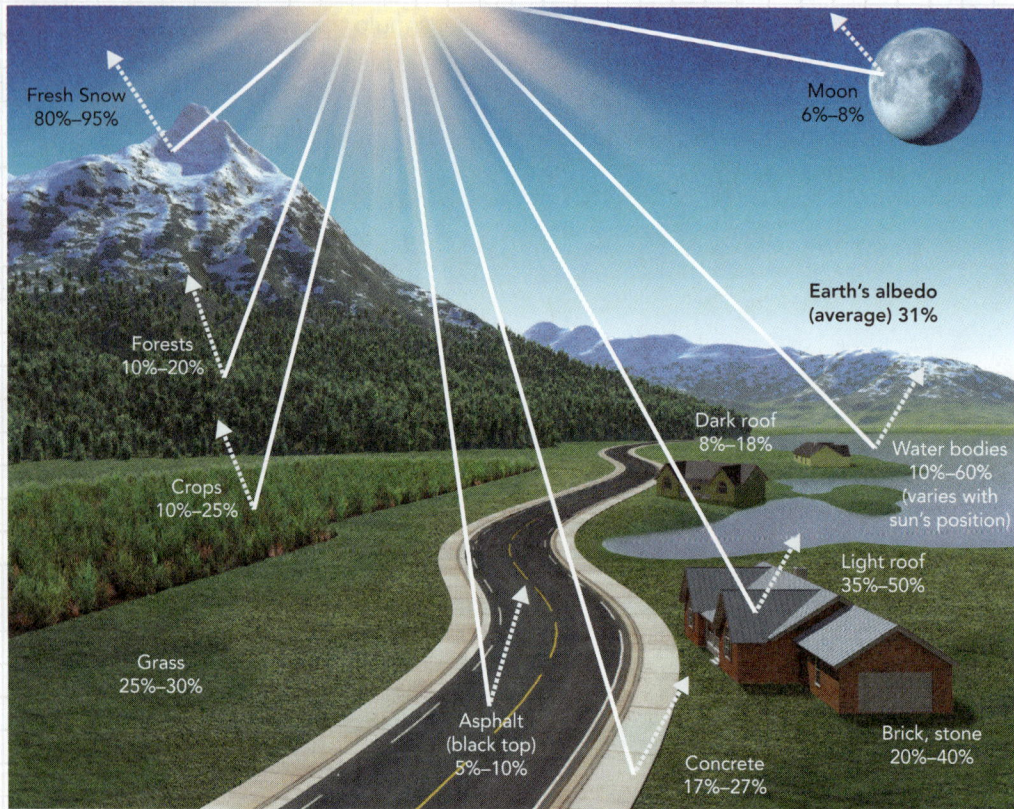

Light surfaces reflect more sunlight than dark surfaces do.

Fresh Snow 80%–95%

Moon 6%–8%

Earth's albedo (average) 31%

Forests 10%–20%

Dark roof 8%–18%

Water bodies 10%–60% (varies with sun's position)

Crops 10%–25%

Light roof 35%–50%

Grass 25%–30%

Asphalt (black top) 5%–10%

Concrete 17%–27%

Brick, stone 20%–40%

Credit: Adapted from Elemental Geosystems by Robert W. Christopherson. Copyright © 2007 by Pearson Education, Inc. Adapted and reproduced by permission of Pearson Education, Inc.

10. When humans build a parking lot of dark asphalt over a grassy field, the albedo of the surface _____. When ice and snow melt due to changes in climate, soil and rock are revealed and the albedo _____.

WORD BANK
- increases
- decreases

Albedo and Climate

A region's surface types affect its climate. In general, the more sunlight that is absorbed, the warmer the area will become. For example, in a city with a lot of dark surfaces, such as asphalt, the temperature can be a few degrees higher than the temperature in a nearby grassland. However, this is not always true. Think about a forest with a sandy desert nearby. You might think the forest would be warmer because the trees are darker than the sand. However, the forest could be cooler because its trees shade the ground and because trees use energy to release water from their leaves, which cools the air. The desert does not have any of these processes to lower temperatures.

EVIDENCE NOTEBOOK

11. How might the surface types in Yosemite and Joshua Tree National Parks affect their climates? Record your evidence.

Analyze Rooftop Albedos in Los Angeles

In cities, there are several human-made surfaces. Roofs, sidewalks, roads, and parking lots are often made up of materials such as asphalt and concrete. In a large city, such as Los Angeles, the colors of rooftops can have an impact on the local climate. Explore the map below to see the albedos of some of Los Angeles' rooftops.

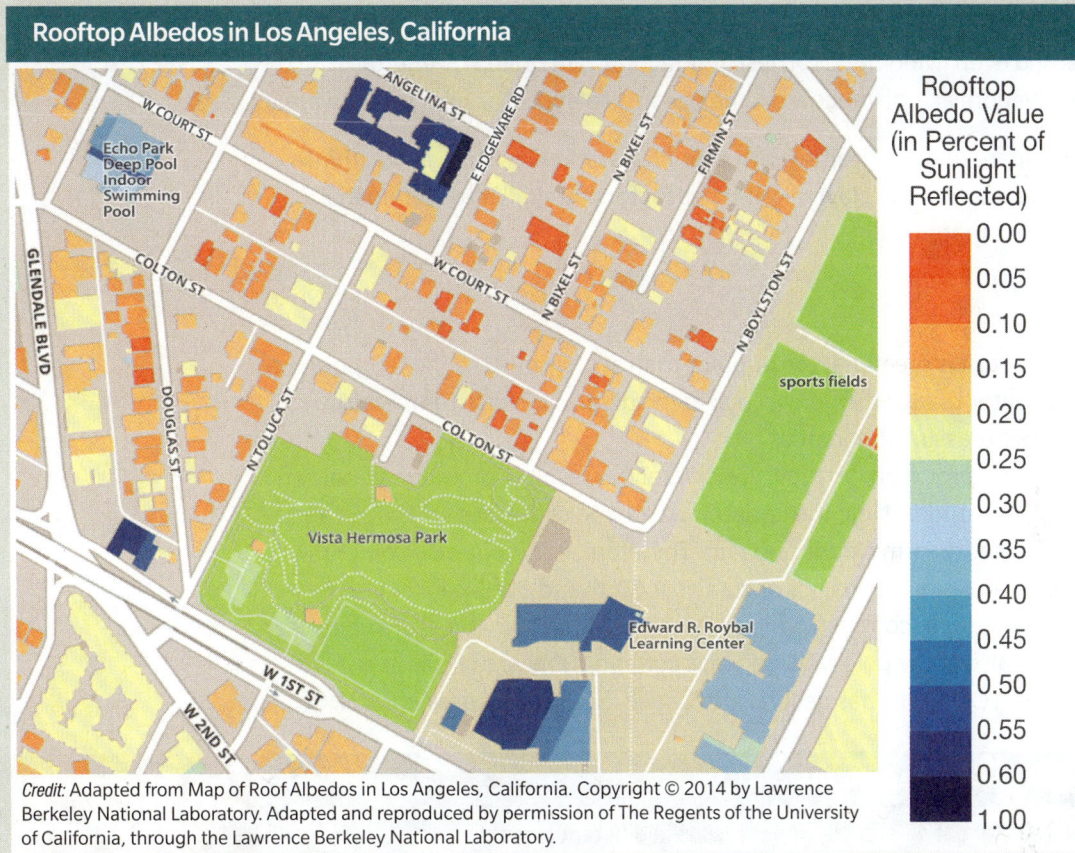

Rooftop Albedos in Los Angeles, California

Rooftop Albedo Value (in Percent of Sunlight Reflected)

0.00
0.05
0.10
0.15
0.20
0.25
0.30
0.35
0.40
0.45
0.50
0.55
0.60
1.00

Credit: Adapted from Map of Roof Albedos in Los Angeles, California. Copyright © 2014 by Lawrence Berkeley National Laboratory. Adapted and reproduced by permission of The Regents of the University of California, through the Lawrence Berkeley National Laboratory.

12. The red, orange, and yellow roofs on the map reflect 0–25% of sunlight. These roofs are likely warmer / cooler than the green and blue roofs.

13. Which of the following is likely true about the air temperatures near the red, orange, and yellow roofs compared to the air temperatures near blue and green roofs?

   A. The air temperatures are the same near all roofs.

   B. The air is slightly warmer near the red, orange, and yellow roofs.

   C. The air is slightly cooler near the red, orange, and yellow roofs.

14. **Engineer It** You are a part of a planning group that wants to make the air temperatures in this part of Los Angeles cooler. Use the data on this map and the information from the text to write a recommendation to help the group achieve this goal.

_____

_____

_____

_____

_____

_____

Explaining What Influences Climate

Factors That Influence Climate

A location's climate is influenced by interactions between the ocean, the atmosphere, ice, landforms, and even living things. These interactions are driven by energy from the sun. Latitude, elevation, and distance from the ocean also affect the climate of an area.

15. **Discuss** Compare today's weather with your area's climate. What do you think caused the weather today? How might those factors be similar to factors that determine the climate?

Latitude

The intensity of sunlight is greater at the equator than at the poles, so the temperature is higher at the equator than at the poles. Look at the diagram. These temperature differences cause air pressure differences.

Along with Earth's rotation, air pressure differences result in different global wind patterns at different latitudes. Near the equator, warm, moist air rises and cools, and water vapor condenses to form clouds and rain. Therefore, rainy climates commonly exist near the equator. A similar process occurs near 60°N and 60°S, causing rainy climates in those regions. In contrast, cool, dry air sinks along high-pressure belts near 30°N and 30°S and also at the poles. These areas commonly have dry climates. One reason why southern California has deserts is because the latitude there is 32°N.

Latitude's Effect on Climate Patterns

The intensity of sunlight at different latitudes results in different climates.

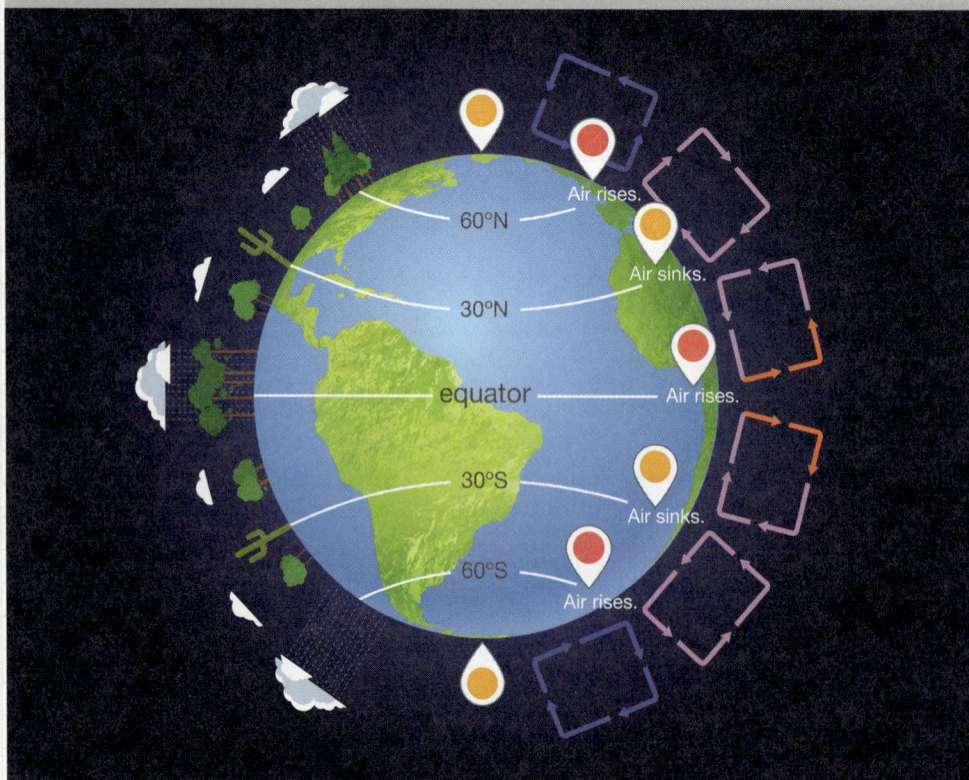

Explore Online

Around low-pressure belts, air rises, cools, and forms clouds and precipitation. Low-pressure belts result in wet climates.

Around high-pressure belts, air sinks and dries, resulting in clear skies and little precipitation. High-pressure belts correspond to dry climates.

Prevailing Winds

Prevailing winds are global patterns of wind that generally move in a certain direction. Prevailing winds affect climate because they move air masses from one place to another. For example, moist air masses that form over the Pacific Ocean are carried to the west coast of the United States by prevailing winds called the *westerlies*. Prevailing winds also drive ocean surface currents that travel the globe and constantly move both warm and cool ocean water.

Distance from the Ocean

Water absorbs and releases energy more slowly than land does. As a result, oceans keep the temperature of nearby land from changing as much as it would if there were no water nearby. Because it is near the Pacific Ocean, California has a milder climate than states further inland, such as Nevada and Arizona.

Nearby bodies of water increase the humidity of nearby air. Because of this, places near large bodies of water often have more clouds and precipitation than they would if the body of water were not present.

16. The average annual high temperature in El Centro varies from about 15 °C to 31 °C. In San Diego, it varies from about 14 °C to 21 °C. The more moderate temperatures in San Diego / El Centro are due to its nearness to the Pacific Ocean.

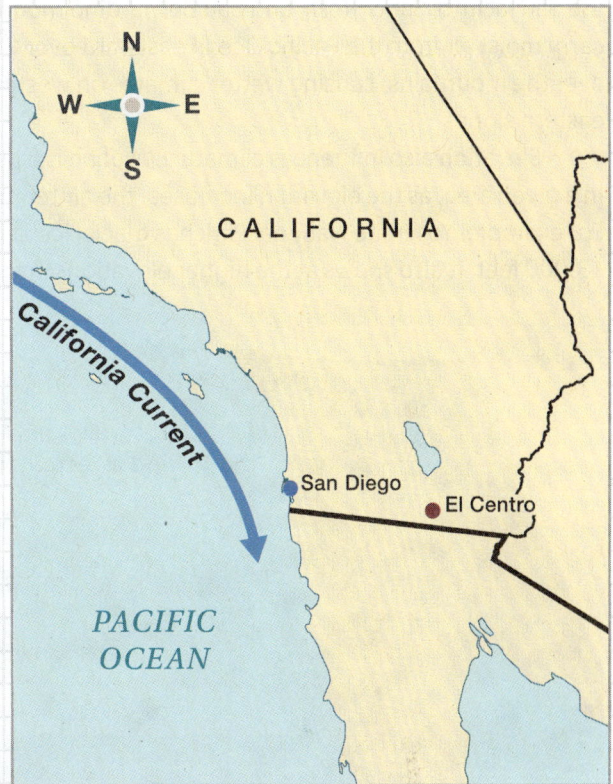

Ocean Currents

Ocean currents move water and distribute energy and nutrients around the globe. *Surface currents* are driven by prevailing winds. They carry warm water away from the equator and cool water away from the poles. Ocean currents moderate the temperatures of coastal cities. Cold ocean currents cool warmer air and warm ocean currents warm cooler air. For example, the waters of the California Current move cool water from the northern Pacific Ocean southward along the western shores of North America. This current has a general cooling effect on the air temperatures of cities near the shoreline.

17. Cool, moist air masses form over the Pacific Ocean where the cold California Current flows. Prevailing winds bring these air masses toward land. How might this process affect San Diego's climate? Explain your reasoning.

Landforms and Elevation

Landforms such as tall mountains can influence an area's climate. In some places, prevailing winds move moist air toward mountains. As the moist air rises, it cools and condenses and may cause rain or snow to fall. The air that reaches the other side of the mountain is drier, causing a rain shadow.

California has several mountain ranges that run north to south through the state. Yosemite National Park is on the western side of the Sierra Nevada mountains. Joshua Tree National Park is located to the east of California's Peninsular Ranges, which include the San Jacinto, Santa Rosa, and San Bernardino mountains. When prevailing winds carry moist air from the Pacific Ocean eastward over California, the air rises to pass over the mountains, causing wetter climates on western slopes and drier climates on eastern slopes.

Elevation also influences climate. *Elevation* is a place's distance above sea level. In a given area, as the elevation increases, the air temperature generally decreases. For example, Yosemite National Park has glacial ice at its highest elevations around 13,000 feet. It also snows at the higher elevations in the park during the winter.

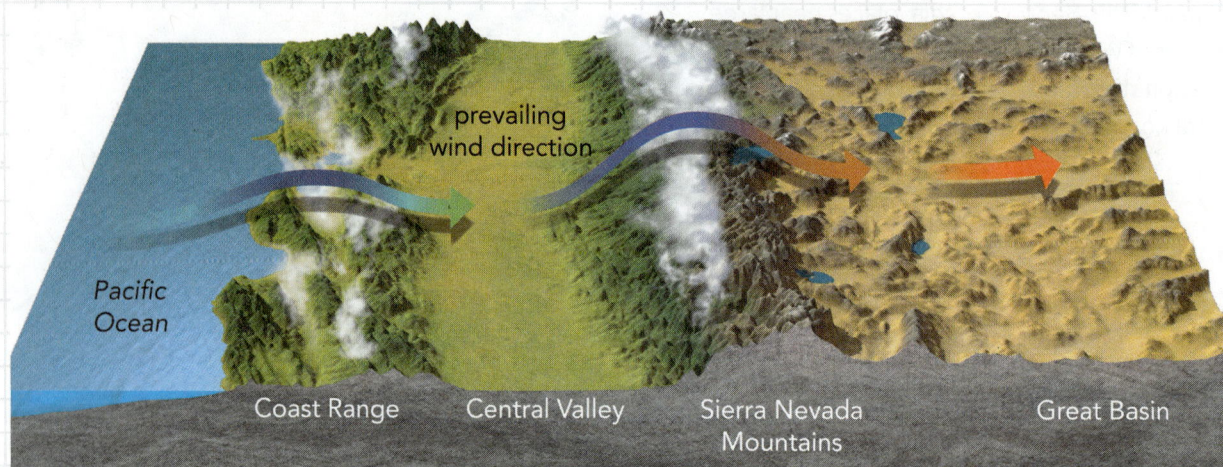

18. **Write** Imagine what it would be like to walk from the California coast to the Great Basin area. Use what you have learned from the text and the diagram to describe the changes in climate during your walk.

EVIDENCE NOTEBOOK

19. What factors influence the climates of Yosemite National Park and Joshua Tree National Park? Record your evidence.

Do the Math

Relate Elevation and Precipitation

Average annual precipitation varies in central California. Elevation also varies. Explore the maps to determine if and how elevation and precipitation are related in this area.

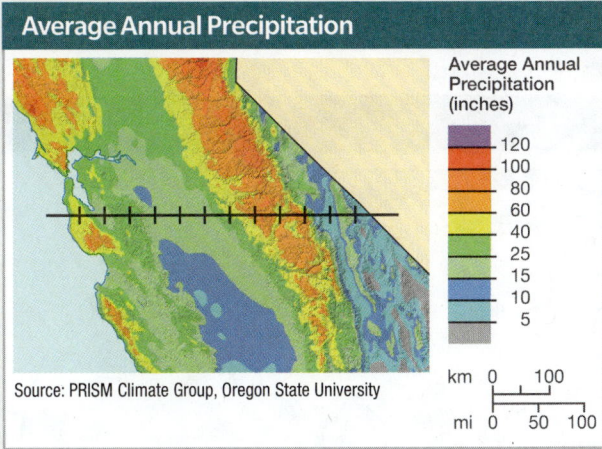

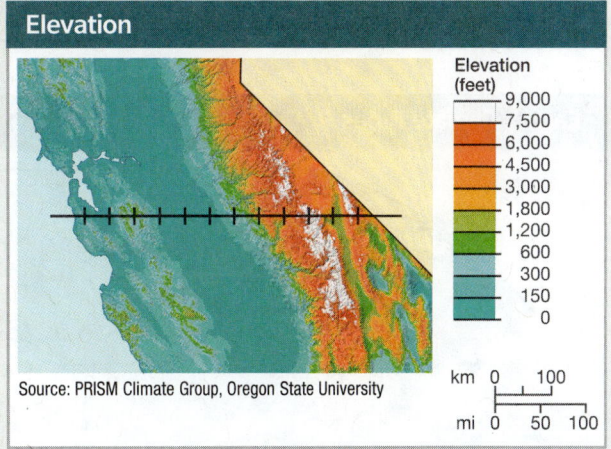

Average Annual Precipitation

Average Annual Precipitation (inches)

- 120
- 100
- 80
- 60
- 40
- 25
- 15
- 10
- 5

Source: PRISM Climate Group, Oregon State University

km 0   100

mi 0   50 100

Elevation

Elevation (feet)

- 9,000
- 7,500
- 6,000
- 4,500
- 3,000
- 1,800
- 1,200
- 600
- 300
- 150
- 0

Source: PRISM Climate Group, Oregon State University

km 0   100

mi 0   50 100

20. Examine the lines with tick marks on each map. These marks are placed at the exact same locations on both maps. Fill in the table by estimating the elevation and precipitation at each tick mark, going from left to right.

Tick mark	1	2	3	4	5	6	7	8	9	10	11
Precipitation (in)											
Elevation (ft)											

21. Construct a graph based on the data in your table.

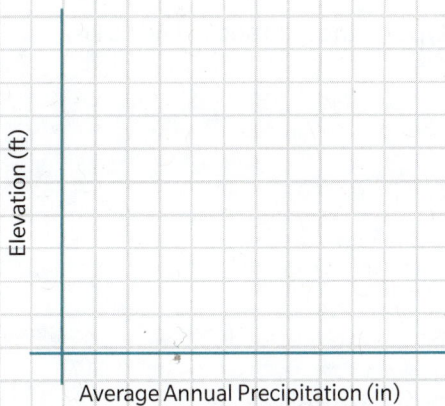

Elevation (ft)

Average Annual Precipitation (in)

22. Analyze the graph to explain the correlation between precipitation and elevation in this part of California.

Using Regional Climate Models

Climate is a complex phenomenon because it is influenced by so many factors. Models of Earth's climate types can be helpful because they make it easy to see patterns, such as latitude's effect on climate.

Earth's Climate Types

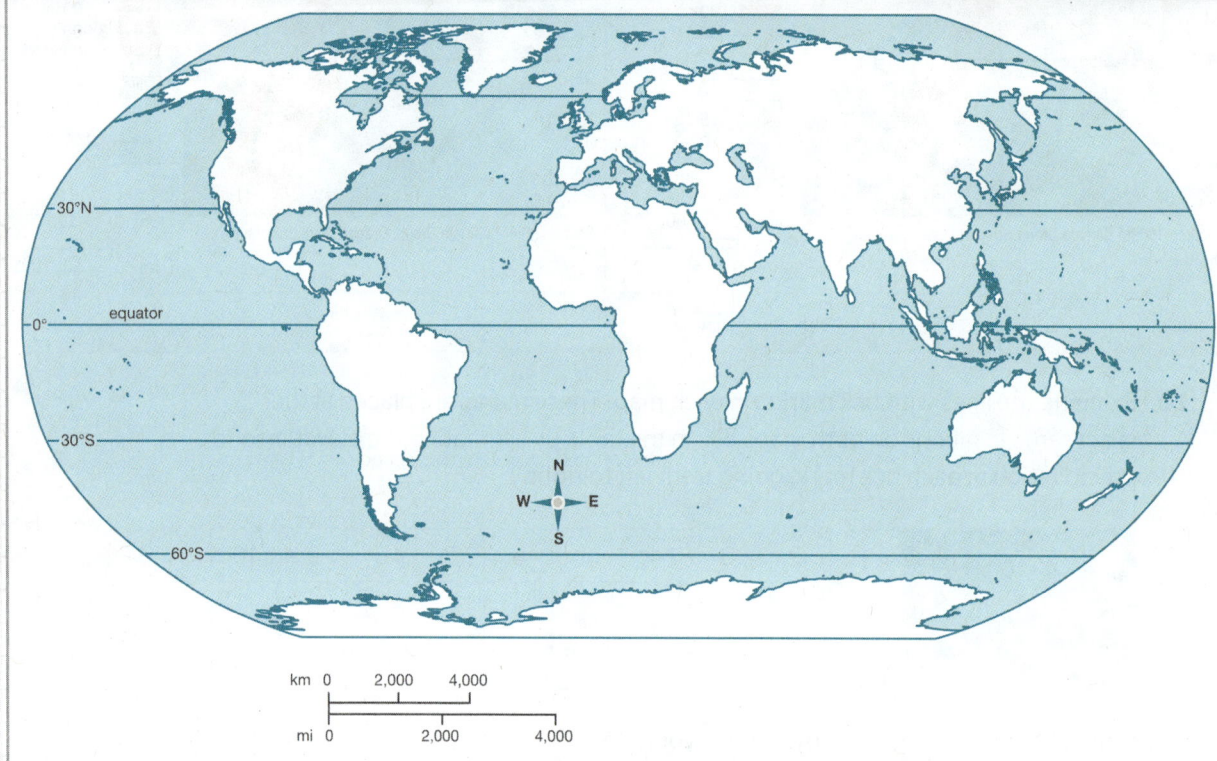

23. Divide Earth into three major climate types. Show each type on the map and include a key. Explain your reasoning for your decisions.

Earth's Regional Climates

There are several different systems used to classify climate. They can be based on different criteria, or they may represent different time periods. For example, Earth can be divided into a few major climate zones, into several regional climate types, or even into hundreds of local climates.

The Köppen-Geiger classification of regional climates is commonly used. This classification is periodically updated in order to reflect the most current data. For example, one version represents climate from 1986 to 2010. Before that version was a version that represented 1951 to 2000.

Hands-On Lab
Model Your Climate

You will develop and use a model to describe your local climate. You will use the model as a visual display in a multimedia presentation to explain the factors that influence your local climate.

MATERIALS
• Materials for climate models will vary.

Procedure and Analysis

STEP 1 Define your area of study. This might be the city you live in or a region.

STEP 2 Collect climate data for your area. Summarize the climate, including temperature and precipitation patterns. Note if there are seasons or winds, and how much and what kind of precipitation falls throughout the year.

STEP 3 Describe what factors influence your climate, or what your model's "inputs" will be. Think about sunlight, latitude, elevation, surface type, prevailing winds, landforms, and ocean currents.

STEP 4 Plan a way to model your climate. How will your model show the inputs to your local climate system?

STEP 5 How will your model show the outputs to your local climate system? For example, how will it represent temperature and precipitation outputs?

STEP 6 Identify the materials you will need to make your model.

STEP 7 Check in with a teacher to describe your plans and materials needed. Get confirmation that you are ready to proceed. Then develop your model.

STEP 8 **Language SmArts** Make a multimedia presentation to help clarify your model and emphasize your main points. Present this to the class.

Earth's Regional Climates

Earth has several regional climates. Explore the map and photos.

Humid tropical
- No dry season
- Short dry season
- Dry winter

Dry
- Semiarid
- Arid

Humid Subtropical
- No dry season
- Dry winter
- Dry summer

Humid Continental
- No dry season
- Dry winter

Highland
- Highlands

Polar
- Tundra and ice

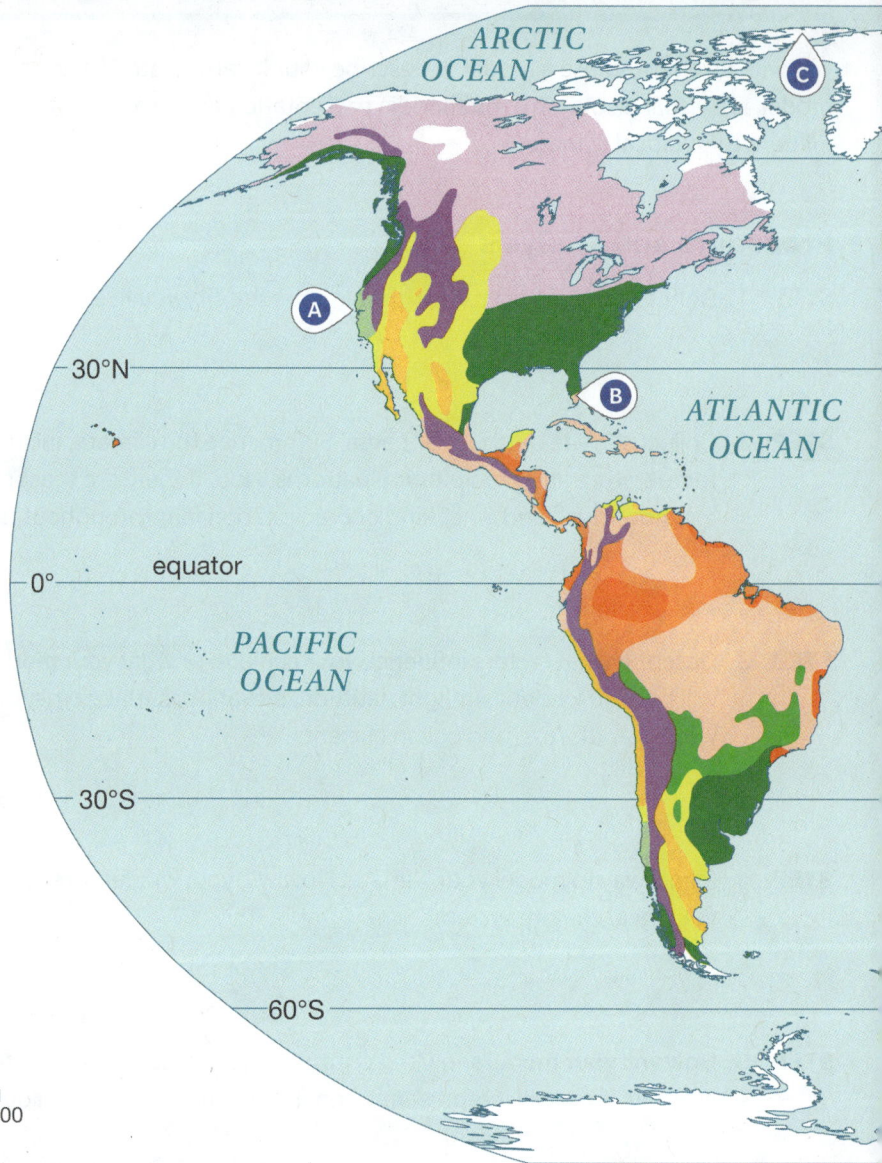

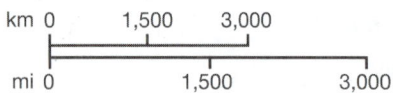

km 0   1,500   3,000

mi 0   1,500   3,000

ARCTIC OCEAN

C

A

30°N

B

ATLANTIC OCEAN

equator

0°

PACIFIC OCEAN

30°S

60°S

A The mild Mediterranean climate of coastal California is influenced by prevailing winds that bring cool, moist air in from the Pacific Ocean.

B This swamp in southern Florida is located in the only tropical climate zone in the continental United States.

C The arctic hares of Ellesmere Island, Canada, thrive in the polar climate of the area with its long, cold winters and brief, cool summers.

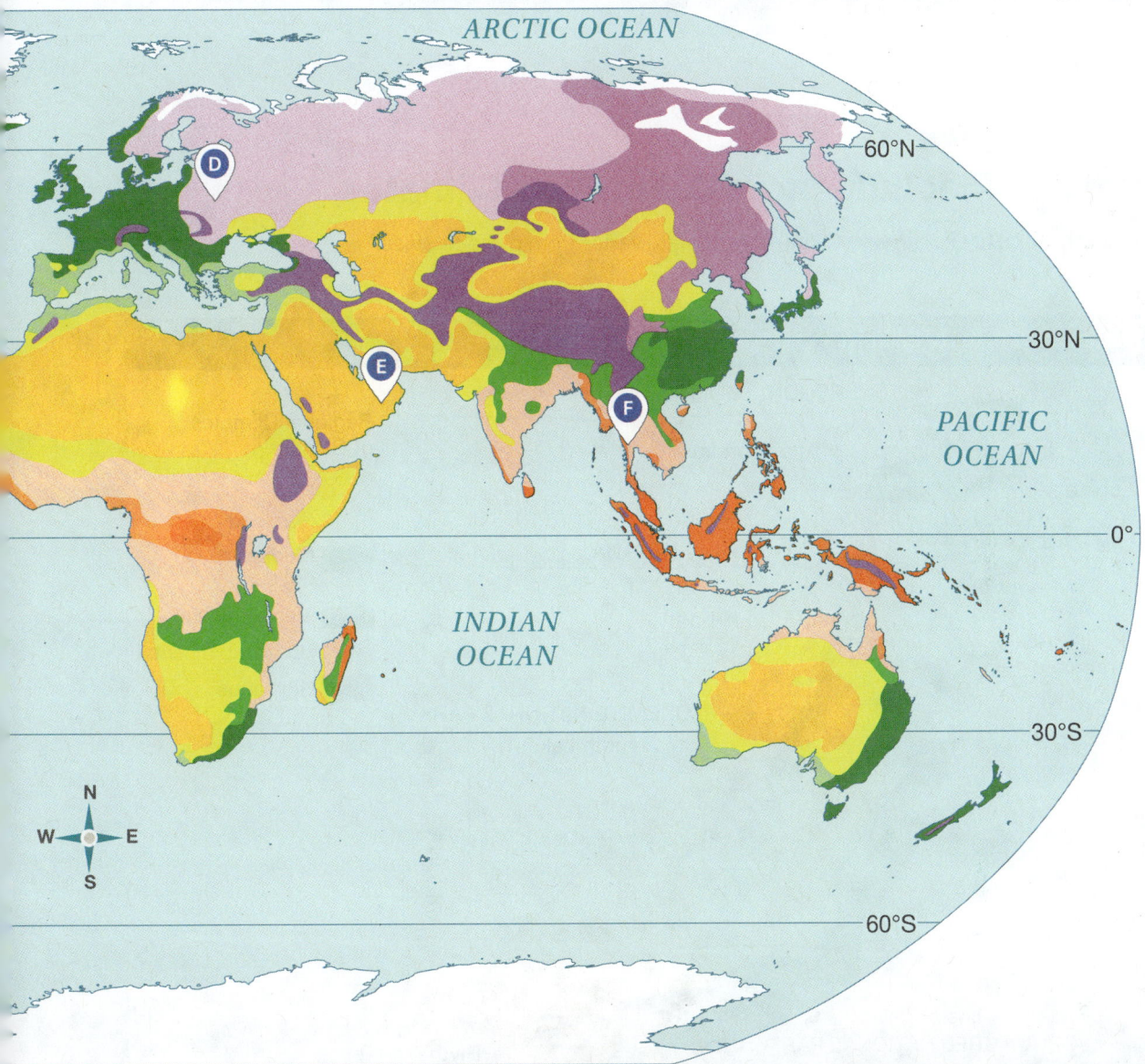

ARCTIC OCEAN

60°N

30°N

PACIFIC
OCEAN

INDIAN
OCEAN

0°

30°S

N
W — E
S

60°S

Moscow, Russia, has a temperate climate with warm summers that can be somewhat humid. Winters are long and cold.

The large, hot desert of Rub' al Khali, located on the Arabian Peninsula, is the result of a high-pressure belt, high temperatures, and lack of precipitation in the arid climate.

The lush vegetation and abundant water in Erawan National Park in Thailand are the result of a humid tropical climate.

EVIDENCE NOTEBOOK

24. What regional climate types are found in the two National Parks? Record your evidence.

Explain What Influences California's Climates

Explore the map to explain why California's climate varies from place to place.

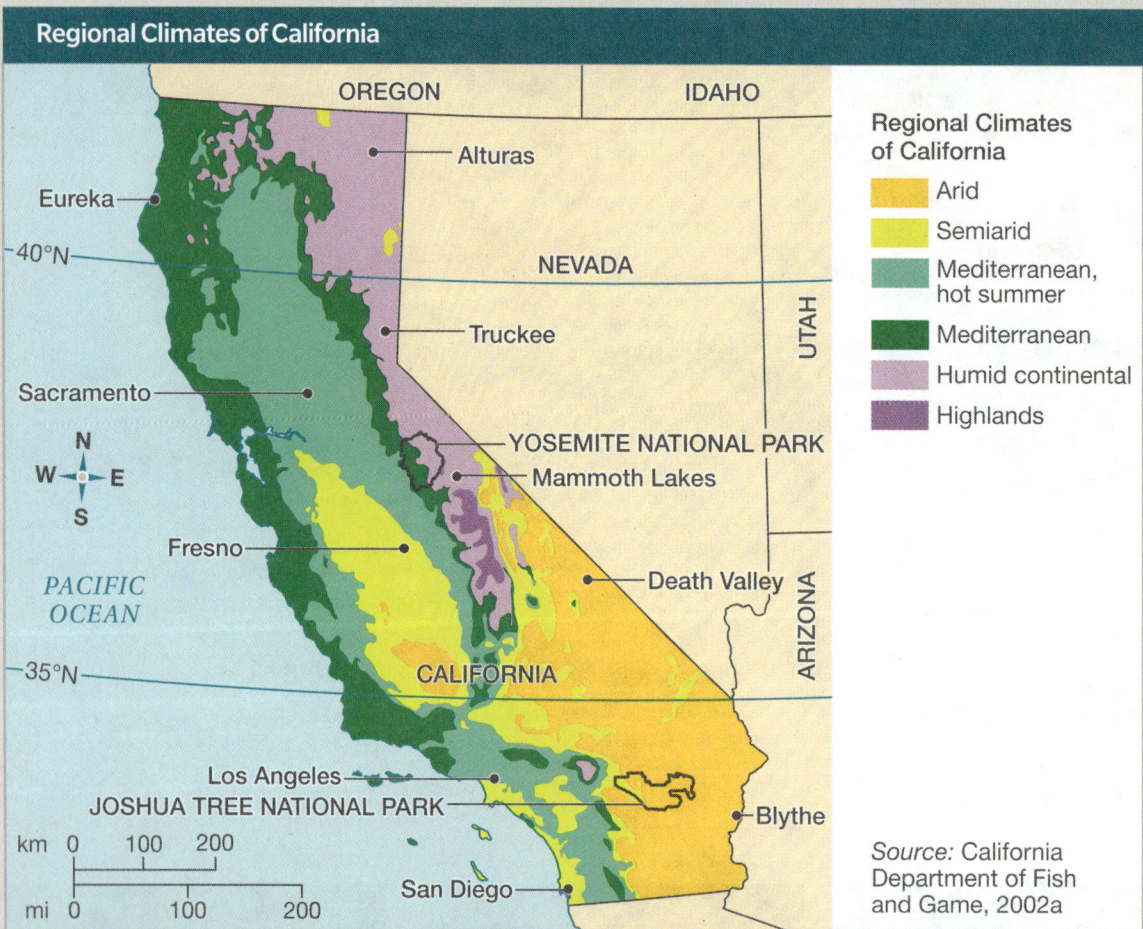

Regional Climates of California

Regional Climates of California

- Arid
- Semiarid
- Mediterranean, hot summer
- Mediterranean
- Humid continental
- Highlands

Source: California Department of Fish and Game, 2002a

25. Eureka and Alturas have different regional climates even though they are at a similar latitude. Part of the reason is due to nearness to Nevada / the equator / the ocean.

26. Truckee and Fresno have different climates that are mainly due to which of the following factors? Choose all that apply:

A. nearness to the Pacific Ocean

B. their latitudes

C. nearness to Nevada

D. their elevations

Continue Your Exploration

Name: _____   Date: _____

Check out the path below or go online to choose one of the other paths shown.

| Exploring the Greenhouse Effect | • Lake Effect
• Hands-On Labs 🖐
• Propose Your Own Path | *Go online to choose one of these other paths.* |

The Greenhouse Effect

How does a greenhouse work? Sunlight passes through the glass and warms the floor and objects inside. In turn, the air inside the greenhouse warms. The warm air is trapped by the glass, so the interior of the greenhouse gets warmer.

The windows in a greenhouse are similar to Earth's atmosphere. Sunlight passes through the atmosphere and warms the surface. This causes the air to warm. Some of the energy is absorbed by *greenhouse gases* in the atmosphere. This phenomenon, called the *greenhouse effect*, is what makes Earth warm enough for humans and many other plants and animals to live. However, human activities have rapidly increased the amount of greenhouse gases in the past few hundred years. This increase has caused Earth's average global temperature to rise. Rising temperatures have some negative effects on the environment, which we depend on for water, food, and other resources.

Greenhouse Gases

Naturally occurring greenhouse gases include water vapor, carbon dioxide, methane, nitrous oxide, and ozone. Human activities have caused their levels to rise. Chlorofluorocarbons (CFCs) are human-made greenhouse gases that come from using refrigerants, aerosols, and cleaning solvents.

Gases in the atmosphere retain heat, which is similar to the way a greenhouse retains heat.

Continue Your Exploration

Common Greenhouse Gases and Their Sources

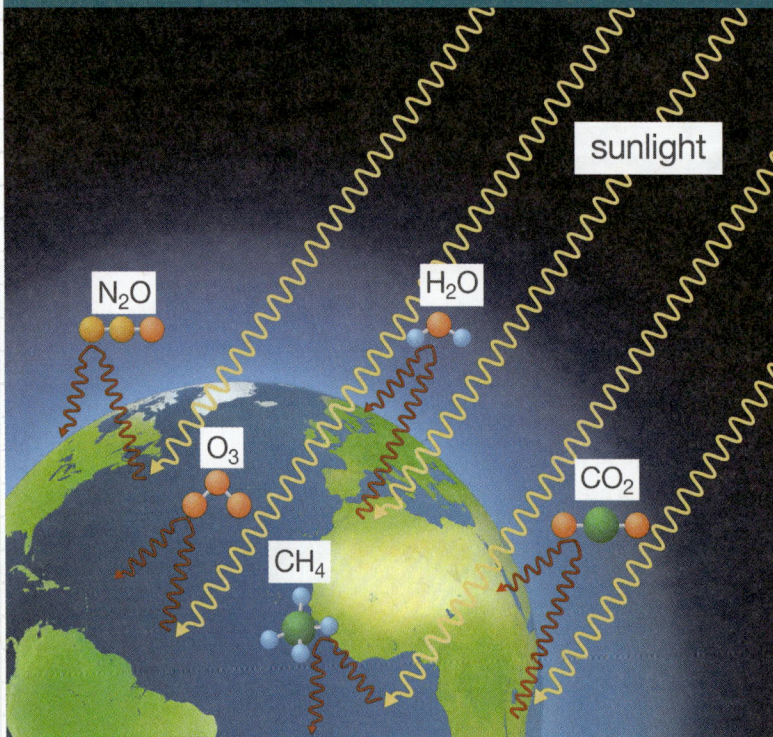

Carbon dioxide (CO_2) occurs naturally in the atmosphere, but humans have increased levels by burning coal, oil, natural gas, and wood.

Nitrous oxide (N_2O) is naturally present in the atmosphere, but human use of fertilizers in agriculture and burning fossil fuels is increasing the amount.

Water vapor (H_2O) occurs naturally in the atmosphere. The amount of water vapor has increased with increasing global temperatures.

Methane (CH_4) occurs naturally in the atmosphere, but humans have increased amounts due to oil and gas production, raising cattle, and producing garbage.

Ozone (O_3) occurs naturally in the atmosphere but can also be produced by automobile exhaust, pollution from factories, and burning vegetation.

1. Complete the description using the word bank. You may use a term more than once.

   As greenhouse gases have _____, the global average temperature has _____. Warmer global temperatures have _____ sea ice and caused sea levels to rise.

   WORD BANK
   • increased
   • decreased

2. Make an *X* next to the actions that would increase levels of greenhouse gases.

   _____ driving a car that burns fossil fuels

   _____ riding a bike and walking

   _____ using fertilizer to grow crops

   _____ eating less meat from cattle

3. Why do you think humans continue to do the activities that increase greenhouse gases in the atmosphere?

4. **Collaborate** Research the increase in the atmosphere's carbon dioxide concentrations over the past 100 years. Compare this to increases from previous time periods, including before humans existed. Use evidence from your research to support a conclusion about human activities and carbon dioxide in the atmosphere.

Can You Explain It?

Name: _____   Date: _____

Why do these regions in California have such different climates?

> **EVIDENCE NOTEBOOK**
>
> Refer to the notes in your Evidence Notebook to help you construct an explanation for the differences between the climates of the two locations.

1. State your claim. Make sure your claim fully explains why the climates of the two locations are so different.

2. Summarize the evidence you have gathered to support your claim and explain your reasoning.

Checkpoints

Answer the following questions to check your understanding of the lesson.

Use the graph to answer Questions 3 and 4.

3. The graph shows the average annual temperatures of four cities, which were calculated from 30 years of data. This graph therefore helps to describe each area's weather / climate.

4. Look at the latitude of each city. Select all that apply.

   A. The cities at higher latitudes have less precipitation.

   B. The cities at lower latitudes are colder.

   C. The cities at lower latitudes are warmer.

   D. The cities at higher latitudes have a greater range in temperatures over the year.

Average Monthly Temperatures at Certain Latitudes

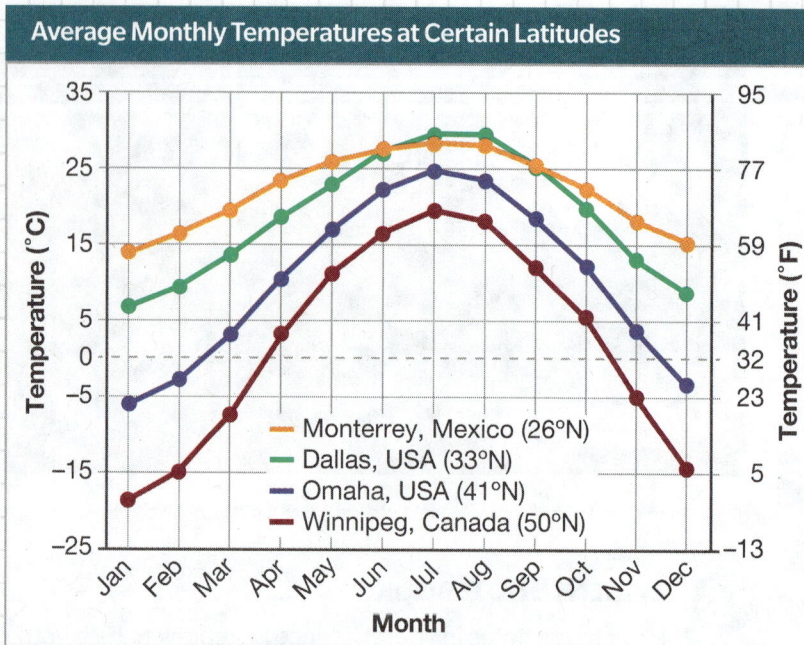

— Monterrey, Mexico (26°N)
— Dallas, USA (33°N)
— Omaha, USA (41°N)
— Winnipeg, Canada (50°N)

Credit: "Latitude's influence on mean monthly temperature, Figure 6.9" from Understanding Physical Geography by Michael Pidwirny. Copyright © 2014-2017 Our Planet Earth Publishing. Adapted and reproduced by permission of Our Planet Earth Publishing.

5. Tobias modeled the albedo effect by laying large white and black T-shirts out in the sun. He measured the temperature / humidity of each shirt for a few hours. The end result was that the white / black shirt was warmer.

Use the map to answer Question 6.

6. London, England has mild temperatures compared to many inland cities around the same latitude. This is because warm air masses form over the warm North Atlantic Current. Prevailing winds that blow east / west to east / west bring the warm air over London.

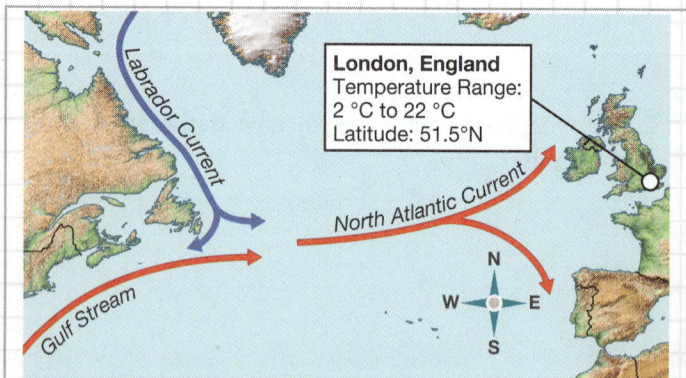

London, England
Temperature Range:
2 °C to 22 °C
Latitude: 51.5°N

Labrador Current

North Atlantic Current

Gulf Stream

7. Snow reflects / absorbs more sunlight than water does because snow has a lower / higher albedo. As snow melts, more / less sunlight is absorbed by the darker soil beneath it. This causes cooling / warming in the local area.

Interactive Review

Complete this section to review the main concepts of the lesson.

An area's climate is described by its average temperature and precipitation patterns over a long period of time.

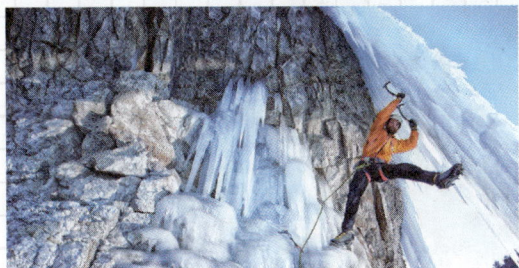

A. Why does describing an area's climate require weather data for more than one or two years?

Areas near the equator receive more direct sunlight than areas near the poles. Sunlight is reflected and absorbed differently by different surfaces.

B. How is climate affected by latitude?

Factors that influence climate include latitude, prevailing winds, ocean currents, elevation, surface type, and landforms.

C. Provide an example of how two or more climate factors can work together and affect California's climate.

Earth has several different regional climates.

D. Explain why regional climates do not follow latitude lines exactly.

Lesson 5 Earth Has Different Regional Climates **371**

Choose one of the activities to explore how this unit connects to other topics.

☐ People in Science

Noelani Puniwai, Conservation Scientist Noelani Puniwai was born and raised in Puna, Hawaii. With a PhD in natural resources and environmental management, Noelani bridges the gaps between science and society to help take care of the lands and waters of Hawaii. As climate changes, Hawaii will see changes in recreation, industries, and day-to-day life of the local people. Noelani studies how surfers, fishermen, and others report and experience changes in weather patterns in Hawaii. This helps her link measurable changes in climate and weather to real-world effects.

Research the effects of climate change in Hawaii. Describe the major concerns people there are facing today. Choose one of these concerns and work with a partner to propose a solution.

☐ Social Studies Connection

Alaskan Inuit Culture The Alaskan Inuit (uh•LAS•kuhn IN•oo•it) people inhabit many western and northern parts of Alaska. In Alaska, the average daytime winter temperature is generally below freezing. The local weather and climate have a great impact on Inuit culture.

Research the Alaskan Inuit people and how they have adapted to this cold climate. Make a multimedia presentation that includes how weather patterns influence the clothing, housing, transportation, and other lifestyle factors of the Inuit people.

☐ Engineering Connection

Building Homes for Different Climates Architects design houses that shelter and protect people from particular environmental conditions. To design homes that are suitable for various climates, architects must understand different climates. They must also understand the types of building materials that are available and sustainable in that environment.

Research home designs and building materials architects use in different climates. Create a visual display explaining the range of materials available to construct homes in various climates and locations.

Name: _____   Date: _____

Complete this review to check your understanding of the unit.

Use the diagram to answer Questions 1 and 2.

1. What process does this image show?

   A. condensation

   B. carbon cycling

   C. convection

   D. Coriolis effect

2. Which of the following is a strength of this model?

   A. Arrows are used to show movement of air.

   B. Explanations of the unseen mechanisms are included.

   C. The relationships between energy, gravity, and cycling are labeled.

   D. The model can be used to predict more processes related to air movement.

---

3. Solar energy is transformed into *potential / kinetic / thermal* energy as the sun warms Earth's surface. Some parts of Earth are warmed more than others, so temperature differences result and drive convection currents in the air and oceans. As convection currents form, thermal energy is transformed into *potential / kinetic / solar* energy.

Use the map to answer Questions 4 and 5.

4. This *weather / climate* map shows the average *type / amount* of precipitation in Colorado during the year.

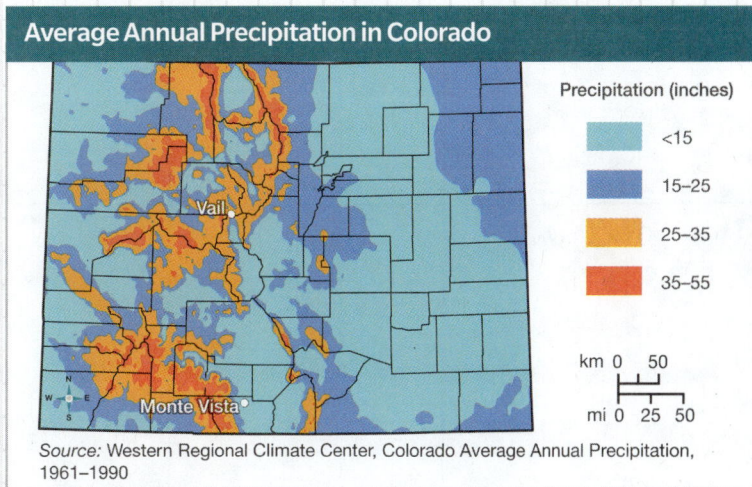

Average Annual Precipitation in Colorado

Precipitation (inches)

<15

15–25

25–35

35–55

km 0   50

mi 0   25 50

Source: Western Regional Climate Center, Colorado Average Annual Precipitation, 1961–1990

5. Which of the following factors could cause the precipitation average in Vail to be higher than the precipitation average in Monte Vista?

   A. Vail is in a different county.

   B. Monte Vista is in a rain shadow.

   C. The temperature is usually hotter in Monte Vista.

   D. Monte Vista is south of Vail.

6. Complete the table by providing examples of how the factors that influence weather and climate relate to each big concept.

Factors that influence weather and climate	Cause and effect	Interactions in the Earth system	System models
Global winds	Global winds are caused by the uneven heating of Earth's surface and the rotation of Earth.		
Ocean currents			
High and low air pressure			

Name: _____   Date: _____

Use the map to answer Questions 7–9.

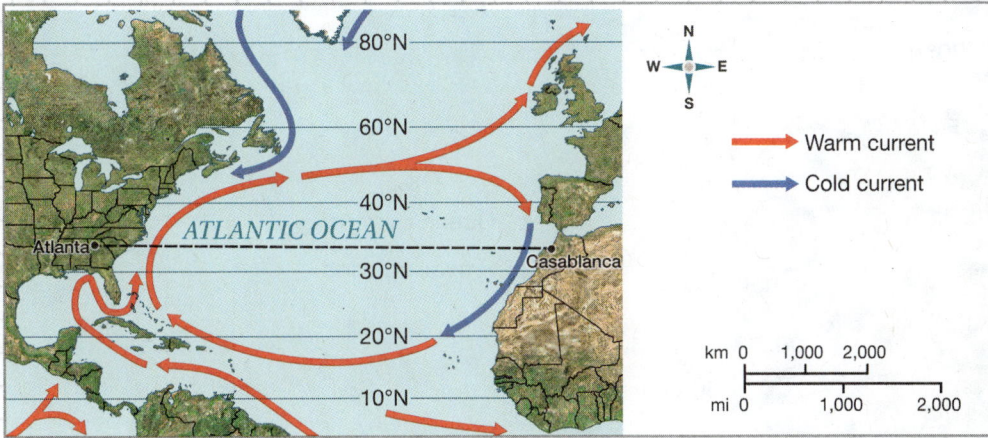

7. Atlanta has very hot and humid summers. During the fall, winter, and spring, Atlanta has milder temperatures. In Casablanca, temperatures remain mild throughout the year. Cite evidence from the map to explain why these cities have such different climates, even though they are at the same latitude.

8. Some hurricanes form near the coast of West Africa in the Atlantic Ocean, south of Casablanca. Atlanta is more likely to be affected by these hurricanes than Casablanca is. Use the map as well as your knowledge of the relationship between prevailing winds and ocean surface currents to explain why this occurs.

9. How could this map help a meteorologist make predictions about weather patterns in cities near the Atlantic Ocean? What other information might a meteorologist need to make reliable weather predictions?

Use the map to answer Questions 10–13.

Eria, an Imaginary Continent on Earth

Examine this map of an imaginary continent to explain weather and climate patterns.

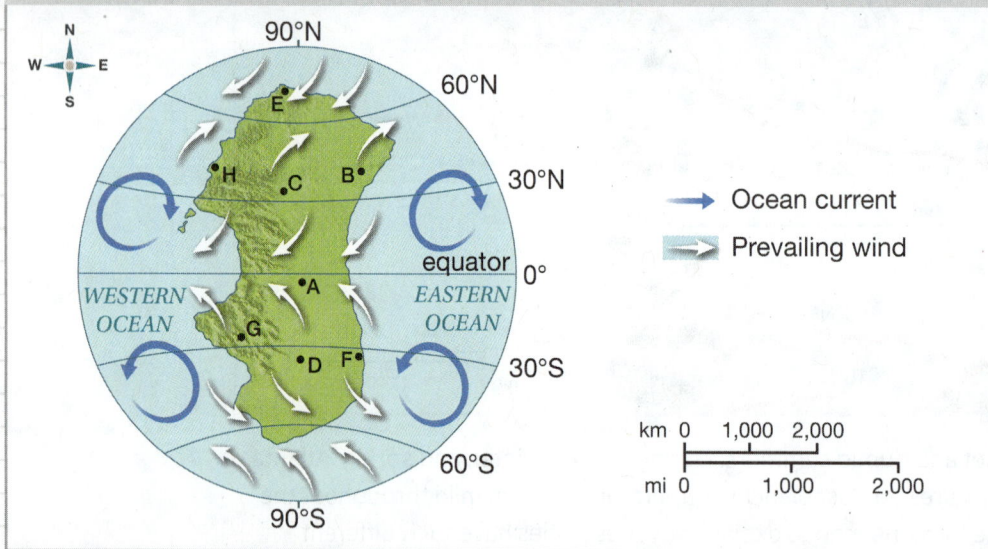

10. What factors are represented on this map that could potentially affect weather and climate on the continent?

11. Identify the location where you would most likely find a rain forest. Support your claim with evidence and reasoning.

12. The Eastern Ocean is warm between 0° and 30°S. What type of air mass likely forms here? How might this affect point A, which is at a low elevation?

13. Why might the climate in location H be different from the climate in location C?

Name: _____   Date: _____

What Influences Marine Layers in California?

Have you ever heard of "May Gray" or "June Gloom"? In certain locations in California, cool mornings filled with heavy clouds and fog are common during these months. This is due to the formation of a *marine layer*. Sometimes, you can travel to an elevation above the marine layer and experience warmer and sunnier weather!

You will collect data to describe how marine layers form, identify where they form, and note the climate types associated with them. You will explain why only certain locations experience marine layers and then explain the effects of marine layers on people and other living things.

The steps below will help guide you in planning an investigation and constructing an explanation.

1. **Ask Questions** Develop a list of questions about the marine layer that develops in California.

2. **Conduct Research** Find information about marine layers that develop in California and describe their effect on weather. Where specifically in California do they form? Describe what influences the development of marine layers, including any local factors and global weather patterns. List other places in the world where marine layers develop and note the climate types associated with each location.

3. **Analyze Data** Compare locations and climate types where marine layers form in the world. Describe any patterns you notice.

4. **Construct an Explanation** Explain why some coastal cities in California experience "May Gray" and "June Gloom" while others do not. Use evidence from your research to support your answer.

5. **Construct an Explanation** Explain how weather associated with marine layers affects people and other living things. Use evidence from your research to support your explanations.

✓ **Self-Check**

	I described both the local factors and global weather patterns that influence the development of marine layers in California.
	I described the weather associated with marine layers and identified where marine layers develop in California.
	I compared locations and climate types where marine layers develop around the world.
	I provided evidence to explain why only certain locations are affected by marine layers.
	I provided evidence to explain how marine layers could affect people and other living things.

Environmental and Genetic Influence on Organisms

How do the environment and genetics influence the traits of organisms?

Unit Project 380
Lesson 1   Organisms Are Adapted to Their Environment. 382
Lesson 2   Organisms Inherit Traits from Their Parents 400
Lesson 3   Reproduction Affects Genetic Diversity 416
Lesson 4   The Environment and Genetics Affect Plant Survival 434
Lesson 5   The Environment and Genetics Affect Animal Survival 456
Unit Review 479
Unit Performance Task 483

This plumage display of a male bird of paradise attracts the female. With their needs met by the rich tropical rain forest, birds of paradise can spend extra time and energy on reproduction.

You Solve It   What Factors Affect Reproductive Success?

Analyze reproduction in a group of peacocks and peahens to see how genetic and environmental factors affect the number of offspring that survive.

Go online and complete the You Solve It to explore ways to solve a real-world problem.

Investigate Unique Reproductive Behaviors

A. Look at the photo. On a separate sheet of paper, write down as many different questions as you can about the photo.

B. **Discuss** With your class or a partner, share your questions. Record any additional questions generated in your discussion. Then choose the most important questions from the list that are related to how the unique reproductive behaviors of an animal are linked to the environment in which it lives. Write them below.

Male seahorses have a brood pouch on their fronts. The female deposits eggs in this pouch, and the male carries the eggs until the baby seahorses are born.

C. Choose an animal with a unique reproductive behavior to research. Here is a list of animals you can consider:

platypus	Monarch butterfly
desert spider	Emperor penguin
coral	Pacific salmon
alligator	brown-headed cowbird

D. Use the information above and your research to create a presentation that describes the unique reproductive behavior of your chosen animal and how that behavior is linked to the environment in which your animal lives.

Discuss the next steps for your Unit Project with your teacher and go online to download the Unit Project Worksheet.

Language Development

Use the lessons in this unit to complete the network and expand your understanding of these key concepts.

■	Similar term
■	Phrase
■	Cognate
■	Example
■	Definition

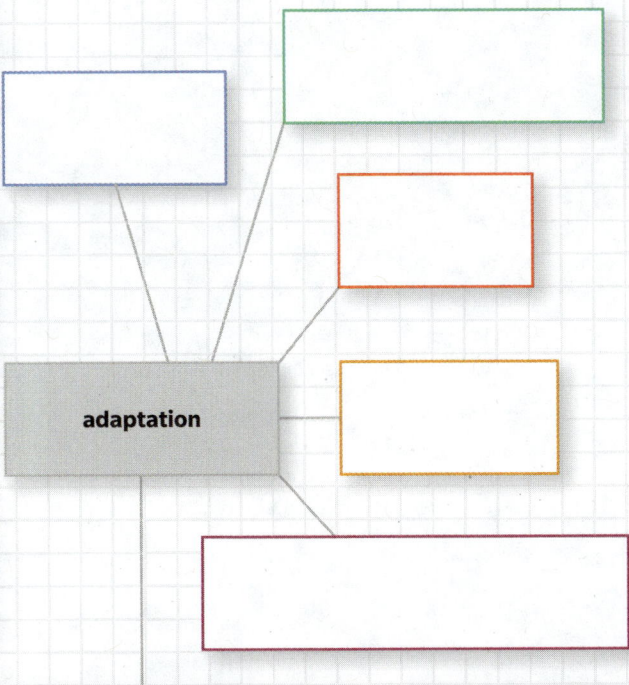

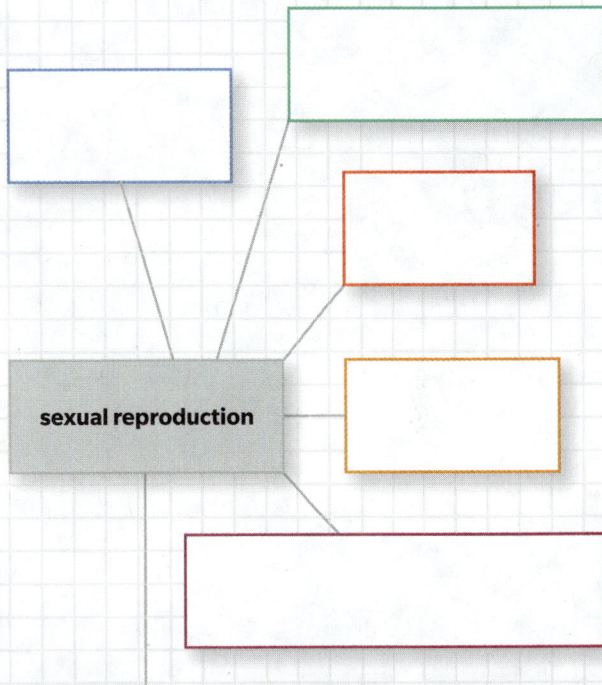

adaptation

sexual reproduction

How do the environment and genetics influence the traits of organisms?

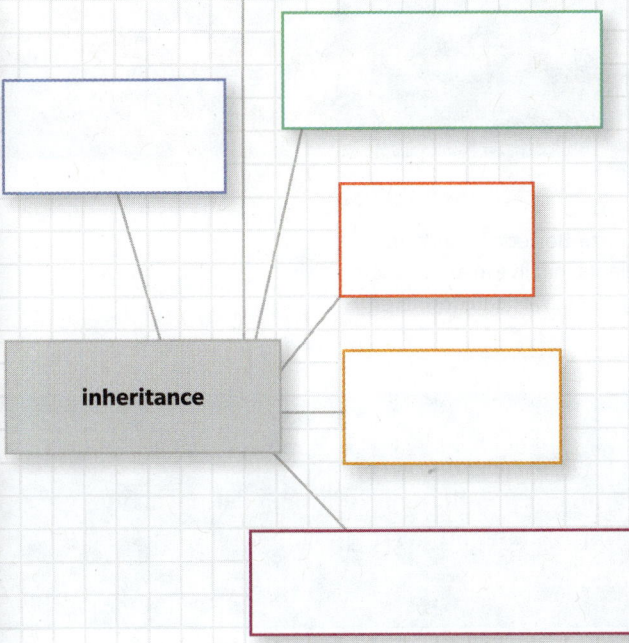

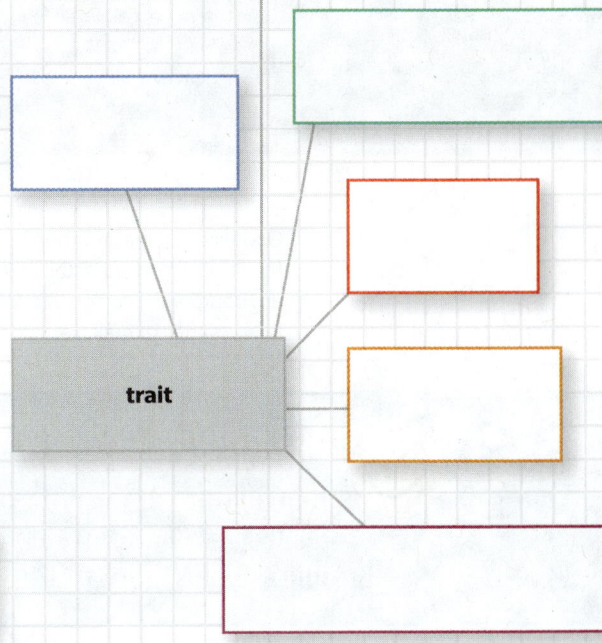

inheritance

trait

Organisms Are Adapted to Their Environment

Ocotillos, such as this one from Anza-Borrego Desert State Park in California, are tall, thin plants that live in a dry desert environment. They grow small green leaves and bright red flowers after rainfall.

Explore First

Contrasting Plant Types Examine a succulent and a nonsucculent plant. List your observations about each plant. Which plant do you think would survive with less water? Why?

Go online to view the digital version of the Hands-On Lab for this lesson and to download additional lab resources.

CAN YOU EXPLAIN IT?

Why do Emperor penguins and roadrunners live in different areas of the world?

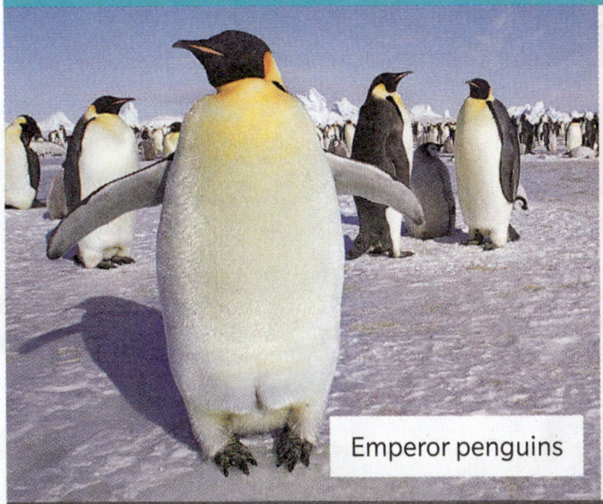

Emperor penguins

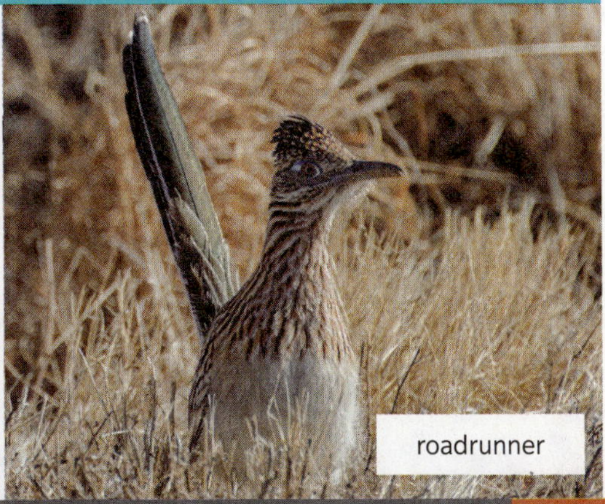

roadrunner

The Emperor penguin has many characteristics that allow it to live in Antarctica and survive some of the coldest temperatures on Earth. For example, the penguins have feathers and fat to conserve body heat. The greater roadrunner has characteristics that allow it to survive in the desert. For example, roadrunners get rid of excess salt through glands near their eyes. This allows them to conserve water and live in dry areas.

Explore Online

1. Describe the conditions where Emperor penguins and roadrunners live. Use the information from the descriptions and what you can observe from the pictures.

2. Describe the characteristics of plants or animals that would help them survive in the conditions you observed.

EVIDENCE NOTEBOOK As you explore the lesson, gather evidence to help explain why Emperor penguins and roadrunners live in different areas of the world.

Analyzing Factors that Determine Climate

If you travel to a new place, you may experience a different climate. Alaska is known for its cold winters and snow. The Sahara Desert in Africa is known for its hot temperatures and lack of rain. Regions on Earth have different combinations of temperature, precipitation, wind patterns, and humidity that make up the climate. The climate of an area depends on where on Earth the area is located.

3. Label each photo with the number that matches the location on Earth where you think that climate occurs.

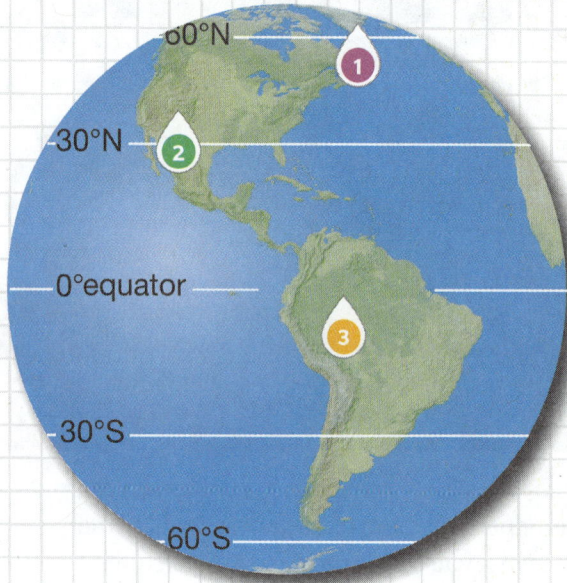

Primary Factors that Determine Climate

Weather refers to short-term conditions in the atmosphere. Climate refers to the long-term weather patterns of an area. Climate is influenced by interactions between sunlight, oceans, the atmosphere, ice, landforms, and living things. It is possible to predict the climate of a region if you know where on Earth it is located.

Latitude and Altitude

Latitude measures how far north or south of the equator a region is located. Locations at high latitudes (far from the equator) receive less sunlight than places at low latitudes (close to the equator) and are typically colder. Altitude is height above sea level. Places at high altitudes are typically colder with more precipitation than places at low altitudes.

Location of Mountains and Oceans

Mountains can cause different climates to form on each side of the mountain range. This is due to a rain shadow effect. Mountains typically have lower temperatures than nearby lowland areas. Oceans affect climate by absorbing energy from the sun, releasing it over time, and redistributing it across the globe through ocean currents. Water absorbs and releases energy more slowly than land does. This means that land near oceans experiences a smaller temperature range (less difference between temperature highs and lows) than land farther from oceans. Oceans and other large bodies of water also increase the amount of water in the air. This often leads to more precipitation in coastal areas.

Elevation Profile across Washington

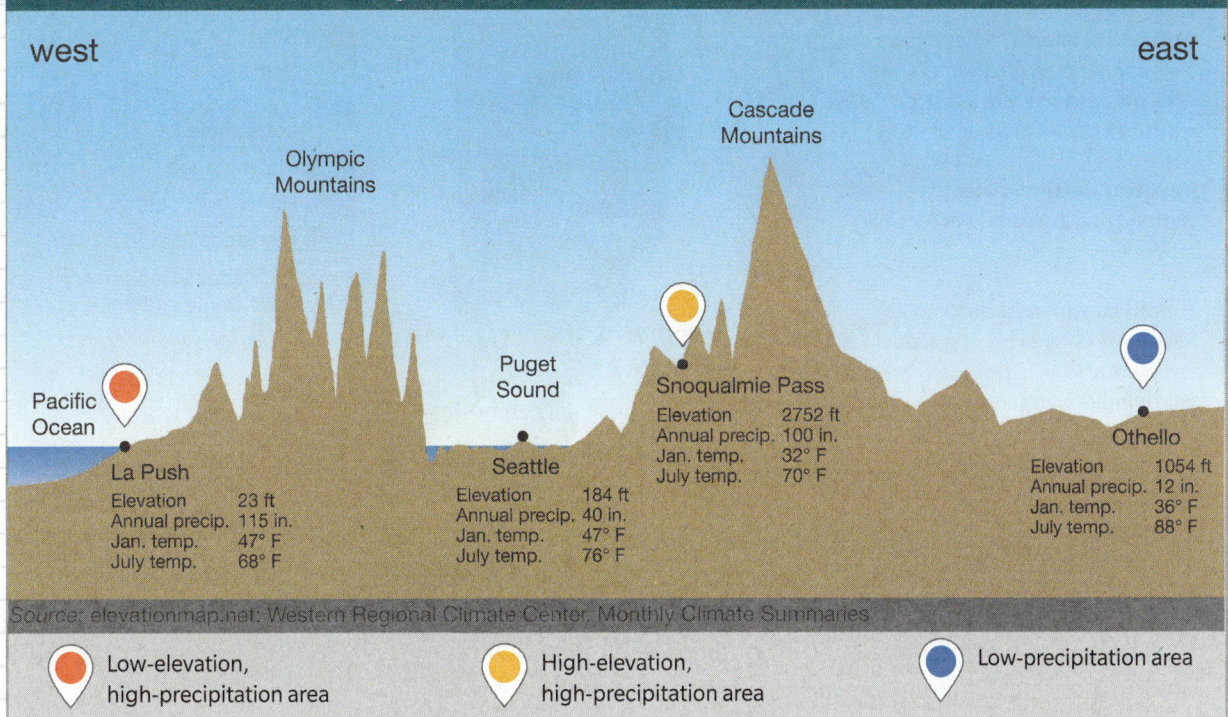

west   east

Cascade Mountains

Olympic Mountains

Puget Sound

Snoqualmie Pass
Elevation   2752 ft
Annual precip.   100 in.
Jan. temp.   32° F
July temp.   70° F

Pacific Ocean

La Push
Elevation   23 ft
Annual precip.   115 in.
Jan. temp.   47° F
July temp.   68° F

Seattle
Elevation   184 ft
Annual precip.   40 in.
Jan. temp.   47° F
July temp.   76° F

Othello
Elevation   1054 ft
Annual precip.   12 in.
Jan. temp.   36° F
July temp.   88° F

Source: elevationmap.net; Western Regional Climate Center, Monthly Climate Summaries

🔴 Low-elevation, high-precipitation area

🟡 High-elevation, high-precipitation area

🔵 Low-precipitation area

4. Low-elevation, high-precipitation areas are *close to / far from* the ocean, where moisture-filled air causes precipitation. Rain shadows occur because the air is *dry / moist* after it crosses the mountains.

Climate Affects the Local Environment

Climate determines how hot or cold, sunny or cloudy, windy or still, and dry or humid a particular place is. This affects the amount of food, light, space, and water in an area. Weather conditions that impact local environments, such as fog, frost, or severe storms, are also related to climate.

5. Match the climate described on the left side (the cause) with the environment shown on the right (the effect).

A temperate rain forest receives lots of sunlight and rain. This allows trees to grow.

coastal climate	hot summers, limited water and plant life
high-latitude climate	cold, low amounts of sunlight and plant life
dry climate in rain shadow	plentiful plant life, water, and sunlight

Grasslands typically get enough rain for grasses and shrubs to grow, but not large trees.

California Regional Climates

Arid and semiarid climates have hot, dry summers and cold winters with very low precipitation. These climates may form as part of a rain shadow.

Mediterranean climates have warm to hot, dry summers and mild, moderately wet winters.

Humid continental climates have large differences in seasonal temperatures, with hot summers and cold winters with snowfall.

Highland climates are cool to cold. Temperatures are typically colder at higher altitudes.

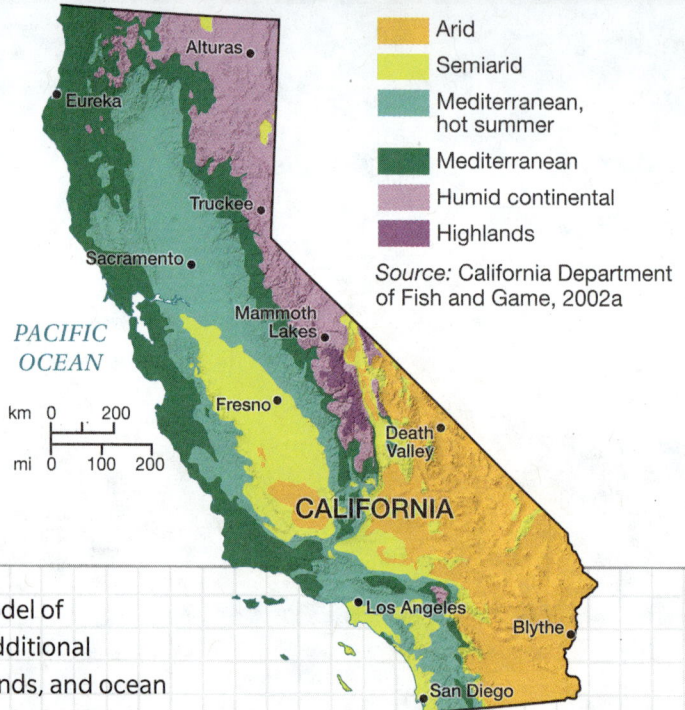

Legend:
- Arid
- Semiarid
- Mediterranean, hot summer
- Mediterranean
- Humid continental
- Highlands

Source: California Department of Fish and Game, 2002a

6. **Collaborate** Develop a topographic model of California. Use your model, along with additional information about latitude, prevailing winds, and ocean currents, to describe the climate patterns in California.

Engineer It
Analyze a Climate Problem

Desert climates can be very hot during the summer. That doesn't stop people from living in these areas, but most humans need help to live comfortably in hot climates. Use the decision matrix to help you evaluate the solutions for living in a hot climate.

7. The criteria are rated based on importance and the solutions have been evaluated for each criterion. Complete the totals by adding the numbers in each column. The highest total indicates the best solution for the stated problem.

Criteria	Criterion rating (1–5)	Solutions			
		Shade	Air conditioner	Swimming pool	Fan
Not expensive	3	2	1	1	3
Easy to maintain	2	2	2	1	2
Comfortable temps	5	2	5	2	2
Totals					

8. What is the best solution for this problem? What is the biggest trade-off for this solution? Provide evidence to support your answer.

_____

_____

_____

_____

Connecting Climate Patterns to Plant and Animal Life

If you mapped all of the world's tropical rain forests, they would exist in a band near the equator. You would see the same pattern if you mapped the location of humid, tropical climates on Earth. This relationship shows how environmental factors can affect where organisms live.

9. Look at the California Regional Climates Map and the California Land Cover Types Map. What questions do you have about how the two maps are related?

California Land Cover Types

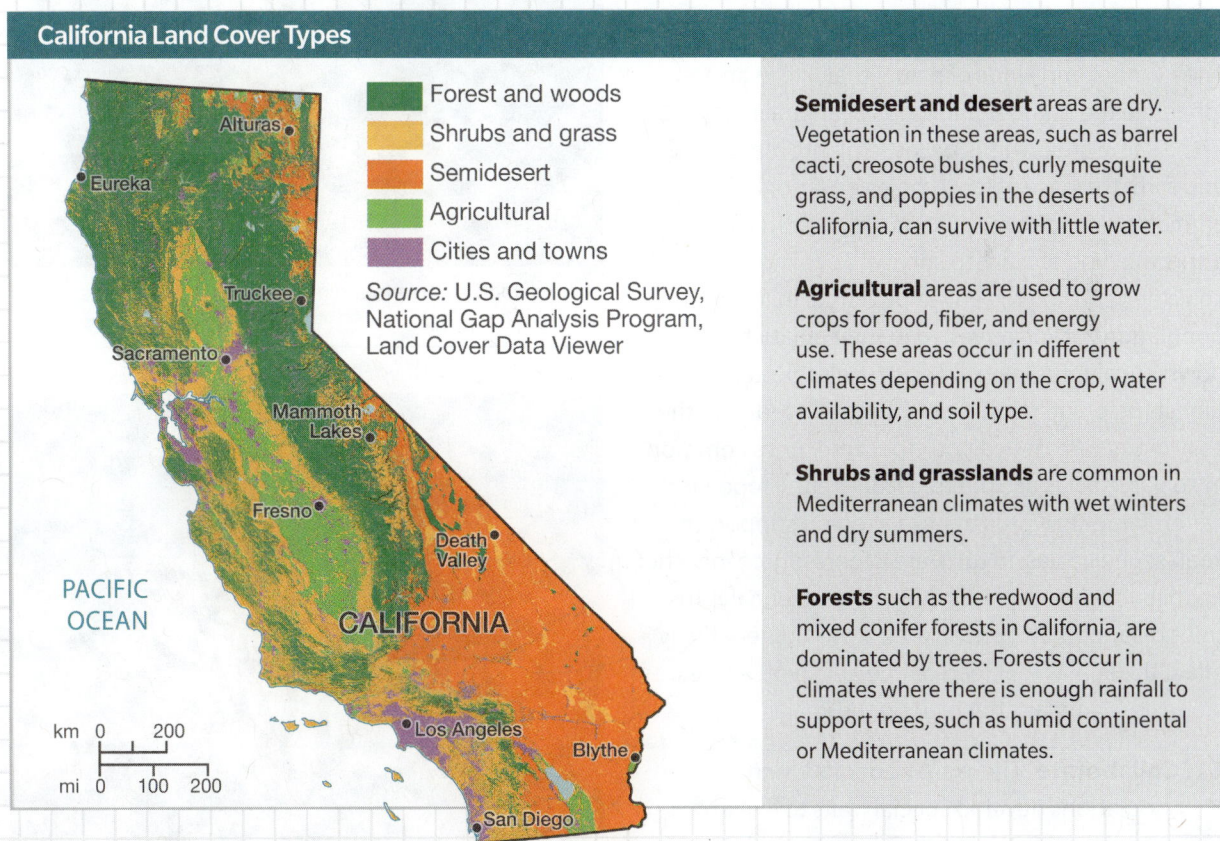

Legend:
- Forest and woods
- Shrubs and grass
- Semidesert
- Agricultural
- Cities and towns

Source: U.S. Geological Survey, National Gap Analysis Program, Land Cover Data Viewer

Semidesert and desert areas are dry. Vegetation in these areas, such as barrel cacti, creosote bushes, curly mesquite grass, and poppies in the deserts of California, can survive with little water.

Agricultural areas are used to grow crops for food, fiber, and energy use. These areas occur in different climates depending on the crop, water availability, and soil type.

Shrubs and grasslands are common in Mediterranean climates with wet winters and dry summers.

Forests such as the redwood and mixed conifer forests in California, are dominated by trees. Forests occur in climates where there is enough rainfall to support trees, such as humid continental or Mediterranean climates.

10. **Language SmArts | Discuss** Work with a partner. You should each select one of the land cover types that you are familiar with. Take turns asking each other questions that can be answered with yes, no, or a simple phrase in order to guess your partner's land cover type. What climate might occur in these areas?

Climate Helps Determine Where Plants and Animals Can Live

All living organisms require food, water, space, and suitable temperatures in which to grow and reproduce. The different climates around the world provide different temperatures and rainfall levels which support many different plant communities.

Plants Live in Specific Climates

Over many generations plants have developed specific characteristics that make them suited to grow and reproduce in specific climates. For example, some plants have adapted to extremely dry climates by developing long roots or the ability to store water in their leaves or cells. Some shrubs have adapted to the windy, salty environment of coastal areas by growing short, wind-resistant branches and leaves and the ability to filter out salt.

Plant Communities Influence Animal Communities

The number and kinds of plants that live in an area influence the number and kinds of animals that live in the same area. This is because plants make food and form the base of food chains on land. Different animals prefer different plants. Some animals need a specific type of plant to survive. For example, the koala depends on the eucalyptus tree. In the past, populations of koalas varied in their ability to break down eucalyptus leaves. Those koalas better able to digest the plants survived and reproduced, and the easy digestion of eucalyptus became more common in koalas. Koalas use the trees for shelter, food, and water. The eucalyptus trees in a region support the koalas. The koalas, in turn, are a food source for other animals, such as pythons and eagles. If eucalyptus trees disappeared from an area, it would negatively affect the koalas that feed on the eucalyptus trees, as well as the animals that feed on the koalas.

11. **Collaborate** There are tradeoffs when populations develop special traits to live in an environment. For example, redwood trees cannot be tall to reach sunlight in a crowded forest *and* be short to avoid strong winds. Select an organism with a partner. Present a poster that explains the tradeoffs that make the organism well-suited to its environment.

Pickleweed is a wetland plant native to California. Pickleweed is salt-tolerant and thrives in sunny conditions.

The redwood is a tree found mainly in the coastal forests of northern California.

The Joshua tree is the largest of the yuccas and thrives in the Mojave Desert.

Hands-On Lab
Compare the Drought Tolerance of Plants

Imagine you live in a dry climate and would like to add a plant to an outdoor garden. The garden is not often watered. Plan an investigation to determine which plant type is better suited to a dry environment.

Procedure

As you develop your investigation, consider these questions:

- How can your observations from the beginning of the lesson help you plan your procedure?
- What data should you measure and record?
- How can you determine the health of a plant?
- How will you handle having a control and more than one plant in a treatment group? (Hint: There may be an opportunity for team work.)

MATERIALS
- graduated cylinder
- light source
- nonsucculent plant, small, potted
- succulent plant, small, potted
- water

STEP 1 Plan and write your procedure to determine which plant is better suited to a dry environment. Your procedure should describe the independent and dependent variables.

STEP 2 Get your teacher's approval before you begin your investigation. Make any changes to your procedure requested by your teacher.

STEP 3 Predict the results of your experiment based on your prior observations.

STEP 4 Perform your investigation following the steps you have written. Record your observations on a separate sheet of paper.

Analysis

STEP 5 Write a short argument that identifies the drought-tolerant plant that you recommend for the garden. Use evidence from your investigation to support your answer and present your argument to the class.

STEP 6 Organisms are influenced by many environmental factors at once, such as the amount of water, nutrients, and sunlight available in an area. Why is it important to change only one variable in an experiment, even if there are many environmental factors that affect a plant in the natural world?

EVIDENCE NOTEBOOK

12. Emperor penguins eat fish, squid, and other animals they catch in the ocean. Roadrunners eat lizards, insects, and other animals they catch in the bushes and grass. How does the climate where these birds live affect the plant and animal life and what the birds eat? Record your evidence.

Do the Math

Analyze Climate Needs

Darwin's orchid (*Angraecum sesquipedale*) is an orchid species from the lowlands of Madagascar. This orchid often occurs in areas that get more than 203.2 cm (80 in.) of rain each year.

13. What information does the climate graph provide about the climate around Antananarivo, Madagascar? How much precipitation does this area receive annually? What is the average temperature in this area?

_____

_____

_____

_____

Climate Graph for Antananarivo, Madagascar

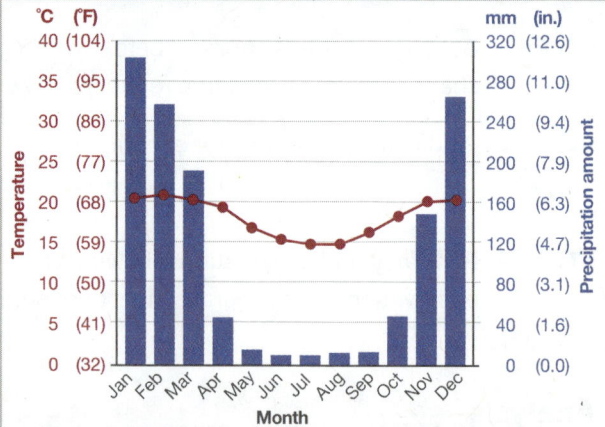

Credit: Adapted from Climate: Antananarivo by AM Online Projects. Copyright © by AM Online Projects. Adapted and reproduced by permission of Alexander Merkel, AM Online Projects, © Climate-Data.org.

14. Is the Darwin's orchid suited for the climate around Antananarivo? Use evidence to support your answer.

_____

_____

_____

Explaining How Adaptations Help Organisms Survive

Seals are as comfortable in water as humans are on land. Seals have flippers and a tail that help them swim and a thick layer of fat to keep them warm. Seals can hold their breath for a long time. This allows them to catch food and avoid predators.

15. Write Use the photo and your knowledge of seals to write a story about how this seal's traits help it survive in its environment.

Seals can live in very cold water. They are agile swimmers, which helps them to avoid predators and catch prey.

Adaptation

An **adaptation** is a trait that helps an organism survive and reproduce in its environment. Sometimes an adaptation helps an organism get food or water. For example, the long neck of a giraffe helps it reach leaves high in the trees. Sometimes an adaptation helps an organism protect itself or hide from predators. For example, stick insects developed traits that made them look like sticks. This makes it hard for other animals to see the insects. A trait that aids survival may become more common in the population as the trait is passed from parent to offspring during reproduction.

Explore Online

Giraffes' long necks allow them to graze on tall trees in the African savanna.

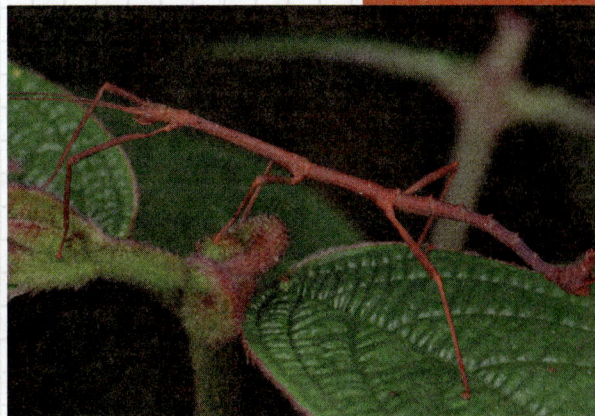

This insect is disguised as a stick. Camouflage is an adaptation that helps organisms avoid detection.

16. Leopards have spots to blend in with the patches of sunlight on the jungle floor. How might a trait like spots become more common in a population of leopards?

A. Leopards get their spots by rubbing against each other. Eventually all leopards in a population will have spots.

B. Blending in helps leopards successfully hunt for food. Leopards with more food are more likely to survive and pass on their spotted trait to offspring.

C. An adult leopard develops more spots during its lifetime in order to compete with other leopards.

Physical Adaptation

Physical adaptations are structures or physical characteristics that help animals survive and reproduce. For example, many animals have adaptations that serve as a disguise. The leaf katydid and the stick insect look like parts of a plant.

Behavioral Adaptation

Behavioral adaptations are actions that animals take in their environments in order to survive. Examples of behavioral adaptations that help animals survive cold weather are bears hibernating during long, cold winters and birds flying south for the winter in order to find more food. Bees store food during the summer to eat during the winter.

Explore Online

The desert beetle has long legs to raise its body up off the hot sand. This helps it to remain cool.

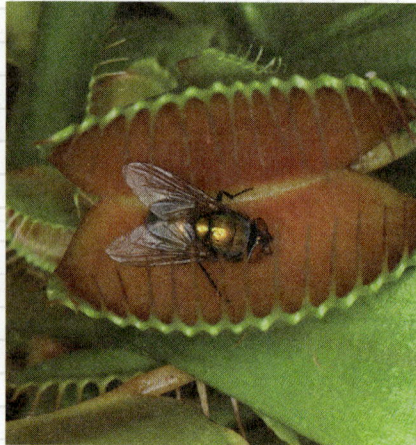

This carnivorous plant has evolved a physical adaptation that attracts and traps small insects for it to feed on.

Some bears hibernate during the winter. This behavior allows the bears to conserve energy when food is scarce and the weather is very cold.

17. Decide whether each adaptation is a physical or a behavioral adaptation.

Adaptation	Physical or Behavioral
Koalas have fur on their rumps which acts as a cushion for hard branches they sit on.	
The opossum "plays" dead for protection from its enemies.	
Coastal redwoods have shallow roots that extend far from the tree to provide support.	
Humpback whales migrate north from Antarctica to breed in warmer water.	

EVIDENCE NOTEBOOK

18. What adaptations do Emperor penguins and roadrunners have? Record your evidence.

Case Study: Sierra Nevada

Banner Peak is part of the Ansel Adams Wilderness in the Sierra Nevada.

Sierra Nevada is a Spanish phrase that means "snow-covered mountain range." This region runs along the eastern side of California. The mid-latitude location and closeness to the Pacific Ocean means that the Sierra Nevada can have unusually mild mountain climates. Snowfall increases with elevation and latitude. Precipitation is heavy on the coastal side of the mountains from November to April.

Bristlecone pines grow slowly in the poor soil and cold weather of the mountains. These trees keep their needles for many years instead of replacing them yearly. This is one way they save energy. Bristlecone pines occur in mountains just east of the Sierra Nevada.

American pikas have thick coats and small, round bodies to conserve heat in cold weather. They gather and store plants in a sheltered pile and eat the dried plants during the winter.

Sky pilot plants grow low to the ground where temperatures are warmer. Sky pilots bloom for a short time in the summer months. The flowers are showy to attract pollinators.

Bighorn sheep have sharp eyesight to spot predators. Their padded hooves help them climb steep terrain. Males clash with their horns to compete for dominance and the chance to breed.

Some butterflies, such as this painted lady, can survive in the mountains. They depend on plants for food and a place to lay their eggs. Some plants depend on butterflies for pollination.

19. Pikas grow thick fur in winter, and their small bodies conserve heat. Kangaroo rats do not sweat, and oily fur helps them conserve moisture. They get water from seeds. Predict what would happen if a pika and a kangaroo rat switched environments.

Similar Adaptations Can Occur in Similar Environments

It is not uncommon for animals and plants that live in similar conditions to develop similar adaptations. For example, many desert-dwelling plants have similar adaptations to conserve water. Some plants have shallow, extensive root systems that allow them to absorb as much surface water as possible.

20. The rubber tree has smooth, thin bark and large, waxy leaves that allow rainwater to run off faster. Which organism is most likely to live in an environment similar to the rubber tree's environment?

    A. Kangaroo paw plants that have tiny hairs to hold on to water droplets.

    B. Giant water lilies with waxy leaves that float on water.

    C. Ocotillos that become dormant, or inactive, between rainfalls.

The *Sinopoda scurion* is an eyeless, cave-dwelling huntsman spider. There is little or no light where this spider lives.

The golden mole cannot see. Its eyes are covered with furred skin. These moles spend most of their time underground.

Identify Suitable Adaptations for Specific Environments

Deserts have extreme temperatures and little rainfall. Reptiles that can survive hot temperatures and cacti with shallow roots to capture water are common. Some animals pass through when the weather is more moderate. The tundra is cold with a short growing season. There is little rainfall and the tundra is snow-covered in the winter. Low-growing plants with shallow roots and migrating animals are common.

WORD BANK
- white winter coat
- migration
- active at night
- shallow roots
- thin fur
- spines, not leaves
- hibernation

21. Identify whether each adaptation is suitable for the desert, the tundra, or both areas. Then write each adaptation in the correct location in the Venn diagram.

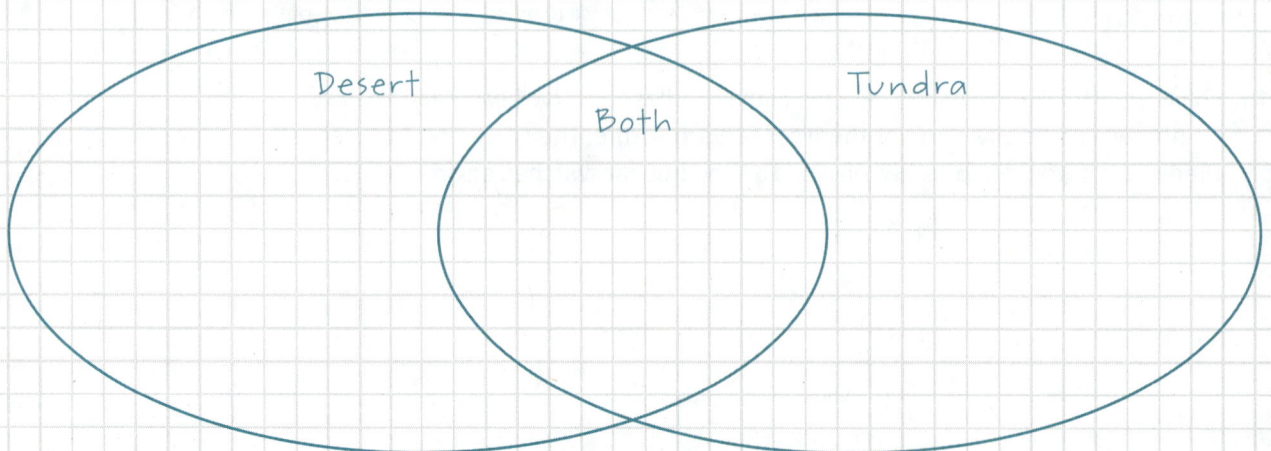

Desert — Both — Tundra

Continue Your Exploration

Name: _____   Date: _____

Check out the path below or go online to choose one of the other paths shown.

People in Science

- **Hibernation, Migration, or Staying Active**
- **Hands-On Labs** 🖐️
- **Propose Your Own Path**

Go online to choose one of these other paths.

Dr. Gary Bañuelos, Soil Scientist

Gary Bañuelos grew up in Red Bluff, California. He studied German, crop science, and international agriculture before earning his PhD in plant nutrition from Hohenhiem University in Germany. During his studies in Germany, Dr. Bañuelos tested vegetables for radioactive contamination. This led to an interest in how some plants remove harmful substances from the environment. Dr. Bañuelos now studies the *phytoremediation* of soils—helping to improve soils through the use of plants—particularly in areas with high levels of selenium, boron, and salt in California.

Gary Bañuelos is a soil scientist at the US Department of Agriculture (USDA) Water Management Research Unit and teaches at several universities.

Selenium is an element that is harmful in large amounts. However, selenium is also a necessary micronutrient for humans and other animals. In other words, people need a little bit of selenium, but a lot of selenium can be harmful. Selenium occurs naturally in some soil. Selenium in farm fields dissolves in irrigation water. It may become part of water runoff from irrigated fields. This can lead to high, harmful levels of selenium in waterways and other ecosystems. As the human population has increased, more wildlands have been cleared for agriculture. This has caused more irrigation runoff and more selenium in waterways and natural areas. Selenium levels may become so high that they threaten aquatic and land-based wildlife. When irrigation runoff is more closely managed, selenium builds up in the soil of farm fields. Traditional crops may be unable to grow in soil with lots of selenium. To reduce threats to ecosystems and human populations, Dr. Bañuelos was asked to use phytoremediation techniques to manage selenium movement in ecosystems.

1. Plants are adapted to different conditions based on the environment in which the plant lives. What characteristics would you look for in a plant to be used in phytoremediation to improve soil with high levels of selenium and salt?

Continue Your Exploration

Dr. Bañuelos has studied many plants that are able to thrive in saline and selenium-rich soil. One of those plants is the prickly pear cactus (*Opuntia ficus-indica*). The prickly pear plant takes up selenium through its roots. The selenium is then stored in the prickly pear fruits and "paddles" of the plant, or the selenium is released into the air as a nontoxic gas. The amount of selenium stored in the cactus tissues is safe for humans and animals to eat. Prickly pear plants don't need a lot of water. This makes it an ideal plant for phytoremediation of selenium in dry areas of California.

2. What effect does phytoremediation with prickly pear cacti have on selenium-rich soil and the cacti? Select all that apply.

   A. more selenium in the soil

   B. less selenium in the soil

   C. more selenium in the prickly pear cacti

   D. less selenium in the prickly pear cacti

3. Develop a model that describes how selenium moves from the environment through the phytoremediation process.

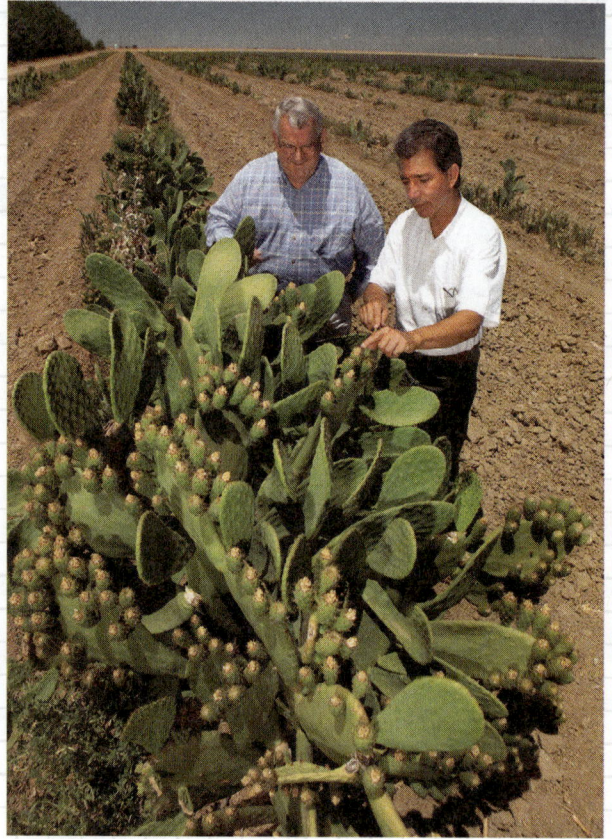

Dr. Bañuelos (right) and collaborator John Diener (left) inspect a prickly pear cactus.

4. **Collaborate** With a partner, develop a multimedia presentation that describes how prickly pear cacti are used in the United States and other places in the world. Explain why farmers need an economic market for the prickly pear cactus in order for this crop to be planted. How does phytoremediation with prickly pear plants demonstrate the interdependence of science and society?

Can You Explain It?

Name: _____   Date: _____

Why do Emperor penguins and roadrunners live in different areas of the world?

Emperor penguins

roadrunner

EVIDENCE NOTEBOOK

Refer to the notes in your Evidence Notebook to help you construct an explanation for why Emperor penguins and roadrunners live in different areas of the world.

1. State your claim. Make sure your claim fully explains why Emperor penguins and roadrunners live in different areas of the world.

2. Summarize the evidence you have gathered to support your claim and explain your reasoning.

Checkpoints

Answer the following questions to check your understanding of the lesson.

Use the map to answer Questions 3–4.

3. In which places would you expect to find organisms with similar adaptations?

    A. 1 and 2

    B. 2 and 3

    C. 1 and 3

    D. 1, 2, and 3

Vegetation Type
- Grassland and savanna
- Tropical forest
- Desert
- Chaparral
- Montane

Credit: Adapted from Population, Landscape and Climate Estimates, V3. Copyright © 2012 by Center for International Earth Science Information Network (CIESIN)/Columbia University, Palisades, NY. NASA Socioeconomic Data and Applications Center (SEDAC). Adapted and reproduced by permission of Center for International Earth Science Information Network.

4. Based on the relationship between plant life, climate, and latitude, which location is closest to the equator?

    A. 1

    B. 2

    C. 3

Use the photo to answer Question 5.

5. Camels store fat in their humps, allowing them to go days without eating. What is a similar adaptation in a different animal?

    A. Cacti store water in their stems to help them live through dry periods.

    B. Bees store honey to feed the colony during the winter.

    C. Seals store fat to keep warm in cold water.

    D. Bears store fat to fuel their bodies during hibernation.

---

6. Adaptations help organisms to survive in specific environments. Match the adaptation with the most likely environment.

extreme heat	store water in stems
high winds	hibernation
extreme cold	active at night
lack of water	low-growing plants

Interactive Review

Complete this section to review the main concepts of the lesson.

Major factors that affect climate are latitude, altitude, closeness to oceans, and closeness to mountains.

A. How do mountain ranges affect regional climate?

The climate in an area helps determine the plants and animals that can survive in the region.

B. What patterns would you expect to see in a climate map and a vegetation map of the same area?

Adaptations help an organism survive and reproduce in its environment.

C. Use an example to illustrate the relationship between adaptations and environment.

Images/Getty Images

Organisms Inherit Traits from Their Parents

These African cichlid fish all have a black stripe over their eyes. Do you think they could be related?

Explore First

Categorizing Traits List five traits that people may have. Then divide the traits into two categories: traits that don't come from parents and traits that do. How did you decide the category for each trait?

Go *online* to view the digital version of the Hands-On Lab for this lesson and to download additional lab resources.

CAN YOU EXPLAIN IT?

How did these kittens get their fur colors?

These kittens are all related because they have the same two parents. However, when you look at the fur colors of the kittens, you'll notice that they are not all the same.

1. Knowing the kittens' fur color, what would you predict the parents' fur looks like?

2. Why do you think these kittens look similar in some ways and different in other ways?

EVIDENCE NOTEBOOK As you explore the lesson, gather evidence to help explain how the kittens got their fur color.

Investigating How Traits Are Passed from Parent to Offspring

More than 150 years ago, an Austrian monk named Gregor Mendel observed that pea plants in his garden had different forms of certain characteristics. Mendel studied the characteristics of pea plants, such as seed color and flower color. Each characteristic that Mendel studied had two different forms. For example, the color of a pea could be green or yellow. These different forms are called **traits**.

Mendel noticed that when the plants reproduced, the next generation of plants did not always share the same traits with their parents. He planned an experiment to investigate how the traits of the parent plants were passed on to the offspring.

3. Discuss What are some differences you notice in these pea plants?

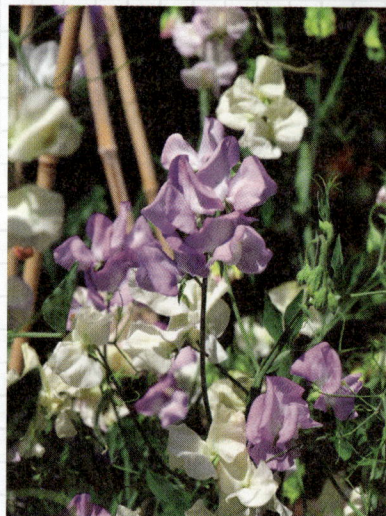

Mendel used pea plants to study how traits are passed from parent to offspring.

Mendel's Pea Plant Investigation

These two plants represent the parent generation. Usually, these pea plants self-pollinate. But instead, Mendel fertilized one parent plant with the pollen from the other parent plant.

These four plants represent the first generation of offspring (F1). In the F1 generation, all of the plants have purple flowers.

These plants represent the second generation of offspring (F2). Most of the F2 generation offspring have purple flowers, but some offspring have white flowers.

4. How does the presence of white flowers change from the parent generation, to the first generation of offspring, to the second generation of offspring?

Mendel's Investigation Methods

Mendel studied each pea plant trait separately, always starting with plants that were true breeding for that trait. A true-breeding plant is one that will always produce offspring with a certain trait when allowed to self-pollinate. The white-flowered and purple-flowered parent plants that Mendel studied were true-breeding plants for the flower color trait. Usually, pea plants self-pollinate, but Mendel *crossed* the two parent plants, meaning he fertilized one parent plant with pollen from the other parent plant. Then, he let the first generation self-pollinate. He used these same methods to study other pea plant traits.

Before Mendel became a monk, he attended a university and studied science and mathematics.

Dominant and Recessive Traits

When Mendel crossed the purple-flowered and white-flowered plants, all first-generation plants had purple flowers. Mendel called this trait the *dominant trait*. Because the white-flower trait seemed to recede, or fade away, he called it the *recessive trait*. For all traits that Mendel studied, a similar pattern occurred. One of the parents' traits would not show up in the first generation. These were all recessive traits. The other trait—that shows up in all first generation offspring—was the dominant trait.

But what about the second generation of offspring? About one-fourth of these plants had white flowers—the recessive trait. The rest had purple flowers. The trait that seemed to disappear in the first generation reappeared in the second generation. Again, for all of the traits that Mendel studied, this same pattern occurred.

Language SmArts
Construct an Explanation of Trait Inheritance

What could explain the mysterious disappearance and reappearance of the recessive traits? Mendel hypothesized that each plant must have two inherited "factors" for each trait, one from each parent. Some traits, such as white flower color, only occurred if a plant received two factors for white flower color. A plant with one white flower factor and one purple flower factor would have the dominant trait: purple flowers. However, this plant could still pass on the white flower factor to the next generation of plants.

5. Explain how Mendel's data supported his hypothesis. Support your answer by citing textual evidence from this lesson.

_____

_____

_____

_____

6. Mendel crossed a true-breeding plant with yellow peas with a true-breeding plant with green peas. All first generation offspring had yellow peas. Explain which trait is recessive.

_____

_____

Relating Genetic Structure to Traits

Mendel's experiments and conclusions were the beginnings of scientific thought about how traits are passed from parents to offspring. Mendel's observations can be further explained by our modern understanding of the molecule called DNA. DNA is short for deoxyribonucleic acid. DNA contains instructions that determine an organism's traits and coordinate the growth and development of an organism.

7. **Discuss** How is DNA similar to a recipe? What happens if a recipe is changed slightly?

Scientists can isolate DNA to investigate the relationship between the structure of DNA and traits in organisms.

Genes Influence Traits

DNA is organized into structures called **chromosomes**. An individual has paired sets of chromosomes. What Mendel called "factors" are now known as genes. A **gene** is a segment of the DNA that makes up a chromosome. Because an individual has pairs of chromosomes, an individual also has pairs of genes.

Each gene can have different forms, or variations. For example, Mendel's pea plants had two variations of the flower color gene, causing purple or white flowers. Each parent contributes one set of genes to its offspring. So, for a particular trait, one gene variation comes from each parent. The different gene forms are called **alleles**. Alleles carry the codes for producing various **proteins**, which are large molecules that do much of the work in a cell and also make up much of the cell's structure. Proteins are responsible for most aspects of how our bodies function, as well as for our physical appearance and behavior.

Mendel's pea plant traits were all controlled by just two alleles: a dominant one and a recessive one. For those pea plants, the allele for purple flowers is the dominant allele, and the allele for white flowers is the recessive allele. Some traits follow this inheritance pattern; however, most do not. Usually there are more than two alleles for a single gene within a population of organisms. Each organism, however, can carry only one or two alleles for one gene. Most traits, such as height and eye color, are determined by more than one gene.

The Structure of DNA

The chemical components that make up DNA are too small to be observed directly. However, experiments and imaging techniques have helped scientists to infer the shape of DNA and the arrangement of its parts. A molecule of DNA is shaped like a twisted ladder, a shape that is called a *double helix.* The rungs of the ladder are made of pairs of bases. A length of base pairs along a DNA molecule is what makes up a gene. The instructions of DNA are coded in specific sequences of base pairs.

8. **Collaborate** Build a model that illustrates the relationships among DNA, chromosomes, and genes. Present your model to the class.

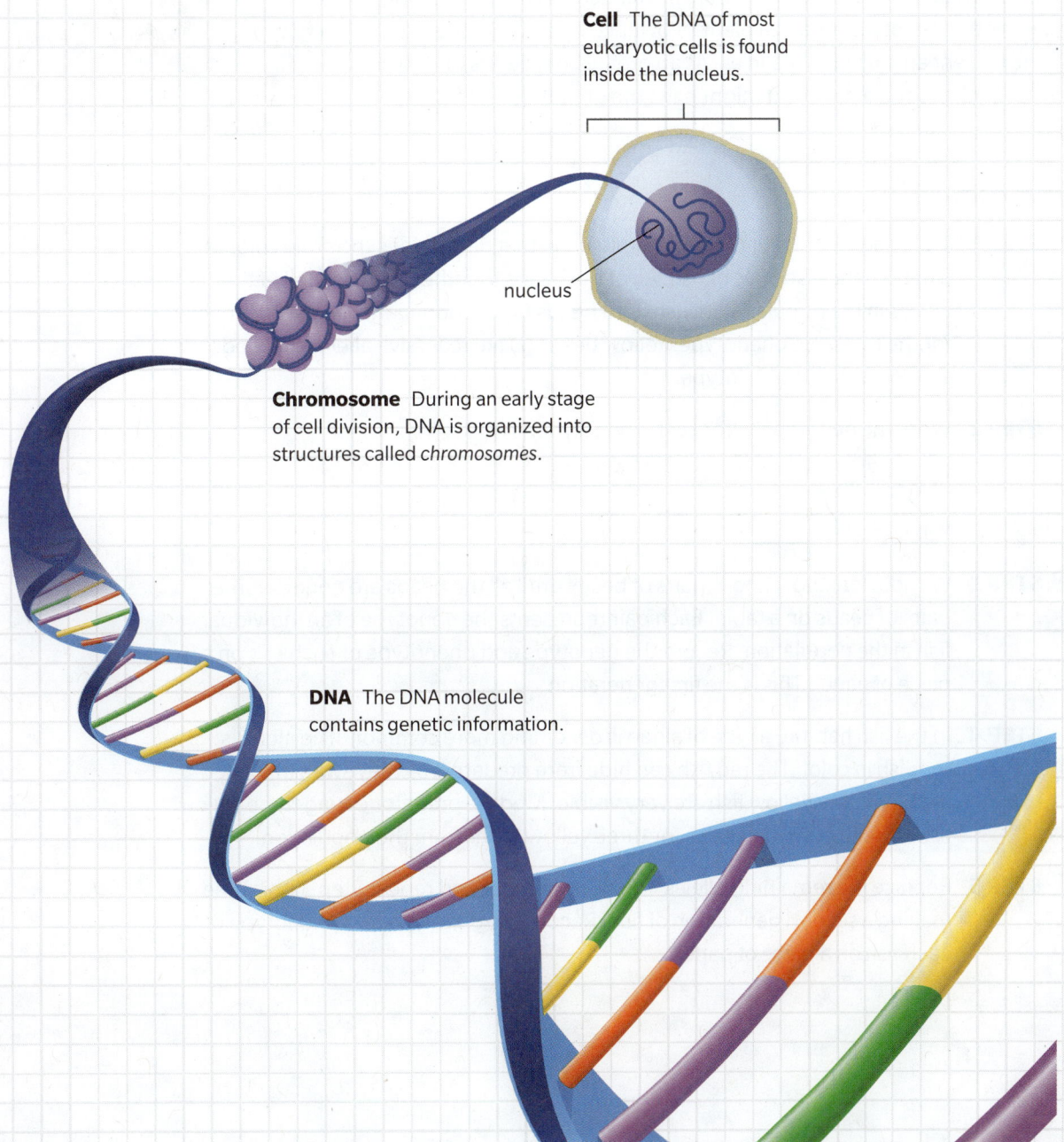

Cell The DNA of most eukaryotic cells is found inside the nucleus.

nucleus

Chromosome During an early stage of cell division, DNA is organized into structures called *chromosomes.*

DNA The DNA molecule contains genetic information.

Hands-On Lab
Model Genes and Traits

Use a model to describe genetic variation for the scale color of a hypothetical fish species. Use evidence to predict, over several generations, the proportions of dominant and recessive alleles in the population. .

The combination of alleles that an organism receives from its parents is called the organism's *genotype*. The observable traits of an organism are its *phenotype*. Genotypes can be represented by letter symbols. Often, dominant alleles are shown with capital letters and recessive alleles are shown with lowercase letters. For example, *F* could represent the dominant allele of purple flower color and *f* could represent the recessive allele of white flower color in pea plants. You can write a genotype for a pea plant's flower color by using the letters to represent an individual's alleles. As an organism receives one allele from each parent, a pea plant might have the genotype *FF, Ff,* or *ff*.

> **MATERIALS**
> - cup
> - red beads (12)
> - yellow beads (10)

Procedure

STEP 1 The beads represent the alleles for a gene that determines the scale color of a hypothetical species of fish. All of the beads together represent all of the alleles in the population of fish. Red beads (*R*) are dominant alleles that code for the red-scale phenotype. Yellow beads (*r*) are recessive alleles that code for the yellow-scale phenotype.

STEP 2 Write the genotype(s) for each phenotype.

Red scales: _____

Yellow scales: _____

STEP 3 Without looking, choose pairs of beads until all the beads are gone. Set the pairs of beads on a table. Each pair represents the genotype of an individual fish in the population. Record the genotype and phenotype of each fish on a piece of paper. This is the first generation.

STEP 4 In the fish habitat, a type of algae is becoming more common. The algae is reddish in color. The red fish can hide from predators as they swim in the red algae, but the yellow fish are very visible. Model a predator eating three yellow fish by removing the alleles for three yellow "fish" from the population.

STEP 5 Replace the remaining alleles into the container and repeat Step 3, this time making a second generation of fish. Record the genotype and phenotype of each fish on a piece of paper.

Analysis

STEP 6 Compare the first- and second-generation phenotypes. Explain the reasons for any differences.

STEP 7 Use evidence from your simulation to explain what would happen after many generations if environmental conditions for these fish remained the same. Justify your response.

STEP 8 Suppose that yellow algae began to outcompete the red algae in the fish environment. Describe how you could model the next two generations of fish in this changed environment.

EVIDENCE NOTEBOOK

9. Think about the different phenotypes of fish scale color in this lab and the phenotypes of fur color in the kittens at the beginning of this lesson. Explain why all of the kittens don't have the same fur color, even though they have the same parents. Record your evidence.

Predict Effects of Mutation

Changes in a section of DNA are known as *mutations*. How do mutations happen? One cause of mutations is random errors that occur when DNA is copied to make new cells.

A mutation in bacteria can make an individual bacterium resistant to antibiotics. Galactosemia in humans is caused by a mutation in one gene and prevents people from digesting a sugar found in dairy foods. This can lead to poor health or death. Mutations that cause a change in human eye or hair color do not affect the health of the individual. Some small changes in DNA do not change the protein that the DNA codes for.

10. Which mutation described in the paragraph is harmful, which is neutral, and which is beneficial? Explain your reasoning.

_____

_____

_____

_____

Modeling Inheritance of Traits

Not all traits are passed on from parent to offspring. Some traits are learned, such as the ability to ride a bicycle or write your name in cursive. Other traits are acquired, or taken on after birth. For example, a person might dye his hair blue, but that is not an inherited trait.

11. Engineer It The three processes below would allow a horticulturist to grow only purple-flowered pea plants for many generations. However, the horticulturist is constrained by time. Which of the following processes would allow the horticulturist to grow only purple-flowered plants in the shortest amount of time? Explain your reasoning below.

A. A horticulturist could start by crossing two plants with purple flowers. In each new generation, they should select plants with purple flowers to cross, until all of the plants for several generations have purple flowers.

B. A horticulturist could send plant specimens to a lab for genotype analysis, which usually takes 1–2 weeks.

C. A horticulturist could allow the purple plants to self-pollinate, then separate purple plants from the first generation and allow those plants to self-pollinate.

Flower color is an inherited trait.

Genes Are Passed from Parents to Offspring

Before anyone knew about DNA or genes, Mendel figured out that "factors"—what we now call genes—were passed from parent to offspring. **Inheritance** is the passing of genes from parents to offspring. In one form of reproduction, offspring inherit all of their genes from one parent, so that the offspring and the parent are genetically identical. For example, you can take a cutting of a houseplant and grow a new individual plant. The new plant is genetically identical to its parent unless mutations occur. In another form of reproduction, two parents contribute genetic material. The offspring of this type of reproduction are genetically different from each of the parents as well as from each other.

Genes and Alleles on Chromosomes

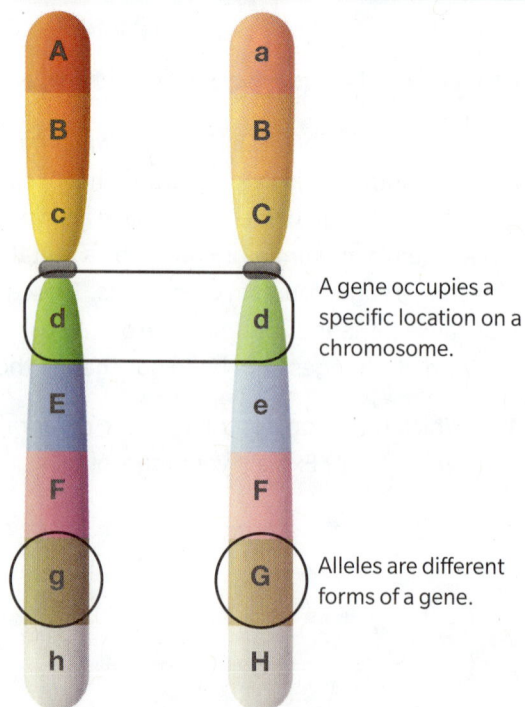

A gene occupies a specific location on a chromosome.

Alleles are different forms of a gene.

12. Mendel's peas had two phenotypes for pod color: yellow pods and green pods. The allele for yellow pod color is *Y* and the allele for green pod color is *y*. On the lines below, write the phenotype for each genotype. Then summarize how these alleles were passed from parent to offspring.

Genotype	Phenotype	Summary
Parent 1: *YY*	A. _____	
Parent 2: *yy*	B. _____	
All offspring: *Yy*	C. _____	

Inheritance Is Modeled with Punnett Squares

Mendel discovered the basic laws of inheritance through his studies of pea plants. His observations confirmed that each parent plant contributes one allele for each gene, offspring randomly receive one allele for each gene from each parent, and dominant alleles are always expressed in offspring.

One tool for understanding the basic patterns of heredity is a Punnett square. A *Punnett square* is a model used to predict the possible genotypes of offspring in a given cross. The example shows a cross between a pea plant with purple flowers (*FF*) and a pea plant with white flowers (*ff*). The top of the Punnett square shows the possible alleles for this trait from one parent (*F* and *F*). The left side shows the possible alleles from the other parent (*f* and *f*). Each square shows a possible allele combination for potential offspring.

Punnett Square for Flower Color

13. Fill in the missing genotype to complete the Punnett square.

This parent plant has the dominant alleles *FF*, giving the plant purple flowers.

This parent plant has the recessive alleles *ff*, giving the plant white flowers.

14. Use the laws of inheritance and the predictions in the Punnett square to explain how genetic factors can influence the traits of organisms.

15. The pea plant traits studied by Mendel were determined by one gene. However, many traits, such as fur color, are determined by more than one gene. How might the influence of multiple genes affect the number of possible phenotypes for cat fur color? Record your evidence.

+ ÷
− ×

Do the Math
Calculate Genotype Probability

A Punnett square shows all possible genotypes for the offspring of a cross, not what the exact results of the cross will be. A Punnett square is used to predict the probability that an offspring will have a certain genotype. *Probability* is the mathematical chance of a specific outcome in relation to the total number of possible outcomes.

Probability can be expressed as a *ratio*, an expression that compares two quantities. A ratio written as 1:4 is read as "one to four." Punnett square ratios show the probability that any one offspring will get certain alleles. Probability can also be expressed as a percentage. A percentage compares a number to 100, stating the number of times a certain outcome might happen out of a hundred chances.

16. Complete the Punnett square. The allele for red feathers (*R*) is dominant and the allele for brown feathers (*r*) is recessive.

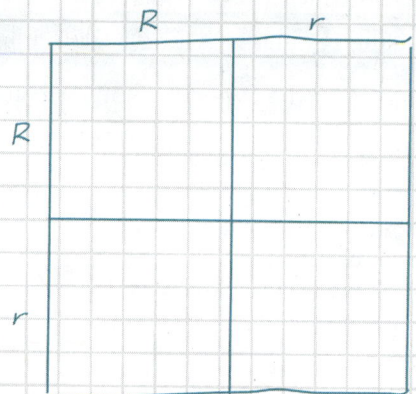

	R	r
R		
r		

17. Use probability to describe the likelihood that an offspring of this cross will have each genotype or phenotype:

Genotype or Phenotype	Probability	Percentage
RR genotype	1:4	$1 \div 4 = 0.25$ $0.25 \times 100 = 25\%$
Rr genotype		
rr genotype		
red feathers		
brown feathers		

Continue Your Exploration

Name: _____   Date: _____

Check out the path below or go online to choose one of the other paths shown.

People in Science

- **Genetic Engineering**
- **Hands-On Labs** 🖐
- **Propose Your Own Path**

Go online to choose one of these other paths.

In the mid-19th century, scientists knew that the DNA molecule existed, but they did not know what it looked like. Many scientists studied DNA's structure, and the combined work of four scientists in particular helped solve the mystery.

DNA is made up of chemical compounds called *nucleotides*. A nucleotide consists of a sugar, a phosphate, and a base: thymine, guanine, adenine, or cytosine. Erwin Chargaff found that in DNA, the amount of adenine equals the amount of thymine and the amount of guanine equals the amount of cytosine.

Rosalind Franklin used x-ray diffraction to make images of the DNA molecule; her research indicated DNA had a spiral shape. James Watson and Francis Crick used Chargaff's and Franklin's research to build a model of DNA. In their model, DNA is in the shape of a double helix, which looks like a twisted ladder. The sugars and phosphates make up the outsides of the ladder, while the "rungs" are made up of joined pairs of nucleotides. Adenine (A) pairs with thymine (T), and guanine (G) pairs with cytosine (C). These paired, or complementary, bases fit together like two pieces of a puzzle.

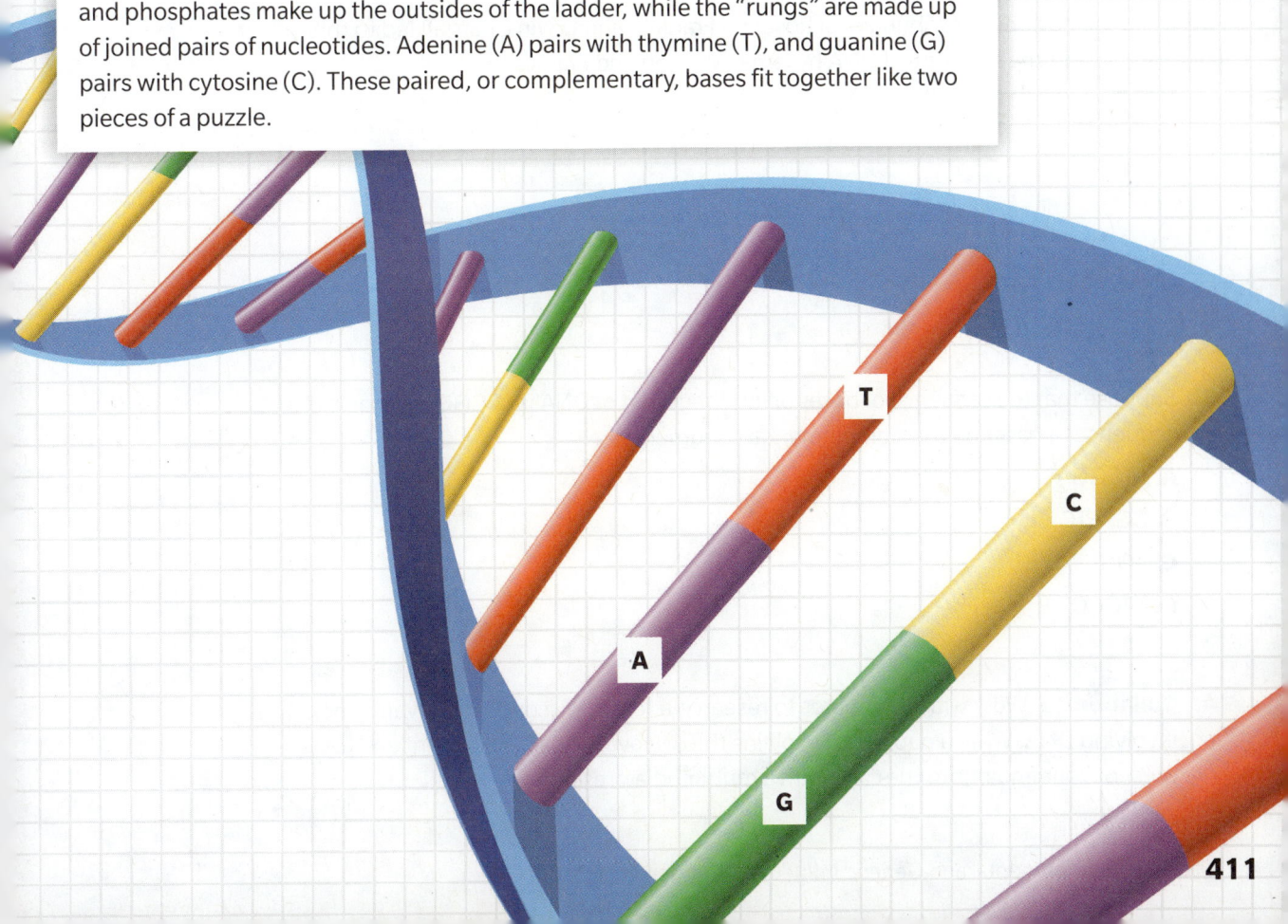

T

C

A

G

411

Continue Your Exploration

1. A scientist knows that a molecule of DNA is 27% cytosine. What else does the scientist know about the DNA molecule?

   A. The DNA molecule is 27% guanine.

   B. The DNA molecule is 27% adenine.

   C. The DNA molecule is 73% guanine.

   D. The DNA molecule is 27% thymine.

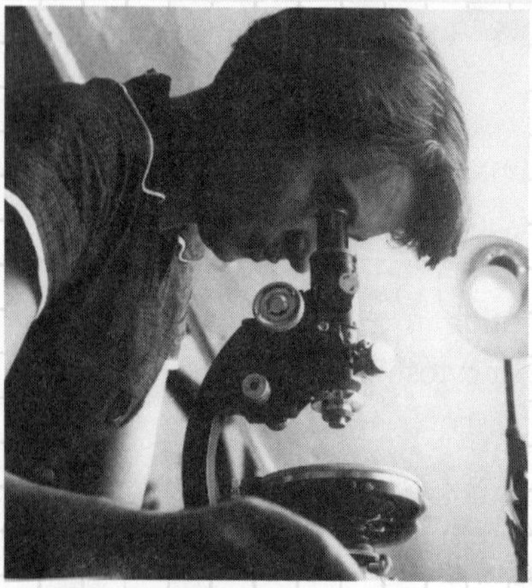

X-ray crystallographer Rosalind Franklin, circa 1942

Biochemist Erwin Chargaff, circa 1970

James Watson (left) and Francis Crick (right), in their laboratory, circa 1953

2. Describe how the contributions of Rosalind Franklin and Erwin Chargaff led to the discovery of the structure of DNA by James Watson and Francis Crick.

3. Suppose that the sequence of bases on one segment of DNA is ATCGGA. What is the sequence of bases on the complementary segment?

   A. ATCGGA

   B. CGATTC

   C. AGGCTA

   D. TAGCCT

4. **Collaborate** Work with classmates to research a recent discovery or advancement involving DNA. Write a paper that explains the discovery or advancement and present your findings to the class with a multimedia presentation.

Can You Explain It?

Name: _____   Date: _____

How did these kittens get their fur colors?

EVIDENCE NOTEBOOK
Refer to the notes in your Evidence Notebook to help you construct an explanation for how these kittens got their fur colors.

1. State your claim. Make sure your claim fully explains how the kittens got their fur colors.

2. Summarize the evidence you have gathered to support your claim and explain your reasoning.

Checkpoints

Answer the following questions to check your understanding of the lesson.

Use the diagram to answer Questions 3–4.

3. For which gene or genes will the recessive trait be expressed in this individual? Choose all that apply.

    A. the Q gene

    B. the S gene

    C. the T gene

    D. the U gene

4. What genotype(s) might the parents of this individual have for the Q gene? Select all that apply.

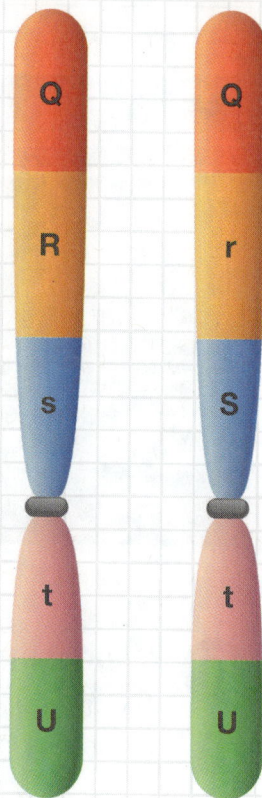

    A. *QQ*

    B. *Qq*

    C. *qq*

Q	Q
R	r
S	S
t	t
U	U

Use the diagram to answer Questions 5–6.

5. For Mendel's peas, seed shape was round (*R*) or wrinkled (*r*). Fill in all of the possible genotypes that could result from the cross shown in this Punnett square.

6. An offspring from this cross has a
0% / 25% / 50% / 75% / 100%
chance of having round peas and a
0% / 25% / 50% / 75% / 100%
chance of having wrinkled peas.

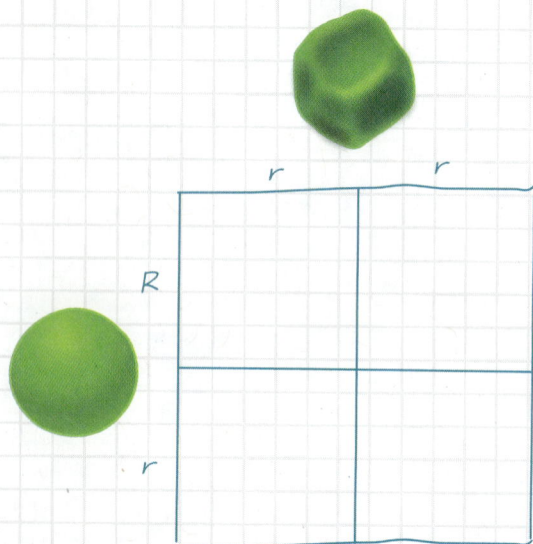

	r	*r*
R		
r		

Interactive Review

Complete this section to review the main concepts of the lesson.

Mendel discovered a basic inheritance pattern by studying pea plants.

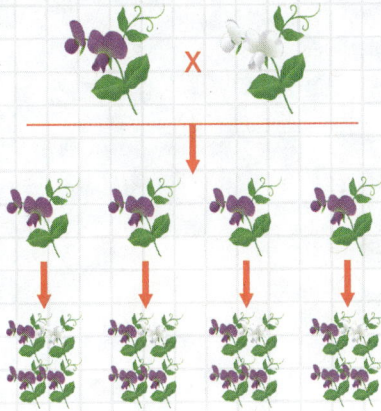

A. Mendel studied seven different features of pea plants, including flower color, seed shape, and seed color. Describe the evidence Mendel used to determine if a particular trait was dominant or recessive.

Genes, which are located on chromosomes, determine traits.

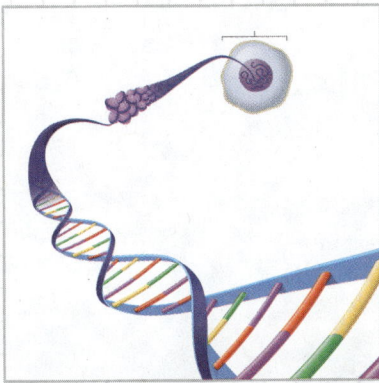

B. Explain how chromosomes, genes, and alleles are related.

The inheritance of some traits can be modeled using a Punnett square.

C. For Mendel's peas, yellow seed color (*G*) is dominant and green seed color (*g*) is recessive. Write and complete a Punnett square to model a cross between a *Gg* parent and a *GG* parent. Use evidence from the Punnett square to explain why the offspring may have different genotypes or phenotypes.

Reproduction Affects Genetic Diversity

Female grizzly bears have a litter of one to four cubs. The cubs will stay with their mother for two to three years.

Explore First

Modeling Variation Use marbles, beads, or other objects to model a population with high genetic diversity and a population with low genetic diversity. What environmental conditions would benefit a genetically diverse population and what environmental conditions would benefit a genetically similar population? Explain your reasoning.

CAN YOU EXPLAIN IT?

Why is the Cavendish banana in danger of extinction?

Banana crops throughout the world are being devastated by a fungal infection commonly known as Panama disease.

Panama disease is caused by a soil fungus, which enters the plant through the roots. The fungus grows in the plant's transport tissue and blocks the flow of water and nutrients throughout the plant. The Cavendish banana is the variety of banana most commonly eaten by people in the United States. The Cavendish banana may become extinct, or no longer living on Earth, because of this widespread disease.

1. Why might this disease spread quickly in banana plantations?

EVIDENCE NOTEBOOK As you explore the lesson, gather evidence to help you explain why the Cavendish banana is facing extinction.

Describing Types of Reproduction

Earth is home to millions of species of plants, animals, and other living things. In order for a species to survive, individual organisms of that species must make more organisms like themselves. Organisms produce **offspring**, or young organisms like themselves. Reproduction—the process by which organisms generate a new individual of the same species—is a characteristic of all living things. During the process of reproduction, organisms pass genetic material to their offspring.

Parents and Offspring

Thornback ray and pup
Males and females mate. Then females lay two eggs in sand in shallow waters. The eggs hatch into pups after 4–6 months. The pups will be fully grown in 5–8 years.

Luna moth and caterpillar
Females mate with a male and then lay hundreds of eggs. Caterpillars hatch, feed for 3–4 weeks, and then spin a cocoon of silk. Adult luna moths emerge after 2–3 weeks.

Teddy bear cactus and clones
Teddy bear cactus branches can stick to the fur of animals. The branches fall off the traveling animal and grow as a clone plant.

Green frog and tadpole
Female frogs lay thousands of eggs that are fertilized by males in water. Tadpoles hatch from the eggs. After developing for 3 months, they can leave the water as adult frogs.

2. Compare and contrast the reproduction and growth of these organisms based on the information provided and your knowledge of reproduction.

Types of Reproduction

There are two types of reproduction: asexual reproduction and sexual reproduction. In **asexual reproduction**, a single individual is the parent. The parent passes copies of its genes to its offspring, so the offspring are genetically identical to the parent unless gene mutations occur. Most unicellular organisms reproduce asexually. Fungi, plants, and some animals can also reproduce asexually. Asexual reproduction allows an organism to reproduce quickly and can produce a large number of offspring in a short period of time.

The New Mexico whiptail lizard is a unique, all-female population that reproduces asexually. These lizards have the ability to reproduce from unfertilized eggs. The offspring that have all of the mother's genetic material are called full clones. It is relatively rare for animals and other multicellular organisms to reproduce only asexually.

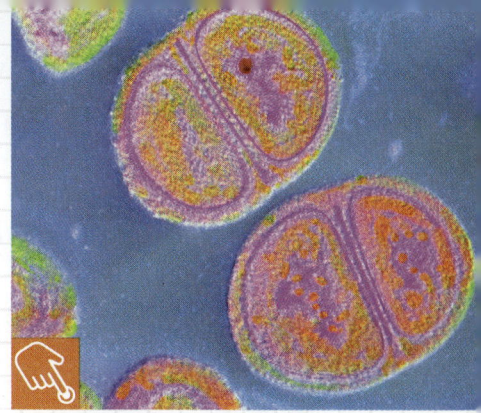

These bacteria reproduce by means of binary fission. During binary fission, an organism makes a copy of its DNA and then splits in two.

3. **Collaborate** With a partner, select an example of a clone from a biological system. Present your example to the class, explain why it is considered a clone, and add an illustration or image of your example to a class collage.

In **sexual reproduction**, there are two parents. Each parent contributes half of its genetic information to the offspring, so the offspring are genetically different from both parents. Most multicellular organisms reproduce sexually, including plants and animals. Sexual reproduction usually takes more time and produces fewer offspring than asexual reproduction. However, sexual reproduction increases genetic variation. This variation increases the chance that some offspring will have new traits that will help them survive in a changing environment.

4. A female elephant typically has one baby after mating and carrying the offspring in her womb for 18–22 months. Amoebas are microscopic aquatic organisms that can divide in half every two days. Which organism reproduces through sexual reproduction? Explain your reasoning.

This coral dahlia flower has male and female parts. The male parts make pollen, which contains male reproductive cells. Pollen from one flower can be transferred to the female part of another flower, beginning the process of reproduction.

📋 **EVIDENCE NOTEBOOK**

5. Banana plants grown for food crops are the result of asexual reproduction. How many parents and how much genetic variation does each banana plant have? Record your evidence.

Some Organisms Can Use Both Types of Reproduction

Some organisms can reproduce both asexually and sexually, depending on environmental conditions and other factors. Organisms that can use both types of reproduction include fungi, many plants, some reptiles and fish, and a few types of insects.

Aphids reproduce asexually at the beginning of the season when the environment is favorable and there is plenty of space on the host plant. Aphids reproduce sexually at the end of the growing season, after they have dispersed from crowded host plants. Reproducing asexually during favorable conditions allows the aphids to pass along all beneficial genes. Reproducing sexually after dispersing provides a higher likelihood that some of the offspring will survive in the new environments.

6. Redwood trees can reproduce both sexually and asexually. Which type of reproduction might give offspring more of an advantage if a large clearing around the tree became available?

Identify Asexual and Sexual Reproduction

7. Read about the reproductive processes of the animals below. Then decide whether the process is an example of *asexual reproduction*, *sexual reproduction*, or *both*.

	Female bullheads lay their eggs under small overhangs or in a pit. The male bullheads fertilize the eggs with their sperm. Male bullheads guard the eggs until they hatch.	
	Male and female jellyfish release sperm and eggs into the water. A fertilized egg develops into a larva that will grow into a polyp. The polyp will release a portion of its body into the water that will grow into an adult jellyfish.	
	Corals can reproduce in a variety of ways. One way is by a process that can produce a new coral from a fragment. A portion of a coral may be broken off by a boat, a person, or an animal. The broken piece can grow into a new coral.	

Environmental Influence on Reproduction

Environmental factors influence the ability of organisms to reproduce and offspring to survive. The quality and availability of food, water, energy, and space are critical to successful reproduction. Many organisms time their reproduction to occur at the same time as favorable environmental conditions. This maximizes the chances of their offspring surviving.

Stable Conditions

Imagine an environment with stable conditions that remain the same year after year. In these environments, it can be beneficial for parents to pass along all of their traits to their offspring. This is because the parents are already well-adapted to the conditions. Because the conditions remain stable, there is less need for further diversity in the population. Organisms that reproduce asexually, such as the bacteria that live in hot springs, are particularly suited to stable environments. Their offspring take on all of the traits of the parent bacterium, which allows the offspring to survive in the extreme temperatures of thermal pools.

Hot springs and other thermal features are home to bacteria that can survive at very high temperatures.

8. _Sexual / Asexual_ reproduction is _more / less_ successful in a(n) _stable / unstable_ environment as it passes on all of one parent's genetic traits that are suited to the environment.

Changing Conditions

In an unstable environment, such as one that is gradually warming, it is important for animals to be able to adapt to changing conditions. For example, sexual reproduction allows birds to develop different beak sizes over generations. Birds can use their beaks to release heat if they get too warm. A bigger beak is able to release more heat than a smaller beak. This can lead to different beak sizes between birds that live in a cooler coastal climate and inland birds of the same species that live in warmer climates.

Song sparrow populations in warm inland areas have larger beaks than populations in cooler coastal areas.

9. What are the most likely effects of human disturbance on stable environments? Select all that apply.

   A. Change the conditions from stable to variable.

   B. Change the conditions from variable to stable.

   C. Positively impact species that reproduce through asexual reproduction.

   D. Negatively impact species that reproduce through asexual reproduction.

Case Study: Joshua Trees

Joshua trees live in the Mojave Desert with hot summers, cold winters, and very little rainfall. Joshua trees reproduce sexually through the pollination of flowers, and asexually through vegetative reproduction from roots or branches. Asexual reproduction in Joshua trees is more common at higher elevations. The colder, windier conditions may make it more difficult for pollinators to successfully pollinate the trees. Joshua trees living at higher elevations may also benefit from asexual reproduction because they can pass along all of their beneficial genes to offspring.

Joshua trees live in harsh conditions that promote both sexual and asexual reproduction.

10. Decide whether *asexual* or *sexual* reproduction would be more beneficial in the following environments.

Environment	Asexual or Sexual
Same average temperature and rainfall for 50 years	
Rain shadow area of a mountain range with similar maximum and minimum temperatures for a century	
Apex predator has been hunted to near extinction	
Pollution is degrading the environment	
Humans are changing plant and animal life	

Engineer It
Develop a Hybrid

Farmers often breed two different varieties of a plant to produce offspring with desirable traits. These plants are called *hybrids*. The farmer selects parents with traits that are desired in the offspring, such as flower color, plant height, fruit yield, or pest resistance.

11. A rose farmer needs to grow plants that produce orange flowers in the colder fall months to meet customer demand. Describe how the farmer might try to produce this hybrid.

There are thousands of rose hybrids in nearly every color and variety of shapes.

Relating Reproduction to Genetic Variation

Reproduction is the process by which organisms inherit genes, which are segments of DNA on a chromosome. The genes inherited from the parent or parents determine the genetic traits of offspring. When an organism reproduces asexually, all the genetic material of the offspring is inherited from one parent. When an organism reproduces sexually, the offspring receives half of its genes from each parent.

Although hydras sometimes reproduce sexually, they reproduce mainly by *budding*, a type of asexual reproduction. A bud begins to grow on an adult's body. When it has developed a mouth and tentacles, the bud breaks off from the adult. Amphibians reproduce sexually. Female adult amphibians lay eggs that are fertilized by sperm from male adult amphibians.

12. **Discuss** Do you think the offspring of each organism are genetically identical to the parent or not genetically identical to the parent? Support your argument with evidence.

A hydra is an animal that lives in freshwater. Its body is shaped like a tube. It has tentacles around its mouth.

An amphibian is an animal that lives both on land and in water.

Inheritance and Asexual Reproduction

Prokaryotes, such as bacteria, are unicellular and reproduce by a type of cell division called *binary fission*. This process results in two unicellular organisms that are genetically identical to the parent. Asexual reproduction in multicellular organisms is more complicated but also usually involves a type of cell division that results in genetically identical cells.

Having offspring that are genetically identical to the parent ensures that any favorable traits that the parent has are passed on to the offspring. However, if the environment changes, a population with low genetic variation is less likely to have individuals with traits that allow them to survive.

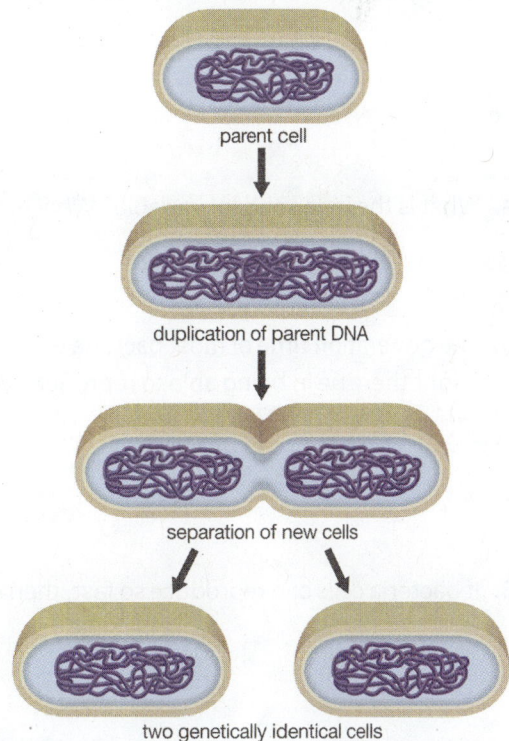

Transfer of DNA in Asexual Reproduction

parent cell

duplication of parent DNA

separation of new cells

two genetically identical cells

Do the Math
Calculate the Rate of Asexual Reproduction

Generation time is the average time between two generations in a population. For example, if a certain type of bacteria reproduces every 20 minutes, then the generation time is 20 minutes. Since bacteria reproduce by dividing into two cells, a bacteria population doubles in a generation time.

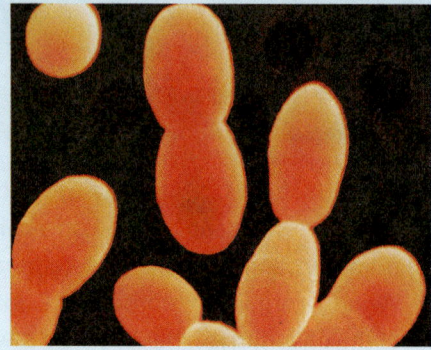

Lactococcus lactis is a bacteria used commonly in the production of cheese.

13. Use the data from the table to create a line graph of the bacteria population over time. What can this model explain about bacteria populations? What information is not provided by this model?

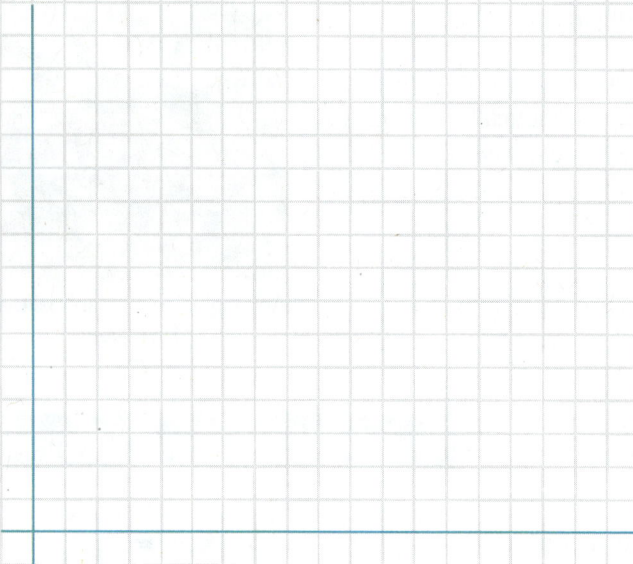

Time (in minutes)	Number of *Lactococcus lactis* Cells
0	1
52	2
104	4
156	8
208	16
260	32
312	64

14. What is the independent variable? What is the dependent variable?

15. The generation time of most bacteria can be measured in minutes. What advantage might there be in being able to reproduce very rapidly?

16. If bacteria cells can reproduce so fast, then why don't bacteria take over the world?

Inheritance and Sexual Reproduction

Sexual reproduction requires two parents. Each parent makes **gametes**, or sex cells. In animals, many plants, algae, and fungi, female organisms produce egg cells, and male organisms produce sperm cells. Gametes have one copy of each chromosome, half the total number of chromosomes of a body cell. The parent gametes are all genetically different.

During sexual reproduction, a sperm cell and an egg cell join in a process called *fertilization*. When an egg cell is fertilized by a sperm cell, a new, genetically different cell is formed. This cell—called a *zygote*—has a complete set of genetic material because it has received half of its chromosomes from one parent and half from the other parent. Thus, the zygote has inherited two copies of each gene, one from each parent. The genes may be identical, or they may differ from one another. The zygote will go through many cell divisions to form an adult organism. The organism that forms is genetically different from both parents.

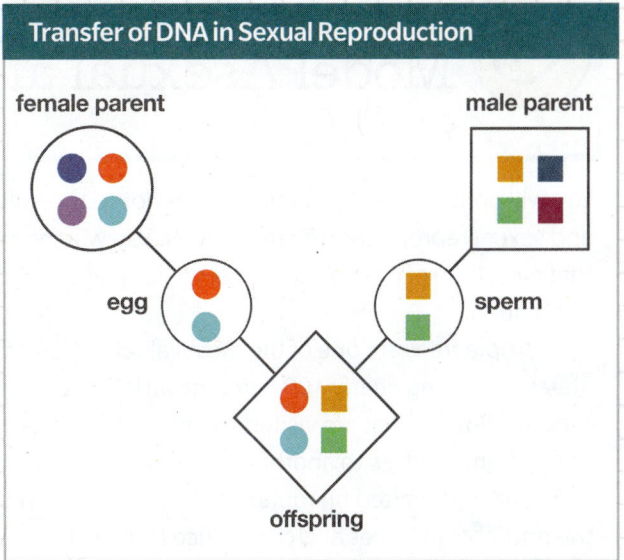

Transfer of DNA in Sexual Reproduction

17. What other genetic combinations might be possible from the parent organisms shown in the diagram? Circle the letter of all possibilities that apply.

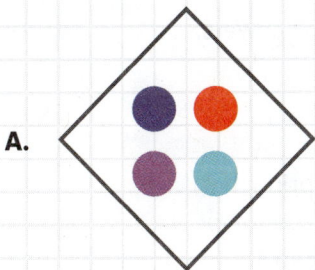

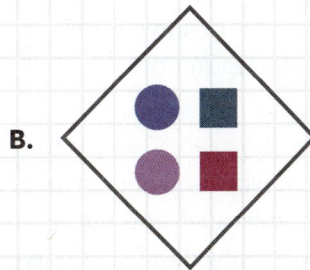

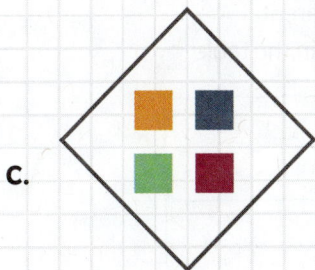

A.

B.

C.

D.

Advantages of Genetic Variation

Sexual reproduction increases genetic variation in a population of organisms. Offspring have different traits from their parents and from each other. This genetic variation improves the chance that at least some individuals will survive. If the environment changes, a population with greater genetic variation is more likely to have individuals with traits that will allow them to survive new conditions.

Hands-On Lab
Model Asexual and Sexual Reproduction

You will predict the genotypes and phenotypes resulting from the asexual and sexual reproduction of apple trees. You will then compare the effects that each type of reproduction has on genetic variation in the apple tree population.

    Apple trees are one of the most valuable fruit crops in the United States, including nearly 100 different varieties, or *cultivars*. Apple trees produce flowers that are visited by animals, such as honeybees, that carry pollen from one tree to another tree. Apple trees can also be grown from stem cuttings grafted on roots. Aphids are common pests of the apple tree. They feed on the nutrients in leaves and can reduce tree growth if present in high numbers.

Procedure and Analysis

STEP 1 Examine the information in the table describing the genetics of several apple tree traits.

Trait	Dominant Allele (Symbol)	Recessive Allele (Symbol)
flower color	pink (F)	white (f)
fruit color	red (C)	green (c)
aphid resistance	not resistant (R)	resistant (r)

STEP 2 What are all the possible genotypes that can result in a tree with pink flowers, green fruit, and aphid resistance?

STEP 3 List all possible genotypes and phenotypes for each trait of the offspring that could result from the asexual reproduction of an apple tree with the genotype *FfCcRr*. Record the genotypes and phenotypes in the table below Step 4.

STEP 4 List all possible genotypes and phenotypes for each trait of the offspring that could result from the sexual reproduction of an apple tree with the parental genotypes *FfCcRr × FfCcRr*. Record the genotypes and phenotypes in the table.

Asexual Reproduction		Sexual Reproduction	
genotypes	phenotypes	genotypes	phenotypes

STEP 5 How do the genotypes and phenotypes of offspring for each type of reproduction compare to each other?

STEP 6 The probability of offspring receiving certain alleles as the result of sexual reproduction can be modeled using a coin toss. Use masking tape and a marker to make a set of three coins to represent the alleles of one parent (*FfCcRr*). For example, one coin should be labeled with *F* on one side and *f* on the other side.

STEP 7 Make another set of coins to represent the other parent (*FfCcRr*).

STEP 8 Toss all six coins to determine the genotype of one offspring. Record the offspring genotype and phenotype in the table.

STEP 9 Repeat the toss two more times. Record the offspring genotype and phenotypes in the table.

Round of Reproduction	Genotype	Phenotype
1		
2		
3		

STEP 10 How do the genotypes and phenotypes of the offspring compare to the parents and to each other?

STEP 11 Is it easier to predict the outcomes of sexual reproduction or asexual reproduction? Explain your answer and describe why it may be useful to predict the genotypes or phenotypes of offspring.

18. Genetic variation can result in differences in many traits, including resistance to diseases. Describe the genetic variation of the banana plants grown for food. How do you think this level of variation relates to the threat of Panama disease in banana crops? Record your evidence.

Language SmArts

Compare Asexual and Sexual Reproduction

19. Compare asexual reproduction and sexual reproduction by completing the Venn diagram with phrases from the word bank.

word bank
- one parent
- two parents
- produces offspring
- genetic variation
- faster
- slower
- many offspring
- few offspring

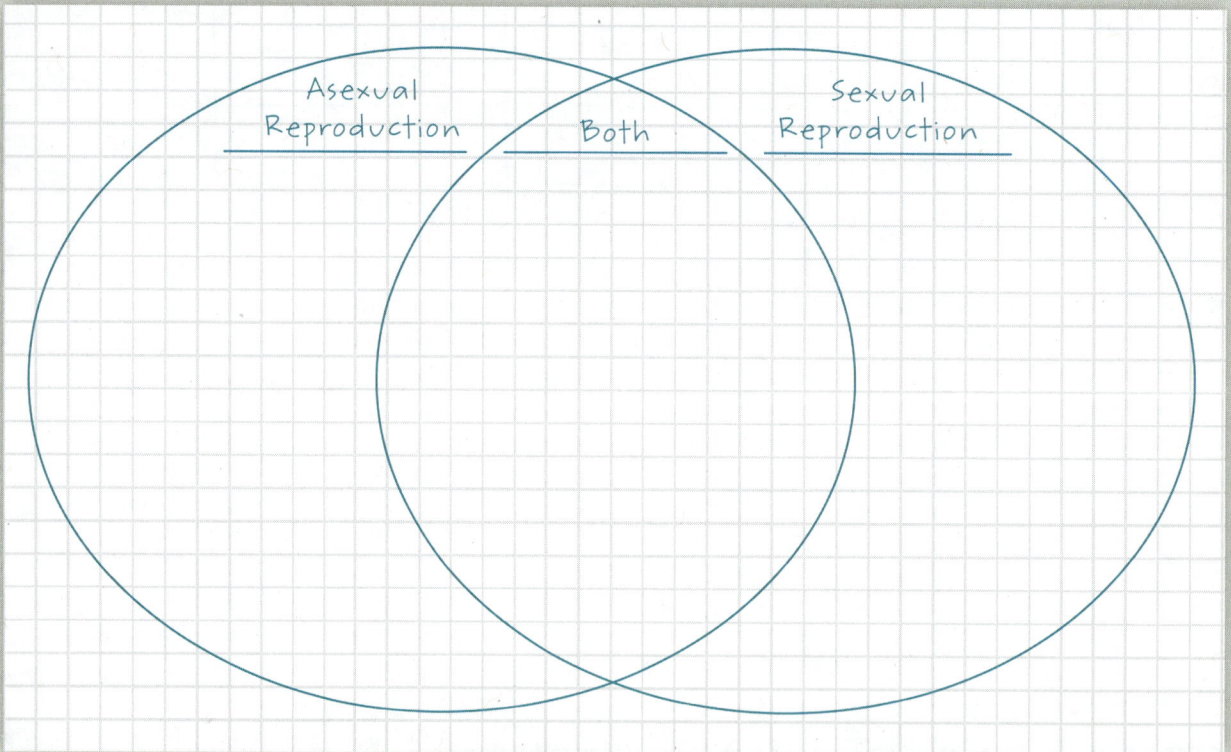

Asexual Reproduction — Both — Sexual Reproduction

20. Using your completed Venn diagram, write a summary detailing the advantages and disadvantages of each type of reproduction.

_____

_____

_____

_____

_____

_____

Continue Your Exploration

Name: _____   Date: _____

Check out the path below or go online to choose one of the other paths shown.

Factors That Influence Reproduction

- **Odd Reproduction**
- **Hands-On Labs** 🖐
- **Propose Your Own Path**

Go online to choose one of these other paths.

Nearly every multicellular organism reproduces sexually, but some can also reproduce asexually. Environmental factors, such as light, temperature, and food supply, can influence the type of reproduction used by these organisms. Organisms that can use both types of reproduction are able to successfully reproduce when conditions are favorable and also when conditions become more challenging.

Honeybee reproduction occurs when a queen bee mates with a male bee, called a drone. The queen is the only female bee that mates. She uses the drone's sperm to fertilize eggs that will develop into female worker bees. An average colony has between 20,000 and 80,000 workers. The queen can also lay unfertilized eggs that will develop into drones. An average colony has between 300 and 800 drones.

1. How is this method of reproduction advantageous to the honeybee colony? Select all that apply.

   A. The queen bee is the only member of the hive that is the result of sexual reproduction.

   B. Sexually produced worker bees have genetic diversity, which could increase their overall fitness.

   C. Male bees can be produced only when needed for mating.

Continue Your Exploration

Fungi are multicellular organisms that can live anywhere there is decaying matter, but many species of fungi are associated with trees. Fungi often reproduce asexually by releasing spores, which are reproductive cells that can develop into a new individual without combining with another reproductive cell. Fungi can also reproduce asexually by budding. Fungi reproduce sexually when cells from two parents fuse.

2. Describe how environmental changes might affect the type of reproduction utilized by fungi. Relate the type of reproduction to genetic variation of offspring in your answer.

Strawberry plants can reproduce sexually by producing fruit or asexually by sending out runners. Runners are extensions of the central stem of the plant that spread out along the ground and grow into new strawberry plants.

3. What is the advantage of sending out many runners from the central stem? What is the disadvantage to the central plant?

4. **Collaborate** Select a scientific paper that investigates environmental factors that affect the reproduction or survival of an organism. Use the sources cited in the paper to explore how the author supported his or her claim with previous scientific studies. Then create a poster that explains the role that science as a body of knowledge plays in current and future scientific discoveries.

Can You Explain It?

Name: _____   **Date:** _____

Why is the Cavendish banana in danger of extinction?

📋 **EVIDENCE NOTEBOOK**

Refer to the notes in your Evidence Notebook to help you construct an explanation for why the Cavendish banana is facing extinction.

1. State your claim. Make sure your claim fully explains why the Cavendish banana is in danger of extinction.

2. Summarize the evidence you have gathered to support your claim and explain your reasoning.

Checkpoints

Answer the following questions to check your understanding of the lesson.

Use the photo to answer Questions 3–4.

3. Marmosets usually give birth to fraternal twins, two offspring that grow from two different fertilized eggs. Marmoset twins are genetically identical / not identical.

4. What advantage does the white-faced marmoset gain by its method of reproduction?

   A. The marmoset population has genetic variation.

   B. The marmoset can reproduce without a mate.

   C. The marmoset can reproduce many offspring at a time.

   D. The marmoset can reproduce by budding.

A white-faced marmoset protects her fraternal twin pups.

Use the photo to answer Questions 5–6.

5. Dandelions can produce seeds by both asexual and sexual reproduction. How does this benefit the dandelion? Select all that apply.

   A. The sexually produced plants provide genetic diversity to the population.

   B. The asexually produced plants ensure that favorable traits are passed to the offspring.

   C. The sexually produced plants do not compete with the asexually produced plants.

   D. The asexually produced plants can rapidly colonize an area.

6. The dandelion seeds seen in the photo are a result of sexual reproduction. What events led to the development of the seeds?

   A. The seeds formed through binary fission.

   B. The seeds formed because of stable conditions.

   C. The fusion of gametes formed the seeds.

   D. Runners from the parent plant grew and formed the seeds.

A young dandelion flower (yellow florets) grows next to a mature flower with a full seed head.

Interactive Review

Complete this section to review the main concepts of the lesson.

Two types of reproduction are asexual reproduction, which involves one parent, and sexual reproduction, which involves two parents.

A. Compare the advantages of each type of reproduction.

Asexual reproduction results in offspring that are genetically identical to the parent. Sexual reproduction results in offspring that have a combination of genes from each parent.

B. Draw a diagram that compares inheritance that results from asexual reproduction to inheritance that results from sexual reproduction.

The Environment and Genetics Affect Plant Survival

The moth orchid, which grows in Southeast Asia and Australia, has flowers that bloom for three months.

Explore First

Modeling Seed Dispersal Use a cotton ball and a hook and loop fastener to model two seed types. Predict which is more likely to be dispersed by wind. Blow on the models to test your prediction. How might the other seed type be dispersed? What environmental factors might plants with these seed types depend upon for dispersal?

Go *online* to view the digital version of the Hands-On Lab for this lesson and to download additional lab resources.

CAN YOU EXPLAIN IT?

How do the characteristics of the sacred lotus flower relate to reproduction?

The sacred lotus grows in soil that is submerged in water. An individual plant can live for a thousand years, and the seeds can remain capable of reproducing for as long as 1,300 years.

Explore Online

Researchers have found that the sacred lotus plant has the ability to regulate the temperature of its flowers. As the air temperature cools, the flower maintains a steady temperature and gives off a fragrant scent.

1. What function do you think a flower that stays warm at night might have for a plant? What function do you think a sweet smelling flower might have for a plant?

EVIDENCE NOTEBOOK As you explore the lesson, gather evidence to help you explain the characteristics of the sacred lotus flower.

Investigating Reproductive Structures of Plants

Like all living organisms, plants produce offspring through reproduction. Different species have different ways of reproducing, but they all have specialized structures for reproduction. These structures come in a wide variety of colors, shapes, and sizes. They can be a source of nutrition for animals, and objects of beauty highly valued by people.

Analyze Plant Structures

2. Examine the plant structures below. Which functions do you think each structure plays in the plant's reproduction? Write the functions for each plant.

| attract animals | disperse seeds |
| protect seeds | |

	Willow trees have flower clusters, called catkins, that can be male or female. The female catkins contain seeds, and they are covered with long, fluffy hairs.	
	Cherry trees have distinctive flowers that range in color from white to pink. The flowers contain sugary nectar and protein-rich pollen.	
	Pomegranate trees grow in warm, dry climates. Their seeds are housed inside colorful, juicy fruits.	
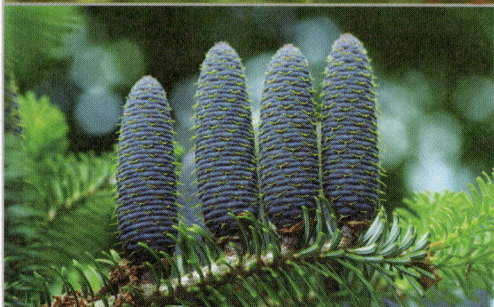	Blue spruce trees have male and female cones, both of which are covered with tough scales. The female cones contain lightweight seeds.	

Sexual Reproduction in Plants

All plants can reproduce sexually. Plants produced by sexual reproduction are genetically different from both parents and from each other. This genetic variation increases the chance that some offspring will have traits that help them survive in a changing environment.

Reproduction of Seedless Plants

Seedless plants do not produce seeds for reproduction. Instead of seeds, the bodies of seedless plants grow from spores. A *spore* of a seedless plant is a tiny structure that is dispersed from the parent plant and can grow into a new plant body. To reproduce, sperm from one plant must swim through water to fertilize the egg of another plant. Because of this requirement for water, many seedless plants live in moist environments. The fertilized egg grows into a stalk-like structure that produces spores. Spores grow into new plants and the life cycle continues.

Reproductive Structures of Seedless Plants

Mosses are seedless plants that grow on rocks, soil, trees, and even between cracks in pavement.

Release of Spores
Under the right conditions, spores are released from this part of the moss plant, called a *capsule*. Spores may land far away from the parent plant and grow into a new plant body.

Fertilization
In this part of the plant, fertilization occurs when a sperm swims to an egg. A fertilized egg then grows into a stalk-like structure, on which spores are produced.

3. **Discuss** How might dry conditions affect the reproductive success of a seedless plant?

Reproduction of Seed Plants

In seed plants, sperm are carried in a microscopic structure called pollen. *Pollen* looks like fine dust and can be transported by wind, water, or animals. Eggs develop inside a structure called an *ovule*. The ovule has a small opening where transported pollen can get inside. When pollen reaches and fertilizes an egg, **pollination** occurs.

A fertilized egg develops into an embryo. The embryo will then grow into a new plant. The ovule becomes the **seed**, the structure that contains the embryo inside a protective coating. Seeds can be carried away from the parent plant by wind, water, or animals. After seed dispersal, the seeds grow into new plants if the conditions are right.

Seed plants can be classified as nonflowering or flowering. Nonflowering plants produce seeds that are not enclosed in a fruit. Most nonflowering seed plants produce seeds enclosed in a structure called a *cone*. Flowering plants produce flowers and fruit. Flowering plants are the largest group within the plant kingdom. They are also the largest group of plants that live on land.

Reproductive Structures of Nonflowering Seed Plants

Conifers are nonflowering plants that produce male and female cones.

Male Cone Pollen sacs are located on the scales of the male cone. Pollen is produced here. Mature male cones release pollen into the air. Pollen often travels by wind.

Female Cone The female cone has a pair of ovules on each scale. Pollination occurs when pollen reaches an egg inside an ovule. After they are pollinated, the fertilized eggs will develop into seeds. The seeds are dispersed when the cone breaks apart.

4. Based on the structure of the seeds below, decide if the method of dispersal is wind, water, or animals. Then describe your evidence. Write the answer in the space provided.

Seed Structure	Dispersal Method
milkweed seedlings	
dry burdock	
palm seed	

EVIDENCE NOTEBOOK

5. The sacred lotus plant has a large seedpod that eventually dries out and causes the flower to bend over. How do you think the sacred lotus flower's seeds are dispersed? Record your evidence.

Asexual Reproduction in Plants

Many plants are also able to reproduce asexually. For example, in some plants, a part of the parent plant, such as a root or a stem, can grow into a new plant. Tubers, such as potatoes, can sprout roots that take hold in the soil and produce a new plant. Other plants, such as spider plants, produce plantlets. *Plantlets* are tiny plants that grow along the edges of a plant's leaves or on special stalks. They eventually break off and develop into new plants. Asexual reproduction in plants results in offspring that are genetically identical to the parent.

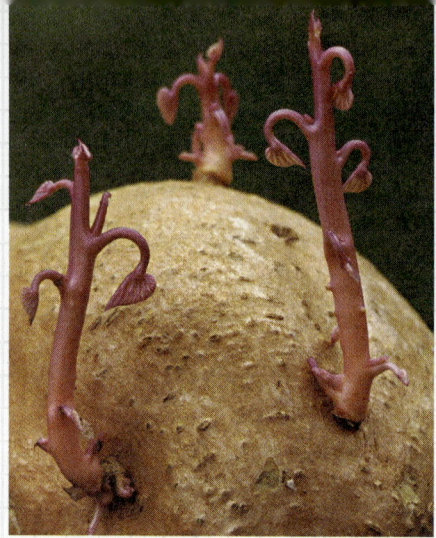

Each "eye" on this potato is an asexual structure that can grow into a new plant.

6. Write asexual reproduction or sexual reproduction to indicate the type of reproduction that would be most advantageous in each environmental condition shown in the table below. Support your answers with reasoning.

Environmental Condition	Type of Reproduction	Reasoning
Sunlight and nutrient levels are stable.	asexual	Since there are plenty of resources, the plant can reproduce quickly and colonize the area.
Water becomes scarce.		
A pest species is introduced.		
A new space for growth becomes available with similar conditions.		

Construct an Argument

7. The majority of plants on Earth are seed plants. Use reasoning and evidence from the text to construct an argument about why producing seeds might be advantageous to the reproductive success of a plant species.

_____

_____

_____

_____

_____

_____

_____

Analyzing Reproductive Success of Flowering Plants

Plants cannot move around to find mates or to deposit their seeds in the perfect spot for growth. Wind and water can assist plant reproduction. However, many plants rely on insects, birds, or mammals to carry their pollen and seeds.

Explore Online

The hawk moth visits flowers at night.

8. Night-blooming plants are usually pollinated by animals that are active at night, such as some species of beetles, moths, and bats. What traits might a night-blooming flower have to attract nighttime feeders?

Pollination in Flowering Plants

The sperm of seed plants is carried in pollen. When pollen reaches an egg of the same kind of plant, it is called *pollination*. Some types of plants self-pollinate. This means that pollen is transferred to the egg of the same plant. Other types of plants cross-pollinate. In this case, the pollen from one plant is transferred to the egg of another plant. Animal pollinators play an important role in cross-pollination of plants.

Flowers contain nectar, a sugar-rich liquid that provides energy and nutrients to animals. Animals attracted to the flowers by their color or scent are rewarded with a tasty meal of nectar. The plant benefits because the animal carries away pollen that sticks to its body. The pollen is deposited on the next flower the animal visits.

9. **Discuss** Why might it be beneficial for a plant to be able to self-pollinate and to also have adaptations that attract animal pollinators?

The structures of the reproductive organs found in a flower relate to their function in pollination.

Pistil The pistil is the female reproductive structure of a flower. A pistil consists of the stigma, the style, and the ovary. The stigma is often sticky or covered in hairs. This makes it easier to collect pollen. The ovary contains the ovules, which produce eggs. After fertilization, the ovules develop into seeds. The ovary develops into a fruit.

Stamen The stamen is a flower's male reproductive structure. A stamen consists of an anther, the pollen-producing part of the flower. The anther sits on top of a thin stalk. The anther produces spores that develop into pollen.

Pollinator As pollinators feed on pollen and nectar, pollen from a flower's anther rubs off on their bodies. When they fly to a second flower, pollen from the first flower rubs off on the second flower's stigma. Meanwhile, pollen from the second flower's anther rubs off on the pollinators' bodies, ready to be delivered to another flower.

heliconia flower

Heliconia is found in the rain forests of Central America and southern Mexico.

10. Based on the structure of the heliconia flower, which animal do you think is its pollinator?

A.

long-nosed bat

B.

Hercules beetle

C.

green hermit hummingbird

Hands-On Lab
Investigate Flower Structures

A flower contains the reproductive structures of a flowering plant. In addition, flowers have specialized leaves called *sepals* and *petals*. Sepals cover and protect the flower while it is budding. Petals are often colorful and can help attract animal pollinators. The pedicel is part of the stem that supports the flower. At the end of the pedicel is the receptacle, which forms the base of the flower.

You will dissect a flower and record drawings of the structures you discover.

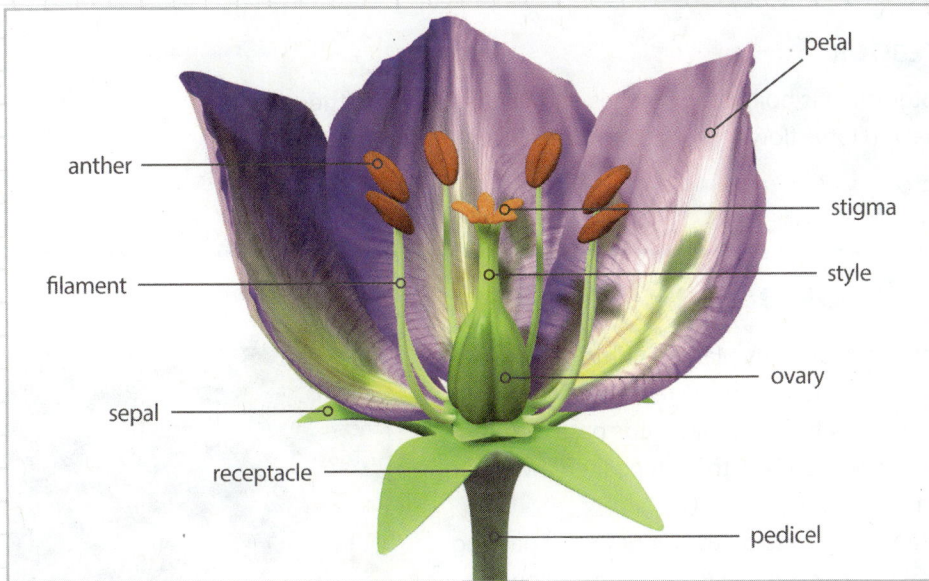

MATERIALS
- flower
- hand lens
- lab gloves (as needed for allergies)
- scalpel
- surgical mask (as needed for allergies)

Procedure

STEP 1 Use the scalpel to carefully dissect the flower. Sort the structures.

STEP 2 **Draw** Use the hand lens to examine each structure. Draw and label one example of each structure. Depending on the type of flower you dissect, the structures of your flower might look different than the structures in the drawing.

Analysis and Conclusions

STEP 3 Describe patterns you observed in the arrangement of the flower parts.

STEP 4 **Collaborate** With a partner, model the body features you would expect of an animal that pollinates the type of flower you dissected. Present your model and explain how structure and function are important for plants and pollinators.

> **EVIDENCE NOTEBOOK**
>
> **11.** The sacred lotus plant is pollinated by bees and beetles. How do the traits of the sacred lotus flower help attract these pollinators? Record your evidence.

Seed Dispersal of Flowering Plants

Wind and water disperse the seeds of many plants. Animals also play a role in seed dispersal. Animals are attracted to the fruits of some flowering plants. When an animal eats a fruit, the seeds pass through the animal's digestive system. The seeds are then deposited away from the parent plant as the animal travels.

Other types of seeds can hitch a ride on the fur or feet of passing animals. The seeds have hooks, barbs, or sticky mucus that allows them to attach to animals.

Some animals bury the seeds of plants, planning to return and eat them later. If an animal does not retrieve the buried seeds, the seeds may germinate where they are buried. Squirrels that bury oak tree acorns are an example of this type of animal-assisted seed dispersal.

This bird will excrete the prickly pear seeds through its digestive system.

12. What are the benefits to the survival of offspring when seeds are dispersed far from the parent plant?

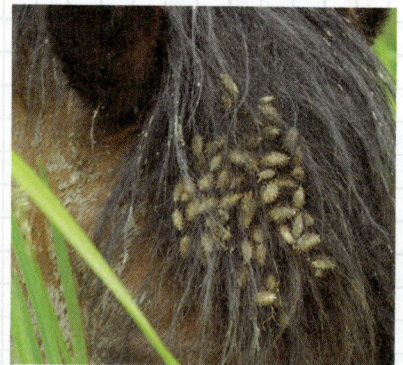

Burrs stick to the fur and feet of mammals, such as this horse.

13. What are the drawbacks to the survival of offspring when seeds are dispersed far from the parent plant?

Do the Math
Analyze Honeybee Colony Loss

Bees are important pollinators for the global food supply. In the United States $15 billion of apples, berries, almonds, and cucumbers are pollinated by bees each year. However, since at least 2006, bees have been suffering from a phenomenon known as *colony collapse disorder* (CCD). Beekeepers have been experiencing higher than expected colony losses since CCD was first reported. Scientists are investigating various causes of CCD including bacteria, parasites, pesticide use, and habitat destruction. Other causes of colony loss include harsh temperatures, poor nutrition, and queen death.

U.S.-Managed Honeybee Colony Loss Estimates

The graph shows the honeybee colony losses reported over a ten-year period. Total annual loss estimates (summer and winter) were not reported between 2006 and 2009.

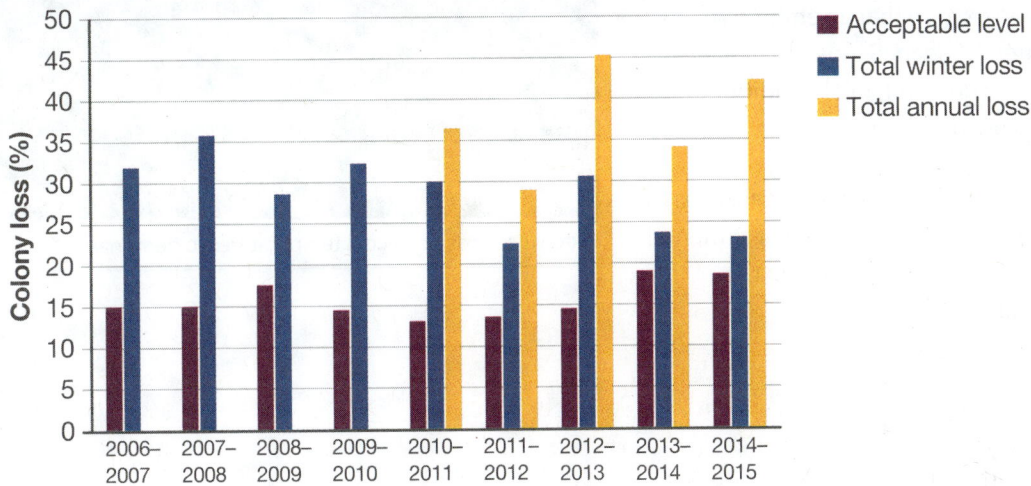

Source: Bee Informed Partnership, 2015,
The Bee Informed Partnership National Management Survey 2014–2015

14. What percentage of acceptable loss was estimated for 2006–2007 and 2007–2008 when CCD was first reported? How much did the total winter loss estimates for these years exceed this expectation? During which year was the difference between acceptable loss and total winter loss the greatest?

15. What was the average total annual loss over the years for which these data were reported? What was the average total winter loss over this same period of time? Use evidence and reasoning to write an argument that supports or refutes the claim that summertime losses account for the majority of annual losses from 2010–2015.

Describing Factors That Affect Plant Growth

Plants need air, sunlight, water, space, and nutrients for growth. Each plant species has its own specific requirements. For example, the seeds of different plants may have different requirements to *germinate*, or develop from a seed into a small plant. Processes controlled by genes inside the seed are triggered by temperature, moisture, and light. These environmental cues indicate that conditions are good for plant growth. Some seeds need extreme temperatures, such as freezing or fire, for germination. Extreme temperatures can help break down a hard seed coat so water and oxygen that an embryo needs to grow can enter the seed. Seeds can delay germination, or go *dormant*, until conditions are right for plant growth.

Dutch iris seeds need cold temperatures to germinate.

16. Explain how seed germination is caused by a combination of genetic and environmental factors. Cite evidence from the text to support your answer.

Genetic Factors Affect Plant Growth

Genes are passed from parent to offspring during reproduction. A plant's genes affect its traits. Therefore, different genes are responsible for the differences in the thousands of plant types, or species, that exist on Earth. For example, ferns grow well in the moist, low-light conditions of the forest floor, and cacti grow well in dry, full-light conditions. The ability of different types of plants to grow in such different conditions is due to genetic differences between plant species.

Individual plants of the same species can also have genetic differences. These differences exist because there can be different forms of the same gene. For example, different varieties of the same plant species may grow at different rates, even if they are planted in the same garden. Different forms of certain plant genes may affect drought tolerance or leaf size, both of which can affect the growth of plants.

Engineer It
Explore Plant Hybrids

Plant breeders cross-pollinate different types of plants in order to produce a desired trait or traits in the offspring. For instance, they might try to introduce resistance to disease, drought, or pests. Breeders also select for flower color, larger fruit, or a seedless variety. (Think seedless grapes and watermelon.) The resulting domesticated plants have genetic differences from the parent plants.

Heirloom tomatoes are valued for their taste, color, and unusual appearance.

Sun Gold tomatoes are very sweet and tolerant of cooler temperatures.

Grape tomatoes are sweet, small, and heat-tolerant.

Juliet tomatoes are sweet, small, and resistant to disease.

---

17. How might a cross between the Sun Gold tomato and the Juliet tomato result in a desirable hybrid?

18. A tomato breeder has noticed that a hybrid is not attracting pollinators to its flowers. What genetic change may have occurred in this hybrid? What does that mean for the long-term survival of the hybrid?

19. Scientists have discovered a gene that affects how many tomatoes an individual plant produces. The gene controls a protein named *florigen*, which affects the number of fruit a plant develops. When a plant has a dominant (*F*) and recessive (*f*) allele for the gene, it produces a high tomato yield. Plants that have two dominant or two recessive alleles for the trait produce a lower tomato yield. Fill out the Punnett square. Use evidence from this and other Punnett squares to support or refute a farmer's claim that this cross will result in the most offspring with high tomato yields when compared to other potential crosses.

	F	*f*
F		
f		

Lesson 4 The Environment and Genetics Affect Plant Survival **447**

Environmental Factors Affect Plant Survival

The mosses and redwoods that inhabit California forests grow quite differently due to differences in their genes. Mosses are very short plants, while redwoods are very tall trees. Environmental conditions also play a role in plant growth. If a redwood seed was planted in soil that was contaminated by pollution, the tree may never reach its full potential height. Mosses thrive in cool, wet environments with plenty of shade. If the temperatures increase or the air becomes dry, moss may fail to grow.

Climate

The term climate refers to the predictable weather patterns of a region over a long period of time. If the climate of the region changes, it could affect a plant's ability to grow and survive. For example, California's dry climate makes the state prone to droughts, which are periods with lower-than-average rainfall. As average global temperatures increase, California may have more frequent droughts. Since plants need water to grow, extreme drought conditions could limit the growth of native California plants.

Local Conditions

Bigleaf hydrangeas produce different flower colors depending on the pH of the soil. The pH scale ranges from 0 to 14. Lower values are acidic, while higher values are alkaline, and 7.0 is neutral. If bigleaf hydrangeas are planted in neutral or alkaline soil, their flowers will be pink. If planted in very acidic soil, they will produce blue flowers. If the soil is only weakly acidic (pH = 5.5–6.5), the flowers will be purple or have a mix of blue and pink petals.

The color differences among these flowers are caused by pH differences in the soil.

20. A gardener wants to grow hydrangeas in his flowerbeds shown in the image. He has three different types of soil. Soil A has a pH of 5.0, Soil B has a pH of 6.0, and Soil C has a pH of 8.0. The gardener wants pink flowers in Bed #3, purple flowers in Bed #2, and blue flowers in Bed #1. Which soil should the gardener put in each flowerbed? Use evidence of environmental and genetic influence on hydrangeas to support your answer.

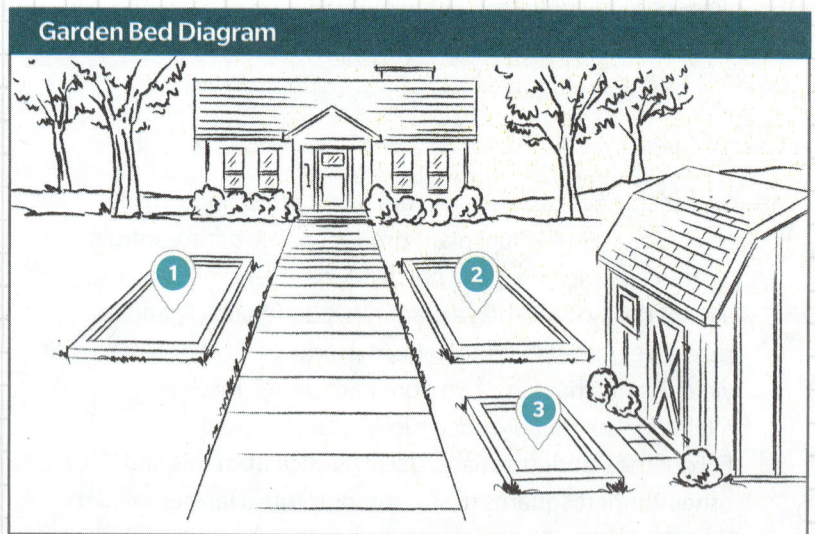

Garden Bed Diagram

Environmental Stimuli

Like all organisms, plants respond to environmental stimuli. Seasonal changes can stimulate a plant to grow, reproduce, or even become dormant until the conditions are more favorable. For example, many trees have green leaves during warmer seasons. In colder months, these leaves change color and fall off. Some seeds can stay dormant for months, or even years, until the conditions are right for growth.

Plants bend toward a light source because they need light to perform photosynthesis.

21. The diagram shows how a tree responds to changing seasons. Identify the environmental cues that cause the tree to change.

word bank
- change from cold to warm
- change from hot to cool
- ~~transition to longest days~~
- transition to shortest days

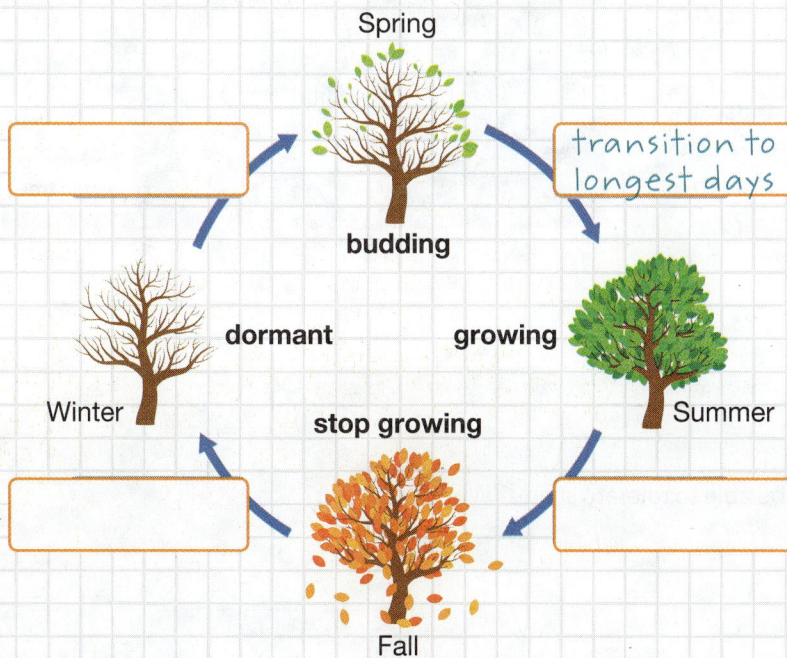

Spring

transition to longest days

budding

dormant   growing

Winter

stop growing   Summer

Fall

22. Read the environmental conditions. Decide whether the condition will result in *increased* or *decreased* growth of the parent plant.

A. Nutrient-rich organic matter was added to the soil. _____

B. The habitat experienced rainfall levels well below normal for the year. _____

C. Tall trees grew around the plant. _____

D. A plant that requires an alkaline soil is planted in soil that has a pH of 5.0. _____

Genetic and Environmental Influence on Plants

Many plants are sensitive to soil salinity, or the sodium content in soil. Saline soil occurs naturally in coastal areas that receive spray from the ocean. It is also caused by human activities, like irrigation and the de-icing of roadways.

Highly saline soil can limit a plant's ability to absorb water and restrict the plant's growth. In slightly saline soil, lettuce and other highly salt-sensitive food crops experience a 25 to 50% decrease in crop yield. Some crops, like sugar beets, carry salt-tolerant genes that allow them to grow even in highly saline soil.

Soil salinity is a problem in areas of California's Central Valley due to poor drainage, irrigation, and other factors. The region grows many profitable, salt-sensitive crops, like almonds and plums. In some areas, the soil salinity is now too high to grow food. Much of this land has been sold for other uses, like the construction of solar energy farms.

Analyze Aspen Growth

aspen trees

Aspen trees are a type of tree native to cold regions. Aspens are often a pioneer species, populating areas that have recently lost vegetation to erosion, fire, or disease. They provide cover for conifer seedlings, but they often die out as the conifers take over the area. Aspens can reproduce sexually but more often reproduce asexually by sending up multiple stems from a single root system.

23. Mountain aspens are often used to landscape homes in lower-elevation suburban or urban areas. What factors might affect the growth of the mountain aspen in the new habitat?

24. Would you expect an aspen tree to be able to tolerate shade? Why or why not?

25. Small groves of aspen trees that appear to be separate trees may be multiple stems attached to one extensive underground root system. Would you expect individuals in a grove to be able to adapt to a change in the environment? Explain.

Continue Your Exploration

Name: _____   Date: _____

Check out the path below or go online to choose one of the other paths shown.

| Capsaicin Levels in Peppers | • **Seed Vaults**
• **Hands-On Labs** ✋
• **Propose Your Own Path** | *Go online to choose one of these other paths.* |

The sensation of "heat" experienced when a person eats a hot pepper is not taste. Instead the pain receptors in the mouth are triggered when a person eats a hot pepper. The Scoville scale is a measurement scale that was created to measure the heat of a pepper, which is caused by a chemical compound called *capsaicin*.

The amount of capsaicin in a chili pepper is determined partially by its genetics and partially by the environmental conditions in which it grows. These conditions include factors, such as temperature, humidity, soil conditions, light, and the availability of water. When chili peppers are grown in less-than-ideal conditions, peppers that genetically should have low heat will become hotter, while peppers that genetically should have high heat will become less hot.

Carolina Reaper

ghost pepper

Red Savina habanero

The Carolina Reaper is currently the hottest chili pepper in the world, with an average measurement of 1,569,300 SHU (Scoville heat units). The Carolina Reaper is thought to be a hybrid of the ghost pepper and the Red Savina.

Continue Your Exploration

1. How could a farmer increase his or her chances of growing a pepper with a certain heat measurement on the Scoville scale?

2. A chili pepper plant that produces fruit with a low heat level is grown in an area that experiences a drought. What might the farmer expect will happen to the plant? Why?

3. A farmer wants to create a chili pepper that has a higher SHU measurement than the Carolina Reaper. What could he or she do to achieve this goal?

4. **Collaborate** Why do you think pepper fruits contain capsaicin? How might capsaicin affect the reproduction or growth of a pepper plant? Research hypotheses about the function of capsaicin. Use multiple, credible sources to collect your data. Write a short paper and present your findings in a multimedia presentation.

Can You Explain It?

Name: _____   Date: _____

How do the characteristics of the sacred lotus flower relate to reproduction?

EVIDENCE NOTEBOOK

Refer to the notes in your Evidence Notebook to help you construct an explanation for how the characteristics of the sacred lotus flower contribute to the reproductive success of the plant.

1. State your claim. Make sure your claim fully explains the characteristics of the sacred lotus flower.

2. Summarize the evidence you have gathered to support your claim and explain your reasoning.

Answer the following questions to check your understanding of the lesson.

Use the photo to answer Questions 3–4.

3. How might this flower contribute to the plant's reproductive success?

   A. The shape of the flower's petals attracts pollinators.

   B. The flower attracts bees that think they are meeting a mate.

   C. The flower scares away birds looking for a meal.

4. Number the statements in order to describe how an animal pollinator aids in the pollination of a flowering plant.

   _____ The ovules develop into seeds.

   _____ The pollinator flies to another flower where the pollen rubs off on the flower's stigma.

   _____ The sperm within the pollen fertilizes the eggs.

   _____ The animal pollinator feeds on nectar, and the flower's pollen attaches to its body.

Use the photo to answer Question 5.

5. Bonsai trees are kept small using the art of trimming and shaping. They can be grown from seeds or cuttings. Which statements are true about bonsai trees? Select all that apply.

   A. Bonsai trees do not need light, water, and nutrients to survive and reproduce.

   B. Bonsai trees need light, water, and nutrients just like the full-sized tree species.

   C. Bonsai trees can reproduce sexually and asexually.

   D. Bonsai trees can only reproduce sexually.

6. Can breeders always know the exact traits that a hybrid will have? Select all that apply.

   A. Yes. People create hybrid plants because they want to combine the desirable traits of one plant with the desirable traits of another plant.

   B. No. People cannot predict every trait that a hybrid will have.

   C. No. A breeder may succeed in breeding a hybrid that has the specific trait they find desirable, but the hybrid may also have another trait that is less desirable.

   D. Yes. The outcome of reproduction can be predicted with 100% certainty.

7. Eucalyptus plants grow in wildfire-prone areas. Their seeds have a thick coating that melts during a fire, releasing the seed into the ground. This coating allows the seed to stay dormant / grow tall until a wildfire occurs. This increases / decreases the chances that the seed will grow after the fire.

Interactive Review

Complete this section to review the main concepts of the lesson.

All plants can reproduce sexually, producing genetically diverse offspring. Many can also reproduce asexually, producing genetically identical offspring.

A. How are non-flowering seed plants and flowering plants similar and different?

All plants have specialized reproductive structures. Plants can be pollinated by wind or water, and they can often self-pollinate. They may also rely on animal pollinators.

B. Describe how animals can contribute to the reproductive success of a plant.

Both environmental and genetic factors have an effect on plant growth.

C. Draw a cause-and-effect diagram with examples of how genetic and environmental factors can affect plant growth.

The Environment and Genetics Affect Animal Survival

An elephant calf develops inside its mother for 18–22 months, longer than any other mammal.

✋ Explore First

Modeling Reproduction Develop a model that shows what might happen in a population if only the males with a certain trait reproduce. Can your model help you explain extravagant traits in males, such as the showy tail feathers of a peacock or the large antlers of a moose?

CAN YOU EXPLAIN IT?

Why are these male zebras fighting?

These zebras live on the grassy plains in Etosha National Park in Namibia. Plains zebras live in family groups that include one male and several females with their offspring.

1. Think of three reasons why these zebras might be fighting with each other.

EVIDENCE NOTEBOOK As you explore the lesson, gather evidence to help you explain why male zebras fight with each other.

Describing Animal Reproduction

Scientists estimate that as many as eight or nine million species of animals may be living on Earth. Although some of these animals can reproduce asexually, sexual reproduction is the dominant form of reproduction in animals. Multiple factors influence the reproductive success of an animal. For example, genetic factors may result in a male bird that has a call that females prefer over the calls of other males. However, the survival of this male's offspring will depend on the available food supply, protection from predators, and weather conditions. Dragonflies are also influenced by multiple factors. Dragonflies reproduce sexually. Fertilized dragonfly eggs hatch into nymphs. The nymphs are aquatic. Therefore, dragonflies require an environment with water in order to reproduce successfully.

These mating dragonflies reproduce sexually.

2. Write asexual reproduction, sexual reproduction, or both in the table to describe the reproductive process of each animal.

Animal	Reproductive Process	Type of Reproduction
Eastern gray squirrel (mammal)	After a male and female squirrel mate, fertilization occurs inside the female's body. She gives birth to two or more offspring that she feeds with milk from her body.	sexual reproduction
Roseate spoonbill (bird)	After a male and female spoonbill mate, fertilization occurs inside the female's body. The female lays eggs that will hatch into chicks.	
New Zealand mud snail (mollusk)	Female mud snails are born with genetically identical embryos inside them. They can also mate with a male to produce young snails from fertilized eggs.	
Tree frog (amphibian)	In all of the many species of tree frogs, the female lays eggs, and then the male fertilizes them.	
Walking stick (insect)	Female stick insects can produce offspring from unfertilized eggs. They can also mate with a male to produce fertilized eggs.	
Pacific salmon (fish)	Salmon eggs are laid by a female and then fertilized by a male.	

Sexual Reproduction in Animals

Sexual reproduction is a type of reproduction that involves two parents. Offspring get one copy of their chromosomes from each parent. As a result, organisms produced by this type of reproduction are genetically different from both parents. This genetic variation increases the chance that some offspring will have traits that may help them survive in a changing environment. The ability of an organism to pass on its genes to healthy offspring is called *reproductive success*.

In sexual reproduction, fertilization can be internal or external. In some species, the male and female mate, and fertilization occurs inside the female's body. In other species, the female lays eggs, and the male fertilizes them outside the female's body. Some animals lay fertilized eggs, and others give birth to live offspring.

This male damselfish is protecting the eggs he fertilized outside the female's body.

This mother robin laid eggs that will develop into young birds that she and her mate will care for.

This mother kangaroo will carry her baby (joey) in her pouch until it is fully developed.

This mother seal gave birth to her pup. She will feed it with milk from her body until it can find its own food.

3. What behavior do all of these animal parents have in common? How do you think this behavior contributes to each animal's reproductive success?

Asexual Reproduction in Animals

Asexual reproduction is a type of reproduction that involves only one parent. The parent passes a copy of its genes to its offspring. Unless there is a mutation, an organism produced by asexual reproduction is genetically identical to its parent and to other offspring produced asexually by the parent.

Environmental conditions can influence the type of reproduction used by an animal that can reproduce asexually or sexually. These animals might reproduce asexually when rapid reproduction is beneficial, such as the opportunity to colonize a large area. They might also reproduce asexually if conditions are unfavorable for sexual reproduction. For example, a shortage of mates or an unsuitable temperature for survival might favor asexual reproduction.

WORD BANK
- lack of mates
- injury
- temperature change

4. Which environmental stimulus might result in asexual reproduction in these animals? Use the terms in the word bank to complete the table.

	Planaria reproduce asexually by regeneration. If the animal is split or cut into pieces, the cut segments can grow into new animals.	
	Male and female sponges can reproduce asexually by producing structures that are able to survive harsh environmental conditions.	
	Female Komodo dragons can reproduce asexually through a process that does not require fertilization of their eggs by a male.	

EVIDENCE NOTEBOOK

5. The zebra is a mammal like the eastern gray squirrel and the seal. How do you think a zebra reproduces and raises young? Record your evidence.

Evaluate Reproductive Strategies

Aggregating anemones are animals that live in shallow ocean reefs. They are usually found in dense colonies that extend across a large, rocky area. *Aggregating* refers to forming a group or cluster. Each colony is a group of genetically identical animals that are hostile to members of other colonies that live on their borders.

Aggregating anemones can reproduce asexually by splitting into two pieces. They can also reproduce sexually by releasing sperm and eggs into the water. A fertilized egg develops into a larvae that will eventually settle to the ocean floor and start a new colony of aggregating anemones.

aggregating anemone

6. How do both types of reproduction influence where aggregating anemone colonies establish and grow? Use reasoning and cite evidence from the text to support your claims.

_____

_____

_____

_____

_____

Relating Animal Behaviors to Reproductive Success

Reproductive success is the ability to produce offspring that are healthy and that survive. Different species of animals use different strategies to increase their chance of reproductive success. These strategies include adult behaviors, such as courtship and parenting.

Strategies for reproductive success also include offspring behaviors. The offspring of some animal species imprint—or trust and follow—one or both parents. Young geese demonstrate this behavior. The offspring of other animals instinctively stop moving to avoid attracting the attention of predators.

These baby cardinals make loud calls and open their mouths wide when a parent is near.

7. How does the behavior of the bird's offspring contribute to reproductive success?

Courtship Behaviors

Courtship behaviors are attempts by animals to attract mates. Securing a healthy mate is one way to increase the odds of reproductive success. Courtship behaviors are exhibited mainly by males to convince females that they are valuable mates. In some species, females also engage in courtship behaviors.

Frogs, deer, bats, whales, and seals vocalize to attract a mate. Some animals, such as many species of birds, vocalize and perform dances. Males sometimes dance alone, although in some species the female joins in.

This male manakin moonwalks across a branch to impress a mate.

The males of many bird species display brightly colored feathers or other body parts in an attempt to attract females. Most females, by contrast, have feathers of neutral colors. They are the ones being courted by the colorful males.

Male animals of some species display their strength or fight with other males to court females or to establish dominance in a group. Male deer fight each other using their antlers. Male elephant seals slam their bodies into each other, while male damselflies ram each other's bodies.

The males of other animal species give presents to females or build structures for them. They do so to persuade the females to mate. Bowerbirds, for example, build intricate nests and show them to females, hoping to win their approval. Male kingfisher birds present females with fish.

8. What qualities do these males have that encourage females to accept them as mates? Use the Word Bank phrases to record your answers.

WORD BANK
- provides a meal
- protects offspring and females
- has good genetic fitness

Male elks' antlers can weigh up to 18 kilograms (40 pounds) and stand as tall as 1.2 meters (4 feet) above their heads. Elk use their antlers to fight with other males and chase off predators.

Male peacocks have long, beautiful tail feathers. The feathers are heavy, and the peacocks must be strong to carry them.

These are male and female spiders. The male, which is the smaller of the two, has a gift for the female––an insect wrapped in silk.

9. Discuss Birds sing for many reasons, but male birds produce particular songs to attract females. What other benefit might these loud vocalizations provide to the male? Talk about your ideas with a partner.

EVIDENCE NOTEBOOK

10. How could the fighting behavior of male zebras provide information to female zebras about reproductive success? Record your evidence.

Parenting Behaviors

Parenting behaviors are attempts by animals to ensure their offspring's survival. These behaviors are another way that animals increase their odds of reproductive success.

Many animal species build nests for their eggs and young. Males or females, or both, gather the materials and construct the nests. One or both parents might guard eggs and offspring in the nest.

Animals feed their young in a variety of ways. Female mammals nurse their young with milk from their bodies. Other species gather or hunt food for their offspring. For example, some birds eat food and then regurgitate it for their young. The offspring are better able to eat the food once it has been partially broken down by the parent bird's digestive system.

Animals care for their young for varying lengths of time. Many reptiles abandon their eggs before they hatch, so the young are on their own. Other species stay with their offspring for a few months (birds) or for years (elephants). Some animals also teach offspring how to fend for themselves. For example, lions teach their young to hunt.

Some animals sacrifice their health or their lives for their offspring. A male emperor penguin holds a single egg on the top of his feet, covered with a layer of skin to keep it warm. He does this for 60–68 days through extremely cold and windy conditions with no access to food. Another example of parent sacrifice is the female of many octopus species that guard and care for their eggs for months—even years—before they hatch. After the eggs hatch, the female dies. After the eggs of the killdeer bird hatch, both parents keep predators away from their offspring by pretending to be injured. A killdeer will drag its "broken wing" along the ground, luring the predators away from the young birds. Adult killdeers sometimes are caught and killed by predators while using this strategy.

> **WORD BANK**
> • building a nest
> • defending offspring
> • feeding offspring
> • teaching offspring

11. What parental behavior is shown by each of these animals?

red squirrel

Bengal tiger and cubs

penguins and caracara

brown bear and cubs

Do the Math

Analyze Female Mate Choice

Guppies are freshwater tropical fish native to South America. Males usually have brightly colored fins and tails. Researchers study the traits that female guppies prefer when choosing mates. The table show the results of experiments that tested female preference for three different tail sizes.

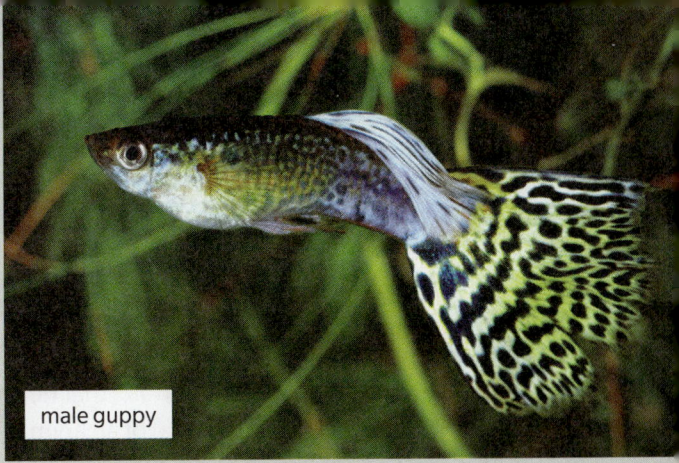

male guppy

12. Use the data from the table to describe the three experiments in your own words. How does female choice function in this system?

Experiment 1

Male Tail Size	Female Choice (%)
Large-tailed male	78
Small-tailed male	22

Experiment 2

Male Tail Size	Female Choice (%)
Large-tailed male	68
Medium-tailed male	32

Experiment 3

Male Tail Size	Female Choice (%)
Medium-tailed male	65
Small-tailed male	35

Source: Bischoff et al., Behavioral Ecology and Sociobiology 17:3

13. Why might the percentage of female preference for medium-sized tails be greater in Experiment 3 than it was in Experiment 2?

14. In a population of guppies, there is an equal number of short-tailed, medium-tailed, and large-tailed males. Based on the data, which group of males would have the highest probability of reproductive success? Why?

Explaining Factors That Influence Animal Growth

Animals face many challenges to survive. Environments can be unpredictable, and many factors that affect health act on animals at the same time. For example, food supply, weather, and disease influence the growth of animals. Animals inherit traits that help them face these challenges. But, the growth and survival of an animal depends on complex interactions between genetic and environmental factors.

15. Do you think the bowl provides a healthy environment for the goldfish? Why or why not?

Common goldfish will eat as much food as they are given and produce large amounts of waste.

16. What factors might limit the growth of a goldfish living in a large pond?

Genetic Factors Affect Animal Survival

Sexual reproduction in animals results in genetic variation of traits in offspring. Differences in traits can give some individuals an advantage over other individuals. Some offspring might have better eyesight or hearing, stronger jaws or teeth, or thicker fur than other offspring. Some might not have inherited diseases that others have.

These genetic differences do not only affect individual offspring. They also affect entire populations. Due to differences in genetic traits, some individuals in an animal population might be able to survive changing environmental conditions better than other individuals. As a result, the population can continue to exist in the community.

Gray wolves have long legs and strong jaws that help them catch and kill prey.

Explain Trait Selection in Dog Breeds

At least 12,000 years ago, humans began to domesticate members of a wolf-like species. Scientists think that this animal is a common ancestor shared by the gray wolf and the dogs of today's world.

Each of the more than 300 different dog breeds was developed over a long period of time. Humans selected the dogs with the traits they wanted and then bred them. For example, the poodle is used during hunting to retrieve birds from the water for the hunter. Its keen intelligence, webbed feet, and curly coat that is almost waterproof make it well-suited to hunting in rivers and marshes. These traits are very different from the traits of the wolf-like ancestor of long ago.

In the past, dogs have been bred for many jobs, including hunting, guarding, herding, and being companions. Today, dogs are also bred and trained to help people who have visual impairments, mobility issues, and mental illnesses. Certain dogs help military and police personnel sniff out explosives and rescue people in distress.

The greyhound was bred as a hunting dog. It chases and captures fast prey, such as rabbits.

The dachshund was also bred as a hunting dog. It captures rats and other small animals that burrow in the ground.

17. Compare and contrast the traits that would be desirable in a dog that helps police locate explosives and a dog that provides companionship for the elderly.

18. Dog breeders choose mates in an effort to produce offspring with desired traits. How does this compare with the way that advantageous traits in wolves get passed on to offspring?

Environmental Factors Affect Animal Growth

Genetics is not the only factor that affects animal growth. The conditions of an animal's environment also affect growth and development. Beneficial environmental conditions include abundant food, water, air, and space. They also include a habitat free from pollution, as well as sufficient shelter from predators.

Harmful environmental conditions include weather, such as drought, that deprives animals of water or that negatively impacts the growth of the plants that the animals eat. Other harmful environmental conditions are overcrowding, pollution, and habitat destruction.

Multiple factors determine the growth of these grass-fed Angus cattle.

Adaptations to the Environment

All animals need the same basic resources to survive and reproduce: food and water, space, and a suitable temperature range. Climate and local conditions affect whether or not animals can find the basic resources they need to survive. Animals have adaptations that help them survive in a particular climate with specific local conditions.

Pronghorn antelope have adaptations that allow them to survive in their environment. Their hair is hollow which helps them control their body temperature in both hot and cold conditions. Pronghorns can survive for days without water in environments where water is scarce. Pronghorns are very fast, an adaptation to avoid predators. These animals also developed adaptations that allow them to take in large amounts of oxygen to fuel their fast runs. Finally, pronghorns have hair that pulls off easily, which allows them to elude the bite of many different predators.

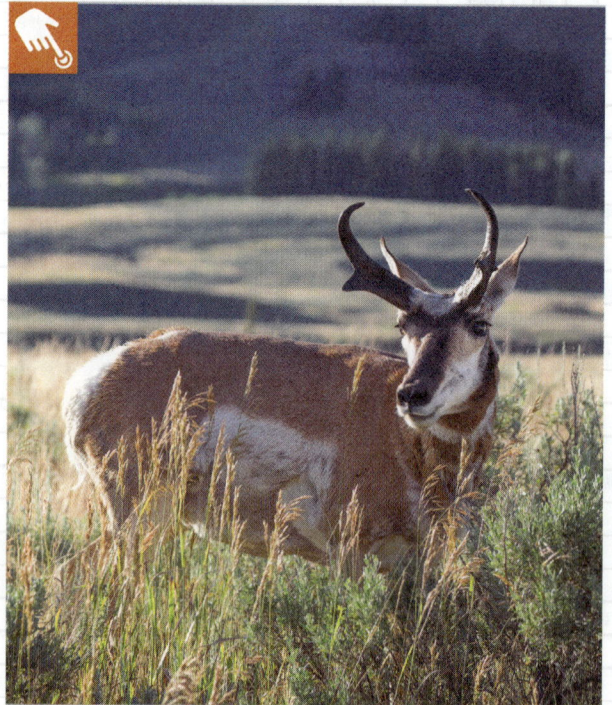

Pronghorns are considered living fossils because the species has remained mostly unchanged for thousands of years.

19. **Collaborate** The Sonoran pronghorn is an endangered species that lives in the Sonoran desert. Work with a partner to identify environmental stressors that threaten the Sonoran pronghorn throughout its range. Organize your research into a graphic organizer that links causes (environmental stressors) with effects (impacts on pronghorns). Share your results with your class.

White-tailed ptarmigans are grayish-brown in the summer and white in the winter. Seasonal changes prompt the change in feather color.

The giant armadillo is nocturnal, or active at night. The sun going down cues these animals to start their day.

EVIDENCE NOTEBOOK

20. Zebras live in groups of one male and several females or groups of young and weaker males. Why does the grouping of the zebras lead to males fighting? Record your evidence.

Case Study: The Pacific Flyway

Millions of birds migrate each year across the Pacific Flyway. Both genetic and environmental factors drive this migration. These birds travel to warmer climates because they lack physical adaptations to survive cold winters. Also, their food supply decreases as insects die off or burrow for the winter.

Some birds depend on the wetlands of California to be their winter nesting grounds, but over 95 percent of these wetlands have disappeared. Most of this land is now farmland. This is particularly true in California's Central Valley, the agricultural hub of California.

21. Collaborate Work with a partner to research solutions to the declining winter habitat in the Central Valley. Write and present an argument that could be used to convince others to accept this solution and put it into action. Support your argument with scientific reasoning and empirical evidence from reliable sources.

Pacific Flyway Routes in California

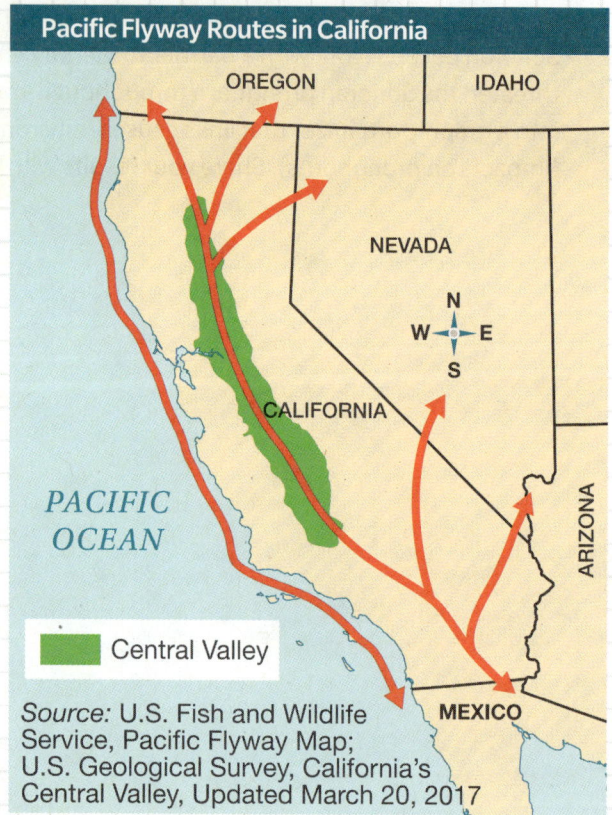

Central Valley

Source: U.S. Fish and Wildlife Service, Pacific Flyway Map; U.S. Geological Survey, California's Central Valley, Updated March 20, 2017

22. Decide if each change in animal growth is caused by a *genetic* or an *environmental* factor.

Causes	Effects
environmental	Bulls, calves, and cows grow weak when the grass is sparse due to drought.
	A cow grows better than other cows when the herd is moved to a colder climate.
	Young cattle do not grow well when a disease kills the grass.
	Calves are not growing well because of a parasite present in the herd.
	A bull grows better than other bulls during an unusually warm summer.

Hands-On Lab
Model the Growth of an Animal

You will work with a group to design a board game that models how genetic and environmental factors affect animals. Then you will create the board game with provided materials. Finally, you will switch games with another group, play the other group's game, and give the group feedback about the game.

MATERIALS
- colored pencils, markers, or crayons
- objects that can be used as tokens
- paper
- poster board
- scissors

Procedure

STEP 1 With your group, brainstorm an idea for a board game that models the growth of an animal over time. The game must also meet the following conditions:

- Your game must incorporate five scenarios of genetic and environmental factors that have an effect on growth.

- Players will receive points or will move forward when there are positive effects on growth. For example, a player lands on a space or draws a card that reads, "Plenty of food this season! Move forward three spaces." Players will move backward or will lose a turn when there are negative effects on growth. For example, a player lands on a space or draws a card that reads, "Drought in progress! Lose a turn."

STEP 2 Once your group has finished brainstorming, discuss with group members the details of your game. Record your scenarios on a separate sheet of paper.

STEP 3 After your group has worked out all the details, create the game using the provided materials.

Analysis

STEP 4 Trade games with another group. Play the other group's game. As you play, write your comments and questions about the game: What did you like about the game? Is there anything the other group could do to improve its depiction of the genetic and environmental factors that influence the growth of animals?

Predict the Growth of Blackbuck Antelope

Blackbuck antelope live in groups on the hot, dry grasslands of India and Pakistan. They mostly eat grasses but will also eat leaves, fruits, and flowers. They are among the fastest animals on earth and have very sharp eyesight. Predators include leopards and wild dogs. Human populations use the blackbuck habitat for agriculture and hunt the antelope for their meat and horns.

The blackbuck antelope is an herbivore native to India and Pakistan.

Blackbuck antelope males compete with each other for territory and mates. They have long, spiraling horns that they use to fight and attract females. A female antelope gives birth to a single fawn that will stay hidden in grasses until it is ready to join the herd.

23. Use the facts about blackbuck antelopes to construct an explanation for how genetic and environmental factors influence the reproduction and growth of these animals. In your explanation be sure to include:

- factors that affect blackbuck reproduction, including the type of reproduction, as well as courtship, parenting, and offspring behaviors

- factors that affect blackbuck growth including weather conditions, predation, food supply, and genetic traits

_____

_____

_____

_____

_____

_____

_____

_____

_____

_____

_____

Continue Your Exploration

Name: _____   Date: _____

Check out the path below or go online to choose one of the other paths shown.

Teaching Offspring	• **Effect of Temperature on Gender** • **Hands-On Labs** ✋ • **Propose Your Own Path**	*Go online to choose one of these other paths.*

Some animals teach their offspring skills that will help them survive when they are ready to live on their own. Parents teach their offspring in a variety of ways. Some parents directly teach skills or train offspring gradually over time. In other species of animals, offspring may simply observe adults and then use trial and error to learn.

Meerkats are prairie dog-like mammals that thrive in large packs. They use direct teaching of skills as a parenting behavior. Parents teach their offspring how to capture and kill dangerous prey, such as scorpions. They bring nearly dead animals to the offspring because the prey is too dangerous to start with for instructional purposes. They might render the prey animals harmless, for instance, by removing the stinger. This teaching behavior is not limited to the actual parents. Other adult meerkats, called helpers, will also teach offspring that are not theirs.

1. What benefit might adult meerkats gain by helping the offspring of others learn how to capture and kill dangerous prey?

meerkats

Continue Your Exploration

River otters are an example of a species in which offspring observe adults and then use trial and error to learn. River otters do not know how to swim at birth. The females teach their offspring by pushing them into the water when the offspring are about two months old. The females will carry the offspring on their backs if help is needed. The offspring learn by doing.

Orangutans are another species in which the offspring learn through observation. They participate in activities with adults and copy their behavior. Offspring remain with their mothers for eight years or more. They learn everything from swinging through trees to finding food to building a nest to sleep in at night.

river otters

orangutans

2. For adult animals, what are the advantages of making the investment of time and resources to teach offspring life skills?

3. For adult animals, what are the disadvantages of making the investment of time and resources to teach offspring life skills?

4. **Collaborate** Research another animal that invests in teaching of their offspring. Summarize your research in a multimedia presentation that describes details of the parenting behaviors. Cite multiple valid sources to support your research.

Can You Explain It?

Name: _____   Date: _____

Why are these male zebras fighting?

EVIDENCE NOTEBOOK

Refer to the notes in your Evidence Notebook to help you construct an explanation for why the male zebras are fighting.

1. State your claim. Make sure your claim fully explains the function of the behavior.

2. Summarize the evidence you have gathered to support your claim and explain your reasoning.

Checkpoints

Answer the following questions to check your understanding of the lesson.

Use the photo to answer Questions 3–4.

3. The male midwife toad will carry the eggs he fertilized until they are ready to hatch. This male midwife toad most likely reproduces asexually / sexually.

4. The eggs will hatch into tadpoles that need water to grow and develop. Which statement includes a factor that might negatively affect the growth and development of the tadpoles?

    A. The tadpoles can grow in very shallow pools.

    B. The tadpoles' habitat is infected with a fungal disease.

    C. The tadpoles are prey for dragonflies.

    D. The tadpoles grow into adult toads in 3–5 weeks.

Use the photo to answer Questions 5–6.

5. The type of behavior shown by this pig-tailed macaque is best described as offspring / courtship / parenting behavior.

6. What is the possible benefit of this behavior to the macaques? Select all that apply.

    A. The reproductive success of the mother may increase.

    B. The offspring might grow and develop into a healthy adult.

    C. The offspring might learn this behavior from its mother.

    D. The reproductive success of the father may decrease.

7. The fishing industry typically captures fish larger than a minimum size. Due to decades of overfishing, the number of large fish in a river has decreased over time. Recently, scientists discovered that some fish in the river have started to reach maturity at a younger age when they are a smaller size. This early development decreases / increases / does not affect the fishes' chances for successful reproduction. This improves / reduces / does not affect the likelihood that the fish population will survive in this environment.

Interactive Review

Complete this section to review the main concepts of the lesson.

Sexual reproduction is the dominant type of reproduction among animals, although some also reproduce asexually.

A. Explain the relationship between sexual reproduction and genetic variation in animals.

Courtship, parenting, and offspring behaviors contribute to the reproductive success of animals.

B. Describe one courtship behavior and one parenting behavior, including how each behavior contributes to the reproductive success of an animal.

Genetic and environmental factors influence the growth of animals.

C. Use a cause-and-effect diagram to illustrate how different factors can influence the growth of organisms.

Choose one of the activities to explore how this unit connects to other topics.

☐ People in Science

Phoebe Snetsinger, Birder Birding consists of viewing and identifying birds, often using binoculars or spotting scopes to see birds from longer distances. Phoebe Snetsinger was a renowned birder who saw over 8,000 different species of birds in her lifetime. Her birding adventures took her all over the world. Snetsinger used her knowledge of birds to help her accurately identify birds in the field. Birding can contribute to citizen science by helping scientists track changes in where bird species live.

Develop a map that shows the ranges of one bird on each continent that you would like to add to your "life list" of bird species. Explain how environmental conditions influence the range of each bird species.

red-shouldered vanga

☐ Earth Science Connection

Climate and Reproduction Patterns in reproduction and growth relate to patterns in biome distribution on Earth. While organisms at the equator may be able to reproduce all year, organisms living at the cold poles may focus more on basic survival needs, leaving little time or energy for growth and reproduction.

Research one organism and the climate from two different land biomes. Compare and contrast the biome climates and the patterns of reproduction and growth for the organisms. Use a multimedia presentation to share what you learn.

polar bear mother and cubs

☐ Art Connection

Landscape Architects Landscape architects use plant knowledge to make outdoor spaces beautiful and functional. They choose plants with a variety of reproductive strategies that can be successful during different seasons. For example, landscape architects for an amusement park might arrange plants according to flowering season to ensure blooms all year long.

Research different plants and design a landscape for an outdoor space in your community. Choose at least five climate-appropriate plants that use a variety of reproductive strategies. Explain the practical and artistic purposes for each plant in a landscape diagram you share with the class.

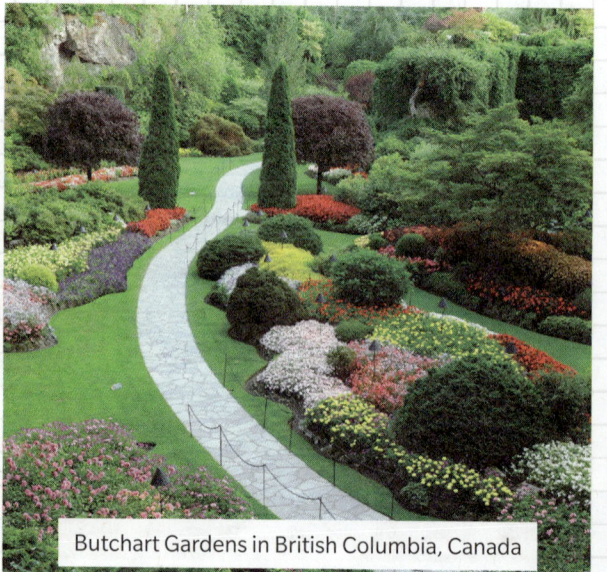
Butchart Gardens in British Columbia, Canada

Name: _____   Date: _____

Complete this review to check your understanding of the unit.

Use the table to answer Questions 1–3.

1. Blood type inheritance involves three alleles, which are shown in the table as A, B, and O. Study the genotypes and resulting blood types of Sam and Heidi's children. Based on this information, which statement about the alleles for blood type is correct?

   A. O is dominant over A and B.

   B. A and B are each dominant over O.

   C. Only A is dominant over O.

   D. A, B, and O alleles are equally dominant.

Blood Types of Sam and Heidi's Children

	Sam	
	A	O
B	**AB** Gabriella (Type AB blood)	**BO** Frank (Type B blood)
O	**AO** Jack (Type A blood)	**OO** Sally (Type O blood)

Heidi

2. Which pieces of evidence from the chart help establish that humans reproduce sexually, not asexually? Select all that apply.

   A. Frank has the same genotype as his mother.

   B. Gabriella has a different blood type than each of her parents.

   C. Sally received one allele from each of her parents.

   D. Heidi and Sam had four children.

3. If Sam and Heidi were to have another child, the probability of that child having Type AB blood is *25 / 50 / 75* percent.

Use the photograph to answer Questions 4–6.

4. Male impala lock horns to compete for mates. The physical advantages that one male has over the other depend on:

   A. genetic factors

   B. environmental factors

   C. both genetic and environmental factors

5. Why is the winning male impala likely to have more reproductive success? Select all that apply.

   A. He is healthier and likely to produce healthy, viable gametes.

   B. He will attract more mates.

   C. He has only beneficial genes.

   D. He will defend the female and offspring more effectively than a weaker male.

6. Impalas may be more territorial during the wet season. Increasing precipitation amounts and the increase in vegetation that follows *increases / decreases / has no effect on* the number of altercations between impalas.

7. Think of an example related to each factor that affects the growth and survival of organisms. Describe the effect that each of your examples has on organisms.

Factors Affecting Survival	Cause	Effect
Climate	rain shadow	organisms adapted to minimal precipitation; plants grow relatively smaller compared to areas with more precipitation
Local conditions		
Genes		
Adaptations		

Use the diagram about reproduction in pine trees to answer Questions 8–11.

1 Wind carries pollen to an egg cell in the female cone.

2 A pollen grain fertilizes the egg, resulting in a seed.

3 A seed falls to the ground and grows into a new pine tree.

8. Do pine trees reproduce sexually or asexually? Use evidence from the diagram to support your answer.

9. Male pine cones contain a large amount of pollen. Why?

10. Pine trees are *gymnosperms*, meaning "naked seeds." Their seeds are not enclosed in fruit, and they do not produce flowers that attract pollinators. How might the reproductive strategy of pine trees be partially responsible for their success in landscapes at high elevation and in cold climates?

11. Are all factors that affect the reproductive success of pine trees pictured in the diagram? Explain.

Use the photo to answer Questions 12–15.

12. The cardon cactus is native to the Sonoran desert in Baja California. It is not found further north because it does not tolerate freezing temperatures. Describe what might happen to the range of the cardon cactus if climate change causes areas north of Baja California to no longer have freezing temperatures.

13. Lesser long-nosed bats use nectar and pollen from the flowers of the cardon cactus as a food source. Bats often pollinate the cacti as they feed. What adaptations would you predict for the lesser long-nosed bat and the cardon cactus?

14. What ensures that the relationship between the cardon cactus and the lesser long-nosed bat will continue between generations?

15. What might happen to the lesser long-nosed bat population during a drought that causes the cardon cacti to produce very few flowers?

Name: _____   **Date:** _____

Save the Whitebark Pines!

The stately whitebark pines of Yellowstone National Park are in trouble! Normally, cold temperatures at the tree line keep away pine beetles, which infect the trees. However, the cold temperature band has shrunk with recent climate change. This leaves more trees at risk of pine-beetle infection. Climate change is influenced by human development, and in this way humans are impacting the range and viability of whitebark pines. A fungus also infects the trees, though scientists are encouraged to see that some pines have an inherited resistance to the fungus. The pines are important to many species in Yellowstone, including other coniferous trees, pine squirrels, birds, and grizzly bears.

As part of an Eco-Task Force, you will develop a plan to increase the number of healthy whitebark pines in Yellowstone. You should consider genetic solutions, as well as actions that might improve reproductive success and enhance sapling growth. Save the whitebark pines!

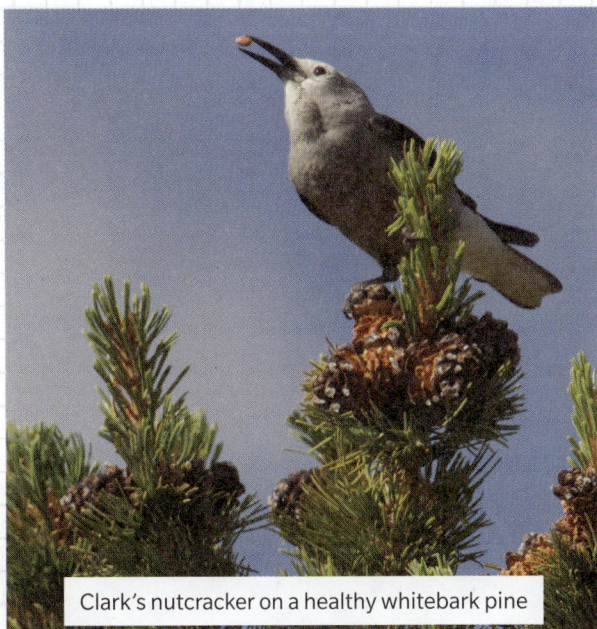
Clark's nutcracker on a healthy whitebark pine

whitebark pine infected with fungus that causes blister rust

The steps below will help guide your research and develop your recommendation.

1. **Define the Problem** Write a statement defining the problem you have been asked to solve. What factors limit the success of the pines?

2. **Conduct Research** Using library or Internet resources, learn more about how environmental scientists help threatened populations. What can your Eco-Task Force do to improve the genetic variation, growth, and reproduction of the whitebark pines in Yellowstone?

3. **Develop a Model** Genetic solutions often require breeding programs. Use Punnett squares to show how you could increase fungus resistance in whitebark populations, depending on whether the allele for resistance is recessive or dominant. Show what crosses would be ideal in each situation. What process will the Eco-Task Force need to use to breed fungus-resistant offspring?

4. **Recommend a Solution** Make a recommendation based on your research. How will you protect adult trees from pine beetles and fungus, as well as ensure successful growth of new saplings?

5. **Communicate** How will you convince officials that your plan will work? Create a multimedia presentation to present your plan to save the whitebark pines in Yellowstone. Use evidence and reasoning to support your claims.

✓ Self-Check

	I listed all factors (genetic, reproductive, and environmental) that limit the number of whitebark pines in Yellowstone.
	I researched how environmental scientists help threatened populations.
	I used a model to consider genetic solutions that could help the whitebark pines.
	My solutions are based on research and a correct understanding of the whitebark pine's pattern of growth and reproduction.
	My presentation used effective scientific argumentation to defend the Eco-Task Force proposal.

Human Impacts on the Environment

How do human activities affect climate change, ecosystems, and living things?

Unit Project 486

Lesson 1   Human Activities Cause Changes in the Environment 488

Lesson 2   Human Activities Influence Climate Change   508

Lesson 3   Climate Change Affects the Survival of Organisms   532

Lesson 4   Engineer It: Reducing Human Impacts on the Environment . . . 552

Unit Review 577

Unit Performance Task 581

A lot of plastic trash ends up in the oceans, where it affects many organisms, such as plankton, corals, fish, and whales.

You Solve It How Can You Grow a Crop Using Water Efficiently?

Design a method for irrigating a melon crop that uses the least amount of water possible while still growing a successful crop.

Go online and complete the You Solve It to explore ways to solve a real-world problem.

Minimize Community Effects on Climate Change

Community projects, such as litter pick-ups, can bring together people of various ages and backgrounds to help protect the environment.

A. Look at the photo. On a separate sheet of paper, write down as many different questions as you can about the photo.

B. Discuss With your class or partner, share your questions. Record any additional questions generated in your discussion. Then choose the most important questions from the list that are related to how communities can work together to reduce climate change. Write them below.

C. Choose a human activity that emits greenhouse gases and that your community or school could focus on to reduce its impact on climate change. What activity will you design a solution to address?

D. Use the information above, along with your research, to plan a multimedia presentation to explain your solution and to convince others to participate in your program.

Discuss the next steps for your Unit Project with your teacher and go online to download the Unit Project Worksheet.

Language Development

Use the lessons in this unit to complete the network and expand your understanding of these key concepts.

- Similar term
- Phrase
- Cognate
- Example
- Definition

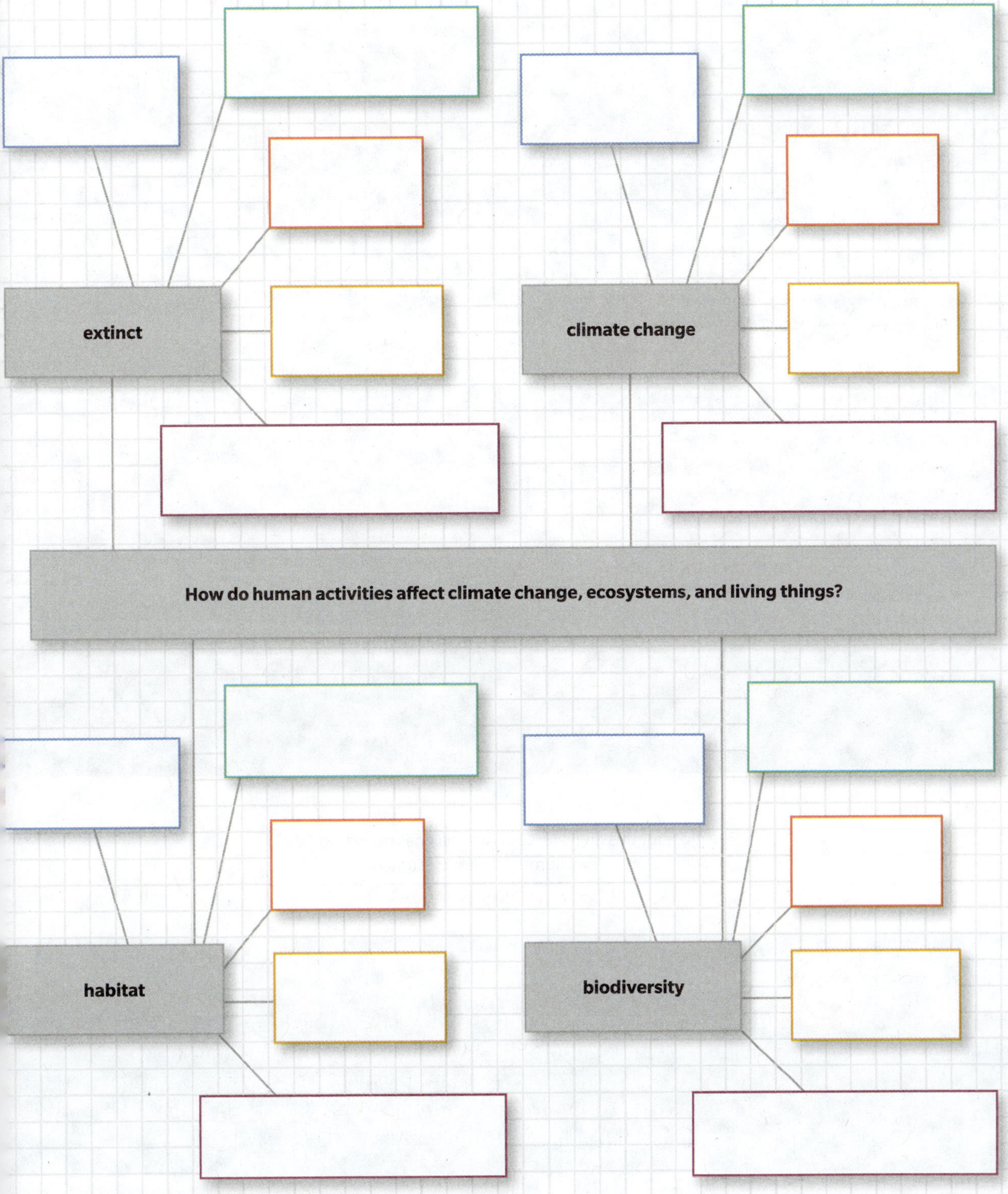
extinct
climate change
How do human activities affect climate change, ecosystems, and living things?
habitat
biodiversity

Human Activities Cause Changes in the Environment

The grass for this golf course in Arizona does not naturally grow in this area. It was brought here by humans.

Explore First

Identifying Human Impacts Choose an area, such as your school campus, your neighborhood, or your town. Make a map that shows which parts of your area are natural and which areas have been altered by humans. How did you determine which areas had been changed by humans and which areas were unaltered?

Go online to view the digital version of the Hands-On Lab for this lesson and to download additional lab resources.

CAN YOU EXPLAIN IT?

How can farming on land contribute to the growth of algal blooms in the ocean?

Algae vary in color. When large amounts of algae are in a body of water, the color of the water may appear to change.

Algae are plant-like organisms that live in fresh water and salt water. Algae get the nutrients they need from the water they live in, and they use the energy from sunlight to make sugars. An algal bloom happens when the population of algae in a body of water increases rapidly. As the algae population grows, more algae also die and decompose. Bacteria that decompose the dead algae use more oxygen, which depletes the amount of dissolved oxygen in the water. Fish and other organisms that need oxygen may die as a result of the algal bloom.

1. Describe how land and oceans are connected.

2. What do you think might cause algae to start growing very rapidly?

EVIDENCE NOTEBOOK As you explore this lesson, gather evidence to help explain how farming on land relates to the growth of algal blooms in the ocean.

Exploring the Environment

All living things need certain materials to stay healthy. Organisms depend on their environment to provide those materials. A **habitat** is the place where an organism lives. It includes the living and nonliving factors that affect the organism, or the *environment* around the organism. The living and nonliving parts of the environment interact. Humans and other organisms rely on the environment for natural resources, such as water and soil. Natural systems also provide ecosystem services, such as the filtering of pollutants from water. These products and services are essential to human life. They are also important to the functioning of human cultures and economies.

3. Identify each factor in the beaver's habitat as *living* or *nonliving*.

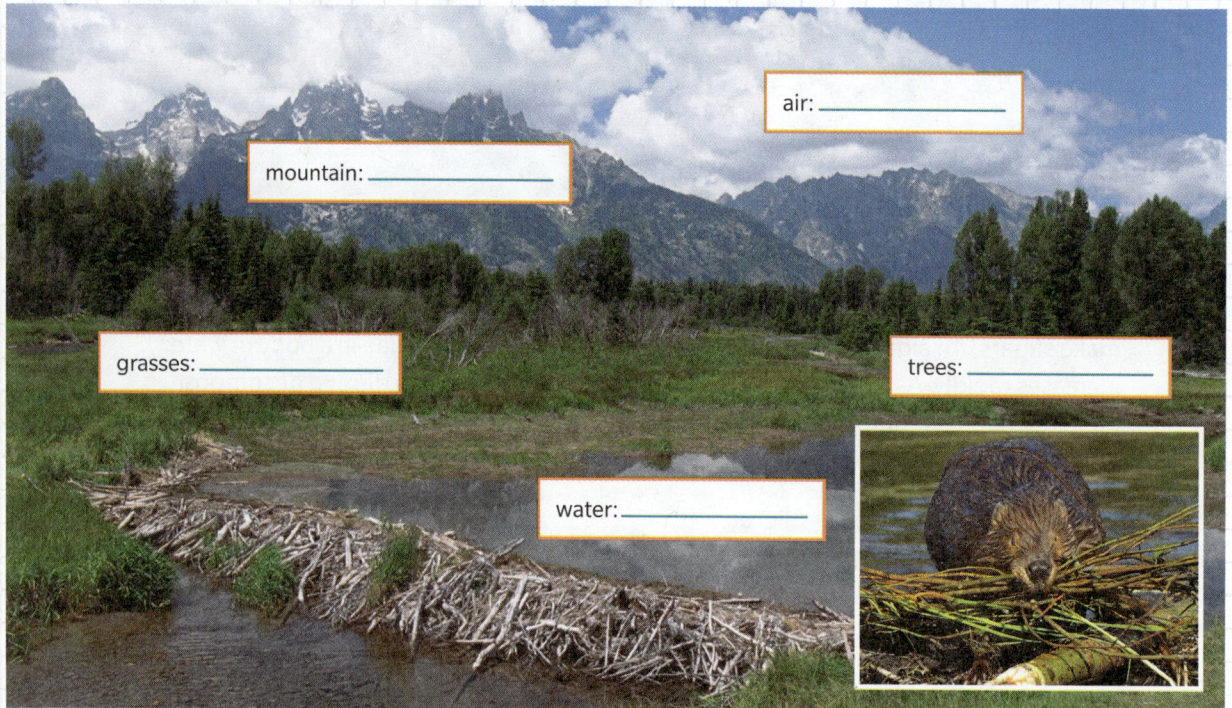

air: _____

mountain: _____

grasses: _____

trees: _____

water: _____

A beaver uses sticks and branches from nearby trees to build a dam in a river.

4. How might the beaver use or depend on at least three of the environmental factors labeled in the photo?

EVIDENCE NOTEBOOK

5. Describe the environment of the algae shown at the beginning of the lesson. How are algae connected to their environment? Record your evidence.

Changes in the Environment

Changes in Earth systems happen all the time. Natural events cause some changes. For example, a flood caused by a severe rainstorm might destroy trees or remove topsoil. Humans can also cause change by actions such as damming a river or removing trees. Natural events and human activities can both disturb the environment. These disturbances can alter resources that living things, including humans, need.

The path of a tornado can easily be seen in this forest. Tornadoes are natural events that disrupt the environment.

Deforestation is the removal of trees and other plants from an area. Humans cut down forests to use the wood or the land.

6. **Discuss** With a partner, look at the images and compare the changes to a forest from a tornado and from deforestation.

Changes Caused by Natural Events

Some natural changes in the environment involve patterns. For example, in some places ocean tides change from high to low twice a day. Weather changes seasonally in many parts of Earth. It can become cooler and then warmer throughout a year. Because these events happen in a repeating pattern, many species have ways to deal with these changes. For example, fur color in Arctic hares changes from brown to white in the winter, an advantage when hiding from predators in the snow. Other natural changes happen suddenly or without a pattern. A forest fire caused by a lightning strike is a sudden natural event that can cause large changes to the environment.

Changes Caused by Human Activity

Human activities can have many different effects on Earth systems. For example, humans can change the shape of the land to meet their needs. Humans may use resources at a faster rate than they can be replaced. This use causes resources to become scarce in the environment and is called *resource depletion*. Humans also affect the environment when they pollute resources. *Pollution* is an undesirable change in a natural environment that is caused by adding substances that are harmful to living organisms.

7. Decide whether each example is caused by human actions or by natural events. Write H for human actions and N for natural events.

   A. asteroid impact flattens a forest _____

   B. flooding from a concrete dam _____

   C. flooding from a severe storm _____

   D. oil spill in the ocean _____

   E. deforestation to clear land for crops _____

Identify Facts

A *fact* is a statement that can be proven. An *opinion* is what someone believes about something. The following is an excerpt from a newspaper article about a dam and its impact on the environment. While you read the article, watch for statements that present facts and statements that present opinions.

The Three Gorges Dam

In 2003, the Three Gorges Dam opened across China's Yangtze River. The dam provides China with a sustainable source of electrical energy for a fast-growing population. It also helps decrease the risk of flooding in the river basin. In 2014, the dam produced 98.8 billion kilowatt-hours of electricity. The dam uses flowing water instead of fossil fuels to produce electrical energy. This process reduced the environmental impact of China's power plants by lowering the amount of carbon dioxide produced by about 120 million tons per year.

Although these results help the Chinese people, the construction of the dam is not as fantastic as it first appears. Building the dam required large amounts of concrete and released harmful chemicals and carbon dioxide into the air. Scientists think that earthquakes may result from water pressure in ground cracks near the dam's reservoir. The worst effect was that people were moved from their villages, and the villages were flooded. Sadly, many natural ecosystems were destroyed, and more than 500 species of rare plants and 300 species of fish were negatively affected. Many living things died because their ecosystems were lost. Building the dam helped the people. However, its effects on certain ecosystems were devastating.

8. Identify each statement as a *fact* or an *opinion* .

   A. The dam provides China with a sustainable energy source for producing electrical energy. _____

   B. The dam is not as fantastic as it first appears. _____

   C. It also helps decrease the risk of flooding in the river basin. _____

   D. The worst effect was that people were moved from their villages. _____

9. Using evidence provided in the article, identify two different cause-effect relationships involving the construction of the Three Gorges Dam and the environment.

   _____
   _____
   _____
   _____
   _____
   _____
   _____
   _____
   _____
   _____

Relating Human Activity to the Environment

Human Activity in Earth Systems

Did you ever see someone throw a plastic cup on the ground and walk away? Some people might say, "Well, it is just one cup." People may not think about how pollution adds up when many people do the same thing.

The Earth system is sometimes divided into four parts, or subsystems. These interconnected subsystems are the hydrosphere, atmosphere, geosphere, and biosphere. The health of each subsystem affects the resources and ecosystem services that individuals and society get from that part of the Earth system. A human activity that directly affects one subsystem may indirectly affect the others. These interconnected changes may affect the quality, quantity, and availability of resources and services that people need.

10. What are three human actions that affect the environment?

Recycling cell phones, which contain metals and plastics, reduces environmental pollution.

Human Impact on the Hydrosphere

All water on Earth is part of the *hydrosphere*, including polar ice caps, snow, groundwater, and surface water. Humans rely on surface water to drink, swim, fish, and transport goods. Farmers might divert water from rivers to give to crops or livestock. Humans also dig wells to pump groundwater to areas where surface water is unavailable. Human use of these water resources can lead to a scarcity of fresh and clean water in the environment.

Water pollution may result from human activities on or near water sources. Water pollution affects organisms that depend on the water supply. **Point-source pollution** occurs when harmful materials enter Earth's hydrosphere from a single, identifiable source such as a factory. **Nonpoint-source pollution** comes from many sources, including rainwater that picks up pollutants as it moves across land.

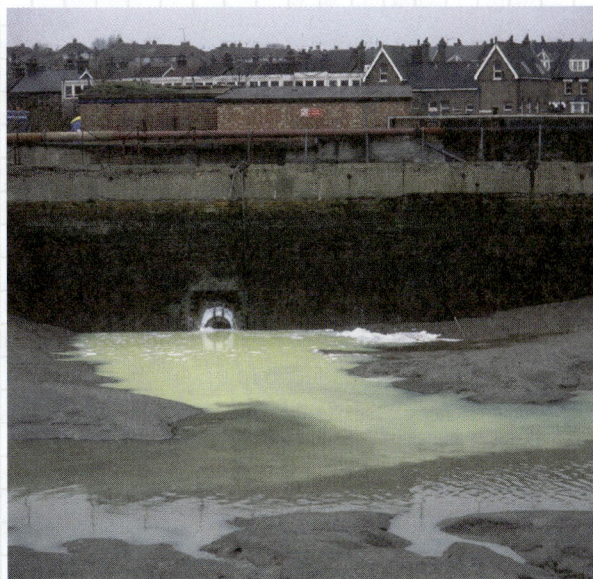

When wastes are dumped into Earth's hydrosphere, pollutants can travel to different parts of the environment.

Hands-On Lab
Model Ocean Pollution from Land

You will make a model to explore how land and ocean pollution are connected.

Procedure and Analysis

STEP 1 Make a prediction about how point-source pollution and nonpoint-source pollution on land may affect water pollution.

STEP 2 Use the materials provided to create a model of either point-source or nonpoint-source pollution on land near an ocean shore.

STEP 3 Explain how your model represents either point-source or nonpoint-source pollution.

STEP 4 Design a method to simulate precipitation with your model. Explore how precipitation affects the land pollution and ocean pollution. Record your observations.

STEP 5 Compare your observations with those of other groups. Is there a difference in how point-source pollution and nonpoint-source pollution on land affect ocean pollution? Explain your reasoning.

STEP 6 **Draw** On a separate sheet of paper, draw a cartoon with three or four frames. Illustrate a human activity that could contribute to the process of pollution that you modeled in this activity. In your cartoon, show at least two effects on the environment of the human activity shown.

MATERIALS
- camera (optional)
- food coloring, blue
- food coloring, red
- metric ruler
- sand, coarse, wet (1/3 volume of washtub)
- spray bottle
- washtub, plastic
- water

EVIDENCE NOTEBOOK
11. Identify the different materials that may enter a body of water by the same process explored in this lab. Record your evidence.

Human Impact on the Atmosphere

The *atmosphere* is the layer of gases that surrounds Earth. If you stand outside and look up, you might see blue sky and some clouds. You may not see air pollution because many air pollutants are colorless gases. Other pollutants may be in liquid or solid form, such as tiny particles suspended in the atmosphere. Air pollution may cause problems for humans and other species alike. Respiratory problems such as asthma can be made worse by air pollution. Many pollutants enter the atmosphere as the result of burning fossil fuels. Other pollutants such as dust may come from construction sites or agriculture as dry soil is carried by the wind.

Burning fossil fuels releases potentially harmful particles and gases into the atmosphere.

Human Impact on the Geosphere

The mostly solid, rocky part of Earth is called the *geosphere*. Humans change the geosphere when they reshape the land to meet their needs. Humans level land to build homes and offices. Humans may also change the land to mine for resources or to farm. Some farming and mining practices can degrade the soil. Degraded soil cannot support plants or crops, leaving the soil exposed. The exposed soil may then be swept away by wind or water, further changing the shape of the land. Humans may change the land to reduce the chance of erosion by planting different types of crops or by terracing sloped lands.

Mining provides people with materials they need, but it also changes the geosphere.

Human Impact on the Biosphere

The *biosphere* is all living things on Earth, including you. Humans affect the biosphere when they hunt, fish, or harvest plants. A species may become extinct if humans remove more organisms than can be replenished. A species is **extinct** when no more individuals remain on Earth. Human activity may also positively impact the biosphere. In many areas, deer populations no longer have natural predators. These deer populations may grow so large that their grazing negatively affects their ecosystem. Hunting deer in these areas can reduce the deer population to protect the forest ecosystem.

Commercial fishing can deplete the food for other species living in the area and add pollution to the water.

Changes to other Earth systems may indirectly affect the biosphere. For example, changes to land or water might degrade or destroy habitats. When an organism's habitat is degraded, the habitat may no longer be able to support the organism. Imagine that a lake is polluted or its water is removed for human use. In this example, organisms that depend on the water in the lake to survive either move to other sources, or, if they cannot move, they may not survive.

Connected Effects of Human Activity

Human activity may affect multiple parts of the Earth system. Burning fossil fuels releases particles and several different gases into the air. Some of these gases pollute the air. For example, gases such as nitrogen oxides and sulfur dioxide, react with water in the air to form acid rain. Acid rain may kill trees or crops and cause surface water to become more acidic. These effects can harm living organisms in the biosphere.

A mine in West Virginia, where the top of a mountain was removed to reach the coal in the ground.

12. Complete the paragraph with the words geosphere, hydrosphere, atmosphere, and biosphere.

Surface mining changes the shape of the land, which affects the _____. These land changes may fragment or destroy habitats in the area, which affects the _____.
Mining exposes new materials to the surface. Rain may carry these materials into rivers and streams, which affects the _____. The process of mining can also cause small particles to enter the _____.

Human Impact on the Florida Panther

In the 1500s, the Florida panther roamed most of what is now the southeastern United States. The Florida panther lives in forested areas, wetlands, and swamps.

13. How might a growing human population have affected the Florida panther population?

Florida panther

    As European settlers arrived in the 1600s, they clear-cut the land so they could grow crops. Today much of the area has been urbanized. The cutting of trees and building of roads and cities fragmented the panther's habitat. It reduced large, connected habitats to smaller, less connected areas. The panther was also hunted to protect livestock.
    In 1967, the Florida panther was listed as an endangered species by the United States government and conservation efforts began. Conservation efforts included protecting and connecting panther habitats and making it illegal to hunt these large cats. In the early 1970s, there were approximately 20 adult wild panthers in southern Florida. Conservation efforts resulted in there being almost 200 in the same area in 2014. Despite the increase in numbers, Florida panthers still face many dangers. For example, 24 panthers were killed by cars while trying to cross roadways in 2014.

Human Impacts on the Florida Panther's Habitat

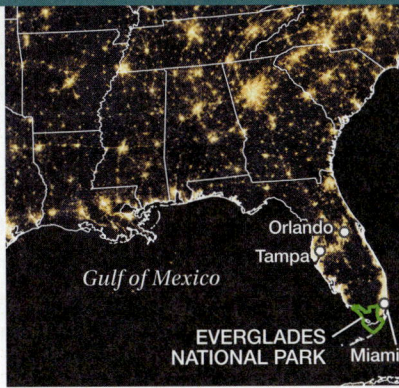

Florida panther historic range

Florida panther current breeding range

Today, Florida panthers in the wild live only in the southwestern tip of Florida. This nighttime image shows light pollution from cities and roads in the southeastern United States. Light pollution is strongly correlated with human activity.

Source: U.S. Fish and Wildlife Service, Florida Panther Recovery Plan, Third Revision, 2008

14. Look at the maps. How do the data in the maps support the claim that human activity has negatively affected the population of Florida panthers?

Engineer It
Evaluate Tradeoffs

Suppose you are an engineer who is designing a new drive system for an automobile. Two criteria for the product are that the design must keep the emission of carbon dioxide (CO_2) low, and that the cost of owning the product must be low. Use the graph to compare ownership costs with yearly CO_2 emissions for three drive system designs.

15. Which design has the greatest release of CO_2 per year in comparison to the others?

_____

16. Based on the design criteria, describe the tradeoff that must be made when choosing one of the three designs. Use the graph to support your argument.

Emissions and Cost of Drive System Designs

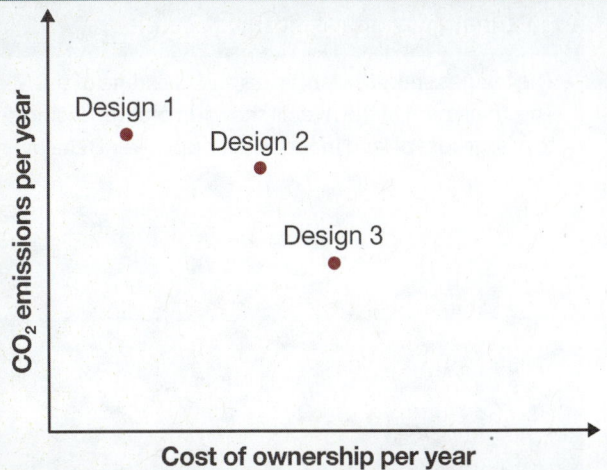

_____
_____
_____

Analyzing the Scale of Human Impacts on the Environment

Human effects on the environment can vary in scale over time and space. Some effects are more noticeable in the long term, such as the increase in the acidity of oceans. Some effects can happen more quickly. For example, developers may fill in a wetland to build a neighborhood, which can impact the environment in the area in a short amount of time. A person cutting down a single tree affects a small area, but when large areas of trees are cut down, a larger area of the environment will be affected. The scale of a human impact on the environment affects the ability of the environment to recover or stabilize.

17. **Discuss** How might a human activity that impacts a small area affect a larger area over time?

Case Study: The Mississippi River

The Mississippi River is one of the largest rivers in the world. The river is an important shipping route and freshwater source for the central United States. Human activity that affects the Mississippi River can have widespread effects due to the size of the river.

Rivers naturally change course over time and occasionally flood due to natural events. The *mouth* of a river is where it empties into a larger body of water. Rivers naturally slow down near their mouths and deposit sediment in a fan-shaped area. This fan-shaped land mass is called the *delta* of the river. To protect cities near the river from floodwaters and to help maintain the course of the river, humans built levees along the river. A *levee* is a raised part of land either naturally occurring or human-built to contain rising river waters. Levees prevent the river waters from spreading out, slowing down, and depositing sediment. Instead, sediment is carried beyond the river's mouth.

The shape of the Mississippi River Delta has changed greatly during the twentieth century. A change this great over a geologically short period of time indicates that human activity has had a role in changing the shape of the delta.

The Changing Mississippi River Delta

The images show the landmass and coastline of the Mississippi River Delta in 1932 and 2011. The main path of the river is shown in orange. Rising sea level and other factors have contributed to a large loss of land in the Mississippi River Delta over 79 years.

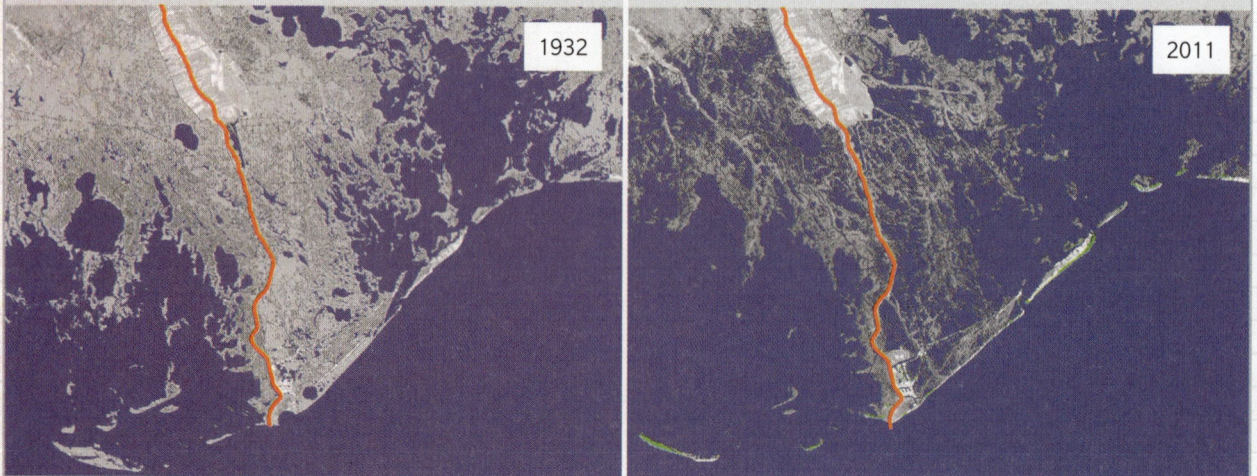

Human-Built Structures to Control the Mississippi River

Humans built several lock-and-dam systems so that larger boats could travel farther upstream on the Mississippi River. The lock portion allows boats passage, and the dam increases the depth of the water. The building of a dam can affect the environment in several ways.

Flow of a River Upstream of a Dam

River water carries sediment downstream. The sediment is suspended in the flowing water and makes the water cloudy or *turbid*. The flow of water slows down as it approaches a dam, and much of the sediment is deposited upstream of the dam.

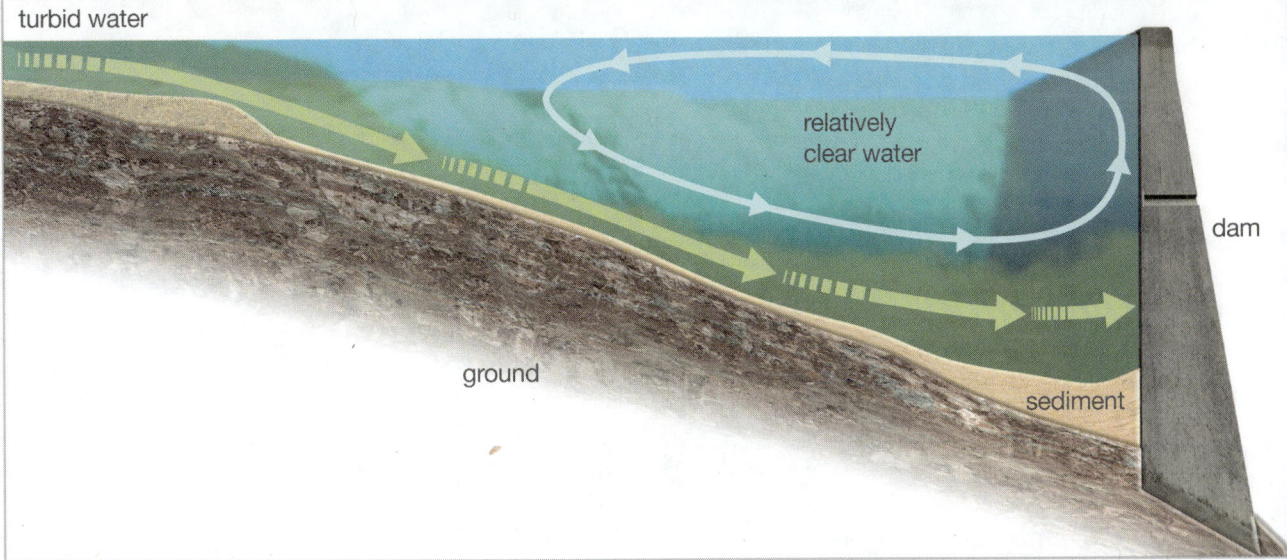

turbid water

relatively clear water

dam

ground

sediment

18. The following are effects of lock-and-dam systems in a river. Which effect will most likely impact the formation of land in the delta?

   A. They prevent the flow of sediments downstream.

   B. They can interfere with fish migration.

   C. They make navigation possible in places.

   D. They can affect water temperature.

For the cities in the Mississippi River Delta, it is important that the path of the Mississippi River does not change, as it would without human intervention. Many levees and other structures have been built to keep most of the flow of the Mississippi River along the same path it followed when cities in the area were established.

19. How might the building of levees have affected the shape of the Mississippi River Delta?

Levees are ridges along riverbanks that prevent rising river waters from overflowing the banks and causing floods.

Navigation and Flood Control Structures on the Mississippi River

Levees help maintain the course of the lower Mississippi River. Locks and dams help boats navigate the upper Mississippi and its tributaries, including the Ohio and Missouri Rivers.

Source: U.S. Army Corp of Engineers

20. How does the number of levees and dams on the Mississippi River affect the scale of human impact on the river and the organisms that depend on it?

Dead Zone at the Mouth of the Mississippi River

In 1972, humans first noticed that a large area in the ocean near the mouth of the Mississippi River appeared "dead." The normally rich community of fish, crustaceans, shellfish, and other animals had disappeared. At first, this happened every few years, but later happened every year. This dead zone appears in the summer when the algae population in the Gulf of Mexico's warm water suddenly increases. The increase in algae reduces the amount of oxygen dissolved in the water. Organisms sensitive to oxygen levels in the water either die or leave the area. More oxygen is removed from the water as dead organisms decay. The result is a *dead zone*, an area where organisms cannot live. Fish leave the area to find waters with more oxygen. Fish-dependent species such as some kinds of birds must look elsewhere for food. The size of the dead zone varies each year. For the last several years, the average size of the dead zone has been almost 6,000 square miles. It is one of the largest dead zones in the world.

Mississippi River Watershed

A *watershed* is an area of land drained by a river system. Forty-one percent of the continental United States is part of the Mississippi River watershed, which drains into the Gulf of Mexico.

Source: NOAA National Centers for Coastal Ocean Science, Hypoxia and Eutrophication

The Mississippi River watershed includes many cities and farms. Human activities in the watershed contribute to pollution in the water. Some pollutants are directly added to the waterways. Other pollutants are picked up from cities and farms by the rain that runs into streams and rivers. The pollutants include contaminants from roadways and fertilizers that farmers apply to crops to help them grow.

21. Explain how wastewater from a manufacturing plant in southern Ohio could affect fish in the Mississippi River. Use the watershed map to support your answer.

22. Farmers often apply extra nutrients to their crops in the form of fertilizer. Describe how these extra nutrients might affect the Mississippi River.

EVIDENCE NOTEBOOK

23. What materials might runoff in the Mississippi watershed contain that could contribute to algae growth in waterways? Record your evidence.

Do the Math
Analyze a Cod Population

Renewable resources must be used carefully to maintain the availability of the resource. For centuries, humans fished for cod off the coast of Newfoundland, Canada. Then, in the mid-twentieth century, new technologies allowed cod to be harvested in much greater numbers than in previous years. Soon after, the cod population declined rapidly. In 1992, Canada introduced a ban on cod fishing in the area. Even after the ban started, the cod population failed to recover as quickly as expected. One possible reason that the cod population remains low is the decrease in phytoplankton, the main food source for cod in the area. Also, the few cod that remain are more susceptible to environmental changes.

Northern Cod Landings

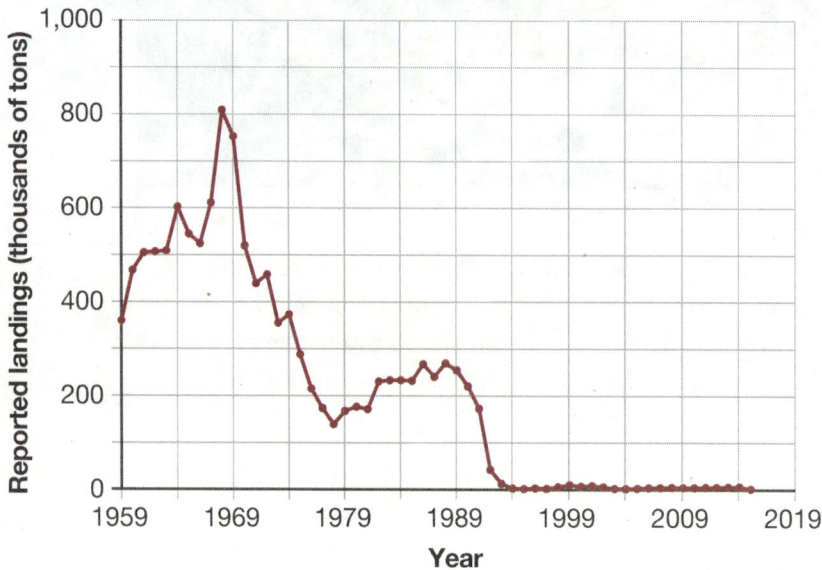

Source: Fisheries and Oceans Canada, DFO Science Newfoundland & Labrador Region

Fish landings are the amount of fish caught at sea and taken to land in any port, even in other countries. Since the sizes and ages of fish caught vary, landings are reported by weight.

24. Use the graph to answer the following questions.

   A. What is the average weight of fish caught per year from 1959–1969, to the nearest 20,000 tons? _____

   B. What is the average weight of fish caught per year from 1979–1989, to the nearest 20,000 tons? _____

   C. About what percentage of the average in part A is the average in part B, to the nearest 5%? _____

25. Why do you think the fishing industry was unable to continue catching the same amount of fish in the decades after the 1960s as had been caught in the 1960s?

_____

_____

_____

_____

_____

_____

Continue Your Exploration

Name: _____   Date: _____

Check out the path below or go online to choose one of the other paths shown.

Chernobyl Nuclear Disaster

- **Impact of *Deepwater Horizon* Oil Well Accident**
- **Hands-On Labs** ✋
- **Propose Your Own Path**

Go online to choose one of these other paths.

Under normal operating conditions, nuclear power generation is safe and releases minimal pollutants into the atmosphere. But in 1986, an accident at the Chernobyl Nuclear Power Plant in Ukraine released huge amounts of radioactive material into the environment. Soon after the incident, the government closed the area within 30 kilometers of the plant and evacuated about 115,000 people. In the following years, 220,000 more people were evacuated to reduce their risk of radiation exposure.

The effects of radiation sickness on people and other organisms vary with the type of radiation, and the level and duration of exposure. Minor exposure may lead to nausea, hair loss, vomiting, headaches, and fevers. More severe exposure may reduce an organism's life span. Within four months after the incident, 28 people had died from severe radiation exposure and thermal burns. About 6,000 cases of thyroid cancer in children have been linked to the accident. Radioactive material is hard to clean up. It continues to be dangerous as it breaks down slowly over time—sometimes over centuries. As of 2017, the Chernobyl area is still closed to the general population.

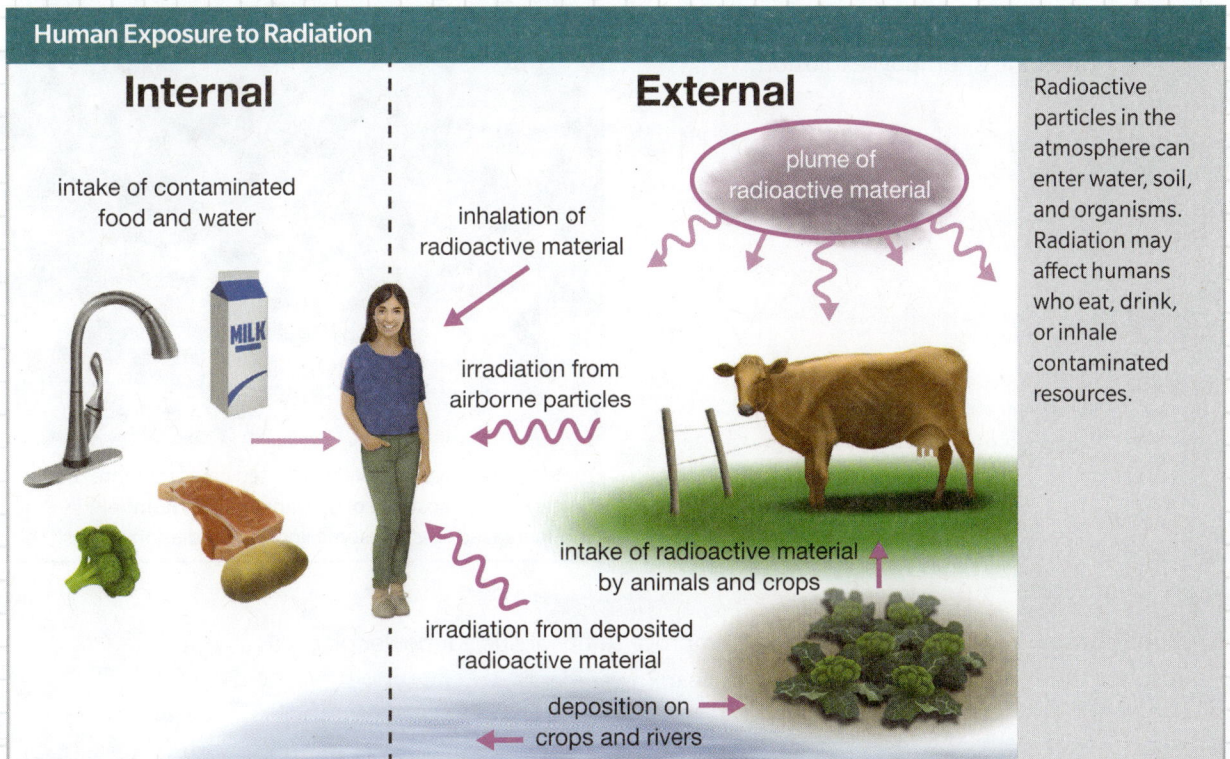

Human Exposure to Radiation

Internal

intake of contaminated food and water

External

plume of radioactive material

inhalation of radioactive material

irradiation from airborne particles

intake of radioactive material by animals and crops

irradiation from deposited radioactive material

deposition on crops and rivers

Radioactive particles in the atmosphere can enter water, soil, and organisms. Radiation may affect humans who eat, drink, or inhale contaminated resources.

Continue Your Exploration

1. Which are some of the effects of radiation poisoning? Select all that apply.

   A. headaches

   B. vomiting

   C. hair loss

   D. death/reduced life span

2. By what process did the radiation spread across such a large area?

3. Why are the effects of the Chernobyl disaster so long lasting?

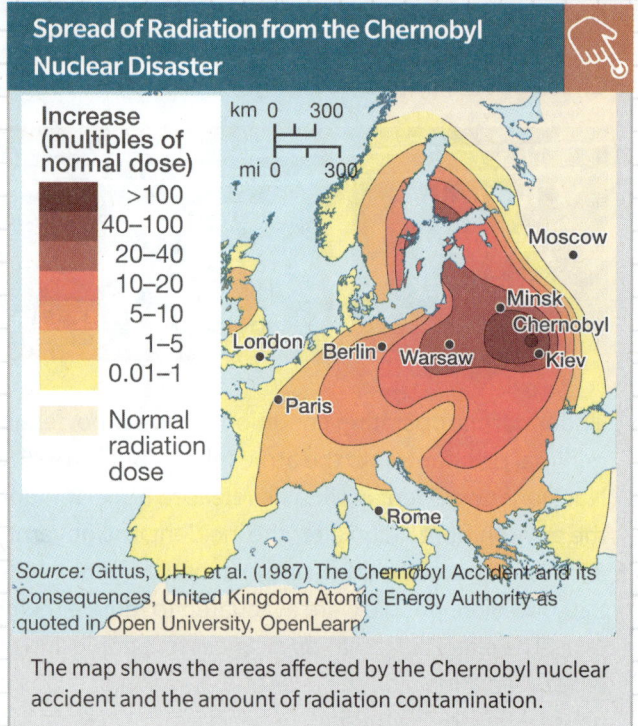

Spread of Radiation from the Chernobyl Nuclear Disaster

Increase (multiples of normal dose)
- >100
- 40–100
- 20–40
- 10–20
- 5–10
- 1–5
- 0.01–1

Normal radiation dose

km 0 — 300
mi 0 — 300

Source: Gittus, J.H., et al. (1987) The Chernobyl Accident and its Consequences, United Kingdom Atomic Energy Authority as quoted in Open University, OpenLearn

The map shows the areas affected by the Chernobyl nuclear accident and the amount of radiation contamination.

4. What are some possible reasons for the increase in the number of wildlife in the affected areas 25 years after the Chernobyl explosion?

Humans have been out of the affected areas for more than 25 years. In the absence of humans, wildlife numbers have increased, despite some lingering radiation effects.

5. **Collaborate** Research changes made to improve safety of nuclear power plants as a result of the accident at the Chernobyl Nuclear Power Plant.

Can You Explain It?

Name: _____ **Date:** _____

How can farming on land contribute to the growth of algal blooms in the ocean?

EVIDENCE NOTEBOOK

Refer to the notes in your Evidence Notebook to help you construct an explanation for how farming on land can contribute to the growth of algal blooms in the ocean.

1. State your claim. Make sure your claim fully explains how farming on land can contribute to algal blooms in the ocean.

2. Summarize the evidence you have gathered to support your claim and explain your reasoning.

Checkpoints

Answer the following questions to check your understanding of the lesson.

Use the photo to answer Question 3.

3. Which subsystems of Earth might these wind turbines affect, and how?

   A. the biosphere by endangering birds in flight

   B. the geosphere by disrupting rock and soil when installed

   C. the atmosphere by polluting the air

   D. the hydrosphere by changing ocean currents

Use the photo to answer Questions 4–5.

4. The area in the photo was originally a forested mountain. Building the structures and ski slopes probably affected the environment in a *positive / negative* way, by *fragmenting / preserving* natural habitats.

5. The snowmakers shown on the left of the image use a freshwater source to create snow for the resort. Which of the following questions should scientists investigate to determine how these snowmakers impact the environment? Select all that apply.

   A. What is the water source for the snowmakers?

   B. Where do the snowmakers get their power?

   C. Are the snowmakers ugly?

   D. Are the snowmakers a danger to birds in the area?

6. Because a change in one part of the Earth system *can / cannot* affect other parts, it may be *easy / difficult* to fully analyze the effects of a human activity. Scientists must collect and analyze data to determine whether a change in the environment is caused by human activity.

7. Creating new roads can alter the biosphere by destroying *rocks / habitats*. Human actions, such as overfishing, can negatively affect the biosphere by causing some species to become *better adapted / extinct*.

Interactive Review

Complete this section to review the main concepts of the lesson.

All living things depend on their environment to provide the things they need. A change in the environment may be caused by natural events or human actions, or both.

A. How could natural events and human actions change a coastline?

Human actions can affect all parts of the Earth system, which include the hydrosphere, atmosphere, geosphere, and biosphere.

B. How might a change to the hydrosphere affect the biosphere?

Human impacts on the environment can be positive or negative and vary in scale over time and space.

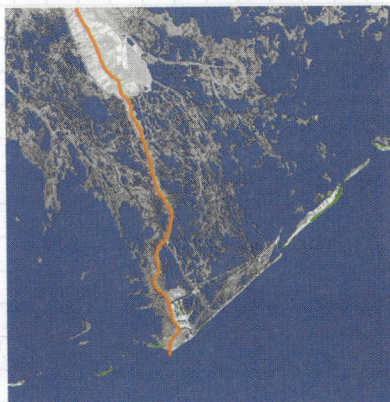

C. Give an example of a human activity that has a greater impact over a longer period of time than it does in the short term.

Human Activities Influence Climate Change

Ice is an important habitat for many seals. When the pack ice breaks up earlier than usual, these seals may starve or drown.

Explore First

Simulating Temperature and Sea Level Fill a graduated flask with 400 mL of water and stopper it. Place a light bulb a few inches from the flask, shining on the flask. Measure the volume of water in the flask every 5 minutes for 20 minutes. How does temperature affect the volume of water in the flask? How can climate change affect sea level?

Go online to view the digital version of the Hands-On Lab for this lesson and to download additional lab resources.

CAN YOU EXPLAIN IT?

What could be causing ice and permafrost to melt in Shishmaref?

The 400-year-old fishing village of Shishmaref, Alaska, used to be surrounded by thick sea ice every winter. Over the last century, less sea ice has been forming and ocean waves have eroded much of the shoreline.

The ground here used to be frozen throughout the year. This *permafrost* has started melting in recent years. The resulting loose soil erodes quickly, damaging buildings and houses in Shishmaref.

1. The amount of sea ice and permafrost have steadily decreased near Shishmaref, Alaska, over the last century. The loss of ice has allowed ocean waves to erode the land and destroy property. What might be causing this melting?

EVIDENCE NOTEBOOK As you explore this lesson, gather evidence to help explain why ice and permafrost are melting in Shishmaref.

Exploring Earth's Climate

Climate

Weather can change from day to day or even several times in one day. *Weather* describes the conditions of the atmosphere over a short period. "A hot, sunny afternoon" or a "cold, snowy day" are descriptions of weather. By contrast, *climate* describes the weather conditions in an area over a long period, such as 30 years. For example, a tropical rain forest climate is warm and rainy throughout the year.

The average climate of Earth can also be described. *Global climate* is often expressed as Earth's average surface temperature, which is currently 16 °C (61°F). Earth's average surface temperature is a combination of the sea surface temperature and the near-surface air temperature.

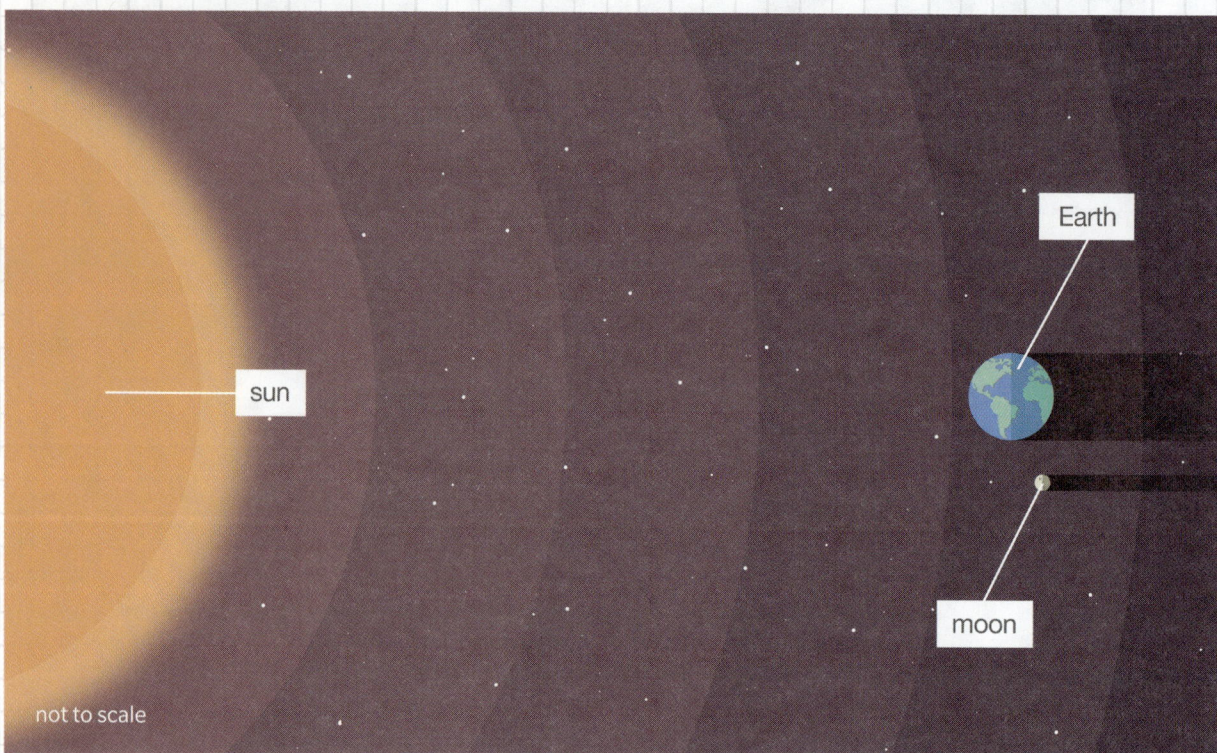

sun

Earth

moon

not to scale

Earth and the moon are about the same distance from the sun. Earth's temperatures range from about −88 °C to 58 °C (−126 °F to 136 °F). The moon's temperatures range from about −178 °C to 117 °C (−290 °F to 240 °F).

2. **Discuss** Why do you think the temperature range on Earth is so different from the temperature range on the moon? Make a list of ideas with a partner.

Earth's Climate System

Earth's climate is the result of complex interactions between the biosphere, geosphere, hydrosphere, and atmosphere. These interactions are driven by energy from the sun. Earth's atmosphere and surface absorb and reflect incoming sunlight. Darker surfaces absorb more sunlight than lighter surfaces do. For example, soil and ocean water absorb more sunlight than clouds, ice, and snow do.

The total amount of energy that enters the Earth system almost exactly equals the total amount of energy released by the Earth system into space. However, solar energy can remain in the Earth system for different periods of time. For example, oceans retain solar energy for a longer period of time than land does. This energy is transferred around the globe by ocean currents and is a major influence on weather and climate patterns.

The Greenhouse Effect

A greenhouse regulates temperatures for plants. Similarly, Earth's atmosphere regulates temperatures on Earth. The **greenhouse effect** is the warming of the surface and lower atmosphere of Earth that occurs when greenhouse gases absorb and reradiate energy. Greenhouse gases include carbon dioxide, methane, water vapor, and other gases. The processes that cause the greenhouse effect are shown in the diagram. Solar energy is absorbed and reflected by Earth's atmosphere and surface. The absorbed energy is eventually radiated back out as infrared radiation. Some infrared radiation goes back out to space, and some is absorbed again by greenhouse gases. The infrared radiation absorbed by greenhouse gases is reradiated and some is reabsorbed. As a result, energy stays in the Earth system longer than it would stay if there were no greenhouse gases.

The greenhouse effect keeps the temperature range on Earth suitable for life as we know it. If the concentration of greenhouse gases increases, more radiation is absorbed and reradiated within the Earth system. As a result, Earth's average surface temperature increases. If the concentration of greenhouse gases decreases, Earth's average surface temperature decreases.

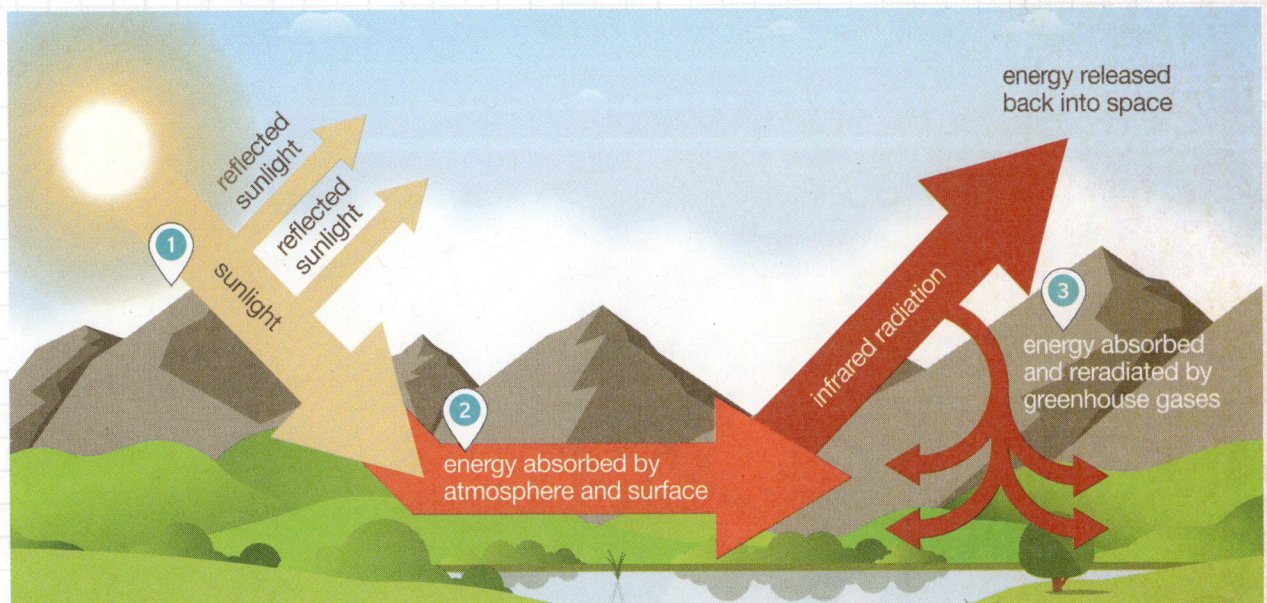

energy released back into space

reflected sunlight

reflected sunlight

sunlight

1

infrared radiation

3

energy absorbed and reradiated by greenhouse gases

2

energy absorbed by atmosphere and surface

1. Sunlight travels through space and reaches Earth. Some solar energy is reflected by the atmosphere and Earth's surface.

2. Some solar energy is absorbed by the atmosphere and surface. It is transformed into infrared radiation and is reradiated.

3. Greenhouse gases absorb some of the outgoing infrared radiation and reradiate it back into the Earth system.

Model the Greenhouse Effect

In this experiment, you will construct and use a physical model to explain how greenhouse gases affect Earth's temperature.

Procedure and Analysis

STEP 1 Pour dark soil into both bottles, so the depth of soil is about 5 cm. Why do you think dark soil is used in this model?

STEP 2 Cover the top of one bottle with clear plastic wrap. Tape the plastic wrap to the bottle, so that air cannot escape.

STEP 3 Set up a data table to record the temperature of the air in each bottle every minute for a total of 15 minutes.

STEP 4 Place the two bottles in direct sunlight. Use the temperature probes to measure and record the temperature of each bottle every minute for a total of 15 minutes. Record your data.

> **MATERIALS**
> • bottle, plastic, 2L, with the top cut off (2)
> • masking tape
> • plastic wrap, clear
> • ruler
> • soil, dark
> • temperature probe (2)

Analysis

STEP 5 The bottle *with / without* the plastic wrap models the greenhouse effect. The air in the bottle *with / without* plastic wrap became warmer than the bottle *with / without* the plastic wrap did.

STEP 6 In this model, the bottle represents the Earth system. The atmosphere is represented by the air and the plastic wrap, and the surface is represented by the soil in the bottle. Models are used to represent the real-world, however, no model is perfect. What are some differences between your model and the real-world?

STEP 7 How could you improve your model to better represent the Earth system?

STEP 8 How might you modify your model to show that changes in the concentration of greenhouse gases in the atmosphere affect temperature over time?

Language SmArts
Explain Temperature Ranges on Earth and the Moon

3. Think about the temperature ranges on Earth and the moon. Unlike Earth, the moon has almost no atmosphere. Explain why the range of temperatures on Earth is so different from that on the moon. Cite evidence to support your explanation.

_____

_____

_____

_____

_____

Identifying Global Climate Change Factors

Global Climate Change

Global climate has changed throughout Earth's history, due to both natural processes and human activities. Some climate scientists study how climate has changed in the past and compare that to how the climate is currently changing.

4. One-hundred-million-year-old fossils of tropical ferns have been found in Antarctica. Tropical ferns grow in tropical climates. Therefore, Antarctica's climate was *warm and rainy / cold and dry* 100 million years ago. Now, Antarctica's climate is *warm and rainy / cold and dry*.

Climate Data

Systematic measurement of temperatures across Earth's surface began around 1880. Today, satellites and other instruments collect detailed data. But how do we know what the climate was like thousands, or even millions, of years ago? This information comes from paleoclimate data. Look at the photos. *Paleoclimate data* contain clues about past climates and are found in rocks, fossils, tree rings, and ice cores. For example, coal commonly forms from plants that grow in swamps. Finding a 150-million-year-old layer of coal provides evidence that the area was likely a swamp 150 million years ago.

Tables, graphs, and maps are made from paleoclimate data to show trends in climate over time and in different areas on Earth. Both paleoclimate data and recent climate data are used in computer models to explore the causes and effects of climate change. Some climate models are used to predict future climate changes.

An ancient glacier passed over this rock and formed these scratches. This is evidence that the climate was very cold when the glacier existed.

Tree rings form each year as a tree grows. Wider rings form when the tree grows faster due to warmer, wetter conditions.

Fossils are the remains of living things from long ago that can give us clues about past climates. This fossil is of an animal that lived in a warm, shallow sea.

Scientists identify different gases trapped in ice that formed thousands of years ago. These data can tell scientists about the levels of greenhouse gases in Earth's past atmosphere.

Paleoclimate Temperature Reconstruction from Antarctic Ice Core Data

These data show how temperature in Antarctica changed over the last 800,000 years. Scientists use these data and others to reconstruct Earth's global climate history.

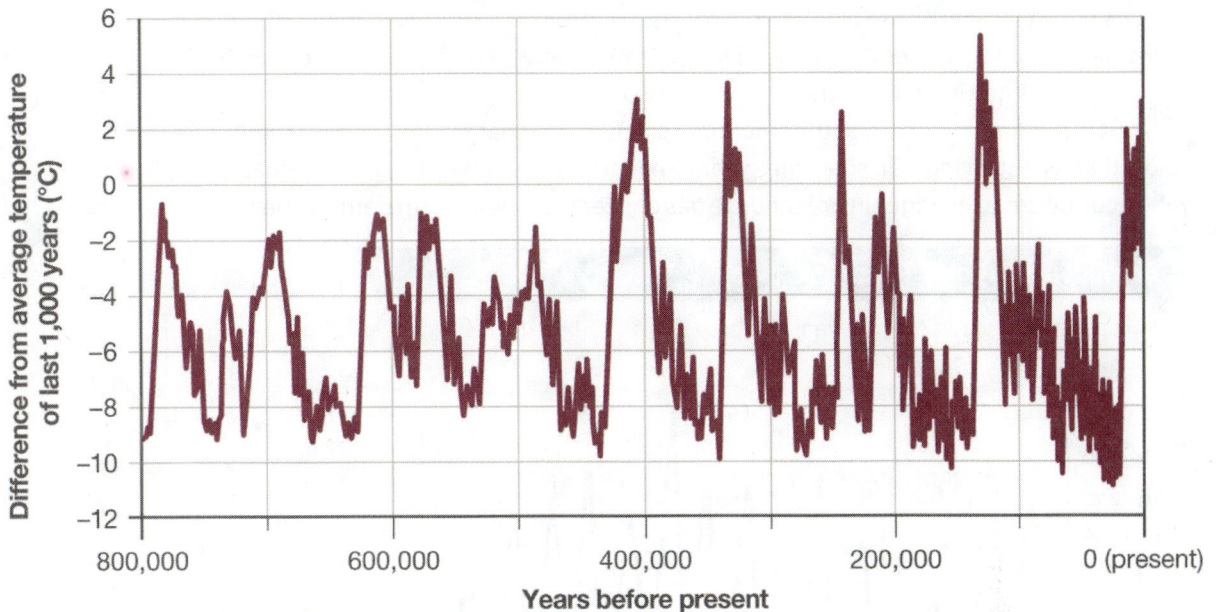

Source: National Oceanic and Atmospheric Administration, Paleoclimatology Program at NOAA's National Centers for Environmental Information

5. The graph shows that the average surface temperature in Antarctica has *changed / not changed* over the last 800,000 years. Scientists think that Earth's average temperature has followed a similar pattern. If so, Earth's average temperature is currently experiencing a *cooling / warming* trend.

Causes of Global Climate Change

The stability of the global climate can be disturbed. Changes can be caused by many different natural processes. Some changes are caused by short-term or sudden events. For example, explosive volcanic eruptions can temporarily lower Earth's average surface temperature for a period of weeks or for a few years. This temperature drop happens because explosive eruptions send ash particles into the atmosphere. The ash particles reflect a portion of incoming sunlight.

Gradual changes also affect global climate. For example, changes in the shape of Earth's orbit occur over a period of about 100,000 years. These changes affect the amount of incoming solar radiation that reaches Earth and its distribution across Earth's surface, which affect global climate.

Human activities also cause global climate change. For example, daily activities such as driving vehicles and raising livestock emit greenhouse gases. The increased concentration of greenhouse gases in the atmosphere results in an increase in global surface temperatures. How long the temperature remains higher depends on how long the greenhouse gases remain in the atmosphere. If greenhouse gas concentrations continue to increase in the atmosphere, the temperature will continue to rise. If concentrations of greenhouse gases decrease, the temperature will stop rising and will begin to decrease.

Astronomical Changes

The shape of Earth's orbit affects global climate, and so do changes in Earth's tilt on its axis. Earth's tilt varies between about 22 to 25 degrees. These changes take place on cycles of about 41,000 years. When the tilt angle is higher, summers are warmer and winters are colder. Earth also wobbles on its axis as it orbits the sun. Over about 26,000 years, this wobble changes the timing of the seasons relative to Earth's distance from the sun. As a result, the intensity of the seasons changes.

Sunspot activity relates to the amount of solar energy that reaches Earth. Studies show that recent changes in solar energy have had very little impact on global climate when compared to changes in greenhouse gas concentrations in Earth's atmosphere.

Sunspot Activity over Time

Sunspot activity varies over 11-year cycles.

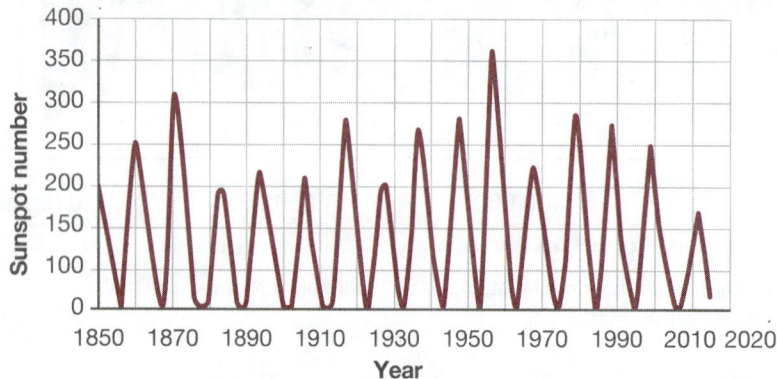

Source: NASA Solar Physics, Marshall Space Flight Center, "The Sunspot Cycle," updated March 15, 2017

Changes on Earth's Surface

Earth's surface is made up of oceans, forests, deserts, ice sheets, rock, and soil. Changes in the materials exposed at Earth's surface affect global climate. Different Earth materials absorb and reflect different amounts of solar energy, and different materials retain solar energy for different amounts of time. For example, rock absorbs more solar energy than water does, but water retains energy longer than land does. In addition, some materials absorb greenhouse gases from the atmosphere. For example, forests, soils, and oceans absorb carbon dioxide from the atmosphere.

1940

2006

6. As Grinnell Glacier in Montana melts, dark soil and rock are exposed. The soil and rock absorb more / less solar energy than the ice absorbed. The result is an increase / decrease in temperature.

Both natural processes and human activities alter Earth's surface. Human activities generally change Earth's surface more quickly than natural processes do. For example, dark pavement and rooftops in a development could replace forested areas in a matter of months or years.

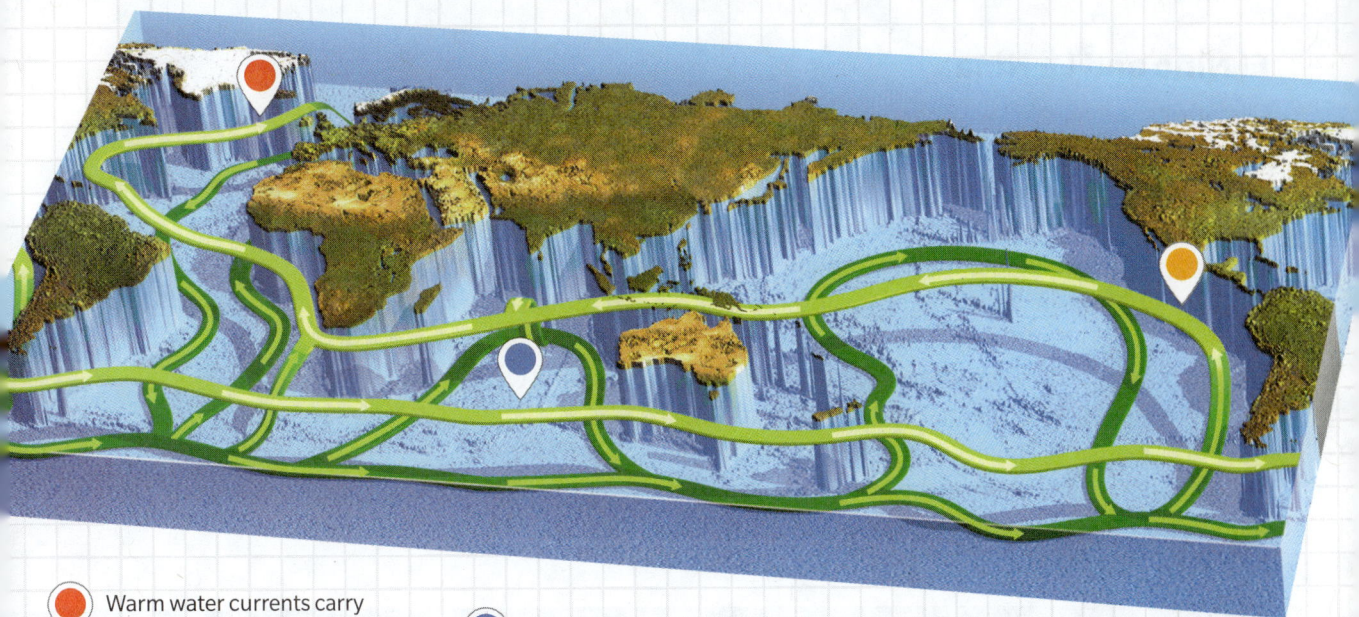

Warm water currents carry thermal energy toward the poles. Cold, deep currents carry thermal energy into the deep ocean. This exchange of energy in polar regions affects regional climates and the formation of polar sea ice and ice caps.

Some surface currents are relatively cold, such as the Antarctic Circumpolar Current. This cold water current keeps temperatures near the pole cold enough to support an ice cap all year round.

In areas where deep water comes up to the surface, climates of nearby land areas are generally cooler. The cold water also carries nutrients and gases to the surface.

Changes in Ocean Circulation

The circulation of ocean waters transports energy and matter around Earth. Warm surface currents carry thermal energy toward the poles, and cold, deep currents flow toward the equator. The movement of water and thermal energy affects both local and global temperatures. For example, the flow of the Antarctic Circumpolar Current isolates the continent of Antarctica and keeps the climate of the South Pole icy.

The Antarctic polar ice cap formed about 23 million years ago, and the Arctic ice cap formed about 3 million years ago. The formation of the ice caps happened well before the recent trend in rising global temperatures. However, since global temperatures have started to rise, the polar ice caps have started to shrink. Scientists think this is related to the amount of thermal energy being transported toward the poles. This suggests that changes in global ocean circulation and in the size or extent of ice caps are likely effects, rather than causes, of recent rises in global temperature.

7. The movement of ocean water transfers thermal energy around the globe. How might an increase in global average temperatures affect the flow of thermal energy around Earth by surface and deep currents?

El Niño and La Niña

Climate is the long-term weather pattern of a region, and some variation in local climates occur over time. Some of these variations happen in short-term or long-term cycles. Short-term climate cycles that affect weather patterns in California include El Niño and La Niña. Because these patterns are predictable cycles, they are generally referred to as ENSO, or the El Niño–Southern Oscillation.

ENSO cycles are important to California's weather and climates because these cycles affect the air and water temperatures in the Pacific Ocean. Over the course of approximately one to seven years, the trade winds strengthen and weaken, changing the flow of energy in the central and eastern Pacific Ocean.

In California, El Niño events are characterized by weaker winds, warmer temperatures, and wetter weather. During La Niña events, the opposite occurs—trade winds are stronger, which brings cooler, drier weather to California. The graph shows the timing of El Niño and La Niña events for a 30-year period.

El Niño and La Niña Events for a 30-Year Period

ENSO events are classified as weak to very strong, depending on the maximum ocean temperatures.

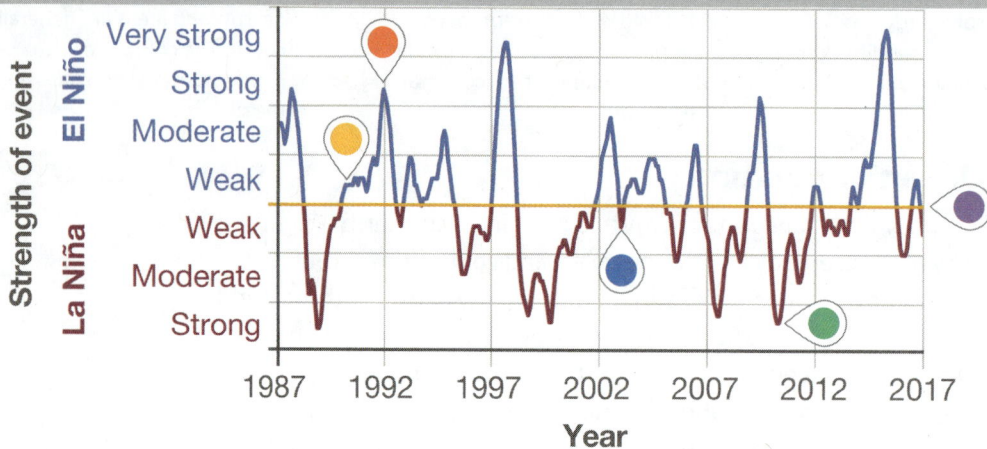

Source: NOAA Climate Prediction Center, Cold & Warm Episodes by Season, 2017

In a weak El Niño event, trade winds weaken slightly, and warmer-than-normal water moves into the central and eastern tropical Pacific Ocean.

In a strong El Niño event, trade winds weaken dramatically and may reverse to blow west-to-east across the tropical Pacific Ocean, drawing warmer-than-normal water into the central and eastern tropical Pacific Ocean.

In a weak La Niña event, trade winds strengthen, blowing strongly from east to west across the topical Pacific Ocean. Warm, moist air and warm surface waters flow to the west, cooling the central and eastern Pacific Ocean.

In a strong La Niña event, trade winds strengthen and carry warm, moist air and waters to the west. The central and eastern Pacific Ocean surface temperatures drop by more than 2 °C.

On average, trade winds blow east to west across the tropical Pacific Ocean. Warm, moist air and warm surface waters flow to the west. The central Pacific Ocean is cool. This is called the "neutral state."

8. Do the patterns in the timing and strength of ENSO events match the timing and trend of recent global temperature change?

Changes in Earth's Atmosphere

Earth's atmosphere plays a large role in global climate. For example, the concentration of greenhouse gases is currently increasing in the atmosphere. The increase in concentration of these gases leads to an increase in the average global temperature.

Greenhouse gases enter the atmosphere from natural and human sources. For example, burning fossil fuels releases greenhouse gases into the atmosphere. Humans burn fossil fuels to power vehicles and to generate electrical energy. Mining, agriculture, and cement production also release greenhouse gases into the atmosphere.

Volcanic eruptions are natural processes that release greenhouse gases into the atmosphere. However, human activities release a larger quantity of greenhouse gases than volcanoes do. Furthermore, explosive eruptions release particles into the atmosphere that reflect sunlight and result in a slight decrease in the global temperature. This effect usually lasts for a period of months or years.

In 1991, Mount Pinatubo erupted in the Philippines. This explosive eruption sent ash into the atmosphere that was spread around the world by global winds. As a result, global temperatures had dropped by about 0.5 °C one year later.

EVIDENCE NOTEBOOK

9. Which climate change factors might be contributing to phenomena occurring in Shishmaref? Think about how changes can be gradual or sudden and natural or human-caused. Record your evidence.

Do the Math

Compare Quantities of Carbon Dioxide

10. Use the word bank to complete the statements to compare the amounts of carbon dioxide released by human activities and by volcanoes.

In 2015, human activities added about 40 trillion kilograms of carbon dioxide into the atmosphere. On average, volcanoes release about 600 billion kilograms of carbon dioxide into the atmosphere every year.

40,000,000,000,000 kg / 600,000,000,000 kg is about 67.

Therefore, _____ release about 67 times more carbon dioxide than _____ do.

WORD BANK
- human activities
- volcanoes

Analyzing Recent Climate Change

The maps below show how Earth's surface temperature has changed over time. The colors on each map show how the temperature in a given time period compares to the average temperature during the years 1951 to 1981.

11. The maps show global temperature changes over time. Different locations have warmed and cooled by different amounts, but the overall global temperature has *increased / decreased / stayed the same*.

Explore Online

Global Temperature Change, 1880–2015

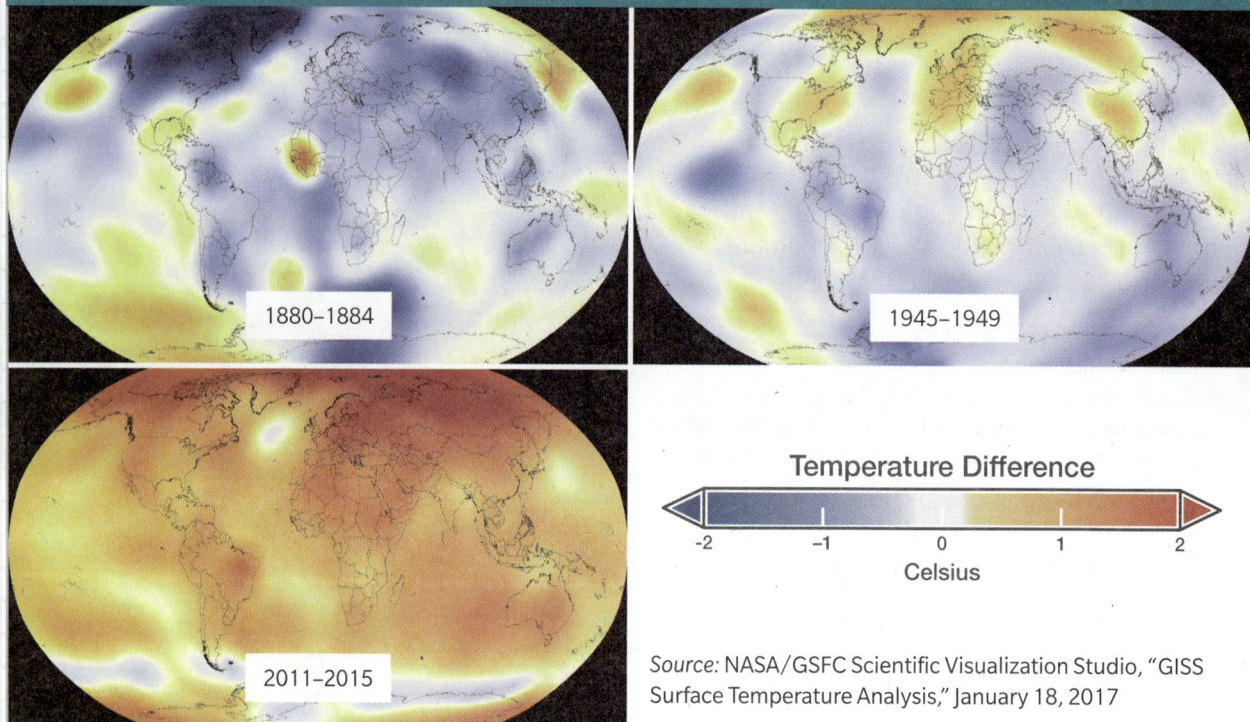

1880–1884

1945–1949

2011–2015

Temperature Difference

-2   -1   0   1   2
Celsius

Source: NASA/GSFC Scientific Visualization Studio, "GISS Surface Temperature Analysis," January 18, 2017

Recent Climate Change

The term *climate change* refers to Earth's increasing global temperature and its effects on natural systems. The recent rise in temperature has been more rapid and has lasted longer than any period of warming over the previous nine centuries. Earth's average global surface temperature has increased over the last century by about 0.6 °C.

This change might seem small, but a change in only a few degrees can completely alter an environment and the things that live there. For example, many organisms in polar regions rely on permafrost. *Permafrost* is a soil that is frozen throughout the year. But small increases in temperatures cause this soil to thaw. When the ice in permafrost melts, the soil becomes more vulnerable to erosion. It no longer supports the trees and other plants that live in the soil. It also releases a greenhouse gas called *methane* into the atmosphere. This gas absorbs solar energy and makes the atmosphere warmer, which thaws more permafrost. These processes form a feedback loop that contributes to the increasing warming of the planet.

Indicators of a Warming World

12. Look at the diagram. Write the words *increasing* or *decreasing* to tell whether the labeled features are increasing or decreasing as a result of climate change.

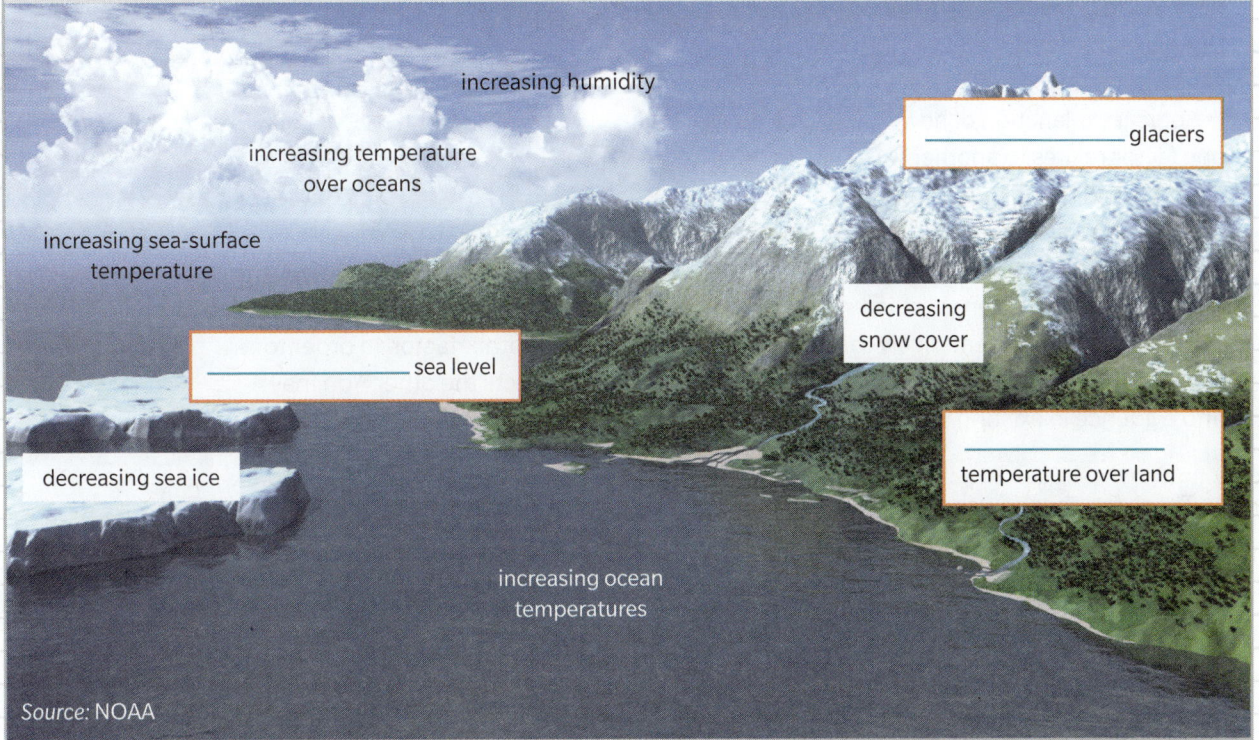

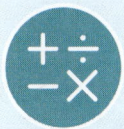

increasing humidity

increasing temperature over oceans

increasing sea-surface temperature

_____ glaciers

decreasing snow cover

_____ sea level

_____ temperature over land

decreasing sea ice

increasing ocean temperatures

Source: NOAA

Do the Math
Identify Correlation and Causation

Correlation with Causation Scientists compare trends in global temperature data to trends in other data to identify whether a correlation exists. A *correlation* means that as one variable increases, another variable increases or decreases in a similar pattern. In these graphs, there is a correlation: temperature and ice cream sales decrease in a similar pattern over the same time period. The goal of many climate scientists is to identify all of the factors that contribute to the recent rapid increase in global temperatures. To do this, more than a correlation between variables is needed.

Causation means that one variable causes the other variable to change. It is reasonable to think that more ice cream is sold when the temperatures are warmer because people want a cold treat. A scientist would gather data to test whether this relationship is true.

Ice Cream Sales and Temperature (Sept. 1–Nov. 1)

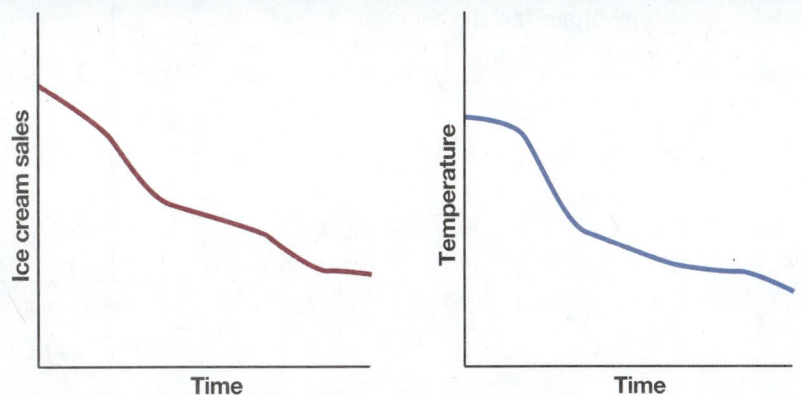

Correlation Without Causation The graphs of pet adoptions and temperature also show a correlation. They both have in the same pattern in the same time period. However, causation is unlikely as there is no logical explanation of how one factor relates to another. A correlation does not always mean that variables are related.

You can investigate whether there is causation when there is a correlation and it seems likely that one factor could affect the other factor. In order to show causation, you must be able to explain why one factor affects the other. You may find evidence in existing scientific knowledge or by conducting your own investigation.

Pet Adoptions and Temperature (May 1–July 1)

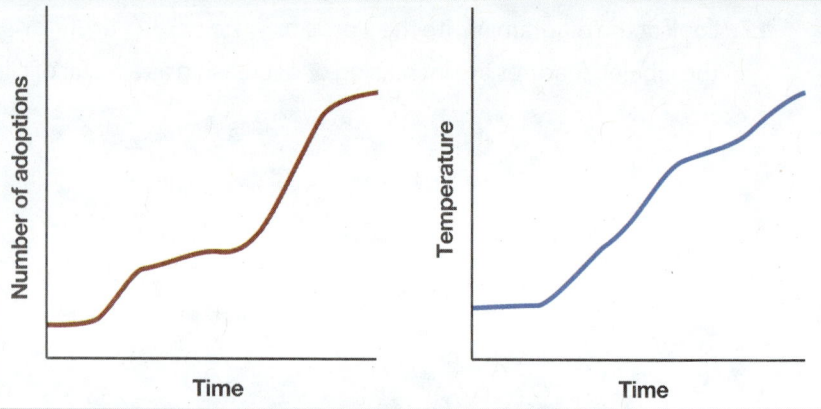

These graphs show the levels of carbon dioxide in the atmosphere and the average global temperature over time.

13. Analyze the data shown in each graph. Is there a correlation? Explain.

Carbon Dioxide Levels in Earth's Atmosphere

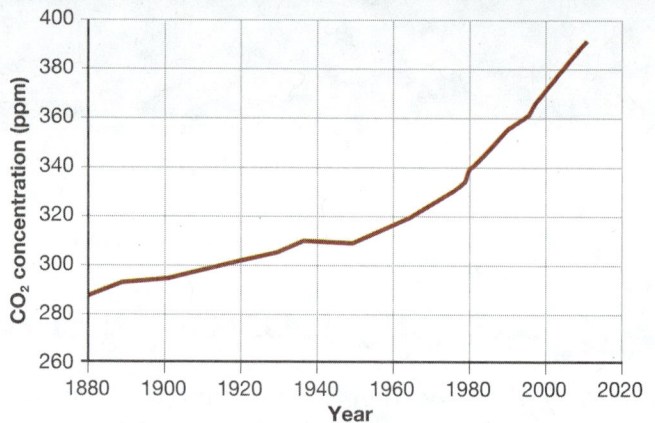

Source: NOAA/NCEI, "Global Climate Change Indicators," Global Temperature and Carbon Dioxide, 1880–2015

14. What questions would you want to investigate to confirm a causal relationship between the concentration of CO_2 in the atmosphere and the average global temperature?

Difference in Global Temperature from Average

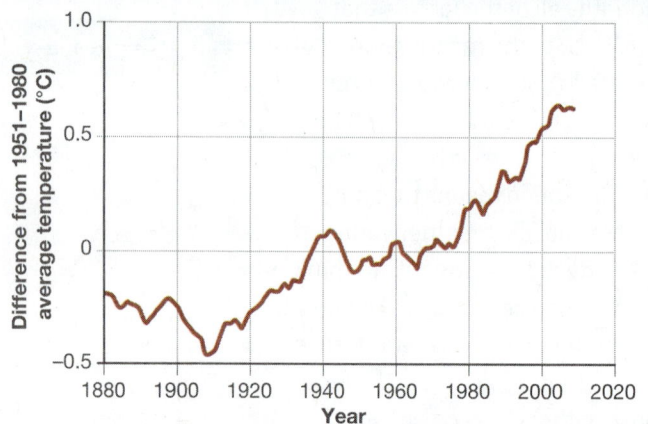

Source: NASA Earth Observatory and GISS, Global Temperature Anomalies, 1880–2010

15. **Discuss** With a partner, discuss your answers to questions on the previous page. Create a list of additional questions you could investigate about other factors that might impact climate change. Identify the evidence you would need to answer those questions.

Causes of Recent Climate Change

Most scientists agree that the primary cause of the recent increase in the average global temperature is a rapid increase in greenhouse gas concentrations. Higher greenhouse gas concentrations intensify the greenhouse effect. This is often referred to as the *enhanced greenhouse effect*.

Many human activities produce greenhouse gases. The rates at which humans perform those activities has been steadily rising over the past few centuries as the human population grows and more people use electrical energy, drive cars, fly in planes, and eat commercially farmed food. People can affect the rate and magnitude of climate change by making wise decisions about resource use. People must decide whether and how to modify their behaviors or technologies to reduce their effects on climate.

Most of the carbon dioxide that has entered the atmosphere in the last century is from the burning of fossil fuels for transportation and to generate electrical energy.

EVIDENCE NOTEBOOK

16. How might human decisions and behaviors be contributing to the erosion in Shishmaref, Alaska? Record your evidence.

Describe Cause and Effect

Positive feedback loops are one cause of rapid climate change. A *positive feedback loop* occurs when a change in one quantity changes a second quantity, and the second quantity then amplifies the changes in the first quantity.

17. As temperatures rapidly increase, sea ice is melting. Ocean water is darker / lighter than ice is. Darker surfaces absorb more / less solar energy than light surfaces do. Therefore, ocean water absorbs more / less solar energy than ice does. This warms / cools ocean water over time, which melts more sea ice.

Understanding the Effects of Climate Change

Climate change is more extreme in some places than in others. For example, the average temperatures near Earth's poles have increased at a more rapid rate than temperatures have increased elsewhere.

The environment in North America was quite different 12,000 years ago. Many animals that thrived in that cooler environment, such as woolly mammoths, no longer exist today.

18. **Draw** During the last "ice age," the average global temperature was about 11 °C (52 °F). Today, it is 16 °C (61 °F). Draw what the area shown might look like now. Describe what it might look like if temperatures were 5 °C (9 °F) warmer than they are today?

Effects of Recent Climate Change

The effects of rapidly changing climate in the past century include sea level rise and changes in habitats. Changes are more extreme in some places. For example, over the past 60 years, the average temperature in Alaska has increased by about 1.5 °C (2.7 °F). That rate of increase is almost twice as fast as that of the rest of the United States.

Changes in the Biosphere

A region's climate affects its organisms. For example, as the climate warms in Alaska, plants begin to grow earlier in the season than they did in the past. This affects any organisms that depend on those plants. As climate changes a habitat, populations of organisms must adapt, move, or die out. In some places, climate is changing so rapidly that some organisms can't adapt or move quickly enough to survive the changes.

Changes in Ice

Earth's ice contains a large volume of water and keeps that water out of the oceans. Recent climate change has caused frozen soil called *permafrost,* continental ice sheets, and glaciers to melt. The meltwater flows into the ocean, and sea level rises. As sea ice melts, animals such as polar bears and seals that rest, breed, and hunt for food on ice lose their habitats. As a result, these organisms may become extinct. Structures built on permafrost can shift and sink into the soil as it thaws.

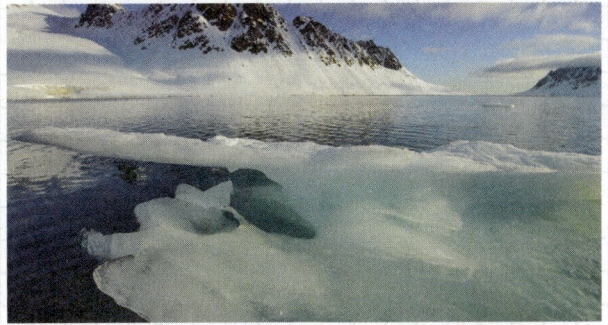

Sea ice protects the coastline. When sea ice melts, the coastline can be exposed to erosion from ocean waves.

Changes in the Oceans

Recent climate change has increased ocean temperatures, which affects ocean currents, weather patterns, and sea level. Warmer surface waters generate more powerful tropical storms, hurricanes, and typhoons. Wave action and high winds erode beaches and damage ocean and coastal ecosystems. Rising sea levels flood low-lying coastal areas with ocean water, which kills organisms. Erosion increases as water reaches farther onto shore during storms, often reaching areas that were once protected.

Thawing permafrost is no longer supported by the solid ice crystals it once contained. As a result, the soil may sink, crack, or collapse. It is also more easily eroded by waves and rain.

Earth's oceans support a diversity of organisms, many of which are important human food sources. Increasing ocean temperatures affect the kinds of organisms that live in particular locations, the migration and breeding patterns of animals, and sensitive marine ecosystems, such as coral reefs and coastal wetlands. As the amount of carbon dioxide in the atmosphere increases, the amount that dissolves in ocean water also increases. This process makes ocean water more acidic, making it difficult for many marine organisms to form hard skeletons or shells.

Increased ocean temperatures harm coral that live in reefs. In a process called *coral bleaching,* algae that the coral needs for food leave, and the coral turns white.

EVIDENCE NOTEBOOK

19. Describe how the increase in global temperatures over the last century could be related to the events in Shishmaref. Record your evidence.

Human Vulnerability to Climate Change

Most human populations live in coastal areas that will be threatened as sea level rises. Changing weather and climate patterns affect the availability of resources and the ability of humans to grow crops for food. Higher global temperatures also affect the way diseases can spread, which affects the health of individual people and of communities. Reducing human vulnerability to climate change depends on understanding climate and climate change, on available engineering and technology, and on human behaviors.

Humans and Greenhouse Gases

To reduce the effects of greenhouse gases on global climate, humans must find ways to reduce the amount of greenhouse gases that are being added to the atmosphere. To help in this effort, scientists and engineers are improving technologies that use wind and solar energy to generate electrical energy. These technologies do not produce greenhouse gases as a byproduct of generating electrical energy. Scientists and engineers are also researching ways to absorb and contain greenhouse gases.

Reducing human impacts on climate change and the impacts of climate change on humans takes a commitment from individuals, businesses, and governments. Individuals and businesses can make choices to use energy and other resources more efficiently. People can use resources in a way that limits the emission of greenhouse gases. Governments can work both domestically and internationally to develop laws and programs to reduce greenhouse gas emissions and to keep people safe from the effects of climate change.

20. Identify two ways that people may be affected by climate change. Then suggest a solution for each problem that could be performed by individuals, businesses, or governments.

Engineer It
Evaluate Solutions for Climate Change

Engineers solve problems by proposing and evaluating solutions.

Engineering Problem: Carbon dioxide in the atmosphere is causing global temperatures to rise. How can the concentration of carbon dioxide in the atmosphere be reduced?

Solution 1: Remove carbon dioxide from the atmosphere by planting trees in deforested areas.

Solution 2: Add fertilizer to ocean water to encourage the growth of green algae that will remove carbon dioxide from the atmosphere.

21. Evaluate the solutions to find strengths and weaknesses. Think about any unwanted effects. Recommend whether each solution should be considered further.

_____
_____
_____
_____
_____

Continue Your Exploration

Name: _____   Date: _____

Check out the path below or go online to choose one of the other paths shown.

Careers in Science

- **Disappearing Coral Reefs**
- **Hands-On Labs** 🖐️
- **Propose Your Own Path**

Go online to choose one of these other paths.

Geeta G. Persad, Postdoctoral Research Scientist

As a freshman in college, Dr. Geeta Persad attended a scientific conference about climate that motivated her to focus on climate science. She believes that one of climate scientists' duties is to inform the public and policymakers about climate research and why it is important.

Scientists like Dr. Persad use computer models to determine how different substances affect the atmosphere and climate. These models include factors such as the amounts of different gases, liquids, and solids in the atmosphere. Scientists change the factors in the climate model to help them understand how each factor may affect climate. Scientists use these models to make predictions about how climate may change in the future.

Dr. Persad's work with climate models has focused on the effects of tiny particles called *aerosols*. These particles affect how clouds form. Dr. Persad has applied what she has learned about aerosols and clouds to computer models so that clouds can be modeled realistically. These data help the computer climate models more accurately recreate the conditions that cause clouds to form and dissipate. These models help scientists understand how clouds, weather, and climate behave and how climate may change in the future.

Dr. Geeta Persad visited the Franz Josef Glacier in New Zealand, which is shrinking as a result of recent climate change.

Continue Your Exploration

1. How does Dr. Persad's work on clouds contribute to our understanding of climate and climate change?

2. Scientists have developed a number of different global climate models. Why do climate scientists use computer models to study changes in climate?

3. A scientist is developing a computer model to study the effects of a certain substance in the atmosphere on climate. Which factors might the scientist need to adjust in the model? Select all that apply.

   A. changes in the sun's output

   B. amount of the substance in the atmosphere

   C. Earth's distance from the sun

   D. whether the substance causes a positive or negative feedback

   E. the source of the substance

4. **Collaborate** With a partner, write at least three questions that you would like to ask Dr. Persad about evidence related to factors that affect climate change.

Can You Explain It?

Name: _____   Date: _____

What could be causing ice and permafrost to melt in Shishmaref?

📋 **EVIDENCE NOTEBOOK**
Refer to the notes in your Evidence Notebook to help you explain why ice and permafrost are melting in Shishmaref.

1. State your claim. Make sure your claim fully explains why sea ice and permafrost are melting and leading to destructive erosion in Shishmaref.

2. Summarize the evidence you have gathered to support your claim and explain your reasoning.

Checkpoints

Answer the following questions to check your understanding of the lesson.

Use the graph to answer Questions 3–5.

3. Which statement is supported by the data in the graph?

   A. The amount of carbon dioxide in the atmosphere does not change.

   B. Melting sea ice is caused by rising levels of carbon dioxide in the atmosphere.

   C. Adding more carbon dioxide to the atmosphere causes Earth's climate to warm.

   D. Carbon dioxide concentration in the atmosphere is higher now than at any other time in the last 400,000 years.

Atmospheric Carbon Dioxide Concentration Over Time

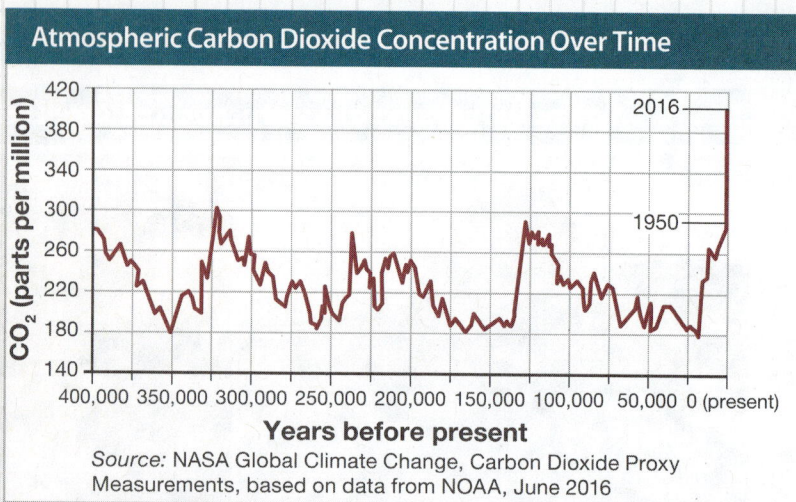

Source: NASA Global Climate Change, Carbon Dioxide Proxy Measurements, based on data from NOAA, June 2016

4. Based on the concentration of carbon dioxide in the atmosphere, Earth's global temperature likely was higher / lower 125,000 years ago than it was 25,000 years ago.

5. The rate at which carbon dioxide is being added to the atmosphere now is higher / lower than ever before.

6. Complete the table by matching the factors provided in the word bank with the effect they have on global temperature.

WORD BANK
- volcanic eruption
- less incoming solar radiation
- more greenhouse gases
- shrinking polar ice caps

Makes Earth Warmer	Makes Earth Cooler

7. When greenhouse gas concentrations in the atmosphere are high, less / more energy is absorbed by the atmosphere. As a result, thermal energy stays in the Earth system for a longer / shorter time, and Earth's average surface temperature rises / drops.

8. Reducing human vulnerability to the effects of climate change requires which of the following? Choose all that apply.

   A. understanding of climate science

   B. improving engineering capabilities

   C. understanding of human behavior

   D. applying knowledge to make wise decisions

Interactive Review

Complete this section to review the main concepts of the lesson.

Climate is driven by energy from the sun and interactions of the Earth system. Greenhouse gases in the atmosphere absorb energy from the sun.

A. How is the temperature range on Earth affected by Earth's atmosphere?

Both natural processes and human activities affect climate. Earth's climate can be changed by sudden events or by gradual changes over time.

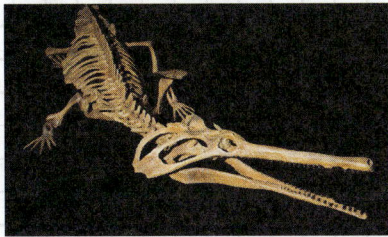

B. Describe how one natural process and one human activity affect climate or cause climate change.

Earth's average global temperature has increased over the last century. The main cause of this increase is carbon dioxide that is released when humans burn fossil fuels as an energy source.

C. How do correlation and causation relate to understanding how natural processes and human activities affect climate or cause climate change?

Minimizing the effects of climate change requires reducing greenhouse gas emissions from human activities and understanding effects of climate change on Earth systems.

D. Give an example of how humans burning fossil fuels affects each of Earth's major systems (atmosphere, biosphere, geosphere, hydrosphere).

Climate Change Affects the Survival of Organisms

When ocean temperatures rise, sea stars, like these ochre sea stars, face a greater risk of contracting diseases. These diseases may cause sea star populations to decline.

Explore First

Modeling Elephant Ears African elephants live on the hot, open savanna. Asian elephants live in cooler, shady jungles. The ears of African elephants are three times larger than the ears of Asian elephants. Model the ears of the two elephants. How does ear size relate to the elephant's environment? How could climate change affect the ears of elephants over many generations?

CAN YOU EXPLAIN IT?

How could climate change affect the survival of koalas?

Koalas are found naturally only in Australia. They have unique adaptations to the cool, moist, eucalyptus forests on that continent. Koalas have thick fur and strong claws, and they eat only eucalyptus tree leaves. In recent years, more and more wild koalas are dying.

1. Koalas spend most of their lives in the branches of eucalyptus trees in cool, coastal and low-elevation forests. What physical and behavioral traits are apparent in the photo and caption that connect the koala to its environment?

2. How do you think climate change might affect the conditions in the koala's environment?

EVIDENCE NOTEBOOK As you explore this lesson, gather evidence to help you explain how climate change may affect the survival of koalas.

Relating the Adaptations of Organisms to their Environments

Living things depend on resources and services that ecosystems provide. An **ecosystem** is all of the living organisms and their nonliving environment in a specific area. The environment shown in the illustration is the chaparral ecosystem in southern California. Organisms interact with each other and with their environment on different levels. A *species* is a group of organisms that are closely related and can mate to produce fertile offspring. A *population* is all of the individuals of a given species in an area. All of the different species that live in an ecosystem make up a *community*.

3. Write the answer that describes each level of the ecosystem in the correct box.

WORD LIST
- community
- ~~ecosystem~~
- individual
- population

ecosystem

Healthy Ecosystems and Habitats

A *habitat* is the place where an organism lives. The quality of a habitat depends on the local environmental conditions. Local conditions include the availability of food, light, space, and water; air or water temperature; and water or soil acidity. For example, in the chaparral ecosystem, the air and soil are dry, and there is a lot of open space. Healthy ecosystems provide natural habitats and other important resources and services that organisms, including humans, depend on. These services include producing food, cleaning air and water, decomposing wastes, and regulating climate and disease.

4. An ecosystem that cannot perform essential services is a(n) healthy / unhealthy ecosystem. Such an ecosystem would be able to support large / small populations of organisms.

Biodiversity

Biodiversity describes the number, type, and variety of all living organisms in a particular area. It includes the genetic and physical variety of individuals within populations, of populations within species, and of species within communities. It also describes the diversity of ecosystems on Earth.

Biodiversity forms the foundation of the ecosystem services that are critically important to human well-being. A higher level of biodiversity generally indicates a stronger, more robust ecosystem that is less likely to be disrupted or destroyed. So, biodiversity can be a measurement of the health of an ecosystem. Wolves are the top predators in the ecosystem of Yellowstone National Park. They affect a number of food webs in the park, including those that include bears, elk, ravens, and even trees and berry-producing shrubs. Because of hunting, there were no wolves in the park area in the early 1900s. The wolves were reintroduced in 1995. By studying the park's ecosystems with and without wolves, scientists have learned about how different species and communities affect the health of the ecosystem.

The reintroduction of gray wolves to Yellowstone National Park has affected the park's biodiversity.

5. Higher biodiversity generally means that an ecosystem is _more / less_ stable because greater variability in the number of species and in the individuals of each species means the ecosystem is _more / less_ susceptible to environmental changes.

6. Based on the data in the table, how do wolves affect the biodiversity and stability of the ecosystems of Yellowstone National Park?

   A. Wolves don't change the stability of the park ecosystem because mule deer populations didn't change after the wolves were reintroduced.

   B. Wolves make the park ecosystem more stable because biodiversity increased after the wolves were reintroduced.

   C. Wolves make the park ecosystem less stable because after they were reintroduced, populations of elk and coyotes went down.

   D. Wolves make the park ecosystem less stable because after their reintroduction, populations of foxes, bears, beavers, and trees went up.

Estimated Populations of Organisms in Parts of Yellowstone National Park		
Organism	Population before wolf reintroduction	Population after wolf reintroduction
Wolves	0	104
Coyotes	1,560	800
Foxes	175	300
Grizzly bears	150	690
Elk	17,000	7,000
Mule deer	2,100	2,200
Beaver colonies	1	12
Willow-dependent bird species	19	33
Cottonwood trees (>5 cm diameter)	<10	175
Berry-producing shrubs (in one research area)	<5	50

Sources: U.S. National Park Service; Ripple et al., Trophic cascades in Yellowstone, Biological Conservation, 2011; Baril, Lisa. Change in Deciduous Woody Vegetation...in Yellowstone National Park's Northern Range, 2017; Newsome, T.M. and Ripple, W.J., A continental scale trophic cascade from wolves through coyotes to foxes, Journal of Animal Ecology, 2014; Jackson, S.G., Relationships among Birds, Willows, and Native Ungulates in and around Yellowstone National Park, 1992

Adaptations to the Environment

Adaptations help organisms survive and reproduce in specific environmental conditions, such as a dry desert or a shallow ocean. Plant adaptations may include flower colors and odors, hard shells on seeds, and timing of budding and blooming. Physical adaptations of animals include feather or fur color and body size or shape. Animal behaviors include nest or den building, foraging and hunting for food, avoiding predators, mating displays or combat, seasonal behaviors like migration and hibernation, and vocalizations.

Adaptations to the California Chaparral Ecosystem

The California chaparral ecosystem is characterized by shrubs, grasses, trees, and animals that are adapted to relatively hot and dry conditions and occasional wildfires.

Coyote brush has thick bark and waxy leaves and can resprout above the ground, which help it to survive wildfires.

The cholla cactus stores water in its fleshy lobes. Other chaparral plants have long, water-seeking roots.

The tarantula hawk hunts tarantulas to provide food and water for its young.

A jackrabbit's large ears release heat to help keep the animal cool.

The cactus wren nests among the cactus spines for protection.

7. How might eucalyptus trees and koalas be adapted to the local environmental conditions where they live? Record your evidence.

Do the Math

Explore a Kelp Forest

Kelp is seaweed, a plant that thrives where sunlight enters cool, clear water. Many organisms feed on kelp. Kelp also provides shelter for many forms of sea life. Forests of kelp are among the most productive ecosystems on Earth.

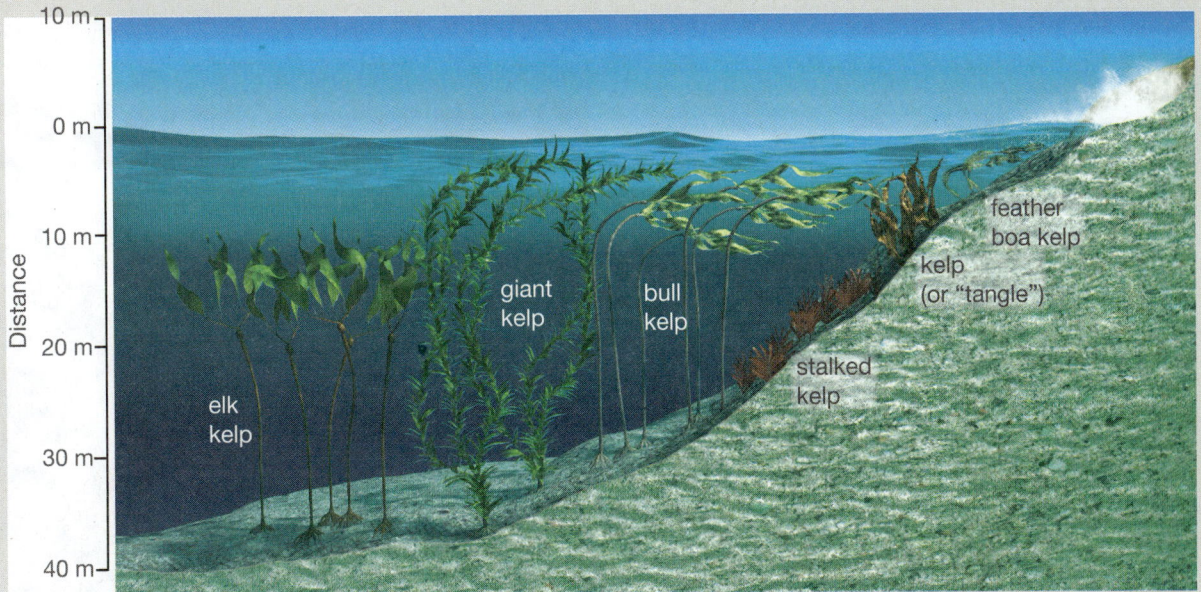

8. How are the different species of kelp adapted to the depths at which each lives?

_____

_____

_____

_____

_____

9. In the space provided, create a number line to plot sea level and the depths at which the different species of kelp live, based on where their roots are.

Analyzing How Organisms Respond to Climate Change

Climate Change Affects the Environment

Climate change disrupts the stability of ecosystems. Climate change affects the nonliving components of ecosystems by changing the temperature of air, water, and soil. Over the past 100 years, average global temperature has risen by 0.6 °C. This increase is primarily a result of the burning of fossil fuels and the raising of livestock for human food. Recent climate change is raising local and regional air, water, and soil temperatures; making water more acidic; and affecting weather patterns.

10. Circle the areas on the maps where the glaciers have changed. Have the lengths of the glaciers shown increased or decreased?

11. Ice and snow reflect more sunlight than dark rock or soil do. How could the melting of glaciers cause changes in the transfer of energy between Earth's surface and atmosphere?

12. How could the changes in the glaciers affect the local environmental conditions to which organisms are adapted?

Shrinking Glaciers in New Zealand

Between 1990 and 2017, the Mueller Glacier, Hooker Glacier, and Tasman Glacier in New Zealand shrank significantly due to rising global temperatures.

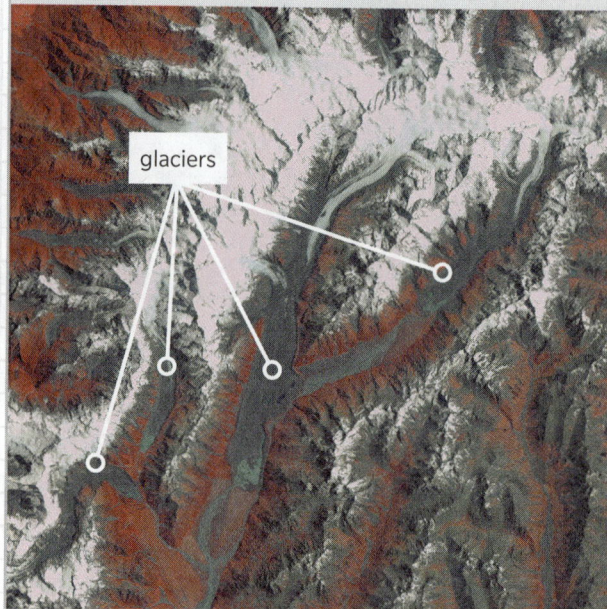

glaciers

Changes to Land Ecosystems

Rising air temperatures affect weather patterns that may lead to heat waves, droughts, and increased wildfire risks. Wildfires can destroy huge areas of habitat and reduce the ability of ecosystems to provide food and clean air and water.

Warming air temperatures also affect the timing of seasonal budding and blooming and of growing seasons. Warmer, drier soil affects the rate of decomposition of organic materials and is also more susceptible to soil erosion. These conditions affect how well plants can grow. Changes in the timing of seasons also affect the migration and reproductive behaviors of animals.

Smoke from a nearby wildfire hangs over the forest in Yosemite National Park.

EVIDENCE NOTEBOOK

13. How could climate change affect the environment in which koalas live? How could koalas respond to that change? Record your evidence.

Changes to Aquatic Ecosystems

As global temperatures rise, ocean and lake water temperatures also rise. Warming waters expand, contributing to sea level rise, which displaces organisms that rely on certain water depths or conditions. Warming oceans also affect weather patterns, which affect regional climates on land. Ocean temperatures are related to severe weather systems, such as hurricanes, and to cyclic climate patterns like El Niño and La Niña. Changes in ocean circulation affect upwelling and cycling of nutrients in the oceans, which affects how and when aquatic organisms get food, migrate, grow, and reproduce.

As carbon dioxide concentration in the atmosphere rises, ocean and lake water absorbs more carbon dioxide from the atmosphere. As a result, the water becomes more acidic. Aquatic organisms are surrounded by the acidic water, which may affect how the organisms grow, move, protect themselves, and reproduce.

14. Climate change *increases / decreases* the acidity of ocean, lake, and river water. Increased acidity *hardens / dissolves* the shells of some marine creatures, *increasing / decreasing* their likelihood of survival or reproduction.

Acidic water dissolves the calcium carbonate shells of some animals. The top photo shows a shell in normal water conditions. The bottom photo shows a shell in acidic water.

Hands-On Lab
Map Monarch Migration

You will map the migration of monarch butterflies between summer breeding and feeding grounds and wintering locations. You will plot data from two different years to model the effects of climate change on the timing of the butterfly migration.

MATERIALS
• colored pencils

Procedure

STEP 1 Color in the key below the maps. Use the same colors for each time interval when plotting the data on both maps.

STEP 2 Look at the table titled "Year 1 Monarch Sightings." Use the location data provided to plot the location for each sighting onto the map for Year 1.

STEP 3 Look at the table titled "Year 2 Monarch Sightings." Use the location data provided to plot the location for each sighting onto the map for Year 2.

Analysis

STEP 4 Year 1 represents an average year, and Year 2 represents a cooler and drier than average year. How did the timing and distance of the migration compare between the two years?

Year 1 Monarch Sightings		
Date	Latitude	Longitude
8/3	38.7	−119.8
8/15	40.5	−122.3
8/16	39.6	−121.8
9/6	36.1	−117.9
9/11	38.6	−121.8
9/12	37.5	−120.7
9/21	37.5	−120.7
9/29	35.4	−120.9
9/30	34.1	−118.8
10/3	34.3	−118.2
10/10	34.1	−117
10/14	34	−117.2
10/18	33.5	−117.7
10/27	33.7	−118
10/29	33.9	−118
11/3	34	−117.2
11/5	33.6	−117.6
12/8	33.9	−118

Year 2 Monarch Sightings		
Date	Latitude	Longitude
8/17	37.8	−122.4
8/18	38.4	−121.8
8/19	38.2	−122.8
8/31	35.1	−120.4
9/1	34.1	−118.1
9/7	34	−117.2
9/16	34	−117.2
9/22	33.7	−117.4
9/25	34.1	−118.1
10/2	33.8	−118.3
10/8	33.7	−118
10/14	33.4	−117.3
10/20	32.7	−117.2
10/24	32.9	−117.2
10/27	32.7	−117.9
11/5	32.8	−116.9
11/10	32.9	−117.2
11/28	32.6	−117.1

Year 1	Year 2
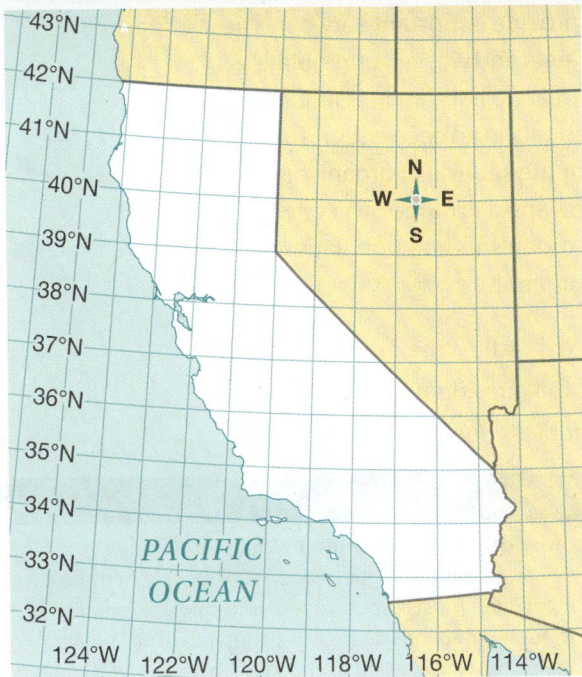	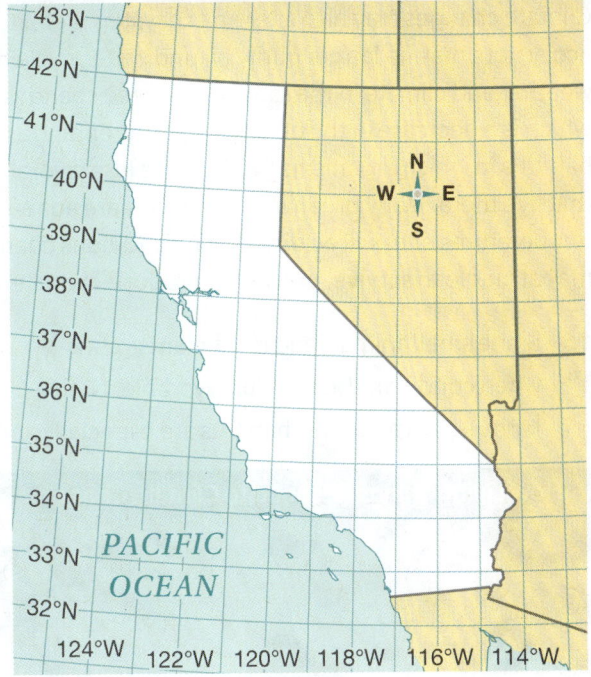

Key

	Before August 30		September 16–September 30		October 16–October 31
	August 30–September 15		October 1–October 15		After October 31

STEP 5 Which year (Year 1 or Year 2) represents what climates in California will be like if the current trend in climate change continues?

STEP 6 Based on this model, how might monarch butterfly populations respond to recent global climate change?

Response, Adaptation, and Extinction

Climate changes may also alter an ecosystem's ability to provide important services. The ecosystem may no longer purify air and water, cycle nutrients and wastes, or regulate weather and climate in the same way. These changes can lead to habitat degradation, which is a decrease in the quality, quantity, or range of habitats in an ecosystem. The habitats in which organisms live become less favorable for the survival of organisms that live there. Many organisms or species are adapted to a specific range of air or water temperatures or of soil acidity. When conditions change, organisms and populations may struggle to survive, grow, or reproduce in that environment.

15. Some small animals and most plants *can / cannot* adjust their range quickly when conditions become unfavorable. Native plants that are adapted to extremely *broad / specific* habitats are especially at risk for loss due to climate change.

How Living Things Respond to Climate Change

Individuals Can Respond to Change Some environmental changes happen very quickly. In these cases, individuals must respond in order to survive. Their ability to survive depends on how well the organisms' bodies or behaviors can respond to changes. To find more favorable habitats, organisms may move, or change ranges, into other locations. They may vary the timing or distances of migrations in order to reach better feeding, breeding, or birthing areas. The quino checkerspot butterfly, a native of California, has shifted its range to higher elevations and changed the host plant on which it lays its eggs.

Populations Can Change over Time Changes to environmental conditions can make certain physical or behavioral traits in a population more or less beneficial. Individuals that have beneficial traits then survive and reproduce to pass those traits on to future generations. The frequency of these traits increases in the population over time, and the population is said to be adapted to its new environment. For example, wild thyme populations in France have been slowly changing so that more of the population produces pungent oils that deter animals who would eat the plants. However, the genes that allow the plants to protect themselves from consumers also make the wild thyme less adapted to cold environments.

Species Survive, Evolve, or Become Extinct As populations adapt, they may survive as a species or may evolve into new species that are better adapted to new local conditions. However, if all populations of a species are unable to reproduce or adapt to new environmental conditions, the species may become extinct. Many large mammals, such as the one-horned rhino, that have long life spans and little genetic variability are at risk of becoming extinct due to climate change. Many uniquely adapted organisms are also at risk of extinction.

Climate Change and Biodiversity

Hawaiian honeycreeper birds are unique to the Hawaiian islands. Many honeycreepers are uniquely adapted to eat specific foods. These rare birds are extremely susceptible to avian malaria. This disease is carried and transmitted by mosquitoes when they bite the birds to consume blood. After the introduction of mosquitoes to the Hawaiian Islands in the 1800s, honeycreeper populations declined. The birds survived only at higher elevations where the temperature was too cool for most mosquitoes to survive. As global temperatures rise, the higher elevations become warmer, and mosquitoes can survive there. But the birds cannot move higher up the mountains because the food sources they rely on cannot easily move. The mosquitoes carry deadly diseases to higher elevations as they invade the last refuges for the birds. Today, native Hawaiian birds face one of the highest rates of extinction in the world. Of 41 honeycreeper species and subspecies known since historic times, 17 are probably extinct, 14 are endangered, and only 3 are thriving.

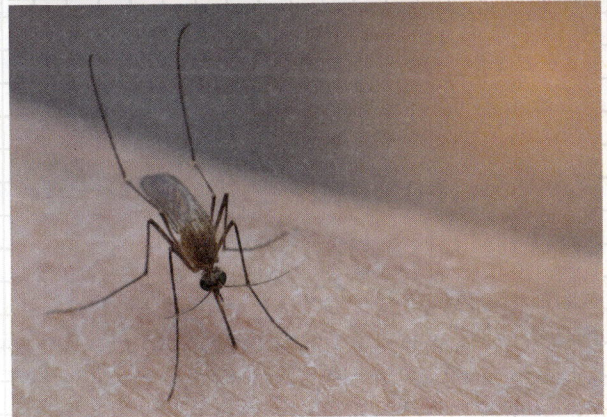

Climate change is expanding the range of mosquitoes, which impacts the scarlet Hawaiian honeycreeper, also known as the i'iwi (ee•EE•vee) in Hawaii.

Do the Math
Evaluate Extinction Probability

The more individuals that are in a population, the more genetically diverse the population is. More diverse populations are more likely to be able to adapt over generations and survive. In a large population, traits that favor the species' survival, such as resistance to disease, could become more common in the population over time. In 2013, the scarlet honeycreeper population was estimated at just over 600,000 birds for all of the islands of Hawaii. However, on some islands, the populations have dropped significantly. On Oahu, for example, scientists estimate that fewer than 50 of the birds remain.

16. Based on the population size and changes to their ecosystems, describe the probability that the scarlet honeycreepers will become extinct in the Hawaiian islands. Does the probability of extinction change if you are looking only at the birds on Oahu? Use scientific reasoning to support your claim.

_____

_____

_____

_____

Monitoring the Effects of Climate Change on Organisms

People and societies can only remain healthy and productive if the surrounding natural ecosystems are healthy and stable. As populations adapt or become extinct, biodiversity changes. In many cases biodiversity decreases, which makes the entire system less able to adapt to future or ongoing changes. Therefore, it is important to monitor and address changes in ecosystems caused by climate change.

17. Coastal wetlands in California are important ecosystems because they stabilize shorelines and *cause / prevent* flooding. These habitats are likely to become *more / less* stable if the populations that live in them move or become extinct in response to climate change.

How Scientists Model Climate Change and Its Effects

Scientists use computer programs to help them model the effects of climate change on different ecosystems and organisms. Scientists use information about the interactions between the atmosphere, land surface, oceans, and biosphere to create computer models that forecast future weather and climate patterns across the globe. Current computer models of climate change project dramatic and rapid environmental changes that are likely to have negative effects on many organisms.

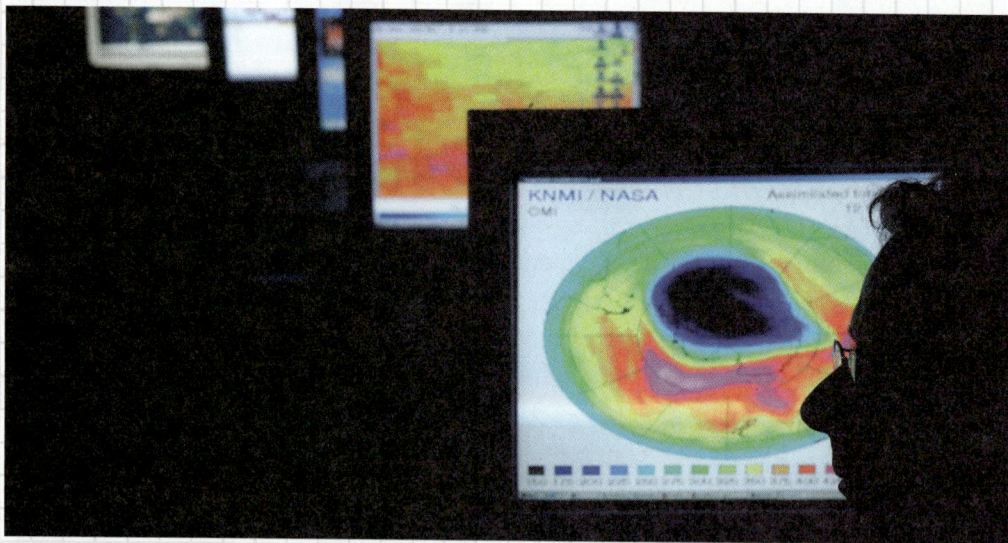

Scientists use several types of computer programs to model the effects of human activity on Earth's atmosphere and oceans. They use computers to analyze data and to predict how changes to Earth's systems will affect humans and other living things.

18. What factors might a computer model need to include for scientists to model the effects of climate change on kelp forest communities off the coast of California?

How Scientists Gather Data about Organisms

Understanding an organism's response to climate change requires *monitoring*. Monitoring involves developing and using technologies and processes to make observations or record data about ecosystem health and biodiversity. Scientists track the responses of individuals, populations, and communities to various nonliving factors and to other organisms in the ecosystem. In some cases, scientists can set up laboratory experiments to investigate ecological changes. But most of the time, scientists have to monitor organisms in their natural environment. How they monitor organisms depends on the particular organism the scientist is studying and the environment in which the organism lives.

Case Study: Using Monitoring Technologies to Study Bats

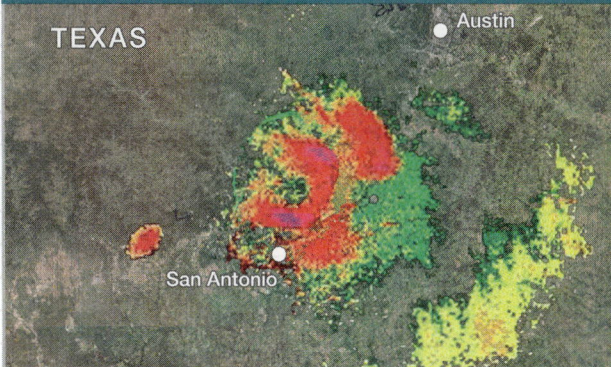

Large numbers of flying bats may form a crescent shape, shown in pink, on weather radar. Scientists use these data to study bat feeding and migrating behaviors.

Scientists can tag bats with radio or satellite transmitters, which send signals that track and record the travel and migration patterns of the bats over time.

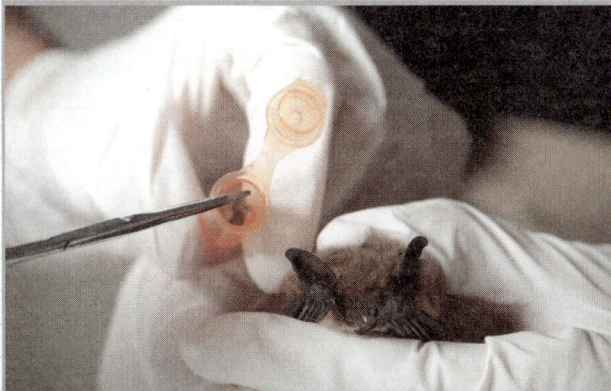

Scientists catch bats to measure their size and weight and to collect hair and blood samples to test the bats' DNA. DNA in bat feces can be tested to find out what the animal has been eating.

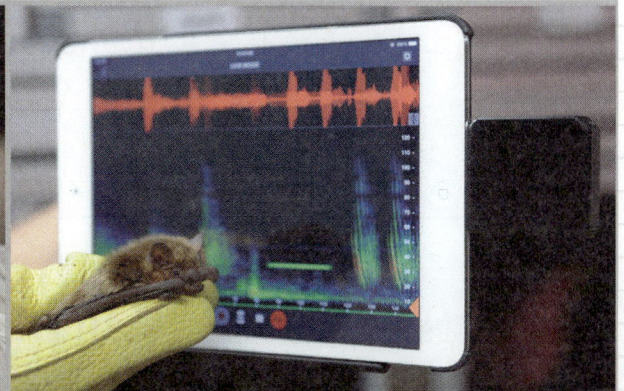

Bats can be tracked by using sound equipment. By recording and analyzing the sounds bats make, scientists can determine whether the bat is traveling, feeding, or mating.

19. How does tracking movements of bats help scientists understand the effects of climate change on bats? Select all that apply.

   A. Tracking movements of bats shows whether bats change their range based on where food is available.

   B. Tracking movements of bat colonies helps explain how bats fly.

   C. Tracking movements of individual bats explains how bats use sound to navigate and communicate.

   D. Tracking movements of bats helps explain why bats may change the timing of their migrations in different years.

Language SmArts | Evaluate Text The following passage was written by a student who was researching the use of satellites and other remote sensing equipment to study biodiversity.

Explore Online

Science and Remote Sensing

1 Remote sensing uses special equipment that can capture images of Earth from high in the atmosphere or from space. 2 Remote sensing equipment gathers data by recording visible and invisible light and sound and radio waves. 3 When the satellite data are analyzed, they can show great detail, such as how much coral or sand is in an area or how many different sizes or types of trees are in a section of forest. 4 Remote sensing using satellites and airplanes is better than gathering data by visiting different locations. 5 Remote sensing allows scientists to observe large areas of Earth that would not be easily observed by a scientist on the ground. 6 As more technology is developed, remote sensing equipment will probably provide more detailed data for scientists to analyze. 7 Because it is so useful, most scientists want to include remote sensing when they plan investigations of biodiversity.

This satellite image shows the extent of the mangrove forest (in black) on the coastlines of Bangladesh and India.

20. Determine whether each numbered sentence is a fact, a reasoned judgment, an opinion, or speculation. Write the number for each sentence in the correct column.

Fact	Reasoned Judgment	Opinion	Speculation

Engineer It
Identify Criteria and Constraints

The Coachella Valley fringe-toed lizard is adapted to life in a dry, hot, sandy environment. The lizards have fringe-like scales on their hind feet that provide traction and enable them to move quickly across sand. They also have adaptations to allow them to burrow quickly into sand.

21. Think about the fringe-toed lizard's lifestyle and environment. What criteria and constraints would apply to a technology that could be used to monitor the fringe-toed lizard's response to climate change?

_____

_____

_____

_____

Continue Your Exploration

Name: _____   Date: _____

Check out the path below or go online to choose one of the other paths shown.

People in Science

- **Superblooms**
- **Hands-On Labs** ✋
- **Propose Your Own Path**

Go online to choose one of these other paths.

Shayle Matsuda, Marine Biologist

Shayle Matsuda is a marine biologist who identifies as biracial and as a member of the LGBTQ+ community. Matsuda's love of the natural world led him to pursue a double major in both the humanities and the sciences. After college, he spent many years working with young people before learning to SCUBA dive. While diving, Matsuda witnessed first-hand the biodiversity and beauty of coral reefs alongside the undeniable impact humans are having on these fragile marine environments. Matsuda became dedicated to studying the ocean and marine biology. He returned to school to earn his Master's degree in ecology, evolution, and conservation biology. He is currently pursuing his PhD in marine biology.

As part of his work at the University of Hawaii Manoa and the Hawaii Institute of Marine Biology, Matsuda studies how corals respond to rising sea-surface temperatures. In addition to this work, he is investigating how different symbionts, both algae and bacteria, may play a role in coral health under stressful conditions.

Shayle Matsuda transplants coral fragments from Kaneohe Bay in Hawaii into a research tank, where the temperature of the water can be controlled.

Continue Your Exploration

Studying How Corals Respond to Climate Change

While individual coral polyps are small in size, together they form huge colonies. Coral reefs form from calcium carbonate deposits left by corals. Corals form a symbiotic partnership with single-celled algae that live inside the coral's tissues. In exchange for a home, the algae provide the coral with energy in the form of sugars from photosynthesis, other essential nutrients, and even the brilliant colors that healthy corals display.

When ocean water becomes too warm, corals react by expelling the tiny algae that live inside their tissues. This process is called *coral bleaching* because the corals become visibly pale, or white, when the algae are expelled. Corals can survive coral bleaching and regain their algal partners if water temperatures return to normal. If the water temperature gets too high or doesn't return to normal quickly, the corals die.

Matsuda's research examines what makes some corals in Hawaii more resistant to bleaching, a trait known as *thermal resiliency*. He compares different traits, such as the types of algae and bacteria that live within a coral and the size and shape of the coral tissue and skeleton. Matsuda thinks that understanding these differences will give him better insight into what makes some corals survive better under stressful conditions. This information can help scientists develop strategies for protecting, conserving, and managing coral reefs for future generations.

1. Describe a healthy coral-algal symbiosis. What might happen to the coral if environmental stressors cause the partnership to break down?

2. Make a flow chart that describes how corals may respond to changes in the temperature of the water they live in. Use your flow chart to model two scenarios: the water temperature rises and then quickly drops to its original level, and the water temperature rises but does not return to normal for several weeks.

3. **Collaborate** With a partner, discuss whether you think all corals in reefs all over the world would respond in the same way to temperature changes. Then make a list of questions that you would like to ask Shayle Matsuda about how corals and algae respond to climate change.

Can You Explain It?

Name: _____   **Date:** _____

How could climate change affect the survival of koalas?

EVIDENCE NOTEBOOK

Refer to the notes in your Evidence Notebook to help you construct an explanation for how climate change may affect the survival of koalas.

1. State your claim. Make sure your claim fully explains how climate change could affect the survival of koalas.

2. Summarize the evidence you have gathered to support your claim and explain your reasoning.

Checkpoints

Answer the following questions to check your understanding of the lesson.

Use the maps of the ranges of aspen trees to answer Questions 3–4.

3. What do the maps indicate will likely happen to the range of aspen? Select all that apply.

  A. It will increase.

  B. It will decrease.

  C. It will disappear completely.

  D. It will shift east.

  E. It will shift north.

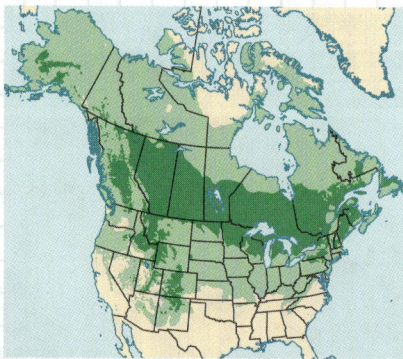

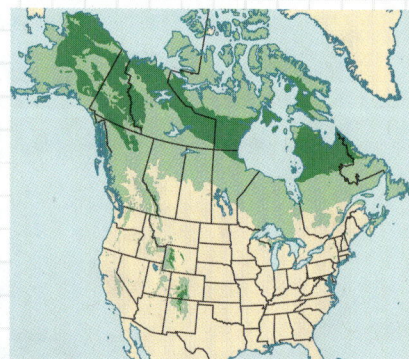

Climate Suitability for Aspen, 1971–2000
    Aspen range   Aspen core range

Projected Climate Suitability for Aspen, 2071–2100
    Aspen range   Aspen core range

Source: Natural Resources Canada, Canadian Forest Service, Forest Change Indicators, Distribution of tree species, 2017

4. Place the letter I or P next to each statement to indicate whether the response of the aspen trees occurs at the individual (I) or population (P) level.

_____ Trees that are better adapted to high temperatures reproduce well.

_____ Young trees do not grow where temperatures have risen but do grow where temperatures remain cooler.

_____ The boundary of the aspen forest shifts to a new location.

---

5. When an organism moves into a new environment, it can *increase / decrease* competition for resources among native organisms, which can cause native organisms to *survive / become extinct*. Extinctions *increase / decrease* the biodiversity and stability of an ecosystem.

Use the photos to answer Questions 6–7.

6. Which of the following is an advantage of seasonal changes in fur color?

  A. It makes hares less likely to be eaten by predators.

  B. It makes hares better able to see each other to find mates.

  C. It makes the biodiversity of the ecosystem greater.

  D. It makes hares better able to respond to climate change.

7. As the climate gets warmer, *more / less* snow is likely to fall in the Arctic, and that snow will melt *sooner / later* in the spring. Individual Arctic hares that get their white winter coats early in the fall and keep their winter coats later into the spring are *more / less* likely to survive, and that trait will likely become *more / less* common in the population.

Interactive Review

Complete this section to review the main concepts of the lesson.

Organisms have physical and behavioral adaptations to the ecosystem in which they live. The diversity of organisms in an ecosystem affects the ecosystem's stability.

A. How is biodiversity related to the ability of an ecosystem to provide essential services?

When climate change affects a habitat, organisms can respond and change, or they may become extinct.

B. Identify two ways that organisms can respond to climate change.

Scientists can monitor changes in ecosystems, organisms, and local and global biodiversity that are caused by climate change.

C. Why do scientists need to understand the interactions of organisms with their environment when studying how climate change affects biodiversity?

Reducing Human Impacts on the Environment

A wildlife overpass allows wildlife to safely move between the parts of their habitat, which has been split by a highway.

Explore First

Comparing Water Quality Gather water samples from one indoor source and one natural source. Place each sample in a clear container and observe them. What criteria would you use to describe the quality of the water in the samples? Which sample do you think humans have affected more?

CAN YOU EXPLAIN IT?

How can human activities be monitored and modified to reduce their effects on salmon?

These Chinook salmon spend most of their life in the ocean, but they swim up freshwater rivers to reproduce. Salmon choose a place to lay eggs based on the depth and temperature of the water and the amount of oxygen in the water.

Explore Online

1. What human activities might change the quality of the water in which salmon live and reproduce?

2. How might climate change affect the water in which salmon live?

EVIDENCE NOTEBOOK As you explore this lesson, gather evidence to explain how human activities that affect salmon can be monitored and minimized.

Describing Methods for Monitoring Human Impacts on the Environment

Humans affect the environment in many ways. Sometimes, our actions have unwanted or even catastrophic effects. In order to prevent or correct effects that harm the environment or human health, people gather data. For example, water quality data can be used to find out if water is safe to drink. Some pollutants may not be visible. So, special tools or methods may be needed to determine water safety.

The quality of water varies depending on where it is from.

3. Think about some of the things that might make water unsafe to drink. How can you decide if the water in each beaker in the photo is safe to drink?

Resource Use

The environment provides many resources for humans, such as land, water, and air. Human use of a resource may make that resource unavailable or unsuitable for other purposes. For example, some land uses can destroy or fragment a habitat. This negatively affects the organisms that live there.

There are organizations around the world that record data about the use of land and water. In the United States, much of this data is collected by the United States Geological Survey (USGS). Water or land use may also be regulated and measured by local governments or organizations.

Collection of Resource Use Data

People may take photos or use specialized sensors to measure and record data. Data may be collected locally or remotely. Meters measure the amount of water that is pumped from an aquifer or the amount used at a specific place. Satellite cameras and instruments remotely collect data about larger areas, such as an area the size of a city or larger.

The satellite photo shows how an area of forest near a river has been cleared by humans.

Analysis of Resource Use Data

Once data are collected, the data must be analyzed. Resource use data may be shown in many ways, such as a photo, map, table, or chart. Scientists look at trends when they analyze data. They also use the data to determine correlations. Data are correlated when two data sets have related trends. For example, if one variable increases, another variable increases or decreases at the same time. When data are strongly correlated, scientists look at the data or collect more data to find out if there is a cause-and-effect relationship between the two variables. For a relationship to be cause-and-effect, there must be a mechanism by which one variable causes change in the other.

Urbanized Land Use in Austin, Texas

Urbanized land is an area of land that is used for cities or for suburban purposes. This land includes buildings and paved surfaces.

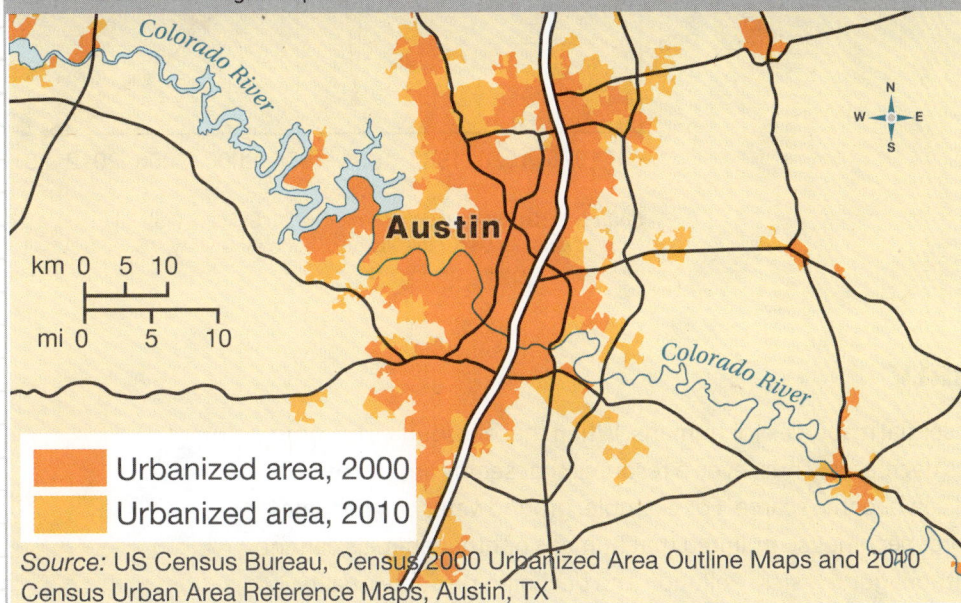

km 0 5 10

mi 0 5 10

Urbanized area, 2000
Urbanized area, 2010

Source: US Census Bureau, Census 2000 Urbanized Area Outline Maps and 2010 Census Urban Area Reference Maps, Austin, TX

4. Analyze the map. What does the change in urbanized area indicate about the change in land use of the city? How might that change affect the environment?

Data about water use are collected so that people can keep track of the amount of water that remains available. Most places on Earth have water beneath the ground in aquifers. People pump this groundwater to the surface for drinking, irrigation, and industrial uses. Groundwater in an aquifer is replaced slowly as water from the surface flows through permeable soil or rock. However, water is not likely to be absorbed if it cannot seep through the land surface or if the land slopes steeply. Impermeable surfaces, such as asphalt, do not allow water to enter soil. Instead, the water runs off the land as surface water, ending up in rivers, lakes, and oceans.

When an aquifer is depleted, it can cause the ground to sink. Another effect of a depleted aquifer is the contamination of the remaining water with salt from nearby oceans or other contaminants. Contaminated or salty groundwater is unusable for most of the purposes for which groundwater is used by humans. People must think about the effects of current resource use and technologies on the long-term health and functioning of societies and ecosystems.

5. Assume the trend of pumping water from the aquifer continues at its current rate. Predict the water level in the aquifer in the years after 2016. Support your claim with evidence and reasoning.

Water Level of a Well in the High Plains Aquifer

This graph shows the water level in a well getting farther from the surface of the ground. This means that the amount of water in the aquifer has decreased.

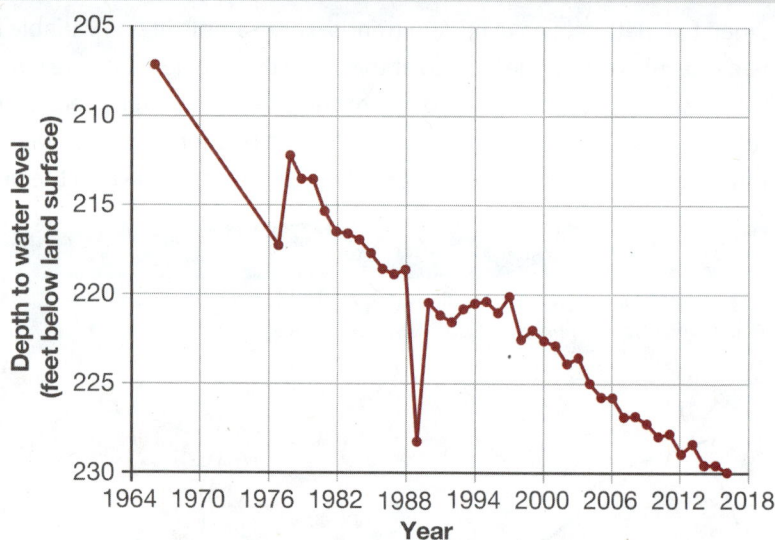

Source: USGS National Water Information System: Web Interface, Groundwater levels for the Nation, Cheyenne County, KS

Resource Quality

Air, soil, and water are essential resources for humans. When these resources become polluted, their usefulness decreases. Thus, even a resource that seems abundant and is widely distributed can become scarce. For example, groundwater can become nonrenewable if the aquifer becomes so polluted that humans or other animals cannot drink or use the water without getting sick. Pollution and declining resource quality can also affect the ability of the ecosystem to provide essential services, such as the production of food or the availability of habitats.

Do the Math
Compare Concentrations

Pollution levels are usually described in terms of concentration. The concentration of a pollutant is the amount of the polluting substance compared to the total amount of the sample. For example, a concentration of 1% is one unit (gram or mL) of pollutant in 100 units total. However, amounts of pollutants much smaller than 1% can be harmful. Therefore, pollution may be measured in parts per million or parts per billion. One part per million (1 ppm) is one unit of pollutant in one million units total. One part per billion (1 ppb) is one unit per one billion units.

6. A concentration of 1% is 10,000 times greater / less than 1 ppm.

   A concentration of 1 ppm is 1,000 times greater / less than 1 ppb.

   A concentration of 1 ppb is 10,000,000 times greater / less than 1%.

Collection of Resource Quality Data

There are different ways to collect data about pollution in the environment. Some pollution can be observed directly, like when you smell smoke in the air or see color changes in water. Some pollution can be monitored by observing the effects it has on living things. For example, pollution might cause the leaves of plants to change color. Scientists also use tools that measure substances in air, water, or soil. They can take a sample to a lab or use instruments to analyze data in the field. Some equipment, such as sensors on satellites, can take measurements from far away and send data to computers at remote locations.

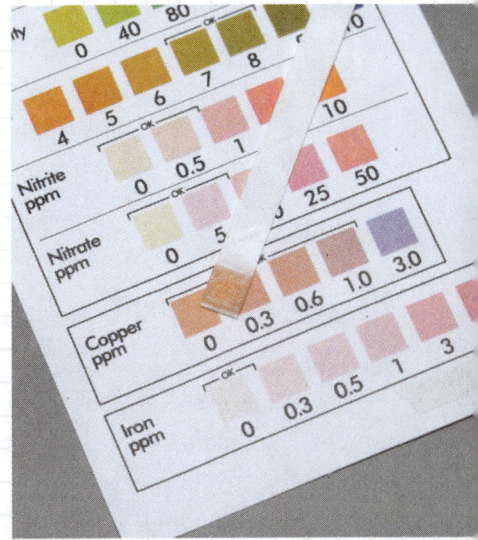

This test result shows the amount of copper in a sample of drinking water.

7. The Environmental Protection Agency (EPA) is a government organization that regulates pollutants. The EPA set the maximum safe amount of copper in drinking water at 1.3 ppm. The test result for a sample of water is shown in the photo. According to this test, the water is / is not safe to drink.

Analysis of Resource Quality Data

The amount of pollution in a resource affects the quality of the resource. Acceptable concentrations of different pollutants are generally set by state or federal agencies, such as the Environmental Protection Agency (EPA). The acceptable concentration of a pollutant depends on the pollutant, its effects on the health of humans or other organisms, and the way the resource is used. For example, drinking water generally has lower acceptable limits for pollutants, metals, and bacteria than water used for irrigating crops does.

Scientists may also measure concentrations of nonpolluting substances to make sure the levels are acceptable. Soil quality measures may include testing for certain nutrients, to make sure the soil can support certain crops.

8. This photo shows water flooding a farm field. How can the effects of runoff from this field be monitored?

Water flows between rows of crops on a farm. As the water flows, it picks up dirt and other substances, including fertilizers or pesticides.

9. What criteria might be useful for determining the quality of water in salmon habitats? What methods could people use to monitor that water quality? Record your evidence.

Propose How to Monitor Human Impacts

Surface and groundwater resources near cities receive pollutants from many different sources. To minimize impacts of urban areas on the environment, city officials must monitor the sources of pollution.

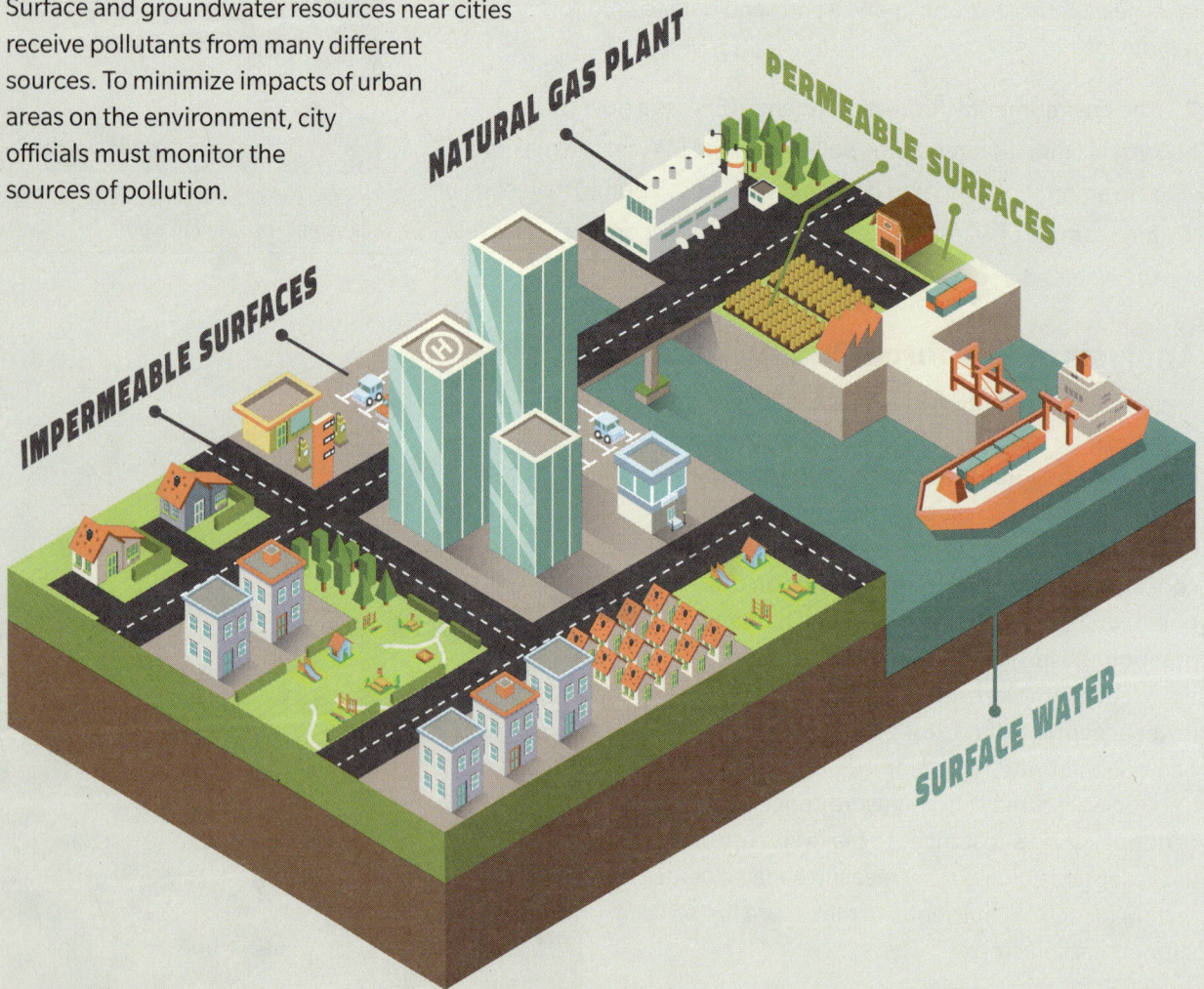

NATURAL GAS PLANT

PERMEABLE SURFACES

IMPERMEABLE SURFACES

SURFACE WATER

10. The town in the drawing formed a committee to work on ways to detect possible problems with the quality of groundwater and surface water. As a member of the committee, propose what sources of pollution should be monitored and how they should be checked.

_____

_____

_____

_____

_____

_____

Developing a Method to Monitor a Human Impact on the Environment

Once scientists know that a human activity impacts the environment, they can develop methods to monitor the activity and its impact. Monitoring is necessary to determine if changes in human activity affect the impact on the environment.

11. Think about some of the things you disposed of today or in the past week. How could you monitor the solid waste you generate in a week?

Some landfills cover large areas of land. Natural processes break down the solid waste over time, which can cause pollution in the area.

Solid Waste

Solid waste includes organic and inorganic materials. Organic materials, such as paper, are found in or made from living things. Some organic materials decay quickly. Sometimes humans change organic materials in ways that make them take longer to decay. For example, pressure-treated wood is chemically treated so that it is more durable. Inorganic materials, such as glass and metals, may take very long periods of time to break down by natural processes.

Under certain conditions, some organic materials, such as plants, decay into compost.

Every day, about 2 kilograms (kg) of solid waste per person is generated in the United States. Solid waste is typically taken to a landfill when it is discarded. Most landfills are designed to prevent pollution, but waste can dissolve and pollute groundwater or surface water. Particularly hazardous solid waste goes to specially designed landfills.

About one-third of the solid waste in the United States is either recycled or composted. Organic materials, such as food waste, paper, or yard waste, can be composted. Composted materials can then be used to improve the quality of soil.

When some organic materials decay without oxygen, as they do in a landfill, they produce methane. Methane is a greenhouse gas. When released to the atmosphere, it can contribute to rising global temperatures. But it can also be burned to produce electrical energy.

The breakdown of wastes in landfills generates the greenhouse gas methane, which is vented into the atmosphere.

Geographic Creative/Alamy

The Engineering Design Process

You can use the engineering design process (EDP) to develop a way to monitor a human activity and determine its environmental impact. The first step of the EDP is identifying the problem, for example "how do we monitor solid waste produced by a school?" Engineering design is an iterative process. That means you might not develop the best solution on the first try. Instead, you assess the results and then adjust your solution. The solution you choose depends on the criteria and constraints. To ensure a solution will solve the problem, you must make sure criteria and constraints are well defined.

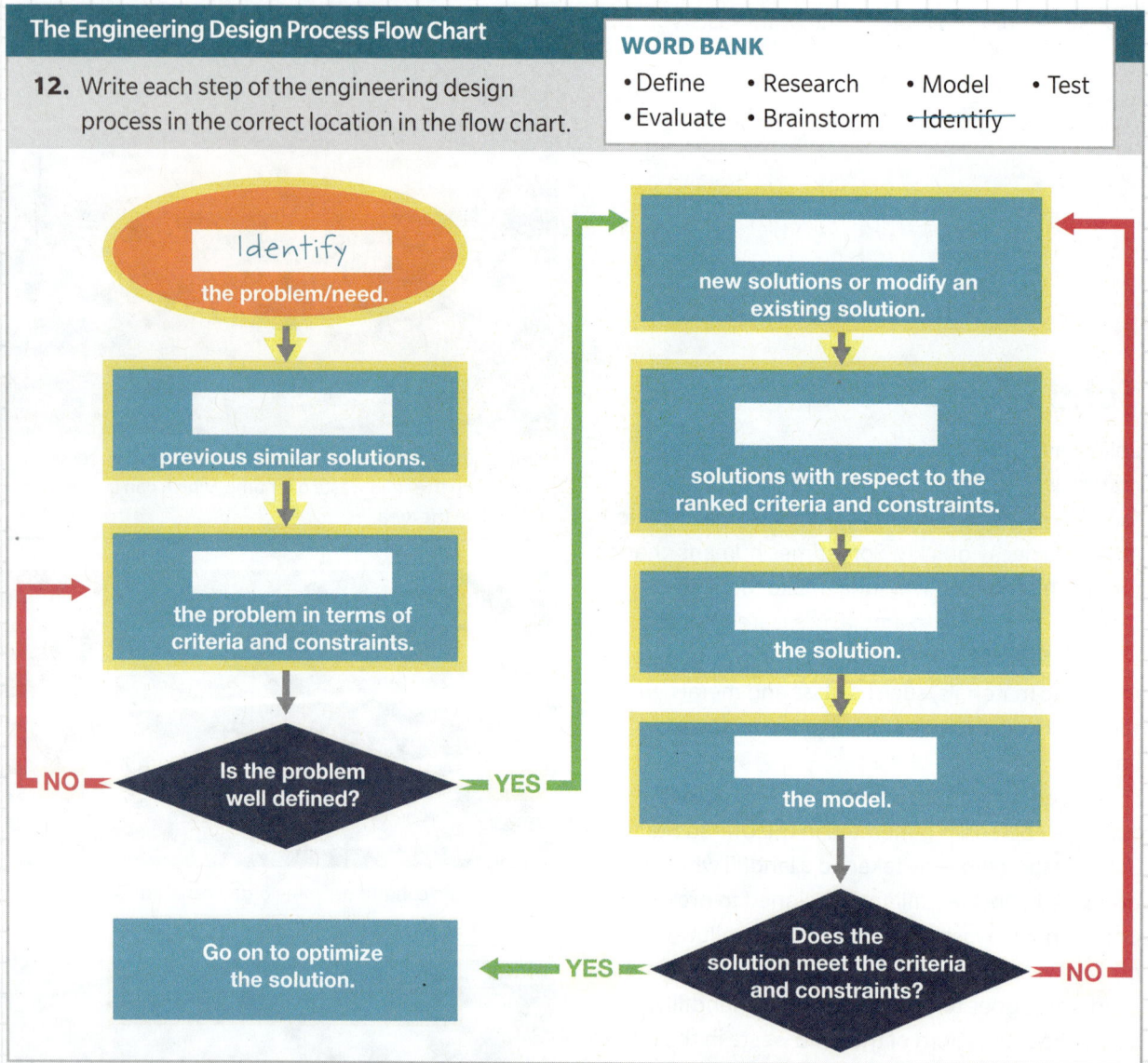

The Engineering Design Process Flow Chart

12. Write each step of the engineering design process in the correct location in the flow chart.

WORD BANK
- Define
- Research
- Model
- Test
- Evaluate
- Brainstorm
- ~~Identify~~

Identify the problem/need.

_____ previous similar solutions.

_____ the problem in terms of criteria and constraints.

Is the problem well defined? — NO / YES

_____ new solutions or modify an existing solution.

_____ solutions with respect to the ranked criteria and constraints.

_____ the solution.

_____ the model.

Does the solution meet the criteria and constraints? — YES / NO

Go on to optimize the solution.

13. Each time the EDP is used, steps may be completed in a different sequence. You may return to any previous step in the process at any time, but you may not skip steps. For example, you must always model / optimize the solution before you can test / identify the model. The problem must be well defined / tested before you research / brainstorm possible solutions.

Design a Method to Monitor Solid Waste from a School

You will use the engineering design process to develop a method to monitor the amount and types of solid waste generated by your school.

Scientists know that solid waste in a landfill has a negative impact on the environment. Reducing the amount of solid waste sent to landfills can reduce the negative impact on the environment.

MATERIALS
- computer, for research (optional)

Procedure and Analysis

STEP 1 **Research the Problem** With your group, research the problem of monitoring the amount and types of solid waste and identify existing solutions for similar problems.

STEP 2 **Define the Problem** State the problem related to monitoring your school's waste. Then add at least one constraint to more completely define the problem of monitoring solid waste from your school.

Problem:

Criterion	Constraint
1. Information is measurable.	1. Students must not handle hazardous waste.
2. Data can be collected by students.	2. All activities must occur during school hours.
3. Waste to be evaluated currently goes to a large trash container outside.	3.

STEP 3 **Brainstorm Solutions** Based on your research, brainstorm possible methods that could be used to monitor the solid waste generated by your school. Record all possible solutions on a separate paper.

STEP 4 **Language SmArts | Evaluate Possible Solutions** On a separate sheet of paper, create a decision matrix for evaluating the possible solutions. Evaluate all of the possible solutions from Step 3 to identify the solution that you think will best satisfy the criteria and constraints of the problem. Be sure to consider any scientific principles and any potential impacts on people or on the natural world that may limit your solutions.

STEP 5 **Choose a Promising Solution to Test** Describe the solution you chose, or draw a diagram of your chosen solution. Explain why you think the solution will work.

STEP 6 **Propose a Test** Before a solution can be implemented, it must be tested. The test results should show whether the solution fully meets the criteria and constraints. In the space below, describe how you would test your solution.

Monitor Solid Waste from a Neighborhood

14. In what ways might the waste from a neighborhood be different from or similar to the waste from a school?

_____

_____

_____

_____

_____

_____

Homes generate many different types of solid waste.

15. Could you use the same method to monitor the waste from your school and the waste from a neighborhood? Explain why or why not.

_____

_____

_____

_____

_____

_____

Describing Methods to Reduce Human Impacts on the Environment

When data show that a human activity impacts the environment in a negative way, scientists and engineers develop ways to reduce these negative impacts. Scientists and engineers rely on their scientific understanding of the problem, as well as on their knowledge of engineering principles and of human behavior. This knowledge allows them to make wise decisions when proposing solutions and deciding whether a change in behavior or a new technology might be needed.

16. You are going on a three-day camping trip with friends. You are able to bring only one gallon of water per person per day. How might you change the way you use water to make sure your supply lasts long enough?

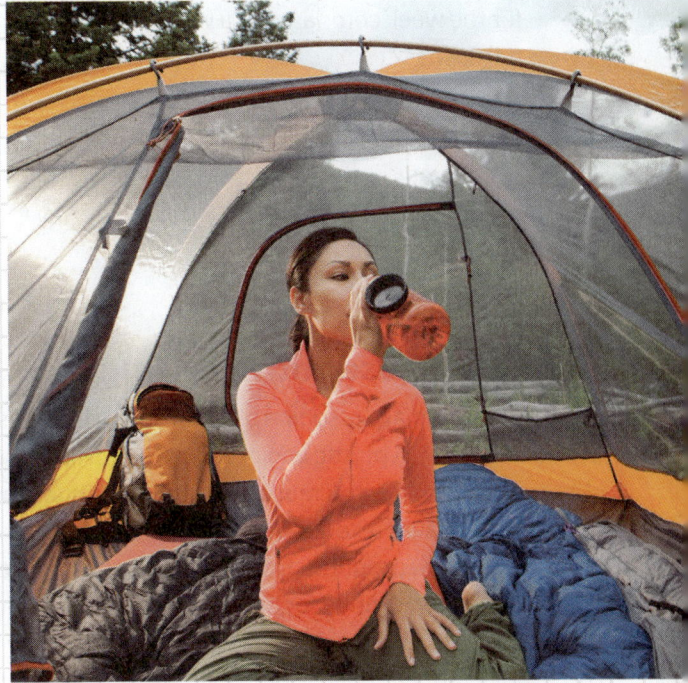

When you are away from a clean water supply, you need to carry drinking water with you. You might also use a tool or process to purify water that you find so that it is safe to drink.

Resource Availability

Using a resource in a sustainable way means that the resource continues to be available. Renewable resources are resources that can, under certain circumstances, be replaced as fast as they are used. For example, new trees can replace a forest when old trees are cut down. In order for these resources to be sustainable, they cannot be used faster than they can be replaced. Other resources, such as metals that are mined or oil that is pumped from the ground, are nonrenewable. It takes millions of years for these materials to form. A nonrenewable resource will eventually be used up. Use of nonrenewable resources must be minimized to make sure the resource is available for as long as possible.

Careful Use of Resources

What are some ways that humans can reduce the rate at which we consume resources and make them more sustainable? It is possible to reduce use by changing the way we behave. For example, you can turn on the faucet only to rinse your mouth and toothbrush. You will use less water this way than if you leave the water running while you brush your teeth. Better technology can also reduce resource use. Modern air conditioning units are more efficient than older ones due to improved technology. They use less energy to cool buildings, so they reduce the use of energy resources. If you monitor how you use resources and are careful to use only the amount you need, you can often reduce your resource use.

17. Do the Math A hotel installs dual-flush toilets to help conserve water. The new toilets use 1.6 gallons for one full flush and 0.9 gallons for one partial flush. Measurements show that in the first week there were 1,190 full flushes and 3,150 partial flushes. How many gallons of water were saved for the week compared to a week in which all the flushes were full flushes?

This toilet has two types of flushes. One uses much less water than the other.

Resource Reuse and Recycling

Another way to make resource use more sustainable is to make products last longer by reusing them. A plastic bag or a sturdy canvas bag can be used many times when shopping. Each time you reuse the bag, you reduce the number of new bags that are needed. That saves resources. Things that cannot be reused can often be recycled as materials for new products. Used paper can be recycled to make new paper to reduce the need for harvesting trees. Recycling metal, plastic, or glass containers provides materials for new products. It reduces the use of resources. The diagram shows how recycling aluminum reduces the amount of aluminum that is mined.

Mining bauxite to produce aluminum has a large impact on the environment. Aluminum is made into many products. These products can be recycled over and over, saving the material and energy resources needed to mine bauxite.

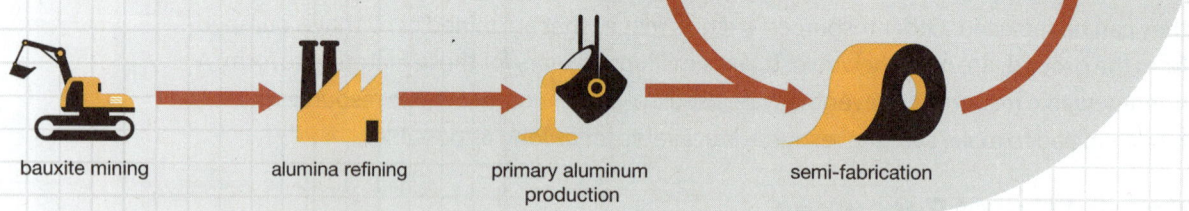

product use

recycling

product manufacturing

bauxite mining

alumina refining

primary aluminum production

semi-fabrication

18. How does recycling aluminum reduce the environmental impact of the human use of aluminum?

Resource Quality

The quality of a resource determines its value and usefulness to people and affects the health of people and the environment. Some human activities affect the quality of resources, such as water or soil. The quality of resources can be negatively affected by overuse, by improper use, and by pollution.

Behavior Change

Sometimes the quality of a resource can be maintained or improved if people change their behavior. A person may choose to buy food grown locally rather than food that is shipped from another state or country. This change in behavior may reduce air pollution because foods are often shipped in vehicles or trains that use fossil fuels for energy. Some people leave trash and other items on beaches. These items may then be washed into the ocean, adding to water pollution. By changing their behavior to make sure that these items are disposed of responsibly, people can reduce water pollution.

19. What are some questions you could investigate to determine if a change in behavior would impact resource quality?

Technology Development and Use

New technologies take time and money to develop. Newer technology often costs more than existing technology. Often, without a catastrophic event, people may not see the need to switch to a newer technology. For years, people dumped raw sewage into the same bodies of water from which they drank. It was not until people started getting sick from the polluted water that communities invested in methods to filter and treat drinking water. Since the 1800s, humans have been burning coal to generate electrical energy. Burning coal adds greenhouse gases and other pollutants to the air. Mining coal may also cause air, water, and soil pollution if it is not done carefully. Due to societal needs and regulations, scientists have worked to develop technologies to reduce the pollution produced by mining and burning coal. Scientists have also developed technologies such as wind turbines. Wind turbines generate clean energy because they do not create air pollution when they are running. However, building wind turbines does require resources. Obtaining those resources may impact the environment negatively.

20. **Discuss** With a partner, discuss reasons that humans may continue to use technology that negatively affects the environment when technology with fewer negative effects exists.

Case Study: The Dust Bowl

The Great Plains in the central part of the United States was once a vast grassland. The grasses had deep roots and were adapted to the climate of the plains. Herds of animals lived on these plains and fed on the grasses. In the 1800s, few people used the land to farm crops. In the early 1900s, new technologies made it easier to farm large areas of land. As the price of grain increased, more farmers began plowing the soil and planting grain crops over large areas of land. The grain plants did not have deep roots like the native grasses. When a long drought happened in the 1930s, the fields became dry and crops died. Heavy winds picked up the dry soil and formed giant dust storms. These dust storms caused respiratory problems. Sometimes humans and animals in the area died. Swarms of grasshoppers ate many remaining crops, leading to even less protection for the soil. The loss of fertile topsoil made it more difficult to grow crops.

Since the lessons of the Dust Bowl period, farmers have begun to implement a variety of soil conservation techniques. These methods include contour planting, cover crops, crop rotation, and the planting of windbreaks.

Native grasses have deep roots that hold soil in place and keep the soil healthy.

Without deep roots to hold the soil in place, the soil was carried away by the wind in massive dust storms.

21. Dust storms occurred after humans changed the environment. Which activities contributed to severe dust storms? Select all that apply.

    A. plowing soil for crop planting

    B. overgrazing herds of cattle

    C. removing native grasses

    D. building towns and dirt roads

22. **Write** In the 1950s, a drought similar to the one in the 1930s was predicted. The United States Congress offered farmers money to turn farmland back into grassland to avoid another dust bowl. Farmers had to decide whether to accept the offer or to continue farming their land as they had been doing. Think about the situation from the farmers' point of view. On a separate sheet of paper, write a letter responding to this offer as a farmer in the area at the time. Say whether you would or would not accept the government offer and explain your reasoning.

Farmers can plow the ground and plant crops in straight lines. They can also use contour farming. Contour farming follows the shape of the land when farmers plow and plant.

Analyze the Environmental Impact of a Power Plant

Conventional power plants burn fuel to heat water and make steam. This steam turns a turbine to generate electrical energy. The steam is then cooled, so that the water can be heated again. This heating and cooling repeats in a cycle. The water used to cool the steam is often drawn from nearby surface water. The steam transfers thermal energy to the water, which makes the water hotter and the steam cooler. The hot water is released into a nearby body of water. It causes thermal pollution that may make the body of water too warm for plants and animals living in it. In a combined heat and power (CHP) plant, shown in the diagram, the hot water heats buildings instead of being discharged into the nearby body of water.

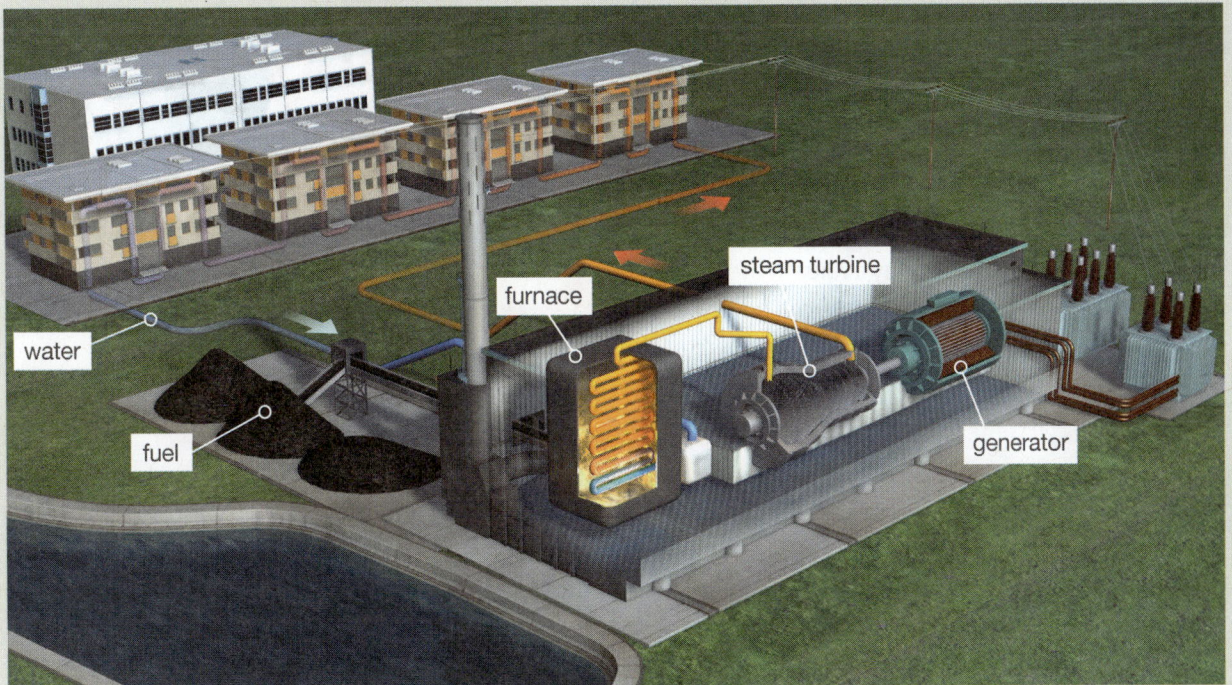

Follow the path of the water through the furnace and steam turbine. Then notice how the hot water passes through the buildings. The water cools down as the buildings are heated. The cool water then returns to the furnace in a continuous cycle.

---

23. Which of the following are ways in which the CHP plant has a lower impact on the environment than a traditional power plant? Select all that apply.

    A. It uses thermal energy more efficiently than the traditional plant.

    B. It causes less thermal pollution in the nearby body of water.

    C. It uses fuel that causes less pollution than a traditional plant.

    D. It does not produce greenhouse gases when fuels are burned.

> **EVIDENCE NOTEBOOK**
> 24. What human activities could have an effect on salmon habitats? How can those activities be modified to reduce their effects on salmon? Record your evidence.

Developing a Method to Reduce a Human Impact on the Environment

Define and Evaluate a Problem Related to Solid Waste

Recall that the engineering design process is a tool that you can use anytime you want to develop a solution for a specific problem. Solutions may be a process or a physical object. The first step of the engineering design process is to identify the problem. An engineering problem must be stated very clearly so that a solution can be developed to address the exact problem. The purpose of the criteria and constraints is to define the problem in a way that makes it possible to measure how well the solution works. Engineers begin with as many ideas as possible, and then they evaluate the ideas to choose a solution they think will be the most successful. A promising solution can then be tested and improved until all of the criteria and constraints are satisfied.

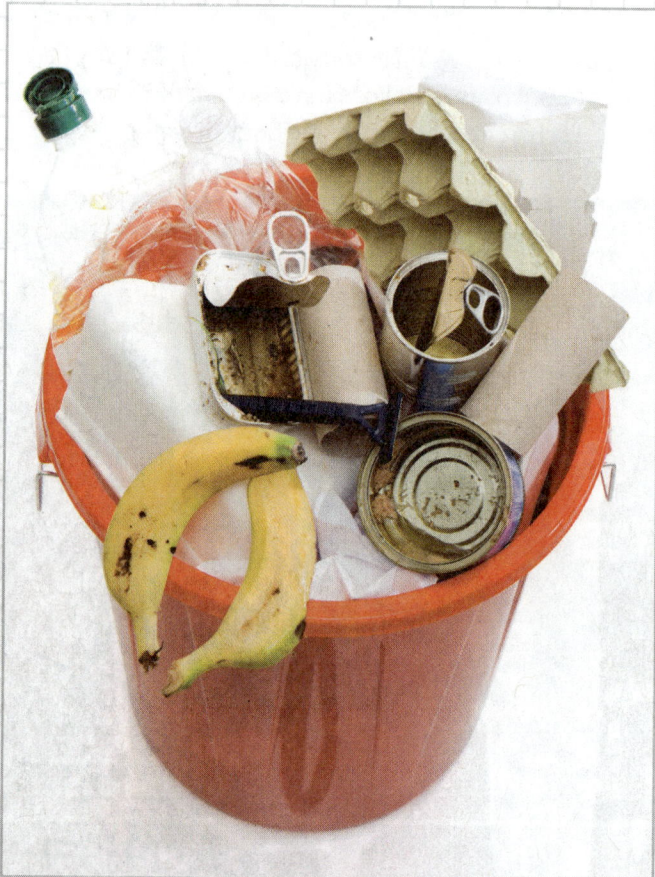

The trash in this can is all going to a landfill. But some of this waste could be disposed of in a different way.

25. Which of the following changes might reduce the impact of your school's solid waste on the environment? Select all that apply.

   A. Start school later in the morning.

   B. Compost food waste to make garden fertilizer.

   C. Reuse the back of worksheets as scratch paper.

   D. Collect plastic bottles for recycling.

26. **Discuss** With a partner or group, discuss the sources and types of solid waste that are generated in your school.

Evaluate a Method to Reduce the Impact of Solid Waste on the Environment

You will use the engineering design process to develop a method for reducing the environmental effects of solid waste generated by your school.

MATERIALS
- camera (optional)
- meterstick (optional)
- scale (optional)

Procedure and Analysis

STEP 1 Research the Problem Research the problem and possible solutions for reducing the impact of solid waste.

STEP 2 Define the Problem State the engineering problem related to reducing the environmental impact of your school's waste. Then determine criteria and constraints for your problem.

Problem:	
Criterion	**Constraint**
1. Can be directed by students	1. Does not require any money
2.	2.
3.	3.
4.	4.

STEP 3 Brainstorm Solutions Based on your research, brainstorm possible methods that you could use to reduce the amount of solid waste that is generated by your school and goes to a landfill. Record all possible solutions on a separate sheet of paper.

STEP 4 Choose a Solution Evaluate the solutions you brainstormed, taking into account any scientific principles and any potential impacts on people or on the natural world that may limit your solution. Choose the most promising solution from your brainstorming step. Describe your solution, and explain how it addresses the engineering problem.

STEP 5 **Design and Implement a Test** Decide the best method for testing your solution. Perform the test and record your test results on a separate sheet of paper.

STEP 6 **Analyze Results** Analyze the results to determine whether your solution would work for the whole school. Use evidence and reasoning to support your claim.

STEP 7 **Evaluate the Solution** Based on your test results, can your chosen solution be used to reduce the environmental impact of solid waste generated by your school? If yes, explain how the solution could be used to reduce the school's environmental impact. If no, how would you change your solution to make it more likely to solve the problem?

Reduce the Energy Use of a School

Schools require electrical energy for many different needs. The environmental impact of the electrical energy used by a school depends on the source of the power.

27. Examine the graph. Brainstorm ways that the school might reduce its energy use. A constraint of this problem is that the recommended change cannot require a lot of money.

_____

_____

_____

_____

_____

_____

_____

_____

Electrical Energy Used by a School

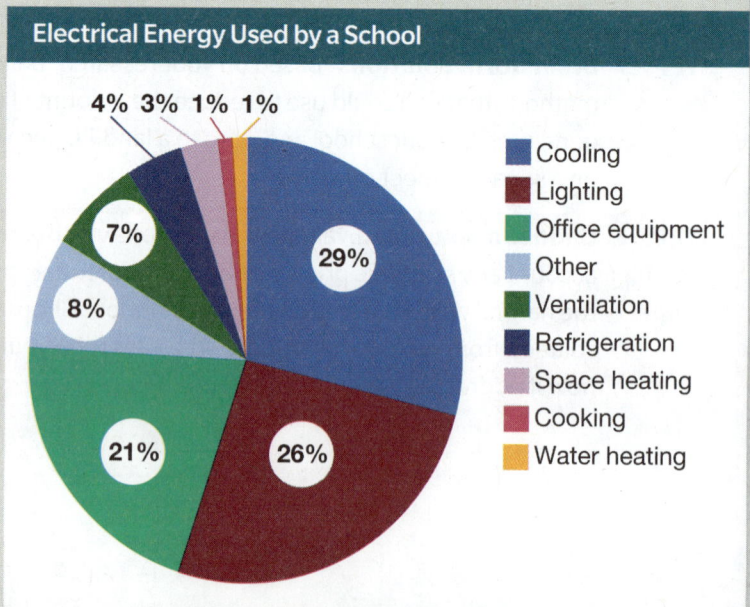

4% 3% 1% 1%

7%

8%

21%

26%

29%

- Cooling
- Lighting
- Office equipment
- Other
- Ventilation
- Refrigeration
- Space heating
- Cooking
- Water heating

Continue Your Exploration

Name: _____   Date: _____

Check out the path below or go online to choose one of the other paths shown.

Urban Planning to Reduce Impact

- **Air Pollution Past and Present**
- **Hands-On Labs** ✋
- **Propose Your Own Path**

Go online to choose one of these other paths.

In 2016, about 54% of the world's population lived in cities. A city can have a large impact on the environment, due to the large human population of the city. Urban planners design transportation systems. They also design systems to provide water, electrical energy, and sewage services to all the people in a city. The design of these systems affects the environmental impact of a city. Planned public transportation, such as trains and buses, helps reduce the use of cars. Some cities, such as Copenhagen, Denmark, build infrastructure to make it easier for people to use bicycles instead of cars to get to and from work.

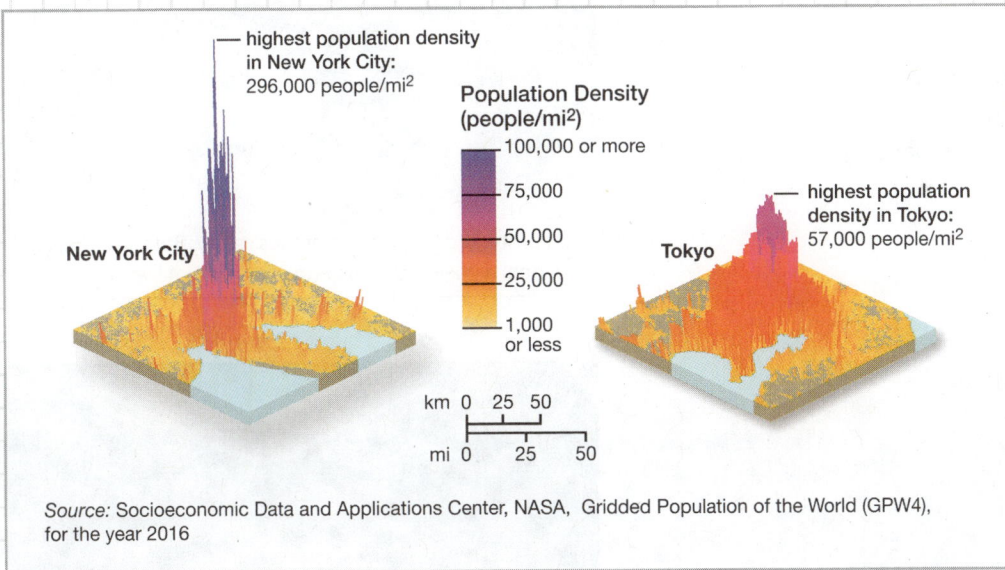

highest population density in New York City: 296,000 people/mi²

Population Density (people/mi²)
- 100,000 or more
- 75,000
- 50,000
- 25,000
- 1,000 or less

New York City

Tokyo

highest population density in Tokyo: 57,000 people/mi²

km 0 25 50
mi 0 25 50

Source: Socioeconomic Data and Applications Center, NASA, Gridded Population of the World (GPW4), for the year 2016

Compare the populations of New York City and Tokyo. How are the people in these cities distributed?

1. The population of Tokyo is a little greater than the population of New York City. Each year, about 1.6 billion people ride the subway in New York City, but about 3.7 billion ride the subway in Tokyo. Can the population distribution for each city be used to explain the large difference in the number of subway riders each year? What other information might you need to explain this difference?

Continue Your Exploration

2. Some urban planners design transportation systems that reduce human impact. How might redesigning a roadway to add a protected bike lane impact the environment?

Riding a bicycle on a busy street is dangerous. Drivers often do not see cyclists, or they drive closer to cyclists than is safe.

3. Urban planners redesign a roadway to encourage people to bike from place to place. How can they monitor or measure environmental impacts related to the new bike lanes?

An unprotected bike lane improves safety. But the cyclist still must deal with vehicles moving in and out of the bike lane.

This protected bike lane is located between parked cars and the sidewalk. The parked cars protect bicyclists from moving vehicles.

4. **Collaborate** With a small group, brainstorm non-transportation-related ways that cities can reduce their environmental impact. Make a brochure to present your ideas to city officials.

Can You Explain It?

Name: _____   Date: _____

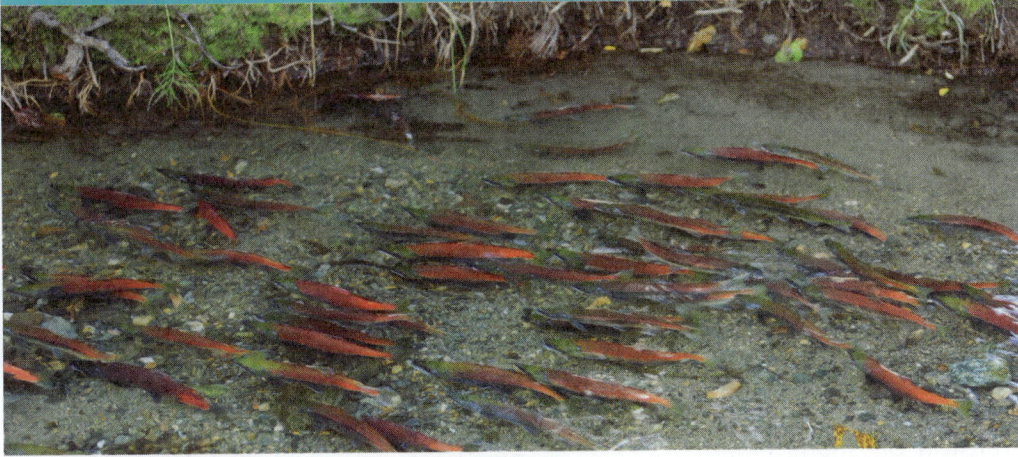

How can human activities be monitored and modified to reduce their effects on salmon?

> **EVIDENCE NOTEBOOK**
>
> Refer to the notes in your Evidence Notebook to help you construct an explanation for how human activities can be monitored and modified to reduce their effects on salmon.

1. State your claim. Make sure your claim fully explains how human activities can be monitored and modified to reduce their effects on salmon.

2. Summarize the evidence you have gathered to support your claim and explain your reasoning.

Checkpoints

Answer the following questions to check your understanding of the lesson.

Use the photo to answer Questions 3–4.

3. Which problem does the storm drain label solve?

   A. It keeps waterways from flooding.

   B. It stops people from overfishing.

   C. It protects groundwater from pollution.

   D. It discourages people from polluting waterways.

4. Which of these criteria appear to be satisfied by the label in the photo? Select all that apply.

   A. It is low cost.

   B. It does not require new technology.

   C. It stops all possible pollution.

   D. It records data on the effectiveness of the solution.

Use the chart to answer Questions 5–6.

5. About how many times more water is needed to produce a pound of beef than a pound of lentils?

   A. 0.5 times

   B. 1.9 times

   C. 13.5 times

   D. 1,450 times

6. A family chooses to eat lentils instead of beef for dinner to reduce the family's impact on the environment. The chart does / does not support this reasoning, because raising beef for food requires less / more water than lentils. Thus, eating less / more beef has a positive impact on the environment, because water is an important and often scarce resource.

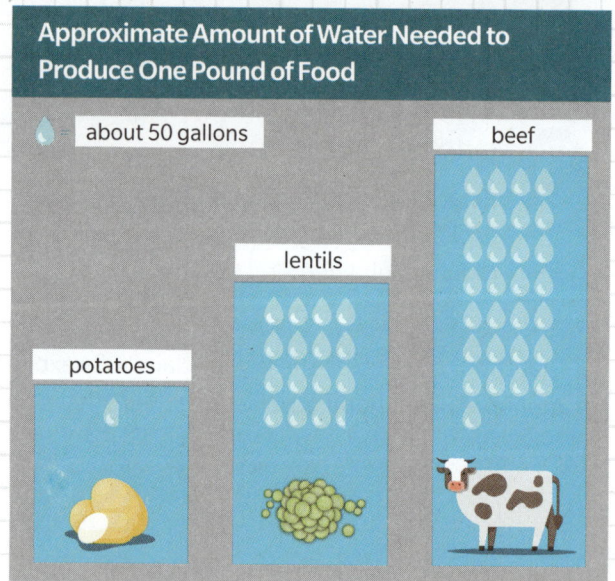

Approximate Amount of Water Needed to Produce One Pound of Food

about 50 gallons

beef

lentils

potatoes

Source: Mekonnen, M.M. and Hoekstra, A.Y. (2010), Value of Water Research Report Series Nos. 47 and 48, UNESCO-IHE, Delft, the Netherlands

7. Which of the following data for monitoring human effects on the environment can be collected by a satellite?

   A. land use in a rural area

   B. quality of a body of water

   C. air quality around a city

   D. water use per person in a city

8. A new city program encourages people to bike rather than drive a car to work. It is hoped that this program will monitor / reduce air pollution in the city and the rate of climate change. The program effectiveness could be monitored / reduced by surveying residents to see how they commute.

Interactive Review

Complete this section to review the main concepts of the lesson.

Scientists monitor resource use and quality to determine how humans impact the environment.

A. Give two examples of resources that scientists monitor, and describe how they monitor the quality and use of each resource.

The engineering design process can be used to develop a method for monitoring human impacts on the environment.

B. How can the engineering design process be used to develop a method for monitoring the environmental impact of a human activity?

People can reduce their impact on the environment by changing their behavior or by using new or different technologies.

C. How might the effect on the environment of the human activity of traveling be reduced?

The engineering design process can be used to develop ways to reduce human impacts on the environment.

D. Why would a community decide to use the engineering design process as they look for a solution for an environmental problem?

Images; (bc) ©MAY/BSIP SA/Alamy; (b) ©Maica/E+/Getty Images

Choose one of the activities to explore how this unit connects to other topics.

People in Science

Dr. Simon Nicholson, International Relations Scholar Dr. Simon Nicholson directs the Global Environmental Politics program in the School of International Service at American University Dr. Nicholson trained first as a lawyer before becoming a professor. He works to develop laws, policies, and regulations related to climate change technologies that balance the risks of climate engineering technologies and the needs of people affected by climate change.

   Research a proposed idea for climate engineering. Create a model that describes the technique, the expected result, potential side effects, and any ethical or regulatory issues.

Music Connection

Songs about Saving Earth Many songwriters and singers have been inspired by human effects on the environment. These artists use music to share information and to encourage action and change regarding issues that are important to them.

   Identify a song that was inspired by human impacts on the environment. Read the lyrics. Then write a brief essay explaining how the song is related to natural resources or environmental conservation. Identify Earth systems and natural resources that are mentioned in the song. Then present your findings by playing the song and leading a group discussion.

Social Studies Connection

Science and Activism Some individuals find an environmental cause they feel strongly about and do bold things to raise awareness. Often these people are called "activists." Some activists walk in marches or plan demonstrations to inform others about environmental causes. These activities can raise awareness about environmental issues and motivate people to help make changes.

   What else would you like to know about science and activism? Research an environmental activist to find out about the activist's cause and efforts. Create a multimedia presentation to share with the class.

Name: _____

Date: _____

Complete this review to check your understanding of the unit.

Use the graph to answer Questions 1–2.

1. Which of the following statements describes how rising global temperature affects the caterpillars?

   A. More caterpillars survive and mate each year.

   B. The caterpillars hatch earlier in the season.

   C. The caterpillars move to a new habitat.

   D. The caterpillars change the food they eat.

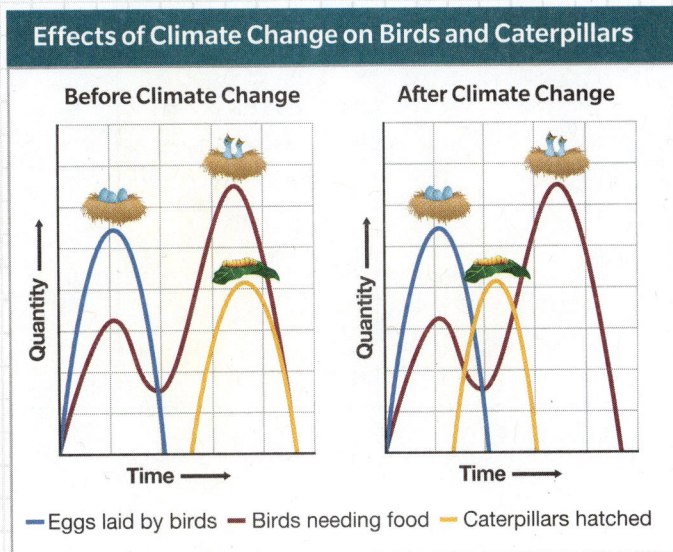

Effects of Climate Change on Birds and Caterpillars

Before Climate Change   After Climate Change

Quantity / Time

— Eggs laid by birds — Birds needing food — Caterpillars hatched

2. What physical or behavioral adaptations will determine how well the birds survive the change in climate? Select all that apply.

   A. the number of eggs the birds lay

   B. the variety of foods the birds can eat

   C. the timing of the birds' mating and laying seasons

   D. the location and size of the birds' range

Use the decision matrix to answer Questions 3–5

3. Complete the decision matrix by calculating the totals for each product.

| Product | Criteria | | | | Totals |
	Can be used for at least 3 days (2)	Inexpensive (3)	Produces little waste (5)	Requires little energy to make (5)	
Liquid soap in plastic bottle	2	2	2	2	
Bar soap in paper wrapper	2	3	4	4	

4. Which product would you choose for the guest rooms of an ecologically friendly hotel?

   A. Liquid soap, because it is the least expensive.

   B. Bar soap, because it has the highest total score in my decision matrix.

   C. Liquid soap, because it has the lowest total score in my decision matrix.

   D. Bar soap, because it produces more waste than liquid soap.

5. If the liquid soap in a plastic bottle produced less waste, would it change your decision?

   A. No, it still scores lower in my decision matrix.

   B. No, it still scores higher in my decision matrix.

   C. Yes, less waste outweighs the other categories.

   D. Yes, bar soap is harder to clean up when the guests leave.

6. Complete the table by explaining how the following categories are related to each concept.

Topic Category	Cause and Effect	Patterns	Stability	Change
Climate	A variety of natural processes and human activities cause changes in Earth's climate.			
Human Activities				
Climate Monitoring Methods				
Biodiversity				

Name: _____   Date: _____

Use the plastic usage diagram to answer Questions 7–10.

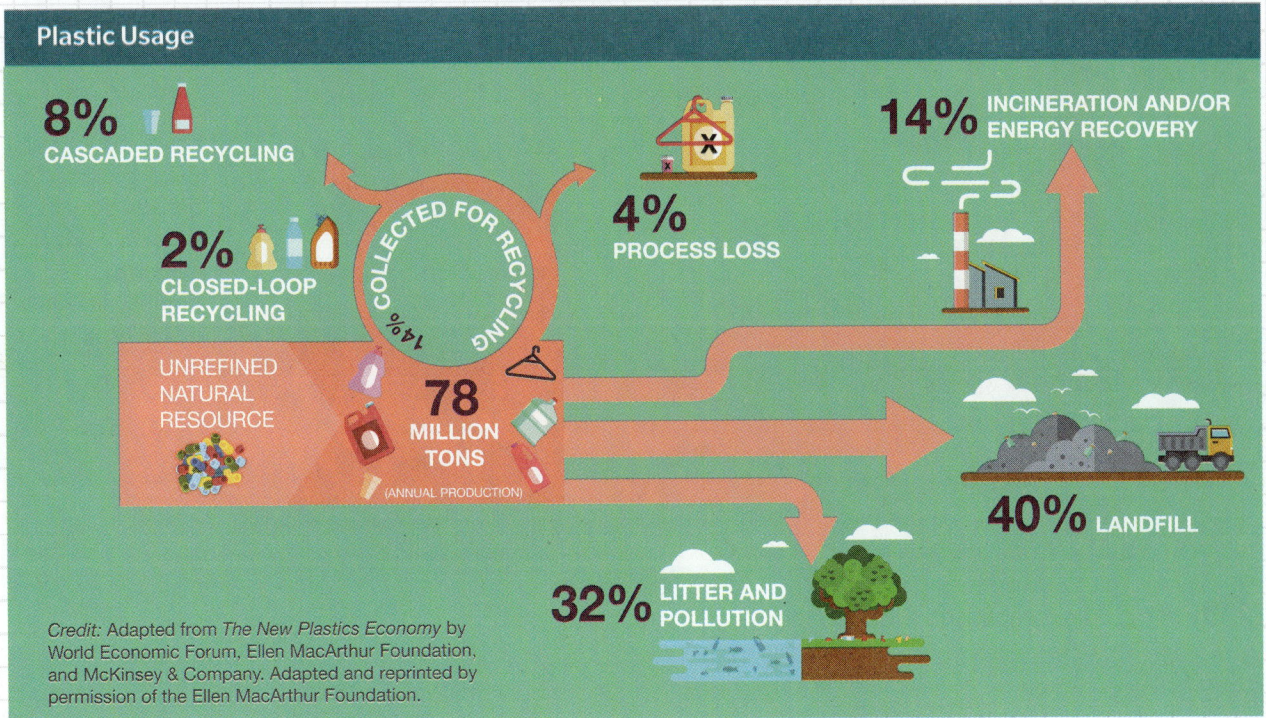

Plastic Usage

8% CASCADED RECYCLING

2% CLOSED-LOOP RECYCLING

14% COLLECTED FOR RECYCLING

UNREFINED NATURAL RESOURCE

78 MILLION TONS (ANNUAL PRODUCTION)

4% PROCESS LOSS

14% INCINERATION AND/OR ENERGY RECOVERY

40% LANDFILL

32% LITTER AND POLLUTION

Credit: Adapted from *The New Plastics Economy* by World Economic Forum, Ellen MacArthur Foundation, and McKinsey & Company. Adapted and reprinted by permission of the Ellen MacArthur Foundation.

7. After a plastic bottle has been discarded, what four outcomes could happen next? List these four outcomes in order from the most likely to the least.

8. Explain why not all of the plastic products that are produced are recycled.

9. Suggest three ways that plastic packaging materials could affect biodiversity in an ocean ecosystem.

10. Suggest at least three ways human behaviors could be changed to minimize the impacts of plastic packaging materials on Earth's systems.

Use the infographic to answer Questions 11–14.

Greenhouse Gas Emissions during Food Production Compared to Car Miles Driven

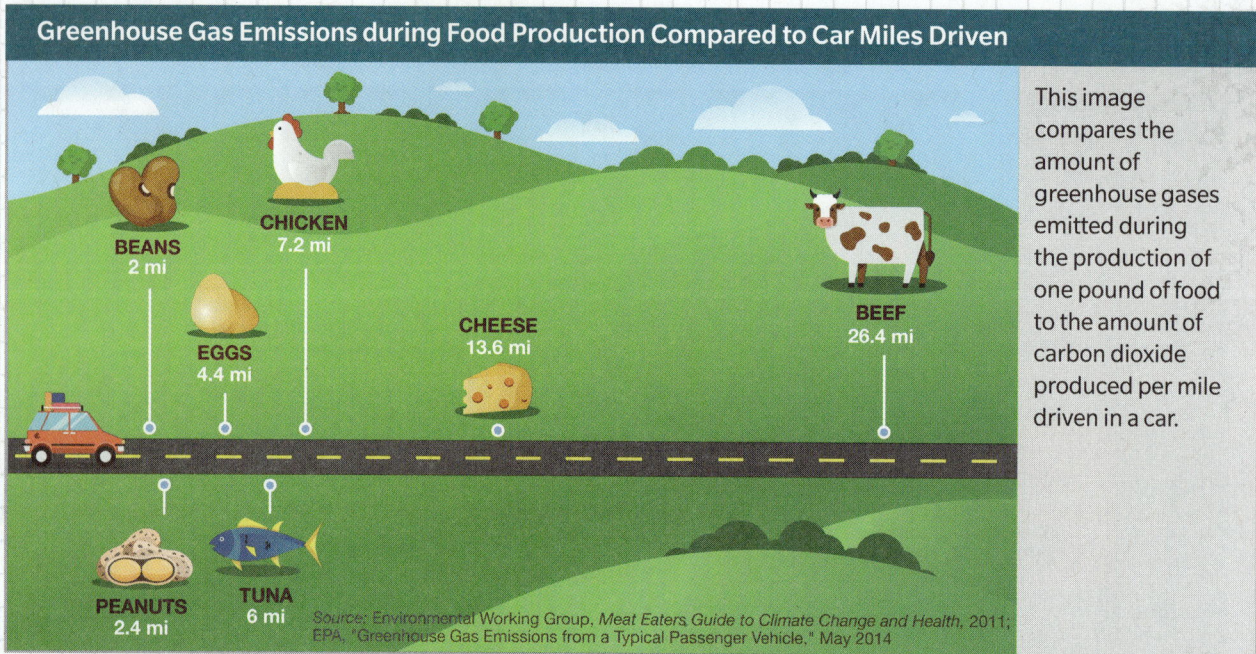

BEANS
2 mi

CHICKEN
7.2 mi

EGGS
4.4 mi

CHEESE
13.6 mi

BEEF
26.4 mi

PEANUTS
2.4 mi

TUNA
6 mi

This image compares the amount of greenhouse gases emitted during the production of one pound of food to the amount of carbon dioxide produced per mile driven in a car.

Source: Environmental Working Group, *Meat Eaters Guide to Climate Change and Health*, 2011; EPA, "Greenhouse Gas Emissions from a Typical Passenger Vehicle," May 2014

11. Why is the comparison shown in the image useful?

12. If a round-trip distance to the grocery store is 20 miles, which would reduce your greenhouse gas emissions more: making one less trip to the store or eating one less pound of beef? Explain your reasoning.

13. Global Warming Potential (GWP) is a measure of how much heat a greenhouse gas absorbs. Higher GWP means the gas absorbs more heat. The GWP of CO_2 is 1 and the GWP of methane is 21. Producing beef and dairy products releases a lot of methane. Driving a car releases a lot of carbon dioxide. What else would you need to know to determine which action has a greater potential impact on global temperature?

14. If you wanted to reduce your greenhouse gas emissions, how might you change your diet to have the greatest impact? Use evidence and scientific reasoning to support your claim.

Name: _____   Date: _____

How can air travel be improved to reduce impacts on Earth systems?

Air travel is an important part of our global culture and economy. However, it causes significant greenhouse gas emissions and requires large amounts of natural resources. Greener Skies is an initiative that is being implemented to help decrease airport emissions. It improves upon existing area navigation (RNAV) procedures. These new procedures direct aircraft to fly a different course to reduce mileage and, therefore, the amount of fuel burned during the flight. Research Greener Skies procedures that have been put into place at Seattle-Tacoma Airport and other airports. Use what you learn to determine whether any of these procedures would benefit an airport near you.

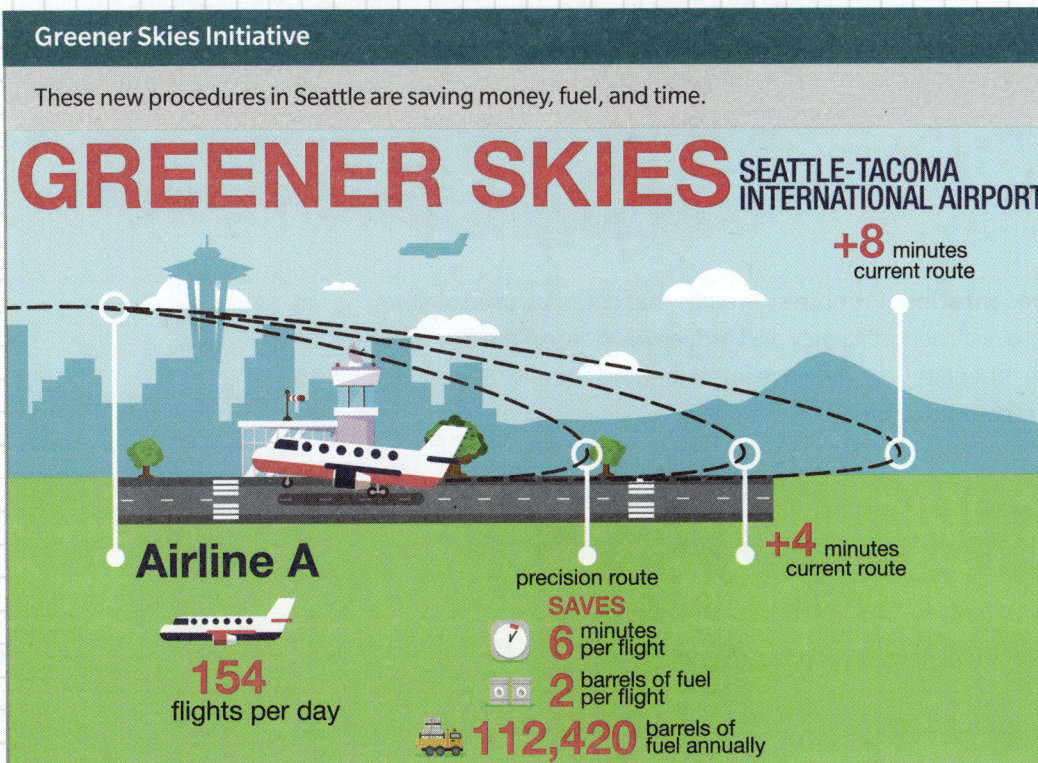

Greener Skies Initiative

These new procedures in Seattle are saving money, fuel, and time.

GREENER SKIES SEATTLE-TACOMA INTERNATIONAL AIRPORT

+8 minutes current route

+4 minutes current route

Airline A

154 flights per day

precision route
SAVES
6 minutes per flight
2 barrels of fuel per flight
112,420 barrels of fuel annually

Source: Federal Aviation Administration, U.S. Department of Transportation, and Alaska Airlines, June 27, 2014

The steps below will help guide your research.

1. **Define the Problem** What questions do you have about the goal of the Greener Skies initiative? Write a statement defining a problem that Greener Skies is trying to solve.

2. **Analyze Data** In a test of the new procedures, a single airline was able to save 87 gallons of fuel per flight and shorten flight times by 9 minutes. As a result, they reduced greenhouse gas emissions by 1 metric ton every time a plane landed at the Seattle-Tacoma Airport. Across all airlines, about 206,085 flights landed at Seattle-Tacoma in 2016. Calculate the amount of fuel and the amount of greenhouse-gas emissions that would be saved using the Greener Skies initiative at Seattle-Tacoma Airport over the course of one year and ten years.

3. **Conduct Research** Research the Greener Skies procedures enacted at the airports in Seattle and other test airports around the country. Consider how the Greener Skies procedures could be implemented at another airport of your choice, taking into consideration the air-traffic patterns at that airport.

4. **Develop a Presentation** Propose strategies that could be used at your chosen airport to improve airport efficiency and reduce impacts on the environment. Use evidence from other airports that have implemented Greener Skies initiatives to support your recommendation.

5. **Communicate** Present your proposal to your class.

✓ Self-Check

	I defined the problem that the Greener Skies program is trying to solve.
	I analyzed data about carbon emissions caused by airplane flights and how Greener Skies procedures can reduce them.
	I researched air traffic patterns and procedures at another airport of my choice in order to evaluate which initiatives could be implemented there.
	I developed a presentation that proposed strategies to improve efficiency at my airport and reduce human impacts on the environment.
	My proposal was supported by evidence and clearly communicated.

Go online to access the **Interactive Glossary**. *You can use this online tool to look up definitions for all the vocabulary terms in this book.*

Pronunciation Key

Sound	Symbol	Example	Respelling	Sound	Symbol	Example	Respelling
ă	a	pat	PAT	ŏ	ah	bottle	BAHT'l
ā	ay	pay	PAY	ō	oh	toe	TOH
âr	air	care	KAIR	ô	aw	caught	KAWT
ä	ah	father	FAH•ther	ôr	ohr	roar	ROHR
är	ar	argue	AR•gyoo	oi	oy	noisy	NOYZ•ee
ch	ch	chase	CHAYS	o͞o	u	book	BUK
ě	e	pet	PET	o͞o	oo	boot	BOOT
ě (at end of a syllable)	eh	settee lessee	seh•TEE leh•SEE	ou	ow	pound	POWND
ěr	ehr	merry	MEHR•ee	s	s	center	SEN•ter
ē	ee	beach	BEECH	sh	sh	cache	CASH
g	g	gas	GAS	ŭ	uh	flood	FLUHD
ĭ	i	pit	PIT	ûr	er	bird	BERD
ĭ (at end of a syllable)	ih	guitar	gih•TAR	z	z	xylophone	ZY•luh•fohn
ī	y eye (only for a complete syllable)	pie island	PY EYE•luhnd	z	z	bags	BAGZ
îr	ir	hear	HIR	zh	zh	decision	dih•SIZH•uhn
j	j	germ	JERM	ə	uh	around broken focus	uh•ROWND BROH•kuhn FOH•kuhs
k	k	kick	KIK	ər	er	winner	WIN•er
ng	ng	thing	THING	th	th	thin they	THIN THAY
ngk	ngk	bank	BANGK	w	w	one	WUHN
				wh	hw	whether	HWETH•er

Index

Page numbers for key terms are in **boldface** type.
Page numbers in *italic* type indicate illustrative material, such as photographs, graphs, charts, and maps.

A

acidic water, 539, *539*
acid rain, 497
Act, 210, 274, 343
adaptation, 391
  in chaparral ecosystem, 536, *536*
  environment affecting, *393, 394*
  of organism, 391, 534–537
  types of, 392
adaptive technologies, 18
adenine, 411
adrenal gland, 171, *171*
advantages, 65
aerodynamics, 8, *8*
aerosols, 527
African cichlid fish, 400, *400*
African elephants, 399, *399*
aggregating anemone, 461, *461*
agricultural areas, 387
agriculture
  geosphere affected by, 495
  modeling runoff, 101
  water needs of, 493
air
  atmosphere as, 270
  circulation of, 275–278, 279–282
  currents, 94, 97
  mass of, 319–320, *319*, 326, 331, 359
  as matter, 279
  movement of, 268–287
  particles of, 294, *312, 314*
  quality of, 556–558
air mass, 319
air pollution, 495
air pressure
  element of weather, 314
  formation of, 271–272
  identifying weather associated with, 316–318
  map of, 316
  prevailing wind and, *324*
  system of, 317–318, *317*

  temperature differences causing, 275
  on weather map, *318*
  wind formation caused by, 315
air temperature
  air pressure changes caused by, 275
  clouds effecting, 313
  cricket chirps estimating, 339, *339*
  differences in cause wind, 272
  differences of changing air density, 272
  affecting precipitation, 313
  pressure affected by, 316, *316*
  thermal energy of, 208
  during water changing states, 240, *240*
air travel, 581–582
Akashi Kaikyo Bridge, 62
Alaska, 384, *384*
Alaskan Inuit Culture, 372, *372*
albedo, 354–357
algae, 90, 101, 425, 489, *489*, 500
allele, 404, 408, *408*
Alpine butterfly, 393, *393*
Alpine wildflower, 350, *350*
alternative energy, 191, 219, *230*, 563
altitude, 360, 361, *361*, 371, 384, *385*, 399
Alturas, California, 366, *366*
alumina refining, 564, *564*
aluminum, 205, 223, 564, *564*
Alvin, 305, *305*
Amazon, 265, *265*, 281, *281*
ambient temperature, 220
American pika, 393, *393*
amoebas, 419
amphibian, 423, *423*, 459, *459*
analysis
  of air mass interaction, 320
  of animal body systems, 146–151
  of board game, 471
  of cells, 113, 115–118, 120–121
  of climate model, 363
  of clouds and rain formation, 243
  of cod population, 502

  of cost-benefit, 45, 65
  of data, 52, 54, 56, 65, 378
  of drought tolerance of plants, 389–390
  of energy transfer, 185
  of factors determining climate, 384–386
  of female mate choice, 465
  of flower parts, 443
  of formation of wind, 271–272
  of greenhouse effect, 512
  of heat, 208–210
  of hibernation, 158
  of honeybee colony loss, 445
  of impact of technology on society, 20
  of insulated lunch container, 229–230
  in investigations, 20
  of models, 88
  of monarch migration, 540–541
  of pine box car, 71–72
  of pollution, 494
  of processes, 248
  of reaction time, 159
  of relationships between structure and function, 20
  of resource quality data, 557
  of resource use data, 555–556
  of risk-benefit analysis, 49
  of shipping costs, *337*
  of solar water heater, *220*
  of solid waste reduction, 569–570
  of system responses to exercise, 150
  of technological influences, *13*
  of thermal energy loss, 201
  of thermal energy transfer, 222
  of tissue, 94
  of water density, 295
  of water on Earth, 238–240
  of weather forecast map, 343, *343*, 344, *344*
  of wind, 274
Analyze Geothermal Heat Pumps, 230

Ancient Roman builders, 188

Angus cattle, 468

animal. *See also* living thing; organism

  adaptation of, 382–394, 421, 468–469

  algal bloom affecting, 500

  asexual reproduction of, 419–420, 423–424, 426–427, 429, 458, 460

  biomimetics, 160

  body system of, 146–151

  brains of, 155, *155*

  cell structure of, 116, *116*

  climate influencing, 387–390

  environment affecting, 454–473, 477

  environment influencing reproduction of, 421

  eukaryotic cells of, 116, *116*

  extinction of, 495

  genetics affecting, 466–467, 477

  homeostasis in, 152–153

  information processing, 152–156

  interaction in systems, 165

  memories of, 158

  migration of, 161–162

  multicellular organism, 110

  need for green plants, 99

  plants influencing, 388

  producing offspring, 418

  reproduction passing genetic material in, 418

  response to information, 157–160

  seed dispersal by, 444, *444*

  selective breeding of, 467

  sexual reproduction of, 419–420, 424, 425–427, 429, 458, 466

  similar environments produce similar adaptation, 394

animal behavior, 157

  courtship behavior, 462–463, 477

  hibernation, 158

  investigating, 86

  parenting, 462, 464, 477

  reproductive success relating to, 462–465

  response to information, 157–160

  warming and cooling, 152, *152*

Ansel Adams Wilderness, 393, *393*

Antarctic ice core data, *515*

Antarctic polar ice cap, 517

antennae, 149

anther, 443, *443*

anthroposphere, 100

Anza-Borrego Desert State Park, 382, *382*

aorta, *151*

aphid, 420

apple trees, 426–427

aquatic ecosystem, 539, *539*

aquatic organism, 539, *539*

aqueduct, 193

aquifer, 555, 556, *556*

Archaean, 110, 115

area navigation (RNAV) procedures, 581

argument

  engage in argument from evidence, 56

  evidence supporting, 96, 136

arid climate, 386, *386*

armadillo, 469, *469*

Art Connection

  Landscape Architects, 478

Artic tern, 162, *162*

artificial reef, 102

asexual reproduction, 419

  of animals, 458

  genetic inheritance in, 423, *423*, 455

  of plants, 419–420, 423–424, 440

  rate of, 424

  transfer of DNA through, 423, *423*

aspen, 450, *450*

assembly line, 68

Assessment

  Lesson Self-Check, 23–25, 41–43, 59–61, 75–77, 105–107, 125–127, 141–143, 163–165, 195–197, 213–215, 233–235, 255–257, 285–287, 307–309, 329–331, 347–349, 369–371, 397–399, 413–415, 431–433, 453–455, 475–477, 505–507, 529–531, 549–551, 573–575

  Unit Performance Task, 83–84, 171–172, 263–264, 377–378, 483–484, 581–582

  Unit Review, 79–81, 167–170, 259–262, 373–376, 479–482, 577–580

assistive technologies, 18

astronaut, 70, 139, *139*

astronomical change, 516

Atlantic Ocean, *299*

atmosphere

  absorbing sunlight, 354, *354*, 511, *511*

  changes in, 519

  cycling of matter in, 280

  defined, 270, 300

  energy flow in, 174, *174*

  flow of energy in, 281, *281*, 287

  greenhouse effect of, 511

  greenhouse gases in, 367–368

  human impact on, 495

  movement of water in, 241–244

  patterns of air movement in, 268–287

  reflecting sunlight, 354, *354*, 511, *511*

  as subsystem of Earth, 97, *97*, 98

  water in, 242–244, 257

atmospheric river, 325, *325*

atrium, *151*

avian malaria, 543, *543*

B

background research, 47

bacteria

  asexual reproduction, 424, *424*

  binary fission reproducing, 419, *419*

  decomposition by, 99

  growth of, 225

  in hot springs and thermal features, 421, *421*

  identifying cell of, 118, *118*

  as living thing, 93

  prokaryotic cell, 115

  unicellular, 110

Baja California, Mexico, 270, *270*

ballpoint pen, 70, *70*

banana crop, 417, *417*, 428, 431, *431*

Banner Peak, 393, *393*

Bañuelos, Gary, 395–396, *395*, *396*

basic life function, 93

bat, 462, 545, *545*, 551, *551*

battery, 190, *190*

bauxite, 564, *564*

bear, 392, *392*, 416, *416*, 464, *464*

beaver habitat, 490, *490, 535*
bee, 429, 445
behavior, 157, 158, 165, 392, *392*
Beijing, China, 353, *353*
Bengal tiger, 464, *464*
bighorn sheep, 393, *393*
bigleaf hydrangea, 448, *448*
bike design, 13, *13*
bike lane, 572, *572*
binary fission, 419, *419*
biodiversity, 535
biologist, 123–124
biomedicine, 78
biomimetics, 160
biomimicry, 19, 160
biosphere, 97, *97,* 99, 300, 495, 511, 524
Biosphere 2, 89, *89, 105*
bird
    migration of, 470, *470*
    reproduction of, 458, *458*
    willow dependent, *535*
blackbuck antelope, 472, *472*
Black Rock Desert, Nevada, *1*
blood, 146
blood vessel, 95, *95*
bluegill, 420, *420*
blue planet, 238, *238*
blue spruce tree, 436, *436*
board game, 471–472
body temperature, 152, *152*
bone
    connective tissue, 146
    marrow of, 103–104
    in skeletal system, 149
    transplantation of, 103
boundary, 10, 97
bowerbird, 462
bowling ball, 178, *178,* 179, 183, *183,* 186, *186*
brain, 149, 155, *155,* 157, 158
brainstorming, 46, 47, 54, 57, 97, 226, 228, 471, 561, 569, 572
brass, 205
bristlecone, 393, *393*
brittle star, 160, *160*
brown bear, 464, *464*
budding of hydra, 423, *423*
buildings, 100
Butchart Gardens, 478, *478*
butterfly, 111, *111*

C

cactus wren, 536, *536*
calcium carbonate shell, 539, *539*
California
    Alturas, 366, *366*
    Ansel Adams Wilderness, 393, *393*
    Anza-Borrego Desert State Park, 382, *382*
    Banner Peak, 393, *393*
    chaparral ecosystem, 534, 536, *536*
    cities and towns in, 387, *387*
    climates in, 359, *359,* 360, *360,* 366, *366,* 369, *369,* 386, *386*
    coastal wetland, 544
    effects of El Niño and La Niña, 518, *518*
    elevation of, 361, *361*
    fresh water in, 247
    Fresno, 366, *366*
    Joshua Tree, 387, *387,* 422, *422*
    Joshua Tree National Park, 351, *351,* 365, *365*
    land cover types in, 387, *387*
    Los Angeles, 357, *357*
    Mojave Desert, 202, *202,* 350, *350,* 369, *369,* 422, *422*
    The Pacific Flyway, 470
    Pacific Ocean effecting weather of, 324
    Point Reyes National Seashore, 268, *268*
    quino checkerspot butterfly, 542, *542*
    redwood tree in, 388, *388*
    regional climates of, 366, *366*
    San Clemente, 352, *352*
    San Diego County, 279, *279*
    San Francisco, 223, *223,* 265, *265,* 352, *352*
    Santa Ana winds, 279, *279,* 282, *282*
    Santa Paula, 270, *270*
    satellite image of, *323*
    Sierra Nevada, 323, 350, *350,* 393, *393*
    soil salinity in, 450
    Truckee, 366, *366*
    weather forecast in, 341, *341,* 342, *342*
    weather patterns in, 323–326
    wildfire in, 270, *270,* 279, *279*
    Yosemite National Park, 347, *351,* 360, 369, *369*
California Current, 223, *223,* 292, 324, 325, 331, 359, *359*
camouflage, 391, *391*
cancer cell, 166
canyon, 98
Can You Explain It? 5, 23, 27, 41, 45, 59, 63, 75, 89, 105, 109, 125, 129, 141, 145, 163, 177, 195, 199, 213, 217, 233, 237, 255, 269, 285, 289, 307, 311, 329, 333, 347, 351, 369, 383, 397, 401, 413, 417, 431, 453, 457, 475, 489, 505, 509, 529, 533, 549, 553, 573
capillaries, *151*
capsaicin, 451–452
caracara, 464, *464*
carbon
    cycle of, 304, *304*
    cycling of in atmosphere, 280
    emissions into atmosphere, 101
    in glucose, 112, *112*
carbon arc light, 32
carbon cycle, 304, *304*
carbon dioxide
    in atmosphere, 241
    in Biosphere 2, 89
    from cellular respiration, 90
    comparing quantities of, 519
    concentrations of, 539
    cycling of in atmosphere, 280
    emissions of, 526, *526*
    exchange of, 304, *304*
    from excretory system, 147
    as greenhouse gas, *368,* 397, 523
    oceans cycling, 303
    plants converting into oxygen, 133
    from respiratory system, 148
carbon monoxide, 28, 29, *29*
car design, 1, 8–9
cardinal bird, 462, *462*
cardinal flower, 388, *388*
cardiovascular system, 29, 148
Careers in Engineering: Electrical Engineer, 73–74
Careers in Engineering, Energy Conservationist, 235, *235*

Careers in Science: Geeta G. Persad, Postdoctoral Research Scientist, 527–528
Careers in Science: Hydrologist, 253–254
Careers in Science: Physical Oceanographer, 305–306
carnivorous plant, 137, 392, *392*
Carolina Reaper pepper, 451, *451*
Case Study
    The Dust Bowl, 566, *566*
    Joshua Tree, 424
    The Mississippi River, 498–501
    The Pacific Flyway, 470
    The Santa Ana Winds, 286
    Sierra Nevada, 393, *393*
cat, 197, *197*, 213, *213*
catkins, 436, *436*
causation, 521–522, *521–522*
cause and effect, 523
cause-and-effect relationship, 555
Cavendish banana, 417, *417*, 431, *431*
cell, 93
    analyzing systems of, 115–118
    division of, 110, *110*
    egg, 425
    gamete (sex), 425
    identifying different systems of, 118, *118*
    as living systems, 108–123
    living things made of, 110
    modeling, 119–121, 127
    of nerve, 108, *108*, 149
    observing under microscope, 111–113
    in organisms, 93
    of plants, 131, *131*
    size of, 120–122
    special junctions connecting, 96
    of sperm, 425
    structure of, 131, *131*
    types and structures of, 115–118, 127
    virus particles attacking, 109, *109*
cell membrane, 115, *115*, 116, *116*, 117, *117*
cell nucleus, 123, 405, *405*
cell phone, 72
cell theory, 110
cell wall, 115, *115*, **116,** 117, *117*, 130

Celsius, 244
central collector, 211
ceramic, 221, 224
chameleon, 154, *154*
change, energy flows causing, 176–196
chaparral ecosystem, 534, 536, *536*
Chargaff, Erwin, 411–412, *412*
Checkpoints, 24, 42, 60, 76, 106, 126, 142, 164, 196, 214, 234, 256, 286, 308, 330, 348, 370, 398, 414, 434, 454, 476, 506, 530, 550, 574
chemical change, 211
chemical composition, 221
chemical energy, 181, 182, 190, *190*
chemical reactions, 182, 303
chemical receptor, 154
Chernobyl Nuclear Disaster, 503–504, *504*
cherry tree, 436, *436*
chili pepper, 451–452
Chinon, France, 216, *216*
Chinook salmon, 553, *553*, 573, *573*
chlorofluorocarbon (CFCs), 367–368
chloroplast, 115, *115*, 116, **116,** 117, *117*, 123
cholla cactus, 536, *536*
chromosome, 404, 405, *405*, 408, *408*, 415, 425
cicada, 149, *149*
cilia, 112, 149
circulation
    of air, 275–278, 279–282
    of oceans, 245–246, 257, 300–305, *302*
    of water, 98, 242
circulatory system, 93, 95, 148, *148*, 151
cities, 345–346, 387, *387*
civil engineers, 16
claim
    making, 275
    stating and supporting, 23, 41, 59, 75, 92, 105, 125, 141, 163, 195, 213, 233, 255, 285, 307, 329, 347, 369, 397, 413, 431, 453, 475, 505, 529, 549, 573
Clark's nutcracker, 483, *483*

climate, 352
    albedo and, 356–357
    animals affected by, 387–390, 399
    in Beijing, China, 353, *353*
    classifying, 362
    data of, 514–515
    description of, 352–353, 510, 531
    differences in, 265
    on Earth, 510–513
    factors determining, 384–386, 399
    graphs of, 353, *353*
    influences on, 358–361, 371
    monitoring effects of, 544–546
    ocean energy flows effecting, 303
    patterns of, 544
    plants affected by, 387–390, 399, 448
    problems of, 386
    recent changes in, 523, 524–526
    regional differences, 350–366
    in San Francisco, 352, *352*
    sunlight affecting, 354–357, 371, 511, *511*
    weather and, 265–383
climate change, 485–582
    biodiversity and, 543
    monitoring organism, 545–546, 551
    organisms responding to, 538–543, 549
    organism's survival affected by, 532–546
    response, adaptation, and extinction, 542, 551
climate scientist, 521
climate zones, 362, *362*
climatologist, 345
clone, 419
cloud
    absorbing solar energy, 313
    element of weather, 313
    formation of, 243, 257
    on weather map, *318*
Coachella Valley fringe-toed lizard, 546
coal, 565
coastal wetland, 544
cold air
    in convection cells, 274, *274*, 276, *276*
    in global wind patterns, 277, *277*
    denser, 272, *272*

cold front, 321

cold ocean current, 223

cold water, density of, 294–296, *294,* 301, *301,* 302

Collaborate, 11, 22, 40, 58, 74, 104, 124, 140, 162, 194, 212, 228, 232, 254, 275, 286, 302, 306, 328, 346, 355, 368, 388, 396, 405, 412, 430, 443, 444, 452, 470, 474, 504, 528, 548, 572

collision, 186–187, 189, 218

colony collapse disorder (CCD), 445

combined heat and power plant, 567, *567*

combustion of fossil fuel, 304, *304*

community in ecosystem, 534, *534*

community project, 486

compact fluorescent lamps (CFLs), 192

compare and contrast
  concentrations, 556
  dog traits, 467
  drought tolerance of plants, 389–390
  hot and cold objects, 200–201
  information, 322
  maps, 387, *387*
  movement of water through stems, 135
  Northern and Southern Hemisphere, 278, *278*
  parents and offspring, 427
  phenotype, 407
  reproduction and growth of organisms, 418
  sexual and asexual reproduction, 428
  temperature, 198
  test data, 228
  thermal conductivity, 210
  thermal energy in objects, 204–205, 206

components
  of Earth systems, 93–98
  of a system, 86, 87

compost solid waste, 559, *559*

computer
  development of, 14
  energy transformation in, 192, *192*
  images generated by, 88

modeling programs, 544
  raw materials needed for, 14
  weather forecasting on, 341

computer model, 11, 91, 92, 510, 523

conceptional model, 11

concrete reef ball, 102, *102*

condensation, 243, 250

conduction transfer, 209, 215, 219, 281, *281,* 303

cone, 436, *436,* 438, *438*

conifer, 438, *438,* 450, *450*

connective tissue, 95, *95,* 146

conservation effects, for Florida panther, 496–497

constraints, 33
  best solutions fitting, 45, 61, 232, 560, *560*
  change in, 34, 36, 38, 43
  identifying, 37, 43, 225, 226, 546
  for lighting city streets, 33
  on lunch line design, 21
  making tradeoff, 65
  for model car design, 37–38
  redefining, 34, 43
  for umbrella, 31

construct an explanation, 138, 378

consumer demand, 15

consumer safety laws, 8

continental deflection, 292, 298

contour farming, 566, *566*

convection, 273
  cells of, 274, *274,* 276, *276*
  cycling matter due to different densities, 273, 281, *281*
  modeling, 270–275
  transfers of energy by, 209, 215, 219, 225, 303

convection current, 300–301, *301*

convective thermal energy loss, 225

conventional power plant, 567, *567*

cooling pool, 216, *216,* 219, *219*

Copenhagen, Denmark, 571

copper, 557

coral
  as animals, 146
  bleaching of, 525, *525*
  in coral reef system, 90, *90*
  reproduction of, 420, *420*

coral dahlia flower, 419

coral reef, 90, *90,* 91, 101, *101*

Coriolis effect, 276–278, **276,** *276,* 287, 292, 298

correlation, 521–522, *521–522*

cost-benefit analysis, 45, 65

courtship behavior, 462–463, 477

cover crop, 566, *566*

coyote, *535*

coyote bush, 536, *536*

crabeater seal, 147, *147*

crabs, 90, *90*

crash testing, 12

Crick, Francis, 411–412, *412*

criteria, 32
  best solutions fitting, 45, 48–49, 51, 61, 226, 228, 560, *560*
  change in, 34, 36, 38
  identifying, 38, 43, 65, 225, 546
  for lighting city streets, 32, *32*
  for lunch line design, 21
  for model car design, 37–38
  redefining, 34, 43
  for umbrella, 31

crop rotation, 566, *566*

cryosphere, 97

CTD instrument, 305, *305*

culture, 100

current
  in Mediterranean Sea, 299, *299*
  pattern of, *302*

cryosphere, 98

cytoplasm, 115, *115,* 116, *116*

cytosine, 411

D

dam, 10, *10,* 251, 490, *490,* 491, 499, *499*

damselfish, 459, *459*

damselfly, 462

Darwin's orchid, 390

data
  analyzing, 65, 378, 555, *555*
  on climate, 514–515
  of climate change, 544
  collecting, 217, 545–546, 551, 554, 557
  evaluate and test, 52, 54, 56, 61

for optimizing solutions, 68–70
scientist gathering, 545–546, 551
weather prediction using, 341–344, *341*

dead zone, 500
decision-making tool, 48
decision matrix, 48, 50, 54
decomposition, 99, 304, *304*
deep ocean current
Coriolis effect, 298, 309
effect of water density on, 298, 309
formation of, 246, 298–299
in Mediterranean Sea, 299, *299, 302*
modeling, 294–299
deer, 462
deforestation, 491, *491*
dehydration, 171, *171*
delta, 498–501
dendrites, 108, *108*
density
of air, 272
of air masses, 321
of hot and cold water, 292–296, *292*
deoxyribonucleic acid (DNA)
in asexual reproduction, 423, *423*
of bats, 545, *545*
in chloroplast, 123
defined, 404
in mitochondria, 123
mutation of, 407
in sexual reproduction, 423, *423*
structure of, 405, *405,* 411–412
dependent variable, 158, 424
deposition, 244, 250, *250*
derby car, 36
dermal tissue, 131, *131*
desert
in California, 202, *202,* 350, *350,* 369, *369,* 387, *387,* 388, *388*
climate of, 386, *386*
plants in, 130, *130,* 141, *141*
Saharan Desert, *384*
semi-arid desert, 387, *387*
specific adaptations for, 394, *394*
desert beetle, 392, *392*
design optimization, 64
design problem, 19, 28–30, 37–38
design video game character, 151

diagram
of air circulation, *276*
of carbon cycle, 304, *304*
of changing seasons, *449*
of convection current, *301*
of dam system, *10*
of deep ocean current, *298, 309*
of energy transfer, *194*
of garden bed, *448*
of heat energy, *200*
of kitchen fires and simple stoves, *29*
of latitude, *358*
of Mediterranean Sea currents, *299*
of models, *92*
of ocean circulation, *245*
of photosynthesis, *133*
of plant body systems, 131, *131*
of plant root systems, 134, *134*
of respiratory system, *151*
of thermal energy flow, *220*
of warming world, *521*
of wind formation, *272*
diatom, *303*
digestive enzyme, 147
digestive system, 90, 147, *147*
digital camera, 72
digital models, 92
digital scale, 7, *7*
dinosaur, 237, *237,* 255
disadvantages, 65
Discuss, 2, 6, 28, 46, 86, 89, 91, 97, 104, 109, 110, 129, 130, 136, 145, 146, 154, 160, 174, 192, 202, 224, 225, 226, 238, 249, 266, 270, 276, 276, 282, 322, 352, 380, 386, 387, 402, 404, 423, 437, 441, 463, 486, 491, 498, 510, 523, 565, 568
dog, 153, *153,* 467, *467*
doldrums, 277, *277*
dolphin, 86, *86*
dominant allele, 426
dominant gene, 404, 409
dominant trait, 403
Donate Life, 104, *104*
donor, soliciting and identifying, 104
donor tissues and organs, 103
dormant, 450

Do the Math, 11, 38, 40, 102, 121, 150, 328, 339, 564
Analyze a Cod Population, 502
Analyze Climate Graphs, 353, *353*
Analyze Climate Needs, 390
Analyze Female Mate Choice, 465
Analyze Hibernation, 158
Analyze Honeybee Colony Loss, 445
Analyze Temperatures, 240, *240*
Analyze Water Density Data, 297
Calculate Genotype Probability, 410
Calculate Stomata Percentage, *137*
Calculate the Rate of Asexual Reproduction, 424
Compare Concentrations, 556
Compare Objects' Thermal Energies, 206
Compare Quantities of Carbon Dioxide, 519
Compare the Hemisphere, 278
Compare Thermal Properties of Different Materials, 227
Describe Relative Humidity, 313
Energy Efficiency, 192
Evaluate Extinction Probability, 543
Evaluate Parachute Designs, 53
Explore a Kelp Forest, 537
Identify Correlation and Causation, 521
Predict Run Times Using a Model, 335, *335*
Relate Elevation and Precipitation, 361
Use Math for Design Improvement, 66
double helix, 405, *405*
dragon blood trees, 128, *128*
dragonfly, 458, *458*
Draw, 30, 54, 100, 143, 151, 187, 191, 195, 252, 272, 311, 346, 443, 494, 524
drinking water, 557, *557,* 563
dry burdock, 439, *439*
dry climate, 362, 364–365
Dungeness River, 245, *245*
dust, movement of, 269, *269*
Dust Bowl, 566, *566*
dust storm, 566, *566*
Dutch iris, 446, *446*

E

ear, 149, 153
Earth
  absorbing and reflecting sunlight, 354, *354*, 511, *511*
  albedo, 356–357
  changes in orbit of, 515, 516
  climates of, 350–366, *362*, *364–365*, 371, 384, *384*
  diversity of living things on, 418
  satellites orbiting, 85
  surface changes of, 516
  surface temperatures changes, 520, *520*
Earth Science Connection
  Climate and Reproduction, 478
Earth's rotation
  causing winds and air current, 98
  Coriolis effect, 276, *276*
  effecting gyres patterns, 292–293, *293*
  effecting pressure system, 317, *317*
  jet streams caused by, 283, *283*
  matter in atmosphere effected by, 275
  Earth System
  air circulation relating to, 279–282
  air movement patterns in atmosphere of, 268–287
  air pressure in, 314, *314*
  analyzing water on, 238–240
  carbon cycle on, *304*
  climate system, 511–513
  cycling of matter in, 303
  energy flow in, 174
  ice on surface of, 248, *248*
  interaction in, 89, 310–327, 511
  modeling of, 97–102
  movement of water on, 245–246, 288–305
  states of water on, 239–240
  subsystems of, 97–102, *97*, 270, 300
Eastern gray squirrel, 458, *458*
E. coli bacteria, 93, *93*
economy, 100

ecosystem, 534
  biodiversity of, 535, 551
  climate change disrupting, 538
  dam system disrupting, 247
  habitat degradation, 542
  health of, 534–535
  importance of, 544
  levels of, 534, *534*
  roads affecting, 16
Eco-Task Force, 483
Edison, Thomas, 44, 57
egg
  of aggregating anemone, 461, *461*
  of birds, 459, *459*, 464
  of dragonflies, 458
  of fish, 420, *420*, 459, *459*, 553, *553*
  of flowering plants, 441
  of octopus, 464
  parents protecting, 464
  of seedless plants, 437, *437*
  of seed plants, 438
elastic potential energy, 181
electrical current, 182
electrical energy
  defined, 181–182
  reducing use of, 570, *570*
  sensory response, 153
  from steam turbines, 567, *567*
  transformation of, 190, *190*
electrical engineer, 73–74
electric circuits in computers, 14
electromagnetic energy, 181, 190, *190*, 219
electromagnetic receptor, 154
electron microscope, 111
elephant, 419, 456, *456*
elephant seal, 462
elevation, 360, 361, *361*, 371, 385, *385*
elk, 463, *463*, 535
Ellesmere Island, Canada, 364, *364*
El Niño, 518, *518*, 539
embryo
  of fish, 118, *118*
  of mollusk, 458
  of plants, 438, 446
Emperor penguin, 383, 397, *397*
endoplasmic reticulum, 116, *116*, 117, *117*

endoskeleton, 149
endosymbiosis, 123
energy
  causing changes, 178
  clouds absorbing, 313
  collision transferring, 186–187
  convection transferring, 300–301
  Earth balancing, 354, *354*, 511, *511*
  in Earth systems, 97
  flowing and causing change, 176–196
  flow of in atmosphere, 281, 287
  flow of in oceans, 303, 309
  flow of in systems, 173–264
  flow of water cycle, 251
  forms of, 181–182
  gravitational potential energy, 180–181
  hydroelectric power station transforming, 176
  identifying forms of, 178–183
  kinetic, 178–179
  law of conservation of energy, 180
  loss in systems, 191–192
  mechanical energy, 181–182
  modeling transformation of, 189–192
  moving through biosphere, 99
  observing transfer of, 184–188
  from photosynthesis, 90, 130
  potential energy, 180–181
  in radiometer, 218
  stored, 180–181
  from sun, 98, 303
  surface wind and surface current transferring, 292
  in systems, 90
  thermal energy, 98, 189
  transfers of within a system, 90, 178
  in water cycle, 98
  from wind, 39–40
energy conservationist, 231–232
energy drive, in water cycle, 236–257
energy efficient, 192
energy-efficient appliance, 563
energy-efficient home, 232, *232*

energy transfer, 186
  in collisions, 186
  conduction, 209
  convection, 209
  direction of, 200–201
  heat as, 208, 215
  observing, 184–188
  between ocean and atmosphere, 251
  radiation, 209
  through systems, 218
  using thermal energy in systems, 216–235
energy transformation, 189–192, **189**
Engage in Argument from Evidence, 56
engineering, 6
  careers in, 73–74
  defined, 6
  looking to nature, 160
  problem solving, 1, 6
  relationship to science and technology, 6–9
  science and society and, 4–23
  solving design problems, 28–30
  tools of, 6, 25
Engineering Connection
  Building Homes for Different Climates, 372, 372
engineering design process
  analyze and revise design, 230
  analyze data, 84, 582
  analyze results, 570
  analyze system response, 172
  ask questions, 2, 22, 29
  background research, 47
  begins with a problem, 28
  brainstorming solutions, 46, 47
  brainstorm solutions, 561, 569
  choose best solution, 67, 226, 228, 560, 560, 562, 569
  collaboration, 22
  communicate solution, 84, 172, 484, 582
  compare solutions, 264
  conduct research, 84, 172, 484, 582
  consider tradeoff, 70, 70

  define the criteria and constraints, 226, 560, 560
  define the problem, 21, 83, 171, 263, 483, 561, 569, 581
  defining problems precisely, 29, 30–34, 41, 225–226
  design and implement test, 570
  design investigation, 264
  design optimization, 64, 70
  develop and test models, 228
  develop and test solutions, 22
  developing and testing solutions, 51, 51
  developing presentations, 582
  develop models, 264, 484
  evaluate and test solutions, 50–56, 61
  evaluate models, 102, 560, 560
  evaluate solutions, 526, 561, 568, 570
  examine needs to be met, 21
  identify and recommend solution, 84, 264
  identifying characteristics of best solution, 67
  identifying problem or need, 102, 560, 560
  identifying the problem, 28–30
  identify the problem, 21
  improving promising solution, 64–67
  making tradeoff, 65
  modeling, 4
  open-mindedness and, 47
  optimizing solutions, 62–72, 75, 77, 560, 560
  propose a test, 562
  propose solutions, 168, 558
  recommend solution, 484
  research the problem, 561, 569
  select solution with decision-making tool, 48–49
  testing many solutions, 57–58, 568
  testing prototypes, 51–53
  testing solutions, 70, 70
  using data to optimize solutions, 68–70

engineering problems
  criteria and constraints of, 32–34, 568
  defining precisely, 26–40, 43, 225, 568, 569
  developing solutions, 46–49
  evaluate test data, 52
  identifying problem or need, 102, 560, 560
  improving promising solution, 64–67
  making tradeoff, 65
  redefining criteria and constraints, 34, 43
  reframing problems, 36–38
  research the problem, 35, 561, 569
  review data and design, 52
Engineer It, 114, 133, 247, 273, 299, 306, 316, 338, 357, 408
  Analyze a Climate Problem, 386
  Analyze Applications of Mechanical Energy, 183
  Analyze Evaporative Cooling, 224
  Develop a Hybrid, 422
  Evaluate a Model, 102
  Evaluate Biomimetics, 160
  Evaluate Solutions for Climate Change, 526
  Evaluate Tradeoffs, 497
  Explain Trait Selection in Dog Breeds, 467
  Explore Plant Hybrids, 447
  Explore Thermal Energy Storage, 207
  Identify Criteria and Constraints, 546
  Unit Performance Task, 83–84, 171–172, 263–264
engineers
  careers in, 231–232, 571–572
  developing solutions, 225
  science practices compared to, 51
  studying and solving problems in natural systems, 91
enhanced greenhouse effect, 523

environment

adaptation of, 536

adjustments for needs of, 39–40

animals affected by, 456–473, 477

animal's response to, 152–156, 165

in changing condition, 421

climate affects, 385, *385*

communities improving, 486

energy-efficient home, 232

exploring, 490–492

habitat depended on, 534–535

human activity changing, 491, 507

human impact on, 488–502

human impact reduction methods,
563–567

influencing reproduction, 421, 429

interaction in, 490

living things responding to, 110

monitoring human impact on, 554–
558, 559–562

natural events changing, 491, 507

organisms adapting to, 382–394,
534–537

organisms influenced by, 379–484

plants affected by, 137–138, 140,
434–450, 455

power plant impact on, 567, *567*

reducing human impact on, 552–
570

reproduction influenced by, 420,
421, 460

scale of human impact on, 498–502

specific adaptations for, 394, *394*

in stable condition, 421

technology influenced by, 14, 16,
17, 25

technology's impact on, 17, 20, 29

**Environmental Protection Agency
(EPA),** 15, 557

Environmental Science Connection

Passive Solar Design, 258

environmental stimulus, 165, 449,
469

epidermal tissue, 95, *95*

epithelial tissue, 95, *95*, 146

equation, 335. *See also* **formula**

equator

in global wind patterns, 277, *277*

sunlight and, 355, *355*

Erawan National Park, Thailand,
364, *364*

erosion

humans causing, 495

ocean levels causing, 525

water's role in, 238, *238*

estimate

air temperature with cricket chirps,
339, *339*

elevation and precipitation, 361,
361

shipping costs, 338

Etosha National Park, Namibia, 457,
457

eucalyptus tree, 388, 533, *533*

eukaryotic cell

endosymbiosis of, 123

evolution of, 123

in plants, 130

structure of, 115, 116, *116*

evaporation, 241, 250

evaporative cooling, 224, *224*

evidence

citing, 16, 303, 344, 461, 513

engage in argument from, 56

recording on graphic organizers, 92

supporting arguments, 96, 136

supporting claims, 23, 41, 59, 75,
92, 105, 125, 141, 163, 195, 213,
233, 255, 285, 296, 307, 329, 347,
369, 389, 397, 413, 431, 453, 475,
505, 529, 549

Evidence Notebook, 5, 12, 16, 18, 23,
27, 31, 36, 41, 45, 48, 53, 59, 63,
67, 70, 75, 89, 91, 99, 101, 105,
109, 112, 118, 122, 125, 129, 132,
138, 141, 145, 156, 160, 163, 177,
182, 188, 191, 195, 199, 205, 209,
213, 217, 218, 222, 224, 233, 237,
239, 242, 252, 255, 269, 278, 280,
285, 289, 293, 303, 307, 311, 314,
317, 322, 329, 333, 341, 342, 347,
351, 356, 360, 366, 369, 383, 390,
392, 397, 401, 407, 410, 413, 417,
419, 428, 431, 435, 439, 444, 453,
457, 460, 463, 469, 475, 489, 490,
494, 501, 505, 509, 519, 523, 525,
529, 533, 537, 539, 549, 553, 558,
567, 573

excretion, 242

excretory system, 147

exercise, system response to, 150

exoskeleton, 149, *149*

explanation

cell size limits, 122

constructing, 138

Exploration

Analyze Reproductive Success of
Flowering Plants, 441–445

Analyzing Animal Responses to
Information, 157–160

Analyzing Animals Body Systems,
146–151

Analyzing Cell Systems, 115–118

Analyzing Factors that Determine
Climate, 384–386

Analyzing Heat, 208–210

Analyzing How Organisms Respond
to Climate Change, 538–543

Analyzing Influences on Technology,
13–16

Analyzing Recent Climate Change,
520–523

Analyzing Systems and Models,
10–12

Analyzing the Scale of Human
Impact on the Environment,
498–502

Analyzing Water on Earth, 238–240

Applying the Concepts of Heat
Transfer, 225–230

Assessing the Impact of Technology
on Society, 17–20

Comparing Hot and Cold Objects,
200–201

Connecting Climate Patterns to
Plant and Animal Life, 387–390

Defining Problems Precisely, 31–34

Defining Systems, 90–92

Describe Weather Patterns in
California, 323–326

Describing Animal Reproduction,
458–461

Describing Climate, 352–353

Describing Factors that Affect Plant
Growth, 446–450

Describing How Plant Systems
Process Nutrients, 133–136

Describing How Plant Systems Respond to the Environment, 137–138

Describing How Sunlight Affects Climate, 354–357

Describing Information Processing in Animals, 152–156

Describing the Movement of Water in Earth's Atmosphere, 241–244

Describing the Movement of Water on Earth's Surface, 245–248

Describing the Thermal Properties of Materials, 221–224

Describing Types of Reproduction, 418–422

Describing Weather, 312–315

Developing a Method to Monitor a Human Impact on the Environment, 559–562

Developing a Method to Reduce a Human Impact on the Environment, 568–570

Developing Solutions, 46–49

Evaluating Solutions, 50–56

Explaining Factors That Influence Animal Growth, 466–472

Explaining How Adaptations Help Organisms Survive, 391–394

Explaining How Fronts Change Weather, 319–322

Explaining the Accuracy of Weather Prediction, 340–344

Explaining the Circulation of Air, 275–278

Explaining What Influences Climate, 358–361

Exploring Earth's Climate, 510

Exploring Plant Body Systems, 130–132

Exploring the Environment, 490–492

Identifying Cells, 110–114

Identifying Different Forms of Energy, 178–183

Identifying Global Climate Change Factors, 514–519

Identifying Weather Associated with Pressure Systems, 316–318

Improving a Promising Design Solution, 64–67

Investigating How Traits Are Passed from Parent to Offspring, 402–403

Investigating Reproductive Structures of Plants, 436–440

Modeling Deep Currents, 294–299

Modeling Earth Systems, 97–102

Modeling Inheritance of Traits, 408–410

Modeling Living Systems, 93–96

Modeling Surface Currents, 290–293

Modeling the Flow of Thermal Energy through Systems, 218–220

Modeling the Water Cycle, 249–252

Modeling Wind and Convection, 270–275

Monitoring the Effects of Climate Change on Organisms, 544–546

Observing Energy Transfer, 184–188

Relating Air Circulation to the Earth System, 279–282

Relating Animal Behavior to Reproductive Success, 462–465

Relating Genetic Structure to Traits, 404–407

Relating Human Activity to the Environment, 493–498

Relating Ocean Circulation to the Flow of Matter and Energy, 300–305

Relating Reproduction to Genetic Variation, 423–428

Relating Science, Engineering, and Technology, 6–9

Relating Temperature and Thermal Energy, 202–207

Relating the Adaptations of Organisms to their Environment, 534–537

Researching to Define Engineering Problems, 35

Solving a Design Problem, 28–30

Understanding the Effects of Climate Change, 524–526

Using Data to Optimize Solutions, 68–70

Using Mathematical Models to Make Predictions, 334–339

Using Models to Analyze Systems, 101–102

Using Regional Climate Models, 362–367

Explore First, 26, 62, 108, 144, 488

Analyze Historical Weather, 332

Categorizing Traits, 400

Collecting Water, 236

Compare and Contrast Plant Types, 382

Compare Wall Structures, 4

Comparing Solution Designs, 44

Comparing Temperatures, 198

Determining Density, 288

Evaluating Models, 88

Measuring Wind Direction, 310

Modeling Elephant Ears, 532

Modeling Leaves, 128

Modeling the Rate of Warming, 268

Modeling Reproduction, 456

Modeling Seed Dispersal, 434

Modeling Variation, 416

Moving Boxes, 176

Observe Organisms, 350

Observing Thermal Energy, 216

Temperature and Sea-Level, 508

Water Quality, 552

Will It Float? 288

Explore ONLINE! 6, 10, 12, 50, 90, 104, 138, 178, 182, 199, 273, 294, 329, 333, 391, 392, 435, 441, 468, 520, 553

external environment, 152–153

extinct, 495

extinction, 495, 542, 543

eye, 149, 153

F

Fahrenheit, 240

farm

affects algal blooms, 489, *489*, 505

agricultural runoff from, 100, 557

contour farming, 566

feedback, 10, 152–153

feedback loop, 520

fertilization, 425, 437, *437,* 459
fertilizer, 557
fibrous root, 134, *134*
filament, 57
fire
    in homes, 28–30
    wildfire, 99, *99,* 270, *270,* 539
    winds moving, 279
fireworks, 190, *190,* 197, *197*
fish
    in coral reef, 90, *90*
    embryo cell of, 118, *118*
    reproduction of, 420, 458, *458*
Fisher, Paul, 70
flagella, 115, *115*
flashlight, 178
floating garbage, 289, *289,* 303, 307, *307,* 485, *485*
flood, 491
flood control, 500, *500*
floragraph, 104, *104*
Florida climate, 364, *364*
Florida panther, 496–497, *496–497*
flow chart, *560*
flower, 131, *131*
flowering seed plant, 437, 441–445
fog
    formation of, 223, *223,* 324
    in San Francisco, 223, *223,* 265, *265*
food
    cooking process, 28–29
    cooking with solar energy, 173
    plants producing, 133
    storage of, 9
    in systems, 90
food web, 334, *334,* 535
force
    of air pressure, 314
    kinetic energy started by, 178, *178*
Ford, Henry, 68
forecasters, 333, 341
forest
    California land cover, 387
    plants in, 130
formation of hail, 244
formula
    cricket chirps, 339, *339*
    density, 295
    relative humidity, 312, 313, *313*

    stomatal percentage, *137*
    surface area-to-volume ratio, 121
    thermal conductivity, 210, 224
    trend lines, 336, *336*
fossil, 514, *514*
fossil fuel, 191, *304,* 496, 519, 523, 531, *531,* 538
fox, *535*
Franklin, Rosalind, 411–412, *412*
Franz Josef Glacier, 527, *527*
fresh water, density of, 295
Fresno, California, 366, *366*
frilled lizard, 96, *96*
frog, 148, *148,* 433, *433,* 462
frontal lobe, 155, *155*
front of weather, 319–32
frozen water, 98, *98*
fruit, 436, *436*
full clone, 419
function
    of cell structures, 115–118
    structure related to, 19–20
    of tissue, 94
fungal infection, 417, *417*
fungi
    decomposition by, 99
    multicellular organism, 110, 430
    sexual and asexual reproduction of, 420, 425, 430
    on whitebark pine, 483, *483*
furnace, 567, *567*

G

gamete, 425
garbage, oceans cycling, 303
gases
    sound energy vibrating particles of, 182
    state of water, 239, *239,* 257
    thermal energy's relationship to, 221
gas lamp, 32
gene, 404
    differences in, 446
    location of, 408, *408*
    modeling, 406–407
    mutation of, 419

    passed from parent to offspring, 408–409
    traits influenced by, 404–407, 415
generator, 191
genetic, 459
genetic material
    in asexual reproduction, 419, 423–424, *424,* 433, 460
    in DNA, 405, *405,* 415
    information for cell function, 115, *115*
    organisms influenced by, 379–484
    passed from parent to offspring, 408–409
    in plant cells, 130
    reproduction passing down, 418
    in sexual reproduction, 419, 425, *425,* 433
    variation in, 425, 428, 437, 459, *459*
    in zygote, 425
genetics
    animal growth affected by, 466–467
    animals affected by, 456–473, 477
    disease caused by, 407, 466
    diversity of, 416–428, 455
    plants affected by, 434–450, 455
    structures of, 404–407
genotype, 406, 409, *409,* 426–427
geosphere, 97, *97,* 98, 300, 495, 511
geothermal heat pumps, 230, *230*
germination, 446
ghost pepper, 451, *455*
giant mirror, 207, *207*
giant sequoia tree, 130
gill, 148
giraffe, 391, *391*
glacier, 98, 248, *248,* 514, *514,* 516, *516,* 538, *538*
glassware, 7
Glen Canyon Dam, 247
global circulation pattern, 301, *301*
global climate, 510, *510*
global climate change, 485–582
    biodiversity, 543
    causes of, 514–519
    monitoring organism, 545–546, 551
    organisms responding, 538–543, 549

organism's survival affected, 532–546

response, adaptation, and extinction, 542, 551

global ocean circulation, 302–303, *302*, 309

global temperature changes, 515, 520, *520*, 538, 539

global wind

belt, 276, *276*

influencing climate, 358

pattern of, 277–278

prevailing wind, 324, 331, 352, *352*, 359

spreading volcanic ash, 280

surface wind, 292

glucose, 112, *112*

Golden Gate Bridge, 223, *223*

golden mole, 394, *394*

goldfish, 466, *466*

golf, 488, *488*

Golgi apparatus, 116, *116*, 117, *117*

grain, *566*

grape tomato, 447, *447*

graph

average weight of adult dormice, *158*

of bacteria population, *424*

Beijing, China's climate, *353*

climate in San Francisco, *352*

of climates, *353*

decision matrix, *48*, *49*, *54*

for developing and testing solutions, *51*

of electrical energy used by a school, *570*

elevation and precipitation, *361*

mathematical models, *337*

of Northern cod landings, *502*

for optimizing solutions, *69*

of run times, *336*

of water levels, *556*

weather forecast, *341*, *342*

graphic organizer

for key concepts, *3*, *87*, *175*, *267*, *381*, *487*

of systems, *92*

grasshopper, 566, *566*

grassland, 130, 385, *385*, 566

gravitational potential energy, 180–181, 187, 246

gravitropism, 140

gravity

deep ocean current affected by, 298

plants responding to, 138

water cycle affected by, 251

gravity racer car, 35, *35*

gray whale, 161, *161*

gray wolf, 466, *466*

Great Basin, 360, *360*

Greener Skies, 581, *581*

Green frog and tadpole, 418, *418*

green hermit hummingbird, 442, *442*

greenhouse, 225, *225*

greenhouse effect, 367–368, 511–513, *511*, *512*–513

greenhouse gases

atmosphere changed by, 519

emissions of, 515, 531

humans increasing, 526

landfill producing, 559, *559*

melting permafrost releasing, 520

naturally occurring, 367–368, *368*

reducing, 486

green rooftop, 224, *224*

gray wolf, 535, *535*

Grinnell Glacier, Montana, 516, *516*

grizzly bear, 416, *416*, 535

ground tissue, 95, *95*, 131, *131*

groundwater, 246, 251, 555

guanine, 411

guitar, 156, *156*

guppy, 465, *465*

gyres, 292–293, *293*

H

habitat, 490, 496–497, 524, 534–535

hail, 244, 313

hailstones, 244

hair, 149

half sphere, 278

hammer, 181, *181*

hand-powered flashlight, 177, *177*

Hands-On Labs

Compare the Drought Tolerance of Plants, 389–390

Compare Thermal Energy in Objects, 204–205

Design a Method to Monitor Solid Waste from a School, 561–562

Design a Model Car, 37–38, 54–55, 71–72

Design and Test an Insulated Container, 229–230

Evaluate a Method to Reduce the Impact of Solid Waste on the Environment, 569–570

Examine the Transfer of Thermal Energy through Radiation, 222

Explore Density of Differences in Water, 295

Investigate a Technology Inspired by Nature, 19–20

Investigate Flower Structures, 443–444

Investigate the Transfer of Energy, 185

Map Monarch Migration, 540–541

Measure Reaction Time, 159

Measure System Response to Exercise, 150

Model an Air Mass Interaction, 320

Model Asexual and Sexual Reproduction, 426–427

Model Genes and Traits, 406–407

Model Ocean Pollution from Land, 494

Model the Formation of Clouds and Rain, 243

Model the Formation of Wind, 271–272

Model the Greenhouse Effect, 512–513

Model the Growth of an Animal, 471–472

Model Tissue Structure and Function, 94

Model Your Climate, 363

Observe Cells with a Microscope, 113

Observe Transport, 135

Hands-On Labs (continued)
  online, 5, 27, 45, 63, 89, 109, 129, 145, 177, 199, 217, 237, 269, 289, 311, 333, 351, 383, 401, 417, 435, 457, 489, 509, 533, 553
  Predict Costs Using a Model, 337–338
  Use Cell Models to Investigate Cell Size, 120–121
Hawaiian honeycreeper bird, 543, 543
hawk moth, 441, 441
Health Connection
  pollution, cancer, and the cell, 166
heart, 96, 96, 103–104, 103, 148, 148, 208–210
heat, 208
  energy flow of, 198–215
  energy transfer of, 200–201
  sensory receptor's response to, 153
heat transfer
  applying concepts of transfer of, 225–230
  designing solutions for, 227–230
heirloom tomato, 447, 447
heliconia flower, 442, 442
Hercules beetle, 442, 442
hibernation, 158, 392, 392
high elevation, 352, 352
highland climate, 362, 364–365, 386, 386
Highlands of Scotland, 246, 246
high-pressure air system
  affecting weather, 317–318, 331
  Earth's rotation effecting, 276, 276
  in global wind patterns, 277, 277
  Santa Ana winds, 282, 282
  wind formation caused by, 271–272, 272, 287
high-pressure belt, 358, 358
homeostasis, 152–153
honeybee colony loss, 445
horse latitudes, 277, 277
hot air
  in convection cells, 274, 274, 276, 276
  density of, 272, 272
  in global wind patterns, 277, 277
hot spring, 421, 421
hot water, density of, 294–296, 294, 301, 301

housefly, 145, 145, 163, 163
human
  analyzing effects of activities of, 90
  in anthroposphere, 100
  body system of, 146–151
  cerebral cortex, 155, 155
  genetic material of, 404
  natural system of, 91
  organ transplants, 103–104
  problems, 28
human activity
  atmosphere pollution caused by, 495, 519
  climate change influenced by, 525–526, 531
  in Earth systems, 492, 507
  environmental impact of, 488–502
  improving resource use during, 565
  influencing climate change, 508–526
  Mississippi River Delta impacted by, 498–501
  monitoring environmental impact of, 554–558, 559–562, 575
  reducing impact of, 552–570, 575
  scale of impact of, 498–502
  water pollution caused by, 493, 494
human-built river controls, 499
human exposure to radiation, 503
human-powered treadwheel, 188, 188
humid continental climate, 362, 364–365, 386, 386
humidity
  in air masses, 319
  as component of weather, 312, 384
  affecting snowflakes, 327–328
  relative, 312, 317
  on weather map, 318
humid subtropical climate, 362, 364–365
humid tropical climate, 362, 364–365
hurricane
  in Baja California, Mexico, 270, 270
  climate change affecting, 525
  lightning during, 266
hybrid, 422, 422
hydra, 423, 423, 433, 433

hydroelectric dam, 191
hydroelectric power station, 176
hydrogen, 112, 112
hydrologist, 253–254
hydrosphere, 97, 97, 98, 300, 493, 511
hyena, 140
hypothalamus gland, 167, 167

ice
  climate data in, 514, 514
  on Earth's surface, 248, 248
  as habitat, 508, 508
  melting of, 509, 529, 529
  movement of, 251
  recent climate change affecting, 525, 525
  state of water, 239, 239
ice age, 524
iceberg, 248
ice climber, 352, 352
immune system, 104, 148
impermeable surfaces, 558, 558
Incan architecture, 4, 4
incandescent light bulb, 32, 44, 44, 57–58, 192
independent variable, 158, 424
indicators of a warming world, 521, 521
individual in ecosystem, 534, 534, 542, 542
infection, viruses causing, 109
infiltration, 246, 250
infographic, 166
information
  animal's response to, 157–160
  processing of, 149, 152–156
  transfers of within a system, 90
infrared photography, 199, 199, 209, 213, 213
infrared radiation, 154
infrared sensors, 293, 293
inheritance, 408
  in asexual reproduction, 423, 423
  modeling, 408–410
  Punnett squares modeling, 409, 409
  of traits, 403

innate behavior, 157

inorganic matter, 280, 559, *559*

input

    into atmosphere, 99, *99*

    into cell systems, 118

    of energy in radiometer, 218

    energy transfer, 186

    flashlight, 177, *177*

    into hydrosphere, 99, *99*

    modeling, 218, 363

    into photosynthesis, 129, *129*

    into systems, 10, 90

insect, 458, *458*

insecticide-treated mosquito net, 5, *5*

insulated coat, 198, *198*

interaction in systems

    causing weather, 310–327, 511

    computer modeling, 544

    digestive and excretory system, 147

    on Earth, 97, 270, 300, 490

    of organism, 534

    respiratory and circulatory system, 148, 151

    skeletal and muscular system, 149

Interactive Review, 25, 43, 61, 77, 107, 127, 143, 165, 197, 215, 235, 257, 287, 309, 331, 349, 371, 399, 415, 433, 455, 477, 507, 531, 551, 575

interior vena cava, *151*

internal environment, 152–153

internal movement, 149

International Space Station, 139–140

investigation method, of Mendel, 403

investigations

    animal behavior, 86

    performing, 389

iterative design process, 77

iterative testing of prototype, 69

J

jackrabbit, 399, *399*, 536, *536*

jellyfish, 420, *420*

jet stream, 283–284, *283*

joey, 459, *459*

Joshua Tree, 388, *388*, 422, *422*

Joshua Tree National Park, 350, *350*, 369, *369*

joule (J), 181, 203

Juliet tomato, 447, *447*

K

kangaroo, 459, *459*

kangaroo rat, 93, *93*

kelp forest, 537, *537*

key concepts, graphic organizer for, 3, *87*, *175*, *267*, *381*, *487*

kidney, 103–104, 147, 171, *171*

killdeer bird, 464

kinetic energy

    of air particles, 312, *312*

    defined, 178–179

    in energy transfer, 184–188

    loss of, *240*

    mass proportional to, 179, 197

    measuring, 182, 202, 203, *219*, 221

    of melting ice cream, 200, *200*

    for sublimation, 242

    transfer of, 281, 287

    transformation of, 189–192, 197

    types of, 181

kingfisher bird, 462

kitten, 401, *401*, 413

koala, 388, 533, *533*, 549, *549*

Komodo dragon, 460, *460*

Köppen-Geiger, 362

Kronotsky Reserve, Russia, 270, *270*

Kwan, Garfield, 166, *166*

L

lactococcus lactis, 424, *424*

lake, 98

Lake City, Colorado, 352, *352*

Lake Tahoe, 98, *98*

land ecosystem, 539

landfill, 559, *559*, 568, *568*

landform

    affecting weather, 325, 331

    influencing climate, 360, 371, 384

landscape architect, 478

Language Development, 3, 87, *175*, 267, *381*, 487

Language SmArts, 185, 205, 230, 252, 275, 282, 301, 344, 363

    Compare and Contrast Information, 322

    Compare Asexual and Sexual Reproduction, 428

    Construct an Argument, 440

    Construct an Explanation of Trait Inheritance, 403

    Describe the Problem Precisely, 30

    Describe Weather, 315

    Discuss, 387

    Evaluate Possible Solutions, 561

    Evaluate Reproductive Strategies, 461

    Evaluate Text, 546

    Explain Limits to Cell Size, 122

    Explain Sensory Receptor Patterns, 156

    Explain Temperature Ranges on Earth and the Moon, 513

    Identify Facts, 492

    Identify Influences on Technology, 16

    Use Evidence to Support an Argument, 96

    Use Observations to Develop an Argument, 136

La Niña, 518, *518*, 539

large intestine, 147, *147*

latitude

    influencing climate, 358, *358*, 384

    of Sierra Nevada, 393, *393*

    sunlight affecting, 3715

    sunlight and, 355, *355*

lava lamp, 273, *273*

law of conservation of energy, 180, 189, 218

laws of inheritance, 409

leaf, 133

    adaptation of, 388

    food production of, 129

    of plants, 127, *127*

learned behavior, 157, 469, 473–474

leatherback turtles, 155

left atrium, *151*

leopard, 144, 391, *391*

Lesson Self-Check, 23–25, 41–43, 59–61, 75–77, 105–107, 125–127, 141–143, 163–165, 195–197, 213–215, 233–235, 255–257, 285–287, 307–309, 329–331, 347–349, 369–371, 397–399, 413–415, 431–433, 453–455, 475–477, 505–507, 529–531, 549–551, 573–575

levee, 498–501, *499*

lever, 183

Life Science Connection
    medical biology, 78

light
    plants responding to, 138
    sensory receptor's response to, 153

light-emitting diode (LED), 32, 192

light energy, 182

light microscope, 7, *7*, 111

lightning, 266

Liles, Kaitlin, 283, *283*

limestone cave, 248, *248*

limitations, 32–34

lion, 157, *157*, 464

liquid
    sound energy vibrating particles of, 182
    state of water, 239, *239*, 257
    thermal energy's relationship to, 221

litter pick up, 486

living donor, 103

living system
    cells as, 108–123
    modeling, 93–96
    organism as, 93
    of plants, 128–138

living thing. *See also* **animal; organism; plant**
    in biosphere, 99
    cells making, 110, 127
    cell theory defining, 110
    characteristics of, 110, 127
    in Earth systems, 97
    needs of, 490
    organisms as, 93
    responding to environment, 110
    water in, 237

local environment
    climate affects, 385, *385*
    plants affected by, 448

lock-and-dam system, 499, *499*, 500, *500*

long-nosed bat, 442, *442*

long-range weather forecast, 342

Los Angeles, 357, *357*

Lower Mississippi River levee system, 500, *500*

low-pressure air system
    affecting weather, 317–318, 331
    Earth's rotation affecting, 276, *276*
    in global wind patterns, 277, *277*
    Santa Ana winds, 282, *282*
    wind formation caused by, 271–272, *272*, 287

low-pressure belt, 358, *358*

luna moth and caterpillar, 418, *418*

lunch carrier, 225–230

lung
    in respiratory system, 148, *148*, *151*
    transplantation of, 103–104

lymphatic system, 148

lysosome, 116, *116*

M

magnetic resonance imaging (MRI), 155, *155*

magnification, 113

Maldives, 236, *236*

mammal
    nursing young, 464
    reproduction of, 458, *458*

manakin bird, 462, *462*

manure, 100

maple tree, 130, *130*

Margulis, Lynn, 123–124, *123*

Mars, 85

mass
    of Earth in geosphere, 98
    kinetic energy directly proportional to, 179, 184, 197
    thermal energy's relationship to, 221

material
    cost and availability of, 33
    criteria for umbrella, 31
    engineers use of, 6
    plants moving, 134
    thermal conductor, 227
    thermal insulator, 227
    thermal properties of, 221–224

mathematical models, 11, 92, 334–339, 349

Matsuda, Shayle, 547-548, *547*

matter
    constant motion of particles of, 202
    convection causing movement of, 300–301
    cycling of in atmosphere, 280, 287
    cycling of in oceans, 303–304, 309
    in Earth systems, 97
    energy flow in, 182
    moving through biosphere, 99
    transfers of within a system, 90

measurement
    of average kinetic energy, 202
    energy in units of joule (J), 181
    of reaction time, 159
    of system responses to exercise, 150
    of total kinetic energy, 203

measuring devices, 7, *7*

mechanical energy, 181–182, *183*

mechanical receptor, 154

Mediterranean climate, 364, *364*, 386, *386*

Mediterranean Sea, *299*

medium-range weather forecast, 344

meerkat, 473, *473*

memory, 152, **158**

Mendel, Gregor, 402–403, *402–403*, 415, *415*

Mendel's Pea Plant Investigation, 402, *402*, 409, 415, *415*

mental model, 11

meteoroid, 188, *188*

meteorologist, 341, 345

methane, *368*, 520, 523

methods for monitoring, 559–562

metric ruler, 114

Michaud-Larivière, Jérôme, 39

microorganisms, 112

microscope, 6, 111–113

microscopic aquatic organism, 419

microwave sensors, 293, *293*

migration, 161–162, 540–541

milkweed seedling, 439, *439*

mining, 495, 496, 565

mirror, 207, *207*

Mississippi River Delta, 498–501, *498*

Mississippi River watershed, 500, *500,* 501, *501*

mitochondria, **116,** *116,* 117, *117,* 123

model

of agricultural runoff, 100

cells, 119–120

climate change, 544

of clouds and rain formation, 243

design a model car, 37–38, 54–55

develop and test lunch containers, 228

of Earth systems, 97–102

effects of Earth's rotation on matter in atmosphere, 275

of elephant ears, 532

energy transformation, 189–192

evaluating, 88

of floating garbage, 289, *289,* 307, *307*

of flow of thermal energy, 219

flow of thermal energy through systems, 218–220

of genes and traits, 406–407

global ocean circulation, 302, *302*

of global winds, 277, *277*

of greenhouse effect, 512–513

helping scientists study natural systems, 88–102, 107

of inheritance of traits, 408–410

mathematical models, 334–339

of nautilus, 334, *334*

of oceans' surface currents, 290–293

physical model, 119

prototype, 51, **65**

of Punnett squares, 409, *409,* 415

regional climate, 362–366

science using, 334–339

sexual and asexual reproduction, 426–427

of stems, 128

of systems, 11, 92

to test design solutions, 65

three-dimensional (3D) model, 119

tissue structure and function, 94

of traits, 456

two-dimensional (2D) model, 119

types of, 11, 92

wall structures, 4

of water cycle, 249

weather forecast, 341–343

weather prediction, 178

wind and convection, 270–275

Mojave Desert, 206, *206,* 354, *354,* 369, *369,* 388, *388,* 422, *422*

mollusk, 458, *458*

monarch butterfly, 161, *161*

monitoring human impact

describing methods for, 554–558

developing methods for, 559–562

in neighborhood, 562

monitoring organism, 545–546, *545, 551, 551*

Moscow, Russia, 364, *364*

mosquito, 543, *543*

mosquito netting, 5, *5,* 16, *23*

moss, 437, *437*

moss leaf cell, 118, *118*

moth orchid, 434, *434*

moulting, 149, *149*

mountain, 384, 399

mountain aspen, 450, *450*

Mount Everest, 314, *314*

Mount Pinatubo, 519, *519*

mouth, 153

movement

of air pressure, 315

of matter through convection, 300–301

muscular system providing, 149

of water on Earth's surface, 245–248, 253–254, 290–305

muffin design, 64–67

mule deer, *535*

multicellular organism

animal, 146

cell specialization in, 93

as living thing, 110

plants as, 130

reproduction of, 419, 429–430

multimedia presentation, 363, 372, 396, 452

muscle tissue, 146

muscular system, 149, *149*

Music Connection

Songs about Saving Earth, 576

mutation of DNA, 407

N

Namib desert, 129, *129,* 141, *141*

National Aeronautics and Space Administration (NASA), 73–74, 290

natural gas plant, 558, *558*

naturally radioactive rocks, 98

natural resource, 490

availability of, 14, 563–564

quality of, 556–558, 565

reuse and recycling of, 564, *564*

technology's use of, 14

use of, 490, 554–556, 563–564

natural system

characteristic of, 91

defining, 91

interactions of, 89

models of, 92

properties of, 91

using models to study, 88–102

nautilus, 146, *146,* 334, *334*

nectar, 441

needs, 28, 31–34

negative feedback, 148–149

negatively charged particles, 182

nerve

in animals, 149

impulses in, 108, *108*

nervous system, **149**

nervous tissue, 146

neuron, 153, *153,* 155, *155*

New Mexico whiptail lizard, 419

Newton's cradle, 187, *187,* 189, *189,* 197, *197*

New York City, 571, *571*
New Zealand mud snail, 458, *458*
Nicholson, Simon, 576
night blooming plant, 441
nitrogen
    in agricultural runoff, 100
    in atmosphere, 98, 241
    cycling of in atmosphere, 280
    plants need of, 133
nitrous oxide, *368*
nonflowering seed plant, 438, *438*
nonliving thing
    cells lacking in, 110
    in Earth systems, 97
nonpoint-source pollution, 493, 494
nonrenewable resource, 563
nonvascular plant, 131
noria, 193–194
northeast trade winds, 277, *277*
North Equatorial Current, 292
Northern cod, 502, *502*
Northern Hemisphere, 278, *278*
North Pacific Current, 292
nose, 153
nuclear cooling pool, 219, *219*
nuclear energy, 181, 182, 219, 503
nuclear fuel rods, 216, *216*, 219, *219*
nucleotide, 411
nucleus, 116, **116**, *116*, 117, *117*
nutrient
    in agricultural runoff, 102
    in algal bloom, 489
    from animals, 132
    in fertilizer, 501
    ocean cycling, 302, 359, 539
    from plants, 441
    plant systems processing, 131,
      133–136, 417
    respiratory and circulatory system
      transporting, 93, 95, 148
    in soil, 133, 143, 557
    water cycling, 542
nymph, 458

O

obelisk, 183, *183*, 188
observation
    of cells under a microscope,
      111–113
    of energy transfer, 184–188
    of thermal energy, 216
occipital lobe, 155, *155*
occluded front, 322
ocean
    absorbing solar energy, 270
    algal blooms in, 489, *489*
    carbon dioxide in, 303, 304, 539
    changes of salinity in, 297–298
    circulation of, 245–246, 257, 300–
      305, *302*, 517, *517*
    convection currents in, 300–301
    currents of, 245, *245*, 250, *250*, 289,
      290, 300–305, 359, *359*, 371
    cycling of matter in, 303–304, 517,
      517
    density of water in, 297–298
    energy flow in, 174, *174*, 517, *517*
    floating garbage in, *289*
    influencing climate, 359, *359*, 384,
      399
    movement of water in, 288–305
    as part of hydrosphere, 300
    patterns in, 290
    physical oceanographer studying,
      305–306
    pollution from land in, 494
    recent climate change affecting,
      525, *525*
    surface currents of, 290–293, 324
    surface temperatures of, 293, *293*
    temperature rising in, 297–298,
      532, *532*, 539, *539*
    volume of, 238, 300
    wind transferring kinetic energy to,
      281
ocean current, 290
Ochoa, Ellen, 73–74, *73*
ochre sea star, 532, *532*
ocotillo, 382, *382*
octopus, 464

odor memory, 158
offspring, 418
    in asexual reproduction, 419, 421,
      422, *422*, 423–424, *424*, 433
    genetic variation in, 425
    as hybrids, *422*
    organisms producing, 418
    parent passing traits to, 400–410,
      421
    parents protecting, 464
    parents teaching, 473–474, *473*
    of plants, 436, *436*
    reproductive success resulting in,
      462–465
    in sexual reproduction, 419, 421,
      422, *422*, 423, 425, *425*, 433, 459,
      459
    survival of, 420
okapi, 146, *146*
olfactory, 162
one-horned rhino, 542, *542*
online activities
    Hands-On Labs, 19, 37, 54, 71, 94,
      113, 120, 135, 150, 159, 185, 204,
      222, 229, 243, 271, 295, 320, 337,
      363, 389, 406, 426, 443, 471, 491,
      512, 540, 561, 569
    Take It Further, 21, 39, 57, 73, 103,
      123, 139, 161, 193, 211, 231, 253,
      283, 305, 327, 345, 367, 395, 411,
      429, 451, 473, 503, 527, 547, 571
    Unit Project Worksheet, 2, 86, 174,
      266, 380, 486
    You Solve It, 1, 85, 173, 265, 379,
      485
onyanga, 129, *129*
open kitchen fires, 28–29
open-mindedness, 47
orangutan, 474, *474*
organ, 95
    of animals, 146
    brain, 149
    ear, 149
    eye, 149
    of plants, 131, *131*, 133, 143
    sensory organ, 153
    subsystem of different tissue types,
      95

organelle, 115, **115**, *115*, 130
organic matter, 280, 559, *559*
organism, 93. *See also* **animal; plant**
  adaptation of, 391, 421
  binary fission reproducing, 419, *419*
  carbon in, 304, *304*
  cells of, 93
  climate change affecting, 532–546
  climate influencing, 387–390
  decomposition of, 304, *304*
  environmental and genetic
    influences on, 379–484
  environment influencing
    reproduction of, 421
  interaction in systems, 90
  as living systems, 93–96, 107
  multicellular, 93, 110
  needs of, 388
  producing offspring, 418
  responding to climate change,
    538–543
  scientist monitoring and tracking,
    545–546, 551
  subsystems of, 93
  tissues of, 93–94
  unicellular, 93, 110
  water needs of, 238
organ system, 95
  of animals, 146
  of frilled lizard, 96, *96*
  of plants, 131, *131*, 143
  subsystem of group of organs, 95
***Origin of Eukaryotic Cells* (Margulis),**
  123
output
  by atmosphere, 99, *99*
  from cell systems, 118
  energy transfer, 186
  flashlight, 177, *177*
  by hydrosphere, 99, *99*
  modeling, 218, 363
  from photosynthesis, 133, *133*
  from systems, 10, 90
ovary, 443, *443*
ovule, 438

oxygen
  during algal bloom, 489, *489*, 500
  in atmosphere, 98, 241
  in Biosphere 2, 89
  in glucose, 112, *112*
  nonliving thing, 110
  oceans cycling, 303
  respiratory system using, 148
  in space station, 139
ozone, *368*

P

Pacific Flyway, 470, *470*
Pacific Ocean
  affecting weather, 324, 325, 331
  surfing in, 352, *352*
Pacific salmon, 458, *458*
paddle boat, 194
paleoclimate data, 514–515, *515*
palm seed, 439, *439*
Panama disease, 417, *417*, 428, 431,
  435
pancreas, 171, *171*
pangolin, 144, *144*
parachute design, 52–53, 56
paramecia
  cilia, 112
  magnification of, 112, *112*
  unicellular, 110
parathyroid, 171, *171*
parent
  in asexual reproduction, 419, 421,
    422, *422*, 423–424, *424*, 433
  behaviors of, 464
  hybrids of, *422*
  passing traits to offspring, 400–410,
    425
  producing offspring, 418
  reproductive success of, 462–465
  in sexual reproduction, 419, 421,
    422, *422*, 423, 425, *425*, 433, 459,
    459
  teaching offspring, 473–474, *473*
parenting behavior, 477
parietal lobe, 155, *155*
parrotfish, 90
patent, 58

pattern
  of air circulation, 275–277
  of air movement in atmosphere,
    268–287
  of deep ocean currents, 298–299
  of global ocean circulation, 302, *302*
  of global winds, 277–278, *277*
  gyres, 292–293, *293*
  in ocean, 290
  of sensory receptors, 156
  of snowflakes, 327–328
  in water density, 296
  of water movement on Earth's
    oceans, 288–305
  on weather map, *318*
  in weather prediction, 332–344
peacock, 463, *463*
pedicel, 443, *443*
pendulum, 180, 186
penguin, 464, *464*
People in Engineering: Liles, Kaitlin,
  283, *283*
People in Engineering: Ochoa, Ellen,
  73-74, *73*
People in Science: Bañuelos, Gary,
  395–396
People in Science: Chargaff, Erwin,
  411–412
People in Science: Crick, Francis,
  411–412
People in Science: Franklin,
  Rosalind, 411–412
People in Science: Kwan, Garfield,
  166, *166*
People in Science: Margulis, Lynn,
  123–124, *123*
People in Science: Matsuda, Shayle,
  547–548, *547*
People in Science: Nicholson,
  Simon, 576
People in Science: Puniwai, Noelani,
  372
People in Science: Shepherd,
  J. Marshall, 345-346, *345*
People in Science: Snetsinger,
  Phoebe, 478
People in Science: von Ahn, Luis,
  78, *78*
People in Science: Watson, James,
  411–412

permafrost, 509, 520, 525, *525*, 529, *529*
Peru Current, 292
pesticide, 557
petal, 443, *443*
phenotype, 406, 409, *409*, 426–427
phloem, 134
phosphate, 411
phosphorus
    in agricultural runoff, 100
    in Amazon jungle, 269, *269*, 285, *2859*
    cycling of in atmosphere, 280
    plants need of, 133
photograph, infrared photography, 199, *199*, 209
photosynthesis
    in biosphere, 99
    in carbon cycle, 304, *304*
    food production of, 133
    of marine organisms, 303
    organ systems performing, 95
    plants performing, 130, 449, *449*
    in space station, 140
phototropism, 138
pH scale, 448, *448*
physical adaptation, 392, *392*
physical disabilities, 15
physical model
    of cities affecting rainfall, 346
    of Earth, 89, *89*, 275
    formation of wind, 271
    of greenhouse effect, 512–513
    prototypes as, 51
    of systems, 92
    three-dimensional (3D) model, 102, 119
    use of, 11
physical oceanographer, 305–306
Physical Science Connection
    transmission electron microscopes, 166
phytoremediation of soil, 395
pineal gland, 171, *171*
Pineapple Express precipitation, 325, *325*
pistil, 442, *442*
pizza, 211–212, *211–212*
pizza stone, 211, *211*

planaria, 460, *460*
plankton, *303*
planned public transportation, 571
planning and carrying out investigations, 377–378
plant. *See also* **living thing; organism**
    adaptation of, 382–394, 421
    algal bloom affecting, 500
    analyze body system of, 132, 143
    animal influence by, 388
    asexual reproduction of, 419–420, 423–424, 440
    body system of, 131–132
    cell structure of, 117, *117*
    cell types of, 131, *131*
    chloroplast in, 116
    climate change affecting, 539
    climate influencing, 387–390
    drought tolerance of, 389–390
    environmental factors affecting, 421, 434–450
    eukaryotic cells of, 116, *116*
    extinction of, 495
    factors affecting, 446–450
    flowering and nonflowering seed plant, 438, *438*
    gravitropism, 140
    growing in space, 139–140
    hybrids of, 447
    as living system, 128–138
    magnification of, 112, *112*
    Mendel's Pea Plant Investigation, 402, *402*
    multicellular organism, 110
    needs of, 388, 446
    organs of, 134
    photosynthesis of, 99
    phototropism, 138
    producing offspring, 418
    reproduction structures in, 436–440, *436*, *442*, *442*, 443–444, *443*, 455
    responding to environment, 137–138, 143
    seedless plant, 437, *437*
    sexual reproduction of, 419–420, 425, 437–439, 455

    similar environments produce similar adaptation, 394
    specialized cell of, 93
    stem of, 95
    vascular and nonvascular, 131
    water vapor from, 242
plant breeder, 447
plantlet, 436
Point Reyes National Seashore, 268, *268*
point-source pollution, 493, 494
polar bear, 478, *478*
polar climate, 362, 364–365
polar easterlies, 277, *277*
polar ice cap, 517
polar jet stream, 283, *283*
pollen, 419, 438, 441, 442
pollination, **438,** 441–444, *442*
pollinator, 442, *442*, 445
pollution
    agricultural runoff, 100
    of carbon into atmosphere, 101
    cells affected by, 166
    concentration levels of, 556
    as harmful input, 90
    human activity causing, 491
    modeling of, 494
    nonpoint-source, 493
    plants removal of, 136
    point-source, 493
    testing for, 557, *557*
    in watershed, 501, *501*
polyp, 420, *420*
pomegranate tree, 436, *436*
Ponderosa pine tree, 93, *93*
population
    adaptation of, 542, *542*
    of ecosystem, 534, *534*
    in New York City and Tokyo, 571, *571*
    in Yellowstone Park, 535, *535*
porcupines, 157, *157*
positive feedback, 152–153, 523
postdoctoral research scientist, 527–528
potato, 436, *436*
potential energy
    changes in, 180–181, 197
    in energy transfer, 184–188
    transformation of, 189–192
    types of, 181
power plant, 567, *567*

precipitation, 244
in California, 361, *361*
cities affecting, 345
as component of weather, 384
formation of, 313
in fronts, 321–322
Pineapple Express, 325, *325*
prediction of, 344, *344*
in San Francisco, 352, *352*
in Sierra Nevada, 393, *393*
in water cycle, 250, *250*, 257
on weather map, *318*
prediction
air mass interaction, 320
with climate graphs, 353
energy transfer, 184
of genotype and phenotype, 426–427
of growth of blackbuck antelope, 472
kinetic energy versus speed, 179
from models, 334, *334*
of mutation, 407
of outcomes, 400
of shipping costs, 337, *337*
using mathematical models, 334–339
of weather based on patterns, 332–344
of weather forecast, 340–344, *340*
pressure, sensory receptor's response to, 153
pressure system, types of, 317
pressure-treated wood, 559
prevailing wind, 324, 331, 352, *352*, 359, 371
prickly pear cactus, 396, *396*, 444, *444*
probability in math, 410, 543
process
iterative design process, 69–70
for optimization, 68
processing information, 155–156, 165
prokaryotic cell, 115, *115*, 123
pronghorn, 468, *468*
property of matter, 210
property of systems, 91
proportions in system models, 11

prosthetics, 18, *18*
protein, 115, **404**
prototype, 51, 65
pulmonary artery, *151*
pulmonary vein, *151*
Puniwai, Noelani, 372
Punnett square, 409, *409*, 410, *410*, 447, *447*, 484

Q

quality of life, 18
quantities in system models, 11
questions
asking, 2, 22, 29, 381
defining engineering problems, 29
generating, 2
quino checkerspot butterfly, 542, *542*

R

radiant thermal energy, 225
radiation
Earth emitting, 354, *354*, 511, *511*
energy transfer by, 209, 210, 215, *215*, 219
from the sun, 281, *281*
warming the ocean, 303
radiation sickness, 503
radioactive contamination, 395
radiometer, 218, *218*
rain
cause of, *310*
cities affecting, 345
formation of, 313
raincoat design, 67
rain-shadow effect, 325
rat, 93, *93*
reaction time, 159
reasoning, 23, 41
recent climate change, 520–523
receptacle, 443, *443*
recessive allele, 426
recessive gene, 404
recessive trait, 403
recycling, 14, 139, 181, *181*, 493, *493*, 564, *564*, 579, *579*
red blood cell, 95, *95*

red rock crab, 146, *146*
Red Savina habanero, 451, *451*
red squirrel, 464, *464*
redwood tree, 388, *388*, 420
reef ball, 102, *102*
reef ecosystem, 90, *90*, 91
refrigerator, 258, *258*
regional climate model, 362–366
relationship
animal behavior and reproductive success, 462–465
between science, engineering, and technology, 6–9
cause and effect, 555
digestive and excretory system, 147
in ecosystem, 334, *334*
elevation and precipitation, 361
hot and cold objects, 200–201
living things and nonliving things in biosphere, 99
models to understand, 11
organism's adaptations and environment, 534–537
plants and environments, 143
reproduction and genetic variation, 427
respiratory and circulatory system, 148, 151
skeletal and muscular system, 149
structure and function, 19–20
surface area-to-volume ratio to movement, 121
surface area-to-volume ratio to time, 121
temperature and thermal energy, 202–207
of traits to genetic structure, 404–407
between variables, 297, *297*
relative humidity, 312, 317
Renault, Michele, 188, *188*
renewable energy, 191, 194
renewable resource, 502, 556, 563
reproduction
animal behaviors affecting, 462–465
of animals, 458–461
of cells, 110, *110*
in changing conditions, 421
defined, 418

reproduction (continued)
environmental influences on, 421
factors influencing, 429–430
genetic diversity in, 416–428
of Joshua Trees, 422, *422*
organs for, 442, *442*
of plants, 437, 441–445
replication of virus particles, 109, *109*
in stable conditions, 421
structures for, 436–440, *436, 442, 442, 443–444, 443, 455*
types of, 418–422, 433
reproductive success, 459, 462
reptile, reproduction of, 420
reservoirs, 247
resource
availability of, 14, 563–564
depletion of, 491
quality of, 556–558, 565
reuse and recycling of, 564, *564*
technology's use of, 14
use of, 490, 554–556, 563–564
respiration, 242, 304, *304*
respiratory system, 92, *92, 93,* 148, 151
review
Interactive Review, 25, 43, 61, 77, 107, 127, 143, 165, 197, 215, 235, 257, 287, 309, 331, 349, 371, 399, 415, 433, 455, 477, 507, 531, 551, 575
Unit Review, 79–82, 167–170, 259–262, 373–376, 479–482, 577–580
ribosome, 115, *115,* 116, *116,* 117, *117*
right atrium, *151*
right ventricle, *151*
Rio Grande, 253, *253,* 254
risk-benefit analysis, 49
river
Mississippi River Delta, 498–501
water and wind shaping, 98
river otter, 474, *474*
roadrunner, 383, 397, *397*
robin, 459, *459*
rock
carbon in, 304, *304*
climate data in, 514, *514*
nonliving thing, 110
rocket car, *1*

rooftop albedo, 357, *357*
root system, 131, *131,* 134, **134,** *134,* 388
roseate spoonbill, 458, *458*
rough endoplasmic reticulum, 116, *116,* 117, *117*
Rub'al Khali desert, 364, *364*
rubber tree, 394, *394*
runoff, **246,** 2504

S

sacred lotus flower, 435, *435*
saguaro cactus, 130, *130*
Sahara, 269, *269,* 285, *285*
Saharan Desert, 384
salivary gland, 147, *147*
salmon, 162, *162*
salt
changes in levels of, 297–298
from excretory system, 147
in soil, 450
salt water
density of, 295
dissolved matter in, 303
large volume of Earth's water, 238, 245
salinity of, 91, 295
San Clemente, 352, *352*
San Diego County, 279, *279*
San Francisco, 352, *352*
San Francisco Bay, 223, *223,* 265, *265*
Santa Ana winds, 279, *279*
Santa Paula, 270, *270*
satellite images
of California, *323*
of deforestation, 554, *554*
ocean surface currents, 288, *288*
scientist using, 334, *334*
of urban heat island, 217, *217*
satellites, 85
scale (on animals), 144, *144*
scale (proportion)
of convection, 274, *274*
drawing to, 114
of health problems, 29
humans' environmental impact, 498–502, 507
under microscope, 113

in system models, 11
of technology, 25
science, 6
careers in, 305–306, 527–528
engineering and society and, 4–23
models in, 334–348
relationship to engineering and technology, 6–9
technology influenced by, 14, 16
scientific models, 11
scientific understanding, 14
scientist
define and study systems, 90–92
engineering practices compared to, 51
gathering data, 545–546, 551, 557
modeling natural systems, 92
monitoring environment, 563, 575
types of microscopes used by, 111
understanding how natural systems function and change, 91
using engineer designed tools, 6
using models to study natural systems, 88–102
Scoville scale, 451
seahorse, 380, *380*
sea ice, 98
seal, 391, *391,* 459, *459,* 462, 508, *508*
sea level, 498, 525
seasons, climate change affecting, 539
sea star, 532, *532*
Seattle, 581, *581*
Seattle-Tacoma Airport, 581, *581*
seed, **438,** 444, *444,* 446
seedless plant, 437
selenium, 395
Self-Check, 84, 172, 264, 378, 484, 582
semiarid climate, 386, *386*
semiarid desert, 387, *387*
sensory information, 153, *153,* 155–156
sensory organ, 153
sensory receptor, **153,** *153,* 154, 156
sepal, 443, *443*
serval, 154, *154*
sex cell, 425

sexual reproduction, 419

of animals, 437–439, 455, 458, 459, *459*, 477

asexual reproduction compared with, 428

defined, 419, *419–420*

environmental influences on, 421–422

genetic variation in, 423, 425, *425*

modeling, 426–427

of plants, 437–439, 455

shake table, 4, 11, *11*

sharks, 90

shelter, 90

Shepherd, J. Marshall, 345–346, *345*

Shishmaref, Alaska, 509, *509*

shoot system, 95, 131, *131*

short-range weather forecast, 344

short-term climate cycle, 518, *518*

shrub, 387, *535*

Sierra Nevada, 323, 350, *350*, 393, *393*

silkworm, 154, *154*

simulation

crash testing, 12

of engineered systems, 10, 11

of natural systems, 11

types of, 11

Sinopoda, 394, *394*

skeletal system, 149, *149*

skin

epithelial tissue, 146

part of nervous system, 149

as sensory organ, 153

transplantation of, 103

sleet, 313

small intestine, 147, *147*

smooth endoplasmic reticulum, 116, *116*, 117, *117*

smooth muscle tissue, 95, *95*

Snetsinger, Phoebe, 478

snow, 98, *98*, 244, *311*

snowflakes, 327–328, *327*

snowy tree cricket chirps, 339, *339*

soapbox car racing, 35

social awareness, 15

Social Studies Connection

Alaskan Inuit Culture, 372, *372*

Chilling Out, 258

Epic Failures, 78

Science and Activism, 576

society

adjustments for needs of, 39–40

engineering and science and, 4–23

technology influenced by, 15, 16, 25, 32

technology's impact on, 17–20, 25

soil

acidity of, *450*

carbon in, 304, *304*

conservation techniques, 566, *566*

during Dust Bowl, 566, *566*

matter from organisms in, 99

quality of, 556–558

salinity of, *450*

soil fungus, 417

soil scientist, 395

solar energy

for cooking food, 173

Earth systems use of, 511, *511*

improving, 525–526

in space station, 139

storing energy of, 207

solar oven, 210, *210*, 215

solar panel, 139, 191

solar power plant, 207

solar system, 90

solar water heater, 220, *220*

solid

sound energy vibrating particles of, 182

state of water, 239, *239*, 257

thermal energy's relationship to, 221

solid waste, 559, 561–562, 568–570

solution

brainstorming, 46, 47, 54, 57, 226, 228

combining best parts of, 72

decision-making tool, 48–49, 50

developing and testing, 44, 46–49, 51–53, *51*

evaluate advantages and disadvantages, 65

evaluating and testing, 50–56, 59

identifying characteristics of, 67, 228

improving, 64–67

making tradeoff, 65

open-mindedness and, 47

optimizing, 62–72, 69, 75, 77

risk-benefit analysis, 49

selecting promising, 49

selecting with decision-making tool, 48–49

tradeoff, 49

using data to optimize, 68–70

song sparrow, 421, *421*

Sonoran Desert, 469, *469*

Sonoran pronghorn, 469, *469*

sound energy, 181, 182, 190, *190*, 191

sound wave, 154

southeast trade winds, 277, *277*

Southern Hemisphere, 278, *278*

space pen, 70, *70*

Space Shuttle Discovery, 73

specialized cell, 93, 94, 112, *112*

special junctions in heart, 96

species, 534, *534*, 542, *542*, 543, *543*

speed, kinetic energy proportional to, 179

sperm

of aggregating anemone, 461, *461*

of flowering plants, 441

of seedless plants, 437, *437*

of seed plants, 438

in sexual reproduction, 425, *425*

spider, 154, *154*, 463, *463*

spider plant, 440

sponge, 146, 460, *460*

spore, 437, *437*

squirrel, 444, 464, *464*

stamen, 442, *442*

state of matter, 221

stationary front, 322

steam turbine, 567, *567*

steel, 223

stem, 134

modeling, 128

of plants, 131, *131*

water movement through, 135

stigma, 443, *443*

stimuli, 153, 157

stoma, 136, *136*, 137, *137*, 143, *143*

stomach, 147, *147*

stored energy, 180–181

storm, causes of, *311*

St. Peter's Square, 183, *183*, 188

Strait of Gibraltar, *299*

Strait of Juan de Fuca, 245, *245*

strawberry plant, 430
street lighting, 32, *32*
structure
    of coral reefs, 90, *90*
    of *E. coli* bacteria, 93, *93*
    function related to, 19–20
    of nerve cells, 108, *108*
    of tissue, 94
style (of flower), 443, *443*
sublimation, 241, **242**, *242*, 250, *250*
subsystem
    of circulatory system, 148
    circulatory system, 93, 95
    of Earth, 97–102, 107
    immune system, 104
    organs as, 95
    respiratory system, 93
    smallest subsystem of organism,
        93–94
    tissue, 93–94
subtropical jet stream, 283, *283*
sugar
    in DNA, 411
    movement of through plants, 134
    from photosynthesis, 133
sun
    atmosphere receives energy from,
        98
    Earth and climate powered by, 354
    energy from, 182, *182*, 281, *281*
    energy from for wind formation, 270
sundew, 132, *132*
Sun Gold tomato, 447, *447*
sunlight
    absorption of, 354, *354*, 511, *511*
    affecting climate, 354–357, 371,
        511, *511*
    hitting Earth's surface, 355, *355*,
        511, *511*
    latitude and, 355, *355*, 371
    plant cells absorbing, *112*, 130
    reflection of, 354, *354*, 511, *511*
    in temperate rain forest, 385, *385*
    water cycle affected by, 251
sunspot activity, 516
superior vena cava, *151*
surface area, calculating, 120–121
surface area-to-volume ratio,
    120–121

surface current
    continents effect on, 292, 309
    Coriolis effect, 309
    Coriolis effect on, 292
    defined, 246
    formation of, 290–291
    gyres patterns of, 292–293, *293*
    modeling, 290–293, *291*
    satellite images of, 288, *288*
    surface wind transferring energy
        to, 292
surface water, 251, 558, *558*
surface wind
    direction of, 276, *276*
    modeling, *291*
    transferring energy to surface
        currents, 292
suspension bridge, 62, *62*
system, 10, 90, 218
    of animals, 146–151
    boundaries of, 91, 218
    of cells, 115–118
    components of, 10
    defining, 90–92
    digestive, 147
    energy flow in, 173–264
    energy loss in, 191–192
    engineered systems, 10, 25
    excretory, 147
    interaction in, 107
    living, 93–96
    modeling, 92
    models of, 11
    muscular, 149, *149*
    natural systems, 10, 25
    nervous system, 149
    nonvascular, 131
    optimizing solutions, 68
    of plants, 128–138
    properties of, 91
    radiometer as, 218
    skeletal, 149, *149*
    using thermal energy in, 216–235
    vascular, 131

T

table
    of adaptations, 392, *392*
    of calculations, 67
    of cause and effect, *470*

    of criteria and constraints, *34, 42,*
        46, 569
    of criteria and solutions, *386*
    of data, 296, 337, *465*
    decision matrix, *48*
    of dispersal method, *439*
    energy used by light bulbs, *192*
    of estimates, *361*
    of facts and opinions, *546*
    of ideas, *526*
    of monarch migration, *540–541*
    of natural system, *91*
    of observations, *294*
    for order of importance of criteria,
        33
    of paleoclimate data, 515, *515*
    of population in Yellowstone
        National Park, *535*
    of precisely stated problems, *30*
    of questions, *35*
    relative humidity, *313*
    of reproduction, *422, 426, 427, 440,*
        458
    of run times, *335*
    snowflake types, 328
    of test data, 54, 56
    thermal conductivity, 224, 227
    of traits, *426*
Take It Further
    Adjustments for Societal and
        Environmental Needs, 39–40
    Capsaicin Levels in Peppers, 451–
        452
    Careers in Science: Physical
        Oceanographer, 305–306
    Careers in Science: Postdoctoral
        Research Scientist, 527–528
    Chernobyl Nuclear Disaster, 503–
        504
    Designing an Efficient Lunch Line,
        21–22
    Developing Solutions by First
        Asking Questions, 22
    Ellen Ochoa, Electrical Engineer,
        73–74
    Energy Conservationist, 231–232
    Exploring the Greenhouse Effect,
        367–368
    Factors That Influence
        Reproduction, 429–430
    Growing Plants in Space, 139–140

Heat and Cooking, 211–212
Hydrologist, 253–254
Jet Streams, 283–284
Lynn Margulis, Biologist, 123–124
Many Solutions Tested, 57–58
Migration, 161–162
Moving Water Uphill, 193–194
People in Science: Bañuelos, Gary, 395–396
People in Science: Chargaff, Erwin, 411–412
People in Science: Crick, Francis, 411–412
People in Science: Franklin, Rosalind, 411–412
People in Science: Shepherd, J. Marshall, 345–346
People in Science: Watson, James, 411–412
Snowflake Size and Patterns, 327–328
Teaching Offspring, 473–474
Transplantation, 103–104
Urban Planning to Reduce Impact, 571–572
taproot, 134, *134*
tarantula, 536, *536*
technology, 6
    development and use of, 565
    influences on, 13–16, 25
    as part of anthroposphere, 100
    reducing human impact with, 563
    relationship to science and engineering, 6–9
    scientific tools, 6–7, 111
    society affected by, 17–20
Teddy bear cactus and clone, 418, *418*
teeth, 147
telescope, 6
temperate rain forest, 385, *385*
temperature, 202
    affecting energy transfer, 200–201, 208, 220, 223
    in air masses, 319, 321
    animal response to, 152, *152*
    average kinetic energy, 202, 215
    in California, 324
    causing movement, 270

changing water density, 294–299, *294*
    comparing, 198
    as component of weather, 312, 384
    for cooking food, 211
    differences in, 208, 215
    on Earth, 513
    affecting snowflakes, 327–328
    of global air and water, 101
    in global climate change, 515, 520, *520*, 538, 539
    greenhouse effect, 367–368
    greenhouse effect regulating, 511
    influencing climate, 358
    infrared photography capturing, 199
    in nuclear cooling pool, 219
    of oceans' surface, 293
    ranges of on moon and Earth, 513
    in San Francisco, 352, *352*
    systematic measurement of, 514
    thermal energy's relationship to, 202–207, 221
    in urban heat island, 217
    on weather map, *318*
temporal lobe, 155, *155*
tensile strength testing, 50, *50*
thermal battery, 207
thermal conductivity, 210, 224, *224*, 227, *227*
thermal conductor, 227, 235
thermal energy, 203
    ambient temperature, 220
    analyze loss of, 201
    applying concepts of transfer of, 225–230
    changes in, 223
    comparing amounts of, 204–205, 206
    conduction transfer, 209
    convection transfer, 209
    for cooking food, 211
    energy form of, 181
    energy transfer of, 189, 191, 208, 224
    for evaporating water, 241
    factors affecting, 205, 235
    flow of, 219, 235
    in geosphere, 98

modeling flow of, 218–220
    of objects, 221–223
    ocean currents effected by, 303
    radiation transfer, 209
    state of water changed by, 239–240, *240*
    temperature's relationship to, 202–207
    total kinetic energy, 203, 215, *219*, 221
    transfer of, 567, *567*
    transfer of in atmosphere, 281, *281*, 287
    uses of, 190, *190*
    using energy transfer in systems, 216–235
    in water cycle, 251
thermal insulator, 227, 235
thermal mass, 225, 235
thermal properties
    of materials, 221–224
    of substances, 223–224
thornback ray, 418, *418*
three-dimensional (3D) model, 119, *119*
3D printed skeletons, 102
Three Gorges Dam hydroelectric power station, 176, *176*, 492, *492*
thunderstorm, 266
thymine, 411
thymus, 171, *171*
thyroid gland, 171, *171*
tidal energy, 191
tiger shark, 147, *147*
tissue, 93
    in heart, 96, *96*
    model structure and function of, 94
    of plants, 131, *131*, 134, 143
    subsystems of an organism, 93–94
    types of, 95, *95*, 146
toilet, 564, *564*
Tokyo, 571, *571*
tomato, 447, *447*
tool
    of animals, 469
    for decision making, 48–49
    engineers developing, 28
    for mechanical energy, 183, *183*
    metric ruler, 114
    microscope, 19, 111–113

tools, 6
Tottori sand dune, 352, *352*
touchscreens, 72
tradeoff, 49, 497
trait, 402
    of animals, 466–467
    inheriting from parent, 400–410, 413
    modeling, 406–407
    modeling inheritance of, 408–410
    of pea plants, 402, *402*
    relating to genetic structure, 404–407, 415
    reproduction passing down, 391
    selective breeding of, 467
transformation of energy, 189–192
transmission electron microscopes, 166
transpiration, 241, **242**, *242*, 250, *250*
transplantation of organ and organ systems, 103–104
transportation system, 16
trebuchet, 26, *26*
tree
    dragon blood tree, 128, *128*
    as living thing, 93
    maple tree, 130, *130*
    rings of, 514, *514*
tree frog, 458, *458*
treehouse design, 27, *27*, 41
trend, 555, *555*, 556, *556*
Truckee, California, 341, *341*, 342, *342*, 366, *366*
tuber, 440, *440*
tufa pinnacles, 98, *98*
tundra, *394*
Tunguska, Siberia, 188, *188*
two-dimensional (2D) model, 119, *119*
typhoon, 525

U

ultraviolet light, 154
umbrella design, 31, *31*, 34
unicellular
    asexual reproduction of, 419
    as living thing, 110
unicellular organism, 93
United States Geological Survey (USGS), 554

Unit Performance Task
    How can air travel be improved to reduce impacts on Earth systems? 581–582
    How can dehydration be prevented? 171–172
    How can you cool water faster? 263–264
    Save the Whitebark Pines! 483–484
    What Influences Marine Layers in California? 377–378
    What is the best feature for a new pool entry ramp? 83–84
Unit Project Worksheet
    Community Climate Change, 486
    Energy Flow in the Earth System, 174
    Investigate an Animal Behavior, 86
    Investigate Severe Weather, 266
    Off to the Races, 2
    Unique Reproductive Behaviors, 380
Unit Review, 79–82, 167–170, 259–262, 373–376, 479–482, 577–580
urban heat island, 217, *217*, 224, *224*, 233, *233*
urbanized land use in Austin, Texas, *555*
urban planners, 571–572, *571*
urchin, 90, *90*
ureter, 171, *171*
urethra, 171, *171*
urinary bladder, 171, *171*
U.S. Clean Air Act, 15
U.S. Clean Water Act, 15

V

vacuole, 117, *117*, 130
variable, 158, 424, 555, *555*
vascular plant, 131
vascular system, 131
vascular tissue, 93, 95, *95*, 131, *131*
Vatican Obelisk, 183, *183*
velocity, 179
Venn diagram, *134*, 394, 428
Venus flytrap, 137
video game character, 151
video game system, 90
virus particle, 109, *109*, 125
visible light, 199
visual memory, 158

volcano
    ash from in atmosphere, 280, 519, *519*
    in carbon cycle, 304, *304*
    scientists studying, 6, *6*
volcanologist, 6, *6*
volume, calculating, 120–121, 295
von Ahn, Luis, 78, *78*

W

walking stick insect, 458, *458*
wall structures, 4
warm front, 321
waste
    from human activities, 559–562, 568–570
    plants removal of, 133, 136
water
    algal bloom affecting, 489, 500
    analyzing, 238–240
    carbon dioxide in, 539
    changing states of, 239–240, *239*
    circulation of, 98, 242
    condensation of, 243
    conservation of, 563
    copper in, 557
    cycling of in atmosphere, 280
    density of, 294–299, *294*, *297*, 301, *301*, 303
    energy flows through, 208, 303
    energy transferring from, 187, 303
    erosion by, 98
    evaporation of, 241
    global warming of, 101
    gravitational potential energy of, 181, 187
    in hydrosphere, 98, *98*
    importance of, 238
    movement of, 98, *98*, 193, 241–244, 246–247, *247*, 257, 288–305, *302*
    nonliving thing, 110
    organism needing, 238
    in plants, 133, 135, 137
    pollution of, 493, *493*
    in power plants, 567, *567*
    as precipitation, 244
    quality of, 556–558
    role on Earth, 238, *238*
    runoff and infiltration of, 246
    in space station, 139
    states of, 239–240, 257

water cycle, 249
    changes in energy drive in, 236–257
    cycling matter in, 251
    flow of energy in, 251
    hydrologist's study of, 253–254
    model of, 249–252
    solar energy driving, 98
    sunlight and gravity driving, 251
water level in High Plains aquifer,
    556, *556*
water lily, 130, *130*
water molecule
    kinetic energy of, 242
    recycling of, 237, 255
    in water cycle, 2571
water pressure, in plants, 138
water quality data, 554, *554*
watershed, 500, *500*, 501, *501*
water supply infrastructure, 17, *17*
water vapor
    in atmosphere, 98, 241, 280, 312
    in cloud formation, 240, *240*, 243,
      358
    in fog formation, 223
    as greenhouse gas, 367, *368*, 511,
      511
    humidity, 312
    humidity measuring, 312–313, *313*
    in lungs, 147
    as precipitation, 244, 322, *322*
    in Space Station, 139
    state of water, 239, *239*
    in water cycle, 240, *240*, 242, 249–
      250, *249*, *250*
water wheel, 187, *187*, 193–194,
    193–194
Watson, James, 411–412, *412*
watts (W), 192
weather, 312
    in California, 323–326
    climate and, 265–383, 539
    elements of, 312–315, 331

global climate change affecting, 539
    interactions causing, 310–327
    ocean energy flows effecting, 303
    prediction accuracy of, 340–344
    predictions based on patterns,
      332–344
    pressure systems associated with,
      316–318
    sun's role in, 182, *182*
    water's influence on, 238, 303
weather forecast, 174, 340–344,
    340, *343*, 349, 544
weather forecaster, 333, *333*, 341
weather forecast map, 343, *343*, 349,
    349
weather forecast model, 341–343,
    349, *349*
weathering, 238, *238*
weather map, 316, *316*, 318, *318*,
    343, *343*
weather prediction model, 178,
    340–344, *341*
westerlies, 277, *277*, 359, *359*
whale, 462
wheat, 20, *20*
whitebark pine, 483–484, *483*
white-tailed ptarmigan, 469, *469*
wildfire, 99, *99*, 270, *270*, 539
wildlife overpass, 552, *552*
wild thyme population, 542, *542*
willow tree, 436, *436*
wind
    as air movement, 270
    air pressure forming, 316
    analyzing, 274
    assisting plant reproduction, 441
    as component of weather, 315, 384
    Coriolis effect, 276–278, *276*, 287
    creation of, 98
    erosion by, 98
    fire moved by, 279
    formation of, 271–272

    harnessing energy of, 39–40
    kinetic energy transferred from, 281
    modeling, 270–275
    prevailing, 324
    sediment moved by, 280
    seed dispersal by, 444
    on weather map, *318*
windbreak, 566, *566*
windmill, 191
Wind Tree, 39–40
wind turbines, 39, 565
Witch Fire, 279, *279*
wolf, 535, *535*
wood, 29
woolly mammoth, 524, *524*
worm, 99, 146
Wright brothers, 78, *78*
Write, 14, 360, 566

X

x-ray crystallographer, 411–412, *412*
x-ray diffraction, 411
xylem, 134

Y

Yellowstone National Park, 483, *483*,
    535, *535*
Yosemite National Park, 350, *350*,
    360, 369, *369*, 539, *539*
You Solve It, 1, 85, 173, 265, 379, 485
yucca, 388, *388*

Z

zebra, 457, *457*, 469, 475, *475*
zygote, 425